Medieval History

THE LIFE AND DEATH
OF A CIVILIZATION

SECOND EDITION

*With "A Reading Guide to Medieval History" prepared
in collaboration with Thomas W. Huber*

Norman F. Cantor

*Distinguished Professor of History
State University of New York at Binghamton*

MACMILLAN PUBLISHING CO., INC.
New York

COLLIER MACMILLAN PUBLISHERS
London

Macmillan Publishing Co., Inc.
866 Third Avenue, New York, New York 10022

Collier-Macmillan Canada, Ltd.

Library of Congress Catalog Card Number: 69–10930

Printing:　　6 7 8　　　Year:　　7 8 9

ISBN　0-02-319020-5

To My Father and Mother

MEDIEVAL HISTORY

PREFACE TO
THE SECOND EDITION

When this book was published in 1963, it differed from the other general histories of medieval civilization available for use as textbooks in American universities in two respects. First, while giving due attention to political, economic, and social developments, the book gave emphasis to thought, religion, and culture and attempted to understand medieval people in terms of their own professed values rather than our own. Secondly, the discussion of thought, religion, and culture was fully integrated with the analysis of political, economic, and social change in order to attempt a genuine synthesis of the pattern of medieval civilization. The important recent scholarship in medieval history has been along the lines of this integrated, synthetic approach, and in preparing the second edition I have tried to take cognizance of these contributions.

In the second edition, I have retained the structure and greater part of the text of the first edition, but I have made significant changes in several places in the book. The most important changes occur in the sections dealing with the following themes:

> The historiograpical introduction.
> The decline of the Roman Empire.
> Feudalism as a system of values.
> The social significance of Romanesque art.
> The impact of the crusading ideal on medieval values.
> Jewish culture and society.
> The social and political implications of romantic literature.
> The significance of the *Romance of the Rose*.
> The "new monarchies" of the late fifteenth century.
> The Italian Renaissance.

I have retained the bibliographical form used in the first edition, because it has been found pedagogically valuable by college teachers of medieval history. I have added many new titles which represent recent studies and the most important works in foreign languages. All the maps have been redrawn to improve their clarity, and the generosity of the publisher has allowed the addition of nine new pages of illustration. I wish to thank Miss Zane Berzins for assistance in choosing these pictures.

N. F. C.

Lexington, Mass.

PREFACE TO
THE FIRST EDITION

During the past eight years I have taught medieval history to students at Columbia, Barnard, Princeton, Johns Hopkins, Yeshiva, and Manitoba. The enthusiasm which I found in all these universities for the study of medieval civilization convinced me that medieval history can be made relevant to contemporary experience and significant to the educated men and women of today. This book has been written to fulfill that aim.

I have benefited greatly from the inspiration and guidance of my teachers, Joseph R. Strayer of Princeton University, R. W. Southern of Oxford, and the late Theodor E. Mommsen. I was fortunate in having the privilege of studying under the direction of these three scholars of outstanding insight and learning. Each adopted a markedly different approach from the others to the understanding of medieval civilization, and this forced me to think through the problems anew and try to work out the answers for myself.

I wish to express my deepest appreciation to Mr. Michael S. Werthman and to my wife for their invaluable assistance in preparing this book for the press. The concluding stage of my work was greatly facilitated by the advice and encouragement of my colleague Herman Ausubel and by a grant from the Dunning Research Fund of the Columbia University History Department.

I wish to acknowledge the help of the following, my students or former students at Columbia and Barnard: Mrs. Elaine G. Robison, who prepared the index; Mr. John W. McKenna, who put together the chronological lists and aided in the choice of illustrations; and Mr. Arthur Klein, who assisted in the preparation of the maps.

Mr. W. Carter Hunter of The Macmillan Company supervised the publication of my manuscript with characteristic intelligence, care, and good taste.

N. F. C.

Columbia University in the City of New York

CONTENTS

MAPS

THE LIFE AND DEATH
OF A CIVILIZATION

Even the heavenly city, while in its state of
pilgrimage, avails itself of the peace of earth
. . . and makes this earthly peace bear upon
the peace of heaven.

ST. AUGUSTINE
The City of God

Prologue

THE USES
OF HISTORY

In beginning the study of any subject we have a right to ask, What are its uses, Why should we apply our time and energy to this subject, Of what use is this study in our own lives? With reference to the study of history, this pragmatic inquiry is sometimes disdained. It is said that we ought to engage in historical study for the same reason that we climb a mountain: "because it is there." It is claimed that everything man has done in the past is immediately of interest to man, and that this natural interest makes all history worthy of study. Anyone who has this natural interest is potentially a professional historian. But while this lofty approach is of course commendable, any college teacher of history knows that, to say the least, a natural interest in history does not appear to be much more universal than a natural interest in chemistry or mathematics. Furthermore, there is a world of difference between the haphazard and leisurely curiosity which leads to pleasant reading about some historical personality or event—such as Mary Queen of Scots or the Battle of Gettysburg, two perennial "popular" favorites—and the systematic, long, arduous investigation and reflection involved in the real study of history.

Therefore it is right to ask, What are the uses of history? At bottom, we study history for the same reason we study any other human subject, namely, to gain human self-knowledge. The study of history fulfills the precept which the Greeks long ago set down as the highest end of human life: know thyself. Socrates tells us that "the unexamined life is not worth living"; it is only, he claims, when we examine our own human nature that we enter into consciousness of our human existence and are set on the road to wisdom. But does the study of human nature involve only the study of the individual human being? The Greeks themselves held this limited view and investigated humanity for the greater part only in the abstract ideal, with little regard for men in their actual historical-social relationships. Only very slowly, in a complex development of ideas that did not reach its final stage until the nineteenth century, was this approach to the study of human nature seen to be inadequate. And indeed, only in western civilization, as distinguished from the various oriental civilizations, did a clear consciousness of humanity in its ever changing historical context arise.

The use of history as human self-knowledge, which nineteenth- and twentieth-century thinkers have clearly perceived, can be readily understood if we begin by asking what kind of person any human being would be if he suddenly lost the memory of everything he had ever learned. Of course he would be nothing; he would be only an animal, in the sense that a newborn child is really only an animal with potential. But can we restrict memory only to the individual human being and ignore the collective memory of mankind? If we are to attain to full self-knowledge, we cannot. "I am part of all that I have met." This quotation from Tennyson's *Ulysses* provides a key to the most important and general use of history. I am indeed part of all that I have met, not only personally but as a member of a distinct group, society, or civilization. For in the development of our distinct personalities we have been conditioned not only by our personal and family relationships but by a multitude of changes in social life, many occurring centuries ago, which we call history.

Whether or not we are conscious of this fact, not only do we have a personal, individual memory, but also we participate in the collective memory of the vicissitudes which mankind has undergone in the past. Therefore, everyone is an historical being whether he recognizes this all-important fact or whether he is totally oblivious of it. The life of each one of us is conditioned, for good or ill, by events which occurred in distant countries hundreds of years ago, and in our day-to-day life we act according to our understanding of these events, however limited it may be. But in regard to this social memory as well as our individual memory we may truly say, with Socrates, "the unexamined life is not worth living." The unexamined memory of the past is myth and prejudice, and however influential myth and prejudice may be in conditioning social action, they are error and not truth. The examined memory of the past is history in the highest and fullest sense. History as a science, as an intellectual discipline, subjects the collective memory of the past to rigorous scrutiny and, through application of scientific methods carefully worked out by scholars in the past century, attempts to reveal what happened in the past as it really happened, and not on the basis of some myth or prejudice which grew up to flatter some group or nation.

Of course, the understanding of the past as it really happened is a counsel of perfection, and in historical writing as in other areas of life perfection is not often attained. Even with the best will in the world, the greatest care, and the most mature attempt to arrive at freedom from bias, the historian himself is still frequently conditioned by the myth and prejudice of his own intellectual background. This fact has led some historians to despair, to fall into an egocentric relativism, to claim that "every man is his own historian" and that there is no absolute truth in history. It is said that one interpretation is as good as another, and that all historical interpretations, whether presented by the man on the street or the learned scholar, are grounded on socially desired ends. But this despair, while it has the salutary effect of disturbing the smugness of professors—always a good thing to do—goes too far. Granted that historians examining the same era of the past may have profound differences in interpretation, may see some very different patterns of cause and effect in the events they examine, they will still agree on many things. And as history has developed as a science in the past century, historians have arrived at many common conclusions on the interpretation of the past, while still disagreeing on others. There *is,* therefore, a universe of discourse among historians, a hard substratum of commonly agreed-on truth about the past as well as a continuing debate on other aspects of the past upon which agreement may and probably will be reached eventually.

The novice student of history will soon be aware of the dialectical debate among historians; he will, if he has any intelligence, find this debate fascinating. But no one ought to lose sight of the fact that after a century of hard work by thousands of scholars we do know a great many things about the past as certainly as the physicist or chemist or biologist knows certain truths about the world of nature. The novice student should not be misled by the bitter debates which sometimes rage among historians into thinking that history is merely sound and fury. On the contrary, the study of history deserves to be approached with the dignity and high seriousness accorded to other realms of truth. And history has a special dignity of its own since it leads to human self-knowledge, and through self-knowledge to freedom from the myths, prejudice, and dreams—some idle, some vicious—which still condition the action of nonwestern peoples among whom the scientific study of history has scarcely yet begun.

A sound knowledge of history will not let us "foretell the future" in a naive and silly way. But it will enable us to act more wisely in the future.

The man who has accurate knowledge of what happened in the past has come much closer to a full understanding of human nature, and is able to act with the wisdom and confidence that comes from knowledge of truth.

Medieval history is a long and complex moment in the experience of western man; it comprises the period roughly from 300 to 1500 A.D. The legacy of the medieval experience in western civilization is vast and profound. By 1500 the middle ages clearly are no more; but they leave to the modern world the rich heritage of many of its dominant institutions, such as the Christian church, representative government, capitalism, the university; some of its most dynamic ideas, including romanticism, rationalism, nationalism, and the scientific method; and the complex and contradictory nature of modern man himself. If the use of history is human self-knowledge, we cannot dispense with a dispassionate and full understanding of the main lines of development in the middle ages. So many aspects of twentieth-century civilization are the consequence of the medieval experience that to understand "how we got this way," we must know medieval history. And if, as the poet and psychologist tell us, the child is indeed the father to the man, the medieval experience still conditions our destiny today for better or worse. The aim of this book is to make clear the leading aspects of that experience—its achievements and its failures, its glories and its shortcomings, its greatness and its limitations.

Finally it must be emphasized that the medieval experience can only be comprehended by us through an understanding and perception of medieval men's consciousness of the great events which determined their destiny. We must see, we must in fact feel, not only the external character of events, but their inner nature, that is, their impress on the thought of contemporaries. To outline the stages of the Germanic invasions, the events of the reign of Charlemagne, or the deeds of the crusaders is not enough; we must understand how these events impinged on the consciousness of the men who lived through them; we must try to understand how these changes became integrated into the experience of medieval men. On the other hand, we must avoid mere surveys of "great ideas" without relationship to the context of the social situation which conditioned their emergence. It is as limiting to outline the theology of Thomas Aquinas without relating it to the society and culture which presented him with the problems he tried to resolve as it is to survey merely the events of Charlemagne's reign without trying to comprehend what the Carolingian empire represented in terms of the hopes, aspirations, and disappointments of contemporaries. This book will try to avoid the snares of both vacuous positivism and delusive intellectualism (the former a very old failing in writing about medieval civilization, the latter a rather new one, especially with those scholars who take the statements of medieval canon law to be the realities of ecclesiastical life). The aim of the historian is indeed to describe "the way it was"—a simple ideal it would seem to the naive, but so hard to realize! This we shall try to do by depicting the mainstreams of development of medieval civilization and what these mainstreams really meant in the lives and thought of medieval men. Our account will not be completely satisfactory; but writing with sympathy for the problems of medieval men, yet with a determination to make clear their failures as well as their triumphs, we hope to come closer than most to a total, and therefore true, picture of medieval society.

Introduction

THE SCOPE OF
MEDIEVAL HISTORY

I. Historiographical Outline

It is possible to designate the precise day on which the study of the middle ages as a branch of historical literature really begins. In autumn of the year 1764 an English gentleman named Edward Gibbon, who was a moderately wealthy country squire and an Oxford alumnus, made a journey to Italy with the intention of touring the archeological remains of the classical world. In his autobiography Gibbon tells us how the evident changes which had overtaken Rome since the days of the great emperors inspired him to undertake a history of the way in which this great historical development had occurred: "It was at Rome, on the fifteenth of October 1764 as I sat musing amidst the ruin of the Capitol, while the barefooted friars were singing Vespers in the temple of Jupiter, that the idea of writing the decline and fall of the City first started to my mind."

All historical writing and research must begin with first a sense of wonder and then a clearly formulated question. The historian, as distinct from the mere antiquarian, begins not with idle and aimless curiosity but with a genuine question about changes in civilization, states, and individual personality. Gibbon was by this test a genuine historian, for he had a real problem: he wanted to know the course and causes of the great changes which had brought about the erection of Roman Catholic monasteries on the ruins of Roman pagan temples. As an historian Gibbon had many defects. His method of analyzing sources was much inferior to that of professional scholars today; because of his own religious wandering from the Anglican church to Roman Catholicism to skepticism, and because of the generally hostile attitude of the eighteenth-century enlightenment toward supernatural religions, he had no sympathy whatsoever with religious beliefs of the more mystical and profound kind. He also had a pathological hatred of women. One critic has remarked that Gibbon was always sympathetic, liberal, and humane except when Christians were being martyred or virgins were being ravished. Yet in spite of the fact that the *Decline and Fall of the Roman Empire* is in many ways an erroneous and misleading book, it is the first great work on medieval history.

In the course of his research Gibbon relied heavily on the antiquarian writings of some learned French and Belgian monks of the late seventeenth and early eighteenth centuries. Using the critical methods of classical scholarship developed in the first half of the seventeenth century, these monastic antiquarians arrived at a scientific way of testing the genuineness of medieval documents, and also succeeded in laying the foundations for the accurate editing and publishing of medieval writings. Their interest, however, was not history but hagiography. These monastic scholars were trying to publish accurate renditions of the lives of the saints. Their careful scholarly method laid the foundations for scientific research into medieval history, but in itself their work was not inspired by genuine historical ideals.

Gibbon's view of the middle ages as a period of steady decline from the grandeur of the Roman Empire during the second century A.D.—the "triumph of barbarism and religion," as he called it—was inspired by the attitude of the Italian humanists of the late fifteenth century. These humanists had reacted against the civilization of western Europe in the period immediately preceding their own in much the same way as many intellectuals in modern Europe and America reacted against the culture and attitudes of the nineteenth century. Just as we sometimes use the term "Victorian" as a term of opprobrium, so the ideologists of the Italian Renaissance invented "the middle age" (*medium aevum*) as a term of hostility toward and disgust with the culture of western Europe from the period of the Roman empire up to their own day. Taken up by writers of similar views in the seventeenth and eighteenth centuries, the term "middle age" became an historical term of abuse directed against the church, scholastic philosophy, and the literature and art of more than a thousand years of European civilization.

Yet if the term "middle age" was first used extensively in polemics directed against the church, it must be noted that the idea of an historical middle age was itself a concept first formulated by medieval ecclesiastical theorists themselves. In their eschatological speculations they conceived of a middle age between the creation and the last judgment. The application of the term "middle age" to a certain historical period was the consequence of the secularization of this concept by Renaissance humanists and eighteenth-century rationalists.

It is only with the coming of the Romantic movement at the end of the eighteenth century that the term "medieval" and the companion pejorative artistic term "Gothic" came to stand for anything other than barbarism and degeneration. Unfortunately, the view which the Romantic poets and dramatists took of the middle ages was perhaps just as fanciful as the attitude of the Renaissance humanists and their rationalist successors. Medieval Europe was now peopled not by wild barbarians and fanatical monks, but by chivalric knights and chaste, moon-struck maidens. Keats' famous poem *The Eve of St. Agnes* is an excellent example of the new enthusiasm for the middle ages generated by the Romantic movement.

The nationalism of the nineteenth century also made an important contribution to the development of the historiography of the middle ages. Fortunately, the nationalists' contribution abetted the rise of the scientific and scholarly study of Western Europe of the period between 300 and 1500. As is well known, the humiliating defeat of the Germans by Napoleon and the French armies stimulated the rise of nationalist sentiment in Germany in the early decades of the nineteenth century. Because the German nationalists could find neither unity nor glory in their country since the middle ages, they turned fondly and with glowing sentiment toward the glorious days of the medieval German empire. And so, to study and to publish books on medieval Germany, the Prussian government set up a research institute devoted to medieval German history. This institute might have become nothing more than a mouthpiece for silly nationalistic propaganda, but fortunately by the middle of the nineteenth century it had become dominated by excellent scholars trained in the methods of classical scholarship. Fortunately also, the study of the medieval German empire entailed as well the study of the medieval papacy and medieval Italy, and so the German institute of medieval history devoted itself to a very great part of the whole field of medieval civilization. In spite of all the vicissitudes through which Germany has passed in the last hundred years, the great German institute of medieval history, located since the Second World War in Munich, continues its work of publishing the *Monumenta Germaniae Historica.* By the end of the nineteenth century the scientific study of medieval civilization, free alike from the prejudices and fanaticisms of Renaissance humanists, Romantic poets, and on the whole even from nationalist propaganda, was well under way in Germany.

During the latter part of the nineteenth century France, too, had seen the rise of a school of medieval historians, who were also trained at a research institute financed by the government. While the volume of the contributions made by the French scholars to medieval history has been considerably less than that of the Germans, the French medievalists have contributed some of the finest minds to the study of medieval history, and several of the more important general interpretations of medieval history have been made by French scholars and by Belgians writing in French.

By the beginning of the twentieth century other European countries were becoming interested in their medieval heritage. The English have been particularly eager to study the origins of their distinctive political and legal institutions against the background of medieval foundations.

The first professor of medieval history in the United States was Henry Adams at Harvard in the 1870's. Like Gibbon, Adams was prepared neither by training nor by disposition for this task, and he soon went on to other things. But like Gibbon, his historical genius was so great that he was capable of almost rising above his imperfections as a scholar. His study of twelfth-century French art and literature is still of some value today. At the end of the nineteenth century American scholars began to study in Europe. Two of these men who brought to Harvard the scientific method of European medievalists were Charles Gross and Charles Haskins. Haskins especially was responsible for the creation of a school of medieval hsitory in the United States. Not only did he make several important contributions to medieval history himself, but at Harvard between 1910 and 1930 he trained a whole generation of scholars in the rigorous method of European historical research. The Haskins school was joined in the 1930's by some very able German medievalists who were forced to leave their homeland because of Nazi persecution. Ironic as it may appear, the United States at the present time can boast of a group of medieval historians second to none in the world, not even in France or Germany. It would be interesting to know what Edward Gibbon would have thought of this turn of events. He held a lucrative government sinecure under the cabinets which imposed on the colonists the various oppressive measures leading to the American revolution, and as an M.P. he always voted for Lord North.

It is never easy to categorize historians, nor should it be. Like the work of any artist, that of each historian deserves to be considered individually, and it always varies a little from the attitude, method, and manner of expression of any other scholar. Historiography, like any form of literary criticism or any exercise in the history of ideas, is an inexact and imprecise study. Nevertheless, with these cautions in mind, it is possible to group historians in terms of their assumptions and methods. Any intellectual discipline is improved by self-consciousness on the part of its practitioners, by evaluation of the criteria which are employed to arrive at interpretive conclusions, and this is true also of the conscious consideration of the attitudes and methods of historians, which we call historiography. It is possible to survey the approaches to the understanding of medieval civilization in the scholarship of the past four decades and to detect five general approaches to medieval historical change.

The first of these approaches, largely characteristic of German scholarship, and best represented by the work of Percy E. Schramm, Gerd Tellenbach and Carl Erdmann, draws upon the typically German attitude of *Geistesgeschichte* and may be termed the dialectical-spiritual approach. The miseries of the political and economic situation in Germany since the First Word War induced its historians to confine themselves to the realm of ideas where the wretched realities of their country's history since the thirteenth century were less painfully apparent, and where truth and beauty could be found. This attitude has strongly conditioned the writing of medieval history in Germany. It was much more gratifying to contemplate medieval historical change in terms of great debates on the nature of a Christian society—the implications of the imperial ideal, the origins of the crusading ideal, the conflicting interpretations of freedom—than to examine closely the institutional defects of the monarchy and the personal failings of the medieval German kings and nobility. The Hegelian influence, reinforced by the work of Wilhelm Dilthey, also lies behind this tendency toward almost exclusive concern with *Geistesgeschichte* among the leading German medievalists between the World Wars. Nor did the German school shrink from a heavily dialectical approach: it drew sharp distinctions between various movements of thought in medieval Europe, and it emphasized the profound impact on subsequent development of certain critical eras when these dialectically conflicting ideas confronted one another. The dialectical-spiritual school was able to carry out its studies of medieval ideas with a superb command of the tools of scholarship developed by classical specialists. The training which the German medieval history seminars provided in the close explication of the text was ideal for the intensive analysis of the documents of medieval intellectual history, and this kind of training was yet another reason for the popularity of *Geistesgeschichte* among German medievalists and for its perpetuation, with only a slight decrease in the fervor of its adherents, after the Second World War and to the present time.

One of the most eminent exponents of the German school of medieval historiography, Ernst Kantorowicz, spent the greater part of his academic career in the United States, after he was driven out by the Nazis. Kantorowicz's studies of medieval political thought have permanently illuminated for us the way in which medieval men conceived of the state and church. His work also reflects the shortcomings of the German school. It has been said that the Germans describe history which happened to nobody. To a degree this is true. The critics of the German dialectical-spiritual school point out that ideas are given too great a causal significance in its work, that the distinctions between ideas are frequently overdrawn and that in the minds of contemporaries such dialectical clarity was lacking. In reply, it would be argued that the understanding of historical change involves more than recounting the passionate confusions of the contemporary actors. The historian finds it both right and necessary to clarify and sharpen differences, even if contemporaries could not see the dialectical pattern so clearly.

Intellectual history has remained since 1945 the overriding concern of German medievalists. But the heir apparent to P. E. Schramm as the outstanding spokesman of the dialectical-spiritual school, H. W. Klewitz, was killed in the war, and outstanding scholars of the current generation of German medievalists, such as Herbert Grundmann and Theodor Schieffer, are more moderate and less dialectical in tone, and more interested in personalities and social change, than were their great predecessors.

In this respect they come close to the attitude of the most outstanding English medieval historians of the past two decades, who may be designated the devotional-personal school. M. D. Knowles at Cambridge and R. W. Southern at Oxford are its leaders and they have created something like a revolution in medieval scholarship in England: for the first time in ninety years the most eminent English medievalists are interested primarily in ecclesiastical and cultural history, rather than political and legal institutions.

For seven decades medieval history in England was largely synonymous with institutional history. The great question which educated society had to ask of historians in late nineteenth-century England was: how did our enlightened national system of government and law come into existence? A series of very able scholars—William Stubbs, F. W. Maitland, T. F. Tout —set out to find the origins of English institutions in the medieval past. Yet in the late 1930's a new trend in medieval English historiography began to appear in the work of F. M. Powicke. This scholar's interest in the facets of medieval piety influenced his detailed biography of the thirteenth century English king Henry III, published in 1947, which marks a radical departure from institutional history. It tries to evaluate Henry III and his contemporaries as real people, not merely as kings, officials, and barons, and it finds the leaders of medieval society bound together by common Christian ideals. It was, however, in M. D. Knowles' four-volume history of the English religious orders, the first volume of which was published in 1940, that the devotional-personal school was most ably presented. His history of the religious orders is one of the greatest historical works produced by an Englishman since Macaulay. Yet its greatness lies not in its avowed purpose of detailing monastic history but in the author's unsurpassed power of capturing the attitudes and mores of medieval religious leaders. He succeeds in fulfilling the criterion set down by R. G. Collingwood, the Oxford philosopher and historian, whose *Idea of History* has had relatively little influence in England, that history must be seen from the inside, that historians must be able to recreate the ideals and attitudes of the personalities of past ages.

The other leading exemplar of the English devotional-personal school is R. W. Southern who has succeeded his teacher Powicke as the leading medievalist at Oxford. Southern's *Making of the Middle Ages* presents, as no book in any language has done, the most important facets of cultural and religious change in the eleventh and twelfth centuries. Here again, as in Knowles' work, the experience of medieval men has been internalized by the author, so that he is able to talk of twelfth-century churchmen as contemporaries and as friends. In Southern's book, for the first time, the deep currents of sentimental piety which brought about the transvaluation of medieval values become real and perceptible to the modern reader.

Considering the work of Powicke, Knowles, and Southern as a whole, it may be said that these scholars, rather than pointing up dialectical differences, portray a civilization in which the different shades of thought and feeling blend together into a common devotion to the Christian commonwealth, and this unity is represented by the attitudes and ideals of the leaders of medieval piety and devotion. In the hands of a great historical artist like Southern, the result is a most attractive picture of a spiritually united civilization. The obvious criticism of this school's work is that its result plays down the material grossness and ugly power drives of medieval life and that it gives to the medieval thought-world an excessively optimistic placidity, in which the fierce debates of the time as to the nature of the true Christian society are all but ignored.

The academic study of medieval history began in the United States only shortly before the First World War. Inevitably it was profoundly influenced by the Anglophilic attitudes so popular at the time among the educated and socially prominent classes, and American medieval scholarship began as an offshoot of the English institutional school, with the work of Charles Gross, C. H. Haskins, and C. H. McIlwain. In a sense, indigenous American medieval historiography has never extricated itself from this beginning. Intellectual history and the study of the early middle ages have been left in American universities largely in the hands of German émigrés. What has attracted native American scholars had been consistently the political and legal institutions of twelfth- and thirteenth-century Europe.

The contribution of the American institutional school to our knowledge of medieval historical change is as great as that of any other group of medieval scholars. Their work has been instrumental in allowing us to understand the pattern of medieval state-building. They approached medieval history not in an antiquarian spirit but with the intention of finding how medieval historical change contributed to the beginnings of the modern state. It must also be said that their labors have been prodigious; it is probably harder to make sense out of a twelfth-century tax roll than out of the sermons of St. Bernard. Yet as a suitable criterion for evaluating medieval historical change, the quest for the origins of the modern state has very definite deficiencies. The work of Haskins and his disciples is marked by a strange and puzzling combination of strong intelligence, great erudition, and yet a decided lack of involvement in many of the issues that most deeply disturbed medieval men themselves. The work of the American institutional school is vitiated by an abstract indifference to the agonizing spiritual struggles of medieval society.

Economic and technological determinism is the fourth approach to the problem of medieval historical change in the historical work of the past four decades. The economic vicissitudes of the twentieth century and the rapid industrialization of underdeveloped areas have made many medieval historians—of whom Henri Pirenne, Robert S. Lopez, Michael Postan, and Lynn White are some of the more outstanding—conscious of similar radical changes in the material environment of medieval Europe. As has generally been the case in European and American historiography during recent decades, the historians of the medieval economy have made more important contributions than writers on any other aspects of medieval civilization. The pattern of change in the medieval business cycle, trade routes, urban life, demography, and technology are now being extensively worked out. The question remains: how important was economic development in a civilization in which the established landed classes and the clerical scholars were at best only half-consciously aware of these changes? How important is economic change in a society which has no economic mind? The relationship between economic change and the other facets of medieval civilization remains to be thoroughly considered. Economic change, at least with relation to medieval civilization, should remain in the background; it provided a limiting and conditioning framework within which medieval men made their choices on religion, government, art, literature, etc., but by itself economic change determined nothing. How much better would we understand the experience of medieval men if some of the ingenuity and time spent on examining town origins had been devoted to studying the Virgin cult!

Of the many distinguished scholars who have worked on medieval economic development, the most important was Marc Bloch, not only because of his contributions to agrarian history, but even more for the methods and historiographical concepts he advocated, and for the influence he has had on a whole new and very able generation of French medievalists. Bloch was a professor at the University of Paris who was killed by the Nazis in 1944 while he was fighting in the French resistance. His work is inspired by the belief that institutions only attain historical significance when examined in terms of their social functions—an insight already applied, at the end of the nineteenth century, by the English scholar F. W. Maitland, in his monumental analysis of medieval English law.

Although Bloch sometimes inclined to economic determinism he nevertheless had a vision of a total, integrated history which would bring together all kinds of historical research in order to understand the pattern of a whole society. In his attempt at a total view of "feudal society," his enjoining of the comparative study of institutions, and in his conviction that a society is more than a sum of individuals and a civilization more than a collection of fragments, he was following in the traditions of Emile Durkheim and French sociology, and Bloch and his disciples may loosely be referred to as the quasi-sociological school of medieval history. There are many more specific suggestions in Bloch's writings which are of great value in approaching the investigation of medieval historical change: that documentary evidence merely shows the "tracks" of medieval men, and that historians must use intuitive imagination to reconstruct the civilization whose tracks remain; that the devotion of the institutional historian to finding origins is a dangerous and unrewarding obsession; and the best unit of historical periodization is according to men who bear a "common stamp," that is, men who belong to the same generation.

Since 1945 the most prolific school of medieval history has consisted of Bloch's French colleagues and disciples—Robert Boutruche, Robert Latouche, Georges Duby, and Philippe Wolff—who have devoted themselves to intensive regional studies and also to some broad comparative studies along the lines of Bloch's work. It is still too early to evaluate the long-range effect of this school on our understanding of medieval historical change, but some general comments do arise from consideration of their books. In the first place, Bloch's disciples seem more interested in social history than in the history of society. There is a tendency to get away from integrated total history towards which Bloch was working in favor of a much more limited endeavor, albeit a most valuable one—the study of class structure. No important book on the medieval French monarchy came out of France in the 1940's and 50's; the only outstanding scholar working in the field, Robert Fawtier, was of an older generation. The history of education and philosophy of twelfth and thirteenth century France seems to have been abandoned by Bloch's disciples to clerical scholars. Recent French scholarship reveals a tendency to collect data for its own sake and an aversion to general speculation drawn from sociological and anthropological theory. The other disturbing feature of the work of the French school is the accentuation of a tendency already apparent in Bloch's work—the carrying over of the sociologist's lack of interest in individuals, the mechanistic tendency to see individuals only as part of a group, which leads to the neglect of real human personality.

The bewildered novice student, comparing the work of these five schools, may conclude that there were five medieval civilizations and lapse into desperate relativism. But confusion is the beginning of wisdom, and out of this variety of approaches to medieval history a much more profound, sophisticated, and subtle synthesis may be drawn than could possibly have been imagined a half-century ago.

The trend toward a synthesis of the traditional schools of modern interpretation of the medieval world is evident in recent scholarship. Robert Lopez's recent work is marked by a concern with the general pattern of social change and achieves the imaginative and sensitive quality of Bloch's finest studies. The Austrian scholars Heinrich Fichtenau and Friedrich Heer relate intellectual history to political and social problems. The history of the classical heritage in the medieval period by the Cambridge scholar R. R. Bolgar blends the approach of Knowles and Southern with a German kind of dialectical intellectual history and a French sensitivity to social realities. In France and Belgium a group of young historians has inaugurated a re-examination of medieval political and legal institutions; this development not only marks a break with the tendency of French and Belgian scholarship to concentrate on economic and social history; it has already, in the studies made by R. C. Van Canegem and J. Dhondt, related political and legal structures to the realities of social and cultural flux. By the late 1960's a new consensus on the complex pattern of medieval change was crystallizing.

II. *The Periods of Medieval History*

The intensive work of more than a century's historical research has shown beyond all doubt that the humanist view of the period between the fourth and fifteenth centuries as one remarkable only for unprogressive and sterile barbarism is erroneous and absurd. This long period in European history, more than twice as long as the era which separates the Renaissance from ourselves, was in fact a period of rapid and sometimes even violent and revolutionary change. Nor does the period itself hang together in complete unity; it can be readily divided into at least three distinct periods. Hence historians today talk not about the middle age but about the "middle ages," and while they do talk about "medieval civilization," they tend to divide the development of medieval civilization into three distinct periods. This division has now become universally accepted and traditional among historians.

The first of these periods is the very long era from the decline of the Roman Empire, let us say 300, to the middle of the eleventh century. It is the era in which a distinctive western civilization emerged out of the background, one might almost say the clash, of Christian, Graeco-Roman, and Germanic institutions and ideas. Depending on the metaphor preferred, the early middle ages is the infancy and youth, or the springtime, of western civilization. It is a period marked by a great deal of chaos and turbulence, as western Europe was racked by internal disunity and frequent invasion from without by alien peoples frequently exhibiting a rather low level of culture. Largely due to the guidance of the church, this incipient European civilization struggled first of all to develop its distinctive ideals; then it faced the task, even more difficult, of developing the institutions which would embody and activate these ideals in everyday life.

These aims were to a large degree achieved by the end of the eleventh century. The result was the remarkable flowering of European art, literature, and philosophy during the twelfth and thirteenth centuries, which together comprised what the historians nowadays call the high middle ages. More and more research discloses that this extremely fruitful, mature, and stable period was very short-lived, and certainly by the second half of the thirteenth century the conflict between old ideals and new practices—which gives evidence of a disintegrating civilization—had made its appearance.

The result of the dichotomy between ideals and actuality is shown in the fourteenth and fifteenth centuries which historians today call the later middle ages and tend to view more as the old age, or autumn and winter, of medieval civilization. In this period western Europe is racked by disorder, pessimism, economic and political decline, until finally at the end of the fifteenth century the characteristic ideals and institutions of the modern world, based upon the sovereign state, nationalism, and individualism, pushes to the fore. The study of medieval history therefore provides us with an excellent case study of the rise, flowering, and disintegration of a civilization. In the case of medieval Europe such a study is better documented than the history of any other civilization whose evolution has been completed and whose whole pattern of growth, maturity, and decay is evident to the student of society and culture.

While not denying the value and general validity of this traditional division of the medieval period, this book will use an additional, more meaningful, and sophisticated division. We shall begin by discussing the disintegration of the Mediterranean civilization and the rise of the Christian church to the end of the fourth century. This is the period of the Latin and Christian foundations of medieval civilization (Part I). Then the emergence of a new, distinct medieval society and government in the period from 400 to 725 will be discussed. We must here concern ourselves with the Germanic foundations of European civilization and the impact of the Moslem expansion (Part II). An age of great promise, not entirely fulfilled, follows from 725 to 900. This is an era of the coming into existence of the first synthesis of Latin, Christian, and Germanic sources to form the First Europe. The characteristics of this First Europe must be examined in comparison with its two competitors among the civilizations of the time, namely the bordering civilizations of Byzantium and Islam (Part III). The failures of the First Europe are avoided in the successful period of equilibrium and progress between 900 and 1050. During this era many characteristic European institutions begin to take shape (Part IV). During the few decades from 1050 to 1130, however, the early medieval equilibrium breaks down largely as a result of a crisis of conscience on the part of several church leaders. The great struggles of this age of the Gregorian reform must be understood as the key turning point in medieval history (Part V). But no sooner have the participants in this struggle given way to a new generation than the period from 1130 to 1200 is marked by an era of fantastic expansion in all aspects of life, especially in the areas of piety, humanism, and secular power. These achievements and the remarkable men who led these advances must be examined in detail (Part VI). But by 1200 the consequences of the expansion and acceleration of the twelfth century were evident, and a desperate attempt now had to be made by the leaders of European thought and action to bring discordant and conflicting tendencies into a new equilibrium and synthesis. This period from 1200 to 1270 was the great age of summing up and organization, rather than creativity (Part VII). But these strenuous efforts to avoid crisis and conflict fail, resulting in the disastrous and violent controversies of the period from 1270 to 1325. Now times are out of joint, and the process of decline and failure becomes evident (Part VIII). The concluding period of medieval history concerns the era from 1325 to 1500. It is marked by war, pestilence, economic depression, bitter religious and intellectual controversies, and also by the foreshadowing of the modern world (Part IX).

In this new division of medieval history Parts I through IV are concerned with the early middle ages, Parts V through VIII with the high middle ages, and Part IX with the later medieval period.

III. The Themes of Early Medieval History

Turning now to the early middle ages, it will be useful to emphasize the three themes which will be stressed in Parts I through IV of this book.

The first theme has already been suggested. The early middle ages was a period of the emergence of a distinctive western European civilization. The characteristic ideals of western European civilization were formulated out of the legacy of the ancient world and under the pressure of new circumstances. We will see the men of the early middle ages struggling to formulate these ideals from the fourth century until the end of the eighth century. The church will take the lead in this work largely because the church was the only institution strong enough to provide the necessary leadership. By 800, during the reign of Charlemagne, the formulation of these ideals is concluded for the most part, and they begin to affect all aspects of political and social life. It is not, however, until the latter part of the eleventh century that the men of western Europe possess the adequate means to put their formulated ideals into reasonably constant and universal practice.

The second theme which we intend to investigate is the impact which the Christian church and Germanic kingship had upon one another, leading to crucial problems of church-state relations, some of which are still with us. We must examine the doctrine and organization of church and kingship and how they affected each other.

Finally we shall be concerned not only with western Europe but also with the whole Mediterranean world. We shall look at the two civilizations which established themselves, along with western Europe, as the successors to the Roman empire in the Mediterranean basin, namely Byzantium and the Islamic states. We shall trace the course of western Europe's struggle against these other civilizations, first for survival and later for ascendancy.

Where do we begin our study of the life and death of medieval civilization? Modern scholarship has left both the beginning and the end of the medieval period indefinite and a matter of dispute. To understand medieval civilization, how it came to be what it was, its origins in the declining stages of the ancient world must be clearly perceived. Therefore medieval history rightly begins with the Roman empire and its decline from its flourishing stage in the second century A.D.

PART ONE

The imperial destiny drives hard, and
fortune has no longer any gift for us than
the disunion of our foes.

—TACITUS

The Roman world is falling; yet we hold
up our heads instead of bowing them.

—ST. JEROME

THE ROMAN DESTINY

Second to Fifth Centuries

Chapter One

DECLINE AND FALL

I. The Roman Empire in the Second Century A.D.

Edward Gibbon believed that men were happiest under the rule of the Roman empire in the second century A.D. A plausible argument for viewing this as the golden age of mankind could be presented. The Romans were not great innovators; they were skillful at adapting and borrowing the best ideas and institutions of the Mediterranean world and synthesizing them into an organic system. From the rulers of the Mediterranean world who preceded them, the Romans adopted ideas and institutions which they fashioned into a new world civilization. The Greeks, Egyptians, Hellenistic empires, and Persians all made important contributions to the Roman civilization of the second century A.D. The poet Virgil, whose *Aeneid* was a careful expression of the ideology of imperial rule, remarked that it was a "great task to build the Roman state." It was indeed, and only the Romans of the old Republic, of all the peoples of the Mediterranean world, were self-sacrificing, efficient, power-mad, ruthless, and cruel enough to create a world empire.

In 100 A.D. the Roman emperor ruled a great world state stretching from the Euphrates to Scotland and from the Danube to the Sahara. Within this area lived a great variety of ethnic, linguistic, and cultural groups, but Hellenistic Greek was the common language in the eastern half of the empire and Latin in the west. At the top of this enormous political edifice was the emperor, by the second century an absolute despot with pretensions to divine qualities. His government was based upon a hard-working bureaucracy of modest size and a large army. On the whole the emperors were

17

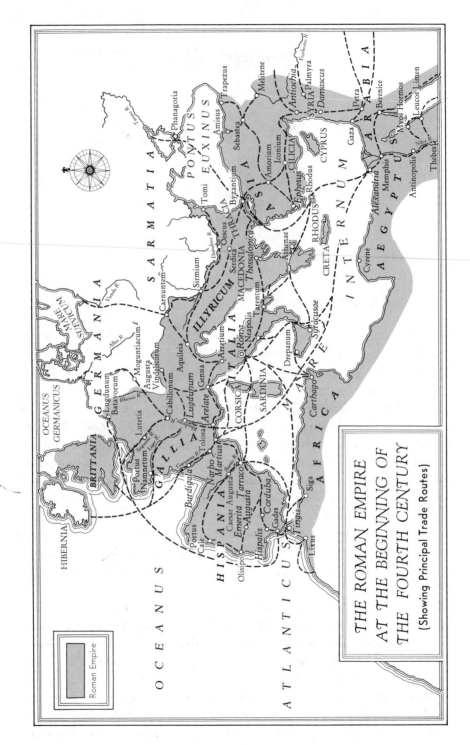

THE ROMAN EMPIRE
AT THE BEGINNING OF
THE FOURTH CENTURY
(Showing Principal Trade Routes)

Roman Empire

18

able men, creating the *Pax Romana,* a vast political and economic unit centered on the Mediterranean Sea, where there were great cities. The western part of the empire, exclusive of Italy, was much less heavily populated and urbanized than the eastern half. To understand the events of the next thousand years, we must initially free ourselves from the preconceptions of Europe-centered history, which was the consequence of medieval development itself. The Roman empire was a Mediterranean-centered civilization. Northern France and Britain, which were to provide so much of the later leadership in western civilization, were mere backward outposts of the Roman world.

Until late in the second century the emperor controlled government and law, but interfered little with economic or religious and intellectual life. This freedom from imperial control encouraged prosperity and all sorts of intellectual experimentation. It must be admitted that the emperor in any case as yet lacked a large-enough bureaucracy to attempt to control economic and intellectual life. But on the positive side, the imperial beneficence was partly conditioned by the spread of ideals of welfare and humanity among the ruling classes of the empire. Already Virgil had proclaimed as the duty of the empire "the raising up of the humble and crushing of the sons of pride," and another imperial ideologist, the poet Horace, spoke in similar terms. There is no chapter in Roman history as glorious as the spread of the ideal of *humanitas* (human decency) among the mean, selfish thugs and near-thugs who had conquered the Mediterranean world. Among the conquered peoples the Greeks, especially, educated their new masters toward the Stoic ideals of universal brotherhood and altruistic duty to the welfare of men and the world state. Stoicism by the second century had become a widespread philosophy among the aristocracy and other educated men, and greatly influenced the development of Roman law. By 212 all *free* people in the empire (there was still a large slave population) were citizens of Rome, and this practice was carried out in Roman law. The Romans were innovators in law, developed one of the world's best law codes, and believed that all citizens, whatever their ethnic background, came under the protection of a uniform legal code.

There were some very ugly sides to the life of the Roman world, which classicists usually prefer to ignore: an enormous slave population, vast urban slums and terrible poverty, the widespread practice of homosexuality. But the fact remains that the Roman empire in the second century presents a picture of a civilization dominated by prosperous cities, good urban sanitation, beneficent and able public administration, an unsurpassed legal system, and vibrant intellectual activity. A peaceful, secure, and energetic way of life was open to members of the middle class and aristocracy in the second-century empire. Nevertheless, by the end of the second century the long "decline and fall" of the Roman empire had begun.

II. *The Crisis of the Roman World*

The problem of the decline of the Roman empire has been called "the greatest problem in history," because it is part of the problem of why any civilization fails. For this reason many historians have attempted to discover the defects of Roman civilization, producing a great variety of conclusions.

Rome was at its height in the second century A.D., but it had a fundamental defect in its political structure: there was no certain principle of succession to the imperial throne. In the second century the means of succession was designation by the preceding emperor, but in the third century this system broke down, bringing about a long struggle in which the army caused much of the instability. Anarchy was the inevitable result when the legions from different provinces tried to place their generals on the imperial throne. It was not until the latter half of the fourth century that the hereditary principle was fully established. This system of succession prevailed in the east into the medieval Byzantine empire; but even then there were periodic civil wars and revolutions, and the emperor was always hampered by the possibility of army revolt.

Though Rome produced great statesmen, politicians, and lawyers, like the other ancient world states it failed to undergo an industrial revolution. Due to this in part, Roman economic problems reached a climax in the latter decades of the second century. Industrial techniques remained primitive, depending mostly on hand labor for production. Few machines were developed past the start of the Christian era. Though the Greeks knew the principle of the steam engine, it was never put to industrial use. Why was there a failure in the application of science to technology? Something was wrong with the prevailing philosophy and with the aristocratic leaders who did not deign to stoop to such lowly practices. Not until the late second century was there pressure to find new sources of power, nor was there a need as long as slave power from conquered areas was plentiful until that time. Productivity could be increased by increasing the number of slaves at work. The availability of slave labor discouraged the invention of new machinery or industrial techniques. Thus it might be said that the primary fault of the Roman economic system was that it was based on slave labor.

In addition to discouraging industrial research and technological improvements, the slave-labor base also limited the quality of the goods produced. The relatively simple production allowed for easy copying, but precluded the production of complex products. For example, the clothes that were produced could be easily imitated because of their simple design. The pottery industry is another example of the ease of imitation of simple goods; in fact, the older Greek pottery industry was faced with competition from southern Gaul in the second century. This kind of situation led to the discouragement of international trade because there were no distinct regional products. Instead of the earlier active and wide trading complex there was growing autarky—production for local consumption and independence of imports from other provinces. There was a partial revival of international trade in the fourth century, but generally from the latter part of the second century the empire slowly disintegrated as an economic unit.

A continuing desire for luxury items maintained trade with the world to the east of the empire. Since Rome had nothing to exchange for these oriental luxury goods, to import them she had to pay with specie. Hence there was a marked drainage of gold to the east, producing a strain on the imperial economic system. Thus the desire for luxury goods from outside the empire, was another failing of the Romans and their economic system. Before this time the Romans had had a stable coinage, but already in the third century the emperors debased the coinage in an effort to stabilize imperial finance. Most emperors were not aware that what they were doing would radically inflate prices. They simply did not understand such things as inflation.

These defects in commerce, industry, and finance were paralleled by crises in agricultural life. In the Roman republic agriculture had been based on the small-scale citizen farmer with his plot of land. These farmers were the backbone of the republic, providing leadership in political and military life. From the first century B.C. the small farms began to give way to the *latifundia*—the large estates worked by slaves, the precursors of the medieval manor. There was great abuse and exploitation of slaves. The small farmers moved into the city, and the slave labor continued to produce while the landlord racked off the profits. This agricultural process had a great effect on the military life of Rome. The citizen-farmer had been the backbone of the republican army and early imperial legions; by the second century A.D. there was a problem of where to get an army.

The later Roman empire appears to have suffered from a decline in population, partly the consequence of the ravages of plague. Nevertheless the military manpower problem was caused more by social than by demographic factors, for in 300 A.D. the empire had between fifty and seventy million people, which was a large enough population to maintain strong armies. But the emperors were afraid to staff their legions with aristocrats lest they attempt to take over the government. The bourgeoisie did not want to leave their businesses and were anything but eager to join the military. There were two remaining sources of manpower: from among the slaves and the city proletariat and from enemies along the northern and western frontiers, the German tribes. The Germans wanted to join Mediterranean life, and late in the second century the emperor began settlements of tribes just across the frontier to act as buffers against the other Germans. For this service these "federates" were given land and privileges. The trouble with this policy lay with the German leaders. These men rose to high positions of command within the imperial army and even approached the power of the imperial throne. They were slow to attack their fellow Germans and, as the history of the German invasions reveals, sometimes betrayed the emperor.

The final problem of the empire was dry rot at its core. The city of Rome itself declined as an economic center while remaining the center of government. In Rome by 200 A.D. there were large, unruly mobs always eager to rebel and riot. Rome was the residence of the emperors, and they met the violence in the streets either with measures of extreme cruelty or by attempting to win over the mobs through entertainments and the dole ("bread and circuses").

After the death of Marcus Aurelius in 180 A.D. a period of chaos and military anarchy, coupled with great economic decline, began. Between 235 and 285 there were eighteen emperors! The policy of the emperors became "Enrich the soldiers, despise the rest," as one emperor advised his successor on his deathbed. The coinage continued to be in a terrible state, and the *Pax Romana* was beginning to fail. The Germans momentarily broke through the frontier defenses, and pirates were active on the inland seas. However, the imperial ideal was so strong that the empire was able to right itself once again, and there was a movement back to centralization in the reigns of Diocletian and Constantine, from 284 to 337 A.D.

Diocletian, a general of Balkan peasant stock, saw that desperate times required desperate measures. He worked to reform the imperial system and produced a great totalitarian structure similar to that of Egyptian despotism, with Constantine putting the finishing touches to this monstrous edifice. The emperor was elevated to a sacred position in the oriental manner, with an elevated throne, diadems, and imperial robes, according to established court rituals of the orientals. The elaborate spiritual and physical elevation of the emperor restored much prestige to him, impressing greatly the people of low education and little sophistication. There was also an extension of the bureaucracy with secret police, informers, torture, and the destruction of the semi-autonomous privileges of cities within the empire. All cities were now ruled from the center. An attempt was made to stabilize prices by imperial decree. Even in church matters the emperor had the final word. All this led to a small economic revival based mostly on a new confidence in the coinage. It slowed down the process of decay, but in so doing destroyed the middle-class prosperity through great taxes used to pay off the armies and the bureaucracy. The harsh tax-collection system required that the more prominent businessmen themselves (the *curiales,* or town councilors) be responsible for the tax collection in their cities and that they make up any deficit from their own pockets if they failed to meet their quotas. With this brutal system and the additional requirement that a man remain in his father's trade and pay a fixed tax no matter what his state of prosperity, the reforming emperors laid the groundwork for the final collapse of the empire. The "reforms" of Diocletian and Constantine did hold the fort for a century until the church was strong enough to take over leadership of society in the fifth century. However, the cure was really worse than the disease as far as the empire was concerned.

In dealing with the many theories of decline and fall of the empire, a definition of terms is required. It must be made clear whether the reference is to decline of a civilization, of an ideal of empire, or of the Roman state itself. The decline of the empire as a civilization has aroused the most controversy among historians. We can dismiss such examples of absurd causation as malaria epidemics and move on to more penetrating theories of the decline of Roman civilization.

Some scholars point out that the spirit of ancient civilization arose in the city-state. With the steady urban decline the civilization was ruined, and its spirit and enterprise disappeared. This interpretation is valid as far as it goes, but it is concerned only with mediate and not ultimate causation. What brought about the urban decline? Another theory is that orientalization caused the Roman breakdown. There *was* a physical orientalization through intermarriage, but the difference does not appear to be significant. Much more important was moral and intellectual orientalization, the intrusion of new spirit and culture from the east. The mystical, otherworldliness of the new spirit turned men away from attention to this world. It is clear that there was a change in values in the Roman world between 150 and 400 A.D. and a consequent loss of leadership. Men of great ability, such as Ambrose and Augustine, would have gone into political life had they not turned to the church, and they would have provided the leadership that the empire lacked.

The greatest historian of the Roman empire, Michael Rostovtzeff, looks to a general revolt of the masses for the cause of decline. The lowest orders, proletarians and slaves, or at least their offspring, rose to the highest places, gaining control of army and government. They were scarcely educated in the classical sense of education. Their perception of the imperial ideal was obscure, and they lacked respect for the freedom of the individual and the law. The new men, who were of humble and obscure origin, came to power in the third and fourth centuries. They did not understand the old traditions of the well-educated minority who had maintained control of the empire through the second century. The elite civilization of the ancient world could not survive absorption by the masses. The weakness of Rostovtzeff's interpretation is that it presents a too clear-cut picture of the "masses" against the "classes." In the later empire men of proletarian and peasant stock *did* advance to power, although many of the aristocracy remained at the center of government. But these new leaders of lower-class derivation did not have any particular class-conscious outlook. They certainly did not regard themselves as engaging in a class revolution.

Recently the views of Arnold Toynbee have been popular. Toynbee presents two interpretations: (1) The decline of ancient civilization began with the Peloponnesian War, and the whole history of the empire is but an epilogue to the failure of Greek civilization; (2) Roman civilization, like all civilizations, failed to "respond" to a "challenge." It "rallied" only long enough to produce the Christian church, the universal religion which was the "chrysallis" of the succeeding civilization. The first of Toynbee's theories is an absurdity, and the second is a tautology, although no doubt a useful and to some extent illuminating one. But merely describing what happened in rather broad terms is not a causal explanation.

Finally we may consider three less obvious theories of the causes of collapse of Roman civilization, but ones which may have the seeds of truth. The first is suggested by the Victorian strictures on the corrupt personal lives of the Roman ruling class as a cause for decay. This thesis was not original with the Victorian moralists. In the late fourth century a lugubrious churchman named Salvian contended that the "vicious lives" of his contemporaries accounted for the imperial decline. It may be replied that it is doubtful if the personal lives of the ruling class became more sordid in the later empire; they were in a great many cases sordid and corrupt in the early empire. Prostitution was one of the most flourishing, and best organized, of Roman industries. Imitating the Greeks, the Roman aristocracy practiced homosexuality and sodomy on a grand scale. Already in the reign of Augustus the staunch aristocrat Horace remarked in one of his poems (not one of those prescribed for modern school children) that when he was in heat he would prefer a boy to a woman anytime. Historians have done little to assess the social consequences of sexual mores. In the case of the Roman empire the question may at least be posed whether prostitution and homosexuality had a debilitating effect on the functioning of the aristocratic family, the institution that had contributed so powerfully to the operation of the old republic. At least it can be said that if not a cause of social malaise, homosexuality is symptomatic of some deep-rooted malfunctioning of the social and moral order. It is worth noting that in two other societies that exhibited quite rapid declines, the medieval Arabic and the twentieth-century English, homosexuality flourished in the ruling elite.

In considering general theories of the decline and fall, we come to a great book, C. N. Cochrane's *Christianity and Classical Culture,* published in 1939 but still not yet given sufficient consideration by historians. Cochrane's neo-Augustinian thesis contends that the fundamental defects of classical thought were themselves the greatest enemies to the survival of ancient civilization. Because of the naive belief in the limitless power of human reason which classical thought propounded, both the political and the intellectual leaders of classical civilization overreached themselves in their political and intellectual structures, trying to create in both instances an ideal, rationally constructed world which foundered on the hard truths of the irrational—the animal and divine instincts in man—which their narrow vision excluded. Cochrane concluded by arguing for the superior merits of the Christian (Augustinian) view of human nature. It is not necessary to be as enthusiastic an Augustinian as Cochrane in order to acknowledge that he rightly pointed out that the false view of human nature upheld by classical culture was a fundamental cause of the inability of the leaders of the Roman world to deal realistically with the political, social, and intellectual problems of the age.

A third highly controversial but illuminating thesis on the decline of Roman civilization has been stressed in recent scholarship: the Roman empire never achieved more than a superficial cultural unification of the Mediterranean world. Particularly in the eastern Mediterranean only a narrow urban elite were genuinely Romanized while the mass of the population remained loyal to centuries-old national linguistic and religious identities. As soon as the imperial government was confronted by military and economic problems and the *pax Romana* became less beneficial, these primordial nationalisms reasserted themselves in a powerfully compelling fashion, gradually won over even the Romanized elite, and in the fourth and fifth centuries steadily alienated the populace from its loyalty to the Roman order. It has also been suggested that even in Rome some members of old aristocratic families had never been reconciled to Caesarian authority and that they subtly undermined devotion to the imperial ideal at the very center of the empire. These nationalist and aristocratic subversions of imperial unity made imperial power and unity a mere façade and turned both rich and poor into internal exiles from the *pax Romana.* When we witness in our own day how shallow was the penetration of European culture into Asia and Africa under the rule of the modern Western empires, we can appreciate that the process of Romanization may, after all, have never made more than a superficial penetration against the resistance of ancient national cultures.

Whatever the validity of these speculations, it must also be stressed that the decline of the Roman empire as an ideal never entirely took place. The ideal of the empire almost disappeared in the west during the fifth, sixth, and seventh centuries, but in the east the ideal remained strong in the Byzantine empire and was revived in the west in the ninth century in the empire of Charlemagne and his successors. The continuation of the idea of Rome in the middle ages is one of the fundamental themes of medieval history. Rome, to Christian people, became synonymous with the political and cultural unity of the world. The Byzantines never gave up the idea, and the emperor in Constantinople thought of himself as the Roman emperor, to whom everyone else was subject. After the sixth century the Byzantine conception of empire had no foundation in reality. The best the eastern monarch could do was to maintain a weak foothold in southern Italy to the early eleventh century.

In the west during the period of the Germanic invasions (450–750) the idea of Rome was very weak. It was preserved by the Christian church and especially by the papacy. The pope, as the bishop of Rome, regarded himself as the successor of the Roman emperor. Because of its conflicts with the Byzantine empire, the papacy looked for a western king who would resurrect the empire in the west and restore political unity and strength to the Latin Catholic countries. Such a revival and reconstruction came in the early ninth century under Charlemagne, and the idea of the empire was very important in the west from the ninth to the fourteenth centuries. It was an especially important idea from the tenth to the thirteenth centuries among the medieval German kings, who regarded themselves as Charlemagne's successors. They were not able to extend their control to England or France, but their rule did bestride the Alps with a relatively weak hold on Italy. But the eventual collapse of the power of the Holy Roman emperor of Germany and Italy in the thirteenth century precluded the fruition of the idea of the empire into the concrete reality of political unity in the medieval west.

The decline of the Roman empire as a state is easily explained. As a state the empire was a tremendous burden on the population. By 400 A.D. it was despotic and oppressive, but offered very little in return. It did not even protect the citizens from the Germanic invaders, and by the beginning of the fifth century there was a visible lack of loyalty to empire and emperor. When the Germans finally broke through the imperial frontiers, few cared to save the Roman state, which had become a monster not worth saving.

III. The Religious Quest of the Roman World

The orientalization of the Roman empire, the bringing in of eastern ideas and values, meant that the people in the empire took religion seriously to an ever increasing degree during the second, third, and fourth centuries. Religion and theology became the staff of intellectual and emotional life for the emperor and aristocracy even as much as for the lower classes. The emperor Diocletian, the master of half the world, would do nothing without first consulting the auguries in the form of livers of dead chickens. In the third century superstition and supernatural religion were widely accepted.

Why did these beliefs enjoy such an increased popularity? People in the third century were suffering from the insecurity of the times. As they became less secure in this world they began to turn to the "other" world. For most people in the late empire life was hard and miserable. The despotism of the emperor and imperial government weighed heavily upon the citizens. A huge urban proletariat lived precariously from day to day, depending on handouts from the government. In addition, large numbers of the population were slaves outright, living under the most terrible conditions. To these people, suffering from the injustices of the social order, this world could not be regarded as rational. Even those who enjoyed a high standard of living greatly feared the power of nature, and the simplest rules of economics were likewise beyond them. They lived desperate lives in an irrational world. Since evil and abuses could not be relieved, the bulk of society sought *soteria*—release, safety, salvation—from the pains of this world. They centered their hopes on a savior god, a dying and reborn god with whom they could associate themselves and also escape from the limitations of mortality. Fascination with the afterlife pushed aside other interests. Rather than the salvation of the state, the universal quest became "What must *I* do to be saved?" By the fourth century the inhabitants of the Roman world had lost faith in both state and civilization, seeking instead individual, personal salvation. A variety of solutions was offered; one approach would borrow from another, and even solutions which gained only a small number of firm adherents had great influence on all others. This blending and mixing together of religions is known as syncretism.

The Romans had had a state religion from the beginning of the empire under Augustus. The religion was based upon the deified emperor, who obtained superhuman and semidivine attributes upon death. In the third century the religion or cult of the divine emperors was less modest. The superhuman qualities were accepted in the living emperor. Certain poets aroused enthusiasm for this movement. Already Horace and Virgil had spoken of Augustus in messianic terms in the early first century. However, most people did not involve themselves emotionally with this emperor cult. It was primarily a state religion designed to maintain the political unity of the Roman world. What interested people in the later empire was a personal religion for personal salvation.

In Alexandria Judaism had long expressed a stern moral code and a monotheistic theology. Secret literature—in this case the Hebrew Bible translated into Hellenistic Greek (the Septuagint)—appealed to the Romans. Although the Jews had rarely gone in for proselytizing, the Alexandrian Jews hoped to win converts, and in the first century A.D., when Judaism was momentarily fashionable in aristocratic circles, they had some success. In the long run, however, very few Romans remained staunch Jews. Judaism was still not clear in its conception of a messiah and the immortality of an afterlife. To the Jews the messiah was a national redeemer and remained such even after the beginning of the Christian era. Judaism was an austere religion with high morality but little worldly reward. It was only because of the oppressiveness of Roman life that the Jews had turned halfheartedly to consideration of an afterlife. Although Philo of Alexandria, in the early first century, attempted to reconcile the Greek philosophical tradition with the Old Testament Jewish tradition, thereby harmonizing science and religion, and although Philo's writings greatly influenced the Christian church fathers, Judaism failed as a universal religion.

Greek philosophy had greater promise as the answer to the religious quest of the Mediterranean world. Of the Greek philosophers, the more scientific and common-sense Aristotle had very little appeal to the thinkers of the Roman era, with whom Plato's writings were very popular. In fact, until the twelfth century some form of Platonism dominated western thought as the basis of theology and philosophy. Plato begins as a rationalist, but ultimately his thought is religious and mystical: the highest Idea of the Good is only achieved by the "flight of the soul." The moral teachings of Platonism became embodied in Stoicism, which was more philosophy than religion and not at all emotional. For this very reason the appeal of Stoicism was quite narrow and confined largely to the aristocracy, although the Stoic ethic of universal brotherhood exercised a wide influence. It was the mystical side of Greek philosophy which had the greatest appeal for the people of the Roman world. The Alexandrian Neoplatonist Plotinus, in the third century, emphasized Plato's mysticism, stating that ultimate truth comes from mystical experience and spiritual exaltation. God was likened to a fountain giving forth holy water, and as the water moved away from the fountain it became less and less pure. People, like impure water, must undergo purification in order to attain communion with god. Thus there must be a catharsis of all intellectual and worldly interests; man must divest himself of the material and emerge pure spirit. But the difficulty of achieving this mystical purification was too great for all but a very few. In addition, the fact that Neoplatonism offered no savior god and demanded that each believer seek god on his own lessened its appeal. Neoplatonism influenced practically all theology, but the ordinary people were more interested in a savior god than in the rigorous spiritual exercises required for Platonic purification.

In their search for a religion to suit their needs, the proletariat, and eventually educated and wealthy men as well, turned to the mystery and sacramental religions which had been circulating in the Roman and Greek worlds for many centuries. The strength and popularity of the mystery religions increased greatly in the first and second centuries as several eastern cults penetrated the Mediterranean world. Their pronouncement that all could attain salvation had overwhelming appeal. In this way they were the first truly universal religions, ignoring national, cultural, and class divisions. Their dramatic and emotional appeal as sacramental religions, full of mysterious ceremony, particularly accounts for their success. The mystery religions all featured a savior god who dies and is reborn, and a sacramental rite which allowed the believer to gain immortality by associating himself with the sufferings and triumphs of the deity. Although these sacramental ceremonies, such as bathing in the blood of a slaughtered bull, may be traced to primitive fertility rites in many cases, mystery religions generally encouraged high moral values and a form of monotheistic godhead.

A bewildering variety of mystery religions had appeared by the end of the third century. The religion of Isis was popular in Egypt, the Great Mother a favorite in Asia Minor. The religion of Mithra (the Unconquerable Sun), probably the most important of the mystery religions, appeared in Persia in the second century and moved steadily westward. It gained many converts among the Roman soldiers and officers of the eastern and even western legions, but never admitted women to its cult, which helps to account for its ultimate failure. Mithra offered a secure salvation and a highly puritanical ethic. Surviving Mithraic prayers are very similar to Jewish and Christian invocations to the deity.

In this seething religious atmosphere Christianity appeared. It was not simply a syncretistic religion, but had an historical concreteness which the other sacramental religions lacked. Jesus had been on earth at an historical time. The Christian savior god had appeared in the flesh; he was not merely a myth. In the third century there was no certainty that Christianity would triumph over all other mystery religions. Mithraism, for instance, was very popular and was supported by several Roman emperors. From the time of the institution of the totalitarian late empire it became clear that one of the mystery religions would sooner or later triumph over the others. As there was one sacred emperor for the whole Roman world, there would sooner or later have to be one universal religion, one god in heaven as there was one ruler on earth. Political totalitarianism implied an eventual religious homogeneity.

Christianity faced stiff competition. In spite of this or because of it, it managed to absorb the best in all the religions of the time. From Judaism it took over the holy scriptures and added the New Testament. It also assimilated the moral code of the Jews. Stoicism supplied the Christians with the belief in the brotherhood of man. Christian thinkers also borrowed heavily from the mystical philosophy and theology of neo-Platonism. They felt, however, that self-purification to attain the union of man with God was impossible due to the corruption of the flesh and that an intercessor was needed to provide ultimate unity with God. Church fathers subscribed to this modified Neoplatonism from the second century on. It is a moot point whether the Christians directly borrowed the sacramental rite from the mystery religions or whether the general religious atmosphere produced a similar manifestation in the form of the Christian sacrament for communion with the savior. In any case, the possession of a sacramental rite of a particularly pure and simple kind, when added to Christianity's other qualities, made it a most attractive religion for the people of the Roman world. But at the beginning of the fourth century Christianity had not yet become the certain and only answer to the Roman religious quest. Not more than a third of the population in the Greek-speaking eastern part of the empire was Christian, and less than 10 per cent of the Latin-speaking population in the west. It was only by gaining the support of the Roman state after 312 that the triumph of Christianity was assured. Diocletian and Constantine staved off the collapse of the Roman empire only long enough for Christianity to become the universal religion of the Mediterranean world. Thus the history of the disintegration of the Roman world is intertwined with the rise and triumph of the Christian church.

Chapter Two

THE CHRISTIAN EMPIRE
AND THE
CHRISTIAN CHURCH

I. The Shaping of the Catholic Church

The history of the early Christian church began to be seriously investigated in the sixteenth century. During this period of the Protestant Reformation both Catholic and Protestant scholars sought to prove that the institutions and doctrines of the early church more clearly conformed to those of their own persuasion. The debate was never settled, not only because of sectarian differences, but also because the sources of our knowledge of the early church are in many cases fragmentary, obscure in information, and even contradictory. To the present day many aspects of the development of the church before the fourth century are in doubt. The student of medieval history need not attempt to settle the controversial problems concerned with the history of the early church. Nevertheless he should have a general view of the ideas and institutions of the church in the first three Christian centuries in order to understand clearly its structure as it appears in the fourth century and later. The early development of the church in many instances predetermined the nature of the medieval church.

At the time of the death of St. Paul, in the middle of the first century, Christianity was widespread in the eastern part of the Roman empire. It had started in Palestine and spread westward, following the trade routes of the eastern Mediterranean. The Jewish diaspora—the dispersion of the Jews to the chief cities of the Mediterranean world—greatly assisted the early spread of Christianity. As early as the fourth century church historians envisioned the Jewish diaspora as a divine plan preparing the way for the spread of Christianity. From the first, Christianity was directed to city dwellers and remained a predominantly urban faith until the later fourth century. Paganism was closely associated with rustic life and farm dwellers; the word *paganus* means a "countryman," a hick, and therefore a non-Christian. When Constantine came to the imperial throne, 20 to 30 per cent of the Greek-speaking eastern empire was Christian and 5 to 10 per cent of the less urbanized Latin West. By 312, perhaps a third of the urban population of the empire followed Christianity.

The nineteenth-century philosopher Nietzsche popularized the idea that Christianity was a slave religion with a slave morality. It is true that it had a powerful attraction for the downtrodden, but by the second century it had certainly gained adherents among the upper classes. It spread slowest among the old Roman aristocracy. As late as 350 many of the old aristocratic families in Rome still resisted Christianity. Nevertheless, it must be emphasized that the Christian religion was not one of slaves alone. It derived most of its leadership from the educated and energetic urban middle class, with men of substance such as St. Paul climbing to greatest prominence.

There were several reasons for the spread of Christianity. As we have seen, it satisfied the religious quest of the people. It also offered the emotionally satisfying fellowship of religious love (*agape*) in the midst of lonely cities. In addition, Christianity rapidly became a highly literate religion attracting educated men to its membership, including many of the best minds of the Roman empire. It accepted classical culture and became philosophical in the best intellectual tradition of the ancient world.

Christians in religious fellowship called themselves *ecclesia,* the word used in the Septuagint to signify God's chosen people of Israel. By calling themselves the *ecclesia,* the early Christians expressed their conviction that they were the new Israel, the new chosen of God. And this meaning of *ecclesia* was taken to include all Christians everywhere. Though there was a particular, physical, local church (*ecclesia*), for example, in Antioch and Alexandria, at the same time Christians believed that the church was a universal and eternal entity stretching from creation to the last judgment. The additional concept of the church as the bride of Christ had a great influence on medieval thought. It eventually led to the doctrine of sacerdotal celibacy and, even more important, encouraged the tension between the view of the church as a mundane, physical reality and the concept of the church as an eternal spiritual entity. If the church was the bride of Christ, to what extent could it become involved with the world? To what extent, if at all, could the bride of Christ be subjected to the domination of secular rulers? There would be many agonizing reappraisals during the middle ages in attempts to answer these fundamental questions.

A church whose self-consciousness was so fundamental had to insist that its teachings be catholic—universal, homogeneous, everywhere the same. This concept of the one catholic church was expressed clearly by St. Irenaeus in the second century. Nevertheless, it must be emphasized that until the eleventh century the church, at least in the west, tended to be permissive with regard to some doctrines and institutions; considerable heterogeneity and variety in belief and practice were allowed.

We know little about the organization of the earliest church. Apparently each ecclesiastical community had a great deal of autonomy, with its own leaders for business and administration. These administrative officials seem to have been first driven to assume religious authority by the pressure of the gnostic movement. The gnostics believed that they could have an inner religious experience and receive *gnosis* (knowledge) directly from God. In reaction to this potential religious anarchy the church developed the authority of a strong hierarchy. Bishops (pastors of the Christian flock) emerged as men of religious and dogmatic, as well as administrative, authority. They defined dogma and exercised absolute control over their flock. The presbyter (priest) emerged as the assistant to the bishop who ruled the church in an important city. Under the authority of the bishop, assisting him in the work of his cathedral and, on the local level, in each individual church, were the priests. The bishops, it was believed, derived their authority through the apostolic succession, a direct succession of spiritual power from Christ himself through the apostles to every bishop. The mysterious spiritual power of the church was seen as emanating from Christ in a direct line to the holder of each episcopal office.

The development of the ecclesiastical hierarchy was also encouraged by the growth of the sacramental system. Through the mysterious rites of the sacraments the believer could gain, or at least prepare for, entrance to the saving grace of God. The modern church has seven sacraments, but until the thirteenth century they were not very well defined in number. A leading eleventh-century theologian enumerated no less than eleven sacraments. The two most important sacraments at all times were baptism and the eucharist. Baptism did not originate with Christianity; it was a common purifying rite in the middle east, as is evidenced by John the Baptist and the practices of the Jewish sect of Essenes. In Christianity baptism became a method of purification by which the believer was prepared for reception into the grace of God; from a more mundane view it was preparation for entry into the fellowship of the church. The sacrament of the eucharist (thanksgiving), or the mass, was a re-enactment of the Lord's Supper—the eating of the bread (body) and drinking of wine (blood) of Christ. This sacrament established the close association with the Lord necessary for reception of God's gracious gift of salvation. Christianity believed that man was innately corrupt and that the eucharist alone made possible participation in the redeeming merits of the Savior so that man could receive grace and achieve salvation. Was this a symbolic or a miraculous ceremony? Nearly all men in the middle ages thought it was a miracle. By a miracle the bread and wine was actually transformed into the body and blood of Jesus Christ (transubstantiation). The ceremony had a great empirical, pragmatic value. It could be performed in a great cathedral by a bishop or in a poor church by a local priest. In any case the official who performed the rite had a special relation to God.

The priesthood (*sacerdotium*) was thus elevated above the position of common members of the church by the performance of the miracle of the eucharist. In the early church *sacerdos* (priest) may have meant any member of the church, implying (so say Protestant scholars) that all believers were priests. With the institution of the hierarchy, the priesthood of the common church members (laity) became potential only; the laity were now placed under the hierarchy, beneath the priests and bishops. The Catholic view held that it was the office and not the quality of the individual priest that made him eligible to perform the sacraments. In the fourth century a great controversy arose over this point. The Donatist heretics claimed that a priest had to be in the state of grace himself—i.e., had to be a saint, had to live a pure life—to perform a valid sacrament. Catholicism of course desires that the priests performing the sacraments lead blameless lives, but nevertheless maintains that without regard to the personal quality of the priest the sacramental rite is valid because the priest performs it as an official of the church and the representative of Christ, not simply as a man. This question was to arise again and again in the history of Latin Christianity and to become the great issue involved in the religious disputes of the fourth century, the high and late middle ages, and also the sixteenth century.

The geographical and political divisions of the empire affected the organization of the church. The area of episcopal jurisdiction became the "diocese," an imperial administrative division instituted by Diocletian. Similarly, the imperial division of the "province" came to designate the area of jurisdiction of the superbishops, or the archbishops, who developed their superior power by virtue of ruling in the larger cities of the empire. In fact, the archbishop was and is alternatively called the metropolitan. Finally, the

Greek-speaking church inevitably recognized the leadership of the bishops of the greatest cities of the eastern empire—Alexandria, Antioch, and Constantinople—who took the title of patriarchs. Similarly, the bishop of overriding prestige, if not of unchallenged authority, in the Latin church was from the beginning, naturally, the bishop of Rome, the pope (*papa*). The Roman church had been founded by St. Peter and St. Paul, who had also suffered martyrdom in the eternal city; no Latin city could match such a great tradition. In addition, the city of Rome was inevitably synonymous with leadership in religious as well as in secular affairs. Furthermore, the bishop of Rome in the first three Christian centuries had the uncanny knack of always coming out on the winning side in any doctrinal dispute. The papal reputation had never been blackened by even momentary heresy. But in spite of these factors contributing to great papal authority by 312, it was not universally accepted even in the west that the pope was the absolute and single leader of Christendom. The Greek patriarchs rejected completely any papal claims in this direction. In the fourth century the bishop of Rome was completely overshadowed by the new Christian Roman emperor. During the first three centuries, however, the pope had gained enormous prestige and had evolved a tradition of his overwhelming importance in the life of the Latin church. In the fifth century, after the collapse of the western empire, the papacy would make great use of this heritage.

Rome as a state did not really care about Christianity until late in the third century. The number of Christian martyrdoms was greatly exaggerated by later legend, and the persecution of Christians was local and infrequent. The Roman state was fairly liberal toward Christians, although it did not approve of them and did not recognize Christianity as a legal religion. The Christians were annoying to the state in their refusal to swear allegiance to the emperor by making formal obeisance to the emperor cult. Nevertheless, Christianity was allowed to develop with very little interference. For example, in the correspondence with Pliny the Younger concerning Christianity in his province in Asia Minor, the emperor Trajan told his governor Pliny to leave the Christians alone. In the middle of the third century there was a change in Roman attitudes. As economic and political conditions deteriorated in the Roman world, sporadic and spontaneous outbreaks of violence against Christians occurred. The church became the scapegoat for the troubled empire. Emperor Diocletian, in trying to form a totalitarian regime, soon became conscious of the Christian church as a state within the Roman state. He believed that its ubiquitous and powerful religious institutions would detract from his efforts to unify and strengthen the empire. For ten years a systematic attempt was made, under orders from the emperor, to destroy the Christian church. Some Christians were martyred, and more abandoned their religion, but the local governors in many areas did not systematically carry out Diocletian's orders.

In any case, the Roman state had turned too late against the church. It was impossible to root out an institution which had the loyalty of perhaps a fifth of the population of the Roman world. The empire could not destroy the church; it would have to live with this new great force in the world. Diocletian retired from office in 306; seven years later the western and eastern emperors proclaimed freedom of religion (the so-called Edict of Milan) in the whole empire. The ruler of the Latin-speaking world, Constantine, who had come to his throne in 312, went further. He proclaimed his active support of the Christian God and His church. Henceforth the Roman empire was to become more and more associated with the church.

II. *Constantine the Christian Emperor*

The character of the eastern Roman empire was largely fashioned by two emperors, Constantine in the fourth century and Justinian I in the sixth. Their social backgrounds were remarkably similar; they were both of Balkan peasant stock. Constantine's father and Justinian's uncle both rose from this humble background to be important generals and later attained imperial power. Constantine's mother Helena (St. Helena in the Greek church) had been a Balkan barmaid and probably a prostitute. Justinian married a circus dancer, Theodora, probably also a prostitute. Constantine and Justinian also resembled each other in great industry, administrative ability, and devotion to the church.

Constantine was born about 280 to Helena and Constantius Chlorus, who was at the time caesar, or assistant emperor, in the western empire in charge of Britain and Gaul. Constantius Chlorus' religion tended toward pagan monotheism in the form of the Unconquerable Sun. Constantine himself, sent to Diocletian's court and traveling extensively in the eastern empire, came to know many Christians quite early in his life. When Diocletian retired in 306, his complex scheme for the imperial succession, consisting of a senior and a junior emperor and two caesars, or assistant emperors, immediately failed. Bitter civil war ensued until, in 310, three generals contended for supremacy. They were Licinius in the East, Maxentius in Italy, and Constantine, his power based in Gaul and Britain, the poorest and least populated part of the Roman world. In 312, although outnumbered by his rival Maxentius, Constantine risked everything in a march over the Alps and upon Rome. At the battle of the Milvian Bridge near Rome—

one of the few really important battles of history—he defeated and killed his enemy. This victory made him ruler of the west and with Licinius in the East Constantine shared the rule of the Roman empire from 312 to 324. In 324 Constantine defeated and deposed his eastern rival and became sole ruler of the Roman world.

Contemporaries wondered at Constantine's apparently miraculous victory at the Milvian Bridge; Constantine himself later claimed that it was no fortuitous event, but rather the result of his adherence to the Christian God before the battle. This conversion of Constantine has become a very controversial subject among historians. Much of the evidence for the conversion of Constantine to Christianity comes from Lactantius, a Latin writer in Asia Minor, who, about 320, wrote the *Death of the Persecutors,* a very popular book in the middle ages. It is a collection of horror stories about the downfall of those rulers who had persecuted the Christians. In the course of this book Lactantius discusses the events which led to the battle of the Milvian Bridge. He tells us in this account that Constantine was instructed in a dream to place the Labarum (standard) of Christ—the crossed chi and rho: that was the Christian monogram—on the shields of his men to bring him victory. Bishop Eusebius of Caesarea, the first great historian of the Christian church and a friend and confidant of Constantine, gives three accounts of the events leading to Constantine's great victory. In 316 he stated vividly that Constantine accepted Christianity and put the chi-rho upon the shield of his legionnaires. In 325, in the *Ecclesiastical History,* Eusebius asserted that Constantine prayed to the Christian God before the battle and later erected in Rome a statue of himself with the Christian standard. No evidence of the statue has ever been found, and the account is probably untrue. Eusebius' *Life of Constantine,* written shortly after the emperor's death in 337, presents the model for the standard life of a Christian monarch which was followed until the eleventh century. In this work Constantine and his army are said to have seen a flaming cross in the sky and the inscription "by this sign thou shalt conquer" before they crossed the Alps to Italy. This demonstrated to Constantine the power of the Christian God, whose standard his army henceforth carried.

There is some numismatic evidence for Constantine's conversion, but it is inconclusive. Both the cross and the Unconquerable Sun are depicted on one coin, while another coin-type shows the chi-rho destroying a serpent, symbolizing Christianity's destruction of paganism. On yet another is depicted Constantine in armor with the chi-rho on the crest of his helmet. A medallion from 330, commemorating the establishment of Constantinople, has distinctly Roman overtones; it shows Victory crowning the emperor. If

Constantine was a sincere Christian, it is evident that he was rather cautious about expressing his full acceptance of Christianity on his coins.

In the course of time many historians have tried to assess the evidence relative to the conversion of Constantine. The great German-Swiss historian Jacob Burckhardt, in *The Age of Constantine the Great* (1852), portrayed Constantine as a Machiavellian prince. Burckhardt was a friend of Nietzsche and a believer in the German theory of the will to power. He pointed out that the empire was in chaos in 312 and that the Christian church was the hope for the restoration of power and stability. Burckhardt depicted Constantine as a strong and ruthless man who wanted to make use of the strength of the Christian church organization, and not being able to beat the Christians, he joined them. He thus used Christianity to enhance the power of his empire. Although Burckhardt tried to discredit Eusebius by denouncing him as a mere propagandist and a big liar, he does not produce any evidence himself to dispel the belief that Constantine was acting from deep-felt religious conviction. Fourth-century men may have been misguided, but they were not cynical in religious matters.

The contemporary French scholar A. Piganiol regards Constantine as a confused syncretist, a semiliterate peasant who thought one religion was like another, and a "muddled man" who groped his way along, not knowing what he was doing. But Constantine certainly understood what he was doing in government and war; why must it be assumed that he was so confused in religion? In the 1920's and 1930's it was common to think of Constantine as either confused or cynical. In the 40's and 50's, as a result of changing historiographical assumptions, there was a pious reaction against these theories. The English historian of Byzantium, N. H. Baynes, portrayed Constantine as a sincere and devout Christian hero, and the French historian J. S. Palanque expounded a theory of the three stages of Constantine's conversion: first, the monotheism of the unconquerable sun, which his father taught him; secondly, the belief in a spiritual deity, which came to him about 310; and finally, the actual acceptance of Christianity before the battle of the Milvian Bridge. Palanque sees a full and true conversion in 312, with Constantine as a firm and devout, if superstitious and not well-informed, member of the church. Palanque's interpretation of Constantine's conversion, while needlessly complex and oversubtle, is the best yet presented.

Constantine, it must be remembered, was not a well-educated man. In his anxiety before the battle of the Milvian Bridge he actually thought he could strike a bargain with God. This gamble on Christianity apparently led to his victory, and he therefore became a supporter of the church. Constantine believed in the great power of a monotheistic deity in any case, and the pressure of the period before the crucial battle concretized his beliefs in the direction of the Christian God. It is true that the emperor was not baptized until he was on his deathbed, but infant baptism was not general in those days; Constantine, for the last twenty-five years of his life, was a sincere Christian. His character was such that he was more active and impulsive than intellectual and spiritual, more subject to fits of temper and violence than to quiet contemplation. Clearly he was no saint, but he looked upon himself as a man with a mission. He felt that he had been called on to save the Roman state and to further the Christian church, and he thought of the two institutions as being tied together. Very early in his imperial career Constantine sensed that the church could act as a backbone for the empire. Hence he made desperate attempts to preserve the unity of the church, believing that God had given him a personal commission for this task. His efforts, religious and political, preserved the empire for another hundred years and blunted the power of such divisive heresies as Arianism and Donatism. In this work Constantine proved himself a man of vision and high ideals and demonstrated his unflagging energy and administrative skill. Constantine's understanding of Christianity was never very sophisticated; yet from his own point of view he was a devout Christian. He had laid the foundation and prepared the way for the Christian church of the middle ages.

From the beginning of his reign Constantine tried to help the church by granting special privileges to the bishops. He apparently intended to act as the representative of the church to the non-Christian population of the empire—he called himself "bishop of those outside the church"—and to allow the bishops to administer the internal affairs of the church. But Constantine soon discovered that this was not possible. From all sides he was immediately called upon by the bishops to settle doctrinal disputes which were threatening to split the church apart. The church had not yet developed a system of universal authority to define dogma. Each bishop was left to decide such questions in and for his own episcopal see. This led to the need for some great council of all bishops of the empire to consider and settle these problems; the Council of Nicaea in 325 was the first such general meeting. Constantine presided and tried, with only momentary success, to impose a dogmatic formula to which all parties could subscribe.

The western participation in the Council of Nicaea was small, because the Arian controversy, which it was summoned to settle, was purely a Greek problem. In the first three centuries of its existence the Christian church had come to adopt the culture of the various areas in which its believers dwelled. Thus there was bound to be a doctrinal and dogmatic split between the east and west. The Christians of the eastern Roman empire, the Greek-speaking part, desired that dogma be defined in logical, philosophical terms.

The Latin world was for the most part free of the Christological heresies that consequently plagued the eastern church. To the western Christians their Greek-speaking fellows were trying to define the indefinable—the trinity of God, Son, and Holy Spirit. The deeply philosophical problems that were of such overriding importance to the easterners gave way in the west to more pragmatic problems of church administration and consideration of the relationship between the deity and man. In the west it was not until the twelfth century that Abelard tried to come to grips with the definition of the trinity, which for centuries had appeared as beyond human reason to the Latin church. In the east, from the fourth century to the late sixth century, the leaders of the church kept unflinchingly to their self-appointed task of analyzing the godhead. The eastern insistence on philosophical and logical definitions led to numerous disputes, which centered themselves in two great heresies: the Arian in the fourth century and the Monophysite heresy in the late fifth and sixth centuries.

Arianism, named after its originator Arius, an Alexandrian priest, insisted on a strong definition of the distinction between God and Christ (God the Father and God the Son). This view reflected the resurgence of Graeco-Roman polytheistic concepts within Christianity; Arius, like the pagan Greek thinkers, tried to make distinctions and levels in the godhead. The western church was immediately anti-Arian, recognizing the danger inherent in such a retrogression to polytheism. The eastern church was badly split on the Arian question, with nationalist feeling aggravating the situation. There had been bitterness of long standing between Alexandria and the other great eastern cities. Not only did Alexandria resent and feel jealous of the new bishop of Constantinople, but also the Egyptians had never been fully satisfied with imperial rule. In the fourth century there was a great resurgence of nationalism in Egypt. It is clear that the Arian religious controversy was based in large part on national and cultural differences. The upshot of the dispute by the later fourth century was that the bishop of Rome and the emperor both took the side of the patriarch of Constantinople, increasing the desire of the Egyptians to break away from the empire. Their nationalist feeling was expressed in Arianism in the fourth century and the Monophysite heresy in the sixth century. More than two centuries of bitterness culminated with only token resistance being offered to the conquering Moslems by the Egyptians in the seventh century.

The Donatist heresy was more important than others to the Christians of the western church. It led to a conflict between Donatism and Catholicism which, with a long hiatus from 700 to 1050, lasted from the fourth to the sixteenth centuries. This is the fundamental doctrinal dispute in western Christianity. In the fourth century Donatism was confined to its birthplace of North Africa (the present Algeria and Tunisia), where it divided the old and militant Christian community into schismatic and orthodox churches. Donatism, named after a certain bishop Donatus, one of its founders, was an indirect outcome of Diocletian's persecutions. The governor of the North African province had been quite lenient, merely requesting the Christians to make a symbolic repudiation of their faith by handing over their scriptures. The wealthier Christians adopted this convenient course of action. But when the persecutions ended, they found themselves branded as "traditores" (betrayers) by a group of zealots, mostly from the poorer classes, who demanded that only the heroic saints who had in no way betrayed their faith be regarded as members of the church.

The Donatist puritans claimed that the traditores had lost grace and were not even Christians any longer. They demanded that the sacramental rites be administered by priests of pure spirit, and held that sacraments administered by unworthy priests were invalid. The Catholic majority maintained their belief that it was the office of the priest and not his personal character or quality that gave sacramental rites their validity. This was the pivotal point of dispute—a church of saints as against the Catholic (universal) church. At the end of the fourth century the great church father and native North African, St. Augustine, mustered all his learning and eloquence against the Donatists in behalf of the Catholic position, but neither the arguments of the Catholics nor even the persecutions waged by the orthodox emperor entirely prevailed against the Donatists. They became an underground church and disappeared only after the Moslem conquest in the seventh century. Donatism reappeared again in the west in the second half of the eleventh century. Its absence from the Christian religious scene for several centuries enabled the Catholic church to assert its leadership in early medieval Europe, a task that could not have been successful had the church followed the Donatist ideals of exclusiveness and not attempted to bring *all* men into the fold and tried to civilize them.

In the high middle ages literate and self-consciously moral laymen demanded, in Donatist fashion, higher standards of morality from members of the clergy. When they were not satisfied in this regard, certain zealots among them denied the distinction between laity and priesthood. In various parts of western Europe heretical theories, all traceable to the Donatist outlook, made their appearance. The church fought the heresies with all the means at its disposal, because they struck at the foundations of Catholicism, but it was never able to root out Donatism completely. By the sixteenth century many people felt that the Donatist position was right. The Reformation, in the instance of Protestant sectarianism, showed its Donatist heritage: to be a full member of the church, you had to have a conversional experience and you had to have a conviction of reception of grace. The problem the Catholic church faced was that in absorbing society there was the chance that, just as society would be civilized and changed by its association with the church, so too could the church be barbarized by society. Had Christianity remained a religion of the elite, this danger from society would have been reduced, and the Donatist ideal of a church of the saints could have been realized. But a church of the saints could not at the same time be a catholic church bringing the means of grace to all mankind. There never could be a compromise between Donatism and Catholicism. Poor Constantine was bewildered by the Donatist dispute. His attempts at peace-making between the two groups inevitably failed.

In his dealings with the church Constantine was advised by his friend and biographer Eusebius, bishop of Caesarea in Palestine. Eusebius' *Life of Constantine* is one of the most important works of medieval literature. It sets the pattern for the ideal life of a medieval king. Medieval kings were by and large hard, brutal, and barbarous men until at least the late eleventh century. The lives of these men were written, however, by clerical ministers of the king who wished to portray their masters as men of noble virtues called to their office by God and as great friends of the church, as well as temperate and kind. Gregory of Tours (sixth century), in his *History of the Franks,* presents a life of the Frankish king Clovis modeled after Eusebius' Constantine. Clovis is even called a second Constantine. In the late tenth century a series of biographies of the early dukes of Normandy, by a French cleric named Dudo, also reflected the Eusebian prototype. This Norman work showed great craftsmanship. Appearing eighty to a hundred years after the fact, it follows the Eusebian tradition of consciously trying to create what should have been, rather than reporting what actually was. The historical facts of these lives are questionable, not because the authors were ignorant of the truth, but because they very cleverly presented what they wanted.

Early medieval historical literature, like hagiography (saints' lives), was based upon the concept of presenting a fulfillment of the ideal and not the actual. This historiography followed the Platonic conception of the *idea* of what a king, emperor, or bishop should be. Medieval historical writing is full of saints performing miracles in fulfillment of the authors' conception of the ideal saint, and of kings likewise conforming to an ideal pattern. This literary emphasis on the ideal lasted at least until the eleventh century. Early medieval literature had no room for the real personality, for individual characteristics. Following on tendencies already evident in late Roman writing, the ideal and the general drove out the real and the particular. In early medieval historiography only occasionally in contradictory passages is there a breakthrough of realism; for example, Gregory sometimes reveals Clovis as the thug he was. There is a question of whether such an occasional departure was due to a weakening of the idealistic conception or simply a lessening of literary craftsmanship.

Eusebius, then, attempted to show Constantine as he should have been but probably was not. Constantine is for Eusebius the fulfillment of the lines of universal development set down when the Roman empire (under Augustus) and the Christian church were inaugurated at the same time. According to this thesis of Eusebius, the world entered its greatest stage with the joint inauguration of the Christian faith and the Roman imperial power, both personified in Constantine. The Roman empire would make sure that Christianity lasted forever, Eusebius believed, and God would reward the empire with yet greater glory and happiness. The deflation of this kind of optimism came only with the failure of the empire at the close of the fourth century. Then the optimism based upon the unity of the empire and the church gave way to the pessimism accompanying the realization that the empire was after all ephemeral, and the destiny of the church was independent of the rest of the empire. This was to be the theme of Augustine's *City of God*. Eusebius lived in a time when great, happy things seemed about to occur. They did not, but we can hardly blame Eusebius for his optimism. All indications in his day were in the direction of an era of unprecedented happiness and progress. Assuredly God would reward the empire for becoming Christian! Augustine's pessimism was no less socially conditioned, because even as he died in 430, the Vandal invaders threw themselves against the walls of his episcopal city.

Eusebius has been badly treated by modern critics; it has been fashionable to compare him unfavorably with Augustine. Medieval writers, while they were deeply indebted to Augustine in many ways, of course, did not find Eusebius' historical views at all shallow, as we have seen. Whenever a king favored the church, he would be hailed as another Constantine, and an optimistic tone would enter into contemporary accounts of the ruler. Assuredly God would bless and reward a devout Christian king with victory and glory!

Constantine's final effort on behalf of the church was the founding of a second Rome at Constantinople. Despite all of his efforts in the first decade of his rule, the Roman aristocracy remained devoted to the ancient rational pagan gods, and most of the old ruling class in the eternal city did not convert until the later fourth century. Constantine did not feel powerful enough to force the old aristocracy into the church, but rather hoped he could undermine the position of Rome in the world and sabotage the influential position of the pagan aristocracy. The Roman aristocracy continued to enjoy wealth and power in the west and in Rome particularly. In building Constantinople, Constantine envisioned a new imperial capital where Christianity would be supreme and unchallenged. Eusebius tells of a miraculous dream bidding Constantine to establish a new capital in the old Greek city of Byzantium on the Hellespont, where it would have the added advantage of not being liable to capture by a frontal attack, due to its impregnable strategic position.

The new capital of Constantinople was, by Constantine's direction, designed in imitation of the original Rome. It was filled with the ancient art work of many Mediterranean cities. He even imported from Rome a proletarian mob, which he called "the Roman people," to give the new city a flavor and appearance of the old. In the long run, despite his efforts and great plans for his new capital, Constantinople only heightened the disintegration of the Roman empire. The creation of a new eastern capital encouraged the division of the empire between an eastern and a western ruler, which had already been tried by Diocletian. Several times in the fourth century there were two emperors, and after 395 the Latin and Greek halves of the Mediterranean world were never politically reunited. By the sixth century Constantinople had become firmly Greek in language and culture. The new capital turned the people of the eastern Mediterranean away from Rome and encouraged their growing separation from the Latin west and its culture. The Justinian code, published in the sixth century, was the last work of Latin literature originating in the eastern part of the empire.

But Constantinople was at least a great new fortress in the east and, in that capacity, was to serve as the savior of Christian western Europe in the early middle ages. In its strategic position at the crossroads of east and west, Constantinople was able to hold back the invasions of various oriental races and religions, blocking them off from the road to Rome and western Europe. The most important instance of this service was the halting of the Moslem advance at the walls of Constantinople in the eighth century. But for Constantinople's role as the fortress of Europe, the people of medieval Europe would have been overwhelmed by the religious determination and military superiority of Moslem armies.

In the short run, the effect of the building of Constantinople did not fulfill Constantine's hopes. The prestige of Rome in the Latin world was not harmed by the new eastern capital. Constantinople was merely an alternate Rome, and there remained the real questions of whether the old Roman aristocracy could be converted to Christianity and whether the full transformation of Rome into a Christian city would be completed. This work was accomplished in the century following Constantine's death by the succeeding Christian emperors and by the bishops of Rome.

III. The Christian Roman Empire

The Roman emperors' acceptance of Christianity in the fourth century raised the problem, for the first time, of the relationship between the church and the Christian monarchy. This was to remain one of the fundamental and characteristic problems of medieval civilization. It would be no exaggeration to maintain that this church-state relationship was the dominant continuing theme in internal European affairs until the twelfth century.

The roots of the relationship lie in the period before the triumph of Christianity. In the ancient world there was a very close identity between royal authority and priestly authority. The authority of kingship was buttressed by association with the divine, and on the other hand, the priesthood was frequently a political as well as a strictly social power. It is well known that the rulers of Mesopotamia and Egypt were associated with the god head. Even the hardheaded Romans of the first two centuries A.D. were partly influenced by these traditions of sacred kingship. The solar theology of the third century went much farther. A full-fledged charismatic basis for the emperor's authority was developed. The idea of the emperor as the vicar of God with semidivine attributes slowly but certainly became influential in political life. The culmination of this intellectual trend was a kind of political monotheism: it was believed that there was one god in heaven and one emperor on earth who was the representative of, and participant in, divinity.

Before Constantine the leaders of the church had perforce to reject this political monotheism because their God was not the god of the imperial propagandists. The most they could say for kings and emperors was that they were a necessary evil. Many early Christians were actively or passively disobedient to the emperor. In accordance with the early church's eschatological bent the authority of the earthly powers (governors, kings, emperor) was regarded as very temporary and limited; it would pass away with the last judgment, which the Christians expected in the not too distant future.

The advance of a Christian to the imperial throne produced an inevitable reconsideration of the church's attitude to kingship. As long as the emperor was a non-Christian, sometimes openly anti-Christian, the theoretical question of church-state relations scarcely arose; the church could take a negative attitude to the state without any doubt or hesitation on the part of its leaders. But the emergence of the Christian king raised a host of new problems, for which the solution was not readily apparent.

The readjustment in the church's conception of kingship was further made inevitable by the close involvement of the emperor and bishops in each other's affairs in the fourth century. Heresies, schisms, and requests for state interference in the life of the church by Christian bishops on the one side, and what J. B. Bury aptly called the emperor's despotic instinct to control all social forces on the other, brought about a close union between church and state.

From the time of Constantine the Christian Roman emperor played a commanding part in the life of the church. The history of the church in the fourth century was largely determined by the fluctuating policies and theological views of the various Christian emperors. We have seen how all this was already obvious in Constantine's reign, which saw the intervention of the state in church disputes, the clash of secular and ecclesiastical aims, and the antagonism of, as well as cooperation between, the emperor and the bishops. The lugubrious and at times ridiculous incidents of church-state relations in Constantine's time were repeated over and over again in the reigns of his successors to the end of the fourth century. We must remember that Arianism was not rooted out simply by being condemned at the Council of Nicaea of 325. The conflict between the orthodox bishops and the Arian party and other heretical groups continued in bitter and frequently violent fashion until the last decade of the fourth century.

The disorders caused by violent divisions in the church on questions of doctrine called for the intervention of the public authorities, and the rival Christian parties in the fourth century—the Arian and Orthodox groups and other such parties—were only too eager to secure the aid of the government to suppress their opponents. Hence, at the very beginning of the Christian Roman empire Constantine had been able to establish the tradition that it devolved upon the emperor to settle questions of doctrine largely at his own discretion, and also to summon general ecclesiastical councils, to preside at them, and to dominate their proceedings.

This situation could not but encourage a general drift to the re-emergence of the third-century political monotheism in a Christian form. Constantine regarded *himself* as divinely commissioned to be emperor. Eusebius thought that the *office* of emperor itself was a divine commission on earth and that the emperor was elevated to a position higher than the church as a whole. Eusebius applied the political ideas of solar theology to the Christian emperor and, in his panegyrics on Constantine, enshrouded imperial power with a sacred aura. Here is the beginning of the later (sixth-century) Byzantine ideal of the king-priest, in which the emperor is indeed both caesar and pope. By the sixth century the emperor conducted ecclesiastical policy in accordance with this caesaropapist doctrine, which proclaimed him the vicar of God on earth and superior in religious authority to the patriarch of Constantinople and all churchmen. This doctrine was not even challenged in Byzantium until the eighth century, and it always remained the dominant tendency in the Greek Christian world, passing eventually from Constantinople to Moscow, the third Rome. In Russia caesaropapism originated an autocratic tradition which, in secularized form, survived even the tsars.

It is not hard to delineate the great harm which came to the empire, the church, and even to western civilization from the adaptation of political monotheism by Christian leaders in the fourth century. The fundamental cause of the failure of the Catholic church to preserve its unity in the middle ages was that different views came to be held in east and west on the validity and usefulness of preserving the fourth-century principles and practices of church-state relations. The Latin bishops, who, out of gratitude to the emperor and because of simple inertia, had gone along with caesaropapism, began to develop other ideas in the last two decades of the fourth century. By the end of the fifth century the bishop of Rome was denying the right of the emperor to interfere in church doctrine and discipline, and the resulting centuries-long dispute was the chief cause of the schism between the Greek and Latin churches. Yet something very much like the Roman-Byzantine idea of sacred monarchy came to be taken up in the west in the eighth century and eventually was the cause of momentous struggles in medieval Europe. And those pernicious and shopworn doctrines of royal absolutism, which were not entirely done away with in the modern world until the twentieth century, have their ultimate origin in the political monotheism of the fourth century.

Even in Byzantium itself the extravagant claims derived from political monotheism had disastrous consequences. Not only did they alienate the bishop of Rome, without whose support the Greek emperor's claim to Italy could not be fully realized, but they also led directly to the loss of the richest provinces of the eastern Empire to the Moslem invaders in the seventh century. The emperor in the fifth and sixth centuries, as the self-designated vicar of God and head of the church, felt compelled to persecute very large groups of heretics in Egypt and Syria who perforce advanced from religious heresy to political treason and welcomed the invading Arabs as their saviors.

If the long-range effects of the absorption of sacred monarchy into Christian thought were in many cases unfortunate, it must be seen that great benefits accrued from the Christian acceptance of political monotheism and its implications. The recovery of imperial unity and authority in the fourth century would have been impossible without the ideology which regained for the emperor the loyalty and devotion of the illiterate masses of the empire. By the time of Constantine it is difficult to see any other basis for the restoration of popular loyalty than the association of the imperial office with divinity. Political monotheism was a political necessity; it was the pressure of political and social need which lay behind the flowering of the doctrine of Christianized sacred monarchy in the late empire. While the new ideology could only uphold popular loyalty for a century in the west, in the more heavily populated and literate eastern empire imperial unity, founded on the autocracy of the sacred emperor, survived the barbarian invasions. Political monotheism had the effect of stilling criticism of the totalitarian ways of the fourth-century emperors, and it could be contended that this despotic system was one which no Christian leader should have tolerated. But through most of the fourth century the alternative to the empire seemed to be the extinction of civilization, and to the Christian leader the empire, with its extreme religious claims, was better than complete anarchy and barbarism.

By the last two decades of the fourth century in the Latin west, the possibility of civilization surviving the empire began to enter the minds of thinking men; this made possible a more critical attitude toward the imperial ideology and prepared the way for the fifth-century rejection of caesaropapism. But by this time the bishops could afford a more independent attitude, because the Christian Roman emperors who succeeded Constantine had destroyed the two most pressing enemies of the fourth-century church, namely Arianism and organized, intellectualized paganism centered in the Roman aristocracy, and they had strengthened the church in other ways as well.

One of the chief problems facing the Christian Roman emperors after the death of Constantine was the settlement of the great Arian controversy. From the first the Arian party had been too strong to be crushed by the orthodox group without the aid of the emperor, and the orthodox bishops appealed to the Roman state to intervene in their behalf. But this dependence of the church on the emperor for the settling of doctrinal issues and the eradication of heresy soon led to a further difficulty. For what if the emperor himself should become sympathetic to the Arian party?

Constantine had been baptized on his deathbed by an Arian bishop, and his sons who succeeded him tended to be sympathetic to the Arian cause. By the fifth decade of the fourth century the situation had become critical for orthodoxy. All the voices which could be raised in favor of the Nicene Creed or in protest against the intrusion of the prince in ecclesiastical matters were silenced by the state. Many of the great episcopacies were vacant—or occupied, if not by Arians, at least by their sympathizers. Only in the seventh decade of the fourth century did a change in the fortunes of the orthodox party occur, simply because the emperors of that period sympathized with their doctrines and became more and more hostile to Arianism.

In the early part of the eighth decade of the century Arianism suffered a condemnation on the part of the orthodox emperor Theodosius I (the Great) and never recovered from this imperial condemnation. Finally, in 383 and 384, Theodosius embarked on a vigorous campaign to destroy the remnants of Arianism in the eastern half of the empire, which he ruled and where Arianism had its stronghold. He promulgated laws forbidding the meetings of the Arian sect, and henceforth the survivors of Arianism formed in the empire only obscure and powerless sects.

Thus the Christian church, in the fourth century, finally settled the great controversy which had so seriously disturbed ecclesiastical life. But it did so only by subordinating itself to the will of the emperor. Furthermore, the destruction of Arianism came too late to prevent the spread of the Arian heresy to the Germanic peoples. It was the Arian rather than the Catholic church which sent missionaries beyond the Danube and Rhine, with the result that several of the Germanic kings of the following century turned out to be favorers of Arianism. While the Arian heresy was extinguished in the empire itself by the end of the fourth century, other Christological controversies arose in the eastern Roman empire in the fifth and sixth centuries. The Byzantine emperor, following the precedent of Theodosius, nearly always took the side of orthodoxy. The result was that the heretical churches welcomed the Moslem invaders in the seventh century. Similarly the heretical church of the Donatists, lingering on in North Africa, favored the Arabic conquest. Thus the heretical controversies of the fourth century and those that succeeded them eventually did great harm to Christianity in Syria, Egypt, and North Africa. Since the state, from the time of Theodosius at least, took the side of the orthodox party, the heretics turned to the invading Moslems for help. Thus, the will of the Roman emperor could not protect the church from all the consequences of the great doctrinal controversies which began in the fourth century.

Similarly, for the eradication of the other great threat to the peace and security of the church in the fourth century, namely, the survival of paganism, the leaders of the church also had to rely upon the power of the emperor. Here the imperial policy was even more successful than in the case of the heresies.

There can be little doubt that the emergence of Christian emperors intimidated many of the enemies of Christianity and encouraged the conversion of pagans to the new religion. Nevertheless, it must be remembered that at the time of the conversion of Constantine no more than 10 per cent of the population of the western half of the empire was Christian. Because of the Roman pagan aristocracy, Constantine had been forced to found a new Christian capital at Constantinople in 330. Throughout the fourth century paganism still had zealous followers and active sympathizers, and more than once the vicissitudes of political developments in the empire led the pagans to hope for a new turn of fortune which would be to their advantage and would once more change the situation.

Paganism found its warmest defenders among the ranks of the Roman aristocracy and the Italian and Greek academic world. In the Roman senate and in the civil service the pagans remained strongly entrenched until the last two decades of the century. During the fourth century pagan piety in the upper classes became more elevated, more ardent, and more mystical. Under the influence of Stoicism and Neoplatonism many of the aristocratic pagans developed a kind of monotheism and abandoned their old lax morality for a more ardent and stern code of ethics reminiscent of the Roman aristocracy in the best days of the republic. Paganism in the fourth century cannot, therefore, be conceived as a dying relic of the past which would have slowly disappeared of its own accord as Christianity advanced. Rather, this reinvigorated, monotheistic paganism had given the old religion a new lease on life, and in the west it constituted a real threat to the security of the Christian church.

The leaders of the church were unable to vanquish of their own accord this reinvigorated paganism, and they looked to the Christian Roman emperors to help them in their missionary work. Constantine and his sons who succeeded him were inclined, however, to be cautious, in view of the strength of paganism among the Roman aristocracy. The little that Constantine's successors did to suppress paganism was interrupted at the end of the year 361 by the succession to the imperial throne of Constantine's nephew, Julian, who immediately set about reversing the religious policy of the emperors since Constantine's conversion.

Julian is generally known as Julian the Apostate. Like his uncle Constantine, he also experienced a conversion, but in the opposite direction—from Christianity to paganism. While Julian had been brought up in the Christian religion, he had acquired a taste for Roman literature and Greek philosophy, and he finally abandoned the Christian religion for that monotheistic kind of paganism already described. As long as his cousin, Constantine's son, was on the throne, he kept his apostasy from the Christian religion to himself, but after his accession to the throne he openly made a profession of paganism.

Julian the Apostate has aroused the interest of many scholars and students of literature, especially those who have a higher regard for classical culture than for Christianity. He is, indeed, a man whose ideas and character were formed by the best that classical culture could offer in the fourth century. He was well educated in Neoplatonic Greek philosophy and learned in the literature of Graeco-Roman culture. He always led a sober, austere, and ascetic life, and he had a grand vision of restoring pagan religion and classical culture to a new, high level. He did not find the means to realize this grandiose conception. Julian actually achieved very little in the way of checking the spread of Christianity and restoring paganism.

Soon after his accession to the throne he began to rebuild and refurbish the old Roman temples, most of which had fallen into decay. He soon began to persecute the Christian clergy and finally prohibited them from engaging in education. But the non-Christian peoples of the empire were more interested in various kinds of mystery religions than in Julian's highly sophisticated and intellectual brand of Roman paganism. When the emperor Julian delivered his long-winded defenses of classical religion and culture to the mobs of the cities of the Mediterranean world, their reaction was either dumb silence or scornful derision. Before he could really do any damage to the Christian church, he was killed in 363 while fighting the Persians, and henceforth the rulers of the Roman empire in both east and west were always Christian.

Julian's rule, however ineffectual, nevertheless encouraged the Roman aristocracy to resist stubbornly the advance of Christianity and left the problem of the survival of paganism in the western half of the empire an even more difficult one than it had been before Julian's apostasy. The emperors in the sixth and seventh decades of the century, while Christian, refused to aid the church in the suppression of paganism and adopted a policy of religious impartiality and tolerance. It was only in the eighth decade of the century that the church again succeeded in obtaining the support of the emperor in suppressing the remnant of paganism.

We have already seen how Theodosius had taken the side of the orthodox party and virtually destroyed the Arian party. Similarly, the leaders of the church were able to obtain his support in crushing paganism. Important steps along this line were already taken by his predecessor as emperor in the west, Gratian (375–383), who brought about the separation of paganism from the Roman state. The pagan title of Pontifex Maximus was finally excluded from the list of the emperor's titles. Gratian had the altar of victory, which had symbolized the association of the Roman state with the pagan gods for centuries, removed from the chamber of the senate at Rome, and he deprived the college of priests of the old religion of their state subsidy. In this way the meetings of the senate and the imperial dignity were removed from any official contact with the old traditional religion.

Gratian's removal of the altar of victory from the senate was the occasion for a great debate between Symmachus, the leader of the pagan aristocracy, and the ablest Italian ecclesiastic, Bishop Ambrose of Milan (St. Ambrose).

The debate makes fascinating and, at the same time, sad reading in view of the subsequent vicissitudes in the history of the freedom of thought. Symmachus is the eternal liberal with all his good and bad qualities: he is tolerant and generous, but weak and not a little naïve. This worthy Roman argues that many roads lead to God—why should the old religion of Rome, under whose aegis the Roman state had prospered, not be left in peace? Ambrose is the hard man who knows that he possesses the Truth—Christianity is the one true religion; all others must be destroyed. The modern reader will make his judgment according to his personal feelings. Two observations may be in order, however: The hard men with the Truth usually prevail over the tolerant liberal who, by his own philosophy, cannot bring himself to destroy his opponent, while his opponent does all in his power to destroy him. Second, it will be noted that the modern totalitarian idea of freedom—that freedom exists only to obey the state—is a secularized version of Ambrose's doctrine, which derives from St. Paul's view that true freedom is the freedom to obey the Truth in Jesus Christ. Is it too far-fetched to see the appeal of modern totalitarian philosophies lying in the fact that they are Christian heresies? To say this, however, is not to say that Christianity is in any way responsible for these heresies. It is to say that Christianity can never accommodate or coexist peacefully with these heresies.

Time was running with St. Ambrose, not Symmachus. Whatever the merits of their arguments, the man they had to convince was the Roman emperor, and, in the person of Theodosius I, he sided fully with the bishop of Milan. Theodosius, who had already destroyed the enemies of the orthodox Christians within the church, went further than Gratian in the matter of paganism and sought to destroy the enemies of orthodox Christianity outside the church. In 392, after he gained control of the whole empire, he issued an official proscription of paganism, forbidding anyone in any place whatsoever, even in private, to exercise any of the rites of the ancient religion.

The very grave character of this legislation led to a dangerous reaction. The remnant of the Roman aristocracy fought desperately to preserve the ancient religion of the Roman state, and finally they gathered around a would-be usurper, a general who had promised to restore paganism. For a time this usurper, this last champion of paganism, gained control of Rome, but finally, in 394, he and his army were completely defeated by Theodosius, and most of those responsible for the pagan reaction perished in the battle.

The victory of Theodosius thus marks the final defeat of paganism. After his death in 395, which followed soon after his military triumph, more laws against paganism were promulgated by his sons, who succeeded him in the east and west. All the sanctuaries and temples of the old Graeco-Roman gods that still remained were ordered destroyed. Freedom of worship was no longer allowed in the Roman empire. The only legal religion in the empire was henceforth Christianity.

After 394 the Christian church thus enjoyed alone the material and moral advantages which Constantine had conferred on the Catholic clergy in order to put it on an equal footing with the pagan priesthoods. And with the grant of new favors to the church by the orthodox emperors of the last two decades of the fourth century, the church received a large number of judicial and fiscal privileges which raised it above the common law of the empire and made it a state within a state. From the time of Constantine the clergy had been exempted from the taxes imposed on all the citizens. In the last two decades of the century the orthodox emperors went further along the line of fiscal exemptions to the church. They allowed men to leave the curial class, and with it all the tax obligations of the urban bourgeoisie, and to enter the ranks of the clergy, where they no longer had any fiscal obligations to the state. In this way the orthodox emperors of the end of the fourth century allowed the tax system erected by Diocletian and Constantine to break down in order to strengthen the ranks of the clergy.

To fiscal exemptions for the clergy were added judicial privileges. The church was allowed to have its own tribunals and to develop its own law— the canon law. Indirectly bishops could mitigate sentences passed by the imperial tribunal through the exercise of the right of sanctuary. Finally the clergy was exempted from the ordinary law courts of the empire, so that the Roman state abandoned entirely its judicial control over the Christian church. The Christian Roman emperors of the fourth century, especially Theodosius, thus made the Christian church fully independent of the jurisdiction of the Roman state.

By the beginning of the fifth century the Christian Roman emperors in the west had freed the church from doctrinal disunity, crushed its pagan enemies, and granted it exclusive privileges which made it a state within a state. It may plausibly be argued that by freeing the church from the jurisdiction of the state, Theodosius and other orthodox Christian emperors destroyed the totalitarian system created by Diocletian and Constantine which managed to preserve the empire in the fourth century. It could be said, therefore, that the policy of the orthodox emperors toward the church was suicidal as to its implications for the Roman state.

In the long-range perspective, however, the policy of the fourth-century Christian emperors toward the Christian church was fortunate for the sake of the survival of western civilization. For in the fifth century the Roman state itself in the west disintegrated before the onslaught of the invading Germanic peoples. By the fourth decade of the fifth century the Roman emperor in the west had no power outside of Italy, and the barbarian kingdoms began to emerge in western Europe. In the seventh decade of the fifth century there was no ruler left in Italy who even called himself by the grandiose, but now empty, title of Roman emperor. If the Christian emperors of the fourth century had not unified, protected, and favored the Christian church to the extent that it became a state within a state, the church might not have been strong enough to withstand the barbarian invasions of the fifth century. And thanks to the Christian Roman emperors, the church in the fifth century was still a strong-enough institution to begin the conversion of the barbarian peoples and their education in the Christian Latin culture. If the power of the church had not been built up in the fourth century, western Europe would have been given over to complete barbarism and cultural darkness in the early middle ages. The Christian Roman empire in the fourth century had built up the power of the Christian church, and now the church was to supplant the Roman state.

The emperors who followed Theodosius were incapable men. Theodosius had managed to pacify the Germans, but his sons antagonized them; in 406 the Rhenish frontiers gave way, and many tribes burst across. There was officially a western Roman empire until 476, but the last emperors had no influence in the course of events. They had even abandoned Rome for Ravenna in the early fifth century. This left the eternal city open to the invaders, and the bishop of Rome emerged as the leader, taking the place of the absent emperor.

As the Roman state disintegrated in the fifth century, the attention of men in the west came more and more to be directed to the only institution which could provide some unity and leadership to religion and education—the bishopric of Rome, the acknowledged leader of the Christian church in the west.

The first pope who seems to have perceived the great role in western civilization which the bishopric of Rome could possibly attain to as a result of the disintegration of the Roman empire was Pope Leo I, usually called St. Leo the Great (440–461). The fourth- and early fifth-century popes were weak and incompetent men who did not take advantage of the prestige of their office. For instance, Constantine asked the bishop of Rome to solve the Donatist dispute, but the pope failed to act and lost a great opportunity to assert papal influence. We must not think of the pope (as the bishop of Rome came to be called) in the early middle ages in terms of the eminent position which the papacy attained during the high middle ages. In the early middle ages the papacy only slowly and painfully, after many vicissitudes and several retrogressions, was able by the latter half of the eleventh century to begin to attain that eminent position which it secured in the twelfth and thirteenth centuries. It was Leo I who clearly formulated the doctrine upon which the papacy could make those claims to jurisdiction which came close to fulfillment in the high middle ages. St. Leo can therefore be said to be the creator of the doctrine of the medieval papacy.

St. Leo was born in the last decade of the fourth century and was elected bishop of Rome in 440 A.D. He was a member of an old aristocratic Roman family, which indicates that the church was beginning to draw upon members of the old ruling class of Rome for its own leadership. The most conspicuous element in Leo's personality, as in that of all the great medieval popes, is his indomitable energy. He worked hard to increase the educational and moral level of the clergy in the west, to improve the liturgy of the church, and he took a leading part in the doctrinal issues that arose in his day. At the Council of Chalcedon in 451 the Greek church accepted Leo's interpretation of the trinity. Finally, he did much to promote the development of canon law.

Twice, in 452 and 455, Leo, aware of the impending collapse of the Roman state, went out from Rome to engage in negotiations with barbarian kings who had invaded Italy and implored them to spare the city of Rome. In at least the first instance, in his negotiations with the Huns, he was successful. In 455 he had less success dealing with the Vandals, but it is significant that the bishop of Rome had taken the place of the Roman emperor as defender of the eternal city. As a scion of the Italian aristocracy, Leo could not conceive of the end of the empire, although there were many indications in his day that imperial authority was sliding to extinction. Yet half-consciously the pope worked to make the Roman episcopate the successor to the Roman state in the west.

The way for this transformation of leadership in the west from the Roman state to the see of Rome was prepared not only by Leo's activities, but even more by the success with which he vindicated the claim of the Roman see to theoretical supremacy in the church. It was a claim which was to prevail in Europe through all the vicissitudes of the early medieval papacy and which constituted a direct challenge to the pretensions of the Byzantine emperor.

The claim made by St. Leo to the primacy of the bishop of Rome in the church was based on the so-called Petrine doctrine. This doctrine can be traced back at least as far as the second century, and Catholics, of course, find it in the New Testament, but it was St. Leo who first gave it a full and forceful expression. The Petrine doctrine is based on the words of Jesus addressing His apostles in Matthew XVI, 15–19.

But whom say ye that I am? And Simon Peter answered and said, Thou art the Christ, the son of the living God. And Jesus answered and said unto him, Blessed art thou, Simon Bar-Jona; for flesh and blood hath not revealed it unto thee, but my father which is in heaven. And I say also unto thee, thou art Peter, and upon this rock [this has been called the most important pun in history, the Greek word for rock being Petros; of course, Christ, speaking Aramaic, said Cephas] I will build my church; and the gates of Hell shall not prevail against it. And I will give unto thee the keys of the kingdom of heaven: and whatsoever thou shalt bind on earth shall be bound in Heaven: and whatsoever thou shalt loose on earth shall be loosed in Heaven.

Interpretations of this gospel text vary greatly, as may be imagined. A common Protestant view holds that Jesus was addressing all the apostles in the person of their leader, Peter. Hence all bishops—or all ministers of Christ—have this God-given power to bind and loose. It was Leo the Great who positively established the Roman Catholic interpretation, which is made plausible by the tradition that Peter was the first bishop of Rome and was martyred there. The tendency of recent archeological work is in the direction of substantiating the historical accuracy of this tradition.

Leo's Petrine doctrine claims that Jesus intended Peter and each of his successors in the chair of Peter to be the primate of the whole church, the rock or foundation of the church, and should have absolute power over faith and morals as Christ's vicar on earth. Thus the bishop of Rome alone possesses the keys to the kingdom of Heaven. He alone is the vicar of Christ on earth. He is the chief shepherd of Christ's flock. This view was never accepted by the Greek bishops; it had, in fact, been denied by North African Latin Christians as late as the third century. In Leo's day the Latin church accepted the validity of the Petrine doctrine, and it was not to be questioned in the west until the twelfth century. But while the bishops of the western half of the empire recognized the validity of the claims made by St. Leo for the Petrine doctrine, the pope's effective power was confined to Italy. France and Spain were on their own, and there were to be great labors and struggles in these other areas in succeeding centuries as the pope tried to extend his jurisdictional influence and make himself the *real* head of the western church. This attempt at turning the Petrine doctrine into a practical reality was to be the main theme in the history of the medieval papacy.

Nevertheless, it is of the greatest importance for medieval civilization that in St. Leo's time the Petrine theory was universally recognized among the churches of the west. Through all the troubles in which the church found itself in the early middle ages, the doctrine set down by St. Leo served as an ideal, calling the papacy to establish an effective jurisdiction over the western church. In the Petrine theory the Roman church found an ideal which gave it the calling of supplanting the collapsing Roman state in the west as the central institution of western civilization. Due to St. Leo the papacy became an institution of such stability and permanence that none of the great changes of the early middle ages could permanently undermine its influence or destroy its prestige. Due to the work of St. Leo the Roman empire in the west found a successor in the Roman pope as the unifying force in western Europe.

In conclusion, we can look back over the whole period between the death of Constantine and the end of the pontificate of Leo the Great and see that, quite unintentionally, the Christian Roman emperors had laid the foundation for the power of the medieval papacy. During the fourth century the bishops of Rome were a succession of rather weak and incompetent men who used the great traditions and inherently vast power of their office to little advantage. Fortunately, the emperors did the popes' work for them. They crushed paganism and made Rome into a Christian city, which Constantine had failed to do and which the popes by their own efforts would almost certainly have never done. The emperors destroyed heresy and assured the doctrinal unity of the western church. They endowed the church with enormous material benefits and corporate privileges.

Then in the middle of the fifth century the Roman state in the west collapsed. All that was necessary was the appearance of a great personality on the throne of Peter, a man of bold ideas and enormous energy, for the bishop of Rome to take over the leadership of the western church from the empire. St. Leo was the right man. Thanks to the work of the Christian emperors, the foundations of papal power had been laid. The edifice would take another five centuries to complete, it is true, but St. Leo now gave the papacy its mission: from the materials provided in large part by the Christian emperors, and following the Petrine ideology of St. Leo, the work of constructing the papal authority in the medieval church could now begin.

Chapter Three

THE MAKING OF
LATIN CHRISTIANITY

I. Athens and Jerusalem

It is of the greatest moment for the history of western civilization that the leaders of the Christian church in the later Roman empire came to terms with classical culture. As a result, a great body of classical literature and philosophy was adopted into the educational canon of medieval Europe, and, even more important, many of the most significant categories of Graeco-Roman thought became central to Latin-Christian culture. This process of adaptation of classical culture by Christianity has been applauded by nearly all modern writers and has even been presented as an inevitable development.

It is readily apparent that the intellectual leaders of the church from at least the second century, if not from the time of St. Paul himself, were men who had received a thorough classical education. Hence it can be argued that these scholars were bound to bring with them the literature and philosophy of Graeco-Roman culture and to impress the fundamental attitudes of classical thought upon Latin Christianity. But this crucial cultural transference was not inevitable; it could have been resisted, albeit with certain sacrifices on the part of educated Christians. And in fact it was resisted by one of the greatest minds in the early church, namely Tertullian, the North African Latin Christian thinker of the early third century.

In the Roman empire the most puritanical wing of the Latin church existed in the large and wealthy cities of what is now Algeria and Tunisia. Perhaps something in the North African milieu made for radical puritanism, for there was later a similar tendency in North Africa when this region had gone over to Islam. Tertullian, the greatest spokesman of North African Christianity before St. Augustine, was a learned lawyer who embraced Christianity in middle age. He had no desire to bring with him his classical background. In fact, he asserted that the church had to maintain its mission by dissociating itself from classical thought. He seems to have realized much more clearly than any other church father that there were profound distinctions between the Judaic and Greek traditions. Alone among the leading patristic writers, he opposed the intrusion of the Greek dualism of body and soul and sought to maintain the Hebrew prophetic view of the *nefesh,* the whole undifferentiated human being. With fanatical zeal he denounced all secular literature as foolishness in the eyes of God and called upon Christians to reject it entirely. He denounced the Graeco-Roman philosophers as "hucksters of wisdom and eloquence," as "animals of self-glorification," and he claimed that the dialectic of "pitiable Aristotle" was the fountain of heresy. "What is there in common," Tertullian concluded, "between Athens and Jerusalem, between the academy and the church? For us, we have no need for curiosity after Jesus Christ, or for investigation after the Gospel."

Tertullian's fundamentalist position had much more to commend it than the modern neo-Thomist, who would have an inevitable synthesis of Christianity and the classical tradition, is willing to admit. The Hebraic conception of *nefesh* and the Greek dualist view of human nature are fundamentally incompatible, and the idea of human existence presented in the first three Gospels and (in the opinion of many scholars) even in the Pauline writings is basically Hebraic. Yet Tertullian's opinions were to have a decidedly minority following among succeeding generations of ecclesiastical thinkers. His radical fundamentalist view was to remain an undercurrent in Christian thought, to worry the more sensitive church leaders concerned about too easy acceptance of the world, and to explode from time to time in puritanical revolts. But the main theme in the history of Christian thought was to be that adaptation of classical culture against which Tertullian struggled so fiercely.

Already in Tertullian's day classical tradition had spent its creative force and was becoming repetitive and derivative. It is no great exaggeration to say that the only original secular work of the later empire was Apuleius' *Golden Ass,* an early form of the picaresque novel. All the important works of Greek and Roman *belles lettres* and philosophy were written before the end of the second century and nearly all before 100 A.D. Henceforth classical culture came to be dominated by academics—always a bad sign—and the classical writings were used mostly as textbooks in the schools.

It was fashionable until the end of the nineteenth century—and in some circles it is still fashionable today—to identify the classical tradition with a liberal education. If by liberal education is meant the education of a "free man," that is, a man of private income who does not have to work for a living in the ordinary sense of the word, this is true. The Roman schools of grammar (elementary education) and rhetoric (secondary and advanced education) were designed to prepare the sons of the aristocracy and the more ambitious middle class for leadership in government and law. For this almost no technical training was required. What was necessary was to be able to read carefully and to write and speak according to the florid standards of eloquence popular in the empire. A student who received this liberal education in that day—as well as in our own—had the advantage over others of being able to read and comprehend and to write and speak clearly. But actually he had—and has—very little to say. Whatever he knew of natural science, mathematics, history, geography, and economics he had to derive from the classical writings. And by the second century, with Aristotle rapidly falling into neglect, not even the most analytical and best-informed aspect of the classical tradition was being taught.

The classical tradition which came to be adopted by Latin Christianity was therefore arid, decadent, and totally bankrupt in new ideas. It was actually the church fathers who gave it a new lease on life; all the important works in Latin and Greek written in the later empire were ecclesiastical products. Why did the church fathers rescue and absorb the classical tradition and ignore Tertullian's profound strictures on the failures and delusions of classical culture? Three answers can be given. In the first place, as products of the schools of grammar and rhetoric themselves the church fathers could visualize no other educational system and curriculum than the one which, originating in Athens, had been universal in the Mediterranean world since Hellenistic times and which the Romans had adopted and spread throughout their empire as a matter of course. For their failure to engage in extensive educational experimentation, the church fathers cannot be faulted. The world had to wait two millennia for John Dewey.

An additional factor determining the adoption of the classical tradition by the church was the consequence of the double-faith doctrine. This doctrine was first clearly outlined by the early third-century Alexandrian theologian Origen and was accepted, although not without some doubt and soul-searching, by most of the church fathers, including St. Augustine. It held that there was a simple uncritical fundamentalist faith for the uneducated masses and another more philosophical and sophisticated body of doctrine for the leaders of the church. In view of the stiff opposition which the church encountered in intellectual circles even in the fourth century, it is not surprising that ecclesiastical spokesmen wanted to demonstrate that their faith was suitable for scholars and philosophers who had read their Virgil and Plato.

In the resulting attempt to achieve a harmony between biblical faith and the classical tradition, the church fathers already had the way opened up for them by the writings of the early first-century Jewish philosopher Philo of Alexandria. The great impression which Philo made upon succeeding Christian theologians may be given as a third reason for the church's rejection of Tertullian's puritan position. The Jews had emigrated to Alexandria almost as soon as it was founded, in the time of Alexander the Great. By the time of the reign of Caesar Augustus, a quarter of the one million inhabitants of Alexandria were Jews. In the face of the prosperous and vigorous milieu of the great metropolis the Jews became rapidly Hellenized. The Jews who had emigrated to Mesopotamia rejected the secular culture with which they came in contact and developed a massive legal code, the Talmud (the foundation of Rabbinical Judaism), to separate themselves completely from secular society and thought. The Alexandrian Jews, on the other hand, tried to demonstrate the compatibility of Judaism with classical culture. They were motivated by the same desire for acceptance by the Gentile world which has inspired modern liberal Judaism. In his numerous works Philo of Alexandria tried to demonstrate that there was a hidden allegorical meaning behind the Biblical text which was compatible with Platonism. He maintained that the obvious historical element in the Old Testament demonstrated the providence of God. Beyond this there was a moral element which favored the same virtues as those propounded by Plato. At the highest level of allegorical meaning, in Philo's view, was to be found a philosophical and theological doctrine which was very similar to the Platonic teachings.

Philo's interpretation of the Bible as containing historical, moral, and philosophical doctrines fitted in very well with the double-faith attitude of the church fathers. It was not necessary for the church intellectuals to be embarrassed by decidedly non-Platonic aspects of the Bible; these could be explained away by allegory. Hence, the prolific Christian school of apologetics and theology which flourished in Alexandria in the second and third centuries drew heavily upon Philo's writings and similarly worked to demonstrate the compatibility of Christianity with the classical tradition. Although another school of Christian biblical interpretation at Antioch advocated as late as the fifth century a more literal, historical approch to the Bible, the Alexandrian method of heavy allegorizing of the Biblical text conformed much better to the double-faith attitude of the church fathers.

It thereby became the characteristic method of Christian Biblical interpretation from the third to the fifteenth centuries.

While the Latin church, put on its guard against the delusions of classicism by Tertullian, had some misgivings about a too-easy acceptance of Graeco-Roman culture, the Greek church, following the lead of Philo, rapidly absorbed the classical tradition, particularly Platonic doctrine. The most prolific and erudite of the earlier Greek church fathers, the Biblical exegete and theologian Origen (died 254), inaugurated in Alexandria a long tradition of interpreting the Christian faith in terms of Platonism. His teacher, Clement of Alexandria, originated the legend, which became very popular in the middle ages, that Greek philosophy derived from Hebraic sources. Clement was thereby able to draw extensively upon Platonic doctrine for explication of the Biblical text. He did not apologize for his wide reading of Greek literature; on the contrary, he put forth the principle, which became almost universally accepted among patristic and medieval writers, that a classical education was a necessary prerequisite for full understanding of the holy scriptures.

The persuasive arguments of the Alexandrian fathers left to be decided by their fourth-century successors, in both the Greek and Latin church, only the question of the quantity of classical culture needed in Christian education. The great leaders of the Greek church in the latter half of the fourth century had little doubt that a liberal adaptation of the classical heritage was necessary. The organizer of Greek monasticism, St. Basil (died 379), while he cautioned that classical education was merely a means to the full comprehension of truth, was nevertheless enthusiastic about the value of Graeco-Roman literature for the inculcation of virtues conforming to the moral precepts of the Gospels and the need to harmonize the principles of Greek science with biblical doctrine. Other Greek fathers were even more enthusiastic about classical culture. St. Gregory Nazianzen, for a short time patriarch of Constantinople (died 390), denounced Christians disparaging the pagan culture as boors and illiterates who did not appreciate the advantages of education to the church. It did not occur to Gregory that Christianity could develop its own distinctive educational methods and doctrine. In his writings and in the eloquent speeches of a later patriarch of Constantinople, St. John Chrysostom ("golden-mouthed") who died in 407, can already be found the attitudes of a genuine Christian humanism which looks upon classical culture not merely as a tool to be used by the church but as something valuable and attractive in its own right. The subsequent cultural history of Byzantium was marked by occasional periods of humanist revival, especially in the tenth century. Byzantine humanism never fulfilled its promise in literature, and Greek *belles lettres* in medieval Constantinople were totally derivative from ancient models and lacking in originality. On the other hand, the classicism interjected into medieval Greek culture by the authoritative opinions of the fourth-century fathers was to exert a strong influence on Byzantine art style, again particularly in the tenth century.

While classical Greek literature was largely philosophic, or at least intellectual in content, Latin literature contained much that was amoral or even pornographic. It was one thing to read Plato; it was another to read Catullus' Lesbian cycle or Ovid's *Art of Love*. This situation, combined with greater deference to the opinions of the earlier Latin father Tertullian, led the fourth-century western church thinkers to be more cautious than their Greek colleagues about the acceptance of the classical tradition. Nevertheless, in varying degrees they abandoned Tertullian's nihilistic attitude and thereby decided the educational, and therefore the intellectual, destiny of Europe for the next thousand years. The opinions of St. Jerome and St. Augustine were decisive in this regard, as R. R. Bolgar has shown in his brilliant study of the classical heritage.

Although Jerome was born into a Christian family, he received a thorough classical education and rapidly went beyond the arid lessons of grammarians and rhetoricians to a deep appreciation of the beauty of language and form in Greek and Latin literature. In middle age, he tells us, when his reputation as a great scholar was already established, he fell ill during a trip to the east and in a dream found himself accused at the divine judgment seat of being not a Christian but a Ciceronian. He seems to have had a severe psychological and moral breakdown; he fled to the Egyptian desert, as was the fashion in more ascetic circles, and spent five years living the life of an abject hermit and in studying Hebrew. Jerome's recovery appears to have been as rapid as his breakdown. He abandoned the Egyptian desert for Constantinople, where he resumed satisfying his old penchant for classical studies, and later for Bethlehem, where in old age he settled down and completed his great translation of the Bible into Latin. It was Jerome's translation, the Vulgate, which became the standard version of the medieval and modern Roman Catholic church. The King James version is heavily indebted to Jerome's translation, a work of the greatest art and extremely high accuracy. The Vulgate could only have been written by a master philologist who at the same time had the keenest sensitivity for the nuances of the Latin language.

When Jerome's ecclesiastical colleagues reminded him of his well-publicized dream, he replied that a dream is, after all, only a dream. St. Jerome's famous dream became a popular theme in medieval literature and art, and it was nearly always thrown in the teeth of medieval scholars by anxious zealots. The primary influence of Jerome's work, however, was to forward the absorption of the classical tradition by the Latin church. His contemporaries, not the least of them Augustine, did not fully appreciate the greatness of the Vulgate. But to the men of the early middle ages the example of Jerome's life and writings demonstrated that the love of classical literature did not necessarily lead a devout Christian away from his faith. On the contrary, St. Jerome revealed not only that Christian humanism was possible and not a contradiction in terms, but also that it could render enormous service to the church in the realms of education and apologetics.

St. Augustine was much less favorably disposed toward the values of classical culture than his great contemporary Jerome. Augustine was a master of the Latin language, and he had been a teacher of rhetoric before his conversion in middle life. But partly on intellectual grounds and partly because he was, like Tertullian, a dour North African, he was highly critical of some salient aspects of the classical tradition. Yet he advocated on pragmatic grounds extensive Christian adoption of the Roman system of education and classical literature. He argued forcefully that the spiritual Israel of the Christian church, setting out on its pilgrimage to the heavenly city, should "spoil the Egyptians"—that is, take from the classical tradition whatever it found necessary and advantageous for the achievement of its ends while abandoning the useless residue. He made specific suggestions on how this program might be carried out. The Roman system and curriculum of education ought, he said, to be preserved in order to maintain a literate church, and he also advocated the preparation of compendia of the liberal arts, textbook summaries of those aspects of classical philosophy and literature which conformed with Christian doctrine. In his theological writings Augustine himself drew heavily upon Platonic philosophy.

The suggestions for the right relationship between Christianity and classical culture set down by Augustine had a tremendous influence in the early middle ages, and between the fifth and eighth centuries Christian education followed the line he had set down: the continued study of grammar and rhetoric as the staple of the educational curriculum, and a drawing-up of compendia of the liberal arts. This was due not only to the force of Augustine's own authoritative influence on Christian education but also to the general cultural circumstances of that period. In the first place, as late classical culture became more and more sterile and academic, there was a general tendency even before Augustine to reduce classical thought to easily read summaries or compendia. But such compendia were exactly what Augustine was urging for Christian education. In the second place, the harassed and relatively ignorant world of the period between the barbarian invasions and the meliorative Carolingian monarchy of the eighth century could not assimilate the full intellectual fare of classical culture. It could only imbibe the classical heritage through the media of compendia, summaries, and encyclopedias.

Thus, both St. Augustine's influence and the circumstances of the intellectual history of the west between the fourth and eighth centuries brought about the Christian church's receiving the classical heritage through the media of summaries and brief treatises on rhetoric and the liberal arts and sciences. The defects of their treatises are more obvious than their merits. They are meager and jejune to the extreme; the scientific knowledge they provided was frequently derived from the realms of fancy and superstition. Yet inadequate as these encyclopedias of classical thought were, they provided the bridge between the fourth century and the flourishing Carolingian schools of the late eighth century.

The first of these encyclopedists and "Latin transmitters," as they have been called, was Martianus Capella, a contemporary of Augustine and a fellow North African. It is uncertain whether Martianus was a Christian— Christianity never enters his treatise—but medieval men certainly believed he was, and his work remained very popular and influential well into the twelfth century. His treatise bears the strange title *The Marriage of Philology and Mercury;* it begins as an allegorical romance and ends as a textbook of the seven liberal arts. It was indeed Martianus Capella's treatise which fixed in the early medieval mind the number of the liberal arts as seven, although, of course, this was supported by a Biblical text from the book of Wisdom: "Wisdom hath builded herself an house, she hath hewn out seven pillars." And even the universities of the high middle ages organized their arts course according to Martianus' division. In Martianus' treatise the seven liberal arts (which appear initially as the seven bridesmaids to Philology) fall into two groups, one of three and the other of four arts. The threefold group (which medieval writers hence called the trivium) were the literary ones: grammar, dialectic, and rhetoric. The fourfold division (the quadrivium) were the "mathematical" or, as we might say, the nonliterary or technical arts: geometry, arithmetic, astronomy, and music. It is highly significant that medicine and law were omitted from the liberal arts by Martianus and hence from the arts faculties by the high medieval universities and even our modern academic institutions. Like Augustine, he argued that medicine and law were not "liberal" studies because they were concerned with "earthly" things—or, as we would say, they were applied, as against pure, sciences. Martianus' treatise on the liberal arts became the foundation of the curriculum of the early medieval schools; his exclusion of medicine and law from the liberal arts had therefore an unfortunate effect on early medieval culture. His rather snobbish attitude to medicine and law, which became typical of early medieval scholars, is a primary reason why the knowledge of medicine was so meager in the early medieval west and why the study of Roman law was scarcely pursued, at least outside of Italy, until the eleventh century. Medicine and law revived as academic subjects in the eleventh and twelfth centuries only as postgraduate studies to be undertaken after completion of studies in the liberal arts. Even our modern American universities seem to be influenced, at least indirectly, by Martianus' treatise. There is really no reason why undergraduates cannot undertake the study of law; it is certainly no less liberal than economics and sociology.

To Martianus' treatise was added the encyclopedic work of two Italian scholars, Cassiodorus and Boethius, in the early sixth century. They were both members of old Roman aristocratic families, and both rose to high positions in the government of the Ostrogothic king Theodoric. It was Cassiodorus' first intention, in working for the preservation of the classical heritage in the Germanic kingdoms, to found a sort of Christian university in Rome. The troubled political and social conditions of the time made this impossible; and he therefore sought to employ the growing monastic movement for this purpose. It was Cassiodorus who founded the first monastery that was a center of scholarship, as so many other monasteries later became. Cassiodorus' summary of the liberal arts was the result of the need to formulate a program of education for his monastic scholars. While Cassiodorus of course believed that the ultimate aim of a monastic education was the study of theology, holy scripture, and church history, he claimed, in the now traditional way among Christian humanists, that for the proper attainment of this end the study of the liberal arts must come first. Consequently Cassiodorus prepared a sketch of the seven liberal arts, a kind of syllabus of universal knowledge, and appended to it a bibliography of classical writings which would further the monks' liberal studies. Cassiodorus' program was the basis of the curriculum of the monastic schools of the early middle ages, and thus it was a very important contribution to the preservation of the classical heritage in the west. To read the classical works he suggested, the monks needed copies; hence the slow emergence of some monasteries as kinds of publishing centers where the selected classical texts were copied either for the libraries of these monasteries themselves or to be sent to monastic houses not so well equipped nor advanced in scholarship.

Cassiodorus' contemporary, the philosopher Boethius, undertook to translate into Latin the entire works of Plato and Aristotle. He did not live to complete this work, but his translation of Aristotle's logic was the only text of the great philosopher available to the early medieval west and was therefore a very important contribution to the preservation of some semblance of Greek philosophy in the early middle ages. Boethius' own treatise, *The Consolation of Philosophy,* is one of the few philosophic works of the period between Augustine and the eleventh century which still has anything to say to modern readers. It was written while Boethius was awaiting execution for treason against the Ostrogothic king, and it provided a neat summary of the classical ethical theories, with a dominant theme of stoicism.

The final great contributor to the classical heritage in the west from the fourth to the eighth century was the early seventh-century bishop of Seville, Isidore, who also came from an old Roman, non-Germanic family which moved from North Africa to Spain in the sixth century. Isidore exercised a great influence on medieval learning through a twenty-book encyclopedia called the *Etymologies.* This strange title reflects Isidore's belief, common in the early middle ages and the result of the prevalent concern with allegory and symbolism, that the road to knowledge lay through the origin of words. Isidore's philological knowledge was very inadequate for etymological inquiries, and his work is riddled with fantasies and superstitions. Yet it was immensely popular and influential because Isidore did not confine himself to the liberal arts, but attempted to survey the whole range of knowledge of the Graeco-Roman world, including medicine, biology, botany, and architecture. For early medieval men his work also had the advantage of systematic arrangement and succinctness. In spite of his numerous errors, he managed to carry over to the early middle ages a great deal of information derived from fields outside the pure liberal arts. He is perhaps not to blame if medieval scholars for several centuries treated his work with unnecessary respect and repeated without critical reflection his fantastic opinions, which he in turn frequently derived from writers of the late Roman empire.

The so-called Latin transmitters were neither original thinkers nor masters of language. They were school teachers and textbook writers. Almost nothing they wrote is still worth reading for its own sake. But their role in the history of culture was a most important one. To these dedicated but mediocre thinkers was given the momentous task of fulfilling the program of Christian preservation of the greater part of the classical tradition. This program had evolved out of the great debate on the values of classicism, which was one of the dominant themes of patristic thought between the second and fifth centuries. The great church fathers had decided in favor of a Latin Christian culture, and rejected the radical puritanism which Tertullian represented. It was left to their humble successors from the fifth to the eighth centuries to put this program into practice with the limited means at their disposal. They did their work just well enough for the church to remain literate and in touch with the classical heritage. There is an enormous falling-off in the level of erudition and intellectual sophistication between Augustine and Isidore of Seville. But the Latin transmitters, however inadequate themselves as writers and thinkers, made possible the cultural revival of the late eighth- and ninth-century Carolingian world which witnessed a partial return, at least, to the rich and vibrant culture of the patristic age.

II. Augustine's Pilgrimage

In 430 A.D. the inhabitants of the North African city of Hippo (near what had been the ancient Carthage and what is today Tunis) realized that civilization as they had known it was in its final days. A few years before, the Vandals, one of the more primitive of the Germanic peoples, had invaded North Africa, and in 430 they were in the midst of obliterating the remaining Roman power in Africa. At this terrible moment only the bishops were left to provide leadership and comfort. The bishop of Hippo, however, who was St. Augustine, the greatest thinker of his age, lay on his deathbed. Some of the North African bishops wanted to flee the country, and they wrote Augustine for advice. He replied that if the spiritual leaders deserted their flocks, the ordinary people would have no guidance in the face of a cataclysmic situation, and the reputation of the church would suffer; the bishops should stay at their posts until the end. It is believed that Augustine died before the Vandals sacked and destroyed his city. His voluminous writings, however, survived to become one of the chief sources of instruction, inspiration, and also dispute among Christians to the present day.

From the eighteenth to the twentieth centuries, during the heyday of liberal religion, Augustine's work fell into disrepute. But since the First World War, as western civilization has experienced enormous changes which parallel the disasters of Augustine's day, many religious thinkers and even sophisticated secular men have again turned to the Augustinian literature for insight into the relationship between the world and the spirit.

It is unlikely that more than a handful of the people of Hippo in the early fifth century realized that their bishop was the most profound and comprehensive thinker the Christian church had yet produced. Augustine's episcopal colleagues recognized his intellectual importance and tried to lighten his pastoral duties, but he never disregarded his flock. Most of Augustine's doctrines were developed as answers to questions of the moment which came up in his pastoral work. He was not a professor of theology who had the leisure to develop systematic theory, but a cleric facing vexing problems of faith and ethics as a daily experience. The effect of this pragmatic nature of the Augustinian writings was that, on the one hand, they not infrequently lacked clarity and contained contradictions, but on the other hand, they were expressed with a passion and a consciousness of the real problems of life such as is rarely matched by any great Christian thinker from his day to this. Toward the end of his life Augustine wrote a little book called the *Retractatio* (Reconsideration). He surveyed the corpus of his work and admitted that he had not been entirely consistent, that he had in fact said things in the heat of argument which were extreme statements of his central position. These inconsistencies and extreme remarks were to be a source of dispute among Christians in the middle ages, during the Reformation, and to the present day. On the other hand, they reveal Augustine as the most human of all Christian theologians, as a thinker whose work reflects not the drab consistency of academe but rather the agonizing day-to-day efforts of a great philosopher and saint to explain the world in terms of the Christian faith.

Augustine's greatest problem as bishop of Hippo was the suppression of the Donatists who, in spite of excommunication and imperial edicts, remained strong and vociferous in North Africa. From this conflict he worked out his doctrine of the nature of the church and the sacraments, which became the orthodox teaching of the Roman Catholic church to the present day. Augustine claimed that the validity of the holy rites was separate from the morality or degree of perfection of the priest administering them. The true validity of the sacraments depended upon the priesthood's divine commission; the sacraments received their effectiveness from God, the giver of all grace, and as long as the priest was officially ordained by the church, the administration of the sacrament was valid. Against the puritan Donatist ideal of an exclusive church of the saints, Augustine went on to define the Christian church as universal, ecumenical, and catholic. He could see no justification in the Donatist claim that the power of the church was vitiated if it allowed some evil men among its membership. Eventually God would judge all men and separate the evil ones from the kingdom of heaven. The church on earth, however, was only an imperfect preliminary form of the heavenly city. The function of the church was to bring the possibility of grace to all men; it was the social body of Christ—the human, and therefore unavoidably imperfect, mundane expression of the holy spirit. There were good men outside the church, Augustine concluded, and bad ones within, but it was the church's duty to try to bring all men into it and thereby advance the realization of the heavenly city. In consequence Augustine, taking as his Biblical text Christ's words "compel them to come in," believed that physical force could be justifiably used to bring about conversion. He knew well enough that force was not sufficient, but on the other hand, he believed that it was far easier to win over people to Christian doctrine once they were formally members of the church. In his desperate struggle with the Donatists he called upon the state to bring the misguided heretics back into the fold, thereby facilitating his task as religious teacher and missionary.

Augustine's doctrine of forced conversion did not avail against the Donatists, because imperial power was too weak, but it was accepted by the medieval church along with his general teaching on the nature of the church and the sacraments. It is a moot point whether Augustine would have approved of the violence used in later centuries against heretics and Jews. It must in any case be remembered that Augustine's doctrine of compulsory church membership reflected his desperation at being unable to win back the Donatists to the fold. It also reflected his Roman background. Like many men heavily influenced by classical thought, Augustine was greatly concerned about the maintenance of order in society, and religious homogeneity was for him not only a religious, but also a social, necessity.

Augustine's flock would thus have known him not only as a pastor to whom they could appeal in trouble, but also as a severe enemy of heretics and even, in a weak and unfortunate moment, as a persecutor. Above all they knew him best as a preacher. In this he excelled, and his sermons became the model for medieval and even later Protestant preachers. Augustine, in fact, wrote a treatise on how to write a sermon—there is no aspect of church life that he did not concern himself with in his writings—and here we can see how his personal experience at Hippo is reflected in the rules he gives for sermonizing: the preacher should always take account of the nature of his audience and of his subject; the language he employs must always be simple enough for his audience to understand, and if the preacher sees from the movement of his audience (in the medieval church the parishioners stood throughout the service) that he is not being understood, he should then rephrase his idea; the sermon should get to the fundamental points and not get lost in unimportant matters; above all, the preacher should make clear his exposition of doctrine by relating it to the actual experience of his audience.

One of the characteristics of Augustine as a Christian teacher was this readiness to speak of the problems of salvation in terms of the experience of his parishioners and himself. He was never reluctant to reveal his own thoughts and his own spiritual crises; few other Christian thinkers have been so frank and outspoken in self-revelation. Augustine was about as far as anyone could get from the stiff-necked, self-righteous Pharisee; far, too, from a disembodied scholastic like Thomas Aquinas. He had suffered all the temptations of Adam's race; he had known the depths of despair; in fact, he did not become a Christian until his thirties. No other Christian theologian has ever spoken so convincingly about the weaknesses of human nature. Sin was not, for Augustine (as it was to be for Aquinas), an intellectual category to be analyzed by the syllogism; it was an ever present reality in human experience. Hence, although we think of Augustine as a pessimist, to his flock in Hippo he appeared as a compassionate teacher who offered them hope. They knew into what depth he himself had fallen; he often reminded them of it. They knew of his agonizing intellectual and spiritual pilgrimage. The only sin against the spirit which shall not be forgiven, Augustine told them in one of his best sermons, is the condition of impenitence. But even

> this impenitence or impenitent heart may not be decided as long as man lives in the flesh. For we are not to despair of any, so long as the Divine Patience leads the godless to repent, and does not hurry him out of his life. God willeth not the death of a sinner, but that he should return from his [evil] ways to live. He is a pagan today; but how do you know whether he may not be a Christian tomorrow? . . . What if they whom you see to be now in any sort of error . . . should before they end this life, this present life, repent and find the true life that is to come? Wherefore, brethren, judge nothing before that time.

In these words Augustine summed up the course of his own life as he saw it.

Born in 354 in a small North African town near Carthage, Augustine was the eldest of three children. His father was a *curiale* and, like other members of this urban middle class, was experiencing genteel poverty. Augustine always disliked his father, who was a pagan. and he was always deeply devoted to his mother, who was a devout Christian and who had the greatest single influence on him during the early part of his life. Like many other great religious leaders, for example John Wesley, Augustine was clearly a mama's boy, and like others of this psychological type he was precocious, painfully introspective, and deeply sensitive. Augustine had no Latin blood; he was a non-Aryan Berber, a race which in his own day, and even more in medieval and modern times, has been noted for its intensive, puritanical religiosity. Augustine's mother wanted him to be a Christian, and his weak father would have agreed to his early baptism, but in his day it was a common practice to postpone this sacrament to early manhood, when it was supposed to erase the sinful consequences of adolescent sexual passion. This was dubious psychology and erroneous theology. In later life Augustine emphasized the necessity of infant baptism and was chiefly responsible for the Catholic church's commitment to this practice.

In his *Confessions* Augustine expatiated on his early wallowing in the sins of the flesh. This, however, is more theology than autobiography. In describing his selfishness as an infant, Augustine was expounding the doctrine of original sin. In the famous story of the theft of pears the child Augustine steals fruit even though he is not hungry, merely to build up his reputation in the eyes of his friends. The purpose of this anecdote is to demonstrate the nature of sin as rebellion. All we know of the young Augustine indicates that he was a studious, serious, and in fact rather priggish lad. Augustine also pictures his young self as deeply bothered by an uncontrollable libido. Here again there is a theological argument, for sex, to Augustine, most clearly reveals both the inability of reason to control will and the resulting weakness of human nature. Yet, if Augustine was ever guilty of sin in the common-sense use of the word, it was in the direction of concupiscence, and this only to a moderate degree. After his ambitious and doting parents had sent the youth to Carthage to study rhetoric, the necessary gateway during the empire to success in law and public life, he acquired a mistress, kept her for fifteen years, fathered a son by her, and abandoned her after his later conversion to Christianity.

At Carthage the God-intoxicated Augustine underwent his first great religious crisis. He had been studying Christian doctrine and preparing for baptism, but his close study of classical literature and philosophy turned him away from his mother's faith. To this young intellectual Christianity seemed too uncouth, irrational, too far removed from the classical tradition. He momentarily solved his spiritual malaise by becoming a Manichee. Manichaeism was an offshoot of the old Persian Zoroastrian religion which emerged in the guise of a Christian heresy because of its absorption of Christ and the Pauline writings. Manichaeism posited an absolute dualism, an eternal struggle between the god of light and the evil god of darkness. In this world there were three divisions of men: the elect, who were ascetics and sons of light; the auditors, who were preparing to be sons of light; and the damned, who were the minions of the god of darkness. The Manichees rejected the cardinal Christian doctrine of the incarnation; Christ was merely another name for the god of light. Similarly they favored only the Pauline writings, the most philosophical part of the Bible, and rejected all else as absurd and illiterate. To a serious young man like Augustine, steeped in classical thought, Manichaeism offered an attractive compromise: it allowed him to keep Christ while rejecting Christianity. And Manichaeism offered a solution to the problem of evil, perhaps the most difficult of all religious problems and one which obsessed Augustine throughout his life: the Manichees simply affirmed evil as an independent substance, the creation of the god of darkness. For ten years Augustine remained a Manichee while he studied and then taught rhetoric at Carthage, and began the slow climb up the ladder of success in his profession. Finally he abandoned Manichaeism, partly due to his mother's persuasion and partly because he concluded that the dualist solution to the problem of evil was too crude.

Although Augustine, as bishop of Hippo, was a bitter opponent of the Manichees, some modern scholars have seen in his mature theology a carry-over of Manichaean attitudes. They point out that Augustine's distinction between the elect and the damned of mankind resembles the Manichaean scheme, and while admitting that Augustine abandoned the absolute dualism of the Manichaean theology, they claim he was sometimes betrayed, in the heat of argument, into writing as if there were an absolute evil as well as an absolute good. It may be replied that a man of Augustine's passionate temperament and deep concern with the problem of evil was bound to make very sharp distinctions which could be interpreted as reflecting Manichaeism, but in fact the Augustinian theology strongly negates the existence of evil as an independent substance.

Augustine's solution to the problem of evil is derived not from Manichaeism but rather from Neoplatonic doctrines which he took up shortly after his arrival in Italy in 383. He was pursuing a successful career as a professor of rhetoric and was destined for a great career in public life when he experienced another of his intellectual earthquakes. He left his job, turned his back on the world, and devoted himself to Neoplatonic spiritual exercises. In the end he found Neoplatonic catharsis impossible; he was too much of a sensual man to become entirely Godlike and enter into mystical union with the deity. But Neoplatonism taught him that all of God's creation was good and that evil was only the perversion of the good, the falling away from God. Later he incorporated this Neoplatonic doctrine into his theology, and it became the common teaching of the medieval and modern church on the nature of evil.

Augustine's conversion from Neoplatonism to Christianity, in view of his inability to achieve a full mystical experience, is not surprising. In his *Confessions* he tells a charming story of how, meditating in the garden, he heard the voice of a child telling him to "take up and read" the Bible. Not surprisingly, he took up the Pauline writings which he had studied even as a Manichee, and St. Paul told him, "put ye on Jesus Christ and make no provisions for the flesh in concupiscence." To Augustine this meant that faith in Christ as savior allowed men to escape the bondage of the flesh and enter into union with God, which otherwise was impossible. In each man,

Augustine later taught, there are two wills: the spiritual and the carnal, the heavenly and the earthly, as the soul is directed either to divine or selfish ends. Only through the mediation of Christ can man escape the bondage of the carnal will and live according to the spiritual will. In this way Augustine explains and emphasizes the Pauline doctrine of justification by faith.

In his *Confessions* Augustine set out to demonstrate his doctrine of salvation by the example of his own experience. All the while he was wandering in the darkness, experimenting with one intellectual system after another, God was leading him to that moment in the garden when he realized the necessity of faith in Christ. Predestination, Augustine implies, cannot be conceived of at every moment in human life; in fact, it may rarely be perceived in the course of a human experience. But years later, as we reflect on our experiences, we can perceive the invisible hand of God leading us to the supreme moment of truth, when in a flash the saving grace of God becomes evident to us. This is what Augustine meant when he told his parishioners, "judge nothing before the end." The saving grace of God is not something we can see at work from day to day; but in the totality of a human life, in balancing up the vicissitudes of experience, we can see that the road we have gone is not an aimless one, but is in conformity with the decree of divine destiny. This is the message of hope which Augustine holds out to his audience, and he implies in his *Confessions* that if the saving grace of God could have come to him, then it can come to every man. Indeed Augustine in the *Confessions* is the symbol of Everyman, of weak, foolish, blind human beings struggling along in desperate lives to which meaning is given only by divine decision.

Shortly after his conversion Augustine became a priest, and in 395 he was chosen bishop of Hippo in his North African homeland. Augustine's role in the history of thought is as the gateway between the ancient and the medieval worlds. He was the last great representative of classical thought and also the creator of medieval theology as H. I. Marrou has shown. Augustine had an abiding faith in nonempirical, purely intellectual construction; he knew little Greek, mathematics, or science. He had a taste for hagiography and miracles. He was a master of the Latin language, and his rhetorical skill was exceeded by very few Latin writers. For his philosophic system he was deeply indebted to the Platonic tradition, but his work sounded the death knell of ancient philosophy. He inaugurated a new world view. Socrates and Plato had identified knowledge with virtue: if a man knows what is good, he will do good. Augustine shows easily that this doctrine violates the realities of human life. It is obvious that men frequently know what good is but are powerless to pursue it. It is obvious, as

Augustine contends, that man is not a rational animal, that will has primacy over reason, that man's emotional, irrational tendencies preclude the following of the dictates of reason. Here Augustine has prefigured many of the teachings of modern psychology. His religious existentialism also makes him a teacher whose doctrines strike a sensitive cord in the modern world. Man seems powerless to control his destiny, yet life must go on in its day-to-day struggle to find the right course. Meaningless as human existence may appear at the moment, to those who are lucky enough or, as Augustine would say, to those chosen by God will come the blinding moment of illumination, the beatific vision.

Every system of thought, whatever its various technical aspects, may be characterized by a certain pervading tone. The Augustinian tone is tragic heroism.

III. Main Themes in Latin Patristic Thought

The higher thought, the intellectual culture of the early middle ages, was the culture of the church; and even when, after the eighth century, the Germanic kings interested themselves in developing certain aspects of higher thought, such as political theory, literary expression remained in the control of churchmen. In early medieval Europe after the sixth century, to be able to write and, with the exception of a few great kings such as Charlemagne and Alfred, even to be able to read meant that you were a churchman. Thus, even when, in the eleventh century, there was a great dispute about the relative powers of pope and king and an extensive polemical literature grew up, churchmen were the ones who presented both points of view. Writings by laymen attacking the church were almost unknown in the early middle ages (indeed, until the end of the twelfth century). Even to attack the church in a written discourse one had to be a churchman, because only churchmen possessed sufficient literacy to accomplish this. For many centuries a common way of deciding whether the accused in a lawsuit was a churchman or a layman was simply to ask him to open the Bible and read. This test was almost infallible.

These considerations indicate that the literary culture of the early middle ages, except for some German folk poetry such as *Beowulf* (which was probably written down by churchmen anyway), was conditioned by the traditions and needs of the church. Perhaps the chief reason why the literature of the early middle ages is so distant from the interests and outlook of most of us is that it is church literature. Most of us would be no more interested in the writings of present-day bishops and abbots than in the writings of their early medieval predecessors.

Because of this ecclesiastical nature of early medieval higher culture, the writers who are known as the church fathers, and whose works are therefore called patristic literature, must be examined as the key to early medieval thought. For until the twelfth century the church scholars worked at all times within the framework of ideas presented in the Bible as interpreted by the church fathers and according to the theology, educational theories, moral doctrines, political philosophy, and philosophy of history found in patristic literature. Before we condemn the early medieval scholars for this conservative and traditionalist intellectual attitude, we must remember that this patristic literature was no meager background. On the contrary, the four great Latin church fathers—Augustine, Jerome, and Ambrose at the end of the fourth century, pope Gregory the Great at the end of the sixth—left behind them a voluminous body of writings which provided authoritative discussions of most of the questions which concerned the life of the medieval church. Not until the end of the eighth century did social circumstances produce scholars whose erudition and intellectual discipline even distantly approximated the culture of the church fathers, and not until the twelfth and thirteenth centuries was there anyone who could come anywhere near equaling it. Even in the twelfth century the church scholars regarded themselves as mere dwarfs sitting on the shoulders of the patristic giants. And, of course, medieval churchmen were not peculiar in the respect, almost veneration, in which they held patristic literature. The church fathers, particularly St. Augustine, continue to exercise a strong influence to the present day. Everyone knows how much Luther and Calvin owed to Augustine; but the same can be said of theologians of our own time, such as Karl Barth and Reinhold Niebuhr. Nor should we forget that the translators of the King James version of the Bible into English in the seventeenth century were greatly indebted to Jerome's Vulgate Latin translation. In general we may say that patristic literature is rich with suggestions, perceptions, and guidance on almost every aspect of life. Medieval men were not foolish or unsophisticated when they regarded Augustine, Jerome, Ambrose, and Gregory as authorities. The Latin church fathers were thinkers of enormous erudition, deepest piety, wisdom, and occasional profundity. It must be remembered that in the early middle ages patristic literature faced no competition in its conditioning of higher culture. There was no higher culture outside the church, and within it there was no Greek scientific revival such as that which brought Aristotelianism to diminish patristic authority in the twelfth and thirteenth centuries.

Thus, if we search for a term which succinctly describes the higher culture of early medieval Europe, we could do no better than to use the phrase, the Biblical-patristic tradition. The text of the Bible was, of course, the starting point for all theory. The Bible was considered the single source and foundation of all faith and thought (history, political thought, science, etc.). Nothing could be incompatible with the Bible and still be respected. For example, no one could believe in the eternity of matter, because Genesis speaks of the creation of the world out of nothing. However, it was the Bible as the church fathers had interpreted it in their voluminous writings which was the fundamental authority. By way of Biblical interpretation, a whole host of intellectual tendencies and attitudes developed by the fathers entered medieval thought.

What were these prevailing tendencies in patristic thought, in addition to the emphasis on the Bible as the foundation of all faith and thought? First of all was a tendency which makes theology possible and the allegorical interpretation of the Bible a necessity: what has been called the double-faith theory. There are two ways of knowing the faith: by the simple faith and creed of the uneducated layman, and by the more sophisticated, philosophically enriched faith of the church scholar. Originating in the Greek church, the double-faith theory was made into a commonplace of the outlook of the early medieval Latin church by the patristic writers, especially Augustine. Although the double-faith theory did not entirely produce beneficial effects in medieval life—sometimes it was taken to imply that there was no necessity to educate laymen, even when social circumstances permitted—it made possible the development of a genuine theology on the basis of Neoplatonist philosophy and the allegorical interpretation of the Bible.

The second characteristic of patristic thought distinguishes Latin Christianity from the outlook of the Greek church. In western Europe the church stressed the moral and legal aspects of religion—the relationship between God and man—as distinguished from the Greek church's emphasis on Christological speculation, which led to so many heresies and schisms. This tendency is already evident in the writings of the first great Latin Christian theologian, Tertullian. In spite of his hostility to classical culture, he could not throw away all the achievements of Roman thought. Tertullian, before his conversion, had been a lawyer, and in his writings Christian thought began to receive a legalistic impress which was to affect deeply the medieval conception of the relationship between the individual and the church on the one hand and the deity on the other. In Tertullian's writings, as in a great deal of early medieval theology in general, God appears as a sort of Roman emperor who makes specific demands upon his subjects and who issues laws that cannot be infringed on pain of severe penalty. The legalistic conception of sin as a debt for which payment of some kind will be exacted by the emperorlike God was the legacy Tertullian left for his successors, and Augustine and Gregory continued this attitude, so fastening it upon the outlook of the medieval church that it became the most frequently expressed view of sin in medieval literature.

This legalistic conception of the deity explains why early medieval men found the Old Testament more attractive than the Gospels. The deity in early medieval art and literature is represented as a judging emperor, as a God of law and wrath. The suffering, self-abnegating Christ and his weeping mother did not appeal to medieval writers and artists until the great romantic upsurge in the twelfth century. Only then do the suffering, loving Jesus of the New Testament and the Virgin Mary eclipse the earlier legalistic (Roman and Hebraic) deity.

The third principle of patristic thought was a distinctive Christian philosophy of history as opposed to Graeco-Roman historiography. In this connection Augustine's *City of God* was the most influential work, although Jerome also made an important contribution.

Fourth, patristic literature offered interpretations of how salvation is obtained through the grace of God. Here there was a variety of opinion, and in this connection it was not Augustine who exercised the greatest influence, but Gregory the Great. It was Gregory's doctrine of merits or good works, holding out the real possibility of salvation to every Christian who obeys the teachings and receives the sacraments of the church, which became a central aspect of early medieval thought.

A fifth theme in patristic thought was a characteristic view of sex and marriage which greatly influenced private life until the modern world, and which is still important in the lives of Roman Catholics. In this area the opinions of the patristic writers were virtually unanimous.

Finally, it was one of the four great Latin church fathers, St. Ambrose, who first clearly rejected the right of the emperor to interfere in ecclesiastical matters and outlined the principles which became the traditional political theory of the early medieval church.

Turning first to the Biblical tradition in medieval thought, it must be recognized that St. Jerome was, in this respect, the greatest contributor among Latin church fathers. As translator, textual critic, and commentator Jerome was the pre-eminent authority for medieval culture. There were two older Latin translations of the Bible, but they were unsatisfactory in many respects, and it was necessary for a scholar well versed in Greek and Hebrew to produce an authoritative text of the divine scriptures. Jerome's greatest task was to translate the Old Testament directly from such Hebrew and Aramaic texts as were obtainable. Although in Jerome's own day many church leaders, including Augustine, were indifferent or even hostile to his work, the Vulgate gradually became authoritative in the Catholic church during the century after his death.

The greater and best part of Jerome's work as a commentator on the Bible was done on the books of the Old Testament. These commentaries exercised a powerful influence on medieval exegesis. Jerome defined the function of the Biblical commentator as erecting a spiritual edifice on the foundation of history. While he made use of the allegorical interpretation made available by Philo and Origen, he avoided extravagant use of this kind of exegesis and frequently confined himself entirely to straightforward historical elucidation of the text. The effect of his commentaries, therefore, was to restrain somewhat the more extreme tendencies of the Alexandrian school of Biblical interpretation. Insofar as he accepted allegorical interpretation, his presentations became authoritative for the medieval church and were repeated endlessly in medieval literature and art. While it is customary to assert that medieval literature and art were heavily devoted to allegorical symbolism, it would be truer to designate this tendency, as far as it existed, as traditionalism. A great number of symbols which appear in art and literature even in the high middle ages constitute merely the traditional perpetuation of allegorical themes delineated originally by St. Jerome and other church fathers. Once set down by patristic authority, allegorical symbols tended to be perpetuated through the medieval centuries. The artist or writer of the twelfth and thirteenth centuries merely employed them as commonly received materials of his craft; it was a matter of traditionalist repetition rather than of novel, conscious symbolizing.

St. Jerome also made an important contribution to medieval historical thinking. Classical historical work tended to be very limited in both space and time. One country within a limited period was the subject of nearly all Greek and Roman historians. Universal history was unknown. But the incarnation of Christ, the most important historical event of all time from a Christian point of view, required universal history; all historical events before and after the life of Christ on earth must be related to this all-important event, and, Christ having died for all men, the history of one country was no longer sufficient. Already Eusebius of Caesarea had attempted to construct a universal chronological table showing where all known historical events lie in relation to the incarnation. Jerome took up Eusebius' chronicle, translated it, and improved and expanded it. The Eusebius-Jerome World Chronicle gave medieval historians the beginnings of a scientific historical chronology. Most early medieval historical works begin with a chronological list or table presenting the important events of world history before Christ and since the Savior's death up until their own time. Until it reached the end of the fourth century, this chronology was simply copied from Jerome's work. Indeed, no monastic library was considered complete without a copy of the Eusebius-Jerome World Chronicle. Following this approach to chronology, it was inevitable that Christians would begin using the year of the incarnation for dating. Isidore of Seville in the seventh century was actually the first writer to employ this Christian time-scheme but Jerome's world chronicle had made this new kind of historical dating inevitable.

The development of a Christian philosophy of history, however, was chiefly the work of Augustine in *The City of God,* probably the single most influential work, aside from the Bible itself, in the history of Christian thought. We should not, however, think that Augustine set out to write an academic treatise on historiography. He aimed initially to provide a Christian explanation for the fall of the Roman empire. But he was sufficiently mature in his historical sense to realize that his explanation would in turn depend on a philosophy of history. Eventually he was led back to consider the whole question of Graeco-Roman historiography. And it eventually appeared necessary to undertake a critique of this historiography in order to present an answer to the original question of the fall of Rome.

The starting point in the chain of events leading to the writing of Augustine's greatest work was the capture of Rome and the sack of Rome for a few days by some invading Visigoths in the year 410 A.D. The emotional impact on the Roman World was equivalent to the result of an H-bomb dropped on New York City. For the first time in several centuries Rome lay at the proud foot of a conqueror, even if it was only for a few days. The imminent collapse of Roman civilization could not be denied any longer.

This event was a great shock to both pagans and Christians. The pagans, of whom there were still many in the western half of the world, seized upon the sack of Rome as a reason to cast aspersions upon Christianity and the Christian God. "Rome has fallen in Christian days" was the cry of those who wanted to make the Christians into scapegoats for the decline of Rome. As long as Rome had remained loyal to its ancient pantheon of deities, the city had gone on from triumph to triumph. The decline of Rome stemmed from the desertion of the altars of Zeus and Apollo.

It is usually said that Augustine wrote *The City of God* in reply to these charges made by the enemies of Christianity. That is partly true, but it is not the whole nor even the most significant part of the story. Many Christians were as dismayed as the pagans on hearing the news of the decline of Rome. Being patriotic citizens of the empire and at the same time members of the church, they had tended to believe that the acceptance of Christianity by the Roman emperors would not impede but, on the contrary, would greatly help to increase the majesty and wealth of the empire. Surely, they had argued, God would reward the Roman emperors for their acceptance of the true faith in the fourth century by dispensing continued and unceasing progress in wealth and power to the Roman state. Had not Christ been born in the reign of the first Roman emperor? Assuredly this indicated that the destinies of the Christian world and the Roman empire were to be connected to the end of the world and the last judgment. This had been the view of Eusebius of Caesarea, writing in the time of Constantine. But now this Christian idea of progress had suffered a stunning rebuttal from the hard facts of the decline of Rome after the emperors had made Christianity the official religion of the Roman state. It was necessary to reconsider the whole question of the relationship between the course of secular affairs and Christian faith. The consequence of Augustine's reflections on these problems was *The City of God,* which took him fifteen years to write. He started in 413 and wrote it in several parts, which accounts for the fact that the work does not hang together too well. There is a general scheme in the book than can be followed if certain irrelevant passages are ignored. Twenty-two books comprise the total work: books one to five attack paganism and discuss the relation of gods to man's present life; six to ten attack those who look to pagan gods for the advantages of life to come; and eleven to twenty-two trace the origin, development, and appointed ends of two cities. Within the last group of books the first four show the origin of the two cities, the next four present their development, and the last four discuss their ultimate destinies.

From the point of view of classical historiography, it would be possible to apply the cyclical theory to this pressing problem of the decline of Rome. It could be argued that the downward phase of the cycle had come and that the world would witness disintegration and collapse, and then the whole wheel of history would begin a new circle. This explanation might satisfy some pagans, but could it be accepted by the Christians? Was not Jesus a real historical individual who had died but once? Could one conceive of an indefinite number of Christs dying and rising through all the cycles of time?

It is obvious that in writing *The City of God* Augustine was faced with just as many questions or more, and undoubtedly more important ones, from the Christian side than from the pagan. However, his friends urged him to answer the pagan attack first, and it is with the pagan claim that Rome had fallen in Christian days that Augustine concerns himself in the first three books of *The City of God.*

Against the pagan critics of Christianity Augustine begins by arguing that the degeneracy of the Romans themselves was enough to bring on the fate which their city had suffered. He admits that the empire was won by men who sacrificed themselves for the good of the state as they saw it, but in the long run the virtues of the Romans even in the best days of Rome had been very limited. Even the Roman virtues, Augustine asserts, were only "splendid vices."

Augustine replies to the charge that Rome had undergone a new period of disaster after the conversion of the emperors to Christianity with the claim that Rome had suffered many setbacks and disasters even when the Romans still worshiped their pagan deities. This argument appears to be trivial and unconvincing to us, and indeed there is ample evidence that Augustine himself was not satisfied with it. After the initial shock of the sack of Rome had passed, Augustine had time to think more carefully about the historical significance of this event. Although his captious and rather trivial argument against the pagans remains in the first three books of *The City of God,* it is clear that in the rest of the work he abandoned this approach and undertook an inquiry into the fundamental problem of a philosophy of history from whose point of view the fall of Rome could rightly be comprehended.

He handed over to an assistant, a Spanish priest named Orosius, the task of writing a detailed history to show what disasters had been inflicted on the various pagan empires, especially the Roman world before the triumph of Christianity. Several years later Augustine's research assistant finally completed this rather absurd task in a lugubrious work called *The Seven Books Against The Pagans,* which presented every conceivable crime and disaster which the world had known before the time of Christianity. Augustine, who had by now advanced to a much more profound historical understanding, was probably appalled by Orosius' catalogue of horrors. But Orosius' collection of horror stories was extremely popular in the middle ages. His crude apology was far more easily understood than Augustine's subtle doctrines.

After his initial weakness in presenting a Christian interpretation of the fall of Rome, Augustine realized that he had to undertake an investigation into the ultimate nature of the historical process. He had to develop a Christian philosophy of history from whose standpoint secular events could be comprehended and put in their proper place. He began with a critique of Graeco-Roman historiography, with emphasis on a consideration of the Greek theory of cyclical regeneration. Before a Christian philosophy of history could be developed, it was necessary to determine the validity of classical historiography.

Christian theologians before Augustine had not been able to free themselves from the influence of the Greek cyclical theory. The greatest theologian among the Greek fathers, the Alexandrian theologian Origen, had given his enormous prestige to a Christian adaptation of the cyclic theory. Origen claimed to find Biblical support for the Greek view of history in the famous aphorism of the book of Ecclesiastes, "there is nothing new under the sun." This is scarcely strange, because the book of Ecclesiastes is the part of the Old Testament which shows the greatest influence of Hellenistic thought. Origen went on to assert that Christ has often suffered and will often suffer, on the grounds that what was beneficial once will always be beneficial. He believed that man dies over and over again, and that Christ suffers over and over again on behalf of man. The incarnation of Christ is thus repeated over and over again through the cycles of history.

It was Augustine who first saw clearly that nothing could be more antagonistic to the Christian dogma of the incarnation than this cyclic theory of history. By the cyclic theory, he warned, "the infidel seeks to undermine our simple faith dragging us from the straight road and compelling us to walk with him on the wheel." Those who believe in such an interpretation of history, he said, "do not know how the human race and the mortal condition of man took its origin, nor how it will be brought to an end. . . . God forbid," Augustine concluded, "that we should swallow this nonsense that the same revolutions of time and temporal things are repeated and are destined to be repeated through countless ages of the future."

Against the cyclical theory Augustine pointed out that the incarnation of Christ, His life on earth, was a unique, single, and never to be repeated event in history: Christ died once and for all for our sins. In the Augustinian view Christian faith implies that, notwithstanding all appearances, human history does not consist of a series of repetitive patterns, but makes a sure, if unsteady, development to an ultimate and final goal. History has a definite beginning, the creation of the world, and a definite end, the last judgment. Within this definite of time the greatest single event was the life of Christ. The incarnation of the Lord inaugurated the sixth, and final, historical era. It was a unique event to which all history before leads up and to which all history must relate.

Important corollaries follow from this linear conception of history centered on the historical life of the Savior. Christ died for all men, and in the sight of God there is neither Jew nor Gentile, barbarian nor Greek. Therefore history comprises the history of the whole human race, from the first man, Adam, to the last judgment. The only possible Christian history is universal history, the history of the entire human race. A history of one people, such as Greece or Rome, which satisfied classical historiography, is no longer sufficient or even valid. Christianity requires a universal history which reveals the workings of God's providence in relation to the destiny of mankind. The Eusebius-Jerome World Chronicle had already taken this view of history.

It also follows from Augustine's conception of history, as pointed out by T. E. Mommsen, that every human life and every human action is in itself of value to the historian, because it plays a part in the providential course of universal history. This attitude, which in the twentieth century is usually called historicism, contradicted the Greek belief in the validity of repeating patterns of identical situations and psychological types, a belief which had not allowed for the unique character and significance of the individual historical event and personality. It is not too much to say that Augustine's conception of history discovered the importance and value of the individual human personality. It is as individual souls that we are judged by God, and it is therefore as individual unique personalities that we take our place in the providential historical process.

From this attack on the classical philosophy of history and its replacement by a Christian theory founded upon the doctrine of the incarnation Augustine proceeds to an attack upon the Christian idea of progress, which had made it so difficult for Christians to understand the fall of Rome. If we begin, Augustine says, with the individual soul, we find that there is a struggle between the spiritual will and the carnal will for mastery. Those men in whom the carnal will predominates love themselves to the point of contempt for God. Those men in whom the spiritual will is predominant love God to the point of contempt for self. Hence we may group humanity into two communities, two societies, two cities. One is the city of God, the community of those in whom the spiritual will is triumphant. The other society is the earthly city, those men in whom the carnal will predominates. Ever since the fall of Satan or, as far as humanity is concerned, the time of Cain and Abel, there have existed these two cities, which are at every point in sharp contrast. The one is the city of Christ, the other of the devil. The one is the city of good, the other of evil. This vast generalization refers to angels as well as men. It comprehends the whole human race, all the numerous peoples gathered throughout the earth, and it takes in also the whole of human history.

The life of the two cities extends from the beginning of the race to the end of the world. During this period of human history the two societies are mixed physically but separated spiritually and morally. Only the life of the inner man, the condition of each individual soul, determines who belongs to the city of God and who to the earthly city. On the day of judgment the citizens of the two cities will be separated physically as well. The citizens of the city of God will attain eternal life; the members of the earthly city will suffer eternal damnation.

It must be emphasized that, in understanding St. Augustine's theory of the two cities, neither the city of God nor the earthly city can be fully identified with any existing state or institution. The pagan Roman empire is not the earthly city, nor is the Christian church the city of God, although in both cases there is a vague relationship similar to the way in which mundane things reflect Plato's pure ideas. The struggle between the heavenly and the earthly cities is a struggle which takes place outside the ordinary level of history. It occurs within the inner man, within the individual soul. We refer collectively to the souls in whom the spiritual will has triumphed as the city of God, and similarly to those in whom the carnal will has triumphed as the earthly city. But salvation remains a matter of individual souls, not of collective groups or organizations. "Mystically we call them the earthly and heavenly cities," says Augustine.

The Augustinian doctrine of the two cities makes a Christian idea of secular progress impossible. History, in the Christian view according to Augustine, must take place at two levels of meaning. The ordinary level of secular affairs has indeed great significance, for the events which take place in human history are determined by providence. They are moments in the line which leads from the creation through the incarnation to the last judgment. The incarnation inaugurated the sixth and final era in history. But while the historian must value each individual event in history as a reflection of the workings of providence, he cannot presume to know God's purpose in ordaining the events which fashion the destiny of mankind. The Christian historian takes note of decline and failure as well as of political and economic success and prosperity. The decline of the Roman empire must have a place in the providential scheme of history as well as the golden age of the empire at its height. It is not, however, for the historian to find God's *purpose* in these changes in the course of the history of civilization. It is not for us to regard the failure of a state or a civilization as a punishment of God, just as it is not for us to regard the success and prosperity of a state or civilization as the reward for human virtue.

All the events of secular history are but the background to the inner and truly significant history of mankind, the history of the two cities. But since this history is founded upon the relationship between God and the individual soul, it is a history which only a divine, not a human, author can presume to write. The most important events that happen in history are beyond historical knowledge. In Augustine's view, therefore, the Christian looked upon the rise and fall of civilization as indeed ordained by providence, without presuming to judge exactly why providence has decreed these drastic changes in the history of mankind. We know only that such changes are related to the incarnation and the last judgment, and therefore ultimately they are ordained for the salvation and welfare of mankind. The Christian knows that civilization may rise and pass away and that the only history which is really important in the eyes of God—fundamental, essential, and not relative—is the history of the two cities. The Christian gets a glimpse of this history in the struggle that goes on within his own soul between the spiritual and the carnal will. But it is only at the last judgment, when the citizens of the earthly city and the heavenly one are separated for all time, that a fuller understanding of the history of the two cities will be made known.

Although Augustine fully answered the Christian doubts and questions on the fall of Rome by showing that the cyclic view of history is incompatible with Christian faith and by demolishing the Christian idea of progress, he did not really answer the pagan critics. He simply shifted the ground of the argument by revealing the proper perspective on the fall of Rome from a Christian viewpoint, an argument which, of course, the pagans could not accept. But Augustine was sufficiently sophisticated to realize that there can be no dispute beyond the level of basic assumption. He is saying to the pagan, Your arguments have no meaning for me since my assumptions are entirely different. Who can blame him for such a mature attitude? Given the assumption of the Christian faith, he is saying, the only possible philosophy of history is the one I have presented in *The City of God.* Augustine's work on *The City of God* must be seen as a great turning point in historical conception. It was Augustine who made clear the theory of history implicit in the Christian Bible. It is a view of history which merits careful consideration even at the present time. But at any time the number of thinkers who have fully adhered to it have been very few, because the Augustinian philosophy of history is ultimately meta-historical.

It is often said that Augustine's *City of God* dominates medieval historical thinking. In point of fact this is not true. Augustine's work was venerated, but his view of history was too subtle and mystical for nearly all medieval writers. The medieval historian tended to identify fully the church with the city of God, which Augustine had refrained from doing. The medieval writer, whenever he described the affairs of a king who favored the church, readily fell into Eusebius' optimistic belief in human progress through union of monarchy and church, a belief which Augustine strongly opposed. Finally, the medieval historian was constantly trying to find the hand of divine providence in the events he described, a quest which Augustine found foolish and dangerous. Augustine's theology of history imposes a self-restraint and demands a profound religiosity which was beyond the grasp of nearly all medieval writers and most modern ones as well. We still tend to identify the interests of our own sovereign state with God's will, and we still believe that the furtherance of our national interests has the support of divine providence. Against these tendencies Augustine had written his greatest work, but few have bothered to listen or have been able to understand his argument.

Similarly, on the questions of predestination and free will, the medieval church departed in practice from the strictly Augustinian position. The problem of reconciling divine omnipotence and human freedom was not invented by Augustine nor even by St. Paul, whose opinions on this question greatly influenced Augustine. The problem is already raised in the Old Testament and is, in fact, bound to arise in any theistic system. Augustine contended that men were responsible for their sins but not for their salvation. He explained damnation more in terms of Adam's fall than as a consequence of individual action. Man's nature was corrupt, and all men were condemned because of that nature. Without divine assistance no man can escape from the limitations of human nature. There is no freedom *from* anything, but only freedom *to* live according to the ways of God, and this freedom is only the consequence of God's gracious gift. In other words, the only free men are those who live in accordance with divine will, who escape from the bondage of the human will because God has chosen them for salvation. This stern doctrine was developed by Augustine in the course of a dispute with the British monk and theologian Pelagius, who claimed that man merited salvation because he freely chose to live the good life, or merited damnation because he chose to live a bad life. Augustine could not accept the Pelagian free-will position because he thought it negated the Christian doctrine of fallen man and detracted from the majesty of God.

But the church, in its pastoral work, found it hard to accept Augustine's position. It was too sophisticated and stern a doctrine to use in converting illiterate masses. It did not seem to make salvation readily available to most members of the church. Already in the century following Augustine's death some French bishops argued for a semi-Pelagian position. They held that salvation was dependent upon the grace of God, but they also said that members of the church could merit that grace. They wanted to be able to promise an immediate reward for moral action. While the church officially accepted the Augustinian doctrine at the synod of Orange in 529, in actual practice the Augustinian teaching was watered down, and the Christian ministers in the middle ages frequently discussed salvation in terms which their parishioners could take as implying an extensive degree of human free will. The medieval Catholic doctrine was set down by St. Gregory the Great at the end of the sixth century. He took the sensible approach that while salvation was a consequence of grace, the individual Christian, in fulfilling the good works which the church advocated, was demonstrating that God's grace had come unto him. In actual practice this meant that if the church member received the sacraments and followed the moral teachings of the church, he need not worry about salvation. This was not a gross violation of Augustine's position, but, on the other hand, it was not fully in accordance with what Augustine had taught. Augustine would never have accepted the performance of good works as a sign of the reception of divine grace. But Gregory was more concerned with the pastoral work of the church than with precise theological definitions. He wanted to assure his audience that any who became moral and practicing Christians merited salvation. It was hard enough to get people to do this; to advocate fulfillment of the church's teachings and still not be able to assure salvation would have placed the church in a most disadvantageous position in its struggle to Christianize European society.

To provide even greater assurance of salvation, the church by the time of Gregory the Great had worked out a scheme of penance by which forgiveness for falling away from the church's teachings could be secured. It was assumed that between heaven and hell there was an intermediary stage called purgatory. Only saints entered heaven immediately; all others had to be purified, and purgatory was the stage and place where this purification of souls, this punishment for the sins of men who on the whole were good and who would eventually enter heaven, could be carried out. But it was possible, so the church taught from the time of Gregory, for this purifying penance to be performed in this life, thereby making easier and shorter the travails of purgatory. Given the fact that the church wanted to assure its members that it possessed all the means for salvation, and given the legalistic conception of the deity, it is easy to see how this idea of purgatory and this doctrine of penance evolved.

Gregory's teaching of penance was institutionalized by the church and became a most important part of church life in the middle ages and is so even at the present time. Penance had four stages: first, a perception of sin and a dread of God's punishment; second—and this is of greatest importance—regret or contrition at having sinned; then third, a confession to an ordained priest, an intentional humiliation to the penitent; and finally, the actual doing of penance, "giving satisfaction" for the sin committed and confessed.

There were many varieties of satisfaction. It could be a contribution to the church, physical toil on behalf of the church, a pilgrimage, or even artistic work which had some religious purpose. It is well known that in the late middle ages certain abuses crept into institutionalized penance, such as the famous indulgences against which Luther fulminated. But it must be seen that, by and large, penance had a sound psychological as well as religious purpose. It allowed a church member to obtain forgiveness for many sins, and it thereby reassured him of the safety of his soul and allowed him to look forward to afterlife with less fear and dread. Through Gregory's doctrine of penance the church qualified Augustine's deep pessimism about the fate of the greater part of mankind. In fact, it played a great role in making Latin Christianity into an optimistic religion and one which was therefore more appealing to early medieval society.

The Latin church fathers were as important in laying the foundations of the political theory of the medieval church as in defining the questions of predestination and free will. From the time of Constantine the Christian emperors had virtually been the rulers of the Christian church. They even took a leading part in defining its dogma. This dominance of the emperor over the church has been given the term "caesaropapism." Slowly, in the fourth century and with a faster pace in the fifth century, the Christian emperors came to develop a theory which would substantiate on grounds of principle their *de facto* control over the life of the church.

The main outlines of this theory are already evident in Eusebius' oration in praise of Constantine in 336. The Roman empire and the Christian church came into existence at approximately the same time; hence the empire was created by providence for the furtherance of the Christian religion and the welfare of the church. Constantine's conversion made the religious significance of the empire explicit. The destinies of the empire and the church are to be intertwined and indeed synonymous. Eusebius concludes by reviving in Christian form the political aspect of the solar theology of the third century: the imperial office has been created by the grace of God, and the emperor is God's vicar on earth for the furtherance of the welfare of the Christian church and empire.

In Eusebius' panegyric it is not yet clear whether the emperor is God's chief vicar on earth or whether the bishops equal him. By the second half of the fifth century the emperor's claim to outrank the bishops because of the nature of his office is presented more and more openly and frequently. During the latter half of the fifth century this theory of caesaropapism had already become full-blown and quite sophisticated.

By that time the empire had distintegrated in the west, but the eastern Roman emperors, or Byzantine emperors, continued the policy of caesaropapism, which was not even questioned in Byzantium until the eighth century. The medieval Byzantine church was a department of the Byzantine state. The head of the Greek church both in practice and theory was the emperor. The patriarch of Constantinople became merely the emperor's assistant in religious matters. And the emperor could, and did at times, dismiss the patriarch if he disobeyed the imperial decrees.

Thus the Byzantine emperors took up and developed a theory to support their authority over the church, a theory which had already made its appearance in the time of Constantine. In spite of Eusebius' panegyric, however, it appears that Constantine thought only that he was personally chosen as the representative of God, that he did not receive this vicarate from the nature of his imperial office. Within two centuries after Constantine this personal vicarate became the official vicarate of God: in consequence of his office the emperor is the ruler of both the universal state and the universal church.

More and more Byzantine caesaropapism takes the form of the doctrine of theocratic monarchy—the idea that the emperor is *ex officio* blessed with sacred attributes. The Byzantine emperor was regarded as *rex et sacerdos* (both king and priest). He was not a mere layman; like the bishop, he also had received sacred attributes from the nature of his office. Nor was this view merely the propaganda of the emperor and the imperial court. The Greek church did not question its validity. The leaders of the Greek church continued to think along the lines evident in Eusebius' panegyric on Constantine. After all, the empire continued to exist for them; was there any reason to question the obvious fact that the destinies of the church and the Christian empire were identical?

As the culture of medieval Constantinople became more influenced with each succeeding century by the culture of the oriental part of the empire, the theory of theocratic monarchy was influenced by conceptions of divine monarchy which had dominated middle-eastern political life for many centuries. The oriental kings, such as the Persian rulers, had always been regarded as sacred and semidivine beings. Persian court ceremonial had already made its appearance in the Roman empire in the reign of Diocletian; the ceremonial of kingship in medieval Byzantium continued to borrow Persian court ceremonial, which made the king a semidivine person elevated above all his subjects, including the bishops.

The idea of theocratic monarchy could, moreover, be readily supported by reference to the Old Testament. Biblical examples and texts to support the claims of the emperor were freely used by the emperor's propagandists. Nor did the eastern church find these Biblical precedents invalid; on the contrary, the Greek churchmen were impressed by the scriptural foundations of the emperor's authority. The Byzantine emperors could, for instance, point to the example of Saul, the anointed of the Lord against whom David would not raise his hand, presumably, so it was argued, because Saul's anointment had given the king a sacred authority. The defenders of the doctrine of theocratic monarchy also pointed to the example of the Old Testament king Melchizedek ("king of righteousness"), who is reported in Genesis to have been a king and a priest at the same time. Melchizedek was held to have prefigured the archetype of the king-priest, Christ himself. Jesus was the scion of the House of David, the king of kings, and at the same time the archpriest.

This theory of theocratic monarchy was carried in the Byzantine empire to ever greater lengths in the fifth and sixth centuries, and around the person of the emperor there grew up a mystique and a religious emotion which seems very oriental in its quality. The emperor was identified with Christ himself. Just as in the heavenly cosmos there was only One who combined all power, so there was in the earthly cosmos only one monarch. This theme was strongly emphasized as a motif in Byzantine art.

Against the theory of theocratic monarchy and the caesaropapist claim of the Byzantine emperors the papacy, in the last decade of the fifth century, put forth a very different conception of church-state relations. This theory of the church on the right relations between church and state goes under the name of the Gelasian theory, after Pope Gelasius I, who gave it its classic formulation. The problem was the one with which political theorists in the early middle ages were chiefly concerned; the concept of theocratic monarchy and the Gelasian theory are hence the two leading political doctrines of the early middle ages. We shall come to trace the history of the conflict between them. For the origins of the Gelasian doctrine we must go back to the fourth century and even earlier.

One reason why the leaders of the church in the fourth century so readily accepted the domination of the Roman emperors was that they had been taught by St. Paul to have respect for the authority of the state. Medieval political theory can be said to have begun with the thirteenth chapter of St. Paul's letter to the Romans. This chapter was quoted over and over again by medieval political writers:

> Let every soul be in subjection to the higher powers: for there is no power but of God; and the powers that be are ordained of God. Therefore he that resisteth the power withstands the ordinance of God: and that they withstand shall receive to themselves judgment. For rulers are not a terror to the good works but to the evil. And wouldst thou have no fear of the power? Do that which is good, and thou shalt have praise from the same: for he is a minister of God to thee for good. But if thou do that which is evil, be afraid; for he beareth not the sword in vain: for he is a minister of God, an avenger for wrath to him that doeth evil. Wherefore ye must needs be in subjection, not only because of the wrath, but also for conscience's sake. For this cause ye pay tribute also; for they are the ministers of God's service, attending continually upon this very thing. Render to all their dues: tribute to whom tribute is due; custom to whom custom; fear to whom fear; honor to whom honor.

This statement, which is of fundamental importance throughout the whole course of medieval political thought, was constantly quoted from the second century onward. Paul held that ordained powers of God (state powers as well as religious) served divine ends and were therefore good. Men should remain in subjugation since the rulers of the world were God's representatives. Paul claimed that the order of civil government was a divine institution. To refuse to submit to the state was to refuse to submit to God. The real purpose of the state was to repress the evil in men that came because of Adam's fall. It is the opinion of some scholars that Paul was here offering only a temporary solution, because he thought the world was soon coming to an end anyway, and all its secular rulers with it. He was also especially concerned that Christians in Rome keep quiet and not gain an unfortunate reputation for subversion. Whatever Paul's intention, the influence of the Pauline teachings inhibited the medieval community's resistance to royal power. But resistance did begin with St. Ambrose.

St. Ambrose was the leader of the Latin church throughout the last two decades of the fourth century down to his death in 397. He was a member of an old Christian Roman family who had risen to a high position in the imperial administration. Sent to Milan as an imperial governor, he had been elected, by popular acclamation and much to his own surprise, archbishop of Milan in 374. For the next two decades he devoted himself to the administration of his see, to theological and devotional writing, and also to building up the power of the church against the domination of the Christian emperors.

Twice Ambrose dared to withstand the great orthodox emperor Theodosius I, condemning Theodosius for his acts and bringing the emperor to surrender and repentance. In both instances he attacked the emperor from his pulpit and denied him the communion of the church until he would follow the policies demanded by Ambrose. And in both instances he reminded the emperor that he was, after all, only a man and that he ought to listen to the representative of Christ so that Christ himself might protect his empire. Ambrose said that it would be impossible for him to offer the holy sacrifice to an unrepentant sinner. Theodosius was, fortunately for Ambrose, a man of very deep piety, and in both instances in which he aroused the wrath of the archbishop of Milan he gave way meekly.

The victory of St. Ambrose over the emperor of the whole Roman world caused a profound stir at the time. And Ambrose's example of resistance to secular power made a great impression on the western church throughout the early middle ages. Very often during the early middle ages, when a leader of the church in the west opposed the will of a king, he cited the example of the resistance given by St. Ambrose to the emperor Theodosius.

It can be said that the capitulation of Theodosius to the demands of the archbishop of Milan marked a turning point in the history of the relations between church and state in western Europe.

Even more influential on later developments than Ambrose's personal example was the theory of church-state relations which he had occasion to enunciate in his letters to Theodosius and in his sermons during the controversy with the emperor. The state, said Ambrose, ought to aid and protect the church. But in religious matters the civil magistrate has no authority over ecclesiastics. "Divine matters are not under the jurisdiction of imperial power." The emperor is a member of the church; hence, "in questions affecting the faith, it is the bishops who are the judges of Christian emperors, and not the emperors who are the judges of the bishops." Ambrose had great admiration for the glory of the Roman empire. Nevertheless, he advocated the autonomy of the church from the jurisdiction of the state. In the final analysis they were two separate institutions. "The palaces concern the emperor, the churches the bishop." In the churches it is the bishop, not the emperor, who rules. Thus St. Ambrose attacked the theory of theocratic monarchy, which became the basis of the system of caesaropapism.

The emperor is the supreme secular ruler, but he is not a sacred person. Ultimately, Ambrose concluded, whenever there is a conflict between divine law and imperial law, it is divine law which must take precedence over the imperial. St. Ambrose clearly formulated the doctrine that the church and the state are two separate institutions. His doctrine contains the further implication, however, that the church is ultimately the superior power because it provides for the salvation of men, including even the salvation of the emperor himself. St. Ambrose made clear, once and for all, that Christ's teaching, "render unto Caesar the things that are Caesar's and unto God the things that are God's," also applied to Caesar when he was a member of the Christian church.

St. Ambrose's boldness in attacking the emperor's authority over the church is all the more remarkable in that he was addressing the last great emperor before the disintegration of the empire, the emperor whose policies so greatly benefited the church, Theodosius the Great. Perhaps only a bishop who was himself from the highest rank of the Roman aristocracy would have dared to limit the emperor's authority in the way Ambrose did. It was Ambrose's letters to Theodosius which outlined the standard political theory of the medieval western church, just as Eusebius' panegyric on Constantine already presented the fundamentals of the political theory of Byzantine caesaropapism.

The collapse of the western empire, already becoming evident two decades after Ambrose's death in 397, made his theory all the more vital for the western church. For the only surviving imperial power was the emperor in Constantinople, who refused to recognize the new situation of the Germanic kingdoms emerging on the ruins of the old western empire, and claimed hegemony over the whole empire since (so the theory went) the entire imperial power had reverted to him. This meant that he would attempt to exercise the same authority over the pope that he was exercising over the Greek patriarchs. And if the emperor would succeed in ever reconquering the western empire, which was his stated intention as soon as he was strong enough, the western church would have to accept the emperor's doctrinal decisions. Against these threats from Constantinople Ambrose's theory offered an excellent counterclaim. In the statements on church-state relations made by Pope Gelasius I at the end of the fifth century, Ambrose's views on church-state relations were taken up, developed, and used against the emperor in Constantinople.

St. Ambrose was not, however, the only church father who helped to shape the political theory of the church. In political theory, as in most other aspects of thought, Augustinianism exercised on the early medieval church a strong general influence, hard to define specifically, but nevertheless prevalent. The disaster of 410 A.D. in Rome meant that Eusebius' exposition of the destinies of the church and the empire had become invalid for the Latin church. Book XIX of *The City of God* was strongly conditioned by this changed political situation. Augustine comforted his fellow Christians in the Latin church by maintaining that the state had no positive function in religious life. Salvation is a matter involving only the relations between God and the individual soul. For this life of the heavenly city the state provides only the necessary law and order—"earthly peace"—as a background. The state is thus, in Augustine's view, only a functional, relative institution designed to provide the proper social and political circumstances for the peaceful exercise of the religious life. But the state, of its own intrinsic nature, makes no contribution to religious life and therefore per se has no moral sanction. Of itself, the state is only "a band of pirates," Augustine concluded.

Therefore, Augustine gives to the state neither the religious and moral ends envisaged by Eusebius nor (what is perhaps a little surprising in view of Augustine's general acceptance of Pauline theology) even the divine sanctions which Paul gives to the state in *Romans.* Political Augustinianism left two legacies for the political ideology of the church. On the one hand, the church will not be inclined to question too closely into the activities of rulers provided they do not interfere in the life of the church and they provide the necessary peace and order so that religious life will not be hindered by social and political disorganization. On the other hand, of course, political Augustinianism finds no divine attributes in the nature of the king; in fact, the state is only a convenient institution having no moral sanction apart from its use to the heavenly city, of which the church is the reflected image. Thus political Augustinianism takes a dim view of the authority of the state.

Now both of these legacies affected, or were at least realized in, the church's attitude to the various rulers of the early middle ages. Speaking generally, we can say that the church followed the first legacy in dealing with the ineffective Germanic kings of the first three centuries after the Germanic invasions. The church urged the kings to maintain law and order without inquiring too closely into the many inadequacies, both personal and institutional, of the early Germanic Christian kingdoms. But when a ruler became so strong as to assume authority over the church, and especially over the papacy, then the church in self-defense proceeded to attack the theoretical foundations of kingship, pointing out that the state possessed no moral sanction aside from what it derived from the church. This principle was first used against the Byzantine emperor by Pope Gelasius I.

In the last decade of the fifth century Pope Gelasius, making use of the opinions of both Ambrose and Augustine, tried to formulate a political theory for the church. Gelasius was pope from 492 to 496. By this time it was clear that there would be a split between the pope and the emperor. The Byzantine church and emperor had adopted an heretical doctrine on the nature of Christ and wanted Gelasius to accept it also. The pope excommunicated the patriarch of Constantinople and attacked the whole foundation of the power of the emperor. He went on to define the relationship between secular and spiritual authority. He said that there could be found in the Bible figures such as Melchizedek and Christ, who were both kings and priests, but that since the time of Christ authority was divided between church and state. There were two institutions of authority in the world: the prelates exercising sacred power, and the kings and emperors holding royal power. The authority of the church was *auctoritas* (legislative), while the authority of the secular rulers was *potestas* (executive power). In Roman law *auctoritas* was superior to *potestas*. In any good state it was thought that the legislative should be supreme over the executive. Therefore Gelasius on the one hand separated church and state, but on the other hand implied that the church was ultimately superior. He wanted to separate church and state because of the immediate problem of keeping the emperor out of church affairs. But Gelasius left a loophole by implying that the legislative institution (church) gave power to the executive (emperor). Ambrose had said that because the pastor was responsible to God for the souls of his flock, he *must* interfere with the king if the state violated the morality of the church. In Gelasius' terms, ultimately the church had *auctoritas*.

At least the Gelasian theory could be used to argue, against the system of caesaropapism, that the spiritual and temporal powers are entrusted to two different orders, each drawing its authority from God, each supreme in its own sphere and independent of the other within its own sphere. But the Gelasian theory had further implications, allowing for its expansion into the doctrine of papal supremacy over the emperor, not merely implying a separation between the spheres of church and state. The Gelasian theory gave to the papacy an organized doctrine which could be made both moderate and radical in its implications, as circumstances permitted. Until the eighth century the papacy was content to draw only the more moderate conclusions from the Gelasian theory. Hard-pressed by the Byzantine emperor, the papacy was content to claim the independence of the jurisdiction of the church from royal control. Its battle to enforce this claim was a long and hard one, and in the end it only met with limited success. But in the eighth and ninth centuries the papacy began to make use of the radical aspect of the Gelasian theory. In the eleventh century Pope Gregory VII fully drew the radical implications from the Gelasian theory, demanding not only the separation of church and state but also the supremacy of papal authority over all kings.

Can we not see in this double aspect of the Gelasian theory the two legacies of political Augustinianism? Augustine implied that the spheres of the heavenly city (reflected in the church) and the state are entirely separate. This, too, is the view of Gelasius in the more moderate aspects of his theory. But Augustine also says that the moral sanction of the state is not intrinsic, but is derived only from the heavenly city (reflected in the church). Thus Gelasius contends that the imperial *potestas* is derived from papal *auctoritas* in the radical version of his theory. The Gelasian theory is political Augustinianism in a simpler, more practical and polemical form.

The foundations for the political thought of the following six centuries were laid down in the patristic period. We shall later have to examine in detail the long struggle between the idea of theocratic monarchy and the Gelasian theory as well as the tension between the moderate and radical aspects of the Gelasian doctrine. Until the Aristotelian revival of the twelfth century all disputes on church-state relations were argued along the lines of these political theories.

It is a moot question whether the Gelasian doctrine is still the political theory of the Catholic church. In view of the tremendous upheaval in Catholic thought in the 1960's, there is also some doubt whether the views on sex and marriage expressed by the patristic writers are still the teachings of the church, but it can at least be said that these views prevailed in the Roman church for fifteen centuries. Consequently, patristic teaching on sex and marriage were destined to affect the lives of millions of people and assuredly are as important in their historical significance as the statements of the church fathers on linear and cyclic history and church-state relationships.

Anybody who reads extensively in patristic literature will be impressed by the frequency with which family and sexual problems are discussed. In view of the fact that the Latin fathers developed their doctrine in most cases out of the need for guiding their parishioners, it is not surprising to find that this subject looms so large in their writings. All the patristic writers agree that sexual intercourse has only one purpose, the procreation of children. They believe emphatically that the fulfillment of sexual desire per se is a sin and a consequence and illustration of human depravity. As St. Gregory expresses this principle, "When not the love of producing offspring but pleasure dominates the act of intercourse, married persons have something to mourn over in their intercourse." He goes on to say that "Holy preaching concedes them this and yet in the very concession shakes the mind with fear." The Hebraic view, the liberal Protestant view, the modern secular view, and also some recent radical Catholic speculation hold that human nature is fulfilled in sexual love. The patristic doctrine is that human nature reaches its culmination by concentrating on the spiritual soul, by negating the physical body, and therefore by refraining from sexual love.

As a consequence, the patristic writers held that virginity is the ideal state for men and women. They supported this claim by both theological and psychological-moral arguments. To the modern reader the almost endless disquisitions of St. Jerome on this subject seem extravagant and perhaps psychotic. But it must be remembered that Augustine, Ambrose, and Gregory, who held the same views on virginity, were whole men, vigorous, and quite experienced with the ways of the world. They argued that the mother of God was a virgin, that the church was the virginal bride of Christ, and that hence the ideal state was to refrain from sexual intercourse and even from marriage. St. Ambrose tells us that those who do not marry "are as the angels in heaven." But there is a further, less doctrinal argument on behalf of virginity. In one of his sermons St. Ambrose makes a very plausible case against marriage in terms of its pain and tribulation, especially for the woman. He expatiates on the agony of childbearing and child rearing; he refers to the humiliating, slavish "ministrations and services due to their husbands from wives." And he concludes with a graphic account of how wives corrupt their souls through their devotion to cosmetics, perfumes, jewels, and clothes in order to remain attractive to their husbands. "What is there left which is her own," the observant bishop of Milan asks, "when so much is changed?" But on the other hand, Ambrose is eager to point out the blessed state of the "happy virgins" who "have indeed your own beauty, furnished by the comeliness of virtue. . . . Let God alone be sought as the judge of loveliness, Who loves even in less beautiful bodies more beautiful souls." It is peculiar that, in discussing virginity, patristic writers nearly always seemed to talk of this ideal state with reference to women, although, of course, they intended virginity as an ideal masculine state as well. The double standard was so commonly practiced in the Roman world that not even the church fathers could entirely free themselves from its assumptions when they came to give their opinions on sexual matters.

The patristic views on sex are still matters for great debate today. It is the historian's task to ask how they came to hold these opinions. Certainly they are not derived from the Old Testament, for the Hebraic view accepts sex as a natural part of life and strongly encourages marriage. In the opinion of many Protestant scholars the patristic denigration of sexual love and marriage cannot even be found in the Gospels. They are derived clearly from the teaching of St. Paul, who urged the Christian flock to emulate his own unmarried state and who asserted that marriage was only better "than to be aflame" (with desire or with sin we are not sure, although with St. Paul there does not seem to have been much difference between sin and a strong sex drive). As to why St. Paul held these views there is no unanimity of opinion among scholars. It could be said that his views on sex, like his political doctrine, were merely an eschatological ethic, a temporary expedient in view of the imminent end of the world. It could also be said that St. Paul was heavily influenced by Greek dualism of soul and body or that he was simply neurotic on the question of sex. In any case, the church fathers followed him very closely on sexual matters, far more closely than they did on questions of political doctrine. And given their tendency to view Christianity from the standpoint of Neoplatonic philosophy—their conviction that if God was spirit, man should become as spiritual as possible—their continuation and amplification of the Pauline hostility to marriage is not surprising.

To understand why the church fathers denigrated sex, we must bear in mind the difference between their social-intellectual milieu and our own. In spite of the excessive concentration upon sexual matters in modern literature and in popular forms of entertainment, the sexual practices of the Roman world were far more lascivious than our own. The Germans only substituted for hypersophisticated lasciviousness crude violence in sexual relations. The church fathers, as educated and sincere men, were inevitably revolted by the sexual practices of their society, and quite naturally they went to the other extreme and could find nothing beautiful or good in copulation—only a necessary way of procreating the species. It can, of course, be plausibly argued that the patristic teaching on sex and marriage was not extreme and erroneous but wise and socially valuable. They knew, as is too often forgotten nowadays, that the sex drive is much weaker than other biological drives such as hunger, thirst, and fear, and it is one of the easiest human drives to inhibit and sublimate. Since medieval men were rarely surfeited with food and drink and for many centuries were rarely free from fear, they had more important things to think about than sexual matters. Thus the patristic teaching fitted in well with the circumstances of early medieval society. This does not mean that most medieval men and women were virgins, but it does mean that men and women who took vows of chastity experienced little desire to violate such vows. Early medieval monks were far more troubled about getting enough to eat than they were about preserving their chaste condition. Even among the comfortable monks of the high and late middle ages the great sin was gluttony, not promiscuity. It can further be argued that the church fathers were good psychologists. It seems that they knew that sexual inhibition and sublimation increased the individual's interest and ability in other aspects of life, such as the intellectual and the religious. Even in our own society, imbued with a heightened sexual consciousness, it is a well-known fact that many men of great intellectual and administrative prowess find little energy and time for family life.

Whatever the ultimate judgment on the patristic view of sex and marriage, it must be seen as a progressive doctrine in terms of the general development of morals in western civilization. One of the most important achievements of the middle ages was a recognition of the dignity of women, an emotionally favorable attitude to feminine qualities. Roman law did something to protect the legal status of women and their right to hold and inherit property, although medieval feudal law was much more liberal in this regard. But in the ancient world, even among the aristocracy, the general conception of woman never passed beyond viewing her as a slave of her husband or father and a sexual tool and breeding machine. To the twentieth-century reader the patristic writers may seen extremely conservative, but in fact they were far more liberal than the ancients on the subject of women. By emphasizing that woman had a soul to protect and by urging women to remain dignified and independent through the virginal state, the patristic writers prepared the way for the romantic elevation and adoration of feminine qualities which came in the twelfth century. Patristic teaching on sex and marriage was the first stage in the emancipation of women from slavery to the male.

In surveying patristic thought, it may finally be asked whether patristic writers took up any of the aspects of the teachings of Jesus w imply a social gospel. From the words of Christ about the poor inheriting the earth and the difficulty of the rich in gaining entry to heaven can be derived a millennial revolutionary sentiment. This was to be a main current in Christian thought from the eleventh to the seventeenth centuries and again in the modern world. Very little of this sentiment can be found in patristic writings. The church fathers were too influenced by the Roman sense of order and by hierarchical principles to develop a social gospel. In St. Ambrose's sermons, however, can be found a limited amount of social criticism and hostility to the rich. The origins of the medieval social gospel which makes its appearance among the Italian urban industrial workers in the eleventh century has not yet been worked out by historians. When it is, Ambrose's social criticism, although it does not loom very large in his writings, may turn out to have been an influential source of this later-medieval Christian social-revolutionary sentiment.

Patristic literature is a vast sea of opinion and information; we have only pointed out certain main currents. In view of the fact that all the intellectuals of the early middle ages were churchmen and that before the twelfth century no writers appeared in Europe whose erudition and intellectual force approached the Latin church fathers', it must be concluded that the history of medieval thought until 1100 is largely a matter of working out the implications and applying in practice the doctrines of Augustine, Ambrose, Jerome, and Gregory. Even in the high and late middle ages the influence of the patristic authorities was very great. Writing in the middle of the twelfth century, John of Salisbury refers to the great scholars and thinkers of his day as merely dwarfs sitting on the shoulders of the patristic giants, and a plausible argument could be made to support this interpretation of the development of medieval thought.

The patristic writers seem far removed from our problems and our thought world. Paperback publishers do not strenuously compete to bring out editions of patristic sermons. Yet if we examine more closely the great body of patristic literature, we can find there ideas on religion, philosophy, ethics, history, politics, and sex which still have relevance to our own world. And whether we agree or not with the patristic doctrines, we must conclude that the Latin fathers, in terms of their erudition, their intellectual power, and their courage in dealing with the problems of a disintegrating society and a new emerging civilization, are among the intellectual giants of the western world.

PART TWO

My heart is mournful as I recount the divers civil wars which so grievously wear down the race and dominion of the Franks.

—GREGORY OF TOURS

Fight against those . . . who refuse allegiance to the True Faith from among those who have received the Book until they humbly pay tribute out of hand.

—THE KORAN

THE TRANSFORMATION OF EUROPEAN GOVERNMENT AND SOCIETY

Fifth to Eighth Centuries

Chapter Four

THE AGE OF THE BARBARIAN INVASIONS

I. The Germans

The second great division of medieval history covers the period from the fifth century to the early part of the eighth. It is marked by the invasion of western Europe and the Mediterranean world by various nomadic and quite primitive peoples: Mongolian, Germanic, and Arabic. The effect was three centuries of enormous upheaval and confusion, which resulted in the transformation of European government and society. The most serious of the invasions were the intrusions into the Roman world by the Germanic peoples—the so-called barbarian invasions—for, unlike the Mongolian and, for the most part, the Arabic invaders, the Germans settled in and determined the destiny of western Europe.

The word "barbarian" was borrowed by the Romans from the Greeks, who used it to designate an alien, and therefore, by definition, someone inferior in culture to a Hellene. The Romans applied the word "barbarian" in the pejorative sense to the people who came to live along the Rhine-Danube frontier. The Romans also generically termed these people *Germani*, which was originally the name of only one of the tribes living beyond the Roman frontier. Another tribe was called the *Allemanni*, which later became the root of the French and Spanish terms for "German." The Germans referred to themselves with a word which has become the root of the modern *Deutsch* and Teuton, that is, *Theut*, which simply means "the folk" or "people."

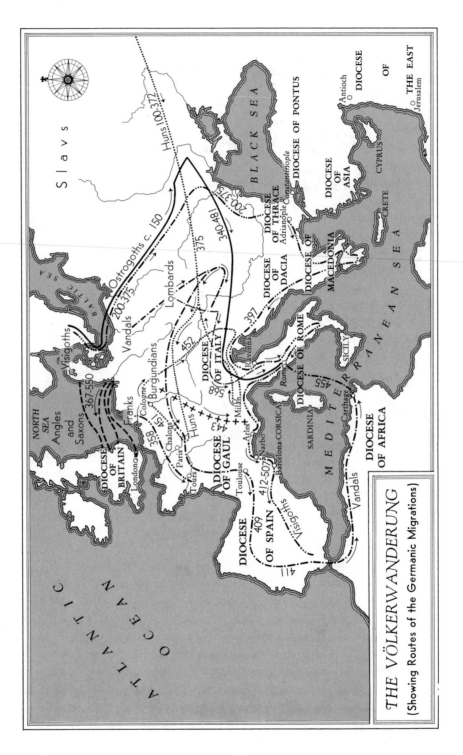

THE VÖLKERWANDERUNG

(Showing Routes of the Germanic Migrations)

Who were the Germans? Where did they come from and why? What were their political and social institutions? These important questions exercised the energy and imagination of many historians, particularly in Germany where naturally the study of the *Völkerwanderungen,* or the migration of the peoples, has been encouraged by nationalist feeling. The literary sources, however, are extremely meager, and all we know about the Germans before the first century B.C. has been derived from archeological research. These studies reveal that the German invaders of the Roman empire originally came from Scandinavia. Therefore, the later Vikings, whose migrations and invasions of western Europe came during the ninth century A.D., were ethnically the same people as the ones whom the Romans called the Germans. About 1000 B.C. the Germans began to move southward from their original homes in Denmark and southern Norway and Sweden. By 100 or so B.C., spreading south and west, they had reached the Rhine river, and somewhat later, perhaps in the first century A.D., they migrated into the Danube basin as well.

As the Germans began to press across the Rhine, they had an easy time pushing back the Celts, who were peaceful people given to agriculture, poetry, and song. The Germans would have conquered Gaul, as they later were to conquer Britain and push the Celts into the Welsh mountains, had it not been for the arrival on the scene in the middle of the first century B.C. of Julius Caesar and the Roman legions. After hard fighting, Caesar pushed the Germans back beyond the Rhine, and the Romans extensively colonized the southern half of Gaul. The Germans temporarily crossed the Rhine in the middle of the third century, during the period of transitory imperial breakdown, but the Rhine frontier was soon reconstructed. Until the final collapse of the Rhine frontier in 406 A.D. the only Germans who crossed the great river into Roman territory were the tribes who were allowed to become federates or mercenaries in the imperial army.

By the second century A.D. the Danube basin was heavily settled with Germans, who pressed on the imperial frontier in this region as well. The Germans along the Danube were dominated by the two great divisions of the Gothic nation: the Visigoths, who lived nearest the frontier, and the Ostrogoths. In the third century A.D. the Danube frontier also was temporarily broken, but the Goths were driven back beyond the Danube before the end of the century. It was not until 376 that any of the Goths were again allowed to cross the Danube river.

There is no positive evidence as to the causes of the *Völkerwanderungen.* We can only surmise the causation a priori. The Germans left Scandinavia partly because of a shortage in food supply due to population growth and partly because of continual wars between the tribes, in which the losers were driven from their homeland to seek a new place to live in the south. As the Germans approached the frontier of the empire, they came in contact with the wealth, advanced technology, and pleasant climate of the Mediterranean. They sought to get into the empire not to destroy it, but rather to participate in its higher standard of living.

The nature of early Germanic political, legal, and social institutions has aroused great interest among historians, and many tomes have been published on the subject. This great interest is due not only to nationalist motivation, but also because so many of the later institutions of medieval Europe seem to have developed out of, or at least are related to, the early Germanic ways of doing things. Particularly in the nineteenth century, when scholars subscribed to the organic view of political and legal development—that the fully developed institution is predetermined by the shape of the microcosmic primitive institutional form—they devoted enormous energy to studying early Germanic institutions.

The sources for the early history of the Germans are, in fact, meager. The most valuable description of Germanic life by any ancient historian is the *Germania* of Tacitus, written in 98 A.D., which comes to about fifty pages in modern print. Tacitus never visited the German frontier, but as a powerful aristocrat he was able to talk to soldiers who had returned from the front, and he had access to government officials and documents. Unfortunately, his purpose in writing the *Germania* was not entirely the impartial dissemination of information. Rather, he wanted to present to his readers the contrast between the primitive, unspoiled, energetic, virtuous Germans and the decadent, oversophisticated, effeminate Romans. His idealized picture of the virtuous German *hausfrau* may be taken with a grain of salt. There is, however, enough circumstantial detail about German political and social institutions in the *Germania* to make Tacitus' work extremely valuable for the historian.

The second group of sources comprises the Germanic folk poetry. Unfortunately, of this group only the Anglo-Saxon poem *Beowulf* has come down to us in a form close enough to the original version to be usable as an historical source. The great German cycle of the *Nibelungenlied,* which inspired the libretti for Wagner's operas, has come down to us only in a thirteenth-century version heavily overlaid by anachronistic chivalric sentiment. *Beowulf,* on the other hand, was written down by a cleric in the late eighth century; the Christian overlay is superficial, and the poem graphically reveals the ideals and mores of the upper strata of Germanic society. The social picture presented in *Beowulf* can be confirmed by comparing the Germanic way of life therein depicted with the mores of Scandinavian society as presented in the Icelandic sagas and eddas. While these depict

Scandinavian society in the high middle ages, they reveal a society at a similar stage of development. This stage can also be found in the Homeric poetry, which similarly is a product of what the English scholar H. Chadwick called the "heroic age." With the exception of Chadwick's pioneering work, published half a century ago, scholars have yet done little to illuminate early Germanic life through application of this comparative method of studying social institutions.

A third group of sources for the early history of the Germans is the so-called Germanic law codes. These are not really law codes at all, but merely written statements designed to amplify the greater part of Germanic law which remained oral and customary. In spite of their drastic limitations, the Germanic laws, such as those of the Burgundians, the Franks (the Salic law), and the Anglo-Saxons (the "dooms"), are extremely valuable for their information on political and legal life.

Finally, archeological evidence has contributed to the historian's reconstruction of early Germanic life. Archeology not only can trace lines of migration, but it also often graphically reveals the level of technology and culture which a particular German people attained. Thus the jewelry and other ornamental work found in the Sutton Hoo ship burial in eastern England in 1939 confirms *Beowulf*'s description of the ship burial of a great king and demonstrates the Germanic skill in metal work. On the other hand, it must be admitted that the results of archeological work on medieval history are often very difficult to interpret. This is partly due to the fact that the medieval archeologist, unlike the digger into the remains of Egyptian and Mesopotamian civilization, is limited in his archeological investigations by the fact that the sites of medieval estates, towns, and roads are still usually very much in use, and therefore systematic excavation is precluded.

The picture of the early Germans has undergone great changes in the past four decades. In the 1920's and 30's it was fashionable to emphasize the similarities of German and Roman life and the continuity of institutions through the fifth and sixth centuries, with the result that the Germanic invasions were viewed as relatively minor in their effect upon European government and society. The leading proponents of this view were the Austrian scholar Alfons Dopsch and the famous Belgian economic historian, Henri Pirenne. Dopsch, in his massive *Economic and Social Foundations of Western Civilization,* by means of dubious archeological evidence, tortured misreading of texts, and special pleading, concluded that there was very little difference in the level of culture and economy between the Germans and the inhabitants of the Roman world. The Germans in Dopsch's work appear as good Austrian burghers ready to sit down for a bit of *Wiener Schnitzel* and Löwenbräu with their fortunate Roman hosts. Likewise,

Pirenne contended that the German invasions did not mark a cataclysmic break in the economic and social development of western Europe. He attributed cataclysmic proportions not to the Germanic invasions but rather to the expansion of Islam in the eighth century.

Since the Second World War, not surprisingly due in great part to the work of French scholars, the Dopsch-Pirenne interpretation of the early Germans has been seriously undermined, and we have returned to the earlier view of the disastrous consequences of the Germanic invasions. E. Salin has presented archeological evidence which directly contradicts the material marshaled by Dopsch in favor of his thesis. P. Courcelle, in his brilliant *Literary History of the Germanic Invasions,* has convincingly argued that we ought to take very seriously the lugubrious views of contemporaries on the significance of the invasions and the actions of the Germans. R. Latouche, relying on the research of other scholars as well, has presented a synthetic view of early medieval economic development which restores the central importance of the German invasions; he has also written the best general history of the barbarian n.igrations and settlements.

From the limited written and archeological evidence that we have about the development of Germanic society from the time the Germans came to settle along the Rhine-Danube frontier to the establishment of the Germanic kingdoms in western Europe—let us say from 100 B.C. to 500 A.D. —two fundamental facts emerge which must be realized if we are to understand correctly the Germanic society in the time of the invasions. The first fact is that the degree to which the Germanic peoples across the Rhine-Danube frontier had been influenced by Roman civilization differed markedly from one tribe to another. Some had reached a stage of civilization about the same as that which they saw across the frontier along the border of the empire. They devoted themselves to agriculture, engaged in extensive commerce with Roman merchants, and accepted Christianity, although by chance it was actually Arian Christianity—they were converted by Arian missionaries in the fourth century. Such Germans only wanted to enter the empire as federates and participate in the life of the Mediterranean world. They greatly respected Roman power and had no intention of bringing harm to it. This level of civilization was reached especially among the Goths living in the Danube basin. They were in contact with the richest and most heavily populated part of the empire.

On the other hand, it appears evident that other Germanic peoples had been little affected by Romanization and were fierce, ignorant, and barbarian in every sense of the word. Most, though not all, of the Germans who invaded the empire from across the Rhine appear to belong to this category. The reasons for this are not very clear. It would seem, however, that the Germans here remained in closer contact with their Scandinavian homeland, which was, of course, closer. Here, too, there were a greater number of German peoples stacked up against the Rhine frontier, so that those who were further back from the frontier tended to be progressively less affected by contact with the empire. Thus the Franks were more violent and less civilized than some of the early invaders, such as the Burgundians. And the Anglo-Saxons, who came directly from the North Sea area, were untouched by Romanization.

Thus it is not easy to generalize about the Germanic peoples. Some were at a social and cultural level equivalent to the peasants of the empire; others indeed impress us as primitives, in spite of attempts by modern German historians to portray them as quite civilized.

The second fundamental fact which should be borne in mind in regard to the Germans of the period of the great invasions is that their political and social institutions did not remain static over the period between 100 B.C. and 500 A.D., but underwent profound changes. Like many primitive peoples Germanic society was at first organized according to blood ties—the family and kindred. While these ties were to a considerable extent preserved up to and through the period of the invasions (as shown by the blood feud in criminal cases), another form of social organization was slowly emerging, and it became central in the period of the invasions (400–600). During this period the bonds of kinship were weakened, a process which shows itself in the prevalence of strife between relatives. The binding force formerly possessed by kinship was increasingly transferred to the relationship between "lord" and "man," between whom no bond of blood relationship was necessary, only the bond of loyalty. Thus during this period there is a decrease in importance of kinship and a great increase in the use of the bond of allegiance or loyalty.

This great change in social organization went along with, and facilitated, a change in political organization, the growth of an irresponsible type of kingship resting not upon the folk but upon military prestige. To the war leader who could provide booty went the allegiance of his followers, but these followers might not even belong to the same kindred or folk as their "king."

Thus, during the period of the Germanic invasions, and at least partly the result of the circumstances of a people on the move and engaging in conquest, there is a great social and political transformation within Germanic society itself. Many of the able-bodied fighters were emancipating themselves from the tribal obligations and bonds by which a society of primitive peoples is usually governed. Furthermore, the princes who emerged among the Germans during this period were freeing themselves, to a large extent, from any public control on the part of the tribe or community. As long as they could feed and enrich their soldiers, they retained the allegiance of these warriors, and neither the king nor war band had any social or political obligation to the folk as a whole. We shall see this situation appear many times among the Germans during the Germanic invasions; the Frankish kingdom of the sixth century arises out of this social and political context.

'The basic German political institution at the end of the fourth century can therefore be said to be the *comitatus,* or *gefolge,* consisting of the chief or king and his war band, who accorded him their loyal service in return for his protection and largess. A chief who reigned for a long time or who achieved great military success was able to create a royal dynasty. The dynasty would claim descent from Woden, put on sacred airs, and possess the kingship as its private property. But succession to the kingship could not be by primogeniture; this was not an early Germanic idea and was restricted by the original power of the war band to give or refuse loyalty. At the death of the king, the leaders of the folk would come together and choose that member of the royal family who was most "throne-worthy," that is, the best fighter. While strict hereditary succession appeared very rapidly in the new Germanic kingdoms of the fifth and sixth centuries, the right of election by the folk remained a strong medieval political tradition for many centuries, especially in areas where the original Germanic institutions remained influential. The election of the king by the leaders of the community was operative in England in the later ninth century in the case of the elevation of the famous King Alfred to the English throne, and as late as 1199 the infamous King John owed his crown in part to the electoral principle. The Germanic electoral principle played havoc with dynastic continuity in the medieval German empire and, in fact, survived to the nineteenth century. The perpetuation of this aspect of early German institutions was due at least in part to the fact that it found favor with the church, which recognized in the principle of throne-worthiness a way of exercising a veto on royal accessions.

The *comitatus* was an extremely weak nucleus for the medieval state. In fact, it can be said that the Germans had no concept of a state, no idea of public authority, and no understanding of loyalty other than the personal loyalty to a chieftain. With some exaggeration, it may be said that the Germanic political theory was not above the level of that held today by marauding street gangs. The distance from the sophisticated Roman idea of public authority and office and of loyalty to an impersonal emperor who represents the state was vast, and the decline in the level of political thinking was precipitous. To understand the disastrous histories of all early medieval kingdoms, it must be remembered that the medieval state had to develop from this abysmal and crude level. Early medieval political construction was constantly challenged and inhibited by the inability of the Germans to conceive of public, as distinct from personal, loyalty. It is not surprising, therefore, that the medieval state did not begin to take shape until the eighth and ninth centuries and did not experience its first era of greatness until the middle years of the eleventh century. And even this late and partial success was only made possible by the addition of ecclesiastical (in part, Roman) conceptions of authority and loyalty to the primitive Germanic political tradition.

The original Germanic legal conceptions were scarcely more advanced than their political ideas. The purpose of the Germanic law courts and forms of procedure was not to establish justice, which the Germans had no way of determining or even of defining, but simply to stop a fight. The aim of Germanic legal process was to inhibit the blood feud, to find an alternative for an aggrieved kin or family seeking vengeance. There were various ways of doing this, and the purpose of the law courts was simply to put these alternatives to the blood feud into operation. The first of these was the payment of *wergeld* (man money), a monetary compensation to a family for the killing of one of its members, or a smaller payment to an individual who had been maimed. The so-called Germanic law code consisted mostly of tables of *wergeld:* so much to be paid for the slaying of a nobleman, so much for a freeman, so much for a serf, so much for an arm, so much for an eye, etc. The compensation required was often very heavy, and even then the aggrieved kinsmen or individual need not always accept it, and might prefer to gain satisfaction by vengeance. It was the court's duty to convince the plaintiff to take the *wergeld* and thereby preclude the outbreak of a blood feud. Nevertheless, blood feuds were frequent in early Germanic society. We know of such a feud in England as late as 1060 which decimated whole families. Anyone who reads early medieval legal records knows that life then was nasty, brutish, and short. It was a violent society in which drunken brawls ending in homicide were extremely common, and the resulting blood feuds a constant possibility.

Early medieval men did not think of a brawl resulting in homicide as murder. Their legal conception resembled that of the American frontier, at least as represented in popular literature and entertainment. To kill a man in a fair fight meant that you had to reckon with his kinsmen, but it was not murder. Murder was killing someone by stealth; murder was a homicide in which the killer was not certainly known. Such a situation put heavy pressure on the Germanic law court, for if the court did not designate the murderer, the slain man's kin would take justice into their own hands and exact vengeance from whomever they suspected. It was therefore necessary to hold a trial and prove the guilt or innocence of the suspect. But neither the methods of proof and assessment of evidence devised by Roman law, which involved a thorough inquiry by a panel of judges, nor the later common-law jury system were available to the Germanic law court. The leaders of the Germanic court would not have known how to assess the evidence even if it were presented to them. This left two methods of proof: the ordeal, involving divine decision, and compurgation, involving the swearing of oaths.

In proof by ordeal the odds were weighted heavily against the defendant. In the ordeal of hot iron the defendant was required to grasp a red-hot piece of metal. His hand was then bandaged, and if after three days the burns had healed, the defendant was innocent; otherwise he was guilty. The ordeal of hot water worked similarly: the defendant was made to put his arm into a caldron of boiling water and lift a stone from the bottom; his arm was then bandaged and in three days it was inspected to decide guilt or innocence. The ordeal of cold water was a favorite in England, where there were numerous rivers and brooks. The defendant was tied hand and foot and thrown into the water; if he sank he was innocent, and if he floated he was guilty, on the premise that water, a divine element, would not receive a guilty person. In the feudal period an additional ordeal, trial by combat between the accuser and the defendant or their "champions" (representatives), was instituted. Because guilt or innocence was decided by the strength of the champion, trial by combat did not leave the question sufficiently to divine judgment; a wealthy man could hire the biggest thug in the country and systematically get rid of his enemies through the bringing of false accusations. Hence, trial by combat was severely limited by the powerful monarchies of the twelfth century, although technically this method of proof was not abolished in England until 1819. While the three common ordeals were rough on the defendant, it must be emphasized that they were intended to be biased in this direction. For the defendant who was put to the ordeal—in England this was called "making his law"—was either someone who was reputed to be a criminal by the opinion of his neighbors or was a person of low social status. A wealthy or highborn person of good reputation in his community was very seldom put to the ordeal. The ordeal, therefore, was a method of providing divine support for popular prejudice. Through the ordeal each folk court was able to cleanse the community of the ill-famed, who sooner or later were bound to be accused of a crime and put to the ordeal.

The church was initially hostile to the Germanic ordeal; but if it was to influence early medieval legal process, it had to accept this common method of proof. After the Germans were converted, the church imposed a religious sanction on the ordeal: before going to the ordeal the defendant appeared in church and swore on the Bible or a holy relic that he was innocent, while the priest admonished him to confess his guilt in order not to damn his soul and lose eternal as well as mortal life. We think that in many cases this brainwashing resulted in confession and that thereby an element of rationality was added to the crude legal process. A defendant convicted by the ordeal was hanged on the spot, hanging being one of the Germanic contributions to civilization. At times in the early middle ages the church succeeded in having kings substitute maiming for the death penalty. Medieval medicine being what it was, the loss of a limb frequently amounted to a slow death in any case. It is also very doubtful that the community courts allowed these humanitarian pronouncements.

Compurgation was a privilege of a defendant who had popular opinion on his side, and this usually meant that he was wealthy or highborn. Compurgation greatly favored the defendant, for by this method of proof the defendant simply denied his guilt under oath and produced a certain number of oath-helpers, preferably of high social status, to swear that his oath was a true and good, or "clean" one. While the church warned about the perils of perjury, we know that this was very common in proof by compurgation. A guilty man who had important relatives or a powerful lord who were willing to lie for him would never be convicted. The conditions of compurgation further attest the underlying fact that Germanic criminal process was very class-biased. The poor, the unfree, the lordless were lucky if they did not end on the gallows, and on the contrary, the rich and well-connected could only come to this end through the most flagrant and repeated crimes, and even then usually only when their victim was himself from the upper strata of society.

It is apparent that very little can be said in favor of early Germanic process. Yet German law made one great contribution to western civilization. It was enormously inferior to Roman law except in the instance of its political implications. Roman law found its origin in the will of the despotic emperor and favored political absolutism. The king had no control over Germanic law; his only legal function was to see that the community courts met and decided cases, and even in this regard his contribution was often negligible. Germanic law was based on the principle that law resided in the folk, that law was the custom of the community, and that the king could not change this law without the assent of the community. Because of this difference between Germanic and Roman law, and because England, even in the high middle ages, remained relatively untouched by Roman law, the Victorian historians found the origin of English parliamentary institutions and the idea of the rule of law in the forests of Germany. While it has been fashionable among twentieth-century writers to scoff at this interpretation, there is an element of truth in it. The Victorians, with their organic conception of institutional development, erred in thinking that the great oak of English liberalism grew *inevitably* out of the acorn of German law. There was nothing inevitable about this development; in 1200 England appeared to be going in the direction of absolutism, and it took centuries of experience and political strife before the legislative supremacy of Parliament triumphed. But it is true that from German law England received a heritage of the legal supremacy of the community over the king. All western European countries could have drawn upon the same legal tradition. But after 1100 the Roman law principle of legal absolutism slowly won out on the continent, whereas England alone preserved the early Germanic idea that law resides in the folk rather than in the will of the king.

II. The First Century of the Invasions

From a simple comparison of the population of the empire and the numbers of the Germans, it would be hard to explain why the Germanic tribes were successful in establishing themselves on Roman soil in the hundred years that followed the Visigothic crossing of the Danube in 376 A.D. The population of the empire at this time was between fifty and seventy million people. Comparatively, the Germans were few in number. The largest of the tribes, such as the Visigoths, had only about a hundred thousand people including women and children and could not have put more than twenty thousand fighting men into the field. The total number of Germans who came into the empire during the first century of the invasions could not have equaled more than 20 per cent of the total population of the Mediterranean world, and it is probable that 10 per cent would be a truer estimate.

It must, of course, be remembered that the Roman government faced a great variety of political, economic, and military problems. The Roman army consisted mostly of proletarians and Germans, and the German generals in the service of the western emperor turned out to be in many cases unreliable. Furthermore, the empire had an extremely long frontier to defend, so that in any one place (west of Constantinople, at least) the German armies were substantial in number compared to the Roman defenders. A very large army had to be maintained in the east in order to hold back the Persians, who steadily threatened the eastern defenses from the third to the seventh centuries. It must also be remembered that those regions of the western empire which were more distant from the Mediterranean coast were thinly populated, and hence German settlement in many regions of the Latin-speaking world did have a very strong impact on the demographic situation.

The impetus to the German invasions came in the 370's from the invasion of the west by Mongolian tribes called the Huns (known as the Hsiung-hu in their Asiatic homeland). Until the seventeenth century, western Europe was to be periodically threatened by nomadic Asian invaders; the Turks were the last of these invaders, and the Huns were the first. It is believed that in the second or third century A.D. the Huns lived in what is today northern China or Mongolia. Certain internal changes in the Chinese political situation forced them to move westward. They tried to invade India, but were repulsed. They then moved with great rapidity westward and passed north of the Caspian and Black seas and down through southern Russia into the Balkans. About the middle of the fourth century they broke into the Danube basin and easily defeated and subjugated the Ostrogoths. They struck terror into the hearts of the Germans, who as yet made only limited use of cavalry and were unable to withstand the Hunnish armies, which apparently fought entirely on horseback. A contemporary Roman historian described the Huns as invincible devils who not only fought but even lived on horseback; he claimed, no doubt on the basis of stories he got from the Germans, that the Huns did not even dismount to eat, but rather warmed raw meat under their saddles and kept going.

The terrified Visigoths, who lived closest to the Danube frontier and who desperately sought a way of avoiding the fate of their Ostrogothic kinsmen, begged the eastern emperor to allow them to cross the river and find refuge on Roman soil. The emperor granted this request and the first large-scale migration of a German folk into the empire took place peacefully in 376. Almost immediately there arose all those problems involving the settling of displaced persons with which we are familiar in the twentieth century. The Visigoths claimed they were being cheated by the Roman governors and businessmen, and the Roman population in northern Greece was scarcely overjoyed by this influx of barbarian immigrants. After two years of bickering, the desperate Visigoths undertook to revolt and fight against the emperor. The overconfident emperor entered into battle with insufficient preparation and without bothering to bring up his cavalry, and in consequence his army was soundly beaten and he was killed. This battle of Adrianople in 378 A.D. can be said to mark the real beginning of the German invasions, for whereas the Visigoths were pacified soon after by Theodosius I and the immediate damage was slight, the Visigoths had demonstrated that a Roman army could be beaten by a Germanic tribe. This ominous fact sounded the death knell of Roman power.

After the death of Theodosius I in 395 the Visigoths again became restless. They were dissatisfied with the lands in Greece which the emperor had given them, and they doubted the good will of Theodosius' sons toward them. The great emperor was succeeded, in the east and west, by his two sons, who were immature and stupid and who were surrounded by venal courtiers incapable of dealing with the explosive situation that was bound to develop. The Visigoths meanwhile had chosen as their king a certain Alaric the Bold, one of the most aggressive and competent of the early Germanic leaders. Alaric had no intention of destroying or even impairing imperial power; he simply wanted good lands for his people. The Visigoths, it might be said, did not want to destroy the empire; they wanted a homestead act, and all the trouble they were to make for the emperor in the following quarter of a century, which had the effect of shattering imperial power in the west, could have been avoided had the emperor initially granted their quite modest requests. But the silly and ill-advised emperor refused to make any concession whatsoever, and Alaric was left only with the recourse of waging war against the Roman authority which in fact he greatly respected.

The Visigothic invasion of Italy, which followed in the first years of the fifth century, was more in the nature of a picketing demonstration than actual warfare. The Visigoths were reluctant to inflict any damage on the Roman power, while, on the other hand, the head of the western imperial army, the German general Stilicho, was very lackadaisical in his dealings with the Visigoths. He prevented them from marching down into Italy, but he made no effort to drive them from the empire or even to push them back beyond the northern boundaries of the Italian province. The terrified emperor fled to the impregnable fortress of Ravenna, which was, however, off the main road into Italy, and hence played very little role in the calamitous events which were to follow. In 406 A.D. Stilicho withdrew his armies from the Rhine frontier in order to bolster the Italian defenses against the Visigoths. A motley group of German tribes poured across the Rhine into France, Spain, and North Africa, and within thirty years these provinces were lost to the emperor. Therefore, the year 406 marks the most important turning point in the first century of the Germanic invasions.

It is not easy to determine what was in Stilicho's mind, but in any case he was murdered in 408 by jealous aristocrats with the approval of the incredibly stupid emperor, and henceforth the road to Italy lay open to the Visigoths. In 410 Alaric's army took Rome and held it for several days in an attempt to blackmail the emperor into acceptance of the Visigothic demands for a homeland. It was this famous "sack of Rome" which so exercised the imagination of contemporaries, including St. Augustine; in fact, as Augustine pointed out, the Visigoths actually inflicted little or no damage on the city. It was Alaric's intention to march his people to the foot of Italy and then to cross over and settle in the rich province of North Africa, but on the Visigothic march beyond Rome their great king died. He was succeeded by his brother-in-law Ataulf, who announced as his policy the reconstruction of the empire under Gothic leadership, a policy which was later put into practice by the Ostrogothic king Theodoric. To symbolize his policy, Ataulf kidnapped and married Theodosius' daughter, a vivacious and brilliant woman who enjoyed herself immensely as a German queen and who played a leading role in the confused diplomacy and politics of the following three decades. Ataulf marched his people back into northern Italy and across into Gaul. Finally, in 418 A.D., the emperor granted the Visigoths their request and allowed them to settle as allies and dependents of the empire in western Gaul, from where they also spread across the Pyrenees into Spain. The Visigothic kingdom in Gaul was conquered and absorbed by the Franks in the early sixth century. In Spain Visigothic rule lasted until the Arab conquest in 711. The story of the Visigothic invasion of the empire is a mixture of farce and tragedy. Its disastrous effects could easily have been avoided, for at no time did the Visigoths wish to harm imperial power. That in the end the Visigothic migrations opened the door for a host of other German invaders was largely the fault of the imperial government.

Of the many German tribes who broke across the Rhine frontier in 406, most important were the Burgundians and the Vandals. The Burgundians settled in the Rhone valley and contributed their name to French geography. They were a peaceful people, apparently quite adept at poetry. The thirteenth-century poetic cycle of the *Nibelungenlied* was ultimately derived from stories which originated in fifth- or sixth-century Burgundy. The Burgundians were absorbed into the Frankish kingdom in the early sixth century.

A much more fierce and primitive people were the Vandals, who, led by their king Gaiseric the Lame, marched across France, through Spain, and into North Africa. It will be remembered that the Vandals were besieging St. Augustine's city when he died. By the fourth decade of the fifth century the rich province of North Africa had become the Vandal kingdom. The Arian Vandals mistreated the Catholic clergy and never gained the loyalty of the North African population. As a consequence North Africa was easily reconquered by the Byzantine emperor in the 530's, and the Vandals' influence on North African development was ephemeral and negligible. Nevertheless, the Vandals' conquest of North Africa was an important turning point in the process of imperial disintegration in the west. The Vandals turned out to be good sailors; almost as soon as they invaded North

Africa they formed piratical fleets and cut off the sea communications between Italy and the rest of western Europe. This made it impossible for the imperial government to reinforce the imperial armies in Gaul and Spain, and it accelerated the establishment of new Germanic kingdoms on Roman soil. Already in the 420's the Roman legions had been withdrawn from Britain, leaving the native Christian Celtic population prey to invasion by savage and heathen German tribes from across the North Sea.

The last victory in western Europe of an army carrying the imperial standard occurred at Chalons in Gaul in 451. At this battle the Hunnish invasion of western Europe, led by their great king Attila, was repulsed, and the Hunnish empire soon after disintegrated. But even this last triumph of Roman arms was misleading, because while the army which defeated Attila was led by a Roman general, most of his soldiers were Visigoths. After 451 the imperial destiny in the west moved steadily toward extinction. In 455 the last descendant of Theodosius died, and for the next twenty years the western emperors were merely the puppets of various German generals and chieftains who contended for mastery in Italy. The victor in this struggle was a certain German general named Odovacar; in 476 he deposed the reigning emperor and chose not to replace him. As he realized that he could not take the imperial title for himself, he ruled the Italian population as the viceroy of the eastern emperor, but he called himself king of the Germans in Italy. Odovacar made use of an old Roman law on the quartering of soldiers to force the Italian landlords to give up part of their estates for the settlement of his heterogeneous German army on Italian soil.

During this first century of the Germanic invasions, what was the attitude of the Roman population to these great upheavals in government and society? Many people, disgusted with the despotism and heavy taxation of the later empire, were either indifferent to the invasions or actually welcomed the invaders. It was hoped that the primitive Germans would not be able to preserve the imperial taxation and police system, and, with few exceptions, their hopes in this direction were fulfilled. We have letters written by Roman aristocrats in the early fifth century in Gaul which show how hard they tried to ignore the momentous changes occurring outside the walls of their estates. But on the other hand, there were aspects of the invasions which immediately struck fear among the ruling class of the empire. There are contemporary reports of the atrocities inflicted on the Roman population, especially by the Arian Vandals in North Africa. Furthermore, when the prospects of imperial collapse became very real, the indifferent aristocracy in some instances experienced a revival of patriotic feeling. The same types of Gallo-Roman nobility who had looked upon the early stages of the invasions with smug indifference suddenly, about the middle of the fifth century, formed armies of their own and maintained pockets of resistance until they were finally crushed by the Franks at the end of the fifth century.

The fact that the Goths and Vandals turned out to be Arians made the invasions a particularly difficult problem for the church. While Augustine and Orosius interpreted the invasions as the result of the providential plan for the eventual assimilation of the Germans into the Catholic church, St. Ambrose and St. Jerome looked upon the invaders with horror. Another Catholic bishop denounced the Germans as vermin who ought to be exterminated.

By the second half of the fifth century the Augustinian view was beginning to prevail, as pessimism and lamentations of disaster were giving way, among the leaders of the church, to growing hope. The work of Pope Leo the Great demonstrated the new opportunity for leadership that had come to the church as a consequence of imperial disintegration. It was becoming apparent that the end of the empire did not mean the end of the world nor even the end of the Latin church.

The mood of the Roman population of the Germanic kingdoms in 480 was therefore one of watchful waiting. What attitude would the German kings finally take toward the church? Could they be converted to Roman Catholic Christianity? And there was always the possibility of reconquest by the eastern emperor, still waiting in the wings and declaring that his war of reconquest was only a matter of time. The Latin churchmen contemplated this possibility with mixed feelings: the emperor would be better than Arian German persecution, but they knew that he would attempt to subordinate the pope to his authority and dictate to the western church on doctrinal questions as he was doing in the eastern empire. Hence the formulation of the Gelasian doctrine at this time, as we have seen. Might not a German king, uncouth and violent but nevertheless a loyal Roman Catholic, be a better ruler for the earthly city? These were the vital questions at the end of the first phase of the Germanic invasions circa 480. The answers to these questions would appear in the following century, during the second phase of the Germanic invasions, and would determine the destiny of western Europe.

III. The Second Phase of the Invasions: The Ostrogothic and Frankish Kingdoms

By 480 A.D. three German kingdoms had been established on the continent of western Europe on the ruins of the Roman empire, but none of these were destined to survive beyond the early eighth century or to have any significant impact on medieval civilization. The kingdom of Odovacar in Italy was an ephemeral institution and collapsed under the force of the Ostrogothic invasions in 489. In the Rhone valley the Burgundian kingdom was absorbed by the Franks and incorporated into their domain in the 520's. The kingdom of the Visigoths stretched through western France and all of Spain. In the early sixth century the Franks also drove the Visigoths out of France.

The Visigothic kingdom in Spain affected Iberian history and culture very little. The Visigoths were originally Arians, but converted to Catholicism in the late sixth century. The seventh-century Catholic bishops tried to glamorize Visigothic monarchy in Spain and to strengthen it with the powers and sanctions of religion. In the eighth century the church adopted the same policy with regard to the Frankish monarchy with far-reaching effects. But the Visigothic kings were so weak and incompetent that not even the support of the church could save them. Despite the efforts of the church the Visigothic kingdom yielded instantaneously to the Moslem invaders in 711. And until the eleventh century the Spanish Christian princes survived only in the Pyrenees. The sole cultural legacy of the Visigoths is found in the work of Bishop Isidore of Seville, who was not even a Visigoth but a scion of the Italian aristocracy.

After the successive failures of all the initial German kingdoms the question arose of whether any permanent German kingdom could be established in western Europe. In the last two decades of the fifth century two new kingdoms were created, and it appeared that the political destiny of Europe would be determined by the shape and fate of these two new entities. The Ostrogoths erected their kingdom in Italy, and the Salian Franks became the masters of Gaul. To anyone who lived in western Europe in the year 500 it would have appeared certain that the future lay with the Ostrogoths. Theodoric, the king of the Ostrogoths, wanted to revive Roman culture and reinvigorate Roman administration under his aegis, and at the beginning of the sixth century it seemed that Theodoric would realize this traditional Gothic policy of synthesizing Gothic and Roman institutions. The Frankish kingdom did not appear to have an equal opportunity for success, for its ruler, Clovis I, seemed to be a barbarian with no appreciation of Latin culture or Roman government. Clovis compared most unfavorably with the great Ostrogothic king as a worthy heir of the Roman emperors. Yet the kingdom of the Franks did survive perpetually while the Ostrogothic state collapsed soon after the death of Theodoric in 526. With Theodoric gone, Italy was reconquered by the Byzantine emperor Justinian, and the Ostrogothic kingdom disappeared from history. The leadership of western Europe therefore passed by default to the Franks. Consequently, Ostrogothic failure

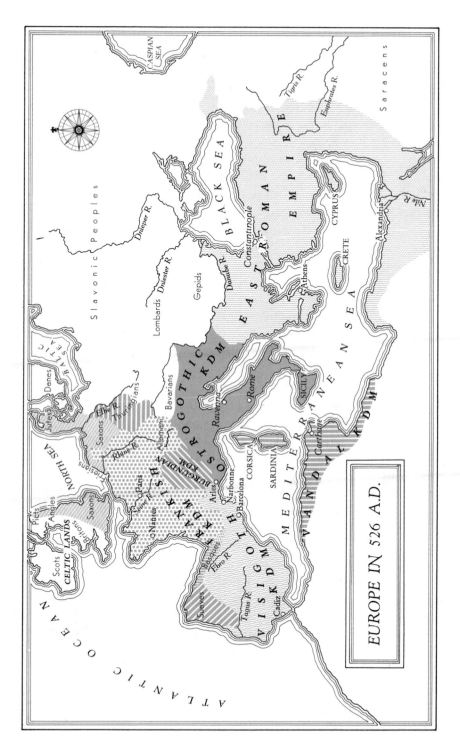

EUROPE IN 526 A.D.

123

and Frankish success were crucial for the development of early medieval Europe, and the causes of these decisive events deserve special consideration.

The Ostrogoths came into the empire from the Danube basin. They had been conquered and enslaved by the Huns in the 370's, but after the death of the Hunnish leader Attila in 453 they gained their freedom. Theodoric, whose name means "leader of the people" and who was one of the Ostrogothic royal family, had been sent while a young boy as a hostage to Constantinople, where he learned to appreciate Roman culture, law, and government. In the 480's he became king of the Ostrogoths through election by the folk. Primogeniture in royal succession was not the early Germanic practice. The throne was regarded as the property of the royal family, but the particular king was chosen from this family by the folk on the principle of throneworthiness.

At the end of the eighth decade of the fifth century Theodoric's policy of establishing a union of Roman and Gothic interests found favor with the emperor in Constantinople. The Ostrogoths had begun to threaten to invade the Byzantine empire. Instead, the wily emperor convinced Theodoric that he should lead his people into Italy, where Odovacar was beginning to assert his independence of the eastern empire. Thereby the emperor could rescue Byzantium from the Ostrogothic peril. At the same time he could bring Italy more firmly under the official jurisdiction of the eastern empire than was the case in Odovacar's reign, for Theodoric went to Italy with the understanding that the rights of the emperor in Italy would be preserved. The emperor considered the Ostrogothic king as his lieutenant, and he expected that the Ostrogothic invasion would do nothing to decrease imperial sovereignty there, but rather would increase its strength.

In four years, between 489 and 493, Theodoric and the Ostrogoths destroyed the kingdom of Odovacar and conquered Italy. Theodoric set up his capital in Ravenna, in northeastern Italy, where several of the fifth-century emperors had already taken up residence. What was the legal position of Theodoric in Italy? It was substantially a continuation of the same system under which Odovacar had ruled. Theodoric's authority consisted of a delegation of imperial power to conduct the general affairs of the government, and at the same time it included a royal title to preserve his prestige over his own people. For a century barbarian generals had been usually the heads of the imperial army in the west. Now that there was no longer an emperor in the west, the civil government also passed into the hands of the leader of the army. The Roman people were becoming habituated to a ruler who was the representative of a distant emperor in Constantinople and who was also the head of the Germanic people quartered on their soil. Thus they came to accept the notion of a barbarian kingdom exercising general powers of government.

For over a decade Theodoric was satisfied with his role as representative of the emperor and as chief of the Germanic federates. Then he began to adopt a new policy, disquieting for the Byzantine emperor. He began to contemplate the eventual establishment of a Germanic kingdom led by the Goths, comprising both Gaul and Italy, perhaps even Spain. He inaugurated a policy of diplomatic marriages, which eventually could have resulted in such a great kingdom. He had, in 493, married the sister of Clovis, and then he gave one of his daughters in marriage to the Burgundian king. He also became the guardian of the Visigothic king, who was a minor. Theodoric seemed, little by little, to be emancipating himself from the distant emperor in the east.

The Byzantines had never renounced Italy because the Roman empire without Rome was an inconceivable thing to them. Now the emperor became concerned that Theodoric would become too strong, and to counterbalance Theodoric's power, he recognized Clovis' hegemony over Gaul and established an alliance with the Frankish king. This was one of the greatest of Theodoric's errors, although it was undoubtedly difficult for anyone at the time to foresee the consequences. His attempt to make the Ostrogoths a Mediterranean power with influence in France and Spain as well as supremacy in Italy brought about the hostility of the Byzantine emperor and the recognition of the legal hegemony of the Franks in Gaul. This situation proved disastrous for the Ostrogoths when the Byzantine empire, under Justinian, regained the military strength to attack Italy.

If we ask why Theodoric dared to undertake such a hazardous foreign policy, which in the end united the Franks and the Byzantine emperor against the Ostrogothic kingdom and resulted in its destruction, the reason for the great risk he took is evident. By the 520's, as a result of his internal policy, he felt that he had obtained the loyalty of the Italian people and at least the neutrality, perhaps even the support, of the pope and the Catholic church.

From the beginning of his reign Theodoric declared that it was his intention to restore the vigor of Roman government and Roman culture and bring benefits to the Italian people. Such a policy was not new among the Goths; Ataulf, the second Visigothic king, had professed similar intentions. The novelty was that Theodoric had the opportunity to carry out this aim and that he took great pains to do so. His shrewdest move was the preservation of the bureaucratic system of the later empire, which had lingered on, in form at least, through most of the fifth century while the worthless last emperors were holding out in Ravenna. Now Theodoric made Ravenna his capital, completely restored the bureaucratic hierarchy, and recruited officials from the ranks of the Roman aristocracy. By 500 he had found the man to implement his internal policy—Cassiodorus, a scion of an old Roman family, a skilled rhetorician, an able administrator, a great "press agent" for the Ostrogothic kingdom. Cassiodorus advised Theodoric on how he might win over the Italian people and set about writing various propaganda works, including an official *History of the Goths,* which would make Theodoric appear in the best possible light to the Italian people.

It was Cassiodorus who coined the slogan for the new regime—*civilitas* —which was stamped on the royal coinage and proclaimed in numerous royal letters written by Cassiodorus. It was claimed that the Goths were not the enemies of civilization; on the contrary, the aim of the new government was to further and preserve Roman civilization. Nor in Cassiodorus' writings are the Goths ever referred to as "barbarians." In fact, in his *History of the Goths* Cassiodorus identifies the Goths with the Scythians, a people mentioned in Greek mythology. Cassiodorus' *History of the Goths,* which has come down to us in Jordanes' abridgment, portrayed the Goths as being "almost equal" to the Greeks in culture. This gross historical misinterpretation was not the result of Cassiodorus' ignorance but rather his ideology. Similarly, the extremely rhetorical style of the letters which Cassiodorus wrote on behalf of Theodoric was the result of a conscious attempt to demonstrate that the Ostrogothic ruler was a defender of the classical tradition.

The program of *civilitas* was given considerable semblance of reality by Theodoric's domestic policies. An extensive program of public works was undertaken, and strict measures against brigandage were enforced; the resulting peace encouraged a return of prosperity in Italy probably to the level of the late fourth century (or at least so we are told by the contemporaries). The Italian population continued to live under Roman law, while only the Ostrogoths used Germanic law. To his court Theodoric summoned the leading scholars of Italy and gave them his patronage—not only Cassiodorus but also Boethius, another Roman aristocrat who became a high government official and began the translation of Plato and Aristotle into Latin. Even a Byzantine court historian admitted that Theodoric treated the Italian population with laudable moderation and generosity.

There were, however, two aspects of Theodoric's policy which could not seem admirable to the Italians and which he was forced by his position as leader of the Ostrogothic war band to maintain: expropriation of Italian land for the Ostrogothic army, and Arianism. The Germans were legally federates and were to be quartered on the land of the native Italian population according to the Roman law of "hospitality." Thus we find Odovacar ordering the Italian landlords to surrender one-third of their land to his soldiers, and Theodoric used the same policy. How else could he provide for his soldiers? We have very little information which allows us to determine how the Italian landlords regarded this policy. Some historians have suggested that in any case there were many vacant estates by this time as a result of the disorders of the previous century, so that the amount of land that Theodoric had to expropriate was small. But the fact that Cassiodorus worked hard to justify this act on the grounds that the Goths were the Roman army indicates that there must have been some resentment on the part of expropriated landlords.

On the question of the continued loyalty of Theodoric to Arianism, the historian is also perplexed by the meager quality of our sources. What did Arianism really mean to Theodoric? He built Arian churches; then who were these Arian priests? Presumably they were native Ostrogoths. About this we know nothing. All we can say is that Arianism had become the folk religion for the Goths, and they could no more give up their customary religion than they could give up their customary law. Theodoric did the next best thing; if he remained an Arian, he did everything he could to appease the Catholic church short of his own conversion. He allowed absolute freedom of religion; he went through a ceremony which implied that he recognized the authority of the pope not only over the Catholic church but also over the city of Rome. By 520 it appeared that the pope had been appeased and that the church would continue to support the authority of the Ostrogothic king even after Theodoric's death. Hence his hazardous foreign policy would succeed because of his skillful domestic policy.

But in the last few years of Theodoric's reign the delicate balance of forces that he had created swung against him, and it was already apparent before his death in 526 that the collapse of the Ostrogothic kingdom could not long be delayed. Unfortunately, here again our sources are very meager, but the dim outline of the changes which occurred is distinguishable. The key to the situation appears to be the policy of the emperor. Through most of Theodoric's reign the emperor had been quarreling with the pope; this produced the denunciation of imperial authority made by Gelasius I in the last decade of the fifth century. The pope felt that the emperor had fallen into heresy and was trying to impose his errors on the church. An Arian who allowed freedom of religion was much to be preferred to the Byzantine emperor as ruler in such instances. Then, in 518 A.D., there was a change of dynasty in Constantinople. The great aim of the ambitious new ruling house was the reconquest of the west. For this end all else must be sacrificed. The emperor Justin I declared his acceptance of the theological dogmas held by the pope (even though he thus alienated many of his subjects), and the emperor and pope appear to have come to a secret understanding while the pope was acting as Theodoric's ambassador in Constantinople. Considerable numbers of the Roman aristocracy threw in their lot with the pope and Byzantine emperor, including the leading official Boethius. Probably they were worried that Visigothic kinsmen of Theodoric, who were still vehemently anti-Catholic, had become leading courtiers at Ravenna.

Theodoric discovered the conspiracy, and his reaction was violent. For some time he had been worried about the succession to the throne; untimely deaths in his family had left only a woman and a child as possible successors, if there was not to be a contest for the throne by the leading Ostrogothic generals. In the last two years of his reign Theodoric abandoned *civilitas*. He imprisoned the pope; he executed Boethius and several leading members of the Roman aristocracy. But his kingdom was doomed. In the decade following his death the Byzantines began their reconquest.

In his personal qualities Theodoric was the greatest German king before Charlemagne, and his policy of *civilitas* parallels in many ways the aims of the Frankish monarchy in 800 A.D. Theodoric's failure to establish a permanent kingdom was therefore of the greatest consequence for medieval Europe. Theodoric was able to establish in his lifetime a *de facto* supreme power in Italy, but he did not destroy the continuity of Roman political ideas and political institutions in Italy; indeed he had no intention of doing so, for he himself had the greatest respect for the glory of Rome. He wished to reconstitute the empire in the west, but under the rule of a Gothic king.

His policy turned out to be a mistaken one. He aroused the fear of the Byzantine emperors that the Ostrogothic kingdom would become so powerful that the reassertion of Byzantine authority in Italy would become impossible and the fear that the Ostrogothic kingdom would emerge as a great Mediterranean power to compete with Byzantium itself for domination of the Mediterranean world. At the same time, because of his respect for Roman institutions and ideas, Theodoric made no attempt to break the continuity of Roman civilization and political organization in Italy. He allowed the Ostrogoths to remain an alien band of Germanic soldiers who played no part in the political and religious life of the country. As powerful as the Ostrogothic monarchy seemed to be in his day, he left his successors in an impossible position. They were left prey to a counterattack by the revived military power of Byzantium under Justinian, but Theodoric had not gained for the Ostrogothic kingdom sufficient loyalty among the Italian people to withstand the Greek reconquest.

The early history of the Franks exhibits marked contrasts in every way with the Ostrogothic development. The Franks were much less influenced by Roman culture—their kings were markedly inferior to Theodoric the Ostrogoth—and yet the Frankish kingdom survived the confusions of the fifth and sixth centuries. It became the largest and most important kingdom to be created on what had been Latin soil, and therefore until the tenth century the political development of western Europe, and to a considerable extent its cultural and ecclesiastical history as well, was determined by the destiny of the Frankish monarchy.

There were at least two important branches of the Frankish people; the one which was to play the important role in history was the Salian Franks, whose original homeland lay in what is today west central Germany. They lived far beyond the Rhenish frontier and had little contact with the Romans, either economically or culturally. Unlike the Visigoths, they had not been converted by Arian missionaries, and when they entered the empire they were savage and violent heathens. In Frankish society the independent free peasant predominated; a class of nobility, if there was any at all, was not powerful, and even in the early sixth century the Frankish army consisted mainly of peasant infantry, with very little use of cavalry. The only civilized aspect of early Frankish society was an interest in agriculture. Because of this interest and because, like all Germans, they wanted to get closer to the wealth of the empire, the Franks obtained from the emperor Julian the Apostate, in the middle of the fourth century, the right to settle along the northern border of the empire in Flanders. Here the outstanding characteristic of Frankish migration immediately became apparent: unlike the other Germanic invaders, the Franks intensively colonized their new homeland. They devoted themselves to agriculture and left a strong demographic, economic, and linguistic impact on the region.

Our only important literary source for the early history of the Franks is the comprehensive and detailed work of Bishop Gregory of Tours written in the late sixth century. Gregory's information was naturally fullest on the period closest to his own day, but from oral traditions he was able to provide fragmentary information on fifth-century Frankish history. Gregory's *History of the Franks,* in spite of certain weaknesses in style and the author's vehement prejudices, is the fullest account we have of any Germanic people. We also have the benefit of place-name evidence for the early history of the Franks. The study of the linguistic roots of the place names of Flanders and northern France allows us to construct the pattern of Frankish migration southward from Flanders into Gaul.

As Roman power disintegrated in the early fifth century, the Franks began to move slowly southward into imperial territory. Here again their settlement consisted not merely of a military occupation, as was the case with other Germanic peoples, but of an actual extensive colonization. It is probably at this time that one family began to exercise leadership in the Frankish folk and was elevated to the privileged position of a royal dynasty. Until the middle of the eighth century the Frankish monarchy was regarded as the private property of this one family, irrespective of the personal

inadequacies of many of its scions. The Frankish royal family, as was common among the Germans, claimed descent from the gods, and in tradition
they ascribed the founding of the family to a certain mythical hero named
Merovech. The fifth-century Merovingians varied in quality; some of them
appeared to have been quite inadequate as warriors and leaders, but what
characterized all the early Frankish rulers as late as 500 A.D. was their intense hostility toward Roman civilization. It is probable that for a decade
or so in the mid-fifth century the Franks came under the domination of one
of the last Roman generals in Gaul. This "very hard yoke of the Romans,"
as it is described in the prologue to the Salic law, when combined with the
native savagery and barbarism of the Franks, accounts for their hatred of
the Romans. This negative attitude finds no parallel among any previous
Germanic invader of the empire, as R. Latouche has emphasized.

By the eighth decade of the fifth century the Franks had intensively
colonized the northern part of Gaul stretching north from the old Roman
city of Paris. As they moved into the central and southern regions, they
encountered a relatively dense Gallo-Roman population, and the Frankish
influence on language and institutions was consequently small in this part
of the country. Because the Gallo-Romans greatly outnumbered the invading Franks, the native vulgar Latin continued to be the language of the
whole country, and even the Franks themselves rapidly adopted the Roman
tongue.

With the disorganized condition of fifth-century Gaul, the Franks
needed only a strong leader to advance from their northern stronghold to
conquer the whole country, and this leader was found in the greatest of the
Merovingian kings, Clovis I (481–511), whose long reign established
Frankish hegemony west of the Rhine. In the pages of Gregory of Tours,
Clovis' crude and savage qualities are painfully evident; at the same time, he
appears as a formidable war leader and a shrewd strategist. After crushing
the Gallo-Roman armies for the last time, Clovis subdued other Germanic
peoples who had been living along the west bank of the Rhine. Clovis then
prepared for his further conquest by receiving baptism along with his whole
army at the hands of the archbishop of Rheims. Although later shrouded
in legend of one sort or another, the reason for Clovis' conversion in 496
was simple: he saw that if he would accept the Catholic religion, he would
be the only orthodox Germanic king in Gaul—in fact, in all of western
Europe. Thereby, as the Catholic champion he would find it easier to gain
the allegiance of the Gallo-Romans as his conquests proceeded. Furthermore, by his conversion he would gain the support of the episcopate, the
only political, economic, and moral power which still existed throughout
Gaul. The enthusiasm of Gregory of Tours, the spokesman for the Frankish

church in the sixth century, shows not only that Clovis had guessed rightly, but also that he had succeeded in surrounding himself with an aura of sanctity. In Gregory's account the savage leader of the Frankish war band is suddenly transformed by his conversion into a new Constantine.

His power reinforced by the support of the church, Clovis proceeded in his conquests. First he moved into the northwest, the land between the Seine and the Loire, and brought it under his allegiance, although this area remained separatist throughout the greater part of medieval French history. Finally Clovis was ready for his great enterprise: the conquest of Visigothic Gaul, Aquitaine. First he neutralized the Burgundians in the year 500, making with them a treaty of alliance. He left it to his sons to conquer Burgundy in the third decade of the sixth century. Although the Visigoths had established a vast kingdom stretching from Spain to Brittany and centered on Toulouse, their kingdom was vulnerable for many of the same reasons which brought down the Ostrogothic kingdom: they were merely military occupiers, not colonizers, and they were Arians. Clovis' victory over the Visigoths was quick and decisive. The church gave him full support in this conquest. In Gregory's account the Frankish conquest of Toulouse is portrayed as a holy war. About the same time, Clovis effected an alliance with the eastern emperor against the Ostrogoths. In 507 the Frankish conquest of Gaul received the sanction of the emperor, who accorded Clovis the titles of consul and Augustus. These titles were purely honorary; they were meant to consecrate under a solemn form the alliance of the emperor and the Frankish king against the Ostrogoths and to recognize the supremacy of Clovis in Gaul. Thus, even while Clovis had no respect for Roman institutions and ideas, he was able to secure imperial approval for his conquests.

One step remained in the foundation of the Frankish kingdom. This was the designation of Paris as the capital. Paris was within the area which had been heavily colonized by the Salian Franks. But the new Gallo-Roman-Frankish church was able to find a greater glory for Paris. At the beginning of the sixth century the tradition that St. Denis, the disciple of St. Paul, had been the first bishop of Paris and had been martyred there took on a new importance. Clovis and the episcopate encouraged this legend; Paris became one of the holy cities of Christianity, and Montmartre the site of a popular shrine. By associating Paris with St. Denis, Clovis emphasized his position as the Germanic champion of Catholic Christianity. He well knew that this role had greatly facilitated the Frankish conquest of Gaul.

It was one thing to conquer Gaul, another to govern it. And the Merovingians turned out to be much less effective as rulers than as leaders of the Frankish war band. Under any circumstances the Merovingian dynasty was bound to run into trouble, given the inadequate political conceptions of the Germanic people. Furthermore, the Merovingians' kingdom, which included not only what is today France but also a large part of the southern half of western Germany, covered far too much territory for the limited institutions of the sixth century. But the mistakes made by Clovis and his successors and the personal inadequacies of most of the Merovingian rulers served to make the situation much worse, with the result that by the early seventh century political power in France was in the hands of the provincial aristocracy, while the royal family held the crown and not much else.

Certainly the Merovingian ruler started out, in Clovis' reign, in a position of apparent strength—even, it could be said, of autocracy—and with enormous material resources. Clovis and his successors regarded the whole country as their personal possession. As a result, whenever a king had more than one son, he decreed that the royal fisc (property) be simply divided among his heirs and that the crown be similarly divided. The Merovingian rulers, holding the crown and its resources as their private property, further affected to rule without consulting anyone. The result was an almost incredible combination of primitive autocracy and anarchy. The Merovingian rulers did nothing for the people except to lead an occasional military expedition. They spent their time satisfying their gross desires and enriching their relatives and dependents. When there was more than one king, as was frequent in the century following Clovis' death, the rulers' chief interest was in fighting and killing each other, so the history of the Merovingian family in the sixth and early seventh centuries is mostly a bewildering tale of carnage and dishonor.

Almost no attempt was made by these primitive chieftains to maintain the Roman administrative system; almost no governmental documents survive from Merovingian France except a few badly drafted charters, and apparently the work of monarchy, so far as there was any, was carried on almost without literacy. The only aspect of Roman government which the Merovingians tried to maintain was the taxation system. But for this they lacked sufficient loyal and able administrators as well as any public feeling that taxes were worth paying. By 600 the vestiges of Roman taxation had all but disappeared, and a Merovingian king who wanted to get rid of one of his officials simply sent him out to collect taxes; he would never be heard from again.

The Frankish and Gallo-Roman nobility, who were rapidly coalescing, were unanimous in their hostility to a monarchy which contributed nothing to their welfare and which presented a miserable spectacle of greed and incompetence. The Merovingians tried to win over some of the nobility to their service by granting them offices accompanied by benefices (benefits), that is, property attached to the office to insure the loyal service of the holder to the king. The favored nobility rapidly made these offices and benefices their private property and established themselves as provincial dynasts. Thus the title of duke, originally the king's local military representative, and count, originally a royal legal representative, were transformed into aristocratic titles inherited along with the accompanying benefices in the great aristocratic families.

By the early seventh century the monarchy was in the process of being robbed blind by the provincial aristocracy, and the Merovingians were left with only a shadow of their original power and only a small part of the enormous royal fisc of the time of Clovis I. Merovingian France presented a picture of an intensely disorganized kingdom politically, with all loyalty going to the local big shot and none to the king. The sixth-century kings, given to fratricidal war, made possible the aristocratic usurpation of the governmental power and wealth of the Merovingian family. Nearly all the seventh-century Merovingian rulers were either children, women, or mental deficients. Such "unthrone-worthy" rulers always signified the death of royal power during the early middle ages.

The church, or rather the bishops of Gaul who provided all the leadership in the church, was greatly disappointed by the Merovingian decline. The episcopate had established an alliance with Clovis, and great hopes were held out for mutual benefit from this union of royal family and Catholic bishops. But Clovis' successors turned out to be so incompetent and savage that by the end of the sixth century the bishops had taken their stand with the great nobility against the monarchy. One of the last of the Gallo-Roman bishops, Gregory of Tours, reveals for us in his *History* the outlook of the late sixth-century episcopate. Although Gregory was better educated than any of his episcopal colleagues, his perspective was nevertheless limited and selfish. He turned away from Clovis' successors in revulsion at their crimes and stupidity and bewailed the breaking up of the alliance between monarchy and church of the early sixth century. If only Clovis' grandchildren would emulate the Frankish "new Constantine"! But since Gregory saw little hope of the happy reconstruction of the old alliance between the royal family and the episcopate, he devoted himself mainly to building up the wealth and prestige of the church of Tours, just as any duke or count would devote himself chiefly to the interests of his own family.

Thus, by the end of the sixth century the political future of the Frankish kingdom, with its effects of localism and provincialism, had driven the episcopate to throw in their lot with the aristocracy. The church, by separating itself from Frankish kingship in the sixth and seventh centuries, made more certain the ever increasing impotence of the Merovingian dynasty. Only the church could have provided sufficient leadership and literacy to have created an effective royal government in France. But the bishops, in pursuing this policy of separation from the monarchy, however justified they may have been in view of the gross personal inadequacies of the Merovingian family, had taken a step which harmed the church itself. The old Gallo-Roman church, which in 400 was renowned for its learning and devotion, in 700 was notorious for its ignorance and lack of energy. A major reason for this development was the tendency of Gregory of Tours and his colleagues to identify their interests with those of the nobility, whose selfishness and provincialism became characteristic of the seventh-century French episcopate. If the Merovingians had produced a few rulers of the caliber of Theodoric the Ostrogoth, the decline of the French church as well as the French monarchy in the later sixth and seventh centuries would certainly have been averted.

The Merovingian monarchy played only a small part in influencing the great social changes which occurred in France in the sixth and seventh centuries. While royal and ecclesiastical leadership between 500 and 700 did very little to establish permanent institutions, the coalescing of Frankish and Gallo-Roman society during this period provided the social context with which later leadership had to contend. Frankish society in the early fifth century was organized along rather simple lines. The royal family and the nobility comprised not more than 10 per cent of the population of the Frankish folk. At the bottom of the Salian social scale was a group, comprising perhaps 20 per cent of the population, in various stages of dependency, including, personal slavery. The largest group in early Frankish society, taking in as much as 70 per cent of the folk, consisted of the free peasants and soldiers. Under the pressure of the invasions and wars of the fifth century this large central group was polarized. A small part emerged as war leaders and joined the ranks of the nobility, while many were pushed down into unfree status.

The coalescence of the native Gallo-Roman population with Frankish society gave added impetus to the decline into dependency of many of the original Frankish freemen. As the Frankish nobility associated themselves with the Gallo-Roman aristocracy, they naturally attempted to force the Frankish peasant soldier into a servile status somewhat paralleling the bottom groups in Gallo-Roman society. About half the population of Gaul in 400 A.D. consisted of people in an unfree status; at least 30 per cent were slaves outright, and another 20 per cent were the semiservile *coloni*. At the top of the social scale in Gaul were the wealthy landlords, from whose ranks also came the bishops and other important churchmen. This lordly class comprised somewhere around 15 per cent of the population. Another

15 per cent consisted of free peasants and the lower clergy. Finally, in 400, especially in the south of France where the Gallo-Roman population was most dense, there were many townsmen who were separate from both the landlord group and the various classes of peasants; these bourgeois who engaged in trade and industry probably constituted 20 per cent of the population of Gaul.

By 600 the Gallo-Roman and Frankish societies had thoroughly mingled, and a new French social structure had appeared. Intermarriage between Frankish and Gallo-Roman families was both rapid and extensive. Gregory of Tours is the last bishop in Gaul who could claim descent entirely from the old Gallo-Roman aristocracy. The new French society was marked by a very large group of dependent serfs at the bottom of the social scale, perhaps as much as 60 per cent of the entire population. The unfree of both Gallo-Roman and early Frankish societies, as well as many depressed free Frankish peasants, went to make up the serf class. The serf was not a personal slave to his lord; rather, he was bound to the land and retained certain legal and economic rights. The lord was supposed to protect him and to provide means of economic sustenance for him, although not infrequently the lord neglected to do both. What he wanted of the serf was labor on his own estates and/or a share of the serf's own crop. There was great gradation within the serf ranks; some serfs were quite prosperous, while others were perpetually on the verge of starvation. Yet, if there was economic heterogeneity among the servile class, there was also legal uniformity: the serf and his family could not leave the lord's estate—the manor, as it came to be called; he owed the lord servile dues and labor, and he was subject to the jurisdiction of the lord's manorial court.

The serf was probably better off than the slave on the Roman *latifundia;* he may often have had less to eat, but he had much greater personal freedom. Hence some historians have talked about the process of "social amelioration" in sixth-century France as the Roman slave system gave way to medieval serfdom. This judgment may be justified; total misery was replaced by partial misery. But this transformation of the economic and legal status of the peasantry did not avail to raise the largest and lowest social group above an animal existence. At least until the twelfth century the life of the medieval peasant differed very little from that of beasts of the field. They toiled, they bred, and they died. In the sixth century they even lacked whatever comfort and inspiration a local curate could provide. There was as yet no parish clergy. The religious needs of the peasantry were met by a priest occasionally sent out from the cathedral clergy of the nearest episcopal center. If a sixth- or seventh-century peasant saw a priest and received the sacraments once a year, he was doing very well. Under these conditions it is not a surprise that the Christianity of the serf class was purely nominal. Whether or not the peasant was baptized, he continued to worship the forces of nature, as he had always done. And even when he thought himself a Christian, his religious outlook was dominated by the grossest superstitions and fertility cults. The Christianity of the early medieval peasant was a hodgepodge of saints, relics, and demons.

By 600 the numbers of the middle group of both early Frankish and Gallo-Roman society had greatly declined. Probably not more than 10 per cent of the peasant population had managed to maintain a free status, and this number included the lower clergy. With the economic decline of France and the rapid de-urbanization which took place following the Frankish invasions, the bourgeois class all but disappeared. Certainly not more than 3 per cent of the French population in 600 were townsmen.

At the top of the social scale was a small group of people who possessed great private wealth and power. This group comprised the royal family and the great provincial aristocracy—the dukes and counts with their vast estates and territorial authority. This class of great lords, in which may be included the bishops and more important abbots, could not have constituted more than 2 per cent of the population. In addition to this great aristocracy there was quite a large group of modest lords and ordinary free soldiers. Some of these were wealthy landlords, but others were merely hired thugs who comprised the armies of kings and aristocrats. It is probable that this class of ordinary lords and soldiers made up as much as 25 per cent of the population of France in 600.

The social structure which had emerged in France, the most important kingdom created on the ruins of the western Roman empire, was dominated by lords and serfs. Urban life had almost entirely disappeared, and all leadership had passed to a very small group of royal princes and great aristocrats. These men were mainly interested in building up the wealth and power of their own families. Most of their life was spent in warfare, they were ignorant of the arts of government, they were blind to the ideals of justice and peace, and they had no understanding of economic problems; Christianity for them was a system of magic, miracles, and hagiography. A comparison of these leaders of French society at the beginning of the seventh century with men of the quality of Theodosius I, Ambrose, Augustine, and Symmachus must lead to the conclusion that the collapse of the western Roman empire was a political, economic, and cultural disaster of the greatest magnitude.

Chapter Five

JUSTINIAN AND MOHAMMED

I. The Nemesis of Byzantine Power

Western government, law, society, and economy had been transformed by the Germanic invasions. But in the sixth and seventh centuries western Europe was not left alone to work out the effects of these great changes. The life of the Mediterranean world was again to be disturbed during these two centuries by the ambitions of Greeks and Arabs. The Byzantine and Moslem impact on western Europe was far less important than the Germanic influence. But the aims of the Byzantine emperor Justinian I and Mohammed, the Prophet of Allah, played significant roles in the shaping of the new European civilization.

The eastern Roman empire had been the first to be invaded by the Germans who initially had broken the Danube frontier, which was defended by the ruler in Constantinople. The first great defeat of Roman arms at the hands of the Germans, at the battle of Adrianople, had been suffered by the eastern emperor. Yet it was the western Roman empire that disintegrated in the fifth century. Why, then, did the Byzantine empire survive the German invasions? Some specific answers can be given to this question. In the first place the population of the eastern empire was much greater and much more urbanized than was the case in the Latin-speaking part of the Mediterranean world. The Germans were not so ignorant as to be unable to realize that they faced an immensely more difficult task if they turned eastward after they crossed the Danube. Second, the eastern Roman empire found the focal point of government, culture, and economy in the impregnable fortress of Constantinople. It took the Arabs, who were militarily far superior to the Germans, seven centuries to take Constantinople. Even in the second decade of the twentieth century a military and naval onslaught on the great fortress of the Dardanelles ended in total failure. Obviously the Germans would have had no chance against Constantinople, and they realized this. And yet there was no other way for the Germans to enter the wealthy part of the Byzantine empire except through Constantinople. The fifth-century western emperors also had an impregnable fortress at Ravenna, but the Germans easily bypassed this city and pushed on unhindered into Italy.

The third reason for the survival of the eastern Roman empire was the ability of the fifth-century Byzantine rulers. They introduced governmental reforms, such as the reduction of the heavy taxation imposed in the preceding century, to gain popular support. They encouraged education and inaugurated the first large-scale codification of Roman law. Following on the work of third-century jurisconsults, the Byzantine legists produced the initial extensive Roman law code in about 425 A.D., which is named after the emperor Theodosius II. Also, the Byzantine rulers were wise enough not to surrender their military powers to German generals, as was done by their western colleagues. Finally, it must be seen that the invasions had a cumulative effect on the power and wealth of the western emperor which was avoided in the east. As the empire lost its territory, it lost its income from taxes, which meant that the government found it harder and harder to maintain the army, and the shrinking of military resources brought about the loss of even more territory, which further reduced imperial income. The government in Constantinople, avoiding this downward spiral, maintained steady tax resources throughout the fifth century. The position of Constantinople as a great center of east-west trade further contributed to the emperor's wealth.

In the fifth century the emperor took great pains to husband resources; he was preparing for the great day of reconquest. Since no emperor remained in the west after 476, the eastern emperor claimed that the Latin countries had reverted to his domain. He maintained that the *imperium* was inalienable, and he looked forward to the time when his resources would be sufficient to restore his effective authority at Rome. In the early sixth century the Ostrogothic attempts to create a pan-Germanic Mediterranean empire appeared to endanger the realization of Byzantine claims. Consequently, in 530 the emperor Justinian the Great launched the reconquest for which his predecessors had been preparing for a century.

Justinian I (527–565) had a greater influence on the development of Byzantium than any other emperor between Constantine and the tenth century. Justinian's uncle was a Macedonian general who had seized the throne. Justin I (518–527) carefully trained his nephew to succeed him on the imperial throne, and of all medieval rulers Justinian was undoubtedly the best educated and possessed the greatest degree of native intelligence. If destiny had not called him to the imperial purple, he would have had a great career as either a lawyer or a theologian. He was a stern, puritanical individual, the hardest-working man in the empire and greatly devoted to the state. His wife Theodora, formerly a circus dancer, turned out to be an intelligent and vigorous woman who helped her husband considerably. The crowd in the Byzantine circus had organized itself into a strange combination of sport-fan clubs and political associations. Early in Justinian's reign, during riots between such rival circus groups which the emperor could not control, he felt compelled to abdicate the throne. Theodora, however, having risen from prostitute to empress, would not let her husband forsake his imperial eminence, and Justinian managed to regain control of the situation. His rule turned out to be both long and memorable on many grounds.

Two monuments of Justinian's reign still survive: the cathedral of St. Sophia (Holy Wisdom) in Constantinople and the *Corpus Juris Civilis*, the Justinian code. St. Sophia is the greatest achievement of Byzantine architecture. Its style is a perpetuation of the church architecture of the later empire, which in turn is modeled on the Roman basilica, but its size and massive quality make the cathedral of Constantinople one of the outstanding examples of medieval art and engineering. The inside of this magnificent structure is adorned with great mosaics which depict the emperor as the representative of God on earth and thereby proclaim the ideology of imperial rule. Only in recent years has the covering which the Turks placed over the mosaics been removed so that we can at last fully appreciate the skill and resources which went into the creation of the great church commissioned by Justinian. The church of San Vitale in Ravenna, also constructed by Justinian, is likewise remarkable for its splendid mosaics.

Of all the emperor's work the making of the *Corpus Juris Civilis* is the best known and most important in its impact on civilization. The Justinian code is perhaps the outstanding accomplishment in the history of jurisprudence. It consists of nothing less than the codification into a few volumes of the legal life of a great world empire over many centuries. It could only have been commissioned by an emperor who firmly believed that "there is nothing to be found in all things so worthy of attention as the authority of the law," who was willing to devote all the necessary resources of his state to the inauguration and realization of this enormous enterprise. Justinian recruited for the making of his *Corpus* the greatest legists of his empire and carefully set down for them a program of preparing a code of all of

Roman law on grounds of rationality, coherence, equity, and furtherance of imperial power. The Justinian code greatly favors absolutism: the emperor is considered as the living law, and his will has the unchallenged force of law. "The emperor alone can make laws [and] it should also be the province of the imperial dignity alone to interpret them." In this autocratic doctrine, as well as in its rationality and organization, its overriding principles of equity, its adherence to a system of legal procedure in which the authority of the judge as the representative of the emperor dominates the court, the Justinian code stands in boldest contrast to Germanic folk law.

While the Justinian code was not studied in the west in the early middle ages, after the middle of the eleventh century it slowly became the basis of the legal systems of all the European countries, with the exception of England. It is true that this reception of the Roman law brought unfortunate consequences politically in that it provided a juristic basis for the absolutism of the later middle ages and early modern times, but the other characteristics of the Justinian code are so much in line with enlightenment and rationality that it deserves to be recognized as an unsurpassed legal system. Furthermore, it must be remembered that if the Justinian code propagated the Roman-Byzantine doctrines of imperial autocracy, it is most unlikely that any but an absolute ruler would have had the power and resources to carry through to its conclusion such a monumental work of codification. Comparison with the other great legal system of western civilization, the English common law, bears out the truth of this statement. Even at the present time the extent of codification of the common law is insignificant when contrasted with the work of legal synthesis and rationalization effected by Justinian I thirteen centuries ago.

St. Sophia and the *Corpus Juris Civilis* would have been monuments enough for most rulers, but they were not enough for Justinian. Partly due to the autocratic tradition of imperial rule, partly because of the febrile atmosphere of the court which adored the emperor as the deputy of Celestial Majesty, and partly, no doubt, because of his own unbounded ambition, he could not rest until he was the ruler of the Eternal City. He never questioned whether an exhausting war of reconquest was in the interests of the welfare of his people; that is not the way Byzantine emperors thought. Justinian did not even consider whether Byzantium really possessed sufficient resources to undertake a costly war of reconquest. He ignored the threats to Byzantine security represented by the Germans, Slavs, and Mongolians, who pressed on the Balkan frontier, and the powerful Persian empire to the east. Aroused by the ambitions of the Ostrogoths, Justinian determined, at his accession, to restore his authority "over the countries which the ancient Romans possessed, to the limits of both oceans, and lost by subsequent neglect." An emperor who could proclaim himelf in his great law code "pious, fortunate, renowned, conqueror, and triumpher, ever Augustus" was not a man to consider the possibility of failure. Placing his "sole reliance upon the providence of the Holy Trinity," he despatched his army and navy to invade North Africa only three years after the beginning of his reign. No more than Phillip II of Spain in a later century could Justinian allow himself to contemplate the far-reaching consequences of the ultimate failure of his armada.

Even before Justinian exhausted the military and economic resources of his empire on Italian battlefields, he had, by his religious policy, dug the grave of Byzantine power. Since the fourth century the eastern empire had been troubled by religious problems. Theodosius the Great had extinguished the Arian heresy, but novel unorthodox theological doctrines again won wide support in Egypt and Syria in the fifth and sixth centuries, inspired in part by Platonic philosophy and in part by nationalistic feeling finding expression in religion. Large masses of the Egyptian and Syrian populations abandoned the traditional doctrine of the incarnation and, following the tenets of Platonism, subscribed to the Monophysite heresy which claimed that Christ had only one spiritual nature. This view was an anathema to the Latin church, which held that in the one person of Christ there were two natures, human and divine. This doctrinal dispute between the Latin church and the Egyptian and Syrian Christians placed the emperor in a very difficult position. If he was to retain the pope's loyalty, without which he could scarcely hope to regain his authority in Italy, he could not afford to agree with the Monophysites. Consequently, at the council of Chalcedon in 451 the emperor forced the Greek bishops to accept the Latin doctrine on the nature of Christ held by Pope Leo I. This did not, however, settle the issue. In the last decade of the fifth century the emperor went over to the Monophysite position, which brought down the wrath of Pope Gelasius I. In the 520's Justin I, preparing for the Byzantine invasion of Italy, reverted to the Latin position in order to gain papal support against the Ostrogoths.

Justinian continued his uncle's policy, but not just for political reasons. As a trained theologian he decided that the Monophysites were wrong on doctrinal grounds, and he launched a severe persecution of the Monophysites which lasted throughout his reign and which was continued by his successors. The result was widespread disaffection in the great cities of Egypt and Syria, which, next to Constantinople, were the most valuable parts of the empire. By the end of Justinian's reign the persecuted Monophysites had been forced into a position of disloyalty to the Byzantine state, and Egypt and Syria were easy prey for any invader who would provide toleration for the heretical churches of the eastern Mediterranean. Whatever might be said of Justinian's doctrinal views on purely theological grounds, they turned out to be disastrous for the unity and security of the empire. As J. B. Bury, the great historian of the Byzantine empire, commented with respect to Justinian's religious policy, "a theologian on the throne is a public danger."

The long-range effects of Justinian's disputes with the Monophysites were thus most unfortunate for Byzantine power. In the short run they made possible the invasion of Italy, with papal support for the imperial army. Justinian, in fact, in the early part of his reign, in order to placate the pope, went so far as to issue a decree acknowledging the separate spheres of jurisdiction of the *sacerdotium* and the *imperium.* Of course, Justinian later abandoned this acceptance of the moderate aspect of the Gelasian doctrine and returned fully to the traditional Byzantine caesaropapist position. But in 530 he was prepared to risk everything for the success of his great venture. To regain Rome he was willing to hazard all the military and economic resources of his state, to antagonize large groups in the greatest cities of his realm, and even to swallow papal political doctrines. With so much at stake, the future of both Byzantium and western Europe hinged on the success of this great gamble.

The initial stage of the Byzantine invasion of the Latin world went well for the Greek armies. Under the command of Belisarius, a military genius, Justinian's forces easily conquered the Vandal kingdom in North Africa. In 533 Belisarius was ready to cross to Italy, pursuing the same invasion route as was to be followed by the allied armies in World War II. The bishop of Rome welcomed the Byzantine invaders, and, following papal leadership, the Italian population abandoned their Arian Ostrogothic rulers. The Ostrogoths had lost their great king, Theodoric, and they were not well led, but unlike the Vandals they had not forgotten how to fight. A quick Byzantine victory in Italy would have seen the fulfillment of Justinian's plan and would have turned the clock back to the fourth century. Instead, it took the Byzantines nearly three decades to destroy Ostrogothic resistance. This Gothic war, as it has been called, ruined Italy economically. Italy suffered a devastating blow from which it did not recover until the tenth century. By the middle of the sixth century a noticeable de-urbanization had taken place; the great cities such as Rome, Naples, and Milan had suffered a catastrophic loss of population, and great Mediterranean cities were transformed into sleepy provincial towns. A contemporary wrote in about 550 that "Nothing remains for the inhabitants of Italy but to die." The Gothic war is the decisive dividing point in the economic and social history of early medieval Italy, a far more important break than the Germanic invasions of the fifth century. Italy declined very rapidly from her traditional position as the cultural and economic leader of Europe and did not begin to regain this place until the late tenth century.

The long Gothic war was as great a disaster for the Byzantine state as it was for Italy. In order to carry through his grandiose policy of reconquest, Justinian was forced to revive Roman financial oppression in its worst form and to exhaust the resources of his empire. By the time his reign finally came to an end in 565, he was hated not only by the persecuted Monophysite groups in Egypt and Syria but even by members of the imperial court who, at the beginning of his reign, had acclaimed him as the greatest of emperors. This widespread disaffection is expressed in the libelous *Secret History* of Procopius, who had been Belisarius' secretary. The emperor who had built St. Sophia and commissioned the *Corpus Juris Civilis* is portrayed by Procopius as "deceitful, devious, false, hypocritical, two-faced, cruel, . . . a faithless friend . . . a treacherous enemy, insane for murder and plunder." Procopius' slanders reflect the inevitable reaction of an exhausted and ruined people against the leader whose excessively ambitious policies have led them to disaster.

While undertaking great campaigns in Africa and Italy, Justinian had done nothing to diminish the power of enemies closer to home. His successors were left to struggle desperately against the Persians on the eastern frontier and a host of Mongolian, Slavic, and German tribes pressing on the Balkan defenses of the empire. Finally the emperor Heraclius I (610–641) decided that a new policy had to be adopted in order to save Constantinople. He allowed the Bulgars, a Hunnish tribe, and various Slavic peoples to settle in the Balkans and in Greece, asserting only a nominal suzerainty over them. The emperor retained under his own authority only the fringe of the peninsula around Constantinople itself, and the ethnic composition of the Balkans changed even more radically than that of western Europe. Heraclius devoted all the remaining resources of his empire to saving Constantinople and Asia Minor from the Persians. In this he was successful. He inflicted a decisive defeat on the Persian empire, which had threatened Rome for several centuries, and the Persian state disintegrated.

Heraclius I was one of the greatest, but also one of the most unfortunate, of the Byzantine emperors. He rescued the empire from destruction and even inaugurated a revivifying organization. It could be said that he also saved Europe from the Persians, for if Constantinople had fallen to its eastern enemy, there was nothing to prevent a Persian advance into Italy. But already at the time of Heraclius' death in 641 a new and even more powerful menace had made its appearance: the Moslems from the Arabian desert. By the end of the fourth decade of the seventh century the Arabs had conquered Syria and were in the process of invading Persia and Egypt. Three decades later they had swept on along the Mediterranean coast and conquered the whole of North Africa.

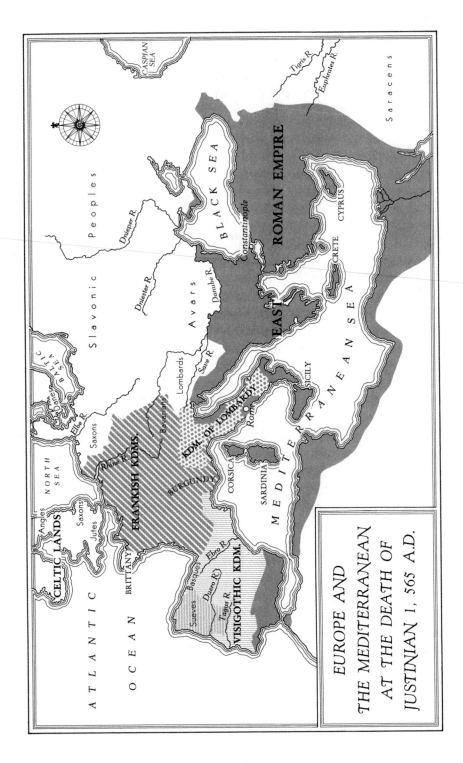

EUROPE AND
THE MEDITERRANEAN
AT THE DEATH OF
JUSTINIAN 1, 565 A.D.

Thus, within a century of Justinian's death the richest and most heavily populated parts of the empire had been lost to the new masters of the Mediterranean world. It is necessary to agree with J. B. Bury's hard judgment that "if any man can be regarded as responsible for this dismemberment of the eastern empire, it is the great emperor Justinian." As a result of his religious policies the east was irrevocably disunited on religious issues. Egypt and Syria were alienated from Constantinople and were disinclined to resist the new invaders, who tolerated their religious beliefs. Furthermore, Justinian had so exhausted the resources of the Byzantine state that his successors did not possess sufficient men and money to maintain the eastern frontier. First the empire had to abandon the Balkans to the Bulgar and Slavs, and then it lost to the Moslems everything else except Constantinople and Asia Minor.

In Italy the reversal of Justinian's work was not as complete and catastrophic as it was in the east, but it came even more rapidly. Italy had hardly passed under Byzantine administration—in fact, Justinian was only three years in his grave—when a new Germanic people broke across the Danube frontier and invaded northern Italy in 568. These were the Langobardi, or the Lombards, one of the crudest and most primitive of all the Germanic invaders. They established a domain very different from the kingdom of Theodoric the Ostrogoth.

The Lombards never ruled the whole of Italy. They dominated the country north of Rome, with the exception of the fortress of Ravenna, which remained in Byzantine hands until the middle of the eighth century. Most of the territory south of Rome continued to be ruled by Constantinople, although the Lombards had some outposts in the south as well, and Sicily was conquered by the Moslems in the seventh century. In this way Italy came to be divided among four rulers—the Byzantines, the Lombards, the pope, and the Moslems—and was not again to be united under one ruler until the latter part of the nineteenth century.

The Lombards organized themselves into two or three large duchies and a few smaller principalities. Like the early Franks, the Lombards condemned Roman culture and government, with the result that the Roman administrative and legal systems disintegrated. The Byzantines had not had enough time to make the Justinian code well known in Italy. Roman law survived in its homeland only as the customary law of the native Italian population and was mixed in with the miserable hodgepodge of Lombard folk law. In addition to their political and legal decrepitude the Lombards remained Arians (for the most part) for a century after their conquest of northern Italy and thus were completely out of touch with the church and the papacy. In fact, even in the eighth century the pope looked upon the

Lombard dukes as his bitter enemies. Perhaps no Germanic people had so little to offer to European civilization as the backward Lombards. They contributed to Italian life only their name and their blood; the former affected the political geography of northern Italy, and the latter made the physical make-up of north Italians rather different from the Mediterranean physiognomy of the southerners. These were meager boons in exchange for Theodoric's policy of *civilitas*. Of course, Justinian had not intended to replace the Ostrogothic with Lombard rule in Italy. But as in the case of his policy in regard to the eastern part of his empire, the risks that he took were so great that failure was bound to result in a worse condition than had existed at the beginning of Justinian's reign.

The emperors after Justinian never possessed the strength to attempt the reconstruction of the Roman empire. Placed on the defensive by the Moslem armies, Byzantium drifted farther and farther away from Europe into a culture of its own. The Justinian code is the last great product of Byzantine letters to be written in Latin. Henceforth the civilization of the eastern Roman empire consisted of a distinctive blending of Greek, Balkan, and oriental qualities.

Justinian's failure demonstrated to the men of the west that, as a result of the barbarian invasions, the Roman empire could not be effectively reunited. Justinian, the greatest Roman emperor since Constantine, was the nemesis of Byzantine power. In the late sixth and seventh centuries Europe turned away from Constantinople, and the European peoples no longer looked to the hard-pressed Byzantine emperors and the essentially alien Byzantine culture for leadership and guidance. Hence, the most important consequence of Justinian's work for sixth- and seventh-century Europe was to bring to the center of the stage the west's own men and institutions. The west was thrown back upon its own resources and had to find leadership in its own ranks. These were the church, led by the papacy and the monastic orders, and the Frankish monarchy. The short-lived alliance between the papacy and the Byzantine emperor had in the end brought only a new disaster for Italy. It remained to be seen whether an alliance between the papacy and the Frankish monarchy could be effected with more fortunate consequences.

II. The Impact of Islam on Early Medieval Europe

The expansion of Islam was a decisive factor in medieval history. It divided the Mediterranean world into three civilizations and power blocks: the Byzantine, the European, and the Islamic. One of the major themes in medieval history from the seventh to the twelfth centuries was the relationship and interaction among these three cultural, economic, linguistic, and religious groupings. In varying degrees each of these civilizations was an heir of the later Roman empire. Byzantium exemplifies the most direct continuation of Roman law, administration, and thought. Western Europe also inherited many Roman traditions, and Islam absorbed some aspects of Roman imperial organization and the better part of the philosophy and science of Greece and Rome. However, Islam was also heavily indebted to oriental traditions, particularly those of Persia and Egypt. Oriental culture had also influenced the later Roman empire, but Islam was the medieval civilization most directly in touch with the eastern heritage.

The triumph of Islam on the eastern and southern shores of the Mediterranean in the seventh century was the consequence of the final and successful attempt made by Arabic tribes to break into the Mediterranean world. There was nothing novel in an Arabic invasion of Egypt and Syria; there had been periodic invasions of the Fertile Crescent by nomads from the Arabian desert since the second millennium B.C., and the appearance of the Hebrews in Palestine was the consequence of one such northward thrust. The organization of the Mediterranean world under Roman rule had, however, put a stop to large-scale Arabic incursion, and the Byzantine empire, until the early seventh century, was successful in blocking the northward migration of the desert tribes.

What difference, then, can be seen in this new Arabic invasion which accounts for its success on a great scale? In the first place, the attack on the Mediterranean world came at a time when the two empires which could have blocked the path of migration and conquest were either dead or exhausted. Heraclius I had just destroyed the Persian empire, but Byzantium's military resources had been fully expended, and the imperial armies were able to offer only token resistance to the Arabs. Furthermore, great masses of the population of Egypt and Syria had been alienated by the religious policy of the orthodox emperor. Not being satisfied with this disaffection, Heraclius had undertaken a large-scale persecution of the Jews, who comprised substantial portions of the population of Alexandria, Antioch, and other great eastern cities. Under these circumstances the Arabic invaders could not but have succeeded, provided that they possessed a modicum of unity and organization.

And for the first time the warlike tribes of the Arabian desert had been harnessed together by a common faith and by religious authority. In this way Islam contributed the vital factor which made possible the rapid Arabic conquest of the richest provinces of the eastern Roman empire. The old myth that the Arabs burst forth with the sword in one hand and the Koran in the other, offering the Mediterranean peoples either conversion or death, has long been discredited. In fact, the Arabs tolerated the religious practices of the Christians and Jews they conquered, only placing a head tax and limitation of political rights on those who would not recognize Mohammed as the Prophet of Allah, and therefore they had a vested interest in not hurrying the conversion of their subjects.

Some scholars have suggested, as an additional reason for the Arabic expansion, economic pressure resulting from an increased desiccation and decline in fertility in the Arabian peninsula. As yet, very little is known about conditions in Arabia in Mohammed's lifetime. There were a few important commercial cities, of which Mecca was the largest and most prosperous, and extensive commerce was carried on with the lands to the east. Great caravan routes stretched across the peninsula, and the picture we build up of Arabia at this time must include areas where urban and agricultural life flourished. However, the fact remains that the greater part of the peninsula was in a desert condition, and the majority of its inhabitants belonged to fierce nomadic tribes.

This economic and social situation is reflected in Mohammed's life and teachings. The Prophet was himself a city dweller. He was a poor member of one of the most prominent families in Mecca, and he made his living as the caravan manager for a wealthy widow many years his senior, whom he subsequently married. Mohammed's doctrine, however, reflects the puritanical revulsion of the simple nomad against the corrupting influence of novel urban mores, in much the same way as the religion of the Hebrew prophets was founded on the revolt of rural ethics against the easier living of Hebrew townsmen. We know very little else about Mohammed that would serve to explain his teachings. He had a passing acquaintance with Judaism and Christianity, which he picked up in his business relations; he was given to epileptic fits in which he experienced visions and received the word of Allah from the archangel Gabriel which he set down in the Koran; and, unlike Jesus of Nazareth, he was an extremely able political organizer and military leader. In his early career, while he was building up his authority, Mohammed did not refrain from following the principle that the end justifies the means. He relied for early support on Jewish tribes in the neighboring city of Medina, but when he no longer needed them, he turned against them. On one occasion he organized bandit attacks on passing caravans in order to finance his religious enterprises. Although many legends have been preserved in Arabic literature about the great Prophet, what we know of his personality comes mainly from the meager facts of his biography and Koranic doctrine. These reveal him to have been an austere, devout, strong, almost violent man with a smattering of learning and a moderate level of intellectual sophistication.

Mohammed may not have been the most sophisticated and learned of religious thinkers, but no spiritual leader has ever founded a faith which has so rapidly appealed to such an enormous number of people. Of all the great religions of mankind, Islam is most suited to serve as a universal religion. The theology presented in the Koran is simple and easily comprehended. It envisions an omniscient deity who makes severe ethical demands on mankind, but who at the same time promises certain reward of eternal life in return for fulfillment of the divine precepts. The all-powerful and all-knowing Allah is a purely monotheistic deity; the Christian idea of the trinity is as much an anathema to the Moslems as to the Jews. Mohammed brings to mankind the word of God, but Mohammed is only the last and the greatest of the prophets, "the seal of the prophets," and he is not in any way a partaker of divinity. In the Koranic view Christ, like Abraham, is one of the great prophets who prepared the way for Mohammed, but the Christian theology of the trinity, with its heavy debt to Platonism, is rejected by Mohammed in favor of the pure monotheism of the Arabian desert.

"Islam" means "submission" to the will of Allah, and Allah demands from His adherents among mankind, if they wish to enjoy the great rewards which He promises, the fulfillment of a stern and puritanical code of conduct. The Moslem is to pray several times a day, and he is to make an attempt to go on a pilgrimage to the fountainhead of the true faith at Mecca at least once in his life. The Koran sets down a long series of regulations on the daily life of the Moslem. The Moslem is to refrain from drinking and gambling, he is not to practice usury in business, and generally he is to deal with his fellow humans according to the highest precepts of justice and mercy. The Moslem is to exercise charity toward his fellow men, and he is to be most generous in assisting the unfortunate and downtrodden of mankind. The Koran emphasizes the value of family life, and while, for the Moslem who can afford it, four wives are allowed, the most rigorous precepts of sexual morality are enjoined upon all members of the Islamic faith. Finally, the Moslem is required to give his life, if necessary, to further and protect the true faith, and for those Moslems who suffer such martyrdom the rewards of eternal life will be the most assured and the greatest. Holy war is one of the pillars of Islam.

The Koranic doctrine presents the most explicit theory of merits among any of the great religions of mankind. Those who follow the word of Allah and who serve God with sincerity and devotion are assured of eternal life and eternal happiness. The agonizing problems raised by the Pauline-Augustinian stream in Christian thought are completely avoided in the

Koranic teachings. And even the occasional doubts which creep into Hebraic thinking on the question of merits and reward, such as are found in the Book of Job, are largely absent from Islamic thought. Furthermore, while the Hebraic concept of heaven is extremely vague and while the Christian concept of heaven is purely ethereal and spiritual, the Koranic picture of heaven is both specific in detail and highly attractive to human desires. In fact, the Moslem is promised a heaven in which he can partake of pleasures denied him in this world; he may drink, gamble, and enjoy the company of beautiful black-eyed maidens, who are mentioned several times in the Koran as rewards promised to the most worthy members of the faith. The Islamic religion, then, is an optimistic one. It conceives of an omnipotent and omniscient God who requires a high and generous level of conduct, and for those who fulfill these precepts it promises the certainty of reward in a heaven which turns out to be a most attractive oasis. It is no mystery why this religion should have proved to be most popular among the warriors of the Arabian desert; but its theology is austere enough and its ethic certainly rigorous enough to appeal also to men of the greatest education and sophistication both in the medieval period and today.

In the seventh and eighth centuries the great majority of the Christian populations who lived along the eastern and southern shores of the Mediterranean went over to this new faith founded by Mohammed. It was a great blow for Christianity that its oldest and most intensive centers should have been lost to Islam. Yet, from the point of view of the history of human values, when the high quality of Islamic theology and ethics is taken into account, it cannot be said that a great disaster had occurred. Why the Christians should have so readily accepted Islam remains something of a mystery in view of the fact that no historian has yet been able to work out the details of this conversion. It is obvious that the Christians were eager to accept the faith of their conquerors and to free themselves from the civil disabilities which were imposed upon those who remained outside the Islamic faith. But the disabilities were not severe, and it is both sad and strange that the great churches of Syria, Palestine, Egypt, and North Africa should so quickly have collapsed before the attractions of conversion to Islam. It is true that the Christian churches did not entirely disappear, and fragmented Christian groups continue to exist in the Islamic countries to the present day, but two hundred years after the death of the Prophet the influence and numbers of the great churches of the eastern and southern Mediterranean had become negligible. And it was not only the orthodox eastern church and the various heretical Greek churches which lost the majority of their followers to Islam; by 900 A.D. the Latin church in North Africa had all but disappeared, and the Spanish Christian church had suffered enormous losses. A Spanish Christian writer of the tenth century tells us that many of his younger contemporaries were converting to Islam not only because of their political ambitions but also because of the attractions of Arabic literature and culture.

The effect of the expansion of Islam on the eastern and southern shores of the Mediterranean may be gauged from the fact that these regions are thought of today as the heartland of Islamic civilization, with attendant distinctive political, economic, and intellectual qualities. In fact, Arab nationalists deny the right of European peoples to rule in these regions. Only those who have benefited from the liberal education of historical studies know that these countries were the birthplace of Christianity and the provenance of the Platonic-Christian tradition which was the mainstream of western culture until the twelfth century. Long before Mohammed received the word of Allah from the archangel Gabriel, the intellectual life of the eastern and southern coasts of the Mediterranean was dominated by St. Paul, Plotinus, Eusebius, and St. Augustine. Yet so complete and irrevocable was the effect of the Arabic expansion and domination that St. Augustine's Tunisian homeland is thought of as the rightful property of Moslem nationalists and not as the place of origin of doctrines indispensable to the development of western civilization.

The expansion of Islam occurred over exactly one hundred years—from the death of the Prophet in 632 until the battle of Tours in 732, when the Arabic armies penetrating into France suffered a defeat at the hands of the Frankish ruler. Many Arabic tribes became violent and restless after Mohammed's death, and the caliph, the "successor" of the Prophet, urged them to resume their marauding expeditions toward the Byzantine empire. By 638 Jerusalem had fallen to the Arabic armies, and in the following three decades they swept on through Syria, Persia, and even reached northern India. Other Arabic armies went into Egypt, conquered Alexandria, and then moved rapidly across the Libyan desert into North Africa, which they easily took from the Byzantine governor. In 711 the Arabic armies, assisted by the fierce Berbers of the North African desert who had rapidly been converted to Islam, inflicted a complete defeat on the Visigothic king and became masters of Spain. The Christian princes managed to hold out in the Pyrenees until the tenth century, when they began the slow reconquest of the Iberian peninsula from the Moslems, which was not completed until the fifteenth century. Until the twelfth century the Moslem position in Spain was secure, and they were masters of the greater part of the peninsula, and until the tenth century, in fact, nothing was heard from the petty Christian lords who barely managed to survive in the mountains.

It may be that the Arabs had now fully expended their resources and that they would not in any case have conquered France, but their defeat at the battle of Tours in 732 put a stop to their further advance to the north, and they remained satisfied with Spain. Meanwhile, in 717 the Arabs had made their last great assault on Constantinople before the fifteenth century and had been unable to take the great fortress on the Bosporus. The Arabs quickly became masters of the Mediterranean and conquered Sicily and Crete, and they were able to attack Constantinople from the sea. But the citadel on the Dardanelles was able to withstand the Moslem onslaught in part because of a new weapon which the Byzantines had developed: the so-called Greek fire, a form of incendiary bomb which the Greeks used to inflict great damage on the Moslem fleets. Constantinople thus managed to survive the Arabic attack and thereby saved western Europe from Moslem conquest via the soft underbelly of the European peninsula. Yet, of all its great and wealthy eastern provinces, Byzantium had managed to hold on to only Asia Minor. The harassed emperor was now forced on the defensive, and there was no possibility of the exhausted Byzantine state undertaking a war of reconquest against the Arabs for another two hundred years.

Until the middle of the eighth century, the extensive territory which the Arabs had conquered was under one rule. The caliph made his capital in Damascus and ruled these vast territories and peoples with an autocratic government modeled on the oriental monarchy of Persia. In the eighth century the non-Arabic peoples who had been conquered and had converted to Islam became dissatisfied with their subject position and demanded a share of the government of the vast Arabic empire and equal citizenship with the warrior caste which had come from Arabia. Finally, in the middle of the eighth century the subject peoples revolted against the caliph of the Omayyad dynasty, who ruled from Damascus, and a new dynasty, mainly Persian in background, the Abbasids, seized the title of caliph and set up a new capital in Baghdad.

The supplanting of the Omayyad by the Abbasid dynasty was a signal for revolt and political decentralization throughout the Islamic world, and by the end of the ninth century, instead of one great Arabic empire, the Islamic world was divided up into several states. The rulers of these states continued to respect the caliph as the successor of the Prophet, but the political power in the Islamic world had now fallen into the hands of various despotic princes. Among these princes was the ruler in Spain where the Omayyad dynasty alone had managed to prevail. The Mediterranean world was now united by the Arabic religion and language, and it formed a great international economic system, but the Arabic civilization was no longer a political entity. From the eighth century the term "Arabic" identifies a great civilization on the eastern and southern shores of the Mediter-

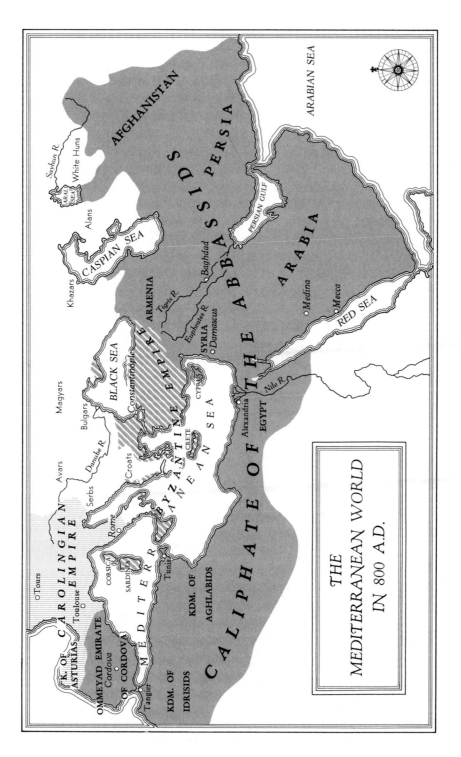

ARABIAN SEA

AFGHANISTAN

Sayhun R.
White Huns

PERSIA

Alans

CASPIAN SEA

Khazars

ARMENIA

Tigris R.
Baghdad

Euphrates R.

ARABIA

PERSIAN GULF

SYRIA
Damascus

Medina

Mecca

RED SEA

Magyars

BLACK SEA

Constantinople

CYPRUS

Nile R.

Bulgars

Danube R.

Croats

Serbs

Avars

CRETE

Alexandria
EGYPT

MEDITERRANEAN SEA

BYZANTINE EMPIRE

CALIPHATE OF THE ABBASSIDS

Tours

CAROLINGIAN EMPIRE

Rome

Toulouse

CORSICA

SARDINIA

Tunis

THE
MEDITERRANEAN WORLD
IN 800 A.D.

K. OF
ASTURIAS

OMMEYAD EMIRATE
OF CORDOVA

Cordova

Tangier

KDM. OF
IDRISIDS

KDM. OF
AGHLABIDS

ranean to which many peoples—Greek, Persian, Syrian, Egyptian, Jewish, Berber, as well as Arab—have contributed.

The caliph's position as the religious leader of Islam became a purely nominal one. By the end of the ninth century three distinct traditions and groups had emerged within the Moslem religious community, which by and large still prevail. There was first of all the orthodox position, which had an overwhelming superiority in the size of its following. The orthodox tradition depended strictly on the Koranic revelation, the Traditions of the Prophet, which were additional doctrinal pronouncements attributed to Mohammed, and a vast complex of religious, moral, and social law derived from the Koran and the semi-canonical Traditions. The caliph was supposed to be the defender of orthodoxy, but this task was actually assumed by a group of religious teachers whose attitude and professional status closely resembled that of the orthodox Jewish rabbis, whom, indeed, they may have originally emulated. There was actually no overriding central authority in the Moslem religious fellowship; there was no pope in Islam. In each Moslem country the orthodox teachers banded together to proclaim the truths of revelation and religious law, and the extent of their power and influence depended largely on whether they could obtain the support of the state. Until the eleventh century the Arabic princes were frequently much more liberal and secular in their attitudes than the leaders of orthodoxy, and hence the latter, while they had great influence, generally lacked the power to persecute those who dissented from their doctrines and legal precepts.

The two other traditions in medieval Islamic religion were the messianic and the mystical. The messianic form of Islamic thought involved belief in a continuing revelation expressed by new prophets who claimed to be descendants of Fatima, the daughter of Mohammed. The supporters of these successor prophets (Shiites) were naturally bitterly opposed by the orthodox community, which regarded Mohammed as the ultimate prophet. But occasionally, in the middle east and northern India, messianic leaders succeeded in transforming their theocratic claims into actual political power and thereby provided isolated areas in which the supporters of a continual revelation found refuge. The Aga Khan is a modern survivor of one of these medieval Moslem messiahs who claimed descent from the Prophet. The mystical tradition in Islam, as in medieval Judaism, was a reaction against the stultifying confines of orthodoxy. The Moslem mystics (Sufists) sought a direct personal relationship with God and an intense religious experience as an escape from the heavy legalism of orthodoxy. After the complete triumph of orthodoxy in the twelfth century Sufism provided the only alternative to the Koranic tradition in Islamic thought.

Before the end of the twelfth century, however, there existed a very rich current of secular thought in the Islamic world, which made Arabic scholars of the tenth and eleventh centuries the greatest philosophers and scientists of their age, from whom the Europeans in the twelfth and thirteenth centuries were to derive a very considerable part of their knowledge in these fields. The Greek philosophic and scientific writings, including the whole of the Aristotelian corpus, which was unknown in Latin Europe before the twelfth century, were translated into Arabic in eighth-century Syria with the assistance of Greek scholars who belonged to heretical Christian sects. The Aristotelian and other Greek scientific writings moved westward through the Islamic world and reached Spain by the end of the ninth century. Tenth-century Cordoba was famous even in hostile Latin-Christian countries as a center of thriving scholarship and science. A nun, writing in distant Germany in the late tenth century, refers to Cordoba as "a fair ornament" of culture, renowned for its seven streams of knowledge. As late as the twelfth century Arabic medicine was far superior to the western variety, and only the opposition of orthodox religious leaders to dissection prevented the Moslem physicians from achieving the medical discoveries which came in the sixteenth and seventeenth centuries in western Europe. In the tenth and eleventh centuries mathematics was almost exclusively an Arabic science, as the perpetuation of the terms "algebra" and "Arabic numerals" in western languages indicates. The Arabic mathematicians were heavily indebted to Chinese scholarship, but they made many original contributions. In the Arabic world before the twelfth century philosophy and science were in the hands of scholars who made their living in secular professions such as medicine, education, and government. Religious and intellectual leadership was separate, and intellectual life was dominated by scholars who had little to do with orthodoxy. This situation contributed to the vitality and boldness of Arabic science, although in the long run it made rational inquiry and speculation vulnerable to attack and subversion on doctrinal grounds during the orthodox reaction of the twelfth and thirteenth centuries.

The Arabic world of the early middle ages was renowned not only for intellectual achievements but also for its agricultural wealth and commercial prosperity. Compared to the Moslem countries, western Europe appears as an underdeveloped area. The favorable economic situation of the Arabic world was, of course, scarcely an Arabic creation, although historians of medieval Islam frequently speak of it in these extravagant terms. The Arabs, however, did have the good sense during the early middle ages to preserve the irrigation systems of the Mediterranean countries, which had been in existence since Roman times and even much earlier in many places, and to perpetuate international trade in the Mediterranean, which had

hitherto been dominated by Byzantine merchants. The Arabs themselves had
nothing to contribute to the economic life of the Mediterranean world, but
they learned commercial and industrial techniques very rapidly from the
peoples they conquered. They turned out to be remarkably good sailors;
they built large fleets and in the eighth and ninth centuries almost completely controlled the Mediterranean. The Moslem princes provided a very
sound coinage, which became the medium of exchange for important commercial transactions not only in the Mediterranean world but in many parts
of western Europe as well. After the Latin-speaking peoples stopped producing their own gold coins in the eighth century, they continued to use Arabic
gold coins in international trade, and these have been discovered all over
western Europe by archeologists. It must always be remembered, however,
in considering Arabic commerce, that the ubiquitous figure of the Arabic
merchant in the early medieval world was often only Arabic speaking;
ethnically he could be an Egyptian, a Syrian, a Jew, a Berber, or one of the
many other peoples who were brought together under Islamic rule.

The impact of the expansion of Islam on the economy of western
Europe has been the subject of enormous controversy among historians.
There can be little doubt about the impact of Islam on the political and
intellectual development of early medieval Europe; it was negligible in both
cases. This is not because western Europe had nothing to learn from Islamic
civilization; on the contrary, both in government, in which the Arabic
countries had absorbed the Roman-Byzantine traditions of bureaucracy, and
in philosophy and science the western Europeans could have benefited
greatly from Arabic instruction. But during the early middle ages there were
no Moslems living under Latin-Christian rule, and, because the western
peoples looked upon the Moslems as perverse and pernicious heretics, they
closed their eyes to the benefits they could derive from association with the
Arabic peoples. In the early middle ages, as in the twentieth century, there
was a price to be paid for iron curtains and cold wars, and the Latin-
Christian peoples deprived themselves of the benefits of Moslem civilization
through their self-imposed political and cultural isolation. Only at the end
of the tenth century did the hatred which the Christians felt for Mohammed's
teachings begin to take second place to the obvious advantages which could
be gained through study at Cordoba. The greatest Latin scholar of the age,
the Frenchman Gerbert of Aurillac, who eventually became pope, went
down into Moslem Spain to study philosophy and mathematics. The education he received from Arabic teachers made him so intellectually superior to
his Christian contemporaries that for many centuries Gerbert was regarded
as the possessor of mysterious powers of sorcery and black magic. It was not
until after 1100 that the iron curtain between Latin Europe and Moslem

Spain was effectively breached; the result was the importation of the Aristotelian corpus from Spain into western Europe, inaugurating an intellectual revolution.

The economic effects of the expansion of Islam are by no means so clear, and for the past twenty-five years historians have hotly disputed the question of the effect of the emergence of the new power block in the Mediterranean in the seventh and eighth centuries on the economic relations between east and west. This controversy was the result of the last work of the very influential Belgian economic historian, Henri Pirenne, entitled *Mohammed and Charlemagne* and published posthumously in 1936. Pirenne was a rarity—a very able and learned scholar who was also an original thinker and the master of a vivacious and persuasive literary style. Most historians tend to become more cautious as they grow older; Pirenne, on the other hand, became more and more inclined to sweeping and radically new generalizations. Pirenne's superb pleading and the great esteem in which he was held by his colleagues everywhere won many converts for his thesis. Indeed, *Mohammed and Charlemagne* had such a profound impact on the general interpretation of early medieval history that many of the older generation of historians find it difficult to abandon or even modify Pirenne's thesis, even in the face of the very powerful criticism directed against it by Robert S. Lopez, Robert Latouche, and other scholars in recent years.

What was Pirenne's thesis? Put briefly, it was that the expansion of Islam brought about the economic disintegration of the Mediterranean world. It was the advance of Islam which produced the final separation of east from west and the end of the Mediterranean unity which, Pirenne claimed, had continued to exist all through the period of the Germanic invasions. Africa and Spain, which had always been part of the Latin world, belonged henceforth to a culture centered on Baghdad. "The western Mediterranean became a Moslem lake; the west was blockaded and forced to live upon its own resources. For the first time in history, the axis of life shifted northward from the Mediterranean." Cut off from Mediterranean life, western Europe reverted to a natural (that is, rural) economy and developed the new institutions of the feudal state and manorial society. The attractions of this clear, incisive, and cosmic thesis are obvious, and Pirenne was able to advance it with a considerable show of evidence. But several scholars, writing in the last twenty years, have contended that the *Mohammed and Charlemagne* thesis is a gross exaggeration and oversimplification of the course of early medieval civilization.

It will be seen that there are two distinct aspects of Pirenne's thesis, both of which must be sustained if his interpretation is to remain valid: first, that the Germanic invasions were *not* a turning point in economic history;

second, that the expansion of Islam *was* the cataclysmic turning point. Both of these aspects deserve careful consideration.

Pirenne contended that, in spite of the Germanic invasions, the economic unity of the Mediterranean world was preserved in the fifth and sixth centuries and Merovingian France remained part of Mediterranean civilization. This view depends on a misreading, intentional or otherwise, of the picture of Merovingian society provided by Gregory of Tours. There had not been a complete break (in Gregory's pages) with Mediterranean trade and culture, but there had been a marked decline of Mediterranean influence. The economy of sixth-century Gaul is not one in which trade and monetary transactions are important. Merovingian France is a society dependent to a very large degree on landed wealth alone. The cities depicted in Gregory of Tours' history are political and episcopal centers, not commercial centers. The Roman *curiales* class has disappeared; the trade with the eastern countries is carried on by easterners—Syrians and Jews. Merovingian France, as compared with Byzantium, is already an underdeveloped area in which agriculture is the basis of the economy and in which commerce is of little importance. It seems impossible to deny the validity of this picture of Merovingian economy, which, furthermore, has been substantiated by archeological evidence. Obviously then, the economic decline of France and the disintegration of the economic unity of the Mediterranean world were well under way before Mohammed.

This is not to say that the Germanic invasions were a sudden catastrophe which alone produced this economic decline. The economic unity of the Mediterranean, and with it the volume of international trade, was declining from the end of the second century. While it is still not completely certain to what degree the Germanic invasions mark a very sharp turn in economic history, it definitely appears that "the meeting of German primitivism with Roman decrepitude," as Lopez described it, markedly accelerated the process of the economic disintegration of the Mediterranean world, whose first symptoms were evident as far back as the second half of the second century A.D.

Recent research by economic historians indicates that toward the end of the sixth century there was a partial restoration of international trade in the Mediterranean under Byzantine auspices. The Syrian merchants in Gregory of Tours' time are evidence of this. By the middle of the seventh century there is evidence of a partial restoration of tin trade between England and the eastern Mediterranean. There is also fragmentary evidence that Ireland and the Baltic countries, which had never been touched by Roman civilization, were now drawn into the nexus of Mediterranean trade.

The second part of Pirenne's *Mohammed and Charlemagne* thesis now remains to be examined: to what extent did the Moslem expansion terminate this partial revival of east-west trade? Pirenne argued that the Moslems and Christians hated each other, and since Moslem sea power dominated the Mediterranean in the eighth and ninth centuries, the continued economic relations between western Europe and the Mediterranean became, a priori, impossible. He then presented a *post hoc, ergo propter hoc* argument, which may be a fallacy in logic, but which is often accepted as plausible by the historian in absence of more certain evidence. He pointed to the moving of centers of European life to northern France and the Rhine valley, the decline of the Mediterranean French ports, and increasing tendency to a purely rural economy in eighth-century France, and concluded that this must have been due to a breakdown of east-west trade as a result of the Arab advance. He was also able to offer some specific and empirical evidence for his thesis. In the late seventh century the western church stopped using Palestinian wine in the Eucharist and published its documents on parchment and no longer on paper imported from Egypt. The highly plausible conclusion is that as a result of the Moslem invasion Palestinian wine and Egyptian papyrus were no longer available to Europeans; at least their importation now involved prohibitive expense.

It has been hard for Pirenne's critics to explain away this empirical evidence. It has been suggested that these oriental commodities were less in demand due simply to changes in taste and methods of production in the eighth century, but this is scarcely a convincing refutation. There is, however, sufficient evidence of another kind to undermine seriously the general validity of Pirenne's thesis. Perhaps for half a century or a little longer east-west trade was almost completely cut off, but certainly from the middle of the ninth century there is ample evidence of a continued trade between western Europe and the Islamic countries. The staple western exports to the Islamic countries consisted of slaves, furs, metal products, and timber. In return, the Moslem merchants offered oriental luxury goods to make the harsh life of the European nobility a little more comfortable. It does seem strange that Pirenne, who was a great authority on medieval commerce, completely overlooked the significance of the thriving slave trade between western Europe and the Mediterranean countries. Jewish merchants initially played an important part in this exchange, and by 900 the Venetians and other Italian merchants had suppressed their religious zeal sufficiently to become the middle men of east-west commerce. Certainly at all times in the early middle ages Mediterranean trade was hampered by Arabic pirates, and this situation made international commerce a risky business and kept the cost of transportation very high. But the European merchant made a very high return on whatever goods did not fall prey to piracy or shipwreck, and since the goods involved were luxury items and raw materials intended to satisfy the tastes of the ruling classes and not for mass consumption, the necessarily inflated cost to the buyer was not a prohibitive factor.

It may be conceded that the expansion of Islam encouraged the commercial disintegration of the Mediterranean world and that it was a factor in the progressive ruralization of the European economy and the transference of the centers of European life to northern France and the Rhine valley. But the actual cutting-off of Europe from Mediterranean trade was only momentary, if it ever occurred at all. The expansion of Islam represents but one stage in an economic process of autarky and de-urbanization which had been going on since the end of the second century A.D. The civil wars of the third century, the Germanic invasions, and finally the Arabic military triumph were the events which accelerated the process and helped to produce the feudal and manorial world of the ninth century. Pirenne contributed greatly to our understanding of medieval history by calling attention to the economic consequences of Islam, but he greatly exaggerated its cataclysmic significance, as well as underrating the impact of the Germanic invasions. Mohammed did not determine the world of Charlemagne, as Pirenne believed; the institutions of eighth- and ninth-century Europe would not have been substantially different had the expansion of Islam never taken place. Nothing is more fundamental in early medieval history than the self-sufficiency of western Europe after Justinian had failed to reconstitute the Roman empire, and the working out in isolation of the destiny of western civilization, with its own institutions and its own leadership.

Chapter Six

THE ADVANCE OF
ECCLESIASTICAL
LEADERSHIP

I. *The Monastic Foundations of Medieval Civilization*

The leadership which was so badly needed by the disorganized western society of the sixth century could come initially only from the church, which had in its ranks almost all the literate men in Europe and the strongest institutions of the age. The church, however, had also suffered severely from the Germanic invasions. The bishops identified their interests with those of the lay nobility and in fact were often relatives of kings and the more powerful aristocrats; the secular clergy in general was ignorant, corrupt, and unable to deal with the problem of Christianizing a society which remained intensely heathen in spite of formal conversion of masses of Germanic warriors to Christianity. The grossest heathen superstitions were grafted onto Latin Christianity: the religiosity of the sixth and seventh centuries was infected with devils, magic, the crudest kind of relic worship, the importation of local nature deities into Christianity in the guise of saints, and a general debasement of the Latin faith by religious primitivism. There was no parish churchman who could go out into the countryside and counter these crudities; at most, a member of the cathedral clergy would occasionally journey out from the episcopal see to administer the sacraments. The secular clergy were neither interested in nor capable of undertaking extensive missionary work. No one even cared about attempting the formal conversion of the German tribes within the Merovingian kingdom who lived east of the Rhine, and they remained heathens until the eighth century. By the beginning of the seventh century church discipline in Gaul was in a state of chaos, and the problem was the most basic one of preserving the sufficient rudiments of literacy to perpetuate the liturgy and doctrines of Latin Christianity. Many priests literally did not know what they were saying at church services, but uttered a mumbo-jumbo which vaguely resembled Latin as a magical incantation in order to impress their near-savage parishioners.

The Latin church was preserved from extinction, and European civilization with it, by the two ecclesiastical institutions which alone had the strength and efficiency to withstand the impress of the surrounding barbarism: the regular clergy (that is, the monks) and the papacy. Of all the institutions in western Europe, only monasticism and the papacy were able to provide leadership for European society, and out of their joint efforts was eventually to come the amelioration of Germanic kingship and its transformation into an additional creative force in early medieval society. But while the papacy and Germanic kingship were ultimately to provide the most dramatic and effective direction to the people of western Europe, it was the monks who were the most continuous force for education, organization, and social amelioration between the sixth and twelfth centuries and a determining factor of the most fundamental kind in the formation of medieval civilization. How did the regular clergy, that is, the clergy living under monastic rule, come to assume these indispensable social obligations? The structure of the new civilization which was created in the early middle ages was determined by the answer to this question.

Monasticism is a form of religious asceticism, which in turn involves the disciplining, limitation, or abnegation of the material and physical aspects of human life in order to assure a saving relationship with a deity conceived of as a purely spiritual being. Asceticism is therefore intended to secure salvation, and this end can be achieved either by the withdrawal of the ascetic from society and its corrupting temptations and distractions or by the severe control of social life so as to make the environment suitable for the ascetic to continue to live in the world. The former manifestation of asceticism is called monasticism, and the latter may be termed puritanism. It is obvious that in the circumstances of the early middle ages, with a violent, disorganized, and fundamentally un-Christianized society, the puritan control of society to make the world safe for asceticism was out of the question. The ascetic had to withdraw from the world in order to assure the triumph of his spiritual will and the salvation of his soul. But the nature of early medieval western monasticism in its ultimate form was such that this flight from the world did not very well succeed; instead, the monastery became a social institution of the utmost importance. The more outstanding monks came to render the greatest services both to the church and monarchy and to give new vitality and leadership to both institutions.

Monasticism is by no means exclusively a western or medieval institution. There are Buddhist monks even today, and there were Jewish monks in Palestine before the Christian era—the radical sect of Essenes, who are believed to have been the authors of the Dead Sea Scrolls. It is possible that St. John the Baptist was influenced by the messianic and eschatological doctrines of this sect. In any case, John certainly practiced the most astringent kind of ascetic life, and Jesus can be said to have supported such a life as the most ideal one when he told his followers that, to enter the fellowship of the kingdom of God, they ought to dissolve all bonds that bind men to the material world, even the love for their own parents. Jesus' warning that "you cannot serve God and Mammon" and the example of his life, in which he rendered obedience to his Father even to death on the cross, were inspirations to all subsequent generations of Christian ascetics to separate themselves from the world and to lead a purely spiritual life as far as is humanly possible. The heavy infusion of Platonist philosophy into Christian thought in the early centuries after Jesus, with its body-soul dualism and its denigration of the material world, engendered the common belief that the soul was most assured of salvation when the spiritual aspects of humanity were cultivated to the exclusion of the physical. Some of the more devout members of the church in the second and third centuries, who interpreted the Gospel in this heavily dualistic manner, sensed a grave danger to their souls from living in society and ran away into wild places in order to pursue purely spiritual exercises. A favorite place of retreat for these holy and contemplative people was the Egyptian desert. But the fathers of the desert, once they had achieved a great reputation for sanctity, found that the world would not let them go; the fathers were literally hounded through the Egyptian desert by admirers seeking to secure their assistance in entreaties to the deity. Thus, almost from the beginning of Christian monasticism, the monks found themselves pursued by the world they had just abandoned in disgust and implored by society to act as its intercessor with God. The tension between the world and the monastery was in evidence from the inauguration of the ascetic movement in Christianity.

The figure of the hermit-saint was a particularly prominent and popular one in the Greek church, and Greek monasticism never entirely overcame the pattern established by its anchoritic origins. The ideal hermit type was established by Athanasius' *Life of St. Antony,* the most famous of the fourth-century desert fathers. Greek anchoritism was liable to go to extremes as the populace confused holiness with extreme physical privation. Such was the case with the early fifth-century Syrian saint, Simeon Stylites, who was reputed to have spent the last thirty years of his life sitting on top of a pillar seventy feet high. The more sensitive and cultured minds in the Greek church discouraged such extreme asceticism. The great fourth-century Christian humanist and Greek church father, St. Basil, contended that the monks ought to obey the commandment to love one's neighbor as well as God. St. Basil was the leader in the creation of a communal type of monasticism in the Greek church which gradually came to predominate over the old anchoritic form. But the Greek cenobitic form of ascetic life remained loose, and the individual monk retained most of his independence. The characteristic Greek monastery was a large community where monks lived together for convenience, but the abbot (*abbas,* father) had very little control over them; he was merely a revered and senior religious.

The development of western monasticism also begins with the anchoritic form. The failure of nerve of western society during the last century of the Roman empire induced some who had lost their faith in civilization but not in God to assure themselves of salvation by undertaking the hermit life in caves and other wild places. Such men frequently achieved great celebrity as saintly miracle workers. The relics of St. Martin, one of these Latin anchorites, were deposited at Tours, which became a popular shrine for pilgrims and accounted largely for the wealth of the bishopric, as Gregory of Tours proudly tells us. Yet extreme anchoritic asceticism never attained the importance that it did in the east, and in the fifth and sixth centuries it gave way to various kinds of cenobitism. This was partly for climatic and partly for social reasons. It was a very different matter to try to be a hermit in the cold climate of northern Europe than to survive by oneself in Egypt. Furthermore, extreme asceticism only appears as a reaction to wealthy urbanized society. There is no point in making dramatic renunciation of worldly fleshpots when nearly everyone is finding it hard to get enough to eat, which was a common situation in early medieval Europe. Anchoritism becomes a powerful movement in western religious life only with the emergence of an urbanized society in the eleventh and twelfth centuries. Until then, western monasticism is distinguished for its attachment to cenobitism.

The earlier kinds of communal monasticism in western Europe closely resembled the loose structure of the Greek religious communities. It was, in fact, this kind of monastery that the Greek churchman St. John Cassian established in Marseilles in the early fifth century. Cassian's *Collations,* his account of conversations with the Egyptian desert fathers, is an important contribution to the development of the western monastic ideal. His work demonstrated both the sanctity of the desert fathers and the dangers which came from the isolation of the hermit life. His book, therefore, became required reading in early medieval monasteries.

The most thriving monasteries of the fifth and sixth centuries were those in Ireland. The Irish monasteries closely resembled the Greek in their form, and this may have been the result of direct influence from the eastern Mediterranean; there is some evidence that Greek churchmen may have come to sixth-century Ireland, presumably following trade routes between Ireland and the east. The Irish monks were exceptionally well educated and zealous; they made excellent missionaries and pioneered in the conversion of the heathen Anglo-Saxons and in attempts to reform the church in Gaul. But the abbot in the Irish monastery had no authority over the brothers, who were free to come and go as they pleased. It was not this loose kind of cenobitic life but a much more strictly controlled and, in fact, corporate monastery which became the institutionalized form of asceticism in western Europe until the eleventh century.

By the end of the ninth century the basic rule for all western monasteries, with the exception of those in Ireland, was the one set down by St. Benedict of Nursia (d. 543) for his own monastery of Monte Cassino near Naples. Western monasticism became identified with the Benedictine order, and because of the indispensable contributions of the black monks (as they were called from the color of their habit) to religion, education, government, and economy, the period from 550 to 1150 has often been called the Benedictine centuries. St. Benedict certainly did not intend to establish an institution which would provide leadership in medieval society. There is even some debate as to whether he intended his rule to be applied universally to all Latin monasteries, but assuredly he hoped that others would imitate the form of the religious life he established at Monte Cassino. He arrived at the final form of his *Rule for Monks* only after many years of careful consideration of the ideal religious life and some painful experiments. St. Benedict was a scion of the old Roman aristocracy, and he brought to the monastic life the Roman corporate sense of order, discipline, and authority. He turned in revulsion from the school at Rome to which his parents had sent him and fled to a wild region to become a hermit, but he found the lonely anchoritic life unsatisfactory and psychologically dangerous. He then became the abbot in a prevailing Greek kind of loose cenobitic community, but he was chagrined by the laxity and disorder he found there. Out of these experiences he derived the severe criticisms of the older forms of monasticism which he presented in the introduction to his *Rule*.

The purpose of the Benedictine community was to assure salvation for the souls of its members. It was a completely self-contained community, economically and politically as well as spiritually, and was not to rely upon the world for anything, except in the extreme case of the notorious corruption of the monastic community. Only when the abbot and the monks were obviously living scandalous lives was there a provision in the Benedictine Rule for outside interference; only then were the bishop or pious laymen of the neighborhood expected to intervene and restore regular life. With the exception of this unusual situation, the Benedictine monastery was to be a completely self-contained, self-supporting, and self-governing world of its own. The abbot was to be elected by the monks for life, and he was to have absolute authority over the lives and souls of the brothers, who were to take unmitigated vows of chastity, poverty, and obedience to the abbot for life. The abbot's absolute authority was predicated on the hierocratic principle: he would be called to account before God for his performance as the divine minister in the monastery, and this superior obligation was the sanction for his absolute rule in the community. The abbot had unchallenged authority to regulate the daily life of the monastery, to assign monks to various duties, and to punish them when necessary. The monks were never to leave the monastery, except under the most unusual circumstances and then only with the abbot's permission, and they were to obey whatever order the abbot gave them, even if they considered it to be wrong; the responsibility for a wrong act would lie with the abbot and not with the monk, who was obeying the regulations set down for him by his hierocratic superior.

The monastic life envisaged by the Benedictine Rule was characterized by a communal life of absolute regularity, with the strictest discipline and unvarying routine. The Rule was not remarkable for extreme forms of asceticism. Benedict had a Roman sense of balance and a keen psychological insight into the possibilities and limitations of human nature. Mortification of the flesh was not to be the rule in his monastery. On the contrary, the abbot was responsible for preserving the health of the brothers: he was to make sure that the monks had two solid meals a day and that the sick, the young, and the old received special care. It is obvious that Benedict did not care much for the extreme forms of asceticism, such as flagellation, hair shirts, or prolonged fasting. He believed in the discipline of the physical appetites but not in self-abnegation and self-destruction.

The order of the monastic day as envisaged by the Benedictine Rule depended somewhat upon the season of the year, but taking an average over the whole year, the twenty-four hours in the daily life of the monk were to be divided into four parts. Four hours of every day were devoted to the *Opus Dei* (divine service), that is, communal liturgical prayer in the chapel. Four hours were provided for individual meditative prayer and the private reading of religious literature. Six hours were to be given to physical labor; the monastery was to provide its own food and to be completely self-supporting. This left ten hours for eating and sleeping, which indicates Benedict's moderation and common sense. The black monks were to live in a constantly devout atmosphere of silence and abstraction from the world. Absolute silence was not required, but needless gossip was prohibited. At mealtimes one of the brothers would read aloud from a religious book—the Psalms, or Cassian's *Collations*—while the other brothers ate in silence.

Benedict realized that some men of even pious inclinations would not be able to endure a life of such strict discipline and routine. Consequently he provided very strict entrance requirements for admission to the monastic community. The candidate for monastic life was to undergo a year-long novitiate before he took his final vows, during which the abbot was to consider carefully the candidate's temperament. St. Benedict regarded his monastery as a microcosm of society and included all classes and age groups: the rich and the poor, the old and the young, the educated and the illiterate, both priests and laymen. The Benedictine Rule allowed for the receiving of children into the monasteries as oblates to God. By no means did Benedict expect that all his monks be educated men and priests. He wanted the brothers who were illiterate or ignorant to be educated, but he certainly did not regard his monastery as a center of learning. His community was to have nothing to do with society and was to perform no services to civilization, not even to the church. This corporate selfishness was justified on the grounds that it provided a refuge where the devout could pursue the highest end of man, the pilgrimage to the City of God.

In the three centuries after Benedict's death the kind of monastery he had created underwent important transformations and became absorbed into society as an institution of the first importance. This was neither what Benedict had wanted nor would have liked, but as M. D. Knowles has suggested, in a sense he had made this development inevitable by the effectiveness of the institution he had created. Early medieval society, so pitifully lacking in workable institutions, had to impose social obligations on the monks. Nor could western society afford to lose the services of literate men and able leaders who were found within the monastic communities; it drafted them out of their religious establishments to render services of the greatest importance. The self-contained nature of the Benedictine monastery made it an institutional unit which was eminently suited to the circumstances of the early middle ages. Only actual physical destruction could disperse the self-supporting and self-governed Benedictine community. In the new world that was coming into being after the Germanic invasions, social and political life was atomized, and the local units in society were the most effective ones. The estate, the village, the province were rapidly replacing the state and the city as the centers of civilization. The Benedictine monastery fitted in completely with the tendency toward localism, and because of its efficiency and self-perpetuating nature it came to assume several important functions: educational, religious, economic, and political.

Even in Benedict's own day the Roman aristocrat and scholar Cassiodorus had envisaged monasteries as the most suitable places for the educational and literary centers of the new society. Cassiodorus tells us that he wanted to found a Christian school of higher study in Rome similar to the rabbinical schools he knew existed in the middle east, but that under the circumstances of the time he found this to be impossible. Instead of such an institute of higher studies, what he devoted himself to was the creation of a more elementary kind of educational institution. He therefore established a large monastery with the conscious purpose of using it as a center for Christian education and scholarship, and in his *Introduction to Divine and Human Readings* Cassiodorus carefully outlines a program for the monastic school. The monks were to cultivate the Biblical-patristic tradition, but in order to obtain the necessary knowledge of Latin for this Christian scholarship, they were also to preserve and study certain classical texts. This educational work, Cassiodorus pointed out, presupposed that the monastery would have a good library of Christian and classical texts, and this in turn involved the creation of a monastic *scriptorium* which would prepare copies of the works to be studied in the monastic school.

In the two centuries after the founding of Cassiodorus' educationally oriented monastery, Benedictine communities all over western Europe similarly established schools, libraries, and *scriptoria.* This was not due so much to Cassiodorus' influence and the impact of his educational treatise, although these were of great importance, as to social need. With the collapse of the Roman state and the de-urbanization of western Europe the state and municipal schools disappeared. The episcopal schools in the early middle ages were only occasionally effective institutions, because they were completely dependent on the patronage of the bishops, who were rarely interested in the life of the mind. Even when a flourishing episcopal school was established, the next bishop was liable to be a semiliterate who would disband the teaching staff and sell off the library. The Benedictine monastery alone, during the early middle ages, had the continuity, the dedication, the library, and the substantial supply of teachers to serve as an effective educational institution. The monks had to undertake this educational task if Christian literature was to be preserved, and all over western Europe by 800 the more important Benedictine monasteries had flourishing schools, large libraries, and *scriptoria* for the production of manuscripts. At a conservative estimate 90 per cent of the literate men between 600 and 1100 received their instruction in a monastic school.

It cannot be said that the Benedictine monasteries were ideal educational institutions. Their attitude to learning was almost entirely functional; they were interested in teaching the Latin language and the dissemination of the Biblical-patristic tradition in order to preserve a literate church. With only few exceptions, the early medieval monastic scholars took a severely functional, Augustinian attitude toward the classical heritage. They were only interested in the Latin literature as a means of educating their students to write serviceable Latin. Such an attitude precluded the monastic school from becoming a center of creative thought. But in any case, early medieval society scarcely had the leisure for intellectual creativity; all literate men were needed for the service of church and monarchy. And although the early medieval monastic scribe usually did not have a deep aesthetic appreciation for the classical texts he was copying, he did preserve nearly all that was valuable in the Latin writings of the ancient world. The earliest manuscripts of all the surviving classical texts are the work of early medieval Benedictine monks.

While St. Benedict had envisaged liturgical prayer as only one distinct part of the monastic day, by the early ninth century the *Opus Dei* had become the major function of many Benedictine monasteries, and service at the altar occupied nearly all the waking hours of the monks in such communities. This development was a consequence of the continued esteem and awe with which ascetic and saintly men were regarded by lay society. Just as the populace of Alexandria had begged St. Antony to pray in their behalf, so the much-admired Benedictine monks were made into the official intercessors with the deity on behalf of early medieval society. Kings and nobles endowed monasteries with lucrative manors in return for monastic masses for the souls of their relatives. By the ninth century many monasteries had become extremely wealthy as a consequence of this endowment of their liturgical function, and the abbot found himself the lord over large estates worked by dependent peasants. Even in this regard the Benedictines made a contribution to medieval society. Their estates were run more efficiently and intelligently than were most of the manors of the lay nobility, and they were the pioneers in whatever rudiments of agrarian science the early middle ages possessed. By the tenth century the black monks owned a very considerable part of the best farmland in western Europe.

This development made many abbots into local powers, and they, like the lay nobility, were given political and judicial functions over the people in their domains. Because of their wealth and influence the abbots of the more important monasteries of northern Europe were also drawn into the developing feudal nexus in the ninth and tenth centuries, were required to become vassals of some king or duke and to send knights to the armies of their lords. The Benedictine abbot of the feudal era was frequently a royal vassal of the greatest importance. One of the English abbatial vassals in the later eleventh century owned a service of sixty knights to the royal army, which made him one of the three or four most important tenants-in-chief in the kingdom. The abbot of Bury-St. Edmunds in the twelfth century ruled more than half of the county of Norfolk. There are even a few instances of French abbots in the tenth and eleventh centuries buckling on armor and going off to fight at the head of their knightly contingent. The political influence of the abbots also emerged as a result of the monastic monopoly of learning. Outstanding Benedictine scholars were recruited in the service of the church, and they became bishops and popes. But others staffed the chancery of a king or duke. They became royal chancellors, the advisors and confidantes of rulers, and from the ninth to the middle of the twelfth century there were several instances of monastic statesmen who were in effect the chief ministers of western monarchs.

The heterogeneous and onerous social obligations undertaken by the Benedictine monasteries only two centuries after Benedict's death could not but affect the internal life and composition of the religious communities. By 800 most monasteries were no longer self-sustaining units, nor did the black monks perform physical labor. They were supported by the labor of serfs on their estates, while they devoted themselves to educational and liturgical work. Nor did the membership of the ninth-century Benedictine community represent any longer a cross section of society. The monks were drawn almost exclusively from the class of the nobility, and the Benedictine abbots, by the tenth century, were usually men of the highest aristocratic and frequently princely origin. The Benedictine convents for women, which had begun to be founded soon after Benedict's day, became particularly homogeneous in their social composition. The nuns of the ninth and tenth centuries were all high-born ladies, and it was almost impossible to be admitted to these convents without being a widowed or maiden relative of an important lord. While the majority of the monks did remain in their monasteries and abided by their vows, the ablest Benedictine monks from the eighth century on frequently left their communities to become missionaries, churchmen, and royal secretaries. This was not the monastery as created by St. Benedict, but it was an institution which was an extremely effective ameliorative force in early medieval society. Monasticism, which had begun as a flight into the desert from the civilized world, became in early medieval Europe not only an integral part of society but a saving force of the greatest significance in the disorganized civilization which followed the Germanic invasions.

II. Gregory the Great and the Early Medieval Papacy

The contribution of Benedictine monasticism to the leadership of the early medieval church may be gauged by the fact that several of the most outstanding popes from the middle of the sixth to the twelfth century were black monks. In the year 590 the first of these monastic popes, Gregory I the Great (d. 604) ascended to the throne of Peter. His pontificate, although not very long, marks one of the most important turning points in the history of the medieval church. This was not because Gregory was able suddenly to overcome the disastrous impact of the Germanic invasions upon the culture and discipline of the Latin church; it was to take five centuries to achieve this end and complete the Christianization of Europe. Gregory I's importance lies in his clear formulation of the program which the papacy was to follow over the next two centuries. He clearly perceived that the historic destiny of the papacy lay in western Europe and that the way to assert papal leadership in European society was through an alliance with the monastic orders and the Frankish monarchy.

Immediately after Gregory's election as pope he sent out letters announcing that he had not wanted the throne of Peter and that he would have preferred to have lived the contemplative life of the monk. While such modest statements became traditional with later popes, even with those who had campaigned for the office for many years, in Gregory's case it was a sincere avowal. He knew that the church at his accession was in a very bad way and that the problems involved in asserting papal leadership in western Europe were almost insuperable. He compared the Latin church of his day to a ship which "creaked shipwreck." Actually the papacy had exercised no effective leadership since the pontificate of Gelasius I almost a century before. The sixth-century popes had done nothing to deal with the consequences of the transformation of European government and society which followed the Germanic invasions. The bishops in Gaul had completely identified their interests with the Merovingian dynasty and then with the provincial aristocracy. In the outlook of even the best of them, Gregory of Tours, there had been a tremendous shrinking of vision, in comparison with the world view of Ambrose and Augustine, toward a narrow parochialism. An eminent German historian of the early medieval church has said, with very little exaggeration, that the history of the Frankish church before the eighth century could easily be written without mentioning Rome at all.

The situation of the church in Visigothic Spain was not much more promising. The Visigoths had abandoned their Arianism for Catholic Christianity,
and the Spanish bishops closely identified themselves with the Visigothic
monarchy. In so doing, they had associated the destiny of the Spanish church
with a decrepit institution whose sole strength was derived from the moral
support given it by the church. This was not to be enough to save Visigothic
Spain from Moslem conquest in the early eighth century.

The situation of the Roman church itself at Gregory's accession was a
most precarious one. The pope was beset by enemies on all sides. To the
north of Rome the primitive Lombards persisted in their devotion to tribal
Arianism, while in Ravenna and to the south of Rome the forces of the
Byzantine emperor were a constant threat to the security of the pope.
The alliance between Rome and Byzantium which had brought about the
destruction of the Ostrogothic kingdom in the first half of the sixth century
had long since collapsed, and in view of the mutually exclusive claims to
be the vicar of God on earth made by pope and emperor, the best relations
that could exist between them involved a situation of uneasy peace. The one
bright spot in this picture of the church at the beginning of the last decade
of the sixth century was Ireland, but Gregory could not rejoice over the
high cultural level of the Celtic monks. For the Irish church had not been
created under Roman direction, with the result that the Celtic churchmen
not only had peculiar practices which differed from the Latin church, but
they seemed to adopt an indifferent attitude toward the Petrine doctrine.
This was at least the conclusion which Gregory had to adopt when he
received letters from the great Irish missionary in Gaul, St. Columban,
haránguing the pope in a severe and not altogether respectful tone on the
proper management of ecclesiastical affairs. When Gregory became pope,
the Irish missionaries already were penetrating northern England, inaugurating the conversion of the heathen English and in Gregory's eyes threatening to foment a schism between the Latin and the Celtic churches.

Gregory by no means fully overcame any of these problems which the
church faced at the time of his accession, but he set down the policy which
his successors were to follow in struggling to resolve them, and he set in
motion the chain of events which began the amelioration of the Latin
church and European society. Gregory is the only pope between the fifth
and the eleventh centuries whose correspondence and other writings have
extensively survived, and we have sufficient documentation to write his
biography and assess his character. He need not be for us, as is the case
with nearly all other early medieval churchmen, a faceless man. But his
character strikes us as an ambiguous and enigmatic one. On the one hand
he was an able and determined administrator, a skilled and clever diplomat,
a leader of the greatest sophistication and vision; but on the other hand,

he appears in his writings as a superstitious and credulous monk, hostile to learning, crudely limited as a theologian, excessively devoted to saints, miracles, and relics. This apparent ambiguity can only be explained in terms of Gregory's background and milieu. Late sixth-century Italy reveals the catastrophic effects of the long Gothic war and Lombard invasion. Its culture is marked by the decline of cities and literacy, the progressive ruralization of the economy, and the advance of ignorance and superstitution. Gregory came from an old Roman family, and he had received a good classical education, but his primary concern as he grew to manhood was the salvation of his soul by a flight from the world. He founded a monastery in which he himself lived as a humble monk, and while he greatly admired St. Benedict, whose biography he wrote, his own attitude to monastic life lacked Benedict's moderation and respect for human nature. As a monk Gregory gave himself over to severe austerities which permanently affected his health, and even as pope his outlook exhibited traces of fanaticism and lack of common sense side by side with the traditional efficiency and effective governance of the Roman aristocrat. At one time Gregory heard that a bishop in Gaul had undertaken to establish a school for the study of liberal arts. Instead of congratulating the Frankish churchman on his effort at improving literacy, the pope castigated him for engaging in a frivolous enterprise! A similar limitation of vision is revealed in Gregory's neglect to learn Greek while he was a papal ambassador for several years in Constantinople. Gregory's personal culture reveals the disastrous consequences of the vicissitudes through which Italy had passed during the sixth century; in his writings there are traces of the pettiness, parochialism, and self-defeating intransigence which marks the work of his contemporary, Bishop Gregory of Tours. Fortunately, Gregory the Great was not allowed to pursue his perverse inclination to become an obscure and ignorant monk. The church needed a man of his education, intelligence, sincerity, and political experience. He was recruited out of the monastery into the papal service, becoming a prototype for many Benedictine monks in the following centuries who undertook similar careers, and against his will was elevated to the throne of Peter. His work as pope falls into three parts: his contribution to the papal office, his attitude to monarchy, and his use of monastic missionaries in the service of the church.

Pope Gregory was first of all conscious of the fact that he was a member of the episcopate, and in his *Book of Pastoral Care* he delineated for his episcopal colleagues their duties as pastors of the Christian flock, contrasting these with the privileges they enjoyed as ecclesiastical princes and nobles, which tended to be their primary concern. It cannot be said that Gregory's treatise on the episcopal office persuaded his colleagues to take a more zealous attitude toward their offices, but at least it served for later centuries as a definitive statement of the nature of the episcopal office. Gregory, however, was conscious of the fact that he was more than just a bishop; as bishop of Rome he was the vicar of Christ on earth. He did not contribute anything new to the evolution of papal ideology, but he carefully summarized the Gelasian doctrine and Leo I's Petrine theory. This view of papal office was summed up in the term *servus servorum Dei,* "servant of the servants of God," which he used as an official appellation and which still appears as a subtitle on papal documents. Gregory thereby expresses the papal authority in terms of the hierocratic principle which St. Benedict had already used to justify the absolute authority of the abbot over the souls of the monks in his monastery. The hierocratic principle found its Biblical support in Christ's statement in the Gospel of Mark: "Whoever is the chief is the servant of all"—that is, he who has the most responsibility has the most power. Since the pope was responsible before God for his ministry as the leader of the Christian church, he required unlimited authority in order to carry out the divine work entrusted to him.

It was one thing to state the papal ideology, but it was a very different matter to assert papal leadership in western Europe. Gregory saw that the first necessity was for the pope to secure his position in Italy itself, and he labored to expand the territory under papal rule beyond the confines of Rome and to build up the "patrimony of St. Peter," the papal state. He was also very conscious of the need for a steady income in order to effect his administrative work in the church, and many of Gregory's letters are devoted to telling his agents how to manage effectively the papal estates in southern Italy.

Even if the pope achieved an independent and secure position in Italy, he had to establish a relationship with the territorial churches in the Germanic countries if he was actually to assert his position as the leader of Christendom. Gregory was far more conscious of this fact than any other previous pope, and herein lies a claim that might be made for him as the real founder of the medieval papacy. He realized that Europe was not just a matter of geography but a distinct culture and spirit contiguous with Latin Christianity, with whose destiny the papacy was ultimately to identify itself. Gregory was respectful toward the emperor in Constantinople, but not because he thought that the bishop of Rome had any longer something to hope for from the Roman emperor; he was merely concerned with maintaining the uneasy peace with Constantinople and leaving the papacy free to pursue its aims in western Europe. And in order to achieve the creation of a European civilization, Gregory saw with a prophetic clarity that the papacy would somehow have to ally itself with the Frankish monarchy, which, while it was a most unpromising institution in Gregory's day, would inevitably dominate the political future of Europe.

Because the Frankish kings ruled, at least nominally, the heartland of Europe and because their kingdom was by far the largest and wealthiest in Latin Christendom, leadership in European society would have to come from the Frankish monarchy working under the direction of the church and revivified by this association. Gregory could not see how it could come in any other way. It was because of his understanding of this extremely fundamental fact in European life that Gregory wrote highly deferential letters to the Merovingian king, Childebert II. Gregory was not blind to the gross inadequacies of the Frankish kings, but he envisioned an alliance between the papacy and the Merovingian dynasty which would transform Germanic kingship into an effective and ameliorative institution.

Gregory's letters to the Merovingian king had no consequences in his own day. It was not until the eighth century that the Frankish rulers were sufficiently intelligent to understand the possibilities for the growth of their own power in an alliance with the papacy. The surprising consequence of Gregory's missionary work was the bringing into existence of a group of churchmen who, in the eighth century, fomented the Frankish-papal alliance on which the new European civilization was to be founded. Shortly after his accession, as a consequence of the challenge from the Celtic church, Gregory felt the need for the conversion of England. As a monk who had been recruited into the service of the church, it was natural for him to employ Benedictine monks as his missionaries to England. He instructed the leader of this mission, Augustine, to begin his work in the kingdom of Kent in southeastern England, because its ruler was known to have married a Frankish Christian princess. At the time of Gregory's death Augustine's mission had achieved its initial success with the conversion of the king of Kent and his nobles and the establishment of the first Latin church at Canterbury (literally, "Kent town"). In the half century after Gregory's death the Latin monks, advancing northward from Canterbury, and the Celtic missionaries at work in the north contended for the adherence of the English people. Finally, in 664, a synod of the English churchmen decided to bring the whole country under Roman rule. This decision not only precluded the schism in the western church which Gregory had struggled to avert; it had much more important consequences. The English Benedictines had the most flourishing schools in late seventh-century Europe, and in the eighth century they sent out missionaries to the continent, inaugurating the transformation of the Frankish church and monarchy. It was an English Benedictine who, in the middle of the eighth century, played a leading role in establishing the Frankish-papal alliance which Gregory regarded as the necessary foundation for the achieving of a new European civilization.

PART THREE

O most sweet Charles, glory of the Christian people, O defense of the churches of Christ, consolation of this present life! . . . It is necessary that all men should exalt your blessedness in their prayers and aid you by their intercessions, since it is through your prosperity that the Christian Empire may be protected, that the Catholic faith may be defended, and that the rule of justice may become known to all.

—ALCUIN

THE FIRST EUROPE

Eighth and Ninth Centuries

Chapter Seven

THE MAKING OF
CAROLINGIAN KINGSHIP

I. Anglo-Irish Culture and the Colonial Phenomenon

Historians have discovered many of the causes of decadence and decline
of a civilization; as yet they have done little to explain the principal
factors leading to the rise and efflorescence of a civilization. We have only
empty tautologies about responding to a challenge. Assuredly, it is easier
to explain failure than success; it is easier to account for the lassitude
and failure of nerve involved in cultural collapse than for the novel energy,
intelligence, and leadership that mark the beginning of a new civilization.
After centuries of disintegration and disorder the first Europe takes shape
in the eighth and ninth centuries; it was an incipient and imperfect
civilization whose leaders overreached themselves and attempted to create a
political structure, the Carolingian empire, which was too ambitious for
their resources. They suffered bitter disappointment and fell prey to deep
disillusionment, but a great many characteristic institutions and ideals of
medieval civilization were defined during these two centuries and served as
the basis for more successful political experiments in the following two
centuries.

In accounting for the formation of the first Europe, economic determinism can be discounted. The improvements in political, ecclesiastical, and
intellectual life were actually contemporary with the acceleration of both
the decline of commerce and the ruralization of the western economy. The
moving force in the rise of European civilization in the eighth century

came from the church. Anglo-Saxon monks and the papacy willed the creation of the first Europe. Working together, they transformed the Frankish church and the nature of Frankish kingship and awoke political and intellectual capacities in the continental peoples, which led to the Carolingian empire and the improvement in educational and intellectual life which distinguishes the eighth and ninth centuries.

The origins of this great historical change are to be found in the culture of sixth- and seventh-century Ireland and seventh- and eighth-century England. It may seem strange that the Irish, who were never part of the Roman world, and the English, who in 590 were savage heathens and similarly out of touch with the traditions of the Mediterranean world, should have played such a great role in the creation of the first Europe. This can be explained as a manifestation of what may be termed the colonial phenomenon in world history. The people on the fringes of an empire or civilization, the frontiersmen or colonials, are frequently the greatest partisans of the system or culture to which they choose to belong. By their hothouse enthusiasm, their conscious efforts at identification with the civilization whose center is so far away, they make their claim to equal citizenship with the people in the heartland of the civilization. The latter often take their world for granted and do little to perpetuate or improve it. The Irish and English monks exhibit the typical zeal of colonials struggling to identify themselves with the center of the civilization. The Irish, who never enjoyed the benefits of Roman civilization, took pains to establish great libraries of classical texts and even became proficient in Greek. The English scholars of the late seventh and early eighth centuries, who were only two or three generations removed from heathenism and savagery, became fanatical supporters of the Roman church. Their great historian, Bede, was such a fanatical Romanist that he even tried to disguise the contributions of Irish missionaries to the conversion of England.

The beginning of Latin-Christian culture in Ireland is shrouded in obscurity, and presumably it will always remain so. It is probable that in the sixth and early seventh centuries three groups of churchmen came to Ireland and brought with them the Christian religion and learning. The first of these consisted of British priests fleeing before the Anglo-Saxon invasions; among them, likely, was a certain St. Patrick. The second group consisted of churchmen who fled from Gaul during the Germanic invasions of the fifth and sixth centuries and sought refuge in Ireland. A third group may have consisted of Greek churchmen from the eastern Mediterranean, who, during the late sixth and seventh centuries, followed the trade routes to Ireland and brought with them their language and certain texts which were not to be found anywhere else in early medieval

Europe. This may help to account for the Irish scholars' singular knowledge of Greek; in the seventh, eighth, and ninth centuries, if a churchman in western Europe knew Greek, he was assumed to be of Irish provenance.

Irish Christianity was distinguished by an intense devotion to learning and missionary zeal. Since it had developed in isolation from Rome, it was also remarkable for certain peculiarities which separated the Celtic and Roman churches. The Celtic church celebrated Easter on a different date than the Roman church, and the clergy was exclusively monastic. The Irish church was not organized into dioceses, and since Ireland had never been part of the Roman empire, there was no reason why the Irish should have developed the diocesan clergy. The leaders of the Celtic church were not the bishops but the abbots of their very large and flourishing monasteries. The Irish monastic schools established great libraries and intensively pursued the study of the trivium and quadrivium. In the early seventh century the Irish monks had the best centers of learning in western Europe, but after 800 they ceased to play an important role in European cultural life, and the Celtic church rapidly declined. When Anglo-Norman barons invaded Ireland in the twelfth century, they found the people whom they conquered uncouth and completely uneducated. Ireland had to wait until the late nineteenth century for another renaissance. Of course, this was not entirely the fault of the Irish; for seven hundred years they were English slaves.

The question remains, however, why the flourishing and enlightened Celtic church rapidly declined after 800. Three reasons can be suggested. By their reluctance to accept the decrees of the Roman church the Irish cut themselves off from medieval western Christendom when it was entering its first creative phase, and thereby condemned themselves to intellectual isolation. This decision proved to be particularly disastrous when Scandinavian invaders destroyed many of the Irish monasteries in the ninth century. Finally, the continued political disunity of Ireland as a result of the perpetuation of primitive tribalism could not but have a long-range deleterious effect on the ecclesiastical and intellectual life of the island.

The Celtic monks found an outlet for their missionary zeal during the late sixth century across the Irish channel, where the Anglo-Saxons remained heathen before Augustine's mission and out of touch with Latin Christianity. Following the withdrawal of the Roman legions from Britain in about 425 A.D., Germanic war bands had come across the North Sea from the Low Countries and penetrated the river estuaries of eastern Britain. They defeated the British Christian princes, possibly including a certain Arthur, subjugating many of the native populace into a slave status and slowly driving the remaining Celts back into the mountains of Wales and Cornwall and across the English channel to that part of northern France which came to be known as Brittany. The slow and piece-meal nature of the English conquest of Britain was reflected in the frag-mented political structure of sixth-century England. The leaders of the war bands established small kingdoms—traditionally seven in number, but the number fluctuated—and contended for hegemony against each other during the next three centuries. In the late sixth century the king of Kent was a prominent lord in southern England; in the seventh century the rulers of Northumbria were powerful for a time; and in the eighth century the king of Mercia, in the rich agricultural midlands, established his ascendency over many of the other chieftains. But even by the eighth century the political and social structure of Anglo-Saxon England had scarcely ad-vanced beyond the institutions described in Tacitus and *Beowulf.* The king's power was dependent upon his effectiveness as a war leader and the extent to which he could reward his "gesiths," or warrior-companions, and the social structure was characterized by large masses of free peasants.

The Celtic missionaries who began the conversion of northern England in the late sixth and early seventh centuries brought with them their deep learning, and the Anglo-Saxon schools of the seventh and eighth centuries were partly indebted to the contributions of Irish scholarship. But the efflorescence.of Anglo-Saxon culture was mainly the result of continental influence. Following the decision of the English churchmen to join the Roman church in the 660's, the pope sent to England, as archbishop of Canterbury, an extremely learned scholar, Theodore of Tarsus, who had originally come from Asia Minor. Theodore established at Canterbury a great school whose students went out to become abbots of Benedictine monasteries in southern England. At about the same time, a native Anglo-Saxon churchman from the noble class, Benedict Biscop, founded the great monastery of Jarrow in Northumbria (Yorkshire). Benedict had traveled extensively on the continent, and he is said to have brought with him to England the nucleus for a library at the monastic school at Jarrow and even some continental art objects.

Jarrow became the center of learning in northern England, as Canter-bury and its satellite monasteries provided leadership in the south, and it produced in Bede (d. 735) the greatest of the Anglo-Saxon scholars. It is a tribute to Northumbrian scholarship, and again evidence of the operation of the colonial phenomenon, that the most learned scholar of the early eighth century spent his whole life as a monk at Jarrow and never left his bleak and thinly populated homeland. Finding the most learned monk of the eighth century in the frontier society of northern England is roughly comparable to locating in the backwoods of Missouri the greatest scholar of the mid-nineteenth century America. It would not be impossible, but it would be surprising.

Bede regarded himself first and foremost a teacher, the head of the monastic school at Jarrow, and a perpetuator of the Biblical-patristic tradition. He used his learning in an empirical way to serve the needs of the church, and he was not interested in philosophic speculation. He applied his knowledge of mathematics and astronomy to deal with the problem of reckoning the date of Easter. He produced a compendium of scientific knowledge which was derived largely from Pliny's natural history. His original scholarship was in the field of history. It was Bede who took up Isidore of Seville's suggestion of a Christian chronology according to the incarnation, and Bede made it the common European way of reckoning historical time. Bede's great historical effort was the *Ecclesiastical History of the English People,* one of the very few works of the early middle ages which is still attractive to the educated public. It is a carefully organized and subtly argued book which gives to the Roman church the decisive role in the making of English civilization. Bede had a more scholarly attitude toward historical writing than any medieval writer between Gregory of Tours and the eleventh century. While in his hagiographical works he is inclined to be as credulous as the authors of most medieval saints' lives, his history is remarkably free from miraculous fantasies. Its tone is factual, restrained, and dry. He took pains to gather whatever information about the Anglo-Saxon invasion that survived in popular memory, and for his account of Augustine's mission he sent a monk to Rome to search the papal archives for Gregory the Great's letters concerning England, which he published extensively in his history. The quality of Bede's thought differs rather markedly from that of the other great Anglo-Saxon scholar of the eighth century, Alcuin, who in the 780's was summoned from his position as head of the school of York to become a prominent assistant to Charlemagne in the reform of the Frankish church. Where Alcuin is imaginative, emotional, and personally involved in the political affairs of his time, Bede appears as an austere and cautious thinker who is involved to a very limited degree with monarchy and the general problems of society.

At the end of his *Ecclesiastical History* Bede makes some lugubrious remarks on the decline of the vitality of Anglo-Saxon culture, and while this may be simply the traditional pessimism of the old commenting on the new generation, the subsequent history of the Anglo-Saxon church confirms his concern about the continued progress of the church to which he was devoted. The later development of Anglo-Saxon England, after the eighth century, is by and large a disappointing story, especially in view of the pre-eminence of the English Benedictines in European culture in the age of Bede and Alcuin. After 800, Anglo-Saxon churchmen were never again to be the intellectual leaders of Europe, and during the tenth and eleventh centuries the English church was indebted to the continent for guidance and inspiraiton. By the year 1000 there is no doubt that England is an intellectual backwater of Europe. The ubiquitous Scandinavians are traditionally blamed for this decline of Anglo-Saxon culture. Jarrow was destroyed by Viking marauders at the end of the eighth century, and for the next two hundred and fifty years there was only occasional respite for the English people, whose energy was dissipated in struggles against successive waves of Scandinavian invaders.

There are two additional reasons for the decline of early medieval England. The Anglo-Saxon kings turned out to be singularly inept. They remained primarily warriors and failed to develop effective royal institutions. By the last quarter of the ninth century, as a result of the Danish invasion, only King Alfred of Wessex remained of all the Anglo-Saxon princes. While Alfred, who was originally intended for the church, was a good scholar and while he fought the Scandinavians to a draw and divided England with them, he made no contribution to the growth of royal leadership in Anglo-Saxon society. His successors in the tenth century established their hegemony over the Danelaw, as the area conquered by the Scandinavians was called, but they were unable to stem the rise of lordship and the passing of real power in society to the earls and thanes who comprised the local nobility. The most effective king in Anglo-Saxon history was the early eleventh-century Danish conqueror Canute. The English clergy of the ninth century tried to buttress the ineffective Anglo-Saxon monarchy with moral and sacred qualities, but with no more effect than that achieved by the bishops of Visigothic Spain. The weakness of Anglo-Saxon kingship and the passing of the leadership in society into the hands of the local nobility were factors contributing to the decline of the Anglo-Saxon church from the flourishing and pre-eminent position it had enjoyed in the age of Bede. The final cause which can be discerned for this development is a relatively simple one. The zealous and dedicated English church of the eighth century sent so many of its outstanding missionaries and scholars to work on the continent that it lost its best potential leaders and dissipated its resources. The devotion of the Anglo-Saxon church to the bishop of Rome was such that it served the interests of the papacy far better than its own.

The Anglo-Saxon missions to the continent began in the last decade of the seventh century. The monastic missionaries began their work among the heathen Frisians in the Low Countries, whence most of the English tribes had originally come. They wished to bring the benefits of salvation to heathens whom they regarded as their kinsmen. Almost immediately Anglo-Saxon missionaries came in contact with the Carolingians, the new dominant family in France. They worked under the direction of Pepin II, the head of the Carolingian family, who wished to extend his influence over the Low Countries and regarded the Anglo-Saxon missionaries as the vanguard of Frankish expansion. The leader of the English mission in the Low Countries also worked under papal aegis and went to Rome, with Pepin's permission, to be consecrated bishop of Friesland. This was the first instance of any kind of definitive relationship between the papacy and the Frankish rulers, and it set the pattern for their increasing association in the first half of the eighth century as a result of their joint support of the efforts of the Anglo-Saxon missionaries.

The rise of the Carolingian family to prominence in France was the ultimate outgrowth of the aristocratic usurpation of royal power in the seventh century. The Merovingian rulers after the 630's were all either women, children, or mental defectives, which meant in each case that they were unable to prevent the seizure of royal property and authority by the provincial aristocracy. The process of disintegration went so far that the Merovingian kings were left with no effective power outside their own private estates. And by the middle of the century they had even lost control over these to the "mayors of the palace," their household officials. In this anomalous situation, however, lay the origins of the revival of royal power in France. The mayors of the palace, having usurped what remained of royal power and property, found it in their interest to regain whatever they could of the royal fisc, which had been usurped by the provincial aristocracy. By the eighth decade of the seventh century an Austrasian, or eastern, family, later known as the Carolingians, were using their control over the office of mayor of the palace to establish their ascendency not only over the aristocracy in the Germanic eastern part of the Merovingian kingdom but also over the dukes and counts of the more Romanic west.

The Carolingians constantly sought ways to reconstruct the royal power in France, which was in their own hands. They welcomed the activities of the Anglo-Saxon missionaries along the frontier of the Frankish realm in the late seventh and first half of the eighth century. The Carolingians' sympathetic attitude toward the Anglo-Saxon missions was motivated by their desire to appear friends of the church, whose moral support could be especially useful in view of their own doubtful legal right to dominate the French monarchy, and because they believed the Christianizing of the frontier Germanic tribes would make their effective absorption into the Frankish monarchy much easier.

Among the Anglo-Saxon missionaries in Friesland in the 690's was a young Benedictine named Wynfrid, better known by his later Latin name of St. Boniface, who came from a prominent noble family in southern England. The importance of Boniface's work was long neglected by historians, but the scholarship of the last quarter of a century has given him his rightful place as one of the truly outstanding creators of the first Europe, as the apostle of Germany, the reformer of the Frankish church, and the chief fomentor of the alliance between the papacy and the Carolingian family. After working for many years as a missionary in the Low Countries, he decided to inaugurate the conversion of the Germanic tribes who lived within the Merovingian kingdom east of the Rhine, in what was to become southwestern Germany. Boniface returned to England, recruited several companions from Benedictine monasteries, and in 718 set out for the continent, where he was to work as a missionary, bishop, and papal envoy until his death in 754.

Boniface's work was carried out with the support of both the Carolingian family and the papacy, as had been the case with the Anglo-Saxon missionary work in the Low Countries. But since Boniface was engaged in bringing a large territory which lay within the Merovingian kingdom into Latin Christian civilization, the significance of this joint direction is much greater in his case. Most of Boniface's missionary work in Germany was accomplished in the reign of Charles Martel, a rough warrior who became the hero of Christian Europe in 732 by his victory over the Moslems. Charles was cautious in his attitude toward Rome and was not prepared to enter into a close alliance with the papacy, but by allowing Boniface to carry out his work directly under papal authority, he opened the way for the entrance of papal influence into the Frankish kingdom and for the league with the papacy which his son, Pepin III, created in the 750's. In his letters Boniface made very clear the extent to which he depended on Charles Martel's assistance. "Without the protection of the prince of the Franks, I can neither rule the people of the church nor defend the priests and clerks, monks and nuns; nor can I prevent the practice of pagan rites and sacrilegious worship of idols without his mandate and the awe inspired by his name."

Boniface made three trips to Rome during the course of his missionary work in Germany, which lasted until 739. On his first visit he received a papal commission to convert the German people and was given his Latin name to symbolize his new position as the representative of the Roman church in Germany. On his second visit to Rome Boniface was made a bishop, and his final interview with the pope resulted in the organization of the German church with the English monk as the archbishop of the primatial see of Mainz.

Boniface's conversion of Germany was a tremendous undertaking. It brought a whole new area of western Europe into Latin Christian civilization and ended with the creation of the German church, which already in the tenth century was remarkable for the intensive quality of its religiosity. Boniface achieved the inauguration of German Christianity through the building of great monasteries, such as his own establishment at Fulda, which became centers of learning and provided the personnel for the new German church organized in the 730's. Even in the tenth and eleventh centuries the great monasteries which Boniface and his assistants had established were the vital centers of German ecclesiastical life. Since the time of Benedict Biscop, in the previous century, all the Anglo-Saxon monks had been Benedictines, and it was the Rule of St. Benedict which Boniface now imposed on the great monasteries he founded in Germany. The constitutional form of his own monastery of Fulda had special significance; for it Boniface obtained a *privilegium* of exemption from episcopal control, thereby subordinating it directly to the papacy as the head of Christendom. This kind of special jurisdiction had been developed by Gregory the Great in order to bring certain Benedictine monasteries into direct association with the papacy, but it had been rarely applied. Fulda and the other German monasteries became famous for their great libraries and *scriptoria*. Some of the greatest works of Carolingian art, in the form of illuminated manuscripts, were the product of the Fulda monastic school.

The effecting of this enormous missionary undertaking required all the resources of the Anglo-Saxon church of the eighth century. We have a letter which Boniface addressed to all the bishops and clergy of the English church, seeking their assistance in his missionary work: "We humbly beseech you . . . that the word of God may go forward and be glorified. We beg you to be instant in prayer that God . . . may turn the hearts of the heathen Saxons to the Catholic Faith . . . and gather them among the children of Mother Church. Take pity on them, for they themselves are now saying, 'We are of one blood and one bone with you'. . . . Be it known to you, moreover, that in making this appeal I have the approval, assent and benediction of two pontiffs of the Apostolic See." This letter shows the peculiar attitude of deep consciousness of their own Germanic background and at the same time a fervent loyalty to the papacy which distinguished the Anglo-Saxon clergy in the seventh and eighth centuries. Boniface's appeals to his countrymen led to a remarkable exodus of priests, monks, and nuns from England to the continent, resulting in the establishment of a large Anglo-Saxon religious colony in Germany.

Boniface's appointment as archbishop of Mainz made him the primate of the church in the eastern half of the Frankish kingdom, and after 739 he turned from his work as the apostle to the Germans to begin the reform of the Frankish church. In this work he was assisted by the support of the two sons of Charles Martel, Pepin III and Carloman, who ruled the western and eastern parts of the Frankish kingdom respectively. Carloman is the first of a new type of saintly king, more interested in religious devotion than in royal power, which will make a frequent appearance in the following three centuries and which is an indication of the growing impact of Christian piety on Germanic society. In 747 he abdicated to become a monk at Monte Cassino; in the previous eight years he and Boniface began the reform of the Frankish clergy. A synod of Frankish churchmen declared their loyalty to the pope. This did not signify the effective papal jurisdiction over the French bishops, but it at least is indicative of a new spirit and attitude on the part of the French clergy, for they had never made such a profession of loyalty to Rome before. Boniface inaugurated the revitalization of the French monasteries, their acceptance of the Benedictine Rule, and the establishment of the first important monastic schools in the Merovingian kingdom. Among the greatest needs of the Frankish church was the creation of a secular clergy on the local parish level, outside the episcopal cities. If the Christianization of Europe was ever to be a reality, the faith would have to be taught by educated priests in each village. The dim beginnings of the medieval parish system, which we can perceive to be a real institution in some parts of ninth-century France, can be traced back to the work of Boniface.

After Pepin III became the ruler of the whole Frankish kingdom in 747, the same kind of reform which Boniface had inaugurated in his own ecclesiastical province was extended to western France with Pepin's assistance. Pepin's relations with the church were not characterized by the deep personal piety which had distinguished his brother. He had discerned in Boniface's work the opportunity and means for the transformation of Frankish kingship and the gaining of the crown from the Merovingians through an alliance with the papacy, for which Pepin prepared by accepting Boniface's program of church reform in his realm. In Rome, at the same time, the results of Boniface's work were believed to open the way to realization of the papal ideology that had developed from the time of Gregory the Great. In the 750's the consequences of long centuries of confused development were coming into sharp focus at last, and the outlines of the first Europe began to take on definitive form. The 750's constitute one of the momentous turning points of medieval history. This decade is characterized by the final emancipation of the papacy from the framework of the east Roman empire, the supplanting of the Merovingian dynasty by the Carolingians, the penetration of the idea of theocratic monarchy into western Europe, and the legal founding of the papal states. Only a half century later was to come the revival of the imperial title in western Europe, which was a direct outgrowth of the events of the 750's. The necessary background to all these decisive achievements lies in the work of St. Boniface and his assistants in their contributions to the Christianization of Europe.

In 754 Boniface returned to the Low Countries as a missionary, taking up the work he had left four decades before, and he suffered martyrdom at the hands of the savage and ungrateful Frisians. In terms of medieval hagiography his life of service to the church thus had a perfect ending. His biographers proclaimed him the "Apòstle to the Germans," and the zealous, Benedictine-dominated German church of the early middle ages was the worthy monument of his service to Latin Christianity. But the Carolingian monarchy of the eighth and ninth centuries was also, to a very considerable extent, a consequence of his work. Carolingian kingship was, however, a monument he would not entirely have appreciated nor have wanted to take credit for. The English Benedictines' heroic struggle for the Christianization of the west had set in motion a complex of ideas and institutions which formed the civilization of the first Europe, and this was to be a world whose tensions, ambiguities, achievements, and disappointments were far beyond the pure and simple ideals and expectations of the English missionaries.

II. The Carolingian Enigma

The course of Carolingian history is enigmatic, and the more research which is done on the period, the more ambiguous it appears and the more difficult it becomes to understand the general pattern of European history in the eighth and ninth centuries. The Carolingian enigma is a twofold one, both in the nature of the events of the period themselves and in the conflicting general interpretations offered by modern scholars. Carolingian history is full of paradoxes, sharp contrasts, and cyclic extremes between idealism and barbarism, intelligence and ignorant violence, apparently rapid achievement and equally rapid collapse. Many historians, particularly of the older school, have found the main theme of the period in its ideological struggles, in the working out of certain very sophisticated ideas, which loom large in the documentary sources of Carolingian history. Others, particularly in recent years, have dismissed these ideological pronouncements as the wishful thinking of monks who produced all the literature of the period, and they have emphasized instead what appears to them to be the realities of social and political life: lordship, an intensely rural economy, and the usual disorders of Germanic society. Out of this interpretation comes a picture of Charlemagne not as the great Christian emperor of a united Europe, but as a typically violent and inept Germanic warrior-king, so that the sharp distinction between the Merovingian and Carolingian worlds is replaced by the common pattern of the "barbarian west" before the tenth century.

The solution to the enigmatic character of Carolingian history lies in perceiving that eighth- and ninth-century Europe belongs to the general form of an underdeveloped, pre-industrial society which is only beginning to benefit from intelligent leadership. Because in such societies power is vested in a very small elite group—in the case of the Carolingian world, the king, the leading churchmen, and a few great aristocrats—it appears that great improvements can be made very quickly. In such a situation the ideology of the elite group is inevitably an extremely important causal factor in the inauguration of social change. If a few top leaders are won over to the cause of progress and enlightenment, a great reversal of the previous conditions of localism and disorder seems to take place immediately. And while this social amelioration rarely conforms to the high ideals of the elite group, real improvement can be effected in a relatively short time, because the leaders have under their control all the intelligence and literacy available in their society. The situation, however, remains a very precarious one in view of the deep traditions of disorder, localism, and violence in the underdeveloped society.

The death of only a few enlightened leaders, or even the sudden loss of one great personality, can cause the whole system to collapse and open the way for an equally rapid reversion to chaos and barbarism. Surrounding the enlightened group of leaders in such a preindustrial society are a mass of wild warriors and bovine peasants totally lacking in comprehension of what the leaders are trying to do. Consequently, as the central direction falters, there is an immediate backsliding into barbarism. In modern industrial, heavily urbanized, thickly populated, and literate societies it is harder for a small group of men to make much of an impression, but on the other hand, cultural breakdown and political anarchy are not so apt to follow removal of one or two important leaders.

The vicissitudes of the Carolingian world become comprehensible in terms of the pattern of an underdeveloped society. The ideals of the elite group, centered in the royal court and the church, were extremely important as causal factors in political and social change. At the same time it must be remembered that this group worked in an intensely ruralized and localized society and that even the great majority of the Frankish lords had no understanding of the greater part of the sophisticated ideology of the ecclesiastical theorists, and they disliked the implications of most of what they could dimly understand. The elite group of kings, bishops, abbots, popes, and dukes were by no means unanimous in their view of the ideal Christian society. But there was a further underlying and irreconcilable conflict between the general attitude and expectations of the leaders of society and the grim realities of political and economic life. This is why Carolingian history is marked by the emergence of sophisticated and complex ideologies on the one hand and the increasing vitality of lordship and manorialism on the other. It explains why Charlemagne appears both as Christian emperor and barbarian overlord. It accounts for the soaring aims, the short-term triumphs, and the disappointments of the leaders of the first Europe. The most significant aspect of Carolingian history, however, is not the perpetuation of Germanic institutions and their inhibiting effect on the realization of the high ideals of the churchmen of the period, but rather the expression of these ideals and the great efforts made to establish a Christian society. These are the novel factors which distinguish the first Europe from the world which immediately followed the Germanic invasions. Although the great expectations of the Carolingian kings and churchmen were not immediately fulfilled, the greater part of their ideology and institutions was perpetuated even after the collapse of the Carolingian empire, and it formed a very considerable portion of the more successful social order of the tenth and eleventh centuries.

III. Monarchy and Papacy

A great part of the history of eighth- and ninth-century Europe is centered on three ideologies, their expression, encounters, and interaction: the concept of papal authority, the doctrine of theocratic monarchy, and the imperial ideal or, more accurately, ideals. The leaders of the Carolingian world were strongly motivated by one or more of these ideologies and the development of royal and papal policies was largely determined by attempts to turn them into practical programs.

The doctrine of papal authority was formulated between 730 and 760, and its expression was partly a consequence of the iconoclastic controversy in Byzantium. In the late 720's the emperor condemned the use of pictures and other representational art objects (icons) as idolatrous and ordered their removal from the churches under his rule. The result was a violent and schismatic quarrel which absorbed the energies of the Greek state and church for two centuries until the iconodules, the defenders of religious images, finally triumphed. The motivation of the emperors who fomented the iconoclastic controversy have been variously interpreted. The emperors who condemned religious images came from Asia Minor, where the Byzantine army was now recruited, and their iconoclastic attitude has been viewed as a consequence of the rise to power in the eastern Roman empire of men influenced by the religious traditions of middle eastern peoples such as the Arabs and Jews, who forbade pictures in their houses of worship. This interpretation regards the iconoclastic controversy as the result of the increasing orientalization of Byzantine civilization. Another view finds the origin of the iconoclastic controversy in eighth-century emperors' attempts to increase the power of the Byzantine state. They found as an obstacle to this end the fanatical popularity of the Greek monks, which the emperors concluded was a result of popular belief in the miracle-working propensities of icons kept in monastic establishments. The emperors, therefore, believed that their iconoclastic policy was a necessary foundation for the revival of imperial power.

Whatever may have been the emperor's motivation in issuing his iconoclastic decrees, they could not be obeyed by the pope, whom he had ordered to conform to his new policy. In the first place, the pope could not concede that the emperor had the right to legislate on such an important doctrinal question. Second, the western church was strongly opposed to the iconoclastic attitude. Its attitude on images in the church had been clearly enunciated by Gregory the Great, who, while of course denying that ecclesiastical images possessed miraculous powers, nevertheless defended their use as a means of education and edification in religious instruction. The pope in 730 was Gregory II; his name was significant, for it was the custom of popes at their accession to assume the name of the previous pope whom they most admired. Gregory II wished to emulate Gregory the Great, and he put into practice his program of papal leadership in Europe. The papacy had not been able to do this during the seventh century, partly because of the weakness of the Frankish monarchy and partly because of its oppression at the hands of the emperor and his army in Italy. The iconoclastic controversy brought matters to a head and gave Gregory II the opportunity to carry out the policy of his namesake. He sent an angry letter to Constantinople denying the right of the emperor to intervene in doctrinal matters and asserting that if the emperor again intended to use force against the bishop of Rome, the whole of the western world stood ready to help the pope. As a matter of fact, Gregory had no way of knowing if this was true, and when in 739 the papacy asked Charles Martel to come down into Italy to protect it against the emperor and the

Lombards, he refused. Charles undoubtedly felt that he had enough to do at home, and in any case the Franks had been on good terms with Constantinople since the time of Clovis. But Gregory II unquestionably believed that the time had come for the papacy to declare its independence of the Roman emperor and to associate itself with the western world and therefore with the Carolingian family, who ruled by far the largest territory in Europe.

In 751 the policy of the two Gregorys came to fruition when Pepin III turned to Rome for assistance in gaining the Frankish crown. The Merovingian king in the eighth century was a complete nonentity. He had no power or property and rode around in an oxcart like a peasant, but he still had the royal title, and by Frankish law there was no way that the Carolingian mayor of the palace could take it away from him. He needed ecclesiastical support, particularly papal authority, to usurp the French crown, and Pepin III was clever enough to do this as soon as possible, because while the Merovingians had been physical and mental defectives for a century, they might still produce another Clovis. The work of Boniface in the Frankish kingdom, the increase of ecclesiastical influence in Frankish society, and the new respect with which the papacy was regarded by the Frankish clergy indicated to Pepin the course of action that he ought to follow. Church law and papal sanctions would be brought in to overrule Frankish traditions. Consequently, he had Boniface transmit to Rome the question whether or not that man ought to be king who actually exercised royal power. The papacy had waited a century and a half for this moment, and the pope could not but give Pepin the answer he wanted. But as a matter of fact, the papal decision that Pepin had the right to displace the reigning Merovingian and assume the French crown was in accordance with the traditions of political theory of the early medieval church. The ecclesiastical theorists had never been impressed by the claims of inheritance. They had always advocated that succession to the throne was contingent on suitability, that is, on the candidate's qualifications to be an effective and just ruler. Pepin seemed eminently suitable in papal eyes. While the Germanic principle of throne-worthiness was very similar to the ecclesiastical doctrine of suitability, Pepin was not able to take advantage of this, because in France the principle of throne-worthiness had died out in the fifth century and had been replaced by the tradition of the exclusive right of the Merovingian family to the throne. The origin of this transformation of the basis of Frankish kingship probably lies, in pre-Christian times, in the Merovingian claim to be descended from the gods. This was reinforced in the early sixth century by Clovis' conquest of Gaul and his claim that the whole kingdom was the private property of his family. It is apparent that only the decision of the vicar of Christ on earth could break the Frankish primordial attachment to the Merovingian house, attested to by their toleration for over a century of a line of royal idiots.

The elevation of Pepin to the Frankish throne in accordance with ecclesiastical law and papal sanction was effected through an elaborate, symbolical, and religious ceremony. St. Boniface, as the papal representative in France, annointed Pepin with holy oil in the same manner as bishops were elevated to the dignity of their offices, and then crowned him king of the Franks. This sacring of the Carolingian ruler had the desired effect of impressing not only the Frankish churchmen but also the lay lords with Pepin's right to the crown. The last Merovingian was sent off to a monastery, and Clovis' dynasty became extinct. Boniface's anointment of Pepin marked a most important turning point in the development of early medieval kingship, for it involved the introduction of the idea of theocratic monarchy into western Europe. There is evidence that the seventh-century Spanish bishops experimented with a similar ideology and ceremony in an attempt to give some moral and religious sanction to the feeble Visigothic monarchy, but this experiment ended with the Moslem conquest of the Iberian peninsula, and does not appear to have served as a precedent for the sacring of the Carolingian ruler.

Why did the papacy introduce royal anointment into western Europe and with it the ideology of theocratic monarchy, against which, in its Byzantine form, the papacy had struggled bitterly since the fifth century? In the long run it must be asserted that the papacy erred in making this innovation; theocratic monarchy became even more troublesome a doctrine to the church in its western form than in its Byzantine form. This was something which could not be seen in the 750's. The fault of Germanic kingship, in ecclesiastical eyes, had been that it was too weak and could give no leadership to society and no protection to the church, not that it was an engine of despotism and a threat to the moral leadership of the church in society. The papacy in 751 finally had the opportunity to put into practice Gregory the Great's programs and to place the Frankish king in debt to Rome. But to do this it had to overrule strong Frankish traditions and secure the crown for its Carolingian allies. The most certain way of achieving this aim was by the full application of religious sanctions, thereby elevating the head of the Carolingian family to a sacred office. It appeared to be a symbolic, dramatic, and glamorous ceremony which would achieve the desired end of securing the Frankish throne for Pepin but which seemed to offer no threat to papal leadership in western society. Ecclesiastical theorists knew about the implications of theocratic kingship and the royal anointing, but the papacy in the 750's did not expect that illiterate

German kings would make use of this in a way disadvantageous to the interests of Rome nor would they even clearly perceive all the implications of the sophisticated doctrines involved.

The papacy was furthermore not concerned about the introduction of theocratic monarchy into western Europe, because it had formulated its own ideology of the papal suzerainty over the kings of western Europe, and it secured from Pepin the apparent recognition of the validity of this doctrine. The idea of papal authority in the western world was formulated in that most famous of medieval documents, the Donation of Constantine, the best-known forgery in history. There is some doubt about the date of the authorship of the Donation of Constantine in the form in which it has come down to us. It is probable that the surviving version was drafted in the middle of the ninth century, but there is ample evidence that the original Donation of Constantine, substantially the same document that has come down to us, was drawn up in the papal chancery in the 750's, personally presented by the pope to Pepin at Paris in 754, and accepted by the Frankish king as a true statement of the valid powers of the papacy.

The papacy felt it necessary to express its ideology through the medium of a forged document attributed to the emperor Constantine because of the nature of legal concepts in the early middle ages. The good law was the old law; law was virtually equivalent to custom, and new claims had to have some customary or historical basis. Given also the respect which men in a largely illiterate society accorded to written documents, it is easy to understand the propensity of churchmen in the early middle ages to forge documents in order to establish a legal basis for their claims. The forged character of the Donation of Constantine does not convict the eighth-century popes of moral turpitude; the document was merely a legal way of expressing papal ideology. It is furthermore probable that the papacy actually regarded as true the peculiar interpretation of the history of Constantine's reign upon which the Donation was predicated and which is summarized in the prologue to the document. The papal court in Rome was not able to find a copy of the document which they really believed Constantine had issued, so they forged their own version in much the same way as many medieval monasteries forged new copies of genuine charters which had been lost.

The author of the Donation of Constantine drew upon the legend of St. Sylvester, which was referred to by Gregory of Tours in his *History of the Franks* and which probably originated in late fifth-century Italy, contemporary with the formulation of the Gelasian doctrine. The legend presents in historical-legal form the radical aspect of Gelasius I's concept of the relationship between papal *auctoritas* and royal *potestas*. According to the legend upon which the Donation of Constantine is based, Pope Sylvester I had cured the Roman emperor of leprosy. In gratitude Constantine not only made the bishop of Rome the head of all the priests in the Roman world, but resigned his imperial crown and all his power to the pope. As an example of his servility to Sylvester the emperor nominally performed the office of the papal groom. The generous pope, in turn, restored to Constantine his imperial crown. The emperor, however, abandoned Rome, Italy, and the western world to the pope and took up residence in Constantinople. The doctrine behind this charming story is a most radical one. The pope is supreme over all rulers, even the Roman emperor, who owes his crown to the pope and therefore may be deposed by papal decree. The pope has the absolute legal right not only to Rome and the patrimony of St. Peter but to Italy and the whole western world if he chooses to exercise his claims.

The boldness and radicalism of the Donation of Constantine may be explained by the papacy's success in realizing the policy of Gregory the Great. The popes of the first half of the eighth century had secured their independence from Constantinople, effected an alliance with the French monarchy, and apparently gained the moral leadership of western Europe. The prospects for papal power seemed endless in the 750's. And furthermore, the papacy was encouraged to express its ideology by the fact that the Frankish king officially performed the services of papal groom—he led the pope's horse a few paces in accordance with the Roman emperor's role in the Donation of Constantine. A great ceremony was then held at the church of St. Denis, the royal monastery of France, which, by its dedication to the disciple of St. Paul, symbolized the association between Rome and Paris. The pope anointed not only Pepin but his wife and children as well and gave the Frankish king the additional title of *patricius Romanorum,* protector of the Romans (that is, of the Roman church), and in fulfillment of this new office Pepin vowed to restore to the papacy the exarchate of Ravenna. The latter territory had fallen to the Lombards in 751, but Pepin swore to return it, not to the Byzantines to whom it had recently belonged but rather to the patrimony of St. Peter, in accordance with the Donation of Constantine's grant of all Italy to St. Sylvester and his successors. In the following year the Carolingian king fulfilled his promise to the pope. He invaded Italy, took Ravenna away from the Lombards, and against the futile protests of the Greeks handed it over to the papacy. Before he returned to France in 756, he deposited on the tomb of St. Peter in Rome a document which has been known as the Donation of Pepin, confirming the independence of the patrimony of St. Peter. Thus, by the end of the 750's the papacy had good cause to believe that it had secured the leadership of the first Europe and that the revitalized Frankish monarchy would be a deferential and useful supporter in the creation of a Christian world order.

Yet within three decades of these momentous events in the 750's, it became apparent that the first Europe was taking shape in a way which did not conform to the papal ideology expressed in the Donation of Constantine. Leadership in western Europe was in the hands not of the bishop of Rome but of Pepin's son, Charlemagne (768–814). The pope more and more found himself taking second place to the Carolingian king. Nor was the Donation of Constantine actually maintained by Charlemagne. He had begun by confirming his father's donation, but in the 770's he destroyed the Lombard kingdom and took for himself the title of king of the Lombards. By laying claim to northern Italy, Charles directly contravened the Donations of Constantine and Pepin. Furthermore, the pope was alarmed to find Charles taking seriously the implications of his anointment. Charlemagne's court scholars addressed him as King David, who was the prototype of a sacred king. It appeared that the ideology of theocratic monarchy was emerging in the Carolingian kingdom for much the same purpose as it had developed in Byzantium. Where the eighth-century papacy had miscalculated was in not understanding that the reformed Frankish church, in spite of its formal professions of loyalty to Rome, would not inevitably be subservient to the papacy. Rather, the bishops and abbots would just as well ally themselves closely with the Carolingian ruler, who could offer them important positions in his government at court and at least provide them with patronage and security, and if the Frankish king now held a sacred office, if he was now *rex et sacerdos,* so much the better; this provided a pretext for the Frankish ecclesiastics' involvement with the monarchy. The papacy had assumed that an educated and thriving Frankish church would look toward Rome; this was a fatal mistake.

Where the pope had also miscalculated was in not making allowance for the rise of a strong personality in the Carolingian family. And no more impressive figure appeared in the early middle ages than that of Charles the Great. He was a prodigious warrior who spent his reign trying to extend the boundaries of his kingdom on all sides. He incorporated northwestern Germany into the Frankish kingdom and in the course of his conquest slew thousands of heathen Saxons in a single day without flinching. The nature of Germanic kingship was such that whatever other admirable qualities a king might have, his ability as a great warrior would gain him enormous admiration and loyalty among lay lords who could respect no other qualities except proficiency on the battlefield. But Charlemagne did have other qualities which gained him the fanatical loyalty, devotion, and service of the ablest churchmen not only in his own vast kingdom but even in England and northern Italy. Altogether, as he appears in the description of his clerical biographer and secretary, Einhard, Charlemagne is a most impressive personality. If Einhard occasionally cribs a line from Suetonius' *Lives of the Twelve Caesars* in order to describe his master and hero, this is in a certain sense justified, for Charlemagne deserves to stand next to the greatest of the Roman emperors. Although only semiliterate—he did not read Latin well and could barely scratch his name—he possessed a keen intelligence which he applied to all problems of government. He was the great warrior of the age, but at the same time he took pains to continue the work of Boniface in the improvement of church discipline and the furtherance of education in the monastic schools of his realm. He recruited the most renowned scholar of the day, the Englishman Alcuin, to improve the Frankish monastic schools, and at his court he surrounded himself with learned and zealous churchmen whose advice he sought and followed. The primitive German chieftain occasionally breaks through the facade of civilization. Charlemagne had a large number of concubines and bastards, he mistreated his daughters, and like the crudest of the Merovingians he planned to divide up his kingdom among his surviving sons as if it were a piece of real estate. But there is enough in Charlemagne's work in the way of intelligence and idealism applied to government to signal a profound transformation in Germanic kingship. He was the first Germanic king since Theodoric the Ostrogoth who consciously and consistently aimed at social amelioration. The churchmen of his day fully realized this and consequently hailed him as the hero of Latin Christianity, leaving the pope in a respected but decidedly inferior position. Charlemagne, unlike the Byzantine emperor, made no claim to be God's prime representative on earth or to legislate on doctrinal matters. But he had a strong sense of his own destiny, and he fully agreed with the churchmen at his court who hailed him as the leader of the new European society.

The papacy had one weapon left in its spiritual armory by which it could assert its authority over the Carolingian monarch. According to the Donation of Constantine, the imperial title had been resigned by the emperor to the pope, and he had received it back from Sylvester. Henceforth, went the papal argument, the imperial title was the pope's to give and to deny. Beginning in the 780's there is evidence that the papacy was preparing to "translate" the imperial title from Constantinople to the Carolingian realm. The pope stopped dating papal documents by the Roman emperor's regnal year and substituted Charlemagne's, and in the 790's the pope sent the official announcement of his election to the Frankish king instead of to the Byzantine ruler, as was the custom. The granting of the imperial title to Charlemagne as a means of reasserting papal authority in western Europe was a desperate expedient but the only recourse open to the papacy. The imperial coronation of Charlemagne would give a new validity to the Donation of Constantine, and since the pope had the right to remove as well as grant the imperial title, it would give the papacy a powerful sanction against the Carolingian king. Of course, Charlemagne would understand the implications of the imperial coronation by the pope. This presented an obstacle to the realization of the pope's plans. At the very end of the eighth century the papacy was forced to accelerate its program of translating the imperial title to the west.

A new menace had come to threaten the security of the bishop of Rome, namely the Roman nobility, who struggled to secure the election of one of their scions to the throne of Peter. As a consequence of this internal squabble Pope Leo III was beaten up by a Roman mob and charged by his enemies in the Roman nobility with moral turpitude. He fled northward to secure the assistance of the official "protector of the Romans," who was engaged at that time in his long war against the Saxons. On the advice of Alcuin, Charlemagne acted very deliberately and slowly in his reply to Leo's entreaties. He sent the pope back to Rome under guard and kept him in protective custody until he himself could cross the Alps toward the end of the year 800. On December 23, at a trial at which Charlemagne presided, Leo finally purged himself of the accusations against him in the German manner. This course of events had signified a dreadful humiliation for the pope and his abnegation before the Carolingian ruler, and he determined to try to regain the prestige and authority of his office by the carrying out of the imperial coronation of Charlemagne. On Christmas day, as Charlemagne rose from prayer before the tomb of St. Peter, Pope Leo suddenly placed the crown on the king's head, and the well-rehearsed Roman clergy and people shouted "Charles Augustus, crowned great and peace-giving emperor of the Romans, life and victory!" Charlemagne was so indignant and chagrined that, according to Einhard, "he said he would never have entered the church on that day, although it was a very important religious festival, if he had known the intention of the pope." Charlemagne did whatever he could to mollify the outraged Byzantines, who claimed that their imperial title had been stolen from them. Charlemagne hardly ever used the title Emperor of the Romans, which the pope had given him. He satisfied himself with the phrase "Emperor, king of the Franks and Lombards" to indicate the real and effective basis of his power.

The imperial coronation of Charlemagne has engendered a considerable controversy among historians, many of whom have dismissed Einhard's statement as excessive modesty on Charlemagne's part. The fact is that

Charlemagne did not want to be crowned emperor of the Romans because in the first place "Roman" meant "Byzantine" to him, and he had no desire to emulate the ruler in Constantinople, and secondly, because he understood the constitutional implications of papal coronation and had no intention of placing himself in a position of debt or weakness with regard to the bishop of Rome. What makes the situation more complex, however, and what has confused many historians is the fact that there was an imperial ideal coming to the fore among the churchmen of the Carolingian realm, but it was not the same concept of the empire which prevailed either at Constantinople or Rome. The letters of Alcuin in particular are full of references to the "Christian empire" and to "Europa," the area contiguous with Latin Christianity whose leader is Charlemagne. In view of Charles' contributions to the welfare of Europe and in view of his position as the greatest king in Europe, Alcuin and other court churchmen were beginning to think that Charlemagne ought to take the title of emperor. This, however, had little to do with emulation of the old Roman emperor or the ruler in Constantinople. It was intended to be the apotheosis of Charlemagne's position as the leader of Christendom. It is likely that an imperial coronation of Charlemagne would have taken place, had not the pope forestalled the Frankish king and his advisers on Christmas day of 800. Certainly Charlemagne would not have allowed himself to be crowned by the pope; the coronation ceremony which Charlemagne preferred was the one used in 813 when he himself crowned his son and heir, Louis, as emperor. Having been crowned by the pope, Charlemagne chose to interpret his imperial title in the way delineated by Alcuin. He refused to think of himself as a Roman emperor, ignored the sanctions which were implied in his coronation by the pope, continued to call himself king of the Franks and Lombards, and regarded the title of emperor as the expression of his position as Christian war hero, theocratic monarch, and leader of the Frankish church.

The imperial idea played a much more important role in the policies of Charles' son and grandson, Louis the Pious and Charles the Bald, and it became a concept whose content was much more heavily influenced by the original papal ideology. The ninth-century Carolingian churchmen moved away from the Christian empire of Charlemagne and in the direction of a political antiquarianism which sought the full revival of Roman imperial ideas by imitating the ornate court ceremony of the Byzantine emperors and by using the full title, Emperor of the Romans. Already in 816 Louis the Pious allowed himself to be anointed by the pope with this title. To the ninth-century Carolingian rulers and their ecclesiastical supporters, emphasis on the imperial title and association of the Carolingian ruler with the Roman emperors was a buttress against the progressive decline of royal power after Charlemagne's death. Ideology became a substitute for Charlemagne's fame as a Germanic war leader. But ideology could do nothing to stem the advancing tide of localism and the rise of feudal lordship. The ninth-century bishops composed treatises on the glories of empire and kingship, and the Carolingian emperors elaborated their court ceremonial, but they were unable to maintain an effective leadership in their kingdom.

The papacy, over the long run, gained no more than the Carolingians from the revival of the imperial title in the west and from the acceptance by the Carolingians of the Romanist ideology. The mid-ninth-century pope Nicholas I aggressively asserted the radical doctrine of the Donation of Constantine, and the popes were adept at using their control over the imperial title to harass the later Carolingians, but this did not save the papacy from disaster in the late ninth century. For the popes needed a strong Carolingian ruler to protect them from the gangster Roman nobility. With the decline of Carolingian power the papacy entered one of its darkest periods, in the late ninth and first half of the tenth century, in which it became the puppet of the ruling Roman nobility and completely lost its position as a leader in European society.

If the history of the ninth-century empire is one of failure on all sides, this should not blind us to the fact that a new element had been introduced into the political life of western Europe. In the latter part of the tenth century the title was taken up again by the German monarchy which rose out of the ruins of the east Carolingian kingdom. The German kings to the middle of the thirteenth century were to make the imperial title a very important part of their policy, and their successors were to preserve the title until 1806.

Chapter Eight

CULTURE AND SOCIETY
IN THE
FIRST EUROPE

I. The Carolingian World

The literary sources and documentary evidence for the Carolingian period
are much more voluminous than for any era since the fourth century.
Whereas our knowledge of sixth-century France is drawn heavily from the
information supplied by Gregory of Tours, and the sources for the seventh-
century Merovingian kingdom are extremely fragmentary, there survive
from the period 750 to 900 hundreds of pages of chronicles, letters, government documents, and treatises. The improvement in literacy is indicative
of the advance of civilization, of the partial overcoming of the effects of
the Germanic invasions and the expansion of Islam, and of the emergence
of a new distinct culture and society in western Europe. In 400 A.D. western
Europe was merely a geographical expression. Roman civilization was
centered on the Mediterranean; and France, England, and the Rhine valley
were mere adjuncts of the Mediterranean world. In 800 Europe signified a
new civilization coextensive with the area of Latin Christianity and created
by the confluence of Germanic traditions and Latin-Christian culture. Compared to Byzantium and Islam, Europe was still poor and backward, but
it had developed distinctive ideas and institutions of its own, had found
leadership within its own ranks, and had become conscious of its own
distinct existence and destiny.

The first Europe included France, England, western Germany, Ireland, central and northern Italy, and the mountain regions of northern Spain. The vital centers of civilization were not on the Mediterranean coast but in the river valleys of northern France and the Rhineland. The culture of the first Europe was unified by the universal language of churchmen, kings, and the aristocracy—Latin. It was the language of both ecclesiastical and secular government and the tongue in which all intellectual matters were discussed or written down. In all cases, whether on behalf of monarchy, church, or duke, the Latin writing was actually executed by clerical scholars who were nearly all products of the flourishing monastic schools of the Carolingian empire. The everyday language of ordinary people, including most of the nobility, varied from region to region. In England Anglo-Saxon was spoken, and in the eighth and ninth centuries it even became a literary language. In Ireland the Celtic tongue was perpetuated. On the continent the north and east were German-speaking areas, while the south and west contained a variety of dialects derived from the vulgar (that is, popular) Latin, the language actually spoken by ordinary people in the Roman empire. These derivatives of vulgar Latin were the precursors of the Romance languages. By the middle of the ninth century German and French were emerging as distinct languages. In the Oath of Strasbourg of 842 the kings of the east and west parts of the Carolingian empire subscribed in what were recognizable French and German dialects. Thus, by the middle of the ninth century there was a growing separation of vernacular tongues between the eastern and western parts of the Carolingian empire. The emergence of French and German contributed to the disintegration of the Carolingian empire, as Latin, on the other hand, was a strong force in uniting the various regions of the first Europe in a common higher culture.

In 400 the church was under the domination of the Roman emperor. By 800 it was freed from the last vestiges of Byzantine control, but the clergy in western Europe were strongly under the influence of the Carolingian rulers and identified their interests with those of the Frankish kingship. The Carolingians did not interfere in matters of doctrine, but they were concerned with the improvement of church discipline and aimed at using the intellectual and even the financial resources of the church in the service of the monarchy. The Carolingians recognized the Petrine theory and the more conservative aspects of the Gelasian doctrine. They conceded that the church belonged to the bishops, but they felt that the bishops belonged to the Carolingians. The clergy of the Frankish realm, in view of the Carolingian ruler's position as anointed king, Christian emperor, and patron of the church, was inclined to agree with this attitude. Typical of the ninth-century higher clergy was Archbishop Hincmar of Rheims (d. 876), who was the friend, adviser, and chief propagandist of Charles the Bald, an expert on government and court ceremonial, and at the same time an aggressive advocate of the privileges of his see and of the episcopal office in general. The secular obligations and interests of the Carolingian clergy and the spiritual claims of the eighth- and ninth-century kings signified the interpenetration of the church and the world, which was to be the distinguishing quality of medieval civilization over the next three centuries. In the first Europe there was already evident that tension between power and spirit, between the ideal and the material, which has been the greatest force for change in European history.

Urban life was still important in 400 A.D., but it played no part in the first Europe. The Carolingian world was an underdeveloped, thinly populated, intensely rural society. Communications were almost incredibly bad, far worse than in the Roman empire, and at least 80 per cent of the population never moved more than ten miles from the place they were born. Famine was a constant danger, violence a fact of everyday life, and average life expectancy not more than thirty years of age. The people of the Carolingian world had very little knowledge of science and hardly any knowledge of medicine. Under these conditions it is not surprising that superstition proliferated among the populace and that the miraculous powers of local saints were the only recourse which ordinary people had against the ravages of nature and physical illness. The educated clergy struggled against superstition and tried to limit the continual emergence of new cults of local saints by requiring episcopal canonization, but to little effect.

The centers of Carolingian life were the castle, the cathedral, and the monastery. Even the so-called cities of the Frankish kingdom, such as Charlemagne's capital at Aachen or the cathedral city of Rheims, consisted only of a governmental edifice surrounded by a few houses and encircled by a wall. There were remains of great Roman cities in northern Italy, such as the Eternal City itself, but many of the streets of the Italian towns were deserted, the houses falling into ruin, and the great Roman systems for water and sewage abandoned. Even the governmental, military, and ecclesiastical buildings of the Carolingian world were extremely modest. The Carolingian castle was usually a wooden stockade, and the churches and other buildings erected in stone were low and squat, modeled ultimately on Roman bathhouses.

At least half of western Europe in 800 either was covered with dense forests or consisted of swampy land unsuited to agriculture. The topography of the agricultural regions and the form of rural economy had been determined by the heavy-wheeled plow, drawn by oxen, which the Germans had brought with them. The furrow driven by the German plow was much deeper than that made by the light plow used in the Roman world. A day's work for the Carolingian peasant would consist of a single long, narrow strip. Consequently, the countryside came to be dominated by large open fields divided into these strips driven by the heavy plow. Because of the lack of fertilizer it was necessary to leave each field fallow every two or three years. By no means all, nor even a great majority, of the peasants of the first Europe were dependent serfs, bound to the land and subordinated to the manorial lord. Especially in Germany and in eastern England villages of free peasants, who held the open fields in common, sharing the strips, were the rule. Here the original Germanic social structure persisted, characterized by a large mass of free peasants. In the Frankish kingdom west of the Rhine and in the wealthy agricultural midlands of England the medieval manor, beloved by textbook writers, was already the basic unit of the economic system. The lord would retain part of the arable land of the village as his demesne, which would similarly be divided into strips. The peasant-serfs were given strips in the open fields in return for working the lord's demesne. They were bound to the land and subject to the lord's judicial authority and various servile dues, such as an inheritance tax called the *heriot*. The open field divided into strips was to remain the basis of the economic system of a great part of rural Europe until the fourteenth century. It was an unprogressive agrarian system of meager productivity, but it was the only one possible in terms of the technology available.

The manor was a self-sufficient economic unit. This was a necessity in view of the overwhelming difficulties of transportation in the period. International trade was carried on only to serve the demands of the very wealthy, and it was largely in the hands of aliens—Greeks, Jews, Moslems. Local society made almost no use of money. To the extent that local exchange was carried on it was conducted by barter. The first Europe came very close to what nineteenth-century writers called a completely "natural" economy. The very small amount of international trade precluded the need for gold coinage. The Carolingians minted only silver coins, which was all that was usually necessary when the smallest silver coin could buy a cow. When gold coins were needed, Byzantine and Moslem currency was used.

The poverty and localism characteristic of the first Europe made it appear insignificant in comparison with the Roman empire and the contemporary civilizations of Byzantium and Islam. But the Carolingian world was marked by the beginnings of the application of intelligence to the problems of society, and while relatively the achievements in this connection may not appear to be great, this development is of the greatest importance in medieval civilization, for it marks the starting point for the political and intellectual growth of later centuries. The work of the Carolingians secured, first of all, a substantial literate class in Germanic society to do the work of church and monarchy. The leader in this great educational movement was the Englishman Alcuin (d. 804) whom Charlemagne had brought from England to improve the monastic schools of his realm and to continue the work which Boniface had begun. Alcuin was eminently successful in accomplishing the tasks set for him by Charlemagne. He established and expanded schools, libraries, and *scriptoria* in monasteries all over France. He wrote textbooks, prepared word lists, and made the trivium and quadrivium a firm part of the curriculum of the Carolingian school. The impact of his work can be seen in the great increase of literary and documentary materials surviving from the Carolingian period. It can be seen in the number of classical texts whose manuscripts are in the Carolingian hand. It can be seen in the spread of Roman liturgy to the French church and in some original contributions made by the Frankish churchmen themselves in this field. It can be seen in the fact that the earliest large collections of canon law, albeit not systematic and containing many forged decretals, date from the middle of the ninth century.

The educational work of Alcuin was decisive for the ninth and tenth centuries. Never again would Europe face the perils of barbarism, illiteracy, and the possible extinction of Latin culture which had been the danger in the seventh century. Alcuin completed the work which Boniface had begun: Latin Christianity became identical with western Europe not only in theory but in practice. An important test of the deep penetration of Latin Christianity into the life of the Carolingian world is the effect which the disintegration of the empire and the Viking invasions had upon education. There was some effect—a decline of some monastic schools due to disturbed local conditions or Viking marauders—but by and large the monastic schools continued their work successfully during this difficult period. Where the Vikings did not penetrate, in the eastern part of the German kingdom, the schools flourished increasingly and took over cultural leadership from the more western monasteries.

We can see, through the ninth century, as one generation of monastic scholars succeeds another, a steady increase in the extent and depth of their learning. Alcuin had been fighting to impose a basic literacy on the Carolingian church; by the middle of the ninth century this was no longer a problem, and with the first line of culture having been gained and secured, the monastic scholars could go on to more profound studies. What they consciously sought to achieve was the recovery of the whole Biblical-patristic tradition of the fourth century, and we can see that they achieved this aim by the end of the ninth century. In a dozen or more great monastic schools in all parts of the Carolingian realm, especially in communities which had been founded or at least invigorated by Anglo-Saxon or Irish monks in the seventh and eighth centuries, there were extensive and active writing offices which preserved and spread the texts of the Bible and all the patristic writers. Augustine, especially, was carefully studied. The care and devotion which the ninth-century scholars gave to Bible study are indicated by the magnificent illuminated manuscripts they prepared. The influence of Byzantine iconography is very evident in the Carolingian illuminations. But their artistic style is marked by a greater degree of classical naturalism and less of the disembodied symbolism of the Byzantine models.

The Carolingian monks' motive for the study of Latin literature was at first exclusively pragmatic, as had been the case with Alcuin following the programs of Cassiodorus and Augustine. By the second half of the century, in isolated cases the monastic scholars went beyond a utilitarian attitude to the classical texts and developed something of a humanist attitude: they admired the style and even the ideas of Cicero and especially Virgil for their own sakes. Such monastic scholars, it must be emphasized, were always a small minority, but the fact that they make their appearance in the ninth century attests the degree of penetration of Latin culture into the life of the French church.

The small currents of humanism which occasionally rose to the surface in the monastic schools joined up with what was in the beginning a quite different stream of culture in the Carolingian age. Charlemagne had gathered around him in his "palace school" a group of eminent scholars, including several from Italy. Alcuin was at times a member of this group as well. They devoted themselves to turning out reams of Latin poetry and playing little court games with the emperor. There were similar groups of court scholars in the reigns of Louis the Pious and Charles the Bald. A note of conscious antiquarianism and imitation of classical motifs runs through their work. This movement has frequently been called the Carolingian Renaissance and its importance greatly exaggerated. The Carolingian court scholars were a little group of educated men (although in quoting classical texts, they had a penchant for relying on anthologies) who gave an aura of Roman culture to the Carolingian court and were well rewarded for their services. It is hard to make more of their work than this. They cannot be likened to the scholars of the twelfth and fifteenth centuries, because as H. Fichtenau and R. R. Bolgar have emphasized, they were largely ignorant of the needs of mankind and they did not use their learning to deal with the problems of society, but only to adorn royal courts and add a façade of antique grandeur. The Carolingian court scholars included only one thinker with any important degree of originality—John the Scot, an Irishman who worked at the court of Charles the Bald. He translated the Neoplatonic philosophy of the fifth-century Syrian monk who wrote under the name of Dionysius, and added some Neoplatonic speculations of his own. But John did not inaugurate a philosophic movement; he had no one to continue his work, and his importance is a very limited one. Alcuin's impact on medieval intellectual development was the result of his educational work and his idea of a Christian empire; his dull poems turned out as a member of the palace school have little or no significance.

Yet, if many of the most learned Carolingian scholars devoted themselves to sterile exercises and did not try to deal with the problems of society, we can nevertheless see in the Carolingian period the beginnings of the application of intelligence to social problems. Charlemagne and his clerical advisors were not content to rely upon Germanic political tradition; they consciously set out to improve the institutional and technical aspects of government. After three centuries of disorder and drift the Carolingian world exhibited sharply contrasting instances of planning and ingenuity. Carolingian script itself is an example of this. Merovingian handwriting is almost impossible to read, but anyone who can read Latin can read most Carolingian documents after a couple of hours' instruction. For the Carolingian script is so sensible and clear that it was received by the first book publishers of the fifteenth century for their type and is therefore substantially in use today. In a sense Carolingian script is even an improvement over the Roman, which employs only capital letters. The Carolingian scribes invented minuscule script, that is, lower-case letters.

The same intelligence is revealed in the operations of Carolingian monetary and legal systems. After three hundred years of numismatic confusion the Carolingian government established a new and reliable currency based on the simplest of principles. They instructed their minters to take a pound of silver and divide it into 240 pieces, out of which the Carolingian coins were manufactured. The name of *denarius* was given to this kind of coin, after one of the units in Constantine's monetary system. The Carolingian coinage worked so well that it was imitated by the English, who still retain it as the basis for their monetary system. A similar element of rationalization enters into the Carolingian impact on the development of the Germanic law. As a way around the inadequacies of Germanic methods of proof, the Carolingian courts devised the inquest, by which a panel of sworn men from the neighborhood gave their opinion in disputes about possession of land. The inquest was perpetuated in tenth- and eleventh-century Normandy and was carried to England in the latter part of the eleventh century by William the Conqueror, where it developed into the jury of English common law.

Carolingian government reveals in many ways the application of intelligence and rationalization to the problems of Germanic kingship. Charlemagne in particular was not satisfied with his position as either warlord or theocratic monarch; he made an effort to establish an effective administration, and he had the best bureaucracy since Theodoric the Ostrogoth. The first step in the reform of Carolingian government involved the establishment of a chancery staffed by monastic scholars and the issuing of documents on several aspects of the life of lay and ecclesiastical society in which the king was interested. The Carolingian royal documents take the form of capitularies, each dealing in turn with various problems of government; the capitularies are reminiscent of Roman imperial decrees. A capitulary on the church ordered ecclesiastics to undertake educational obligations and to live up to the discipline and rule required of them. Another capitulary is addressed to the stewards of the royal manors, instructing them on the management of the estates under their responsibility. This was a necessity in view of the fact that the Carolingian king's domainal lands were his chief source of income. Still another capitulary applies intelligence to the problem of raising an army. The military system of the Frankish empire was still based on the principle of the Germanic folk-in-arms; when the king, as war leader, summoned them, all able-bodied men were supposed to join the royal army. Charlemagne and his ministers sensed the wastefulness and general unsatisfactory nature of this system. Hence the king published a capitulary allowing villages to band together to support one knight on horseback who would be much more useful than a motley mob of peasants carrying sticks and scythes.

Perhaps the most important of all of Charlemagne's decrees dealt with the problem of local government. When the king, with his chancery, court, and army, was in any given area, there was no problem of obtaining the loyalty of the local population. But given the bad communications and the atomized nature of social relations, the problem was to maintain royal influence in areas beyond the possible impact of the king's personality. How were the duke (the local military official) and the count (the king's local representative in matters of law and finance) to be controlled in the areas away from the immediate influence of the royal court? This question had bedeviled the Merovingians, and their inability to solve it greatly contributed to the collapse of royal power in the sixth and seventh centuries. It remained a stumbling block to the Carolingians. Indeed, it may be said to be the most continuous, difficult problem of medieval monarchy. The Carolingian solution was to send out representatives from the royal court, the *missi,* on periodic tours of inspection in the provinces in the hope of maintaining control over the local royal officials and preventing their integration into the provincial aristocracy.

The system of the *missi* was a highly intelligent and plausible innovation in Carolingian government and a tribute to the administrative skill of the ecclesiastics such as Alcuin and Einhard, who served Charles the Great. But already in Charlemagne's later years, the central government was having trouble preventing the rise of a new provincial aristocracy. Nobles might be sent out from the royal court to act as duke or count, and they would be carefully chosen from among loyal men, but once they got to Aquitaine or some other distant province, they tended to strike roots in local society and turn their title and the royal estates which were bound to it into hereditary property. This process of political disintegration was greatly intensified after Charlemagne's death, and the *missi* or any other expedient could not have countered the new factors which brought about the decline of Carolingian power in the ninth century. Charlemagne's surviving legitimate son and successor, Louis the Pious (814–840), was an intelligent and well-meaning man but completely unable to serve as the leader of a Germanic society. He was completely inept as a soldier, and this lost him the respect of the lay nobility, who felt themselves free to do what they wanted and so set about expanding their patrimonies. The situation was made worse by the bitter struggles of Louis' children for the royal title, which were well under way before his death. It was in many ways a repetition of the worst moments of the Merovingian monarchy. Finally, in 843 the three sons of Louis the Pious decided on the partition of the empire by the Treaty of Verdun. There were to be three Carolingian realms: the western, the eastern, and an anomalous middle kingdom which stretched a thousand miles from the Low Countries, along the Rhine, and over the Alps to include northern Italy. The middle kingdom almost immediately collapsed, leaving a maze of petty principalities from Flanders to Lombardy. Remnants of the middle kingdom along the Rhine were to be incorporated into the German empire in the tenth and eleventh centuries; their conquest was to be aimed at by the powerful French monarchy of the thirteenth century, and they were thence to be the cause of frequent war between France and Germany well into the twentieth century.

The Carolingian line did not end in Germany until 911, and in France the Carolingians held on until 987, but from the last quarter of the ninth century the Carolingian king was a nonentity. The power in Germany was in the hands of tribal chieftains whose position had been strengthened by the Carolingians, who gave them the title of duke. In France the power of the central government had been usurped by the dukes and the counts, who were to remain the leaders of French society until the middle of the twelfth century.

The situation in the west Carolingian kingdom was acerbated by the incursion of Viking marauders up the Loire and Seine valleys. The Scan-

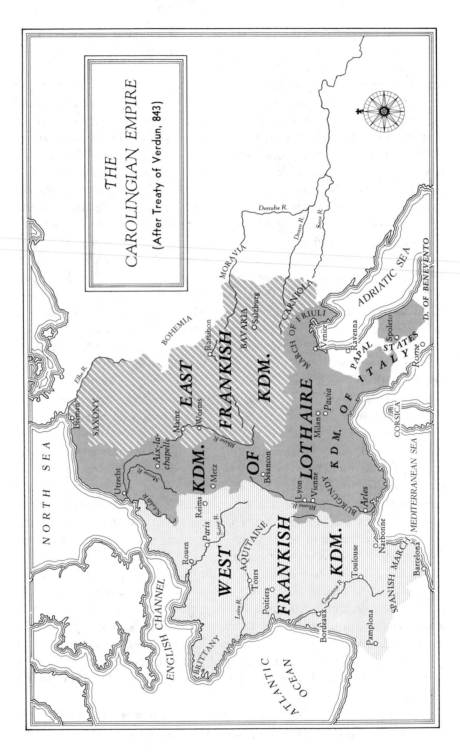

THE
CAROLINGIAN EMPIRE
(After Treaty of Verdun, 843)

NORTH SEA

ENGLISH CHANNEL

ATLANTIC
OCEAN

MEDITERRANEAN SEA

ADRIATIC SEA

Danube R.

Drave R.

Save R.

BOHEMIA

MORAVIA

CARNIOLA

MARCH OF FRIULI

SAXONY

Elbe R.

Bremen

Utrecht

Scheldt R.

Meuse R.

Aix-la-chapelle

Mainz

Worms

Ratisbon

BAVARIA

Salzburg

EAST
FRANKISH
KDM.

Rhine R.

Metz

Reims

Paris

Rouen

Seine R.

BRITTANY

Loire R.

Tours

Poitiers

Bordeaux

Garonne R.

Toulouse

Pamplona

Barcelona

Narbonne

SPANISH MARCH

WEST
FRANKISH
KDM.

AQUITAINE

OF

Besançon

BURGUNDY

Lyon

Vienne

Rhone R.

Arles

LOTHAIRE

K D M. OF

ITALY

Milano

Pavia

Venice

Ravenna

PAPAL
STATES

Spoleto

Rome

D. OF BENEVENTO

CORSICA

dinavian attack on western Europe was the consequence of obscure struggles in Denmark and Norway which resulted in the expulsion of the defeated war bands. The latter either escaped into Russia or took to their long ships and pillaged the river valleys of western Europe. Some went through the straits of Gibraltar and attacked ports in Italy. But it was northern France which, except for the British Isles, felt most heavily the brunt of the Viking invasion. The Scandinavians had nothing to contribute to western European civilization. Their level of culture was no higher than that of the more primitive tribes among their German kinsmen who invaded western Europe in the fifth and sixth centuries. The unit of Scandinavian society was the same kind of war band which is depicted in *Beowulf*. The bounty-giving chieftain alone could gain the loyalty of these savage warriors. The Danish and Norwegian kings had very little authority; in fact, the Scandinavians had a penchant for drowning their rulers in wells. The Northmen were untouched by Latin Christianity until the tenth century; they were heathens who were particularly fond of sacking great monasteries, which they soon discovered were very wealthy.

The later Carolingians were completely incapable of dealing with these new invaders. These descendents of Charlemagne were pious and frequently sophisticated men but nearly always cowards as well. In most cases they did not even attempt to engage the Vikings in battle, but offered the invaders bribes, which only satisfied them for a short while. The Scandinavians who attacked France in the ninth century were very small in number, and their incursion did not represent a cataclysmic event comparable to the Germanic invasions. But their attacks produced fear and disorder, which further encouraged men to look to the most powerful lord in their own neighborhood for protection and to offer him loyal service in return for security. The Scandinavian invasions further emphasized what had been apparent since the 830's—that the Carolingians were no longer great warriors and that the provincial aristocracy need not concern themselves any longer with obeying the royal capitularies.

The Frankish churchmen who witnessed these lugubrious events were deeply chagrined and disappointed. The literature of the last three quarters of the ninth century is extremely pessimistic and bitter in tone. This is not because of any complete collapse of social order, but rather because the world which the bishops found coming into existence was so strongly at variance with their high ideals. They had dreamed of the political unity of Christian Europe under the Carolingian empire, in which a sacred and beneficent king, in accordance with their understanding of Augustinian teaching, would establish earthly peace and dispense justice with the advice of ecclesiastical leaders. This dream had been shattered. The empire was divided, real power had passed into the hands of the aristocracy, and the Carolingian kings were less and less able to either maintain control over government and law within their realm or withstand the incursion of savage invaders from without who pillaged churches with impunity. The disillusioned and embittered churchmen of the ninth century resorted to desperate expedients. Some tried to gain new prestige for the monarchy by heightening its sacred qualities and by elaborating the ceremonial aspects of kingship. Others turned in disgust from the impotent Carolingians and threw in their lot with the papacy. They published a vast compendium of canon law, including many forged decretals attributed to St. Isidore, exalting papal authority over the kings and metropolitans in accordance with the Donation of Constantine. This expedient was of course no help to the Frankish clergy, in view of the growing domination of the Roman nobility over the papacy.

After 900 the ecclesiastics' despairing and bitter tone subsided. The churchmen of what had been the east Carolingian realm associated themselves with the creation of the new German monarchy and found in the Ottonian dynasty very worthy successors to Charlemagne. The bishops and abbots of France in the tenth century turned away from imperial dreams and came to terms with the new feudal order.

II. The Feudal Organization of Society

The great English legal historian F. W. Maitland was wont to amuse his classes at Cambridge by remarking that feudalism was introduced to England in the eighteenth century. By this he meant that the word "feudalism" was not a medieval term. It was invented by English and French lawyers in the seventeenth and eighteenth centuries and was popularized by the political philosopher Montesquieu. At the time of the French Revolution the word was often identified with the *ancien régime* and the privileges of the French aristocracy, which aroused the wrath of the French bourgeoisie. The term "feudalism," therefore, is frequently used in the late eighteenth century in a pejorative sense. From the French radicals it was adopted by Karl Marx, who used the term to signify pre-capitalistic economy. In the late nineteenth century medieval scholars, particularly in France and Germany, began the definition of feudalism with reference to western Europe in the middle ages and tried to work out its history. In view of the fact that feudalism was not a medieval term and that it had already been given certain meanings by modern social philosophy, it might have been wise for medieval historians to avoid using the term and use instead

medieval words such as "vassalage" and "lordship." They were not, however, able to be so reticent on this matter; the educated public demanded
a scholarly definition of feudalism, and a host of authorities came forward
with their interpretations.

In the vast scholarship of the past half century on the nature of feudalism
there have been sharply conflicting interpretations. One school regards
feudalism as a group of political and legal institutions, as a system of decentralized government—public power in private hands, in J. R. Strayer's
excellent phrase. It maintains that feudalism emerged in the second half of
the ninth century with the disintegration of the Carolingian empire. This
school does not believe that feudalism was necessarily bound up with any
specific kind of economic system. It points out that there were still feudal
institutions in the expanding money economy of the thirteenth century and
that, instead of being rewarded with real estate, vassals received *fief-rentes,*
or money fiefs, that is, pensions. This view very sharply distinguishes feudalism from manorialism. It points out that feudalism was a system of
political and legal relationhips involving free men, while manorialism was
an agrarian system involving dependent peasants. The advocates of the
political-legal interpretation of feudalism, or the strict interpretation, as it
may be called, tend to be skeptical about the use of the term "feudalism"
with reference to non-European history. Feudalism is a specific kind of
decentralized government which prevailed in western Europe from the
ninth century into the thirteenth. The outstanding scholars who have
adopted this interpretation of feudalism have been Heinrich Mitteis in
Germany, F. L. Ganshof in Belgium, F. M. Stenton in England, and C. H.
Haskins, J. R. Strayer, and Bryce Lyon in the United States.

The alternative prevailing interpretation of feudalism was largely the
work of Marc Bloch and his disciples in France. This view was presented in
Bloch's classic study, *Feudal Study,* published in 1940. As an economic
and social historian Bloch was not prepared to define feudalism purely in
political and legal terms. He regarded it rather in terms of a whole system
in which all aspects of life—not only political but also economic, ecclesiastical, and cultural—were centered on lordship. Feudalism was a
political system, an economic system, and a system of values. We can speak
of feudal economy, a feudalized church, and a feudal literature in much
the same way as we can use the term capitalism to refer not only to a
certain kind of production and exchange, but also to government, thought,
and "spirit." Bloch's broad interpretation of feudalism comes close to the
Marxist view, but it differs fundamentally from the latter in making the
determinant of the nature of feudalism not the economic system but rather
a multiplicity of factors of which manorialism was only one. Those who

lean toward this broad definition of feudalism are inclined to regard it as a stage in social development which at various times has existed in non-European parts of the world, such as Japan, Byzantium, and Russia.

Drawing upon the intensive scholarship of the past half century and relying upon the work of both schools of interpretation, but leaning more in the direction of Bloch's view, we may identify lordship as the indispensable element in feudalism and attempt a definition. Feudalism is a form of social organization in which most, or at least a great part, of the political, economic, and military power is in the hands of an hereditary nobility. The economic power of the nobility is based primarily on their lordship over large estates and a dependent peasant class. The political and military power of the nobility is based on the control which they gain over freeman soldiers and decentralized governmental and legal institutions. This is the form of social organization which was characteristic of France from the later ninth century to the later twelfth. It did not appear in England until the later eleventh century and not in Germany until about 1100. It never emerged in Italy at all. This does not mean that in the nonfeudal areas of western Europe there were not any lords, but it does mean that they did not gain an almost exclusive control of political, economic, and military power. Nor does the definition imply that the hereditary nobility was no longer important in Europe after 1200. On the contrary, the nobility continued to be important in political, economic, and military life, and in the fourteenth and fifteenth centuries the great aristocrats enjoyed throughout Europe an enormous amount of political influence. But the power of the nobility was no longer based primarily on its lordship over serfs and manors and its control over decentralized governmental and legal institutions. In medieval history feudalism existed at certain times and in certain places. As to whether feudalism has existed in other areas of the world, this is entirely plausible, but the validity of this hypothesis must be based on empirical evidence assessed by the historians of these civilizations.

How did feudalism as we have defined it come to exist in tenth-century France? This is a very difficult question to answer. It is hard to trace the origins and rise of feudal institutions because of fragmentary evidence before the ninth century, which in turn was the result partly of the general illiteracy of European society and partly of the fact that the arrangements made by lords were often initially temporary expedients, not permanent legal establishments attested by documents.

In the classical feudalism of tenth- and eleventh-century France three elements can be distinguished: the personal (lordship and vassalage), the real or property element (fief), and the decentralization of government and law. The development of feudalism until the tenth century involves the process by which the latter two elements were associated with lordship and vassalage. In addition feudalism came to comprise a system of social ideals and values.

Nineteenth-century historians wasted a great deal of energy and paper debating whether feudal institutions were German or Roman in "origin." Most scholars today would say that this is a badly conceived, and essentially false, problem. The nexus of feudal institutions of the tenth century developed out of certain political, legal, and economic forms, in some cases German, in some cases Roman, in response to social need after the collapse of the Roman empire in the West.

Lordship was the basic social and political institution in Germanic society. The *comitatus,* or *gefolge,* the Germanic war band as described by Tacitus and in *Beowulf,* was based on loyalty of warriors to their chieftain in return for the latter's protection and generosity. This is the embryo of medieval feudalism. The perpetuation of this kind of loyalty in the fifth and sixth centuries was made easier by the existence of a similar institution in the later Roman empire, the *patrocinium* (clientage). In the disturbed conditions of the later empire, certain aristocrats gathered around them young men of fighting age whom they rewarded and protected in return for their loyalty and service. The vassals of the sixth and seventh centuries were simply the perpetuation of the German *gefolge* and the Latin *patrocinium.* The vassals were free men who voluntarily subjected themselves to some prominent warlord in their locality, but otherwise their only quality was their fighting ability. The term "vassal" comes from the Celtic word meaning "boy." As is implied by the etymology, the vassals of the sixth and seventh centuries were simply "the boys," gangs of thugs who fought on behalf of certain big men in the neighborhood. They were as far removed as possible from the chivalric knights pictured in the romantic literature of the twelfth and thirteenth centuries. These vassals were simply toughs who beat up people and destroyed property at the behest of their warlord in return for protection, maintenance, and a share of the booty. The social status of the vassals, beyond the basic fact that they were all freemen, depended on the lord they served. Those, for instance, who comprised the personal bodyguards of the Merovingian kings had greater prestige and wealth and were dignified by the special appellation of *antrustiones.*

As yet, vassalage had nothing to do with holding land; the vassals lived in a stockade provided by the lord and were fed, clothed, and armed by him. The next stage in the emergence of feudal institutions involved the association between vassalage and landed wealth, which was intended to reward the vassals for their service and support them. It is a fact of the greatest importance that this "realization of the feudal relationship," as it has been called by Ganshof, was an extremely slow and far from uniform development. Even in the tenth century the majority of vassals in France held no land and continued to live in their lord's household, and even in the early twelfth century, in the intensely feudalized areas of northern France and England, there were many landless vassals, although by this time they were definitely in the minority. In Merovingian times it appears that the only vassals who received estates were men very prominent in society. The Frankish dukes and counts were given "benefices" (benefits), gifts of land, by the Merovingian rulers in order to secure their loyalty and maintain them while they performed their services to the royal government. But the great aristocrats who received these benefices proceeded to treat them as hereditary estates. This is the beginning of the association of hereditary estates with loyalty and service to the lord. The system of benefices was imitated on a smaller scale in the relationship between some of the great aristocrats and their more important vassals.

A slow but fundamental change in military methods between the fifth and eighth centuries increased the necessity for associating vassalage with the benefice, or the fief as it came to be called after the eighth century. The Germans had used mostly infantry, and they had followed the military principle of the folk-in-arms, with the king summoning the mass of free peasantry to come to his aid in war. But the superiority of the armed cavalry, which had already been employed during the period of the Germanic invasions by the Roman emperor, the Huns, and some of the Germanic tribes, became more and more evident. By the eighth century more enlightened warlords in western Europe were seeking to build their armies around the mailed and mounted soldier—the *chevalier,* or *cniht* (knight). The introduction of the stirrup into western Europe from the Mediterranean world in the early eighth century markedly increased the effectiveness of cavalry. But the knight's equipment was a heavy expense, and a lord who wanted a formidable army of knights among his vassals found it expedient to enfeoff (invest) his chevaliers with manorial estates from which they might obtain the income necessary to array themselves for battle.

The granting of a fief did not involve the giving of complete property rights over the estate to the vassal. He had the use of the income of the land as a reward for service and in order to make possible his outfitting as a knight. But technically the ultimate ownership of the land was still the lord's, who could recover it if the vassal ceased to be loyal, and when the vassal died, the fief automatically reverted to the lord. It is believed that the precedent for feudal tenure was a system of landholding called the *precarium,* which existed especially on church lands in the seventh and eighth centuries. By this precarious tenure an abbot or a bishop who had more land than he could profitably manage himself allowed laymen to have the use of such lands, usually on the payment of a rent and with the understanding that the estate was recoverable at will.

With their accustomed intelligence and ingenuity the Carolingian family early realized the military advantages accruing from the enfeoffment of their vassals. Thus, when Charles Martel raised an army to encounter the invading Arabs in the fourth decade of the eighth century, he sought to obtain as large a knightly contingent as possible. He succeeded in carving out fiefs for his vassals from church lands, probably on the basis of precarious tenures. During the second half of the eighth century the Carolingian ruler was rewarding his aristocratic vassals with large fiefs granted from the royal demesne itself. And the great lords of the western part of the Carolingian realm were quick to imitate the king and transformed some of their own vassals into enfeoffed knights. This growing association of fief and vassalage had the effect of generally elevating the social status of the vassal. From the hired thug he was himself becoming, in many instances, an important local lord, enjoying control over one or more manors. There was, of course, a great disparity between the duke or count, who was the vassal of the king, and the common run of knightly vassals, who were, for many centuries to come, violent and uncouth people.

The increasing involvement of vassalage and fief inspired a land hunger on the part of all vassals in feudal society which persisted well into the twelfth century. Whereas previously the fief was regarded as a reward for loyalty, now vassals sought out lords who were prepared to offer them landed estates. Those vassals who already had fiefs set about obtaining more and sought to assure the hereditary character of the land which they held of their lord. Although technically the fief was not inheritable and reverted back into the lord's hands at the vassal's death, by the middle of the tenth century the fief had already become an hereditary patrimony for all practical purposes. On payment of an inheritance tax called the "relief," the deceased vassal's son professed his loyalty to the lord and entered into possession of the fief. The land hunger of the ninth- and tenth-century vassals is well illustrated by the great feudal epic *Raoul de Cambrai,* which, while it has come down to us in a twelfth-century version, dimly reflects a true incident which occurred in the ninth century and admirably mirrors the mores of the feudal class of that period. In the poem the emperor neglects to give Raoul the fief which his father had held, whereupon Raoul takes up arms against his lord in an attempt to force him to grant what he considers his rightful inheritance.

The final stage in the development of feudalism was the passing of governmental and legal authority to the king's great feudal vassals, who in turn passed some of this authority on to their own vassals. This stage is the product of the ninth century and was the consequence of the inability of the later Carolingians to maintain control over the dukes and counts who usurped the royal power over their duchies and counties and turned them into enormous hereditary fiefs. Lordship over manorial estates had always involved political and legal control over the dependent peasantry, but this authority was negligible compared to the passing of public power into private hands in the ninth century. The feudal princes won from the feeble monarchy the right to collect taxes and to hold courts for the hearing of important pleas—the right of "high justice," the power to hang criminals —in their duchies and counties. Similarly, all lesser lords strove to gain pieces of public power and to exercise some political and legal authority within their own fiefs. By the middle of the tenth century in France the powers of the Carolingian king had been swallowed up in the private feudal courts, which exercised overlapping and conflicting jurisdictions in a crazy patchwork of decentralized authority.

The emergence of the feudal kind of social organization was followed by the refinement and rationalization of several aspects of lordship and the entrenchment of a group of social values based on the ideal of loyalty. An involved ceremony by which the vassal declared his loyalty or homage to the lord was worked out. The candidate for vassalage knelt before the lord and the latter clasped his hands around the former's. The church added the usual Christian façade in the appended ceremony of fealty by which the vassal made a sacred vow of loyalty to his lord.

In enfeoffing his vassal, the lord usually handed over a symbol of the estate, such as a grain stalk or a knife. It became customary (in a society where literacy was increasing) to attest the grant of land by a deed called simply a "charter," i.e., document. The medieval charter generally had five parts: the salutation, usually addressed to the leading men of the neighborhood in which the fief lay; the harangue, which gave the reason for the grant and which was often elaborate if the grantee was an ecclesiastic; the dispository clause, which listed, often in very great detail, the location and boundaries of the estate or estates granted; and then the curse, which inflicted an ecclesiastical anathema on anyone who dared to contravene the terms of the charter, again very elaborate if the beneficiary were an ecclesiastic; and finally the witness list, to which those who had witnessed the grant attested their private seals. In royal charters the scribe frequently wrote down the names of everyone present at court until he came to the end of the parchment. The medieval charter was thus an impressive document which, at least until the twelfth century, was apt to be decisive evidence in a lawsuit over possession of land; it is not surprising that ecclesiastics frequently forged charters to help their claim to an estate. It is surprising how negligent lay lords were about preserving them. They rarely could produce the charter when they had to, which encouraged interminable lawsuits over possession of estates.

By the end of the tenth century the respective rights and duties of lord and vassal had been fully worked out. The vassal owed military service to his lord, not to exceed forty days in a year. If he was an important vassal who held a large fief, he owed in addition the military service of a contingent of knights to his lord's army. Furthermore, the vassal owed suit at court—that is, he had to turn up at the lord's private court to participate in lawsuits between his peers, the other vassals of the lord, and to give the lord advice if the latter asked for it. In addition, the vassal was subject to feudal taxation—the relief, the money obtained from the vassal's property through wardship when the vassal died leaving no male heirs of age, and the regular "feudal aids," which the vassal had to pay the lord when the latter knighted his eldest son, married off his eldest daughter, or had to be ransomed from captivity. In return the lord was to maintain his vassal, but by no means did he have to give him a fief, and he was not to "disparage" the vassal by insulting him in one way or another. When the vassal failed to fulfill his vow of loyalty to the lord, he was subject, after trial in the lord's court, to forfeiture of his fief. If the lord acted improperly toward the vassal, the latter had the right of *diffidatio,* the dissolution of the feudal bond, usually inaugurated by the breaking of the symbolic grain stalk or knife that represented the transfer of the fief. The former eventuality usually, and the latter always, meant war, but war was in any case a fact of everyday life in feudal society.

By the end of the tenth century subinfeudation—the process by which a vassal enfeoffed part of his own fief—had become common and had been frequently carried down through several degrees in the feudal scale from king or duke to lowly "vavasour," as the humblest subvassal was called. It was a question of whether the subvassals owed loyalty to the ultimate lord or only to their immediate overlords. There was no general answer to this; it was a matter of whether the original lord was sufficiently strong and energetic to compel the subvassals to take oaths of homage and fealty to him as their liege, or chief, lord. A similar problem arose out of the fact that land-hungry knights became the vassals of two or more lords in order to gain additional fiefs. The anomaly might be solved by one of the lords asserting his rights to be the liege lord. If this did not happen and if the vassal's two lords should go to war against each other and summon the vassal to render them military service, he would solve his predicament by joining the lord who seemed most likely to win.

The Carolingian churchmen had initially been bitterly critical of the advance of lordship, which they believed, and with justice, to be a cause of the disintegration of the Christian empire. But they were not long in coming to terms with the new social order by integrating themselves within it. The bishops and abbots became lords and vassals like the lay nobility and were involved in all aspects of the life of feudal society, except personal participation in feudal warfare. The churchmen did their best to pacify feudal society and to Christianize and idealize the feudal relationship. They added the religious ceremony of fealty to the act of homage and became adept at enumerating the mutual obligations of lord and vassal in terms which presupposed a level of conduct far more civilized and moral than the rough fighters who still composed 95 per cent of the feudal class were capable of achieving. The church tried its best to limit war in feudal society during the eleventh century by the spread of the Peace of God movement, by which the feudal nobility were to form leagues to preserve the peace and to promise not to fight on certain days. Generally the peace movement was a failure; it was only successful when a strong ruler got behind it because he saw in it advantages for himself.

As a general rule feudalism was antagonistic to royal power. As we have seen, it involved decentralized government and the passing of public power into private hands. The feudal pyramid beloved by textbook writers, with the king on the pinnacle, actually gives a false impression of the nature of feudalism. The king of France in the tenth and eleventh centuries was indeed the lord over the great feudal princes, but he had no real power over the dukes and counts who were his vassals, because he was not the liege lord over their subvassals. As long as he could not defeat the duke of Normandy or the count of Toulouse, the king in Paris had no control over them, although he had a right to their formal homage. The duke of Normandy had a much better army than the king had, and the Norman knights did not in any way recognize the king as their overlord. For all practical purposes, the monarch of France, whether he was a Carolingian or, after 987, of the new Capetian house, was only the duke of Paris. A similar situation prevailed in the feudal organization of Germany in the twelfth century.

Where the feudal pyramid actually did operate was in England after the Norman conquest in 1066. This was because the Norman duke in the tenth and the first half of the eleventh centuries learned how to use feudal institutions in a special way—to increase the power of the central government, which was not the way feudalism had worked in the later Carolingian empire.

All social systems are founded upon a set of assumptions about what is good and what is bad in human relationships, and these assumptions have a tendency to be perpetuated and adhered to long after the precise social needs they served have ceased to operate. The values that served feudalism and the feudal lords were these three: first, that military prowess is a social good because only the strong man can provide peace and protection; second, that the bonds of personal loyalty are the sinews of the social order and only the relationship of one man to another can give sanction to political and legal obligations; third, that these bonds of loyalty are arranged in an ascending and descending order, stretching through society and on to heavenly regions.

The third of these assumptions allowed feudal relationships to receive the approval of ecclesiastics trained in the old doctrines of hierarchy. Indeed, it is likely that the churchman gave a much greater emphasis to this feudal value and made hierarchy both more central and more rigid in feudal society. The second of these assumptions, that of loyalty, was useful to ambitious kings and dukes who sought to impose a sovereign power over landed society in the eleventh and twelfth centuries. The ideal of loyalty also inspired, to a degree, a new sensitivity to personal relationships, a sentimental view of the attachment of one human being to another; it became a constituent of the medieval idea of love and an inspiration for the romantic movement of the twelfth century.

The first assumption, on the social value of military prowess, became transmuted into the ideal of aristocratic leadership in society and the belief, which prevailed into the twentieth century, that the man on horseback was the natural leader, whereas others stood and served. Feudal recognition of the intrinsic goodness of physical strength was perpetuated in the moral sanction of the stronger over the weaker that became essential to the operation of the European states system from the twelfth century to the twentieth. And this vestige of feudality still lingers to work its cursed mischief and grind down the arts of peace and deprive mankind of peace and happiness.

PART FOUR

*By divine authority and the institution of
the holy fathers, kings are consecrated in
God's Church before the sacred altar and
are anointed with holy oil and sacred
benediction to exercise the ruling power
over Christians, the Lord's people, . . .
[and] the Holy Church of God.*

— ANONYMOUS OF YORK

THE EARLY MEDIEVAL
EQUILIBRIUM

Tenth and Earlier Eleventh Centuries

Chapter Nine

ECCLESIA AND MUNDUS

I. The Nature of the Early Medieval Equilibrium

By 900 it was certain that the ideal of the political unity of the new Latin Christian civilization could not be realized. The European peoples would have to be satisfied with more limited political structures. During the tenth century these states began to take shape; the political decentralization and social chaos of the late ninth century was reversed, and two successful examples of political leadership appeared in northwestern France and in Germany. The feudal duchy of Normandy and the Ottonian German empire were, to a considerable degree, founded upon strongly contrasting kinds of institutions. But they had in common a fundamental quality of new European civilization: ecclesiastical and secular political ideas, leadership, and resources were inextricably joined together in the creation and progress of these states. The same interpenetration of *ecclesia* and *mundus,* the church and world, can be seen at work all over tenth-century Europe, even in the disappointing later Anglo-Saxon monarchy with its ineffective central government and in the even weaker Capetian monarchy.

This equilibrium between the church and the world was the outcome of the long struggle to achieve the Christianization of European society. Gregory the Great and St. Boniface had been the founders of this movement, which in the later eighth and ninth centuries had been greatly advanced by the Carolingian kings and higher clergy. The failure of Merovingian monarchy had demonstrated Germanic kingship's great need of the moral and religious sanctions and other assistance which the church could provide. The efforts made by the leaders of the Carolingian world to create a world order in which church and kingship worked together had resulted in a bitter and painful failure. The same interpenetration and identification of the church and the world was used, however, by the Norman dukes and German emperors to create more limited political structures, but ones which exhibited outstanding qualities of strength and endurance and which gave to European civilization its first examples of successful political leadership.

The power of both the German emperors and the Norman dukes of the tenth and eleventh centuries was founded to a very substantial degree, on the control they were able to exercise over the church in their territories, especially over the Benedictine monasteries, and by the aid and support given them by the church in the form of revenues, knights, administrative personnel, and the fostering of popular veneration for the pious ruler who affected to be a friend of the church. On its side the church gained its patron's protection against the unruly lay nobility, the endowment of monasteries and bishoprics with great estates and magnificent Romanesque religious houses and cathedrals, the raising of the higher clergy to the front rank of the nobility, and frequent opportunities for the leading ecclesiastics to attend the courts and councils of the ruler and thereby to influence his policy. This kind of relationship between ecclesiastical and secular leaders was supported by the learned doctrine of the identification of the *ecclesia* and *mundus* which was popular precisely at the period when the early medieval equilibrium came to fruition. Since the ninth century there had been a growing tendency for ecclesiastical writers to describe the church, regarded as the mystical Body of Christ, as embracing the whole world. In this view there were not separate spheres for the *ecclesia* and the *mundus*, but rather the church was one, indivisible, universal Body of Christ encompassing the whole world. By the eleventh century this theory had become a commonplace among the leading thinkers and even less prominent writers of the Latin church. "The church" and "the world" were treated as identical and synonymous terms, and hence empires and kingdoms had to be regarded as entities not outside the church but rather within its universal bounds. This theory of the absorption of the secular into the spiritual realm was inspired by the actual prevailing relationship between church and kingship in western Europe in the tenth and first half of the eleventh centuries.

II. The Norman Feudal State

In 987 the Carolingian line finally lost the royal title west of the Rhine. The descendants of Charlemagne had exercised no effective control over the great feudal princes for a hundred years, and the monarchy had no resources of its own. But the persistence of Germanic and Christian traditions of kingship made the French crown still a prized possession, and the most powerful lord in the Île-de-France, Hugh Capet, pushing aside the Carolingians, took pains to secure his elevation to the French throne by the formal Germanic process of election. The church legitimized his rule by anointment, and the abbot of the royal monastery of St. Denis was as devoted to Hugh as he had been toward the Carolingians. With clerical support Hugh Capet was able to pass the royal title on to his son, and, in fact, the Capetian family was to hold the French throne by direct line of hereditary succession until the fourteenth century. As far as the tenth and eleventh centuries are concerned, nothing important had happened; one weak dynasty had merely been supplanted by another. Before the twelfth century the Capetian kings were famous for only two things: extreme piety and sexual promiscuity. This somewhat paradoxical combination of qualities may be due to the fact that all we know about the earlier Capetians comes from the description of monastic chroniclers whose judgment of character was based on severely limited criteria. But it is significant that the tenth- and eleventh-century Capetians only attracted notice by their devout exercises and adulterous scandals. These are purely personal enterprises; the Capetians had no effect on the government and society of France. The great feudal princes who were nominally their vassals acted independently and gave them no support. In fact, these kings were not even secure in their own domain of the Île-de-France, which was infested with the castles of robber barons. It is true that the Capetians did have the royal title and, with the aid of the abbot of St. Denis and the archbishop of Rheims, they cultivated the traditions of sacred kingship. While these traditions would eventually be useful to the later Capetians, they availed the kings of France in the tenth and eleventh centuries very little. Theocratic monarchy could be an extremely powerful moral force, but only when combined with power derived from effective institutions, and of these the earlier Capetians had not a shred.

Among the leaders of feudal France of the tenth century the count of Flanders and the duke of Aquitaine stand out for their effective control over the vassals of their principalities. The counts of Champagne, Toulouse, and Anjou were also figures of prominence in the new feudal society, but it was the dukes of Normandy who stand pre-eminent among the vassals of the king of France. In the late tenth century and first half of the eleventh they made of the hitherto backward frontier, Neustria, in northwestern France, a country renowned for its great monasteries and schools, and they manipulated feudal institutions in an unprecedented manner to create the strongest state in Europe west of the Rhine.

Normandy came into existence as a feudal duchy in 911 when a certain Rollo, the savage leader of a group of Viking war bands, wrested from the terrified Carolingian king the area contiguous with the ecclesiastical province of Rouen. Rollo became the vassal of the French king and received the title of duke, but he proceeded to act in an entirely independent manner and to expand the original size of his fief. The size of the Scandinavian settlement was small, and the Northmen rapidly intermarried with the native population and adopted the French language. Rollo and his companions allowed themselves to be received into the church by the archbishop of Rouen, but their conversion no more altered their way of life than it had that of Clovis and his companions. For seven decades Normandy was the scene of interminable wars and blood feuds among the Norman lords, and the power of the early dukes was simply dependent on their ability as warriors. There is nothing in the history of Normandy before 980 to account for the subsequent development of Norman institutions. How, then, did the Norman dukes between 980 and 1050 create the most powerful feudal duchy in western Europe?

Three stages can be distinguished in the creation of the power of the Norman dukes. In the 980's they helped to place Hugh Capet on the French throne, and as a consequence the Capetians did not attempt to interfere in the affairs of the duchy during the crucial period of Norman state-building. By the time the Capetian king in the 1030's finally realized the significance of the rise of a new kind of feudal state in the duchy contiguous to the Île-de-France, it was too late to remove this danger. The second and most decisive stage in the emergence of Normandy was involved in the relationship between the Norman dukes and the church in their territory. The dukes of the late tenth and early eleventh centuries were much more sophisticated men than their predecessors. They were aware of Normandy's cultural backwardness, and they brought into the duchy from the Rhineland and northern Italy outstanding monastic scholars to inaugurate the improvement of the Norman church. The dukes built and endowed monasteries, supported the monastic schools, and allowed these able scholars to establish some of the most thriving centers of learning in western Europe. Their relationship with the church was not, however, confined to this worthy patronage; they proceeded to use the ecclesiastical resources and personnel to advance their effective power in their territory. It is probable that the leaders of Norman monasticism gave them valuable advice and encouragement in this connection. For these churchmen had come to Normandy in most cases from areas which lay within the confines of the German empire, whose rulers were using the German church for a similar purpose. Certainly the higher clergy in

Normandy did not question the kind of church-state relations which the dukes proceeded to establish before 1035, but rather consciously accepted it.

The dukes' plan was to impose heavy feudal obligations on the higher clergy and to use the knights enfeoffed on ecclesiastical lands as the nucleus of an army which could overcome the unruly lay nobility. By the middle of the eleventh century the Norman duke could, in fact, obtain the military service of more than three hundred knights from his ecclesiastical vassals, which was more than sufficient to destroy the power of the lay nobility. Certain advantages accrued to the duke from his inauguration of the feudalization of Normandy by imposing vassalage on the clergy and only then turning to the lay nobility. The clergy could not legally marry; though many had children, these were bastards who could not inherit fiefs under feudal law. Hence no bishop or abbot could pursue a dynastic interest with regard to his fiefs. The fiefs, in any case, were attached to the ecclesiastical office and were not the personal possession of the bishop or abbot. Furthermore, the duke had control over the election of the higher clergy. He was the venerated patron of the Norman church, whose opinion would be sought before the monks or cathedral clergy proceeded with the election of abbot or bishop. The duke possessed in addition a veto power over the selection of the higher clergy, because unless he were willing to receive the bishop or abbot-elect as his vassal, the latter could not take possession of the lands associated with his office.

The final stage in the rise of ducal power began in the 1020's with the imposition of vassalage and feudal obligations on the lay nobility. This work was made easier by land hunger and overpopulation among the knightly class in Normandy. A few of the restless Norman lords had already departed in the second decade of the eleventh century for southern Italy to carve out domains for themselves in that wealthy land. The landless knights who remained at home could only obtain fiefs from the duke if they were prepared to undertake onerous feudal obligations. The greater lords in Normandy, who already were substantial landowners, found themselves driven to the wall by the dukes' military power and forced into vassalage. This successful final stage in the building of the Norman feudal state suddenly stopped when one of the dukes, in a fit of piety, departed on a pilgrimage to Jerusalem and died en route, leaving as his heir a child whose legitimacy was clouded by the fact that he had been born before his parents' marriage. The early part of the reign of William II, the Bastard (1035–1087), was marked by a desperate attempt by the enemies of ducal power—namely, the Capetian king and the lay nobility—to undo the work of the previous half century. The alliance between the ducal family and the Norman churchmen remained firm, however, and the union of the strength of the ecclesiastical vassals with William's precocious military ability resulted in the complete victory of the duke over his enemies by the end of the 1040's. William then set about continuing his predecessors' policy, establishing the strongest feudal power in Europe by the end of the 1050's. He not only imposed vassalage on all the lay nobility, but was able to demand from them military service of a particularly well-defined and onerous kind. He overcame the debilitating effects of subinfeudation by making himself the liege lord of every vassal in the duchy. In Normandy the amount of feudal service which the tenants-in-chief owed their lord was specifically set down, proceeding in multiples of five knights to as large a feudal contingent as 120 chevaliers, according roughly to the amount and value of land which the vassals held of the duke. By 1060 the Norman duke could command an army of one thousand knights, which was by far the largest available to any ruler west of the Rhine. William prohibited the building of castles without his license on pain of forfeiture, and he was very strict in demanding suit at court from his vassals. His local official, the viscount, was effectively employed to draw the jurisdiction of law and taxation away from the feudal lords and into ducal authority.

The moral sanction for this effective military and administrative power was provided by the support which William received from the church. Like his predecessors, he was a great patron and endower of monasteries, and the Norman schools continued to attract some of the finest minds in Europe. Among them was Lanfranc, a former teacher of law at Pavia in northern Italy who became a monk in Normandy and won renown as one of the foremost theologians of the mid-eleventh century. He became one of William's strongest admirers. The Norman duke gained the plaudits of churchmen all over Europe for taking seriously the Peace of God movement. William saw in it a way of giving religious sanction to centralized ducal authority and of limiting still further the traditional indiscriminate warfare of feudal society, which had no place in his conception of a feudal state. He made himself the president of the Peace of God movement in Normandy and forced its vows upon his vassals. By 1060 a Norman lord who thought of revolting against the duke faced the prospect of ignominious defeat and forfeiture and ecclesiastical condemnation as well.

The completion of the structure of ducal power gave William the freedom to look for new fields of conquest and triumph. He had behind him a magnificent army and an aggressive nobility who sought a satisfactory outlet for both their love of fighting and land hunger. Consequently, in the 1050's William began to turn his attention to events across the channel and to scheme for the eventual gaining of the English throne. The situation in England offered a dramatic contrast to that which existed in Normandy.

The power of the later Anglo-Saxon monarchy was in the course of being drained by the rise of lordship in a manner which paralleled that of the ninth-century Carolingian monarchy. The great earls had gained for themselves not only enormous estates but also control over royal legal, administrative, and finanical institutions in their regions. Compared to England, Normandy was a small, thinly populated, and poor country. But the Norman dukes had succeeded in bringing all the resources of their land under their own control, whereas in England public power was rapidly passing into private hands and the authority of the king was on the verge of extinction. Compared to the Anglo-Saxon king, who was an offspring of the house of Wessex, which had ruled part or all of England for five centuries, the Norman duke was an upstart. Nor could the Norman duke make use of the doctrine of theocratic kingship which had been popular in England since the middle of the tenth century. He had, however, what the Anglo-Saxons, like the later Carolingians, lacked: effective institutions, a strong personality, and military ability. This combination marks a new departure in the development of medieval monarchy.

III. The Ottonian Empire

East of the Rhine, as compared with France, feudal institutions did not comprise the basis of social organization. The political and social structure of the east Carolingian kingdom was still dominated by pristine Germanic traditions. Each of the various tribes, or "stems" as they were called—the Franks, Saxons, Swabians, Bavarians, Lotharingians, and Thuringians—recognized the leadership of a great warrior chieftain who in the Carolingian period had acquired the administrative title of duke and had made it into a sign of his superiority. Below the stem dukes on the social scale there was a small group of great nobles and a large mass of free peasants. In the south and west both manorialism and feudal lordship were making their appearance, but in a degree too limited and embryonic to have any effect on political authority. The leaders of Germanic society were the stem dukes, the great nobles, and the bishops and abbots of the German church. The latter were very influential because they controlled all the literacy and a very considerable part of the landed wealth of the country. In a sense the German church had existed before there was any effective royal leadership in Germany, because the great abbeys which Boniface and his disciples had established in the river valleys of what is today western Germany had been the vanguard of Carolingian expansion. Only after the monks had converted the people, established centers of learning and civilization, and created

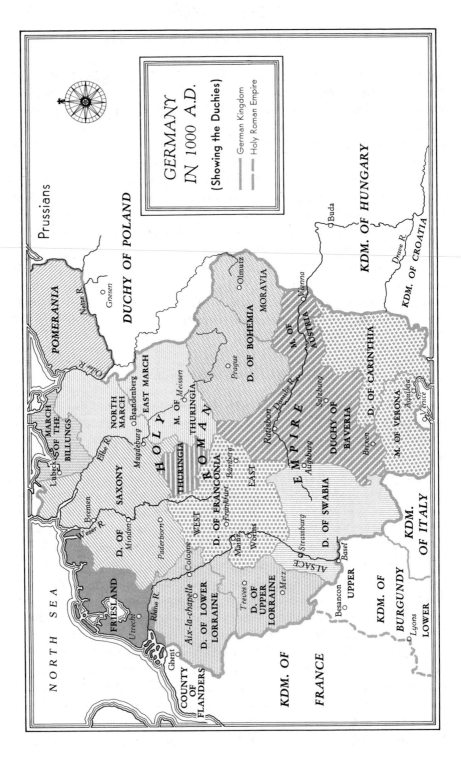

GERMANY
IN 1000 A.D.
(Showing the Duchies)

German Kingdom
Holy Roman Empire

the German church did the Frankish kings begin to exercise an effective rule east of the Rhine.

By the end of the ninth century the Carolingian kings had become nonentities and could offer no leadership to the tribes in their struggles to hold back invaders along their borders. To the west the Scandinavians offered a threat. To the east the incursions of Magyars (Hungarians)— another invader of Europe from Central Asia—and Slavs were very dangerous to the survival of the German duchies. In 911 the last of the Carolingians died, and the stem dukes, asserting the German electoral principle, chose Conrad I, duke of Franconia, as king. This cannot be said to have marked an important change in the history of the German monarchy. Conrad was unable to exercise any authority over the other stem dukes, who remained independent. At Conrad's death in 918 the dukes elected as king his chief tormentor, Henry I the Fowler, the duke of Saxony. Henry's family, which later came to be known as the Ottonians, was to rule in Germany for more than a century, and consequently the beginning of his reign has frequently been said to mark the real beginning of the German monarchy. But as a matter of fact, he was not much more successful than his predecessor, and at the accession of his son Otto I in 936 the German monarchy had found neither the institutions nor the ideology to give it any control over the great dukes. In fact, the duke of Bavaria was attempting to join his duchy with Lombardy, which would have made him more powerful than the Saxon dukes and would have demolished whatever unity the German realm possessed.

The creation of the German monarchy was the work of Otto I the Great (936–973). He consciously symbolized the policy he intended to follow by the manner of his coronation. He insisted on being anointed and crowned by the archbishop of Mainz, the primate of the German church, at Charlemagne's old capital of Aachen. He thereby signified that he regarded himself as the successor of the great emperor and that he intended to associate himself with the powerful German church and to make use of the ideology of theocratic monarchy. His father had feared the powerful bishops and abbots and had refused even to be crowned by an ecclesiastic. Otto determined to dominate the church and to use its resources and personnel in the interests of establishing the institutional basis of royal power in Germany. There was no other way by which the German monarchy could obtain the wealth, military support, and the administrators it needed to overcome the entrenched power of the stem dukes. The German clergy were willing to cooperate with the king, who offered them protection against the nobility, rich endowments for ecclesiastical establishments, and the opportunity to serve in his chancery and act as royal ministers.

A threefold institutional basis for the Ottonian control over the German church can be distinguished. Most important was the institution which came to be called "lay investiture" by its critics in the late eleventh century, but which until then was simply referred to as the royal investiture of churches. The king asserted the right to invest bishops and abbots with the symbols of their office, finding theoretical support for this claim in his sacred quality as an anointed king. Without royal investiture the bishop and abbot-elect could not enter into office; the effect was to give the king control over the election of the higher clergy. To make the king's control of ecclesiastical appointments even more secure, ecclesiastical homage was joined to lay investiture so that the bishop or abbot could only enter into possession of the property belonging to his office after becoming the king's vassal. Under these conditions clerical election became a mere formality in the Ottonian empire, and the king filled up the ranks of the episcopate with his own relatives and with his loyal chancery clerks, who were also appointed to head the great German monasteries.

The Ottonian domination over the church was aided by the persistence of the Germanic legal ideas on property which form the background to the institution of proprietary churches (*Eigenkirchen*). This institution was by no means exclusively confined to Germany; it existed all over Europe and still exists in the Anglican church in the form of the advowson. But it was in the German empire of the tenth and eleventh centuries that the proprietary church system assumed its greatest importance, for it became one of the foundations of royal power. German law held that any structure, including a church, erected on a proprietor's land legally belonged to him. Thus, whoever owned the lands on which churches and monasteries were built could act as the lord over them and appoint the ecclesiastical officials. This was not very important if the church was a parish church, but it was significant if a monastery with great estates was involved. The Ottonian house, partly because of its benefactions to the church and partly by more violent means, gained proprietary rights over many of the German bishoprics and abbeys, thereby acquiring the right of appointing important members of the higher clergy and the control of the ecclesiastical revenue.

The third institutional basis of the Ottonian control over the German church was the system of the "advocacy." The advocate was a secular manager of the estates belonging to a cathedral or monastery who thereby gained a large share of the revenues and lordship over the people on the ecclesiastical estates. The Ottonian family was adept at gathering the majority of advocacies in Germany into their hands.

By the middle of the tenth century the wealth and military power of the German monarchy was steadily on the increase as a result of these ways of establishing close control over the church. It is known that almost half the army which Otto II used in Italy in 981 came from monastic lands. The higher clergy were also used extensively as royal administrators, and not only in the royal chancery. The abbots were granted the power of counts in many cases and given onerous tasks of local administration on behalf of the monarch. With the political, military, and economic support of the church, Otto did not find it difficult to beat the stem duchies, including Lorraine, into submission. By 955 he had begun to meddle in the chaotic affairs of northern Italy through his marriage to Adelaide, an Italian "queen," and his claiming of the Lombard crown.

That year marked the turning point in Otto's reign. He inflicted a crushing defeat on the Magyars at the Battle of the Lechfeld and became the hero of western Europe. To the German nobility he appeared to have fulfilled the claim he made at his coronation to be the successor of Charlemagne. On the field of his victory over the Magyars the great lords raised him on their shields in the Germanic manner and proclaimed him emperor. A few years later, in 962, Otto went to Rome and had himself crowned emperor by the pope.

Modern historians of Germany have engaged in a great debate as to the motives behind Otto's imperial coronation. It is clear that several were involved. He wanted to bring remnants of the old middle kingdom under his control, particularly Lorraine and northern Italy, and he needed the imperial title to provide the legal basis for such claims. He was especially concerned with northern Italy, whose political condition was chaotic, and he wished to preclude further attempts on the part of the south German dukes to conquer Lombardy. Another motive was his need to emulate Charlemagne as much as possible in order to strengthen the legal foundation for his control over the German church. A third reason for Otto's taking the imperial crown was the potential danger of the renovation of the imperial title outside Germany by the French king or a French duke. Another thesis, strongly favored by German historians in the 1930's, is that Otto wanted the imperial title in order to be the moral leader of a German drive into the Slavic lands beyond the Elbe. All or most of these motives were involved in Otto's imperial coronation, but whatever special reasons Otto had for reviving the imperial title, it was the natural consequence of his position as the most outstanding ruler in Europe. He commanded the greatest military power since Charlemagne, he was a theocratic monarch who dominated the church in his territory, and he was the warrior-hero of Germanic society. These qualities made Otto appear, both to himself and to contemporaries, as the worthy successor of Charlemagne, and if the great Frankish king was an emperor, then Otto had to be also. His imperial title was simply the apotheosis of his rule over Germany and northern Italy.

There was nothing Roman in Otto's conception of the imperial title. The nineteenth-century *Kleindeutsch* historians blamed the Saxon king for getting the German monarchy involved with the fatal and debilitating charms of Italy, which they believed to have been the source of all the later troubles of the medieval German monarchy. But Otto hardly spent any time there and did not even make any effective contribution to rescuing the papacy from its subversion by the Roman nobility. Otto the Great was a hard, tough soldier and administrator; he was intelligent enough to make use of ideology, but he was not the kind of man who was actually inspired by ideas. He did, however, fall prey to the proclivity of the *arriviste* to obtain social recognition for his heir. And the only recognition which seemed suitable for the son of the German emperor was marriage to a Byzantine princess. The Greeks initially dismissed Otto as a barbarian upstart, but after a change in dynasty, the new Byzantine emperor finally allowed the Ottonians to have one of his distant relatives. Otto II's marriage inaugurated a kind of political antiquarianism which had marked the Carolingian empire after Charlemagne. Under his Greek wife's influence he directed his attention to establishing effective authority south of the Alps. Otto II allowed the Slavs to destroy the German settlements east of the Elbe, while he used his army to undertake an expedition into southern Italy, where he was killed fighting the Moslems in 983.

During the reign of Otto II's son, Otto III (983–1002), the association of the German empire with Rome became predominant, and the policy of Otto I was abandoned in a fundamental way. It is a tribute to the strength of the institutions which Otto the Great had created that the German monarchy did not completely collapse during his grandson's reign. For Otto III succeeded to the throne as a child, and until 995 the empire was ruled first by his Byzantine mother Theophano, and then by his grandmother Adelaide. During the seven years of his own rule Otto was rarely in Germany, but rather devoted himself to the achievement of a far-flung imperial plan centering on Rome. This program was a consequence of the influence exerted on the youthful Otto III by his teacher, the French churchman Gerbert of Aurillac, who had studied in Moslem Spain and who had become the greatest western scholar of his age. Gerbert and other churchmen who predominated at the court of Otto III talked about a "renewal of the Roman empire." Gerbert easily won over the young and impressionable Otto to his plans for a new empire, with Rome once again the center of the western world. Accordingly Otto took up residence in Rome and set Gerbert on the papal throne as Sylvester II. It was intended that this would be the most important moment in the history of the Roman empire since the time of Constantine. The coins, illuminated manuscripts, and poems coming from Otto's court proclaim an involved and sophisticated imperial ideology going far beyond the political antiquarianism of the later Carolingian empire. To the Ottonian court theorists the city of Rome symbolized both the political unity of the world and the unity of the church. One of Otto's documents begins, "Otto, slave of the Apostles and according to the will of the Lord Savior, august emperor of the Romans. We proclaim Rome capital of the world. We recognize that the Latin church is the mother of all churches." These ideas are depicted in the extremely well-executed Ottonian illuminations. One picture shows Otto seated on his throne and flanked by the Apostles Peter and Paul. Another shows the countries of Europe bringing him gifts of homage.

Gerbert's plans were confined not only to ideology, art, and court ceremonial; Rome as the head of the world and as the head of the church implied some specific policies which, if they could have been executed, would have had a profound impact on the development of Europe. The first of these involved the creation of a great federal empire embracing east central Europe in order to obviate a renewal of the struggle between Germans and Slavs. Otto, in fact, made a trip to Poland to grant the Christian duke of Poland an honorary title and to receive him within the renovated Roman empire. A similar kind of federal arrangement was made with the king of Hungary. The second policy which Gerbert induced Otto to support was in the area of papal-imperial relations. For almost a century the papacy had played no part in European life because of its subjection to the Roman nobility, and as Pope Sylvester II he was conscious of the conflicts that might arise between the German emperor and a revived papacy. In his view the papacy ought not to assert temporal claims, but ought to become a purely spiritual institution. Gerbert did not believe that the Donation of Constantine was genuine, and he persuaded the emperor to condemn it as "lies forged by certain popes and attributed to the name of the great Constantine."

Otto III died in 1002 and Sylvester II one year later, and their ambitious program expired with them. Already in the last years of Otto's reign the Saxon nobles were beginning to rebel against him on the grounds that Otto's imperial ideology neglected Germany and went against their interests. Otto's successor, his cousin Henry II (1002–1024), completely abandoned Otto's plans and confined himself to maintaining the royal power in Germany. This was certainly a more realistic approach to the problems of the German monarchy than those adopted by Otto II and Otto III, and it is doubtful if the institutions created by Otto the Great could have sustained another reign like his son's and grandson's. Nevertheless, it is remarkable that Gerbert had foreseen two of the bitterest conflicts that marked later medieval German history: the struggle of the Germans against the Slavs, and the conflict between empire and papacy. Many aspects of the renewal of the "Roman empire" appear as useless and as empty of real significance as the political antiquarianism of the later Carolingians. But in these two respects Gerbert and his disciple Otto had exhibited a keen perception of two fundamental problems which were as yet in their incipient stage.

The Ottonian empire has sometimes been interpreted as merely a continuation of Carolingian kingship. It has been pointed out that the Ottonian kings relied for their power on their association with the church, that they made use of the doctrine of theocratic monarchy, that they cultivated the imperial ideology; all of these ideas and institutions can be found in the age of Charlemagne and his successors. It is true that the Ottonians were not great innovators, as were the Norman dukes. It is true that the essentials of Ottonian government were already delineated by Carolingian monarchy. But the Ottonians used these precedents to establish a successful and long-lived monarchy, whereas the Carolingian efforts resulted in bitter disappointment. The Ottonians did not have to deal with such a large area, nor were they as troubled by the decentralizing effects of lordship. In addition to these initial advantages, the success of the Ottonian empire must be attributed to the very firm hold over the resources of the church which Otto the Great established and which served as the foundation of effective royal power even when the presence of a strong royal personality was wanting in Germany during the two successive reigns. The Salian rulers of the second and third quarters of the eleventh century were able to build on the achievements of their Ottonian kinsmen, to go beyond Carolingian precedents, and to strengthen the institutional foundations of the German empire.

The Ottonian period, which inaugurated German history, sets the tone and in some ways acts as a microcosm of all the later vicissitudes of German civilization. In the Ottonian empire we see that peculiar combination of aggressive, ruthless efficiency on the one hand and the expression of a childlike, lyrical idealism on the other, or, as the German writers call it, that union of *Macht* and *Geist* that so often distinguishes the later history of the lands between the Rhine and the Elbe.

IV. The Cluniac Ideal

The interpenetration of *ecclesia* and *mundus* which characterized the institutional foundations of both the Ottonian empire and the Norman duchy depended heavily on the resources and activities of the Benedictine order. The relations between church and kingship in the tenth and eleventh centuries and the contemporary theory of the identification of *ecclesia* and *mundus* were, in effect, founded upon the ubiquitous Benedictine cooperation with the leaders of lay society. The monastic order was the keystone of the early medieval equilibrium.

This equilibrium, as it came to be firmly established in the late tenth and first half of the eleventh century, was particularly identified with the ideals and activities of the Burgundian monastery of Cluny and her dependencies and affiliates. As the ideal of the acknowledged leader of western monasticism in the first half of the eleventh century, the Cluniac program became the intellectual expression of the prevailing world order. The abbot of Cluny was the elder statesman of mid-eleventh-century Europe. Cluniac monks were closely involved with the government of the German Salian dynasty, which succeeded to the German throne in 1024, and they played an important role in the creation of the Norman church. The monastery of Cluny itself was the largest, best endowed, and most prestigious in Europe. It held the admiration of churchmen and the devotion of laymen, and the kind of religious life it inculcated was at the heart of early eleventh-century piety.

The monastic life as envisaged by Cluny was, on the whole, not original; it was a perpetuation and intensification of the Benedictine form as it had come to exist by the ninth century. Carolingian monasticism had been given official form in the monastic constitutions of 817, which had been drawn up by St. Benedict of Aniane, who had been placed at the head of all the Carolingian monasteries by Louis the Pious. The aim of the second Benedict was to supplement the rule of the first Benedict and to acknowledge the changes that had taken place in western monasticism over the previous three centuries as the communities of the black monks had come to undertake their indispensable social duties. Benedict of Aniane recognized that the monks no longer supported themselves with their physical labor; instead, they acted as official intercessors for lay society with the deity through liturgical prayer and also performed educational, political, and economic functions. This was the kind of monastic life which came to be identified with Cluny during the tenth and eleventh centuries.

The actual beginnings of the monastery in 910 were extremely modest. It was founded in an obscure corner of Burgundy by a duke of Aquitaine on the site of his hunting lodge, and for a while the duke even neglected to remove his hunting dogs to make room for the monks. Yet within a century Cluny had become the leading monastery in Europe and had formed a loose kind of special order of its own. Several monasteries were directly subject to the abbot of Cluny, particularly daughter houses founded by Cluny itself; and other Benedictine communities, many of which were much older than Cluny, were loosely affiliated with it and recognized the leadership of its abbot. Cluny exercised a strong influence over the great monastery of Gorze in Lorraine; the Cluniacs reformed and then dominated the important French royal monastery of Fleury on the Loire; there was a strong Cluniac influence at work in the revitalization of English monasticism undertaken by St. Dunstan in the late tenth century; and it was a Cluniac abbot from Dijon whom the duke of Normandy in the early eleventh century brought to his duchy to inaugurate the expansion of the Norman church.

Cluny's success must be partly attributed to the fact that it had obtained immunity from both lay and episcopal interference and was directly subject to the pope, and since the papacy, until the middle of the eleventh century, was in a condition of complete decrepitude, the monks of Cluny were entirely free to work out the destiny of their community. They chose a succession of extremely able abbots, usually men with the highest aristocratic, or even princely, backgrounds, who led the Burgundian religious house to its position of eminence in the affairs of Europe. This was particularly true of the two abbots who between them ruled Cluny for most of the eleventh century: Odilo (d. 1049) and Hugh the Great (d. 1109). Cluny demanded of its own brothers and of dependent and affiliated monasteries the full observance of the Benedictine Rule as amended by Benedict of Aniane. The monks at Cluny became famous for the extent and beauty of their liturgical devotions. Kings and nobles all over Europe who had come to take seriously the teachings of the church and who were concerned for the salvation of their own souls and those of their relatives were eager to give Cluny rich endowments in order to be named in Cluniac prayers. But neither its enforcement of monastic discipline nor its association with popular piety accounts for Cluny's leadership in the world order of the early eleventh century. While Cluny was herself free of any lay control, her abbots did not make this a requirement for Cluny's daughter houses or affiliates. On the contrary, the Cluniac monks, who worked all over western Europe, exhibited the greatest eagerness to accept kings and dukes as the patron lords of their establishments. The abbot of Cluny looked with respect, gratitude, and admiration on the friends of the church who ruled in Germany, the Île-de-France, Normandy, England, and other states in western Europe. The Cluniac monks were eager to offer their services to royal chanceries and were not loath to receive the usual rewards for this work—appointments to bishoprics. The Cluniacs readily accepted, and certain of them even encouraged, the entrenchment of the doctrine of theocratic kingship in Germany, and they took the lead in spreading the veneration of the ruler as the patron and friend of the church even in Normandy, where such traditions had hitherto been lacking.

The Cluniac movement entered Germany from Burgundy and Lorraine at the beginning of the eleventh century; the attitude of the German rulers was from the first sympathetic to the spread of the Cluniac movement in Germany. The first of the Salian dynasty, Conrad II (1024–1039), was a harsh soldier and administrator who exploited the German clergy severely, but he favored the spread of the Cluniac movement in his realm. But the great advance of Cluniac influence in Germany came during the reign of Conrad's son, Henry III (1039–1056), who acted as the patron and protector of the order in his realm. Henry had married the daughter of the duke of Aquitaine, whose house had founded Cluny in the early tenth century, but Henry's affinity for the Cluniac order was based on much deeper motives than his wife's special association with the leading monastery in western Europe. In the character and ideals of Henry III can be seen what appears also in the outlook and conduct of the rulers of France, England, and Normandy in the middle of the eleventh century—the completion of the Christianization of Europe. The leaders of western society, nearly all the rulers of the period, and many of the ordinary nobility themselves had come to take very seriously the teachings of the church and to allow these teachings to govern their lives. Contemporaries sensed that Henry III of Germany was a monk in worldly garb, and Edward the Confessor of England, as his appellation implies, later was canonized as a saint. All over Europe in the middle of the eleventh century kings, dukes, and nobles were building churches and endowing monasteries. The regular clergy in particular had come to receive fanatical devotion and respect from the leaders of lay society. Monastic intercession was deemed to be almost indispensable for achieving heavenly grace, and nobles, when they felt mortality creeping on, got themselves off to the nearest monastery to die clothed in the monastic habit. Gifts were made to monasteries not only to secure the salvation of certain named relatives but, in more general terms, for the welfare of all believers living and dead. It is during the eleventh century that the holy day of All Souls was fixed in the church calendar.

The spread of lay piety did not, however, imply the willingness of kings and dukes to subject themselves to ecclesiastical authority. On the contrary, it provided a further intellectual basis for royal control over the church, for it made kings feel as spiritual as churchmen. In no case is this more marked than in that of the great German emperor Henry III. He was not only a great patron of the Cluniac order in Germany, but he was inclined himself to adopt monastic attitudes. His greatest delight was participating in the translation of relics to a new shrine. He was fond of making speeches in which he declared that he forgave all his enemies. At the same time, how-ever, he believed that he had received a sacramental office at his coronation and that he had full spiritual authority to bestow the symbols of ecclesi-astical office on bishop or abbot and to order the affairs of the church. He believed that Christ was working through his royal power just as He did through a priest at the celebration of the mass. As the representative of Christ on earth Henry felt compelled not only to govern the German church but also to order the affairs of the papacy, which had been in a scandalous condition for more than a century. In 1045 there were no less than three rival popes in Rome, corrupt scions of the gangster Roman nobility. The synod of Sutri of 1045, which Henry called and presided over, marked the first step in the reform of the eleventh-century papacy. In two years Henry appointed three German bishops to the throne of Peter, and the pontificate of the last of these, Leo IX (1049–1054), who was the emperor's kinsman, became the turning point in the development of the eleventh-century papacy.

Henry's piety and ecclesiastical interests by no means precluded his con-tinuing the work of the Ottonians and adding to the institutional founda-tions of royal power in Germany. As a strong personality, able warrior, theocratic monarch, and great administrator Henry III represents the apotheosis of early medieval kingship. He brought together all the qualities which made for successful medieval monarchy. Henry realized that the German monarchy was still short of strong and permanent institutions and that it still relied too exclusively on the personnel, resources, and doctrine of the church. He discovered a new kind of royal soldier and administrator in the institution of the *ministerialis*. The latter was a serf-knight, a soldier who was given the best training and equipment of the day but did not have the legal status of a freeman. He did not voluntarily enter into vassal-age, but was entirely dependent on his lord. Serf-knights were by no means exclusively a German institution, but they never played any important role in feudal societies outside the Salian empire. It appears that German church-men were the first to recruit serfs from their estates and to train them as knights, but it was Henry III who made the *ministerialis* into an important royal institution. He used *ministeriales* to garrison the castles which he was building all over northern Germany. It was his plan to join Saxony to Franconia, the homeland of the Salian dynasty, and to make these duchies into the permanent crown lands of the German monarchy. Thus Henry had discovered a new kind of personnel for his army and local government, and in his concern to build up the German crown lands he had laid the foundations for a policy similar to that which the Capetian kings were to pursue with enormous success in the late twelfth and thirteenth centuries. He set up his capital at the great fortress of Goslar in Saxony, which was situated close to the silver mines discovered in Otto I's reign, and he proceeded to use his ecclesiastical knights and the new *ministeriales* to bring the recalcitrant Saxon nobility and free peasantry under the full authority of the Salian dynasty.

In 1050 it appeared that the political destiny of Germany, as much as that of the feudal duchy of Normandy, would be marked by the ever increasing power of the central government. The world in which Cluny was the leading spiritual force was marked not only by the final stage in the Christianization of Europe but also, in Normandy and the German empire, by the achievement of a degree of political and social order which western Europe had not known since the collapse of the Roman empire.

Early eleventh-century ideals of church and kingship were given monumental form in the style of architecture that modern art historians have chosen to call Romanesque. In the river valleys of western Germany, France, and northern Spain by the middle of the eleventh century many stone churches had been built to serve the needs of the monarchical, feudal, and ecclesiastical elite. The churches that have been designated as Romanesque in style exhibit strong regional and local differences in their structure. They have, however, certain things in common. These ecclesiastical structures tend to be small as compared with the grandiose churches of the twelfth and thirteenth centuries. The Romanesque churches were chapels for the lay and sacerdotal hierarchies while the later Gothic churches were designed to bring in the masses for public worship. Second, the Romanesque churches were ecclesiastical fortresses; they were built by the same architects and artisans who erected the feudal fortresses of the eleventh century. The Romanesque church was God's fortress and it reflects a view of Jesus as head of the feudal hierarchy and the prototype of theocratic kings. Thirdly, the Romanesque churches tend to be dark inside; the walls have few windows to let in the light. This is a consequence not only of technological limitation in architectural engineering, but also of the elitist and rather private character of this kind of house of worship. Finally, the Romanesque style is marked by a richness in ornamentation and sculpture, often individual in character and much less universal in style than the Gothic of the thirteenth century. This quality again reflects the elitist and private character of Romanesque art; but it also reveals the increasing self-consciousness and confidence that prevailed in the Cluniac world of the mid-eleventh century. Considered as feats of structural engineering, the Romanesque stone churches mark a tremendous advance upon Carolingian churches. In the Rhine valley, southern France, and northern Spain many of these imposing buildings still stand as monuments to the increasing rationality, piety, wealth, and public power that marked the age of Henry III and the leadership of Cluny in European culture.

Chapter Ten

BYZANTIUM, ISLAM, AND THE WEST

I. The Limitations of the Byzantine and Islamic Civilizations

In the 960's the German emperor Otto I sent a Lombard bishop, Liudprand of Cremona, as his ambassador to Constantinople to obtain a Byzantine princess for his son. The embassy was not successful, but Liudprand has left us an account of his experiences which offers an illuminating insight into the relations between the still new European civilization and the old and wealthy culture of the Mediterranean world. The Greeks regarded the Germans as impoverished barbarian upstarts, and Liudprand was conscious of the fact that there was nothing in the west that even distantly resembled the wealth and luxury of Constantinople. He had to compensate for his sense of inferiority by depicting the Greeks as effeminate and corrupt and living off the glories of a vanished age. His hero, Otto, is bold and honest, the Byzantine emperor cowardly and devious. Liudprand's report of his embassy to Constantinople reflects the encounter of the old and the new, the meeting of a civilization just beginning to develop its characteristic form and one which had reached its ultimate limits. Compared to Byzantium and the other Mediterranean civilization, Islam, western Europe was indeed impoverished and backward in the middle of the tenth century. A hundred years later Byzantium had begun to enter its long eclipse—the Arab world had reached the limits of its cultural, political, and economic growth—while medieval Europe was at the beginning of its greatest period of creativity and improvement, and the Latin peoples had begun their economic and political penetration of the Mediterranean world. This fundamental change in the relative situations of Byzantium, Islam, and the west marks the conclusion of the early midde ages.

In the middle of the tenth century Byzantium entered into its last golden age under the wise and aggressive Macedonian dynasty, particularly during the reign of Basil II (963–1025). The government, economy, and cultural life of the east Roman empire exhibited its greatest vigor since the reign of Justinian in the sixth century. The Macedonians finally brought the divisive iconoclastic controversy that had intermittently raged since the first half of the eighth century to an end by subscribing to the orthodox view on images. They protected the peasant class against the depredations of the wealthy landlords, who aimed at achieving a decentralization of political authority similar to that which had ruined the Carolingian empire. Basil II destroyed the power of the Asiatic Bulgars, who had pressed on the Balkan frontier of Byzantium, and he undertook a counterattack against the Islamic power in the middle east, bringing back Antioch, Cyprus, and Crete under Greek rule. The emperor benefited from his control over the commerce of Constantinople, which in the tenth century was probably the wealthiest city in the world. These political and economic achievements were paralleled by a cultural efflorescence which art historians, at least, have called the Macedonian Renaissance. The magnificent illuminated manuscripts which were produced in the Byzantine court and monasteries during Basil's reign are marked by a greater degree of classical naturalism in their depiction of the human figure.

But the Macedonian age turned out to be the last achievement of Byzantium before the long twilight of Byzantine civilization set in. The rise of lordship after the first quarter of the eleventh century weakened the power of the Byzantine state from within, and in the middle of the eleventh century a new Asiatic invader of the Mediterranean world, the Moslem Seljuk Turks, again forced the Greeks to engage in a bitter struggle for survival. By the beginning of the 1070's the conquests of Basil II had once more been lost to the Moslems, and the desperate emperor was forced to appeal to the pope for aid in preventing the fall of Constantinople.

The history of Byzantium is a study in disappointment. The empire centering on Constantinople had begun with all the advantages obtained from its inheritance of the political, economic, and intellectual life of the fourth-century Roman empire. Except in the realm of art, in which the Greeks excelled, Byzantium added scarcely anything to this superb foundation. The east Roman empire of the middle ages made no important contributions to philosophy, theology, science, or literature. Its political institutions remained fundamentally unchanged from those which existed in the reign of Theodosius the Great at the end of the fourth century; while the Byzantines continued to enjoy an active urban and commercial life, they made no substantial advance in the technology of industry and trade as developed by the cities of the ancient world. Modern historians of the medieval eastern Roman empire have strongly criticized the tendency of nineteenth-century scholars to write off Byzantium as the example of an atrophied civilization. Yet it is hard to find, outside the field of art, any contributions by way of either original ideas or institutions which the medieval Greek-speaking peoples made to civilization. Perhaps the unprogressive nature of medieval Byzantium was precisely the consequence of the vast legacy of the Roman world which the Greeks received inviolate. The Byzantine world apparently had already answered for it all problems of government, economy, and higher thought, and therefore the task to which the Byzantines dedicated themselves was merely one of preserving the satisfactory and comfortable existence they had inherited. The limitations of Byzantine civilization must, of course, also be attributed to the tremendous pressures which were exerted almost incessantly on the frontiers of the empire from the sixth century onward. The Byzantines had to apply all the resources at their command to hold back the Arabs and their other enemies, and in so doing they dissipated their best energies and allowed their culture to become more and more rigid.

The penetration of the Mediterranean world by the Seljuk Turks was by no means a boon to eleventh-century Islamic civilization. The level of Turkish culture was much more primitive than that which prevailed among the sophisticated Arabic-speaking peoples of the eastern Mediterranean. The Turks' attempt to seize political power in the middle east deeply divided the Moslem world for more than a century. At the western end of the Mediterranean a similar incursion took place in the eleventh century by nomadic Berber tribesmen from the North African desert, who crossed the straits of Gibraltar and gained control of Moslem Spain. At both ends of the Mediterranean Moslem world by the middle of the eleventh century, political authority was passing to unsophisticated, fanatical puritans who cared nothing for the great achievements of Arabic thought and who were willing to listen to the hysterical strictures of the orthodox against philosophy and science. After the tenth century the weakness of the Arabic political tradition became more and more evident. The political institutions of Islam were strictly those of oriental despotism, and the later political history of medieval Islam is marked by the irresponsibility of the rulers towards the welfare of the people and the recurrent palace revolutions which are endemic to this kind of political system. The political instability which begins to distinguish the Islamic world in the first half of the eleventh century caused the increasing neglect of the Mediterranean irrigation system, which had been in existence in some cases for three millennia and upon which the prosperity of the Arabic countries was ultimately based. The Islamic world had not yet entered its deep decline in 1050. Some of its greatest military and intellectual achievements were yet to come, and the Moslem merchant was still a dominant figure in Mediterranean life in the eleventh century, but by and large the greatest days of Islam had ended, and the strength of Islamic civilization was leveling off from its pinnacle of creativity. These limitations of Islamic civilization account for the inability of the Arabs to prevent the political and economic penetration of the Mediterranean by the European peoples in the tenth and eleventh centuries.

II. The Rise of Europe

Compared with the Byzantine and Islamic worlds, tenth-century western Europe was still an underdeveloped area, impoverished, intensely ruralized, and thinly populated. But whereas the Greeks and Arabs had reached the ultimate extent of their economic development, western Europe was just beginning a demographic and technological revolution which was to carry the Latin world, within two centuries, to a commercial and industrial level surpassing the economic achievements of any area and period of the early middle ages and probably also of the ancient world. Western Europe between 900 and 1050 conforms to the second stage of W. W. Rostow's theory of the *Stages of Economic Growth,* a definitive interpretation of economic history published in 1960. According to Rostow, the first stage in economic growth is the traditional, largely agricultural one, such as characterized the European economy between 550 and 900. The society next attains the preconditions for "take-off": "improved agricultural methods release more of the population from agrarian pursuits," and "techniques are applied to the processing of some natural resource for export and outlays are made for transport, education and sources of power." This description summarizes the economic history of Europe between 900 and 1050. The development of population, technology, commerce, and industry during this century and a half produced the next period of take-off, during which rapid growth was made in a limited number of key sectors of the economy. This third stage, during which "growth becomes self-sustained, investment rises and remains sufficient to make an increase in output per capita a regular condition," characterizes the European economy from the middle of the eleventh to the latter part of the thirteenth century.

The second stage of economic growth, the precondition for takeoff, was made possible by the early medieval equilibrium. The new political and social order, the improved degree of peace and good government, the Christianization of Europe, and the increase in literacy and social intelligence created an environment which encouraged optimism, enterprise, improved communications, and technological innovation. There was still a great deal of violence in European life, but there was sufficient peace and order in many areas to allow men to use their energies for something beyond the war of all against all—improvement in their material condition. In the tenth century the European people adopted improvements in technology which had been available in the Mediterranean world for centuries. The importation of the horse collar and stirrup gave them a much greater use of available horsepower. Some historians have said that the stirrup made possible the emergence of the knight who was able to stand up in the stirrups and tilt a lance against his adversary, but this advanced form of military horsemanship did not actually appear until the twelfth century. Until then, as contemporary illustrations demonstrate, the medieval knights threw their metal-tipped wooden lances in the manner of nineteenth-century Comanche warriors. The innovations in the control of horsepower were mainly useful in improving transportation in tenth-century Europe. Europeans also began to make use of water power in the tenth century on land and wind power, to a greater degree than before, on the sea. The introduction of watermills greatly facilitated the grinding of grain and contributed to an increase in food supply. Waterpower was also used to operate sawmills and this contributed to an increase in the amount of good lumber available for construction. The development of the lateen sail made it possible for ships in the Atlantic and Baltic coastal trade to tack against the wind, which the old square sails did not permit. For naval warfare and long-distance commerce in the Mediterranean, where the winds were unreliable and inadequate, the Italians employed a Byzantine-type galley which was the descendant of the oared ships of antiquity.

These social and technological changes go a long way toward explaining the steady growth in the population of Europe from the middle of the tenth century. There was no alteration in the extremely primitive conditions of European medicine and no apparent improvement in the pitifully short average life expectancy, but the increased food supply must have resulted in a marked decrease in infant mortality. For all classes in society there was a greater hope of controlling the physical environment and greater expectations of a better life. Greater confidence in the future, joined with the impress of Christian teachings on all classes, increased respect for the value of human life and created a favorable milieu for the raising of larger families.

Nothing demonstrates more dramatically the impact of social and technological change in western Europe than the eagerness of the more numerous younger sons of lord, knight, peasant, and other people dissatisfied with their too meager lot to move around in search of a better life. The scions of aristocratic families could establish large domains of their own in areas where central authority was weakest inside Europe, or they could move to the frontier regions or even overseas and try to carve out fiefs for themselves. The young knights competed with each other to become the vassals of some established great lord, and, failing this, they could follow enterprising nobility in their freebooting new ventures. The opportunity for the younger and poorer peasants was similarly promising and probably greater in the tenth century than either before or after, at least for another four hundred years. The tenth century was the great age of the internal colonization of Europe, turning some of the immense stretches of forest and swamp into agricultural regions. The peasants learned how to clear wooded land, reclaim marshes, and make greater use of field rotation, leaving one of the two or three open fields of the village fallow each year in order to restore its fertility and thereby increase the yield. In Germany the more robust sons of the peasants had a special kind of opportunity for improving their condition; some became royal *ministeriales* and ended up as the captains of royal castles.

In many parts of Europe in the tenth century some of the poorer knights and more intelligent peasants followed an unprecedented avenue of economic advancement. They took up residence in towns and became merchants and craftsmen. The process of the rise of urban life in tenth-century Europe has been somewhat obscured by the categorical thesis which Henri Pirenne presented in his brilliant essay, *Medieval Cities*. Pirenne, in this and other well-written and highly plausible works, insisted that the origin of the tenth-century cities lay exclusively in international trade. He contended that the merchants engaged in this large-scale enterprise gathered for protection under the walls of a "burgh," a fortress belonging to some lay or ecclesiastical prince, and such "burghers" proceeded to make their town into a center for international trade. Eventually, as the bourgeois grew in number, they built a wall around themselves. As the suburbs developed, a new wall became necessary fifty or a hundred years later. Thus Pirenne, measuring the surviving walls of his native Belgian cities, was able to demonstrate their growth in concentric circles, which served as indices of ever expanding commercial activity. This neat pattern of medieval urban growth existed in Flanders and the Rhineland, but there were cities in other parts of Europe whose beginnings and nature were rather different. Most of the cities of Italy had been there since Roman times, but they had been neglected and underpopulated for centuries. In the tenth century people from the surrounding countryside moved into the cities for purposes of engaging in commerce and industry, making them again into centers of urban life instead of mainly centers for ecclesiastical and political administration. There were many towns in England and northern France which began as burghs and ended as centers of only local trade. And all over Europe there had appeared, by 1050, towns which were merely overgrown villages, places in which a few wealthy and enterprising peasants set up a market for the immediate neighborhood. There are many small towns in England whose main street is still called the Corn Market.

An English churchman of the late tenth century distinguished three classes in society: those who fought, those who prayed, and those who worked. He did not mention the bourgeois, for whom there was no place in the traditional social structure. The burgher did not even have a *wergeld* in Germanic law. Was he a freeman or unfree? Was he subject to the bishop or lord whose fortress or cathedral he nestled against for protection? In northern Europe there was no clear answer to these questions, and it was to take three centuries before many cities would gain the right to administer their internal affairs and the bourgeois would achieve the full status of freeman in royal and ducal law courts. These rights were usually obtained by purchase, at exorbitant prices, of a charter of urban liberties from king, lord, or bishop.

The dominant class in society looked with suspicion upon a group of men whose provenance was frequently humble and obscure and who made their living in ways which hitherto had been associated with social outcasts and aliens such as Jews and Arabs. The landed class enjoyed the benefits of commercial exchange and industrial production which the burghers provided. But kings, dukes, bishops, and lords did not regard even the wealthiest burghers as their social equals, and they refused to give the city people their freedom. The burghers of the tenth and eleventh centuries were ruthlessly harassed, blackmailed, subjected to oppressive taxes, and humiliated. This drove the bourgeois back upon their own resources, and it accounts for the intensely corporate and excessively organized character of medieval cities. The city people living in their dark little houses in their crooked and dirty streets, surrounded by an indifferent and frequently hostile world, began in the tenth century to regulate every aspect of urban life with a compulsive efficiency.

In the late tenth century there were already guilds of merchants and craftsmen in Italy and even along the Rhine, which carefully regulated commerce and industry. The merchant guilds were corporations of entrepreneurs engaged in international commerce. The craft guilds were dominated by the master craftsmen who regulated the standard of industrial products, fixed prices, and strictly controlled the journeymen and apprentices who worked in their shops. In the first half of the eleventh century the Italian cities took up the institution of the commune—sworn association of men banded together for some purpose—which had existed in rural areas, and used it as the legal basis for turning their cities into self-governing corporations. By 1050 another common characteristic of medieval life had appeared in the commercial centers of Flanders and northern Italy: the real power among the bourgeois was in the hands of a small oligarchy of great entrepreneurs who controlled the merchant guilds in each city and dominated the town government. In the old episcopal center of Milan there was a bitter feud not only between the bishop and the bourgeois but also between the wealthier people and those of more modest means, "the ragpickers." The class struggle in Milan already indicated what would be a common characteristic of the medieval townsmen: they hated each other even more than they hated everybody else.

The second stage of economic growth, which Europe was experiencing between 900 and 1050, involved the processing of some natural resource for export. It was the Flemish cities which discovered the first staple of medieval European international trade. Having drained the marshes of Flanders, the late tenth-century peasants found the recovered land unsuitable for agriculture and instead used it for raising sheep. They obtained enough wool to make cloth for export, and it was on the basis of this commerce that the Flemish weaving towns of Ghent and Ypres prospered in the eleventh century. By 1050 the first internal trade routes had come into existence, stretching from Flanders across the heart of Europe to northern Italy, whose merchants were willing to exchange Mediterranean luxuries for Flemish textiles. The meeting ground for the Flemish and Italian merchants was the county of Champagne, whose ruler in the twelfth century was to sponsor an annual international fair in his territory.

The north Italian cities had initially become wealthy as interlopers in Byzantine and Moslem trade. The Venetians, who were technically part of the Byzantine empire in the tenth century, were given special trading privileges at Constantinople which allowed them to become the intermediaries between Byzantium and Europe. Not satisfied with this enormously profitable commerce, the ruthless Venetians established relations with all the important Moslem commercial centers of the Mediterranean world. In the later decades of the tenth century Genoa and Pisa, on the west coast of Italy, also sought a share of Moslem wealth, which they attained by a subtle mixture of commerce and piracy. It was the Genoese and Pisan merchants who brought the Rhone valley back into the Mediterranean orbit and who inaugurated the use of the Alpine passes for trade with northern Europe.

The revival of western Europe's participation in Mediterranean economic life was followed, during the first two decades of the eleventh century, by political and military penetration. The more enterprising or land-hungry French knights followed the lead of the Italian merchants in trying to gain a share of the fabulous wealth of the Moslem lands. Norman freebooters appeared in Sicily in the second decade of the eleventh century and began a long struggle to carve out domains for themselves in southern Italy, a country wealthy beyond the dreams of feudal avarice. Similarly, Norman and other French adventurers joined the struggle against the Moslems in northern Spain. This advance of the western European nobility was to culminate, at the end of the eleventh century, in the first crusade of 1095.

Bourgeois, nobles, and peasants were not the only people who were seeking out new opportunities in the late tenth and early eleventh centuries. The churchmen, who in any case had always had a much more international outlook, also now exhibited a greater degree of mobility. A Frenchman and several Germans went to Italy to become the bishop of Rome. A Norman Frenchman was for a time archbishop of Canterbury in the 1050's. The leaders of the Cluniac order moved around Europe, founding monasteries and advising rulers. What was unprecedented in the early medieval church was the emergence of a new kind of itinerant scholar, who traveled great distances to find a suitable intellectual milieu and to study under renowned teachers. The great monastic schools of Normandy drew a steady stream of outstanding Italian scholars. Others, however, were making their way to cathedral cities in northern France and Lorraine to study theology and canon law. A few intrepid souls had even dared to cross over into Moslem territory to study mathematics and science at Cordoba. These usually obscure and impecunious scholars were preparing the ground for a tremendous upheaval in European intellectual life.

In the year 1050, in every country in western Europe, there were groups of people engrossed in some kind of novel enterprise. Europe in no way any longer lagged far behind Byzantium and Islam, and in some respects it had surpassed the greatest achievements of the two civilizations with which the Latin-speaking peoples now competed for hegemony in the Mediterranean. In all areas of human activity new aims were being pursued and new methods tested in the western Europe of 1050. The civilization formed out of the union of Latin Christian and Germanic cultures was entering an era of unprecedented creativity and achievement. The question which remained to be answered was whether the social order of the early medieval equilibrium, which had provided the background for political, economic, and cultural success, could prevail in the changed world which was at the dawn of its existence.

PART FIVE

As if we received our kingdom from
thee! As if the kingdom and the empire
were in thine and not in God's hand!
. . . On me, who, although unworthy to
be among the anointed, have nevertheless been anointed to the kingdom, thou
hast lain thy hand. . . .

—HENRY IV TO GREGORY VII

All know that kings and princes are
descendants of men who are ignorant of
God. . . .

—GREGORY VII

THE AGE OF THE
GREGORIAN REFORM

*Late Eleventh and
Early Twelfth Centuries*

Chapter Eleven

ON THE THRESHOLD
OF THE
HIGH MIDDLE AGES

I. High Medieval Civilization in Historical Perspective

The two and a half centuries of European history, extending from the middle of the eleventh to the early fourteenth century, have been more intensively studied than any other era of the middle ages. It is customary for textbooks of medieval history to view the much longer antecedent period as merely preparatory to the two hundred and fifty or so years which comprised the high middle ages. The general historiographical approach to medieval civilization has tended to regard the high middle ages as the creative and mature segment of medieval culture, the period before as merely immature and promising, and the period after 1300 as a decadent, declining, and disintegrating phase. In fact, the high middle ages are frequently viewed as the *real* middle ages, the period which exhibits those characteristics, attitudes, mores, and ideals which are truly implied by the term and concept of medieval.

The period 1050 to 1325 originally attracted the attention of scholars and belletristic writers because the remains of its civilization are so readily visible in western Europe, as, for instance, the French cathedrals, which even today represent medieval culture to the American tourist. The Romantic writers of the early nineteenth century inaugurated this kind of veneration for medieval monuments in sharp contrast with the attitudes of the Italian humanists and the writers of the eighteenth-century Enlightenment, who contemned what they considered to be the barbarism and superstition implicit in "Gothic" architecture. The Romantic litterateurs and their subsequent intellectual heirs, who, like them, detested the manifestations of the industrial revolution and mechanical civilization, found an ideal world of beauty, devotion, and mystery in the artistic monuments of the medieval past. Compared with a cotton mill or an iron foundry, Notre Dame, Chartres, Salisbury, and Cologne, the surviving ecclesiastical buildings of the twelfth and thirteenth centuries, do indeed appear to reflect a civilization which was more placid, idealistic, and humane.

The discovery of the attractions of high-medieval literature and music followed the new appreciation for the great architectural monuments of the Gothic age. How noble and devoted the common sentiments of a society must have been which produced the literary heroes of the Arthurian cycle, and how exalted and yet ordered the piety of a civilization whose greatest musical effort was the incomparable Gregorian chant! Many sensitive minds in the nineteenth century, and not a few in the twentieth, turning in revulsion from the industrial society and the greed and corruption of the modern state, found refuge and solace in the medieval past. Typical of such work was Henry Adams' *Mont St. Michel and Chartres,* which finds the culture of twelfth-century France dominated by the symbolic figure of the Virgin and contrasting so favorably with the America of President Grant. As an early expression of similar attitudes toward the high middle ages we have H. O. Taylor's *The Medieval Mind,* which, while still highly recommended by certain professors of medieval history even today, in fact tells us very little about medieval intellectual history and a great deal about the personal taste and attitudes of a genial, moderately intelligent Boston Brahmin of the late nineteenth century.

Other groups have also been strongly attracted by high-medieval civilization. Scholars of the Catholic church have in general been more interested in the twelfth and thirteenth centuries than in the early middle ages; this is not surprising, for they could see therein the flowering of medieval Christianity and the fulfillment of the leadership of the church in western society. The important roles which Thomistic philosophy and canon law play in the intellectual and administrative life of the modern Catholic church inevitably have led Roman scholars to an intensive study of the origins and formative growth of these philosophic and legal systems in the period between 1050 and 1300. Our understanding of the intellectual life of the twelfth and thirteenth centuries has been greatly deepened by the work of clerical scholars, who pursue their researches with an intensity and devotion not commonly exhibited among secular historians of medieval

Europe. Certain Catholic publicists have gone beyond this careful scholarship and have proclaimed the thirteenth as the "greatest of centuries," the happiest era in history, marked by unity, harmony, peace, progress, and contentment.

National historians have also found the high middle ages a fertile field for study. German historians have looked to the period between 1050 and 1300 for the glorious achievements of the medieval German empire and also for the determining factors which decided (and, in the opinion of some, apologize for) the subsequent pattern of German history. To historians of France the high middle ages must be very important, for these centuries comprise nothing less than the making of France. France in 1050 was little more than a geographical expression, and out of this disorganization in the following two hundred and fifty years came the French state, the French language, and French culture. How did this great transformation take place among the feudal provinces west of the Rhine? French historians are still intensively engaged in answering this question. To the historians of England the twelfth and thirteenth centuries are no less critical than to historians of France. It was suggested by publicists in the seventeenth century and affirmed by historians in the nineteenth century that the two hundred and fifty years following the battle of Hastings in 1066 comprised the formative period of the distinctive English political traditions of the common law and Parliament. Given the tendency, derived from social Darwinism, to define the nature of an institution by its origins, English historians from the mid-nineteenth century to the present day have felt compelled to make an extremely minute analysis of the political and legal developments of their country during the high middle ages.

American medievalists have tended to study the twelfth and thirteenth centuries to the exclusion of the early middle ages, which in American universities has been studied mostly by German emigrés. To the Romantic escapism of Henry Adams and H. O. Taylor was added, in the 1920's, a new motive for intensive study of the twelfth and thirteenth centuries by American scholars. Hardheaded realists such as Charles Haskins and his many disciples and imitators were fascinated by the growth of medieval institutions. The early middle ages was marked by an agrarian society and political disintegration. By 1300 the historian can find strong evidence of an emerging, modern-seeming, bureaucratic state and more-than-incipient forms of capitalism as well. American medievalists therefore found in the period from 1050 to 1300 the beginnings of the modern world, and they sought to uncover the earliest tracks of bureaucratic government and capitalist society through an analysis of governmental, legal, administrative, and financial institutions. The heroes of the middle ages, in their pages, become not the saints, troubadours, and artists of the Romantic writers but rather the great administrators, legists, and tax collectors. It might be said that the American school, in its approach to the high middle ages, reflected social experience and needs as much as any historiographical school in Europe. They mirrored the average educated American's extreme interest in all forms of political activity, and they were perhaps attracted to a study of high-medieval Europe because in this period could be seen the same rapid development from political disorganization to the centralized state which marked the history of the United States. It is not surprising to find that Haskins and one of his most outstanding disciples, J. R. Strayer, did some of their earliest work in American colonial history.

The values which these various groups of writers have found in the high middle ages cannot be gainsaid, although each must be evaluated in a total picture. That beauty, piety, order, creativity, and political achievement existed in the twelfth and thirteenth centuries no one would deny; the question is to what extent did these qualities exist and how central were they to the whole structure of medieval civilization? Furthermore—and this is of the greatest importance—the favorable qualities and achievements of high-medieval civilization must be set over against its limitations and failures. It must be remembered that in the end medieval civilization disintegrated. The church could not maintain its leadership, and even the new national states faltered, at least momentarily. Alongside beauty and order were violence and chaos. To read the writings of the men of the eleventh, twelfth, and thirteenth centuries is to realize that even the most devoted of them were not plaster saints; they were real men deeply concerned about agonizing and often bewildering problems. Behind the facade of Notre Dame or Chartres lies not much more peace or contentment than behind Versailles, the Palace of Nations at Geneva, or the United Nations Building—perhaps even less. The high middle ages offer the historian the prospect of a very complex society, and a true picture involves a full picture, not merely a superficial view of the outstanding achievements. The full significance for medieval society of this creativity must be assessed and its long-range implications delineated, as they so often are not by those who are simply inspired by medieval philosophy and art. It is, of course, difficult to make this rounded judgment of high-medieval civilization, which has so frequently been interpreted by some one-dimensional scale of values. But the historian must ask why a civilization which could achieve so much could also be unable to solve some cardinal problems visible early in its development, and why it should disintegrate so rapidly.

While the period from the middle of the eleventh to the early fourteenth century exhibits certain unifying qualities and therefore stands out as a distinct era in European history, on closer examination these two hundred and fifty years readily break down into four divisions. The first of these is the age of the Gregorian reform from about 1050 to about 1130. It was similar in many ways to the eras of world revolution of modern times— the Protestant, French, and Communist revolutions—and is distinguished by a great debate on the nature of a Christian society. The second division of the high middle ages is marked by the growth of learning, piety, and power from 1130 to 1200. Although this growth was under way well before 1130, its significance was obscured by the controversies of the Gregorian reform, and it was not until the beginning of the seven long decades of relative quiescence which followed the ending of the Gregorian revolution that the tremendous forces of twelfth-century creativity and achievement fully manifested themselves.

All aspects of life were affected by this creative expansion: religion, art, literature, philosophy, economy, and government. But this creativity also brought with it very grave problems, and toward the end of the twelfth century European civilization had to face up to the fundamental problem of whether the consequences of learning, piety, and power could be reconciled with one another, or whether their conflicting impulses would not undermine and destroy the unity and stability of medieval civilization. The third division of the high middle ages, from about 1200 to 1270, was marked by strenuous, even desperate, efforts to resolve this fundamental problem and to establish a new equilibrium in medieval society. The era is dominated by the aims and program of Pope Innocent III, and the relative renewed stability and calm which prevailed in the middle years of the thirteenth century may with some justice be called the Peace of Innocent III. This era is also marked by some of the greatest achievements in medieval piety and theology which we associate with the names of St. Francis of Assisi and St. Thomas Aquinas. The final division of the high middle ages comprises the half century following the death of St. Louis of France in 1270. At first slowly, and then very rapidly, there was a breakdown of leadership, a failure of consensus, and the inauguration of a new age of violence. But this violence is no longer the individual brutality of the early middle ages but a new, more sophisticated, corporate violence carried out by state against state and by the state against the church. The historian of the high middle ages, then, must account for the origins and must assess the consequences of the Gregorian world revolution, must make clear the implications of twelfth-century creativity and achievement, must delineate the new order which Innocent III established, and must account for the rapid collapse of this order in the late thirteenth century.

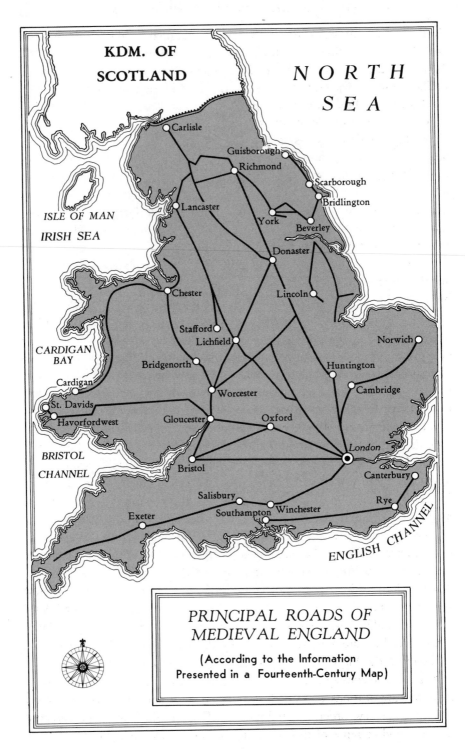

KDM. OF
SCOTLAND

NORTH
SEA

Carlisle

Guisborough
Richmond

Scarborough
Bridlington

ISLE OF MAN

IRISH SEA

Lancaster
York
Beverley

Donaster

Chester

Lincoln

Stafford
Lichfield

Norwich

CARDIGAN
BAY

Bridgenorth
Huntington

Cardigan
Cambridge

St. Davids
Havorfordwest

Worcester

Gloucester
Oxford

London

BRISTOL
CHANNEL

Bristol

Canterbury

Salisbury
Rye

Exeter
Southampton Winchester

ENGLISH CHANNEL

PRINCIPAL ROADS OF
MEDIEVAL ENGLAND

(According to the Information
Presented in a Fourteenth-Century Map)

II. Europe in 1050

What was Europe like in the year 1050? What were the remarkable sights and sounds of the age? What would have caught the eye of a traveler through Europe in this year? We may get some insights into the answers to these questions by accompanying an Anglo-Saxon monk on a journey from his monastery in bleak and distant Yorkshire to the Eternal City in the year 1050.

One day, while our monk was at work in the scriptorium of his monastery, copying manuscripts, he was summoned by his abbot and told that he had been chosen to go on a journey to Rome for two purposes. First of all, he was to pay the abbot's respects to the great Pope Leo IX, who was making far-reaching changes in papal administration and greatly increasing the prestige of the papacy, which had been very low for two centuries. Second, the abbot wanted the young monk to obtain a divorce, or technically an annulment, for the abbot's cousin, a great earl, and for this a papal dispensation was necessary. At this time annulments could be obtained on grounds of consanguinity within the seventh degree (changed in the thirteenth century to fourth degree), and since many of the European nobility had married relatives within the proscribed degree, it was not hard to obtain a divorce provided the pope gave his approval.

Our young monk set off on the old Roman road southward through the wild frontier province of Yorkshire, where most of the thriving religious settlements of the eighth century now lay in ruins as a result of the Viking invasions. When he reached the more southern part of England, he was impressed by the amount of construction and building going on. In fact, throughout Europe in the year 1050 the man-made sounds that one heard most often were the sounds of an axe chopping down trees or hammers and saws at work on new buildings. In a few places, particularly in the great cathedral cities on the continent, buildings of stone were replacing the customary wooden structures, although European craftsmen were still very inexperienced in the handling of stone construction. In 1050 Europe was still very heavily forested, many times more than it is today, with a steadily expanding population and a growing pressure on the food supply. It was necessary to clear the forests and colonize new lands. In any case, the timber provided by the deforestation was greatly needed in building homes, castles, and churches in both urban and rural areas.

The young Yorkshire monk, after several days' journey, arrived at Canterbury, which had been the first Roman church in England and whose bishop was consequently the primate of the English church. When our monk arrived at the cathedral of Christ Church, Canterbury, he was not very surprised to find a great assemblage of people there, including the king, Edward the Confessor. Edward, as his name implies—he was later canonized—was an extremely saintly and pious man although, as was common with saints on the throne, a weak and ineffectual ruler. The monk from Yorkshire found Edward in his favorite occupation—installing new relics in the cathedral of Christ Church. The monk could not help but notice the contempt with which the English nobility regarded the king because of his disinclination to fulfill the Germanic kingly function of war leader. As he had traveled south he had also noticed the disorder and petty wars among the English nobility, which gave evidence of a kingdom on the verge of disintegration.

The Yorkshire monk crossed the channel and landed in Normandy. Here he found a world remarkably different from England, especially with regard to governmental organization and cultural vitality. Normandy was ruled by a man who was by no means a saint, Duke William the Bastard, although he affected to be a great friend and patron of the church and was on very good terms with the papal court. In strong contrast to his kinsman Edward the Confessor, William exercised a very strong control over the nobility of his duchy and used feudal institutions to enhance the ducal power and to unify the territory under his jurisdiction. In Normandy the Yorkshire monk was greatly impressed by the building under way, particularly the construction of great cathedrals and monasteries. The monk was quick to notice that many of the leading churchmen in Normandy were of Italian or Rhenish descent; in either case they had come from regions which were, at least nominally, under the rule of the German emperor. They had been recruited by the duke himself, or by his predecessors, to improve the intellectual and moral qualities of the Norman clergy and to assist him in administrative and legal work. The monk was accustomed to wooden churches in England, and to the extent that there were any stone churches in his homeland, they were squalid little things. He was somewhat taken aback by the attempts to put up ecclesiastical buildings of considerable height and with a new emphasis on the perpendicular line. Certainly this was something new in church architecture in northern Europe, and nothing like it existed in England, although similar architectural styles could be seen in northern Italy, whence many of the leading Norman churchmen had come.

The English monk encountered in Normandy a clerk who had just returned from southern Italy, where he had gone as the chaplain of a Norman baron. The latter had joined a freebooting expedition some years before and was now engaged in conquering this fabulously wealthy land.

From the Norman chaplain the Anglo-Saxon monk heard about an alien world, the distant and unfamiliar Mediterranean lands, inhabited by the feared and hated Moslem infidels and the wrong-headed Byzantine Greeks and distinguished by a comfortable urban way of life beyond the dreams of northern greed. Now, in 1050 A.D., the Moslem and Byzantine control over these fabled lands was being challenged for the first time by the uncouth race of the Franks. It was also known that the Christian princes were beginning to push back the hated Moslem foe even in Spain, where for so long the Cross had ruled over only tiny principalities in the mountains, while the stiff-necked followers of the arch-heretic Mohammed had enjoyed the riches and comforts of Cordoba and the other golden cities of Iberia.

From Normandy the English monk crossed into Flanders, where there were several great monasteries which he visited. It was while he was in Flanders that he became aware for the first time of the existence of a kind of people he had not known before, people who lived in walled towns and who were called *bourgeois*. They were neither adjunct to the cathedral clergy nor the servants of the lords; in industrial cities such as Ghent and Ypres they comprised a new group in medieval society. The English monk had known of only three social classes—those who fought, those who prayed, and those who labored—but these bourgeois people made their living from the manufacture and sale of woolen cloth, some of which was taken by merchants to fairs in Champagne where it was sold and exported to Italy and other distant countries. The background of many bourgeois was obscure; some came from the lower ranks of the knightly class, while others were said to be of servile origin. The bourgeois were not a pleasant people. They were insecure, fearful, and at the same time clever and determined. Their psychological and intellectual make-up was much more complex than that of the old nobility and knightly class and even of most churchmen. They appeared avaricious and not a little dishonest but at the same time extremely devout and pious in an intense, individual way that puzzled the simple monk from Yorkshire. These bourgeois, who stood outside the whole traditional social structure, had no political power, and their precise standing in the law courts was still not settled. One thing they did have was an enormous amount of hard cash, and they used this money not only to build strong walls around their urban enclaves, to erect municipal churches, and to build moderately comfortable houses in the crowded, narrow, and filthy streets of their cities, but also to buy from the count of Flanders extensive rights of self-government.

The English monk realized that he still had a long way to go on his journey to Rome, and it was time to leave the comfortable monasteries and curious cities of Flanders. Even if he could follow the most direct route to Rome via central France—which he could not do because the central part of the country was a no man's land infested with robber barons—the journey would take him two months. He headed from Flanders to Paris with the intention of eventually following the Rhenish route southward via the great ecclesiastical center of Lyons.

What impressed him now as he pursued his journey was the number of lords, merchants, and churchmen whom he encountered on the road. Eighty per cent of Europe's population still did not move more than twenty miles from their places of birth in their whole lifetimes, but the European upper classes were becoming mobile. Any travel was still very dangerous; the roads were incredibly bad, and robbers and brigands might be encountered around almost any bend. But in a civilization in which the pace of life was accelerating, men, and even women occasionally, found it necessary to travel considerable distances. The harnessing and shoeing of the horse one or two hundred years previously had greatly facilitated this travel.

Paris was in some ways a strange city, reflecting the peculiar condition of the French monarchy. As close as ten miles to the city the countryside was dominated by the castles of robber barons, and it is said that the Capetian king feared to go outside the walls of his own city. What impressed the Yorkshire monk most on his visit to Paris was the great royal abbey of St. Denis, which was even more closely associated with the destinies of the Capetian monarchy than its cross-channel counterpart, Westminster Abbey, with the fortunes of the Anglo-Saxon kings. At St. Denis were kept the regalia, the symbols of office of the French crown, which signified the sacred qualities of the Capetian monarchy. But the magnificent ceremony of anointment and coronation, while it convinced the Capetian king of his obligation to the church, had no influence on the great feudal princes of France, who went their separate ways and recognized the hegemony of Paris only in the emptiest, most formal way.

The abbot of St. Denis urged his English visitor to stop on his journey to Rome at the great monastery of Cluny, near Lyons. The abbot himself had originally been a monk of Cluny, as were many of the ecclesiastics in Normandy. Indeed, the English monk had already heard wonderful reports about Cluny, which was the largest monastery of the time and which came to represent the outlook of the whole church in the middle years of the eleventh century. The English monk was not disappointed; Cluny was all that it was supposed to be, and he, like other visitors, came away impressed by the splendor of the buildings, the sophistication of the liturgy, and the discipline and devotion of the monks. It is true that these monks lived much more comfortably and ate much better than the rustic Benedictines of Yorkshire. The Cluniac monks did not undertake any kind of physical labor, nor did they even devote much effort to education and scholarship. They were content to live off the estates and endowments they had received from the admiring rulers of Europe, such as the contemporary German Salian emperor, Henry III, who was particularly devoted to the Cluniac order. Was it not time that the life of the regular clergy reflected the monastic leadership in society? Were not the Cluniac monks truly the princes of the church? Indeed, many of the Cluniac monks were of princely and aristocratic lineage, and did they not deserve even more princely accoutrements as leaders of the church? The Cluniacs answered these questions in the affirmative, and even monks who were devoted to simpler and more rigorous lives were for a long time inclined to agree with them. The Cluniacs were content with the world as it was; it was apparently a perfected world, one in which religious like themselves exercised strong political influence and the German, French, and English rulers fulfilled the implications of their anointments to the office of theocratic monarchy.

The one man-made sound which had been heard most often by the English monk on his journey, next to the sound of peasants' axes in the forest, was the sound of the bells ringing from the rapidly increasing number of monasteries and churches. Everywhere he had gone the English monk had seen new parish churches erected on their own lands and endowed by great nobles. Piety was taking hold in society; it was delightful to find everywhere not only dedicated churchmen but also nobles, bourgeois, and even peasants who understood and regarded with utmost seriousness the doctrines of the faith which had so long ago been carried to the frontiers of Europe by the intrepid disciples of St. Benedict.

These happy musings of the Yorkshire monk were interrupted by his arrival at the great city of Milan after his journey through the Alpine passes. As in the time of St. Ambrose, Milan was dominated by its bishop, but new elements had entered into the life of the great cathedral center which the English monk found surprising and not a little disturbing. Here there existed not only a large bourgeois class, hostile to the traditional political prerogatives of the bishop, but also a disaffected industrial proletariat seething with bitterness against all constituted authority and easily transformed by millennial and apocalyptic doctrines into a revolutionary mob. Here the English monk found the same individualistic and intense lay piety that he had encountered among the Flemish city dwellers, but in Milan this piety was magnified to the point of becoming a grave problem for the church. The literate bourgeois looked with contempt upon many of the cathedral clergy, who indeed were often corrupt and unworthy men, and the general religious atmosphere of the city was one of deep spiritual yearning running off at the edges into rebellion and heresy and not to be easily satisfied or turned aside.

The simple English monk was glad that he did not have to minister to the pastoral cares of the Milanese bourgeois and the proletariat; he was relieved to hear that the reformed papacy of Leo IX was hastening to give attention to such explosive situations. But when he finally had arrived in Rome and traversed its ruined and deserted suburbs and passed along its dirty, stinking streets, coming ultimately to the basilica of St. Peter, the northern monk found even more disturbing ideas in circulation. Leo IX was a kinsman of the great German emperor Henry III and was devoted to the reformation of the papacy under the imperial aegis, but the young cardinals whom he had brought to Rome seemed to be men of rather different outlook. They not only spoke in scathing terms of the decadence and corruption of the secular clergy; they not only questioned the ultimate authority of the emperor over the papacy; they even made occasional critical remarks about the validity of the Cluniac approach to the religious life. Here was a new and disturbing tone which seemed to run contrary to everything that the English monk had admired in his journey southward. He found in the speech and attitudes of the young cardinals a note of intensity and recklessness which in some ways was not dissimilar to the lack of restraint of the Milanese and Flemish bourgeois. The simple Yorkshire monk was happy to plead his suit as quickly as possible and to obtain the annulment on behalf of the earl. He was eager to begin the long journey homeward—through a Europe whose perfected state was not acknowledged by all and whose felicity and contentment seemed possibly transient.

Chapter Twelve

THE GREGORIAN WORLD
REVOLUTION

I. The Nature and Origin of the Gregorian Reform

The eight decades from the middle of the eleventh century to the end of
the third decade of the twelfth constitute one of the great turning points
in European history. It was one of those periods during which vitally important changes in all aspects of life occur simultaneously and with such
great rapidity that no contemporary could foresee the far-reaching consequences of many of them. Nor can the historian, with all the advantages
of hindsight and even after the most painstaking labors, disentangle all the
causal relationships which then inaugurated great upheavals in political,
economic, religious, and intellectual life. Hence, from this point of view
alone, these eight medieval decades resemble the critical eras of the modern
world: the first half of the sixteenth century, the second half of the
eighteenth, and the first half of the twentieth. In all these crucial periods
in the history of the west the forces of change for better or worse, frustrated
so long, burst forth over the land like a flood, leaving behind them the
wrecked structure of an old order and the foundation of a changed pattern
of social life. At most times western man appears to be like a sleepwalker,
accepting passively the social framework built up over the centuries that
have gone before. But during these critical periods of change he appears
more like a daydreamer, pursuing an only partly defined ideal which now
inspires his intellect, and with the novelty of now moving forward with
eyes open instead of closed but still with only partial consciousness of the
direction of his movement.

271

Such a period of fundamental and, at the same time, rapid change was the age of the Gregorian reform and the investiture controversy. It was the period of enormous commercial expansion, of the well-known rise of urban communities, of the first expression of political influence on the part of the new burgher class. It was an age in which the first really successful medieval monarchy was created in Anglo-Norman England on the basis of the feudal institutions and administrative methods and personnel created by the energetic and far-seeing Norman dukes. It was an age in which the long separation of the new western European civilization from the life of the Mediterranean world came to an end. This isolation, in existence since the eighth century, was now replaced by the political and economic penetration of the west European peoples into the Mediterranean basin to the detriment of the Moslems and Byzantines, who had long ruled the Mediterranean lands and controlled Mediterranean trade without a challenge from the north. It was an age of tremendous intellectual vitality which witnessed the most important contributions to the Latin Christian theology since Augustine and the slow transformation of some of the cathedral schools of northern France and the municipal schools of northern Italy into the universities of the following centuries. It was an age of great vitality in legal thought, in which Roman law came to be carefully studied for the first time since the German invasion of the fifth century, and great strides were made in the codification of the canon law.

But as in the eras of fundamental change in modern history, these achievements must be given second place in importance by the historian in favor of an ideological struggle. Out of a far-reaching controversy on the nature of the right order to be established in the world the pattern of civilization of the following centuries was to emerge. The period from 1050 to 1130 was dominated by an attempt at world revolution which influenced in highly effective ways the other aspects of social change. It seems, in retrospect, that it was almost necessary for a revolutionary onslaught to shake to its foundations the order of the early middle ages, in order that the new political, economic, and intellectual forces be given the opportunity to develop in the face of the old institutions and ideas.

It has been characteristic of the history of the west that its destiny has been shaped by four world revolutions in which previous tendencies culminated and from which new ideas and systems emerged. A world revolution is a widespread and thoroughgoing revolution in world view, the emergence of a new ideology which rejects the results of several centuries of development organized into the prevailing system and calls for a new right order in the world. In modern history these world revolutions are well known: the Protestant Revolution of the sixteenth century, the liberal revolution of the eighteenth century, the Communist revolution of the twentieth. The investiture controversy, which the Gregorian reform engendered, constitutes the first of the great world revolutions of western history, and its course follows the same pattern as the well-known revolutions of modern times.

Each of the world revolutions has begun with some just complaint about moral wrongs in the prevailing political, social, or religious system. In the investiture controversy the leaders of the revolution, who have been called the Gregorian reformers, complained about the domination of the church by laymen and the involvement of the church in feudal obligations. This system had led to severe abuses, especially that of simony, which came to be defined in its most general sense as the interference of laymen with the right ordering of church offices and sacraments. In their condemnation of simony as heresy the Gregorians had a perfectly valid complaint.

It has been characteristic of all the world revolutions, however, that while each has begun by complaining about abuses in the prevailing world order, the ultimate aim of the revolutionary ideologists has been not the reform of the prevailing system but rather its abolition and replacement by a new order. In the case of the investiture controversy, complete freedom of the church from control by the state, the negation of the sacramental character of kingship, and the domination of the papacy over secular rulers constituted the ideal new order.

As in all other world revolutions, the ideology of the Gregorians called forth violent opposition on the part of both vested interests and sincere theoretical defenders of the old order. After many acrimonious disputes and a flood of propaganda literature, bitter and protracted warfare resulted. The polarization of educated society into revolutionary and conservative left a large group of uncommitted moderates, including some of the best minds of the age, who could see right and wrong on both sides.

As in all other world revolutions, the ideologists of the investiture controversy were only partially successful in creating the new order. They succeeded in destroying the old system, but the new world was not the revolutionary utopia. Rather, it was a reconstruction of the political and religious system which took into account both old and new elements and left room for the human limitations of greed and power. The church gained a large measure of freedom from secular control, and there was a noticeable improvement in the moral and intellectual level of the clergy. But the church itself, from the time of the investiture controversy, became more and more interested in secular affairs, and so the papacy of the high middle ages competed successfully for wealth and power with kings and emperors. The church itself became a great superstate governed by the papal administration.

As in all other world revolutions, the ideologists during the investiture controversy were themselves united only upon the most immediate and more limited aims of the revolution. As the revolution proceeded, the Gregorians divided into a moderate and a radical wing, each led by eminent cardinals. The radicals were headed by Humbert and Hildebrand, the moderates by Peter Damiani. As in the modern world revolutions, the radicals were for a short period in control of the Gregorian reform movement, a period which was long enough to destroy the old order. But as the conservatives and moderates of various complexions perceived at last the real aim of the radicals and their reckless disregard for consequences, the radicals lost their leadership and were unable to realize their utopian ideals.

As in the modern world revolution, the radicals lost their leadership not to the moderates of their own group, whom they had earlier swept aside, but rather to the politicians, the practical statesmen who called a halt to the revolution and tried to reconstruct from the shattered pieces of the old system and the achievements of the revolution a new and workable synthesis which would again make progress possible. This tendency is already evident during the pontificate of Urban II in the last decade of the eleventh century, and it became dominant in the papacy during the 1120's.

Like all world revolutions, the investiture controversy never reached a final and complete solution. New ideas in a new generation made former issues less meaningful, and the men of the new generation turned to other interests and new problems. Just as Voltaire and Hume could not understand why the men of the sixteenth and seventeenth centuries should have fought over abstruse theological principles, likewise in the 1130's, educated churchmen could not understand why popes and kings should have quarreled over lay investiture only two or three decades before.

The age of the investiture controversy may rightly be regarded as the turning point in medieval civilization. It was the fulfillment of the early middle ages, because in it the acceptance of the Christian religion by the Germanic peoples reached a final and decisive stage. On the other hand, the pattern of the religious and political system of the high middle ages emerged out of the events and ideas of the investiture controversy.

The older view, now largely discredited, that the Cluniac movement directly inspired the Gregorian reform was not only naive but almost the complete opposite of the truth. The Gregorians revolted against the medieval equilibrium and hence against many things that eleventh-century Cluny and its allies represented. What, then, were the origin and cause of the Gregorian reform movement which brought about the decisive turning point in medieval history? Anyone who has tried to comprehend the causes and initial stages of the modern world revolutions will not be surprised at the difficulty of determining those of the medieval world revolution. Many aspects of this problem have not yet been subjected to intensive research. In particular, very few eleventh-century ecclesiastical leaders have been accorded definitive biographical studies. But knowledge of the period has advanced far enough to reveal, at least in outline, the revolution's origins.

The Gregorian reform movement was the logical outcome, but by no means the inevitable and absolutely necessary outcome, of the early medieval equilibrium itself. As the church in the late tenth and eleventh centuries penetrated more and more into the world, imposing its ideals on lay society, it began to face the dangerous possibility of losing its distinctive identity and hence its leadership in western society. For as lay piety steadily increased throughout western Europe, the special qualities of the clergy stood out less clearly. No longer did a devout attitude toward dogma and ritual and the veneration of the saints and their relics suffice to distinguish the outlook of ecclesiastic and layman. By the middle of the eleventh century it was apparent that lay piety had in many cases attained the level of religious devotion hitherto exhibited only by the more conscientious among the clergy. Cardinal Peter Damiani, so frequently serving in his writings as a sort of barometric indicator of eleventh-century attitudes, observed that every faithful Christian was a microcosm of the whole church: "Each of the faithful seems to be, as it were, a lesser church." If the Holy Spirit, Damiani asserted, raised some of the faithful to the ministry of ecclesiastical dignity, it was to be expected that these ministers of God would reveal their special divine gifts by a superior form of religious life. Above all, the monks, who had professed the most perfect religious life, should at least act as the militia of Christ.

The great increase in lay piety created a new problem for the church, and its own traditional hierocratic doctrine, here reflected in Damiani's statement, made the problem particularly urgent. The power of the priesthood and the papacy had been built upon the principle that "him to whom more is given, from him more will be demanded." Previously there was no doubt that more in the way of the spirit was demanded from the clergy; hence the justification of sacerdotal powers in the popular mind. Now doubts were arising on this issue. To many eleventh-century churchmen it seemed that only a greatly improved morality and heightened religious fervor among the clergy could continue to justify the exclusive powers of the *sacerdotium.* Otherwise the *ecclesia* would be absorbed into the thoroughly Christianized *mundus,* and the clergy would lose its distinctive position in society.

By the middle of the eleventh century churchmen everywhere in western Europe were encountering this new, critical problem. They knew that

kings such as Henry III of Germany and Edward the Confessor were monks
in worldly garb, always eager to lead the procession in a translation of
holy relics. They found many nobles who took seriously the Peace of God,
who endowed monasteries and cathedrals, undertook arduous pilgrimages,
and hoped to be accorded the privilege of dying enshrouded in the monastic
habit. Even the scurvy bourgeois gave glimpses of falling in with this new
tendency, with their support of municipal churches and their devotion to
religious festivals. Such laymen would expect a clergy to be still as morally
superior to themselves as it was in the old days when society was savage
and heathen, save in the most nominal sense. The hold of the church over
lay society, the universal respect that the monks especially received from
laymen, could only be maintained by a greatly enhanced piety and morality
among the monks themselves.

The Benedictine order provided the greater part of the leadership for
the eleventh-century church, and consequently the regular clergy was most
sensitive to the consequences of the rise of lay piety. The origins of the
Gregorian reform movement lay in novel tendencies which developed in
eleventh-century monasticism, in a new spirit which made many monks
dissatisfied with the prevailing Cluniac religious life and led them to advocate different and more stringent monastic ideals. The roots of Gregorianism are therefore to be found in the eleventh-century crisis of western
monasticism.

The first stirrings of a new attitude toward monastic life (or, perhaps
more accurately, a very old attitude which was revived) came in northern
Italy about the year 1000. For the first time, at least since the fourth century, the eremitic form of monastic life made its appearance to an appreciable degree in western Europe. It is not surprising to find that these
hermits appeared first in northern Italy. Extreme asceticism is not a
characteristic of an underdeveloped agrarian society where the general
standard of life is marginal and frugal in any case. Asceticism must have a
wealthy society, the fleshpots and temptations of urban economy, to revolt
against. This was true of the eastern Mediterranean in the fourth century,
where the fathers of the desert flourished, and it was true of northern Italy
at the beginning of the eleventh century, where for the first time in the
development of medieval western Europe an urban society existed. North
of the Alps new ascetic movements made their appearance in the second
half of the eleventh century. Particularly in northern France, Flanders, and
the Rhineland do we hear of devoted monks turning away from the comforts and security of the Cluniac type of monasticism and going out into
frontier regions in small groups to form new, strongly ascetic communities.
These isolated new monastic establishments coalesced in the twelfth cen-

tury into the great Cistercian movement and other new religious orders. In northern Italy, however, while new and more stringent cenobitic communities also appeared, the figure of the itinerant hermit-saint remained a powerful catalytic force in religious life into the thirteenth century, culminating in the Franciscan movement.

Whether cenobitic or eremitic in their inclinations, the leading spirits of the new ascetic movement within western monasticism were unanimous in their criticism of the prevailing Cluniac type of religious life. They believed that Cluny and the other great Benedictine monasteries of the day were sadly deficient in observing the rule which the founder of their order had set down and which they were professing. Far from applauding the worldly influence and possessions of the great Benedictine communities, the ascetic leaders complained that the abbeys' wealth and power were a source of temptation to their members, leading them away from realization of the monastic ideal. The solution then for the hermits of the new, more ascetic communities was a strict subjection to the vow of poverty: they must live as the monks in Monte Cassino had lived in the time of St. Benedict, or, expressed in its full doctrinal form, they must return to the spiritual ideal of the apostolic church. In this respect, as in most others, Peter Damiani spoke for the new generation of puritanically inclined churchmen: "We not only abandon nobler occupations and worldly gain, but we have made profession of a perpetual renunciation of these things." Only by adopting this great reform of the regular clergy, it was felt, could the monks preserve, and deserve to maintain, their position of leadership in Christian society.

How did these critical changes in monastic life result in the Gregorian revolution and the monumental struggle over the right order in the world? It was not inevitable that one should have led to the other, but under the circumstances of the era it was a natural progression. The men who came to prominence in the papal court in the 1050's were all monks, and it was natural for them to carry their ascetic and purifying interests one step beyond the monastery and apply it to the whole church. Thus Damiani devoted many years attempting to reform the corrupt clergy in northern Italy. The final step, logical though not inevitable, was to carry over the ascetic and purifying impulse into the world itself. This was the origin of the radical Gregorians' attack on the whole prevailing Christian world order, and is explained by the circumstances of the medieval equilibrium itself—the interpenetration of the *ecclesia* and the *mundus*. If the church and the world were identical and synonymous, as many contemporaries said, then how could asceticism and reform stop within the limits of the church? For the church had no limits, or at least its limits were those of the world itself; the Gregorian radical felt compelled to apply his puritan ideals to all aspects of social life and to establish a unified Christian world system—*Christianitas,* Gregory VII called it. The Gregorians accepted the common eleventh-century identification of the church and the world with complete seriousness, and their ideology therefore required them to carry the ascetic, reforming, purifying impulse from the hermitage and the new monastic community into the most vital aspects of contemporary life outside the monastery. The institutional structure of their world confirmed the lessons of ideology. The regular clergy was so central to the life of the eleventh-century church that it was hard to conceive of a critical change in monastic life that would not affect and reform the whole church. Similarly, in most parts of Europe church and kingship were so involved with each other that radical church reform necessitated political and social revolution.

II. *The Debate on the Essentials of a Christian Society*

By the 1050's the chief assistants of the pope were organized into the "college" (i.e., corporation) of cardinals. The term "cardinal" comes from the Latin word for the hinge of a door; the cardinals were the hinges on which the great papal door moved. The term "cardinal" was singularly appropriate for the men who dominated the papacy in the second half of the eleventh century and attempted to carry out the Gregorian reforms. They were remarkably few in number—not more than a dozen all together over a period of more than half a century were important in the Gregorian movement. Actually, for only two pontificates, that of Gregory VII himself (1073–1085) and Paschal II (1099–1118), was there a real radical on the papal throne. The other two prominent Gregorian reformers were the cardinals Peter Damiani (d. 1072) and Humbert (d. 1061). The latter is often called Humbert of Silva Candida, after the small church in Rome whose pastorate he nominally held in conjunction with his cardinalate, as was customary.

The four leading Gregorian reformers were as remarkable a group of men as ever appeared in European history. They not only dominated the life of the eleventh-century church, but they also participated in, and in many ways contributed to, the leading intellectual currents of the period. In every case the doctrines they propounded did not die with them or even with the eleventh or early twelfth centuries, but rather entered into the mainstreams of medieval thought. The implications of the Gregorians' thought-world reach out in many directions and by no means only within the bounds of orthodox Catholicism. The Gregorians inaugurated a great debate on the nature of a Christian society. Their doctrines were challenged by other learned and devout churchmen, and out of this intellectual conflict emerged at last the outlines of almost every ideological position which was to develop more fully in the following five centuries. Many of the arguments propounded during the Gregorian reform period are still relevant to our own experience and problems.

Of the men we call the Gregorian reformers the one who was most universally loved and respected and least controversial in his own day was St. Peter Damiani. Nevertheless, the inspiration, the pattern, and the implications of his doctrines are in some respects the most difficult for us to grasp of any of the Gregorian reformers' because of their diffuse nature and because they penetrated and affected almost the whole culture and literature of the high middle ages. With justice did Dante, in his *Divine Comedy,* place Damiani in one of the highest circles of heaven and regard him as the predecessor of St. Francis. It might, in fact, be said that St. Francis was only the ultimate development of a religious movement of which Damiani is the most outstanding and identifiable originator.

Damiani's voluminous writings reflect the spiritual conditions of northern Italy in the first half of the eleventh century, whence he was brought to the papal court. Damiani was born in about the year 1007. He was an orphan of poor family, but was adopted by a priest and received a good education in both theology and canon law. He found the prevailing Cluniac life, while in some respects admirable, too much involved with the world, and he became one of the leaders of the new eremitic movement in northern Italy. His vehement denunciation of the corruption of the secular clergy in the Italian cities brought him to the attention of Leo IX, who made him a cardinal and tried to channel his energies in the service of Rome. Damiani was never very happy as a cardinal; he was more the type of the itinerant hermit-saint and preacher than an institutional reformer. Damiani was sent to Milan to try to reform the church there, but his success was not very great. He found himself at odds with Hildebrand (the later Gregory VII) and Humbert, his colleagues in the college of cardinals, whom he admired but considered reckless and dangerous. He was the kind of man who inspired revolutionaries, but his saintly and charitable disposition precluded his being a revolutionary himself. His death the year before Hildebrand became pope is very significant, for it removed from the scene the one man who could have restrained Gregory.

Damiani was the leader of the more moderate group in the college of cardinals who tried to avoid a final break between the reforming papacy and the German emperor. But his teaching was revolutionary enough, in the sense that it reached to the foundations of the medieval religious experience and helped to bring about a transformation of spiritual values. A great change was under way in the eleventh century in the medieval conception of the relationship between the deity and humanity. The judging, wrathful, distant God of the Old Testament, which predominated in early medieval religiosity, was coming to be replaced by the loving, self-abnegating Son of the New Testament, with his weeping and charitable Mother. Religion was becoming less a matter of formal worship and obedience and much more a personal experience. It was in the ascetic and eremitic monasticism in northern Italy and the intense religious experience of the Italian urban communities that this new spiritual outlook made its first appearance. By the middle of the twelfth century the new piety, as it has been called, had spread throughout Europe, had penetrated into the inmost reaches of the European consciousness, and had spilled over and enriched and ennobled the art and literature of medieval civilization. St. Francis was the ultimate figure in this development, and St. Bernard played a tremendous role in advancing and maturing this new religiosity in the twelfth century, but St. Peter Damiani was the first writer to express clearly this new piety. He was the founder of that mystical strain of personal identification of the self-abnegating, loving deity and the hopeful, ascending human spirit which sharply distinguished the religion of the high middle ages from what had gone before.

If Damiani thus played a primary role in the enrichment and fulfillment of medieval Catholicism, at the same time he must be seen as an originator of an uncontrollable emotionalism which is not so praiseworthy as this new conception of the deity, nor in the long run was it easy for the church to control. The new intense emotional religiosity brought with it an irrational fanaticism which, if inculcated in the masses, could produce violent manifestations which no public authority could control. The popular reaction to the first crusade was to be an early example of this. It is not surprising to find that the massacre of Jews in 1096 as a popular response to the crusading appeal found its ultimate authority in the writings of Damiani himself. Even in the opinions of the great saint and mystic of the early eleventh century, fanaticism made its appearance as the reverse side of the new personal, intense religiosity which he did so much to foment. The great increase of anti-Semitic literature in the late eleventh century began with two pamphlets written by Damiani himself, whose passionate charity did not extend to those outside the Christian church.

The ultimate ambiguity and tension of Damiani's doctrine lay in the fact that while, on the one hand, he was the most orthodox defender of the validity and necessity of the sacraments as the means of divine grace and the authority of the priesthood alone to administer them to the laity, on the other hand the central mystical inclinations of his teachings tended to lessen the indispensability of both sacraments and priesthood. For if personal identification is ultimately possible between the human soul and the loving Christ (at least in the popular mind, if not in theological argument), an alternative route to the deity has been opened up. The implications of this underlying dilemma were not seen in the eleventh century, but in the following two hundred years they were to become more and more a source of confusion, doubt, and agonizing conflict in Christendom. It is not too much to conclude, therefore, that the long-range extrapolation from Damiani's teachings was in the direction of that religious individualism which was to dissolve the fabric of medieval Christendom. This is not to say that Damiani was *responsible* for this later tendency in the mystical and emotional aspects of medieval religiosity, but it is to point out that if this mainstream of radical thought is followed back from the fourteenth century to its ultimate sources in the eleventh, the saintly figure of the north Italian eremite will loom very large. Thus, considered against the whole structure of medieval culture, the doctrines of Damiani, who was in his personal inclinations the least radical of the Gregorian reformers, were potentially as revolutionary as anything ever said or done by Humbert or Hildebrand.

Damiani's competitor for the intellectual leadership of the Gregorian papacy was Cardinal Humbert of Silva Candida, a thinker fully as learned and forceful as the great Italian mystic and in some ways more subtle, original, and complex. Humbert came from Lorraine, where Leo IX had been a bishop. It has been established that Humbert had been a monk at Cluny and came to feel strongly that Cluny had betrayed the ideals of its founder. Otherwise his early biography is obscure. Like nearly all the Cluniacs, Humbert of Lorraine was probably a product of the high nobility; this class background would help to explain his consistent hatred of the German monarchy which had asserted its authority over Lorraine against strong local opposition. It is certain that Humbert had studied in the new schools of the canon law which flourished in Lorraine and that he had obtained a vast knowledge of theology and church history. He was likely an intellectual prodigy—he had a good knowledge of Greek, which was most unusual in western Europe at the time—and in spite of his acidulous and critical disposition and his extreme intellectual arrogance, which are revealed in almost every page he wrote, the church could not afford to dispense with his services. Leo IX was glad to have him in the papal service, where his erudition and daimonic energy made him an outstanding figure. Only his premature death—he could not have been much more than fifty in 1061—kept him from the throne of Peter.

Humbert's knowledge of Greek fitted him for the role of papal ambassador to Constantinople. The revitalized and aggressive attitude of the papacy was leading to a reconsideration of papal relations with the Greek church, and the age-old conflicting claims of pope and emperor were again becoming an important issue. The Norman conquest of southern Italy, where many Greek Christians lived, also served to remind the papal court of the problems of Latin-Greek relations. Humbert was not the man to be either cautious or subservient in his negotiations with the Greek church. He ended his legation in 1054 by excommunicating the patriarch of Constantinople, thereby officially declaring a schism which had been developing since the fifth century. This schism has not been ended to the present day, although several attempts have been made at reconciliation over the centuries.

On his return to Rome Humbert became the theoretician of the reform movement and the leader of the radical wing in the college of cardinals. The crucial date, when the effects of his planning and theorizing became evident, was 1059. In this year he was responsible for the publication of two works which signaled the beginnings of the Gregorian revolution. The first was the papal election decree, setting forth the legal manner of electing popes. It placed the election fully in the hands of the cardinals and excluded the interference of both the German emperor and the Roman people. In view of the fact that less than twenty years before Henry III had made popes with almost annual regularity, it marked a very great change in the relations between Rome and the German emperor. But Henry IV (1056–1106) was at the time a minor, and his family was fighting off the rebellion of the German nobility; Humbert was able to carry out his *coup d'état* with impunity, as he had expected. The second work which Humbert published in 1059 was his great treatise on church-state relations, *The Three Books Against the Simoniacs,* the ideological formulation of the Gregorian revolution. It is suffused with violent hatred of the German emperor and calls forcefully for the complete freedom of the papacy from secular control. But there is much more to Humbert's masterpiece than this; it is essentially an attack on the whole early medieval equilibrium between the church and the world.

Just as Damiani's work reflects one of the leading intellectual currents of the time, the new piety, so does Humbert's book reflect the new logic, or dialectic—the new emphasis on the formulation of argument according to the strict canons of whatever was known of Aristotelian logic at the time. Humbert was a pioneer in this controlled manner of debate, which contrasted markedly with the shapeless, or at least purely rhetorical, kind of didactic prose in the early middle ages. And he uses this new intellectual tool in combination with his vast erudition to undermine the existing world order. He argues that simony is not merely the buying and selling of church offices; simony is any interference by laymen in the affairs of the church. By this definition much of the prevailing institutional organization of western society—lay investiture, proprietary churches, royal influence over ecclesiastical appointments—stood condemned as errors in the faith. By Humbert's argument no king or nobleman in western Europe, and not many churchmen, were at that very moment free from participating in acts which condemned their souls.

This was strong medicine, but Humbert was not content to stop at even this radical position. The fatal charms of dialectic, which were to lead so many other brilliant medieval minds into the uncharted swamps of heresy in the following three hundred years, claimed Humbert as an early victim. His puritanism compelled him by logical steps to the conclusion that if the clergy could be reformed in no other way, then the people should examine the moral character of their priest, and if they found it unsatisfactory, they should refuse to take the sacraments from him. Thus was Humbert led to a revival of the Donatist doctrine that the ministration of the sacraments by an unworthy priest was invalid, and to its corollary that the laity had a right to judge the priesthood. It was against these very principles that St. Augustine had labored so hard more than six centuries before, with the outcome that the church had proclaimed Donatism as the most dangerous of errors. It had been decided that the priest, in administering the sacraments, acted as the representative of God, that the efficacy of the sacrament was not dependent upon the personal qualities of the priest but upon the divinely constituted office which he held, and that the laity could not sit in judgment on the priesthood. Humbert's revival of Donatism must be seen as an indirect consequence of the development of lay piety. It is apparent that he had greater respect for the opinion of many laymen than he had for the views of their official pastors.

Humbert had clearly fallen into doctrinal error, and the effect of his teaching, if widely accepted, could only be the undermining of the authority of the priesthood and the negation of the Catholic concept of the predominance of the office over the individual moral character of ecclesiastics. Put simply, it would lead to the substitution of a proto-Protestant church of the saints for the Catholic church. Damiani was quick to point out the Donatist tendencies in Humbert's treatise; to him it was a lesson in the dangers of dialectic, whose value to the church he greatly doubted. Yet others in the papal circle, fired by puritanical fanaticism and no doubt not a little influenced by Cardinal Humbert's strong personality and tremendous intellectual force, were not so quick to see the dangerous and in fact explosive consequences of Humbert's argument. Hildebrand, who was strongly under Humbert's influence and who derived a great part of his ideology from Humbert's writings, was slow to reject Humbert's neo-Donatism and came round to condemning it only in the latter part of his pontificate.

While finally again denounced by the papacy as the severest of errors in the faith, a position which the Catholic church has not altered to the present day, the revival of the Donatist ideology by Humbert, a prominent cardinal and the most subtle theoretician of the eleventh century, was an event of momentous significance for the development of the medieval church. Never again was Donatism to disappear completely from the medieval thought-world. In the second half of the twelfth century it was to be the fruitful source from which heretical movements and doctrines were to evolve into the sectarian Protestantism of the sixteenth century. No scholar has yet established the precise line of continuity between Humbert's treatise *Against the Simoniacs* and the Donatist heretics who appeared in large numbers in northern Italy in the last half of the twelfth century. It seems not too much to postulate, however, that Humbert's teachings, while eventually condemned by the papacy, were taken up into the intense religiosity of the north Italian urban communities and played a leading role in turning the new lay piety in the direction of popular heresy.

In comparison with Damiani and Humbert, Hildebrand was not an original theoretician. He was, however, unsurpassed as an ideologist, which is not necessarily the same thing. He pulled together, from many sources, the novel and radical ideas of his day and synthesized them into a formidable, total program of revolution. As Pope Gregory VII he attempted to implement these doctrines, and in so doing he inaugurated the great struggle between pope and emperor which shook western society to its foundations. Whatever the judgment on the merits of his ideology and the achievements of his pontificate, Gregory VII must be regarded as one of the three greatest medieval popes. Among all the holders of the throne of Peter before the sixteenth century, only Gregory I and Innocent III are comparable in stature. And no pope was ever as controversial as Gregory VII. No one in Europe in the 1070's and 80's could hold for long a moderate and neutral opinion of him. He was greatly admired and loved by some, and at the same time he aroused more hatred and contempt in his own time than probably any other bishop of Rome.

Gregory's controversial quality makes it difficult to establish some of the key facts of his biography and the salient aspects of his character. So many stories and legends, favorable and unfavorable, were told about him that his personality remains somewhat obscured. He was a native Roman who literally grew up in the shadow of the basilica of St. Peter's, took monastic vows, and entered into the service of the papacy in early manhood. Even before Leo IX became pope in 1049, Hildebrand was already an important man in papal circles, and although for a quarter of a century he was passed over for less able candidates in papal elections, he was a dominant force in the college of cardinals and the effective chief of the papal administration. Hildebrand's attitude to the Roman see can be termed almost nationalistic, or at least parochial. Irrespective of the ideological questions involved, he detested the German emperor as an alien interloper who had no business interfering in Italian affairs, let alone in papal policy. As R. W. Southern has well pointed out, Hildebrand's last words when he died in southern Italy in 1085, after being driven from Rome by an imperial army, are highly significant: "I have loved justice and hated iniquity; therefore I die in exile." Any place outside of the Eternal City was exile to this native Roman.

It is difficult to establish Hildebrand's family background. Some contemporaries claimed that he was of bourgeois provenance; this may be a canard, but if it is true, it would help to explain his almost paranoiac hatred of the established order. Beyond doubt, Hildebrand was a hard man to get along with. His prodigious ability as an administrator, his puritanical zeal, and his fantastic energy made him a great leader but a difficult colleague. Even the charitable Damiani referred to him as the "holy Satan." Abbot Hugh of Cluny, the fastidious elder statesman of the eleventh-century church, detested Hildebrand on sight, regarded him as a crass careerist, and did everything he could to block the implementation of Gregory's programs.

Without being either a great scholar or a systematic thinker, Hildebrand was well versed in canon law, theology, and church history. Lacking the true scholar's interest in knowledge per se, he was nevertheless quick to make use of the new learning of the eleventh century to support his point of view. Even before he became pope, Hildebrand had directed some leading Italian scholars to undertake the collection and organization of the canon law, a scholarly work which was being pursued at the same time in northern France and Lorraine. The canon law was such a vast, unorganized body of contradictory propositions that he wanted to make sure that its codification was worked out in directions favorable to papal power. If he had done nothing else, Hildebrand would thereby have made a great contribution to the rise of papal authority, for when the codification that he had inaugurated came to fruition in the mid-twelfth century, it resulted in a canon law which emphasized papal absolutism and rejected alternative early-medieval traditions.

Immediately after his elevation to the throne of Peter, in 1073, Hildebrand drew upon this papal-oriented research in canon law for the propositions which he published as the *Dictatus Papae,* a statement of papal power. The *Dictatus Papae* asserted that the Roman church was founded by God alone, that only the papal office was universal in its authority, and that the pope alone could depose bishops, reinstate them, or transfer them from one see to another. No church council was canonical without papal approval. No one could condemn an appellant to the apostolic see, which was the supreme court of Christendom. No decree or book was to be considered canonical without papal assent. Furthermore, the pope was said to be beyond the judgment of any human being; his actions were to be judged by God alone. The Roman church, by which is presumably meant the papacy, had never erred, and according to the Scriptures it never would err. The Roman pontiff was sanctified by the merits of St. Peter. No one could be a true Catholic unless he agreed with the pope. A final group of propositions in the *Dictatus Papae* dealt with church-state relations. It was asserted that only the pope could use the imperial insignia, implying that the pope was the true successor to Constantine. The pope had the power to depose emperors, and it was lawful for subjects to bring accusations against their rulers to the papal see.

The *Dictatus Papae* was a sensational and extremely radical document, and it is inconceivable to think that Hildebrand was so naive as not to realize that it would make this impression. It was a statement of the revolutionary program that Gregory intended to implement: the creation of a new world order for Christian society founded on the principle that papal authority alone was universal and plenary, while all other powers in the world, whether emperors, kings, or bishops, were particular and dependent. This idea of the plenitude of papal power was by no means novel. It could be found in the radical aspects of the Gelasian doctrine, in the Donation of Constantine, and in the pronouncements of the ninth-century pope, Nicholas I. Gregory could claim with justice that every proposition in the *Dictatus Papae* was merely a quotation from one or another early medieval canon-law text. But the revolutionary quality of a program is not lessened by the fact that at distant points in the past other people had said the same thing. The *Dictatus Papae* was a revolutionary document in view of the comprehensiveness and intransigence of its assertion of papal absolutism and its contradiction of the prevailing world order. For two hundred years papal power had been in abeyance and the great bishoprics and abbeys of western Europe had flourished with little or no assistance from Rome, and certainly with no effective papal jurisdiction over their affairs. The great ecclesiastics of northern Europe could not but feel greatly disturbed by this unmitigated assertion of their absolute subservience to Rome, which went so contrary to common experience. They could not deny the legal, and perhaps even the theological, basis for Gregory's claims, but they would have been less than human if they had not felt that Gregory's program was unnecessary and imprudent and a threat to their whole way of life. The church in Germany, France, and England had done well enough for two centuries without the benefit of papal assistance. To many, and probably to most, of the great churchmen of Europe the *Dictatus Papae* appeared to be the shrill assertion of long-forgotten and rarely exercised theoretical papal authority in the interests of the personal ambitions of Hildebrand.

To the kings of western Europe the *Dictatus Papae* necessarily seemed even more revolutionary and upsetting. It claimed a papal supremacy over monarchy which had never been practiced in European history. Granted that the Donation of Constantine made such claims, no important medieval ruler had ever allowed a pope to interfere in the affairs of his realm. The assertion of this supreme papal monarchy in the world seemed all the more shocking in view of the successful leadership in western society and the unchallenged authority over territorial churches which the great western kings had exercised since the days of Charlemagne.

The churchmen and kings of western Europe were to learn very rapidly that Gregory intended to carry out the program he enunciated in the *Dictatus Papae* at the beginning of his pontificate. They were also to learn that his ideology was, if anything, more radical than was evident from the simple legal propositions of his initial programmatic statement. Drawing upon Augustinian theology, tapping the emotional resources of the new popular piety, and strongly influenced by the teachings of Humbert, Gregory proceeded during the stormy twelve years of his pontificate to refine and formulate his revolutionary ideology. Almost every letter of his voluminous official correspondence contains some part of this doctrine, but his ultimate theory of a Christian social order was drawn together and presented with tremendously persuasive force in his famous *Letter to Hermann of Metz* in 1082. Ostensibly a reply to certain questions put to him by the bishop of Metz, the *Letter* was actually a public pamphlet. It was published in many copies and sent to royal courts and important churches all over Europe.

Since the ninth century political Augustinianism had been on the wane. The social amelioration effected by the government of Charlemagne, Otto I, and Henry III visibly contradicted the bishop of Hippo's strictures on the moral quality of the state. The theocratic kings of the tenth and eleventh centuries were, in the eyes of the churchmen who assisted them, not the pirates whom Augustine had talked about but, rather, divinely commissioned leaders who did the work of the Lord. The common identification of the *ecclesia* and the *mundus* was an attitude very different from Augustine's sharp distinction between the heavenly and earthly cities. The Augustinian view that the state had no moral sanction in and for itself but derived its sanction only from its position as a servant of the church was a meaningless and irrelevant proposition in a world in which there was no clear line of distinction between church and state. But it was this political Augustinianism that Gregory VII now revived in its fullest and most intransigent form. In his *Letter to Hermann of Metz* he contended that royal power was originated by murderers and thugs and that the state continued to bear the stamp of Cain. In the whole history of the world, he said, there were scarcely half a dozen kings who had avoided the damnation of their souls, and these, such as Constantine and Theodosius the Great, had saved themselves from the fatal temptations of secular power only by their subservience to the church. Many simple and ordinary Christians, he said, were more certain recipients of divine grace than the mighty and powerful holders of royal power, who were in most cases really the instruments of the devil.

Continuing in the Augustinian vein, Gregory concluded that the only legitimate power in the world resided in the priesthood, particularly in the bishop of Rome as the vicar of Christ on earth. Only those who subjected themselves to this divinely constituted authority could hope to be included in the heavenly city. Strongly emphasizing the Pauline-Augustinian conception of liberty, he boldly asserted that the freedom of the Christian man consisted in the subjection of his selfish will to the divine ends which the papacy pursued in the world. Only a world order in which these doctrines were realized could be called just and right. Justice, Gregory insisted, was a matter not of custom or tradition or usage but one of fulfillment of the Christian ideal as he saw it. No claims of convenience or custom could be made against his doctrine. He reminded his critics that the Lord had not said, "I am tradition," but rather, "I am the Word." With an apocalyptic zeal he demanded a new right order which would fulfill the ideals of Christian justice and liberty as he had defined them. Nothing less than this total *Christianitas* was acceptable; there could be no compromise with the devil.

The new piety and emotional religiosity of the eleventh century influenced Gregory VII's outlook almost as much as Damiani's. His writings are full of references to the Virgin and to the *pauperes Christi*, "Christ's poor ones," whose assistance he summoned and whose welfare he sought. In Gregory's view this Christian poverty is not an economic or class matter—or at least it is only incidentally so. He is on the side of the poor in spirit, the meek, the humble, and the downtrodden of whatever class or group, and he is the enemy of the rich, the proud, and the powerful, whoever or where-ever they may be. His hatred for the most powerful men in Europe is based not upon a class consciousness but upon a psychological and emotional sympathy for the underdog and hostility to their lords and oppressors. Gregory's conception of Christian poverty is thus in part an attempt to read the sermon on the mount to the class-stratified society of the eleventh cen-tury. At the same time, his violent hatred for the leaders of contemporary society and his highly emotional concern for the *pauperes Christi* are probably symptoms of a paranoiac hysteria and manifestations of a deep neurosis.

Whatever the roots of Gregory's emotionally charged concept of Christian poverty, he was here opening up an important, but as yet tenuous, and hitherto almost unknown avenue in medieval thought. With the minor exception of the sermons of St. Ambrose, social criticism and a Christian social gospel had not yet made an appearance in medieval civilization. This was not to be expected in the agrarian society of the early middle ages, in which all literate forms of expression were the preserve of the landed classes. The emergence in the eleventh century, especially in northern Italy, of new bourgeois and proletarian groups, affected as they were by the new emotional piety, was bound to change all this. Whatever Gregory's inten-tions in his emphasis upon the spiritual superiority of the poor Christians, his teachings were bound to give encouragement to the underprivileged and ambitious classes of the European cities. Given the religious orientation of all forms of thought in the eleventh century and the pietistic outlook of the city dwellers, their social disaffection was bound to be expressed in mil-lennial and apocalyptic doctrines. They, the underprivileged, were the poor who deserved to inherit the earth, or at least much more of it than the established landed classes were willing to allow them. Gregory's emotional attitude toward Christian poverty therefore found a fertile seed-bed in the social disaffection and millennial yearnings of the new urban classes.

The ambiguous meaning of poverty, referring both to lack of wealth and to spiritual qualities, was encouraged by the Gospel itself, for the first Christians, the members of the apostolic church, the original disciples of the Lord, were poor in all senses of the word, both spiritually and eco-nomically. Was this a necessary relationship? To achieve that ideal state of poverty of the soul, that humility which was a sign of Divine Grace, was it necessary to divest oneself of worldly goods? This question was to become an agonizing dilemma for the church in the high middle ages. Gregory's enthusiasm for Christian poverty accentuated the central im-portance of this problem in medieval thought without doing much to resolve it.

The last of the four Gregorian reformers, Pope Paschal II, the only radical Gregorian aside from Hildebrand himself to obtain the papal throne, carried the debate much further and provided a definite answer, although one unpalatable to the great majority of the leading churchmen of his time. Paschal had been a monk in the monastery of Vallombrosa, near Florence, one of the new ascetic and reform communities. He entered into the papal service as an ardent disciple of Gregory VII and remained to the end of his days, long after the high tide of revolutionary ardor had begun to ebb at Rome, an intransigent high Gregorian. After serving as papal legate in Spain, where the fanaticism of the warrior Iberian Christians engaged in the *Reconquista* gave him no cause to lessen his puritanical zeal, he was elected pope in 1099. The nineteen years of his pontificate were marked by his stubborn continuance of the struggle with the German emperor Henry V, by a conflict over church-state relations with the English king, and by his support of a reckless and bootless scheme for a crusade against Byzantium. In 1111 he startled Europe by announcing that he had arrived at a concordat with the German emperor, ending the long conflict between empire and papacy. But when the terms of the peace treaty were published, his rebellious and angry cardinals forced him to repudiate the settlement.

Paschal's solution of the debate over church-state relations was both simple and radical. Since the origin of the controversy lay in the question of the relative jurisdictions of *regnum* and *sacerdotium,* he proposed to the emperor that the German churchmen surrender to the imperial crown their lands and secular offices and constitute themselves a purely spiritual church. In return, Henry V promised not to interfere with the affairs of the German bishops and abbots; of course, the delighted emperor could afford to do this in view of the tremendous accretion of landed wealth and public offices he was given by Paschal's proposal.

Historians have generally failed to perceive the significance of Paschal's concession. It was neither the unaccountable act of an eccentric old man, as some have thought, nor was it the consequence of *force majeure* on the part of the emperor, as the papal court later claimed in repudiating Paschal's treaty. The Concordat of 1111 was fully in accord with Paschal's ideological position, which was in turn an offshoot of radical Gregorianism. Just as the new ascetic monastic orders had taken inflexible vows of poverty in imitation of the apostolic church, so Paschal, who was a product of this puritanical movement, had moved in the direction of the idea of the apostolic poverty of the whole church and the doctrine of a purely spiritual church "poor" in every sense of the term. This may be said to be a logical development of Gregory VII's emotional, if ambiguous, advocacy of Christian poverty.

The provocative doctrine of the apostolic poverty of the church thus makes its first clear appearance in the policy of the last of the Gregorian popes. Rejected by the high medieval papacy, looked upon with horror by the wealthy and powerful ecclesiastics of western Europe, this doctrine was to find favor with the popular heretical movements of the twelfth, thirteenth, and fourteenth centuries. It was to be advocated at the end of the thirteenth century by the radical wing of the Franciscan order, whose own religious heritage is derived ultimately from that same north Italian asceticism of the eleventh century that produced Paschal II. The doctrine of apostolic poverty was condemned by the papacy as a heresy in 1323, but it continued for many decades thereafter to be a source of debate and confusion in the life of the medieval church. Frequently, in the indistinct thought-world of medieval popular heresy, the doctrine of the apostolic poverty of the church is found to be held jointly with that millennial social gospel which also has roots in the teachings of Gregory VII.

The intellectual consequences of the Gregorian reform must be seen as extremely heterogeneous and complex. The Gregorians propounded doctrines which built up papal authority, the centralized organization of the church, and the power of the sacerdotal office—and at the same time undermined them. The doctrines of plenitude of power, papal infallibility, and subservience of monarchy to the priesthood were Gregorian. But from the teachings of the Gregorian reformers also came those ideas which eventually played a leading role in the dissolution of the medieval world order: religious individualism, Donatism, the millennial social gospel, and the doctrine of the apostolic poverty of the church.

In their own day the Gregorians by no means had the forum of public debate to themselves. On the contrary, their discussions of the nature of a Christian world order called forth a variety of comments, critiques, and treatises reflecting almost every shade of opinion. It is indicative of both the intense feelings which the Gregorian reform aroused and the increase of literacy in the eleventh century that the surviving treatises of the period on church-state relations fill more than two thousand pages when printed in modern folio. It is not much of an exaggeration to say that it seems that around the year 1100 almost every monk in western Europe was writing a pamphlet on church and kingship.

Three representative and typical expressions of the criticisms directed against the Gregorians may be considered. There was first of all the reactionary position expatiating on the early medieval tradition of theocratic kingship and asserting that the king was the anointed of the Lord, "and through Grace he is God," as the English churchman who wrote the treatises that are commonly called the *Anonymous of York* tractates contended in the year 1104. Second, there was the conservative Cluniac position exemplified by the *Treatise on Royal and Sacerdotal Power* by Hugh of Fleury, the French royal abbey allied with Cluny. Hugh directly attacks Gregory's denigration of the moral sanctions of kingship and concludes that, for the sake of right order in society, monarchy must continue to be superior to priesthood. The final position, and one of the most interesting and important of the period, was taken by the great canon lawyer, Bishop Ivo of Chartres. This wise and shrewd scholar expressed his doubts that the prevailing social order was actually contrary to the canon law and the demands of church dogma. But even if it were, he said, the sanction of social custom had to predominate even over the exigencies of written law and theology. Since the prevailing order had such wide support among the laity and even among the clergy that it could not be abolished without a schism, Ivo concluded, the reformers had better be content with a discreet protestation and hope for slow reform. The ideologists of the Gregorian papacy, however, were no more willing to listen to the moderate opinion of Ivo of Chartres—who was told by Rome to keep silent—than to the fulminations of royalist reactionaries and the bitter protests of Cluniac conservatives.

To many contemporary churchmen, sincere and devout in their calling, the Gregorians were not so much doctrinally wrong as imprudent, naive, provincial. In countries where kingship was strong, especially in Anglo-Norman England and the German empire, the higher clergy had come to respect monarchy, in whose presence they literally stood with great frequency as royal councilors and ministers. The Gregorians, in contrast with such churchmen, were indeed naive and provincial. Nearly all of them came from Lorraine and northern Italy, where royal power was weak and disorganized and where no one, least of all a monk, could gain much respect for kingship. None of them had the opportunity to work in a royal chancery and to become acquainted with the personality of a Henry III or a William the Conqueror or to gain insight into the tremendous problems of eleventh-century government. Kingship was an idea for the Gregorians, something to be studied in Augustine or Gelasius; it was neither a brutal fact of everyday life nor a glorious sentiment (as it was to the higher clergy of England and Germany). The Gregorians were learned, devout, brave, and even intellectually brilliant men, but they were profoundly lacking in the wisdom and moderation that came from years of intimacy with power and majesty—knowledge that could not be gained in patristic literature, in canon-law collections, by devotions in a monastic oratory, or even by drawing upon the rich intellectual resources of the new piety and the new logic.

III. The German Investiture Controversy

In 1075 the Salian German emperor Henry IV was the most powerful ruler in Europe, at least east of Normandy. Yet the "holy Satan," Gregory VII, setting out to implement his program of justice and liberty, did not fear to demand that the German king immediately give up the institution of lay investiture by which he controlled the appointment of the great churchmen of his realm, and the pope threatened to depose Henry if he did not obey this decree. Gregory's attack on the institutional basis of Salian power came at a crucial time in the development of the empire; it precipitated a fifty-year struggle which, in the opinion of many German historians, decided the fate of Germany.

Henry IV had ascended to the throne on his father's premature death in 1056, but for nine years he was a minor, and until he attained his majority in 1056 his hold on the crown was very insecure. The aggressive policy of centralization which Henry III had pursued had frightened the German nobility, and they determined to take advantage of the sudden reversal of fortune of the Salian house to strip the crown of its powers. Following along the lines set down by the tenth-century Ottonians, Henry had based his power on his control of the resources and personnel of the church, exercised through the doctrines of theocratic monarchy and the institutions of lay investiture, the proprietary church system, and advocacy over the great monasteries of the realm. In addition, Henry III had made use of royal *ministeriales* to garrison the crown castles which he had built all over the realm and especially in the northern duchy of Saxony, whose nobility and free peasantry had continued to exhibit a strong separatist tendency. It appears to have been Henry's intention to incorporate the recalcitrant Saxon duchy into the family possessions of the Salian house, adding this territory to the native Salian duchy of Franconia to form extensive crown lands. The fulfillment of this dynastic policy would have placed the Salian monarchy in a position of overwhelming superiority with reference to the German nobility and would have been the capstone in the building of royal authority in Germany which had begun with the work of Otto I in the middle of the tenth century. It was through the expansion of their crown lands that the Capetian monarchs were able to ascend to supreme authority in France in the twelfth and thirteenth centuries.

The German nobility, led by the recalcitrant Saxons, determined to take advantage of the sudden death of the great emperor Henry III in 1056 and the succession of a minor. The result was nine years of rebellion and civil war in Germany, in which the duchies exhibited the traditional centrifugal tendencies. But the German episcopate, even in Saxony, remained loyal to the monarchy and saved the throne for the young Henry IV. The wisdom of Otto I's alliance with the German church thus received fresh confirmation.

When Henry IV became king in fact in 1065, he brought this decentralizing tendency to an immediate halt and set about continuing the work of his father. Henry was perhaps the ablest and wisest German ruler of the middle ages. Certainly no other German king exhibited more cunning, energy, and inflexible determination in advancing the cause of royal authority. Henry believed that the key to the problem was the duchy of Saxony, where he continued his father's building of castles and embarked upon a policy of not only stripping the nobility of their autonomous privileges but also pushing down the mass of free peasantry into a status of manorial serfdom completely dependent upon the crown. The inevitable consequence was another great rebellion in Germany, in which the aroused nobility and peasantry of the north were supported by dissident aristocrats in the rest of the realm and even by a few disaffected bishops. The struggle, however, was an unequal one, for on the king's side were the great majority of the bishops, the royal *ministeriales,* many of the lower nobility, the wealthy monasteries under royal control, and the new burgher class of the Rhenish cities. By 1075 Henry IV had won a complete victory. The rebel leaders of the aristocracy had been humbled, and the Saxon peasantry had lost great numbers in battle and had come to feel that they had been betrayed by the nobility. The way now appeared to be open for the creation of a strong and unified state in Germany, paralleling the degree of central authority in the lands under the rule of the duke of Normandy and anticipating the French monarchy of the thirteenth century.

At this critical juncture the German king received the papal decree against lay investiture with the accompanying threat of deposition if he did not obey immediately. Henry had not been unaware of the great changes taking place at Rome. During his minority the papal election decree of 1059 had divested him of the prerogative of dominating the papal elections which his predecessors had enjoyed for a century. But, engaged as he was in pressing domestic concerns, he had been prepared to let Italian affairs take their course at least until he could give them his undivided attention. Henry's natural disposition toward Rome appears to have been cautious and moderate, and it is likely that, if let alone, he would not have interfered with the new independence of the papacy. But given the aggressive policy which Gregory undertook from the very beginning of his pontificate, it was impossible for Henry to avoid a conflict with Rome. The initial dispute between the pope and the emperor was over a relatively minor issue, but one indicative of a much deeper underlying conflict. Shortly after Hilde-brand became pope, the episcopal see of the febrile community of Milan fell vacant, and Henry and Gregory each maneuvered to secure the election of his own candidate. Gregory regarded this as an indication of the fact that the German king had not given up his claim to dominate the affairs of northern Italy, and perhaps it caused Gregory to accelerate his attack on the institutional basis of imperial power—its alliance with the German church—by means of the papal ultimatum of 1075. Flushed with his great triumph over the nobility, Henry decided to take the strongest possible line in replying to Gregory's demands, and he found enthusiastic support for this policy among the German churchmen. For a long time they had been more aware than the king of the revolutionary course of the Hildebrandine papacy, and they were no more eager than Henry himself to abandon the prevailing system of church-state relations in Germany.

Consequently, at the beginning of 1076 the clerical scholars at the royal court prepared a letter to be sent in the king's name to Rome in reply to the papal decree on investiture, damning "Hildebrand, at present not pope but false monk," in the strongest possible terms. One of the outstanding examples of medieval Latin rhetoric and reflecting the learning and literary skill of the Salian chancery, Henry's letter constituted nothing less than a defense of the prevailing world order and a declaration of war on the pope who had presumed to dissolve this beneficent system. Henry informed Gregory that his conduct as pope had brought confusion and malediction upon the church, that he had dared to rise up against the royal power conferred on Henry by God, and that he had threatened to divest the Lord's anointed of his kingdom, which Henry had received from the hand of God. Gregory, it was claimed, had usurped the apostolic chair; he had practiced violence under the cloak of religion and betrayed the teachings of St. Peter. The letter concluded with the stirring peroration that Hilde-brand was now called upon by Henry, king by the Grace of God, and by all the imperial bishops, to come down from the throne of Peter. Some of the surviving copies of the letter add an eternal damnation for the pope.

Henry IV's letter to Gregory VII was the desperate cry of self-justification upon the part of early medieval kingship, which had reached its culmination in the Salian empire of Henry III and his son. But Hildebrand seems to have anticipated such a reply. He was not afraid of the imperial army, because in the preceding two decades the papacy had found powerful allies in Italy to serve as a balance of power against the great northern king—namely, the new Norman rulers of southern Italy and Sicily. At first the papacy had been hostile to the Norman invasion of the territory south of Rome, but by the end of the 1050's the papal court had come to realize that the

Normans could be made into a counterweight against the troublesome Roman nobility and ultimately even against the German emperor, whose vague claims to hegemony in Italy the Normans as well as the papacy could be expected to oppose. The Norman-Italian rulers in turn needed papal sanction to give an aura of legitimacy to their naked seizure of the south Italian realms, which had previously been held by a motley crew of Moslem, Byzantine, and Latin princes. This recognition was gladly given by the papacy in order to cement an alliance with the Norman rulers, whose armies provided the necessary military support which the papacy hitherto lacked. In addition to this southern support Gregory could look for assistance in the north to the wealthy and powerful countess Matilda of Tuscany, a pious widow on friendly terms with Gregory himself. Matilda is the earliest example of that new type of independent aristocratic lady of great power and prestige which was to play an occasionally significant role in the politics and society of the high middle ages. Although she was a distant relative of the German king, the pope apparently felt that Matilda could be relied upon to protect him from Henry IV's wrath if the occasion arose.

Acting with characteristic speed and determination, Gregory deposed Henry on receipt of his contumacious and insulting letter and sent papal agents into Germany to stir the ashes of the recent rebellion into a new flame of civil war. Every dissident element in Germany was now accorded a new and unprecedented pretext for attacking royal authority, and rebellion in self-interest was given divine sanction. It is likely, however, that Henry could have weathered this storm if Gregory had not taken the precaution of trying to preclude the continuance of the traditional support given by the great German ecclesiastics of the crown.

The bishops and abbots were informed by the papal agents and by letters sent directly from Rome that on pain of excommunication they were no longer to recognize Henry IV as their king. Excommunication was still a very powerful instrument in the spiritual armory of the papacy; Europe was still a long way from the time when the force of this weapon was to be blunted by excessive use. Furthermore, there was a real possibility that Gregory would triumph in his struggle with the German king, and the ecclesiastics of the empire, fearing for their own security, hesitated to risk their offices and status by openly siding with Henry IV. The immediate effect, therefore, of the papal decree of deposition was a stunning collapse of royal power. Since at least two-thirds of Henry's army came from ecclesiastical lands, he had lost the greater part of his military power without a blow being struck. By the end of 1076 the king found himself almost completely isolated, as the bewildered and frightened German ecclesiastics withdrew their support of the Salian house. The German nobility exulted in this unexpected reversal of their fortunes, and reasserting the old electoral principle in the German monarchy at papal suggestion, they set in motion the constitutional process of electing a new king from outside the Salian dynasty.

The court clerics convinced the king that only his surrender to Gregory and papal forgiveness of his purported sinful acts could save his throne. He determined to go to Italy and personally seek absolution from the pope. It was necessary for Henry to do this as quickly as possible, for Gregory had announced his intention of going to Germany to preside at the assembly of the German nobility which would formally divest Henry of his crown and elect a new king.

A contemporary German monastic chronicler of royalist sympathies has given us a probably romanticized account of how the desperate Henry IV rushed southward, accompanied by only a handful of retainers, through lands infested with his enemies. At the same time Gregory, traveling in a slower and more ceremonial manner, had set out from Rome with the intention of getting into Germany before the king could seek an audience with him. This melodramatic race, which held the attention of all Europe, was won by Henry. He encountered the pope at Matilda of Tuscany's castle of Canossa, in northern Italy, where Gregory had been received as a guest by the countess.

The events which occurred at Canossa in the winter of 1077 constitute one of the great dramas of European history. Contemporary royalist chroniclers describe, with pardonable exaggeration, how Henry stood in the snow for three days until at last the pope was willing to give him an audience and receive his penitent pleas for forgiveness and absolution. Actually, the events that occurred at Canossa were not only high drama but a crucial political encounter of great consequence for the subsequent development of the German investiture controversy, as both king and pope well knew. Henry needed papal absolution if he was to hold his throne, and Gregory was most unwilling to grant this at the very moment of the collapse of Henry's power, when the pope was on his way to attend a great assembly which would elect a papally approved candidate as German king. By the tradition and law of the church, however, no priest, let alone the vicar of Christ on earth, could refuse the comforts of absolution to a sincerely penitent and confessed sinner. Gregory very much doubted, and with good reason, that Henry was genuinely penitent, but it was difficult for him to proclaim this publicly in view of Henry's great show of remorse. Consequently, the pope ignored the king's plea for an audience for three days. Matilda of Tuscany interceded with the pope on behalf of her kinsman; no ruler or great lord, at least outside of Germany, enjoyed seeing the continued humiliation of one of the great anointed kings of Christendom.

Probably not even Matilda's entreaties would have moved Gregory in his moment of triumph. It was only the unwelcome appearance at Canossa of abbot Hugh of Cluny and his unrelenting intercession on Henry's behalf that forced Gregory's hand. Abbot Hugh was the most widely respected and beloved churchman of his day. He and Hildebrand had always disliked each other, and the Gregorian and Cluniac world views strongly clashed, but Gregory could not afford to ignore the advice of the revered and saintly abbot. To have done so would have endangered his own position in Europe, for Gregory well realized that the crowned heads of Europe stood aghast at such novel events as were transpiring at Canossa. He knew that the active opposition of the Cluniac elder statesman of the church would have sufficed to turn public opinion against him and bring about the alignment of the other kings and rulers of Europe alongside the now vanquished Salian monarch. Hence Gregory finally gave Henry the audience he sought, heard his confession, and absolved him; he then made him promise to obey the papal decrees and restored him to his royal status.

In the pope's eyes, if not in the opinion of the disappointed German nobility, there was now no need for electing a new king. Gregory abandoned his planned transalpine journey and dispatched a triumphant letter to the German nobility informing them of the events that had transpired at Canossa and of his peace with the penitent king, who had vowed to be henceforth a loyal servant of the papacy. But Henry, returning to his kingdom, also departed from Canossa in a victorious mood. He had saved his throne and had been given time to re-establish his power. It is most unlikely that he ever intended to observe the oath he had taken at Canossa, and within a year, as he made his intentions public, he was again deposed by the pope. But Henry was never again to be in the helpless position in which he had found himself at the end of 1076, and in fact, in the half century of the German investiture controversy, the papacy was never again to be anywhere as close to total victory as it had been on the morrow of Gregory's initial attack on the German monarchy. After Canossa some German ecclesiasticals had second thoughts and once again threw in their lot with the Salian house. For example, the abbot of the great monastery of Fulda, founded by St. Boniface, was in Henry's later years the head of the royal chancery. With some ecclesiastical support and with the aid of the royal *ministeriales* and armies raised from the crown lands, the German king held his own in the long and bitter war with the German nobility. In 1085 Henry was momentarily powerful enough to take vengeance by driving his papal archenemy from Rome to refuge among his Norman allies in southern Italy, an humiliating exile from which Gregory did not return. Henry IV's last years were embittered by the rebellion of his son, who joined the German nobility against him, but this was mainly a personal and dynastic matter. On his succession to the German throne in 1106, Henry V continued the war against the papacy and its allies in Germany.

Both contemporaries and many modern writers have debated the question of whether it was the pope or the emperor who gained the most from the dramatic confrontation at Canossa. It was clear that both parties gained and lost something and that neither won a total victory. Canossa restored the German crown to Henry, but considering his abnegation before the pope, it also dealt a fatal blow to the ideology of theocratic kingship, upon which the Salian dynasty had relied so extensively. Furthermore, in being forced to obtain papal absolution, Henry gave substance to the Gregorian claim that the papacy had the right to judge and depose even the most prestigious ruler in Europe. Certainly Gregory had cause to exult that the moral power of the papacy had been demonstrated when the greatest ruler of the west was literally forced to become a penitent at his feet. Canossa signified that the bishop of Rome, who had played an insignificant role in the political affairs of Europe for two centuries, would now be a central figure in the affairs of European states.

Gregory's triumph, however, was not unmitigated. Canossa sowed those seeds of doubt and concern about the good intentions and moral standards of the papacy which were to grow rapidly in the following century. The kings of western Europe had been put on their guard and were reluctantly forced to undertake a careful reappraisal of their relations with the church. Canossa made archaic the equilibrium of the early eleventh century. Even conscientious and devout churchmen now had to ask themselves why as sincere and able a ruler as Henry should have been put in such a miserable position. In discussing Canossa a century later, the church historian and imperial prince bishop Otto of Freising refused to see absolute right or wrong on either side. He felt that Gregory had gone to extremes, and he doubted the pope's prudence and, by implication, his good intentions. Thus the magnificent demonstration of papal authority at Canossa had a far-reaching and complex influence on the moral consciousness of medieval society. It signaled the sudden resurgence of Roman leadership in Europe and at the same time set in motion that long chain of disillusionment and controversy which was to end two and a quarter centuries later in another little Italian town with the demise of the medieval papacy.

After Canossa Gregory and Henry fought each other with relentless hatred and all the resources, both moral and physical, that they could summon. The pope again announced the deposition of the Salian ruler and joined with the rebellious German nobility in setting up an anti-king. Similarly, Henry found a north Italian bishop who was willing to take the gamble of being installed as the anti-pope. These maneuvers had little or no effect, and the investiture conflict turned out to be a draw. After Gregory's death in 1085, and particularly during the pontificate of the former Cluniac monk Urban II (1088–1099), the papacy's determination began to slacken. While officially asserting his loyalty to Gregory's policies, Urban began to seek for a way out of the war of attrition in which the papacy had become involved. He tried to unite Europe behind the Roman pontiff through the preaching of the first crusade. Urban's departure from Gregorian ideology was indicated by his willingness to grant the Norman rulers of England and southern Italy the same domination over their territorial churches which Gregory had condemned in the case of Germany. But the ending of the German investiture conflict had become a most difficult matter involving the necessity of saving face on both sides, and Urban was not able to find a way out of this impasse. It needed hardly be said that no supporter of the German king joined the first crusade.

Urban's successor, Paschal II, renewed the struggle, but after a decade even this intransigent high Gregorian wanted to call a halt to the seemingly endless conflict. His radical solution, as we have seen, while it pleased Henry V, was unacceptable to almost everyone else. By the latter part of the second decade of the twelfth century a new generation of cardinals had come to dominate the papal government. Their experience in law and administration conditioned them to view the world from the standpoint of careful bureaucrats rather than that of aggressive ideologists. To these new men the all-or-nothing policy of the Gregorian papacy seemed both dangerous and unnecessary. They envisioned the enhancement of papal authority through the institutional means of legal and administrative centralization of the church rather than by a desperate war with the rulers of Europe. The new leaders at Rome agreed in general with Gregory's ultimate aims, but emotionally they were not inclined to adopt the means he employed. What they wanted to preserve in Gregory's program was the institutional reforms he had inaugurated: the increase in the bureaucracy of the papal court, the sending of legates, or papal ambassadors, to all parts of Europe, and the establishment of the Roman Curia as the effective high court of the church. But they were willing to work slowly for the fulfillment of these ends, to come to terms with the kings of western Europe where necessary, and to bargain hard and continuously for limited concessions rather than dare to risk all on a fundamental conflict. It is this moderate, bureaucratic, legalistic spirit, contrasting markedly with the apocalyptic frenzy of Humbert and Hildebrand, which distinguishes the papacy of the twelfth century from the Gregorian revolution. A policy of "thorough" was replaced by a policy of "piecemeal."

The new generation of cardinals regarded the German investiture controversy as an embarrassing vestige of a now vanished age, and they were willing to make extensive concessions in order to achieve a compromise with Henry V. The principle upon which the short-lived English investiture controversy of 1103–1107 had been terminated was consequently resurrected and embodied in the Concordat of Worms of 1122 between Calixtus II and Henry V. The emperor abandoned the institution of lay investiture with its overtones of the now discredited doctrine of theocratic kingship. But he was allowed to require the homage of bishops and abbots in his domains before they were invested with the symbols of their offices. Thus the papacy granted to the German king the right to exercise a veto over the appointment of German ecclesiastics and, by implication, to maintain the decisive voice in their selection.

This compromise had allowed the English king to maintain his practical control over the affairs of the church in his realm. But the effect of the Concordat of Worms was by no means a simple return to the *status quo ante bellum,* because the half century of the investiture controversy had brought about such vast changes in the German political and social structure that the king was unable to take full advantage of the papal concessions. In many parts of the realm the great dukes had gained a semi-autonomous territorial sovereignty, and it was they and not the king who benefited from the Concordat's grant of jurisdiction over ecclesiastical appointments in their duchies. In still other parts of Germany, particularly in the Rhineland, the great bishops themselves had become territorial princes whom the monarchy could no longer dominate. Thus, as far as Henry V and his successors were concerned, the Concordat of Worms in effect gave them the right to control the appointments of bishops and abbots only in the territories belonging to their own families.

This cataclysmic decline in the German crown's traditional domination over the resources and personnel of the church was paralleled by its losses in other directions. Many of the royal *ministeriales* on whom the eleventh-century German monarchy had so heavily depended proved unreliable. They took advantage of the confusions of the long civil war to usurp control over the royal castles they were guarding and to bargain for their legal freedom with king or anti-king, thereby becoming lords in their own right. By the early twelfth century some of these former *ministeriales* were marrying into the old noble families, and not a few of the great aristocrats of modern Germany are descendants of Salian serf-knights. This weakening of royal institutions was contemporaneous with the advancing power of the territorial princes. In German history the period of the investiture conflict signifies a tremendous growth in the territorial sovereignty of the dukes and other great lords and the creation of provincial autonomy, which was not overcome until the second half of the nineteenth century. It is therefore with considerable justice that many German historians claim that the period between 1075 and 1122 determined the German fate.

The growth of territorial sovereignty and aristocratic power in Germany was greatly abetted by the extensive feudalization of the country for the first time. Vassalage was not unknown in Germany before the investiture conflict, but the feudal pattern was fragmentary and relatively unimportant, especially in the northern half of the land. Fifty years of civil war produced far-reaching political and social changes. The great lords imposed homage on their knights and placed themselves at the head of feudal armies. By the 1120's the bonds of vassalage had proliferated among the landed classes. This extensive feudalization of German society was a catastrophe for the monarchy, because the feudal pyramid in Germany, as in France before 1150, was truncated. The feudal bonds did not ascend to the king's level; they terminated in the suzerainty of the great aristocrats. The vassals of the great lords were bound by no feudal relationship to the king, and their loyalty was henceforth given to the territorial princes, who now had large and well-trained armies to use against the monarchy. The king's military power was derived only from his position as feudal overlord in his native family duchy. But circumscribed as he now was by the virtually independent territorial princes, his private resources were inadequate to restore the shattered structure of central authority. Many great lords, taking advantage of their new autonomy, usurped the king's former control of ecclesiastical property by assuming the advocacy of the great monasteries and the lordship over proprietary churches. Thus the nobility adopted for their own benefit and to the detriment of royal power some of the favorite Ottonian-Salian institutions.

To insure the continued weakness of the monarchy, the nobility perpetuated the electoral nature of German kingship. While, in constitutional theory, the electoral principle had never entirely died out and the Ottonian and Salian rulers had taken the precaution of having their sons elected before the royal deaths, in actual practice the tenth and eleventh centuries witnessed the substitution of hereditary succession. But under the urgings of the Gregorian papacy the nobility revivified the electoral idea. The clerical theorist Manegold of Lautenbach produced a treatise presenting a purely functionalized view of the German monarchy in which the king was compared to a swineherd, employed for a specific purpose, who could be dismissed if he displeased his employer. This radical Augustinian view of the German monarchy pleased the territorial princes, who naturally saw the king as a functionary of very limited powers, chosen and, if necessary, removed from office by themselves. For a quarter of a century following Henry V's death in 1125 the German monarchy conformed to Manegold's swineherd principle. The king was chosen by the princes, given no resources outside those of his own duchy, and prevented from exercising any real authority or leadership in the realm. The royal title was furthermore passed from one family to another to preclude the development of any dynastic interest in the German crown.

Thus, when Frederick I of Hohenstaufen was chosen as king in 1152, the royal power had been in effective abeyance for a quarter of a century and to a very considerable degree for eighty years. The only untapped resources of the crown lay in northern Italy, over whose wealthy cities the emperor had a nominal claim of suzerainty. As a consequence of the investiture conflict, any king bent on regaining the authority which the Salians had exercised had to look to Italy. But the age of the investiture conflict had also witnessed great changes in northern Italy, which made any attempt at the real exercise of imperial power there highly problematical. Since the time of Henry III the Italian cities had experienced no effective rule by their nominal German overlord. And this was precisely the period of their tremendous expansion in wealth and population and the development of their communal institutions. The northern Italian cities, by the middle of the twelfth century, were dominated by narrow oligarchies of merchant and industrial entrepreneurs, ready and able to fight for the preservation of their status and power. They were the natural allies of the papal court, which greatly feared the reappearance of the emperor in Italy. The emperor could see no way of restoring royal authority in Germany except by conquest of northern Italy, but the pope felt that if the emperor should triumph in Italy, he would destroy the independence of the papacy. The investiture controversy, by decimating the resources of the German crown, paradoxically brought the papacy into inevitable conflict with the first ambitious and able prince to come to the Roman throne after the Concordat of Worms. The transformation of northern Italy during the period of the investiture controversy, however, made unlikely the success of such an imperial venture.

To these catastrophic political consequences of the struggle between pope and emperor may be added a cultural disaster: Germany's loss of the intellectual leadership of western Europe. In 1050 the German monasteries were great centers of learning and art, and the German schools of theology and canon law were unsurpassed and probably unmatched anywhere in Europe. The long civil war and the acrimonious disputes between church and state seem to have syphoned off the energy and diverted the attention of the German churchmen. They were assiduous in producing treatises on church-state relations, but they ignored the tremendous advances in philosophy, law, literature, and art which were taking place during the same period west of the Rhine and south of the Alps. Thus German intellectual life fell out of step with the times and slowly became backward and archaic. At the beginning of the twelfth century French and Italian scholars were in the process of creating a new institution for higher thought and education which was to play the central role in the intellectual life of the high middle ages, but the first such university was not established in Germany until the fourteenth century. Culturally as well as politically the Germans fell behind during the investiture conflict and never quite caught up, at least not during the middle ages.

Chapter Thirteen

THE ANGLO-NORMAN
MONARCHY AND
THE EMERGENCE OF THE
BUREAUCRATIC STATE

I. The Triumph of William the Bastard

In his later years Gregory VII seems to have wondered at times whether he had undertaken to fight the real enemy. He became concerned with the ecclesiastical policy of the new Anglo-Norman monarchy, but he was not able to diminish in any way the authority of William the Bastard, now usually called the Conqueror, over the English church. With the decline of the Salian monarchy the Anglo-Norman ruler's position as the most powerful king in Europe was unchallenged. William and his sons were able to advance English royal institutions to a point of perfection and efficiency hitherto unknown in medieval Europe. They ended by developing a new kind of medieval kingship which relied upon administration and law to unify the realm, allowing them to dispense with the traditional ideological basis of monarchy. At the very time that the Gregorian revolution was undermining the old religious foundation of kingship, the Anglo-Norman rulers were fashioning a most effective substitution which was relatively invulnerable to papal condemnations. The Norman conquest, therefore, is of the greatest significance for medieval civilization, because it made possible the creation of a new kind of state, initiating the movement toward the secularism and absolutism which was to mark the twelfth and thirteenth centuries.

In 1066 England was what the economic historian Reginald Lennard has called an "old land." Although the northern part of the country, being unsuited for agriculture, was very sparsely settled, the southern half, particularly the fertile central region, was intensively colonized. The total population of England at the time of the Norman conquest was a million people, which made it a rather thickly settled country; five centuries later the English population was still less than four million. In 1066 London was already an important commercial city, and there were other ports in the south and the east carrying on extensive trade with the continent. Later Anglo-Saxon England appears to have been a very wealthy country. The Anglo-Saxon coinage was among the best in Europe, and the Danegeld, a tax levied by the English king to fight the Scandinavian invaders, brought in enormous amounts of specie. The Anglo-Saxons were furthermore a devout and intelligent people. They had renowned saints, good poets, and skillful artists working on illuminated manuscripts and jewelry.

In spite of all these promising conditions England was ripe for foreign conquest in the middle of the eleventh century. The Anglo-Saxons offer a prime example of a people who were good at everything except government and warfare, and this lack was the undoing of the Anglo-Saxon monarchy. The local English shire and hundred courts, which were a continuation of the old Germanic folk moots, were reasonably effective, but the central government's administrative institutions were weak and primitive, and the great lords, or earls, easily usurped the legal and financial prerogatives of the crown. This political backwardness was accompanied by military weakness. While the armed and mounted knight had become the mainstay of continental armies, the English in 1066 had still not learned to fight on horseback. For thirty years in the early eleventh century England had been part of a great Danish empire, and it was the Scandinavian ruler Canute who was probably the most effective king in Anglo-Saxon history. After Canute's death his great northern empire disintegrated, and the English lay and ecclesiastical nobility found in a continental monastery a surviving member of Alfred's line and placed him on the English throne. The resulting reign of Edward the Confessor (1042–1066) was marked by the incipient political disintegration of the kingdom in the face of the advancing territorial power of the great earls. The childless Edward's death precipitated a succession crisis, and the king of Norway prepared his fleet for the invasion of England. The Anglo-Saxon nobility, in line with the old Germanic electoral tradition, chose the most powerful of the earls, Harold Godwinson, as king of the English folk. But William the Bastard, the ambitious duke of Normandy, claimed the throne by right of succession through his great-aunt and furthermore maintained that both Edward and Harold had promised him the throne on the Confessor's death.

The American historian of Norman institutions, C. H. Haskins, called the Normans the supermen of the eleventh century. A more judicious description is that of Ordericus Vitalis, a contemporary Anglo-Norman writer who said that the Normans were a good and able people when ruled by a strong man, but inclined to a natural violence and disorder when their ruler was weak. William the Bastard had been able to channel the aggressive characteristics of his people in a constructive direction. Following lines already set down by his predecessors and with the advice and support of experienced and learned churchmen, many of whom came from territories at least nominally within the Salian empire, he had created the most centralized feudal state in Europe and at the same time succeeded in winning an enviable reputation as a friend and patron of the church, which stood him in good stead at Rome.

William was able to make good use of both of these feudal and ecclesiastical foundations of his power in preparing for the invasion of England. He summoned out almost the whole feudal army of the duchy, which constituted a thousand knights. The continued rise in population among the landed classes in the duchy, which had not been significantly diminished by the departure of Norman freebooters to southern Italy, meant a shortage of fiefs in Normandy and made the warrior class extremely eager for foreign ventures. In addition, William recruited mercenaries from among the landless knights of Flanders and Brittany, and he was able to cross the channel with an army of as many as 1,500 knights together with the necessary bowmen and supporting infantry. By eleventh-century standards it was an enormous military force.

The probability of William's success was enhanced by the moral support which he received from Rome. At the urging of cardinal Hildebrand the supreme pontiff had sent the duke a papal banner, which he carried with him to England. Why did the papacy support William's conquest? The Norman duke had an hereditary claim to the throne, which Harold lacked, and it might be argued that he was more throne-worthy than the English earl, that is, more able to provide effective rule. But such traditional reasons were only peripheral in papal consideration. The Roman Curia was dissatisfied with the condition of the Anglo-Saxon church, which it believed had conducted its affairs too independently and which it held to be retrograde and corrupt. In fact, in 1066 a scandalous situation prevailed in the see of Canterbury; the papacy claimed that the incumbent archbishop had not been canonically elected and deposed him, but Harold Godwinson was reckless enough to refuse to carry out the papal decision. The papal administration under Hildebrand's direction expected that William's conquest of England would bring about the reform of the English church and its close association with Rome. This turned out to be an only partially correct assumption as a consequence of Hildebrand's failure to assess realistically the ecclesiastical policy of the Norman duke. He had been greatly impressed by William's reputation as a pious friend and supporter of the church, but he did not take into account the nature of church-state relations in Normandy, which were markedly similar to those that prevailed in the Salian empire. Hildebrand's pardonable error in judgment opened the way for the establishment of the Norman system of church-state relations in England.

The pictorial account of the Bayeux tapestry and the vivid, if somewhat confused, details given by contemporary writers depict for us the Battle of Hastings, which decided the fate of England. They showed that the Anglo-Saxons put up a good fight—better than could be expected under the circumstances, for Harold's army was exhausted after having just defeated the invading Norwegians in the north and having been forced to march the length of England in order to encounter the formidable Norman forces. William won his great victory through more advanced armaments and superior tactics. The Anglo-Saxons fought with their accustomed bravery, and the Battle of Hastings was a very bloody encounter by medieval standards. A great many of the Anglo-Saxon nobility were killed on the field, and most of those who survived were deposed from their lands and probably made serfs. Thus the Norman conquest, while not affecting the status and condition of the English peasantry, resulted in the elimination of the English ruling class and the substitution of French lords. The Anglo-Saxon bishops and abbots did not fare much better than the lay nobility. William made his friend and adviser, the Italian-Norman monastic leader and scholar Lanfranc, the archbishop of Canterbury, and the latter was not loath to bring probably trumped-up charges against the Anglo-Saxon higher clergy and replace them with Norman and other French churchmen.

For four decades after the conquest the Normans exhibited an unmitigated contempt for all Anglo-Saxon culture. During this period some of the greatest works of Anglo-Saxon art were probably destroyed; some of the best Anglo-Saxon illuminated manuscripts survived only in continental libraries, having been sent as gifts to rulers or churchmen across the channel. The cosmopolitan Norman nobility spoke French and were representatives of French culture and civilization. The Anglo-Saxon language became a peasant dialect, and it was revived in literary form only in the fourteenth century. For at least a century and a half after the Norman conquest England was culturally a province of France. In spite of the losses to native vernacular literature and art, the Norman conquest was a great benefit to England, which in any case was bound to lose its independence in the 1060's. England was on the verge of political disintegration, an easy prey for foreign conquest. It was bound to become an adjunct either of Scandinavia or of France. The Norman invasion produced the political unification of the country and allowed England to participate in the thriving intellectual, religious, and artistic life of eleventh- and twelfth-century France. Scandinavian conquest would have cut England off from all these achievements.

With characteristic political skill William salvaged whatever was viable in Anglo-Saxon institutions. He preserved the local shire and hundred courts and the Anglo-Saxon royal writ, the official written communication sent out by the royal chancery to its local agents, and the Anglo-Saxon coronation order with its stirring overtones of theocratic kingship. But this religious ideology was only a peripheral matter, for the Anglo-Norman monarchy established its power upon a whole new framework of institutions borrowed from Normandy. Even the preconquest institutions which were continued were given a new vitality and importance by their place in the comprehensive political and legal system.

The complete feudalization of the realm was undertaken by the Conqueror and for the most part completed by the end of his reign in 1087. As the supreme lord of every fief in England by right of conquest, he was able to work out a careful scheme of feudalization which centered in the king as the liege lord of every knight in the realm. As in Normandy, the bishops and abbots were first placed under heavy feudal obligations, and then the lay nobility was enfeoffed. With the exception of the frontier lords, who were given special privileges and large blocks of territory, the estates of any particular great lord were spread over two or more counties to preclude the development of provincial autonomy. As in Normandy also, the precise amount of knight service was established for every royal tenant-in-chief, proceeding in multiples of five to a maximum of sixty knights owed to the royal army. The feudal military service owed by vassals to the Anglo-Norman king amounted to five thousand knights, a vast number for the period. No castles could be built in the country without royal permission, and at least three times a year the royal vassals had to come to the *curia regis,* the king's court, to hear the king announce his plans, to advise him on policy, and to participate in important law suits involving the royal tenants-in-chief. The day-to-day affairs of the government were conducted by a small group of lay and ecclesiastical nobles and monastic clerks who staffed the chancery. The local agents of the Anglo-Norman monarchy maintained the old English title of sheriff ("shire reeve"), but he was actually the Norman viscount, by which title he is often referred to in official royal documents. He was no longer the weak and ineffective royal agent of preconquest times who had been dominated by the great earls, but the leading voice in the government and law of the shire. A middling landholder in his private capacity, the sheriff was given enormous influence and authority by his status as the representative of an efficient and determined royal government which brooked no recalcitrance on the part of even the greatest lords in the country. The sheriff presided over the shire court, and he was the local agent of the royal treasury.

William the Conqueror and his sons amazed continental contemporaries by the extent of their financial resources. This was not only because of England's wealth, for certainly, taken as a whole, the kingdoms of France and Germany were much richer, but because the Anglo-Norman king was able to tax the resources of his realm to a degree far exceeding that of any ruler in Europe. Money was needed to support the king and his family, his central administration, his local representatives, and his military establishment. The relative effectiveness of English royal taxation inaugurated by William the Conqueror is a most important key to the political history of the middle ages. It helps to account for the fact that as late as the fifteenth century the king of England was able to inflict crushing defeats upon French kings, who ruled a country with three times the population of England and whose landed, commercial, and industrial wealth, if we could estimate it precisely, would be even greater. In the middle ages, no less than in the twentieth century, wars cost money, and the power of any particular king was greatly dependent upon the comprehensiveness and efficiency of his taxation system. In this regard the Anglo-Norman king was at least a century ahead of the Capetian monarchy, and no German ruler of the twelfth and thirteenth centuries ever had any comparable command of the financial resources of his country.

The chief source of income of early medieval kings had been their own estates, and William naturally drew a substantial part of his income from the royal demesne, whose administration was the sheriff's responsibility. The law courts were also a very lucrative source of income, but it was their clever and unrelenting use of the feudal possibilities for taxation that accounts for the great financial resources of the Anglo-Norman rulers. Like any other feudal lord, William enjoyed the prerogatives of relief, wardship, and the regular aids, and his treasury found that these old institutions could be made to produce great sums. Not only the lay vassals but also the bishoprics and abbeys which owed feudal obligations to the crown, were subjected to this kind of taxation. In addition to all these sources of royal income William inaugurated the practice of allowing his vassals the option of not sending their knights to serve in the feudal host on payment of a certain sum per knight's fee; the practice came to be called scutage (literally, "shield money") in the early twelfth century. William's tenants-in-chief were glad to be freed of the burden of keeping their knights trained and equipped for war, and William preferred to use the income he obtained from scutage to hire mercenaries for his continental wars. Paradoxically, the same king who brought feudal institutions to their highest refinement and used them most effectively for enhancing royal power was the earliest to realize the inefficiency of the feudal method of raising armies. By feudal law the vassals were required to serve only forty days a year, which was a tremendous nuisance in a long campaign; the knights who were provided to his feudal host were not always adequately prepared and armed; it was advisable to leave most of the English army at home in case of another Scandinavian invasion, which threatened during most of the Conqueror's reign; and in addition, William had the special problem of transporting the knights and horses across the channel, which was both expensive and risky. He preferred to hire mercenaries among the landless knights of Normandy, Flanders, and Brittany for his frontier campaigns against various French princes. The Anglo-Norman monarch's envious continental enemies were not slow to realize the significance of this military innovation. A chief minister of the French king in the first half of the twelfth century referred to the English ruler as "that wealthy man, a marvelous buyer and collector of knights." William initiated the slow substitution of mercenary forces for feudal armies, which is one of the central military developments of the high middle ages.

The enterprise and ingenuity of William's government is demonstrated by legal as well as political and military innovations. For the settling of land disputes among the great barons he commissioned the shire courts to empanel inquests of sworn men of the neighborhood, or juries as they later came to be called. The Anglo-Saxons had occasionally used similar juries to bring criminal accusations in the folk courts, but the preconquest kings were politically so incompetent that they did not realize the value of this institution, and it died out before the eleventh century. The inquest, which can be traced back through Norman legal development to its origins in Carolingian times, was introduced anew into England by the Conqueror, who was not aware of the abortive Anglo-Saxon experiments with it. In the second half of the twelfth century the sworn inquest, or jury, came to be used in criminal as well as civil suits and became the central institution in English legal procedure.

The intelligence and energy of the Anglo-Norman monarchy was magnificently revealed in the last year of William's life by a complete survey of the property and proprietors of England as they existed before the conquest and in 1086. No other government in Europe before the thirteenth century could have carried out such an investigation, the results of which were summarized in two huge volumes which came to be known as Domesday Book. It provided the royal government and law courts with a complete record of the wealth and landholders in England for purposes of taxation and litigation. Domesday Book was put together by royal commissioners working with information derived from the testimony of literally hundreds of local juries. It provides the most detailed record of medieval social and economic life which had yet been made, and its values as a source of statistical information was not surpassed in Europe until the nineteenth century. It remains the most remarkable monument of the work of William the Conqueror and his clerical assistants, who in two decades transformed England from one of the most backward states to one of the most advanced in Europe.

II. *The Significance of the English Investiture Controversy*

Even disgruntled Anglo-Saxon churchmen admired and stood in awe of the achievements of William the Conqueror, but Gregory VII found little cause to rejoice in his protégé's success. As the power of the German emperor declined under papal attack, a new secular leader of much greater potential emerged on the European political scene. Gregory was not blind to the significance of this development. In the long run here lay a greater threat to the achievement of the new world order he envisioned than even the Salian emperor could have offered. Furthermore, the Anglo-Norman church-state system bore disquieting similarities to the situation in Germany on the eve of the investiture controversy. William did not bother to emphasize the traditions of theocratic kingship, but through lay investiture and the vassalage of bishops and abbots he completely controlled the affairs of the English church. And yet, as in Germany, the churchmen were completely loyal to the monarchy, and the king was not only feared but respected and admired by them. The literate work of his government was in the hands of passionately loyal monastic clerks who were promoted for their valuable service through royal appointments to vacant episcopal and abbatial offices. The archbishop of Canterbury, Lanfranc, who was renowned throughout Europe as a theologian and canon lawyer, strongly approved of this close association between the king and the church, and as William's confidant and adviser he seems to have been responsible for many of its refinements.

The Norman conquest brought about a great improvement in the moral and intellectual level of the higher clergy of England. Under royal patronage the monasteries prospered, canon-law collections of a conservative, pre-Gregorian kind were introduced and studied, great monastic libraries were established, and liturgical studies and historical writing were actively pursued. Impressive new stone churches in the Norman perpendicular style were erected, of which Durham cathedral is an outstanding example, and the number and quality of the parish clergy were augmented.

But Gregory discovered that the English church after the conquest was no more in contact with Rome than before. William issued a decree forbidding any of his clergy to go to Rome, to receive papal legates, or to appeal to the papal curia without his permission. Such provisions were in flagrant violation of the policies of the Gregorian papacy, and yet Gregory was powerless to intervene. England lacked a rebellious nobility which he could use as a lever against the monarchy, the widely esteemed Lanfranc of Canterbury clearly lacked enthusiasm for the Gregorian reform, and Gregory was not so foolish as to come to an open break with the English king while Henry IV was not yet vanquished. However, the pope could not resist trying to assert his authority over the English king and archbishop. Gregory claimed that William's conquest of England under the papal banner and the general provisions of the Donation of Constantine required that the Conqueror become his vassal. William, of course, would not hear of it. The pope then demanded that Lanfranc come to Rome and personally make his subservience to the supreme pontiff, but the archbishop prevaricated, refused to leave England, and as a precaution entered into secret negotiations with the imperial anti-pope. Gregory was thus unable to influence the English situation in any way.

The monolithic alliance between the monarchy and the church in England began to show signs of strain after the Conqueror's death in 1087 and Lanfranc's in 1089. William's successor in England, his second son William II, Rufus (1087–1100), used the feudal prerogatives of the crown to tax the church mercilessly. He furthermore exhibited homosexual qualities and a strange sympathy for Jews, which made him unpopular. The new archbishop of Canterbury, the elderly St. Anselm, another Italian-Norman monk and the greatest theologian of his day, was much more sympathetic to the Gregorian-reform program than his teacher Lanfranc had been. A bitter dispute between the king and Anselm ensued in which the English higher clergy sympathized with the venerable archbishop personally but would not support him, partly because they feared Rufus' wrath and partly because they were hostile to the introduction of the Gregorian-reform program in England. Anselm was left with the sole alternative of going to Rome to appeal for papal intervention. Gregory VII would have jumped at the chance, but the occupant of the throne of Peter was now the moderate and wily Cluniac monk Urban II, who had no taste for bitter conflicts. Urban had just completed an agreement with the Norman ruler of Sicily which gave the latter effective control over the church in his domains, and to Anselm's chagrin the pope proceeded to complete a similar concordat with the English king. It was a simple *quid pro quo;* Rufus recognized Urban instead of the anti-pope, and Urban gave papal sanction to the Anglo-Norman church-state system.

The accession of Rufus' younger brother, Henry I (1100–1135), who in every way resembled his father, and of Paschal II changed the situation radically. By 1103 the pope and king were embroiled in a bitter dispute over lay investiture. A Norman count who was Henry's chief adviser was excommunicated by the pope, and the excommunication of the king was threatened as the next step. Not even the bewildered Anselm's appeal for moderation seemed to be able to head off a long and protracted struggle. The resourceful Anglo-Norman king commissioned his chief ecclesiastical supporter, Archbishop Gerard of York, to dredge up the traditions of Anglo-Saxon theocratic kingship in defense of royal investiture of ecclesiastics. The resulting *Anonymous of York* treatises are a delight to students of early-medieval political theory, but they in no way typify the outlook of the Anglo-Norman monarchy, which had substituted the secure foundation of administrative and legal bureaucracy for outmoded religious ideology. In case of a long struggle with the papacy, however, Henry considered that even the antiquated traditions of theocratic kingship might prove useful.

The English investiture controversy proved to be short-lived, however. Anselm withdrew into exile to let the pope and king fight it out between themselves, and the English bishops and abbots remained steadfast in their loyalty to the prevailing church-state system. Paschal's attention was diverted in 1106 by a projected crusade against Constantinople which he was supporting and in which he vainly hoped Henry I would participate. He agreed to the king's proposal for a compromise based upon the principle, which the Anglo-Norman government had long followed, of making a distinction between the religious and the feudal-political capacities of the great churchmen. By the Concordat of London in 1107, which was the model for the later Concordat of Worms, Henry made the token surrender to Rome of abandoning lay investiture, but he maintained inviolate his authority over his bishops and abbots through ecclesiastical homage.

The English investiture controversy was by no means without consequence. It warned Henry of the dangers implicit in the English monarchy's alliance with the church, which could be threatened by papal intervention, and encouraged him to expand his purely secular power through the continued building up of the administrative bureaucracy. After the investiture controversy Henry abandoned his father's policy of using monastic scholars in his administration, because the regular clergy had proved to be most infected by Gregorian ideas and influenced by Rome. Instead he employed secular clerks, who, while nominally churchmen—no other kind of literate men were available in England—pursued the king's interests with the attitude of dedicated professional bureaucrats. Such harsh, ruthless, but extremely able servants the king rewarded with appointments to lucrative bishoprics. Henry expanded his father's practice of scutage in order to make the Anglo-Norman monarchy even less reliant than before on knight service from church lands. The effectiveness of the English treasury was increased through the founding of a controlling accounting body called the exchequer, which borrowed from the continent the system of reckoning with a variant of the abacus. The exchequer kept the extensive annual records of the income and expenditures of the crown, which came to be called the pipe rolls; nothing like this sophisticated accounting system existed in the Capetian realm until the early thirteenth century. The effectiveness of the law courts and the increase of royal jurisdiction over the shire courts was achieved by sending out, on circuit, panels of itinerant justices from the *curia regis* to preside over the county courts. By 1135 the institutions of the English monarchy were so far ahead of the continental kingdoms that royal clerks could plausibly attribute to Henry I the qualities of the emperor in Roman law "from whom law and power [likewise] radiated through the whole kingdom." The same situation existed in Normandy, which Henry had conquered from his incompetent brother Robert.

At a time when the nobility of France and Germany were in the heyday of territorial sovereignty, the English barons found themselves completely circumscribed by the expanding royal institutions, and their feudal privileges were evaporating before the advance of crown bureaucracy. The only possibility of interrupting the expansion of royal power seemed to be in a succession crisis which would allow the English lords to play off one candidate against another, and, to Henry's great disappointment, this prospect became a real possibility through the early death of his only son. His only other legitimate heir was his daughter Matilda, who had once been married to the German emperor Henry V and was now the wife of the count of Anjou. There was no principle in English law which excluded a woman from ascending to the throne, but Matilda was an arrogant and foolish

woman who offended everybody, and in any case the nobility was determined to take advantage of this rare opportunity to stem the tide of advancing royal power. After Henry's death many of the ambitious barons
resurrected the Germanic electoral principle from desuetude and gave their
allegiance to Henry's nephew (a son of the Conqueror's daughter), the
feckless adventurer Stephen of Blois, who appeared in England to assert his
claim. The two decades of desultory civil war which followed have sometimes been called "the anarchy," which they certainly were not, because the
central political, legal, and financial machinery of the monarchy, while
weakened by the removal of strong direction, in no case disappeared. By
the end of the 1140's the lesser nobility in England, who were coming to
be called the knightly class, could see no point in perpetuating a struggle
which benefited only the private interests of the great baronial families, and
even many of these more prominent lords longed for peace and the security
of royal justice. A compromise was reached which brought Matilda's son
to the throne as Henry II, the first of the Angevin line, when Stephen of
Blois died in 1154.

Henry II and his administrators had to work hard to recover the ground
which had been lost in the previous two decades, but in this work of re-
establishing the royal institutions of his grandfather's day and then carrying
further the power of the royal bureaucracy, the king was in fact aided by
the lessons of the civil war itself. After more than six decades of increasing
centralization the English landed classes had been given a taste of continental feudal disorder. By 1154 they were firmly convinced of the benefits
which William the Conqueror and his sons had brought to England and
prepared to acquiesce in the Angevin refinements of the Anglo-Norman
state.

Chapter Fourteen

THE FIRST CRUSADE
AND AFTER

I. Origins of the Crusading Ideal

In the popular historiographical conception, medieval civilization is virtually identified with the crusades. The only event of the eleventh century known to the average graduate of American universities would be the first crusade of 1095, which he would visualize in terms of gigantic warriors dressed in burnished plate armor and riding magnificent steeds, following the standards of the cross to victory over the swarthy hordes of pusillanimous Arabs. No aspect of this picture is quite accurate. The average stature of the late eleventh-century knight, due to improper nourishment in infancy and generally bad diet and medicine, was not above five feet three inches. The knights of the first crusade still, for the most part, wore chain mail rather than plate armor, which did not come into general use until the latter part of the twelfth century. Their horses, by modern standards or even by those of the thirteenth century, were distinctly puny; it was increased crossbreeding with the superior Arab strains that improved the western breed in the following two centuries. It is true that the knights of the first crusade followed the cross, but by no means entirely for religious purposes. Finally, the Arabs were every bit as valiant and skilled in combat as the western knights, and it was the internal political weakness of the Islamic world and not personal inadequacies of Arab warriors that accounted for the success of the first crusade.

What is wrong in the popular historiographical conception of the first crusade is not so much these errors in detail as a tendency to exaggerate greatly the importance of the crusading ideal in medieval life. Even many professional historians of the middle ages, particularly in the United States, have tended to see the crusades as a central factor in historical change from the eleventh to thirteenth centuries and to write with such enthusiastic imprecision that the unwary reader would be led to identify them with medieval civilization itself. Such views are palpable nonsense. The crusades *are* a significant chapter in medieval development, but mainly because they express fundamental patterns of thought and action. They did have some slight effect on the course of European development, but not enough to alter the direction which government, economy, and culture would have taken in any case. The crusades are mainly a manifestation, albeit a most dramatic and significant one, of the major facets of medieval civilization; they are only to a very limited degree a causal factor in historical change during the period. In general, it might be said that the crusades reveal medieval men at their best and at their worst; they are a grand stage on which their characteristics were exhibited in somewhat abnormal and exaggerated form, and this is mainly why they are worth studying.

The origins of the crusading ideal were brilliantly analyzed in the 1930's by the great German medievalist Carl Erdmann, whose controversial book —probably because it places the crusades within the general perspective of medieval culture—has largely been ignored by the crusade buffs in American universities. It is necessary to look for the idea of the crusades in the struggle between Christians and Moslems in Spain and consider how the Latin idea of a holy war emerged from this background. When the Moslems conquered the Iberian peninsula in the eighth century, a few of the Spanish Christian princes and their followers fled into the northern mountains, from which in the tenth century they launched the *Reconquista.* In the eleventh century these Spanish Christians, greatly assisted by the growing political disunity of the Spanish Moslems, gained their initial successes, and by 1100 they held somewhere between a fifth and a quarter of the whole country. The tide of reconquest crept slowly and relentlessly southward, and while the final expulsion of the Moslems was achieved only in 1492, the greater part of the peninsula from the middle of the thirteenth century was ruled by Christian kings. The *Reconquista* was the dominant, almost the exclusive, theme of medieval Christian Spanish history, and some historians have seen it as the determining factor in the molding of the peculiar Spanish character. All Iberian society originated in a grim war of five centuries against Islam, and the Spanish institutional structure was organized around the warlord and the necessities of aggressive warfare. The Spanish Christians eventually, and probably unconsciously, imitated the

Moslem *jihad,* or holy war, with its doctrine that the highest morality was to die fighting on behalf of the deity. Religious fanaticism and military valor became the dominant socially approved values in Spanish society, and it has been said that herein lies the key to the enigmas of Spanish history. The Christian ruling class never learned to do anything but fight, and while this pugnacious energy and military skill led directly to the great overseas Iberian empires, Spain lacked the political and economic experience, the institutions and arts of peace, to take long-range advantage of these initial triumphs.

The Gregorian papacy, through its legates, maintained a careful watch on the progress of the *Reconquista* and for several reasons, both intellectual and strategic, found it worthy of more general imitation. The doctrinal validity of a holy war and the shedding of blood on behalf of the Lord was a moot question. Apostolic Christianity had exhibited strong pacifistic tendencies, but St. Augustine of Hippo had justified the use of force in the church's interest, and we have seen that Hildebrand's outlook was strongly neo-Augustinian. Erdmann emphasized that the strongly militant quality of eleventh-century Christianity, which is reflected in the attitudes of the leaders of the reform papacy, made a war against Islam an attractive proposition. These are the intellectual factors which inspired Gregory VII to project an oriental expedition, directed by the papacy, against the Moslem heretics. There were, however, other motives involved. Such a crusade would be an expression of the supreme pontiff's moral leadership of the western world (which was one of Gregory's cardinal doctrines) and would bring the peoples of the north into closer relations with Rome. Finally, the Latin invasion of the orient could be expected to take a long step toward the assertion of papal hegemony in Greek Christian lands. The Roman curia was deeply concerned by the continuation of the schism of 1054 and regarded a crusade as an effective instrument for affirming the long-claimed papal supremacy over the Greek church.

The situation in the middle east in the 1070's provided an excellent opportunity for this Latin intervention. The Byzantine state was weakened by the rise of feudal lordship and proved itself unable to withstand the advancing armies of the Moslem Seljuk Turks, the latest wave of Asian invaders to penetrate the long-suffering Mediterranean world. The Turks had regained Antioch from the Greeks, and they inflicted a crushing defeat on the Byzantine armies at the Battle of Manzikert in 1071. They now advanced deep into Asia Minor, and the highly intelligent but rather timid emperor, Alexius Comnenus, feared that Constantinople itself was in imminent danger. The extent of the emperor's panic may be gauged by the fact that he appealed to the traditional papal enemy to send him military aid. If Gregory could have vanquished Henry IV, he would have undoubtedly tried to turn Alexis' plight to the immediate advantage of the papacy by dispatching an army designed to serve the Latin cause more than the Greeks. But the perpetuation of the German investiture conflict precluded the organization of a crusade during Gregory's pontificate. It was left for the more moderate, but no less ambitious, Urban II to achieve this.

To Urban the crusade served four ends in addition to the obvious one of regaining the Holy Land for the cross. First of all, it would help to reunite Christendom after the bitter and divisive disputes over the Gregorian reform, and second, it would increase papal prestige at a time when there were supporters of the German emperor even in the city of Rome. Third, it would work toward the ending of the schism between the western and eastern churches. Urban had tried to bring the Greek church in southern Italy under papal authority, but his plan had foundered on a theological dispute about the relationship between the Son and the Holy Ghost (the so-called *Filioque* controversy). A crusade might go to the heart of the matter by making the Byzantine emperor dependent upon, or even subservient to, a Latin army. The fourth value which Urban saw in a crusade was a consequence of his own French background. He well knew that the Germans would not join his enterprise and that the powerful Anglo-Norman ruler would not be inclined to participate. The backbone of the crusading army, aside from a contingent of Norman Italians, would have to come from the French feudal principalities, and Urban realized that an eastern expedition would fit in with the needs of many French lords and knights and at the same time would employ their energies in the service of the church. By the end of the eleventh century the boundaries of the French duchies and counties had become stabilized, and a primitive balance of power existed among them. The great French feudal princes, therefore, had little opportunity for conquest at home, and many were restless and potentially eager for foreign ventures. Furthermore, the rising population curve meant an ever increasing number of landless knights in France ready to cast their lot in an expedition which would allow them to gain domains in the middle east. In addition, Urban well knew that lay piety was having its effect on the French nobility. Their devotion to at least the external accoutrements of the Christian faith indicated that the idea of a holy war would appeal to them.

The pope planned his proclamation of the crusade with great care. He summoned a council at Clermont in central France for 1095 and urged the French bishops and abbots to bring with them the prominent lords of their provinces. Before he arrived at Clermont he already knew that one of the leading French princes, Raymond of St. Giles, count of Toulouse, would take the cross. As Urban began his highly emotional appeal to the "Race of the Franks" to join the crusade, he already anticipated a favorable response. His speech was one of the most skillful and effective examples of rhetoric in European history. He touched upon every motive which a French knight might have, both religious and otherwise, for taking the cross. Urban expatiated on the sufferings of Christians in the Holy Land at the hands of the Seljuk Turks. He mentioned the imminent danger to Byzantium of the Moslem advance. He reminded the French knights of their reputation for courage and piety and called upon them to rescue the Holy Sepulchre from infidel hands. He offered his listeners the prospect of carving out kingdoms in Palestine, "a land flowing with milk and honey." He promised papal protection for the property and family of any crusader, and finally, as the keeper of the keys to the kingdom of heaven, he promised the crusaders plenary indulgence for their sins.

This last inducement closely resembled the Koranic assurance of heaven for any Moslem warrior who died fighting for the faith. The crusading indulgence was to be abused greatly in later centuries, and its ultimate form was attacked in the sixteenth century not only by Martin Luther but also by the Council of Trent. In the twelfth century the church developed the institution of indulgence for vicarious crusading, that is, for supporting crusaders through monetary assistance. By the fourteenth century the papacy allowed the outright selling of indulgences without even this crusading pretext, as is vividly described in Chaucer's *Canterbury Tales*. But there was nothing abusive in Urban's original idea of a crusading indulgence. In his view it was merely an exemplary form of penance, and, of course, its effectiveness was dependent upon genuine contrition. However, he left these theological aspects of the crusading indulgence rather vague, and it is likely that many French knights were led to believe that taking the cross by itself secured heavenly reward. While self-interested motives played a very considerable role in launching the crusading movement— and Urban by his speech in fact encouraged this—it was nevertheless true that many took the cross for primarily religious reasons. We are told by eyewitnesses that at the conclusion of Urban's speech at the Council of Clermont a great shout of *Deus Vult* ("God wills it") arose from the assembly, and many lords and knights came forward to take the cross. Red cloaks were cut up into strips which were sewn in the form of crucifixes on the fronts of tunics.

This emotional scene was repeated all over France and southern Italy in response to the spreading of Urban's message by papal legates. Indeed, it seems that Urban had underrated the effect of his proclamation at Clermont. He was not prepared for the immediate organization of the various groups of knights now clamoring to set out for the Holy Land, and it was not until the following year that the first crusade began. Certainly no one at the papal court anticipated the explosive effect of Urban's appeal at Clermont on the Rhenish cities. Before the French knights could set out on their expedition, a "people's crusade," consisting of unruly mobs from the slums of the Rhineland urban communities, blindly set out in the general direction of the Holy Land. Led by popular preachers such as Peter the Hermit, they committed pogroms on the prosperous Jewish population in their own cities and then moved through Germany and the Balkans like a plague of locusts until they arrived at the gates of Constantinople. The frightened emperor immediately transported them across the Hellespont, where they were exterminated by the Turks. This popular reaction was one of the most significant aspects of the first crusade, because it demonstrated the millennial and apocalyptic outlook of the lower and middle classes of European cities. The papacy had already encountered this millennial feeling in Milan, where social disaffection had also sought an escape through emotional religion. To the participants in the people's crusade Urban's preaching had a significance which the pope himself did not understand. They yearned for release from the frustration and poverty of their unhappy lives, and they found in the pope's pronouncements apocalyptic and eschatological overtones which were in fact beyond the world view of the sensible Cluniac pope. The people's crusade offers a remarkable glimpse of the highly emotional and revolutionary forms which the new piety was taking in urban areas, out of which the popular heresy of the late twelfth century and the papacy's impotence in the face of this mass religiosity were to emerge. The brilliant English historian Norman Cohn has perceived an even broader significance in the "pursuit of the millennium" which inspired the people's crusade; he regards it as the first manifestation in European history of that popular fanaticism of the lower classes which comes to fruition in modern fascism. This interpretation has some merit, but we may also see in the followers of Peter the Hermit the precursors of the Anabaptists and Levellers and other religiously oriented democrats of the sixteenth and seventeenth centuries.

The papacy, however, dismissed the momentary social earthquake of the people's crusade with a bewildered shrug and set about organizing the French feudal princes and knights into a crusading army. The varied motives of the leaders of the first crusade indicate a growing sophistication on the part of the European nobility which distinguishes their attitudes from the brutish outlook prevailing among this class in the tenth century. Genuine piety inspired most of them, but they also had other reasons for setting out for the Holy Land. Some, such as Raymond of Toulouse and

Godfrey, duke of Lorraine, were bored by the lack of opportunity for valor and adventure at home. Others, such as Robert Curthose, duke of Normandy, the incompetent eldest son of William the Conqueror, wanted to restore the prestige they had lost at home by winning a great victory in the east. Count Stephen of Blois joined the expedition because his wife, the ambitious daughter of William the Conqueror, made him go. The Norman Italians were motivated by the genuine hatred for the Byzantine empire and a desire to carve out territories for themselves in the middle east at the emperor's expense. They looked upon the first crusade more as an expedition against Constantinople than as a war against Islam. Their most outstanding leader, Bohemund, had already led an abortive expedition against the Greek empire, and he was to attempt a similar unsuccessful venture, with papal encouragement, in 1106. The north Italian mercantile cities, especially Venice, were enthusiastic for the crusade, and not primarily for religious reasons. They regarded it as another step in their economic penetration of the Mediterranean world. They hoped to gain seaports in the eastern Mediterranean in order to compete more effectively with the Arabic merchants. And the Venetians were awarded the lucrative work of supplying the crusaders once they had reached Syria and Palestine.

Although no European king joined the first crusade, its leaders were, on the average, able and valorous princes. Their great weakness was an inability to agree upon a single leader, mainly because they were of the same social status. The pope finally appointed a French bishop as the nominal leader of the expedition, but from the beginning to the end the first crusade was marked by bickering among the princes and their vassals. Another, and pardonable, deficiency in the direction of the crusade was the leaders' gross ignorance of the geography, climate, and political organization of the Moslem countries, but it is remarkable how quickly the crusaders adjusted to their novel environment. Alexius Comnenus gave them some valuable information, and more was furnished by the Venetians.

The crusaders finally set out in 1096 on the land route through Germany and the Balkans to Byzantium, the jumping-off point for their attack on Islam. This route had already been traversed by the people's crusade, and the Franks, as the Greeks and Arabs called all the crusaders, acted similarly. They massacred Jews in the Rhenish cities and abused and robbed the Balkan peoples whose lands they crossed. Alexius Comnenus greeted them with apprehension. He was glad to receive Latin support, but it was certainly not the kind of aid he had envisaged, and he feared that the crusaders were just as keen on the dismemberment of what remained of the Byzantine empire as they were in attacking the Moslems, especially when he saw his old enemy Bohemund in their midst. He transported them across

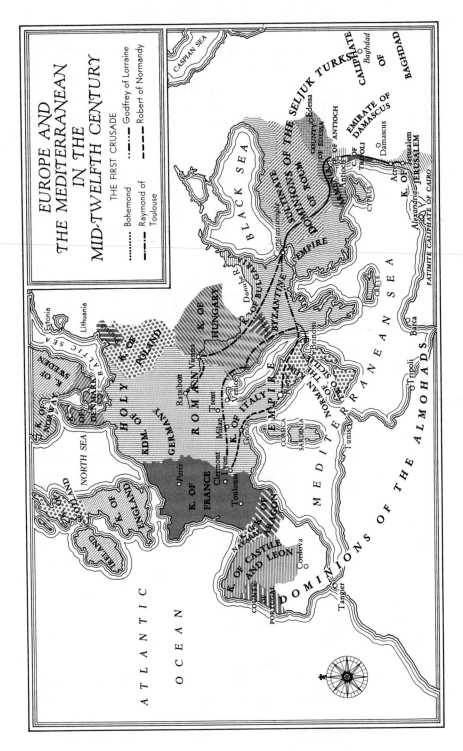

EUROPE AND
THE MEDITERRANEAN
IN THE
MID-TWELFTH CENTURY

THE FIRST CRUSADE

.... Bohemond .... Godfrey of Lorraine
— · — Raymond of Toulouse — — — Robert of Normandy

CASPIAN SEA

SULTANATE OF THE SELJUK TURKS

CALIPHATE OF BAGHDAD
Baghdad
BAGHDAD

SULTANATE OF ROUM

EMIRATE OF DAMASCUS

BLACK SEA

COUNTY OF EDESSA
Edessa
ANTIOCH

Damascus

Constantinople

BYZANTINE EMPIRE

K. OF BULGARIA

Antioch
C. OF TRIPOLI
Acre
Jerusalem
K. OF JERUSALEM

CYPRUS

Alexandria
FATIMITE CALIPHATE OF CAIRO

Danube R.

K. OF HUNGARY

Vienna
Ratisbon

Trent

Milan
K. OF ITALY
Venice

Brindisi

CRETE

MEDITERRANEAN SEA

Barca
Tripoli

Estonia
Lithuania

K. OF POLAND

HOLY ROMAN EMPIRE

KDM. OF GERMANY

NORMAN KDM. OF SICILY

K. OF SWEDEN
K. OF NORWAY
K. OF DENMARK
BALTIC SEA

NORTH SEA

K. OF SCOTLAND
K. OF ENGLAND
IRELAND

ATLANTIC OCEAN

K. OF FRANCE
Paris
Clermont
Lyon
Toulouse

CORSICA
SARDINIA

Tunis

K. OF NAVARRE
K. OF ARAGON
K. OF CASTILE AND LEON
COUNTY OF PORTUGAL
Cordova

Tangier

DOMINIONS OF THE ALMOHADS

the straits to Asia Minor as quickly as possible. The Frankish reaction to Constantinople was not very different from the attitudes of Liudprand of Cremona a century and a half before. When they came face to face with the wealth and military forces of Byzantium, the leaders of the crusade realized that they would have little chance of taking the golden city on the Hellespont. They would have to content themselves with carving out feudal domains in Syria and Palestine and thereby humiliate the emperor by establishing Latin principalities on territory claimed by Constantinople and by providing a foothold for the Roman church in the eastern Mediterranean.

In the face of Byzantine grandeur and culture the Franks had a strong sense of inferiority, and they compensated for their rusticity and crudeness by condemning the Greeks as effeminate and corrupt. Actually the mannered Greek courtiers rightly found the Frankish princes boors by comparison with themselves. There was merit in each party's criticism of the other, but the Franks were representatives of a still youthful and extremely vital civilization, while Byzantium was sterile and decadent and had to rely on its western enemies for salvation from the more pressing Arabic foe. This fascinating encounter between the Byzantine imperial court, the citadel of oversophistication, and the uncouth but enterprising French feudatories was thus highly significant, for it symbolized the meeting of the dawning and the dying day.

The naïveté of the leaders of the first crusade prevented them from realizing the magnitude of the task they had undertaken. The whole western force could not have numbered more than five thousand people, probably less, and the united Moslem world would have had little difficulty in destroying the invaders. But the advance of the Seljuk Turks into the eastern Mediterranean had upset the prevailing political order and had brought about bitter internal disputes among the Arabic princes. The crusaders showed unsurpassed bravery and considerable military skill, and at a critical moment, when their spirits flagged, the discovery of what was purported to be a very important relic rallied them to pursue their invasion. But the fact remains that it was the temporary disunity of the Moslems and their inability to present a united front which played the indispensable role in the triumph of the crusaders. They marched through Asia Minor into Syria and took Antioch after a long siege. Bohemund usurped authority over the city and made himself, for a short time, prince of Antioch; one other crusading leader also fell away from the expedition to carve out his own middle eastern fief. But the others pressed on, and after a bitter struggle they took Jerusalem and characteristically massacred the Moslem and Jewish civilians in the Holy City.

The success of the first crusade was the end result of that penetration of the Mediterranean world which had been initiated by the north Italian cities in the tenth century and furthered by the Norman conquest of southern Italy. It was the consequence, but scarcely a cause, of this and other important changes in European civilization. While the first crusade undoubtedly increased European awareness of the riches of the middle east and enriched European taste for spices and other oriental products, it certainly did not bring about the opening of economic relations between west and east; that development had already been effected on an extensive scale in the previous century. Nor did the first crusade play a part in establishing the intellectual and cultural relations between the Islamic and Latin worlds which brought about the revolution in western philosophy and science in the twelfth and thirteenth centuries. None of the Latin translations of the writings of the Greek thinkers and their Arabic interpreters were made in the crusading states; these made no contribution whatever to western learning. The translations were carried out in the old centers of Latin-Arabic intercourse in Spain and Sicily. The only long-range impact of the establishment of a Latin outpost in the middle east was slowly to teach the European peoples a tolerance for men of another culture and religion. The Latin knights who lived in the crusading states found that their Moslem neighbors were at least as intelligent and moral as themselves, a discovery which inevitably undermined their original fanaticism and hatred for peoples they had known only as stereotyped, monstrous infidels. The lords of the crusading states quickly adopted the dress, food, and many of the private mores of the neighboring Emirs. It was not, however, until the second half of the thirteenth century that these more realistic and tolerant attitudes toward the Moslem people penetrated into the consciousness of western Europe.

II. Vicissitudes and Decline of the Crusading Movement

The first crusade of 1096 created the Latin Kingdom of Jerusalem, a small Palestinian principality centering on Jerusalem and Acre and tightly organized along feudal lines. Godfrey of Lorraine was its first ruler, although without calling himself king, and he was succeeded by his brother Baldwin who was allowed by the clergy and other crusaders to use the royal title. From the beginning of its days the Latin Kingdom was threatened by Moslem reconquest, and in the following two centuries its territory suffered slow but irreversible attrition. Periodically the papacy and other important churchmen inspired European rulers to undertake expeditions in aid of the Latin Kingdom, none of which were ever very successful and several of which, in fact, were disastrous. Actually, the western outpost in the eastern Mediterranean achieved its greatest size at the beginning of its history. By the start of the thirteenth century it had been shrunk, by counterattacks of the great Egyptian ruler Saladin, to a very slim belt of territory. Jerusalem itself was lost to the Moslems in 1187 and the Latin Kingdom was finally extinguished in 1291. The lugubrious history of the later crusades of the twelfth and thirteenth centuries—comprising traditionally six in number, although there were a few smaller expeditions—raises the important question of why western Europe was apparently unable to preserve the Latin Kingdom of Jerusalem.

It was more a matter of lack of interest than of inability. There is no doubt that if at any time in the twelfth and thirteenth centuries the total resources of the papacy and the European monarchies had been applied to the crusading movement, a crushing defeat could have been inflicted on the Moslem armies which encircled the Latin Kingdom. The fact remains, however, that the leaders of western society had many other more pressing interests, and the crusading movement, however worthy they deemed it in their public pronouncements, was to them a rather peripheral matter. Many of the kings and the great feudal princes of western Europe took the cross during the twelfth and thirteenth centuries, but of these only a fraction actually departed for the Holy Land. Frequently the papacy did not mind this backsliding, because it placed the vowed crusader in a spiritual debt to Rome and allowed the pope to demand some other form of service to the church as the price of dispensation from the crusading oath. Even when a great king actually went on a crusade, he more often than not simply went through the motions of fighting the Moslems, taking only a small part of his army with him, staying only a few months in the Holy Land, engaging in only perfunctory skirmishes, and finally reaching some face-saving treaty with a sultan in order to appear back home as a hero of the Christian faith. Paradoxically, the crusading leaders of the twelfth and thirteenth centuries who took their tasks most seriously were the worst soldiers and accomplished nothing except the massacre of their knights at Arabic hands. The crusading ideal during the twelfth and thirteenth centuries was a popular outlet for the intense and widespread piety of the period, but it was only one form among many. To the kings and princes of western Europe, taking the cross was a necessary duty encouraged by the pope and other important churchmen. It was something they had to do as an expression of their status in society and in order to appease public opinion; but nearly all of them took it as a formal matter which required only a small part of their energy and resources.

The second crusade of 1144 was preached by St. Bernard of Clairvaux, the moral leader of the mid-twelfth-century church, in response to urgent entreaties from the Latin Kingdom of Jerusalem for aid against the resurgent Arabic power. St. Bernard succeeded in inducing two of the crowned heads of Europe, Louis VII of France and Conrad III of Germany, to take the cross. This provided more prestige than the first crusade had enjoyed but no more military prowess, for Louis and Conrad were not renowned for their skill on the battlefield or the size of their armies. They never reached Palestine, their forces being cut to pieces in Asia Minor. The sole consequence of the second crusade was the strain it placed on the relations between Louis and his queen, Eleanor of Aquitaine, who accompanied him on the expedition and whom Louis accused of infidelity with one of his generals. The resulting divorce of the Capetian king and the duchess of Aquitaine and her subsequent marriage to Henry II of England had an important effect upon the political development of twelfth-century Europe.

The mixture of tragedy and farce which characterized the second crusade was repeated in the third crusade of 1190, the most ambitious, at least in its inception, of all the Latin expeditions to the Holy Land. The power of Saladin was to be challenged by a crusading army which, at least on paper, commanded the greater part of the military resources of Europe. The three greatest rulers of western Europe at the time, Richard the Lionhearted of England, Philip Augustus of France, and Frederick Barbarossa of Germany, set off for the Holy Land with formidable armies. Barbarossa drowned en route, and the Germans ended by participating only in a token manner. It soon appeared that the cynical Philip Augustus intended only to go through the motions of fighting the Moslems; he was eager to get back home to continue his plotting against the English king. Richard Coeur de Lion took the expedition and himself with great seriousness. He was renowned for his gigantic stature and strength, being six feet tall, and was eager to demonstrate both his individual valor and prowess, which were undoubtedly great, and his skill as a general, which was another matter entirely. An overgrown and spoiled child, Richard had antagonized almost every ruler in Europe by the time he got to the Holy Land, and once there, he not only succeeded in increasing the hostility of the French king toward him, but also incurred the hatred of the Germans. The expedition rapidly disintegrated, and after the English king had satisfied his vanity in a few battles, the wily Saladin accepted a peace treaty which simply preserved the status quo. Then Richard discovered that he had no way to get home, because every route he could possibly take was blocked by his enemies. Characteristically, he chose the most roundabout route, via

Germany, and was imprisoned and held for ransom by the emperor Henry VI. These dramatic events enhanced Richard's stature as a chivalric knight, but they indicate the steady decline of a genuine interest in the crusading movement. The European kings were too busy pursuing their dynastic and territorial interests to give more than perfunctory support to the Latin Kingdom.

The fourth crusade of 1204 was undoubtedly the most successful of all the later oriental expeditions, but it was directed against Byzantium rather than the Moslem world. Pope Innocent III, who preached the crusade, did not originally intend it to take this form. But the Venetians, who provided the fleet for the crusading army (a motley collection of French knights), insisted upon this change of plans, and since they had advanced loans to the crusaders, they were able to extract compliance from them. Innocent readily aquiesced in this change of plans as a means of asserting papal authority over Constantinople. The anti-Byzantine tendencies of the crusading movement, which had been evident from its inception in the eleventh century, came to fruition in the fourth crusade. Constantinople had withstood Moslem armies for five centuries, but it now fell to the Venetians and the French knights, who pillaged the city, abused the Greek churchmen, and set up the Latin Kingdom of Constantinople with papal blessings. For six decades Latin princes ruled in Constantinople, and the papacy used this opportunity to try to bring the Greek Christians under the authority of Rome. In 1261 a Greek prince finally regained the imperial throne, with the schism between the Latin and Greek churches not yet healed. Imperial power never recovered from the disaster of the fourth crusade, and while Constantinople did not fall to the Moslems until 1453, it henceforth played a negligible role in the affairs of the Mediterranean world.

The fourth crusade demonstrated to the papacy how the crusading movement might be used for other purposes than the succor of the Latin Kingdom of Jerusalem. In the thirteenth century crusades were directed more against the enemies of the pope within Europe than against the Moslems. The older kind of crusading venture was perpetuated in two crusades led by the saint-monarch, Louis IX of France, and one expedition conducted by the German emperor Frederick II of Hohenstaufen. None of these three last crusades helped the declining Latin Kingdom of Jerusalem. St. Louis boldly attacked the Moslems in their strongholds, first in Egypt and at the end of his reign in Tunisia. In both cases he was defeated. Frederick II's crusade was a perfunctory exhibition with farcical qualities, since he was actually under papal excommunication at the time of his crusade. Insofar as the crusading movement played a significant role in the life of thirteenth-century Europe it was in the novel and perverted form of wars against papal enemies. The first instance, the crusade against the Albigensian heretics of southern France preached by Innocent III, was generally approved of in western Europe, although the way in which it provided a pretext for the invasion of Toulouse by the avaricious nobility of northern France was reprehensible. But the further uses which the papacy made of the crusading movement discredited it as a spiritual force by flagrantly contradicting its original ideals. In the 1240's Frederick II was branded a heretic on questionable grounds, and the French army, which was invited to seize his south Italian territories, was given the status of crusaders. By the 1280's the crusades had become a purely political institution. The crusading label was granted to Philip III of France for his attack on the king of Aragon, who by no stretch of the imagination could be called a heretic, but whose conquest of Sicily had displeased the papacy. This purely political use of the crusades occurred at the very time when the Latin Kingdom of Jerusalem, lacking reinforcement from western Europe, was sinking to its extinction.

The fact was that in the second half of the thirteenth century the leaders of European society were not enthusiastic for new wars against Islam. In part this was due to a more tolerant and enlightened attitude. They had come to share the discovery of the residents of the Latin Kingdom of Jerusalem that the Arabs were an intelligent and able people. By 1200 there was a greater interest in converting than fighting the eastern peoples. The Franciscan order took the lead in this missionary work. They were especially concerned with the attempted conversion of the Mongols, the latest Asian horde to threaten the eastern Mediterranean. By heading off the Mongols' conversion to Islam and by getting them to accept Latin Christianity, the Franciscans, with the support of the papacy, hoped to destroy Moslem control of the Holy Land. But not even to this peaceful endeavor did the European peoples devote much energy. The sending of two Franciscan friars to the court of the khan scarcely indicates that much attention was devoted to this abortive scheme. The western European peoples should have been greatly interested in converting the Mongols, but the fact remains that the ruling class of Europe, including the pope, was too concerned with pressing domestic matters to give much thought to the conversion of eastern peoples. The meeting of east and west is a worthy ideal, but it is not one which greatly appealed to the men of the high middle ages. The problems of European government, economy, and culture absorbed all their energy, and what little was left of crusading fervor in the thirteenth century was directed by the papacy against its enemies inside Europe.

The crusading movement was a legacy to the twelfth and thirteenth centuries of the fanaticism and zeal of the age of the Gregorian reform. It was bound to become outmoded, to undergo great vicissitudes, and ultimately to decline as European civilization itself experienced profound changes.

Nevertheless, the crusading ideal, as distinct from the crusades as a military and political venture, had a profound and not altogether fortunate impact on medieval life. The crusades gave an absolute moral and religious sanction to the union of military force and religious devotion. The external crusades, those feckless ventures against the Moslem world in the eastern Mediterranean, had very little significance for the social and political life of the western world. The internal crusades, those fought within the confines of western Europe, had greater immediate effects. But by far the most important legacy of the crusades was the lesson that it taught Europeans—that it is right and fitting to kill and destroy in the service of Christian ideals. The immediate sufferers from this belief during the twelfth and thirteenth centuries were Jews and heretics. The long-range sufferer was European society as a whole. For righteous militarism was taken over during the thirteenth century by the new European bureaucratic states and became central to the doctrine and style of the absolutist and national states of the succeeding six centuries. Nor has the belief in killing and destruction in the service of a higher cause suffered any diminution in the twentieth century.

Part Six

My old companions on the Mount [at Paris] . . . whom dialectic still detained . . . had only progressed in one point, they had unlearned moderation.

—JOHN OF SALISBURY

The plague of the church is inward; it is incurable.

—ST. BERNARD

The authority of the Roman empire prevails so greatly by reason of the virtues of our most victorious prince. . . . Things have changed for the better.

—OTTO OF FREISING

LEARNING, PIETY, AND POWER

Twelfth Century

Chapter Fifteen

THE INTELLECTUAL
EXPANSION OF EUROPE

I. The Acceleration of Cultural Change

The ending of the divisive and exhausting investiture conflict allowed
medieval scholars and thinkers to concentrate their energies on the tremendous changes which were already taking place in higher culture. This
acceleration of cultural change and creativity and improvement in all facets
of medieval civilization involving the life of the mind has often been called
"the Renaissance of the twelfth century." The term was popularized by
Charles Haskins in a book by that title published in 1928. Haskins used
the term with the polemical purpose of proclaiming that twelfth-century
thinkers were as devoted to the classical heritage and as fecund in important
ideas as were the Italian Humanists of the well-known Renaissance of the
fourteenth and fifteenth centuries. In Haskins' day it was necessary to
justify medieval history in American universities by pretending that the
middle ages were as worthy of study as the Italian Renaissance. Fortunately
such naive and question-begging efforts are no longer needed, and the study
of the intellectual history of the twelfth century may now be undertaken
without drawing procrustean parallels with the age of Petrarch or Leonardo
da Vinci.

The term "Renaissance of the twelfth century" is in fact rather inadequate
on several grounds. It does not fit the intellectual history of the period, being
in some respects too broad and in several others too narrow. The twelfth-
century Renaissance, if it did take place, was almost half over by 1100.

335

The alleged intellectual rebirth actually began about 1050 and would more appropriately be called "the Renaissance of the eleventh century." The period of greatest intellectual vitality and originality came to an end in the middle of the twelfth century and was followed by the absorption, digestion, and consolidation of the consequences of creativity.

What exactly was supposed to have been reborn in the twelfth century? If it is the European contribution to philosophy and science that is being considered, this would be more correctly described as a birth rather than a renaissance, since many intellectual movements of the twelfth century created something new; they did not simply recover an older tradition. It is this creativity and improvement which distinguishes twelfth-century culture from the late medieval Italian Renaissance. The twelfth-century thinkers were not concerned with the simple recovery of the classical style in literature and art. In so far as they drew upon the classical heritage it was to provide a starting point for new directions and dimensions in all facets of civilized life: religion, law, government, economy, ethics, and education as well as in art, literature, philosophy, and science. The tremendous efflorescence of twelfth-century thought was marked by a much broader spectrum of interest than that of the Italian Renaissance of the fourteenth and fifteenth centuries. To apply the term "renaissance" to this development is to belittle the magnitude and variety of its achievements. The manifestations of twelfth-century creativity deeply affected all aspects of social life in which some intellectual endeavor was required; it was not merely a movement supported by a group of littérateurs or the advocates of a certain type of artistic style, but it was as broad, complex, and heterogeneous as medieval civilization itself. This unprecedented acceleration and proliferation of medieval cultural change is not adequately conceptualized by the term "Renaissance of the twelfth century."

The cultural growth was not limited to one country, as tended to be the case with the Renaissance of the fourteenth and fifteenth centuries. Although France provided the leadership, England, Italy, and to a lesser degree Germany participated in the achievements of twelfth-century thought. John of Salisbury, one of the great figures of the twelfth century, was born in England, educated in France, worked in Italy, later returned to England, and ended his career again in France as bishop of Chartres. The intellectual creativity of the twelfth century was an international movement. It had very little national feeling and no sense at all of divisions by political boundaries. This unselfconscious cosmopolitanism was no longer true of the intellectual leaders of the fifteenth century, not even of good Europeans like Erasmus.

The Italian Renaissance was critical of Aristotelian philosophy and fundamentally antiscientific in spirit. It made no lasting contribution to theology or to the development of piety in western Europe. On the contrary, the cultural changes of the twelfth century were responsible for the introduction of Aristotelianism—the best science available at the time—into European thought, and the twelfth century also witnessed the intensification of the new popular piety and the fulfillment of the trend toward an emotional religion, which brought with it new theological insights and enhanced the western consciousness of the dignity of man. The leaders of the Italian Renaissance are famed for their energy and broad interests. But the vitality and boldness of the intellectual leaders of the twelfth century could scarcely be surpassed. They exhibited a marvelous desire to experiment with new intellectual systems, to investigate new problems, and to follow new methods and avenues of thought, and they had an extremely optimistic belief in their ability to do new things in a short space of time. A prime example of this is the invention and extensive spread of a new architectural style within a single generation. Not since the fifth century B.C. had the history of architecture seen such inventiveness, and not until the twentieth century was it again to reveal such rapid proliferation of a new style.

The optimistic and bold characteristics of twelfth-century culture are reflected in the attempt to apply intelligence to the problems of society. Learning and higher thought reached out from exclusive concern with theology and literature to concern for the amelioration of the contemporary political and social structure. The most outstanding instance of this development is the transformation of European law during the twelfth century, which had momentous consequences for the medieval state. Because it was concerned with social need, because it drew upon but was not enslaved by the classical heritage, because it was involved with the institutionalization of higher education, and because it produced a distinctive new group in society, the growth of law typifies the most important aspects of intellectual creativity and improvement during the period and is probably the best introduction to understanding the characteristics of cultural change in the twelfth century.

II. The Legal Constituents of High Medieval Civilization

The twelfth century contributed to western civilization the central and ubiquitous figure of the professional lawyer. In the ancient world lawyers were no more than semiprofessional; their training was mainly in rhetoric, and only a few great jurisconsults were masters of legal science. Customary

Germanic folk law knew no professional lawyer; the legal tradition was declared by the old men of the folk, and even the judges were laymen in the sense that they had no special training. Only at the end of the eleventh century did there appear the professional lawyer, trained by a rigorous education in legal science, ready to apply his knowledge and discipline to the rationalization of human relationships, suited to engage in public life and to do the work of government. At least until the emergence of the professional scientist in the nineteenth century, the law was the most socially valuable learned profession in European civilization, and the lawyer still plays a great role in our contemporary way of life. By 1200 lawyers had become indispensable to the work of both the western monarchies and the church, and the course of medieval political development was strongly conditioned by the attitudes and ambitions of this new group of social leaders. During the twelfth century also the legal systems of the various European states and the Roman Catholic church began to take on institutional forms which have been largely perpetuated to the present day and which became powerful determinants of their characteristic political attitudes.

The twelfth-century innovations in legal institutions and personnel were a consequence of the new, more peaceful conditions of medieval European society. A greater degree of political order and stability allowed the European governments to consider the morass of confused and contradictory legal traditions which was the heritage of the upheavals of the early middle ages. In no European country in 1100, and not even in the church, was there anything approaching a comprehensive and organized legal system. In attempts to assert their authority in society and to provide a measure of order and justice the secular governments of western Europe were hampered by limitations of and conflicts among the various German customary legal traditions. In Mediterranean countries Germanic legal procedures and principles further clashed with debased fragments of the much more sophisticated Roman legal system. In northern France and England feudal law presented yet another group of competing juristic traditions. Political and social progress could no longer tolerate this legal anarchy. A new political order and the slow shift toward a money economy demanded legal rationalization and codification. The task involved, however, was enormous and bound to strain the resources of legal scholars and royal servants. In the reign of Henry I the skill and intelligence of the Anglo-Norman monarchy, the most advanced secular government in western Europe, was directed toward the beginnings of English legal codification. The results were not encouraging, for even Henry's scholars were unable to synthesize a comprehensive system out of the welter of Germanic, feudal, and ecclesiastical traditions.

The social need for legal reform and codification, and the enormity of the task, made the beginnings of the study of the Justinian code in northern Italy a momentous event in the history of European government and law. It accounts for both the dedicated zeal with which the north Italian scholars pursued their study of the civil law and the rapid spread of this Roman law revival north of the Alps. At the beginning of the twelfth century the work of legal scholars was considered to be as socially useful and as much in the interest of the state or the church as the discoveries of the atomic scientists are held to be socially valuable in the twentieth century.

Historians of medieval law are uncertain as to the precise way in which the Justinian code was discovered in northern Italy and its study begun. It has been suggested that the legal studies on behalf of papal authority which were commissioned by Gregory VII led to the accidental discovery in some Italian library of a long-forgotten copy of the *Corpus Juris Civilis*. On the other hand, it is obvious that the merchants of the north Italian cities, where the study of Roman law was centered, could have imported a copy of the Justinian code directly from Constantinople. It is of course possible that there was more than one source for the civil law text which in the 1070's first began to be intensively studied by scholars in the north Italian cities. It is not important how they came by the text; it was not hard to come by, and it had been ignored in western Europe for five centuries because it was irrelevant to the circumstances of early medieval society. What is significant is the great social value which these pioneering legal scholars of the late eleventh century attributed to the Justinian code and which impelled them to begin its intensive study. The codification of the legal system of an advanced civilization into a summary which was written, systematic, comprehensive, and rational suited ideally the legal needs of western Europe at this time. The strong governments toward which European political development was moving were supported by the absolutist doctrine of the Justinian code. In addition, the commercial leaders of the Italian cities were attracted by the law code of an urbanized society which dealt with areas of life unknown to the rural primitivism that lay behind the Germanic customs. The fact that the Justinian code was a summary of the law of the great Roman emperors enhanced its attraction for certain groups, particularly scholars conditioned by a strong sense of the classical heritage and enthusiasts for the Holy Roman Empire. But the intensive study of the Justinian code which began in northern Italy in the second half of the eleventh century was not primarily the consequence of either literary or political antiquarianism but rather the direct result of the pressing needs of European society.

The *Corpus Juris Civilis* was the greatest legal code ever devised. It envisaged the law of the state as a reflection of natural law, the principle of rationality in the universe. The absolute power over the promulgation and operation of the law was held by the Justinian Code to reside in the will of the emperor. The law, it was claimed, originally resided in the Roman people, but by the so-called *lex regia,* "the royal law," the people surrendered their legislative power to the wise and beneficent emperor. The aim of the law is the achievement of equity, or justice, and in order to attain this the law court may alter or suspend the prevailing statutes in a particular case before it and proceed to decide the issue by abstract ethical principles. The Roman law court is judge-centered. The jurists are supposed to be learned and experienced men, above corruption and even above sentiment. Their power is derived from their position as representatives of the emperor, "the living law," who appoints them. In order to get at the truth, the judges request and receive written depositions from the prosecuting and defense attorneys, they interrogate witnesses themselves, and if necessary they employ torture—"put the question," in the terminology of the civil law. Aside from this debatable use of torture the Roman legal system has only two weaknesses. No provision is made for incompetence or bias on the part of the judges; they are always assumed to be men of the highest wisdom, probity, and good will. Such paragons of legal virtue are hard to come by. The final and the greatest weakness of the Roman legal system is the position of the court and the judiciary as the instruments of the state. In questions involving ordinary criminal matters Roman law is liable to work very well, but defendants charged with sedition and other crimes against the state are not likely to receive impartial treatment from judges who are civil servants. In other words, the Roman law system is at its worst in matters of conscience, and the Roman law court is easily turned into a engine of despotism.

At the end of the eleventh century the weaknesses of the civil law were scarcely evident when compared with the great services which its reception could render to European government and society. It appeared to be enormously superior to the Germanic legal system, which had no concept of equity, no rational canons of evidence, and no professional judiciary, and which was an uncodified and largely unwritten body of confused traditions. Hence the discovery of the text of the Justinian code inaugurated immediately its intensive study in the cities of northern Italy. This study was carried out under municipal auspices, for the wealthy businessmen who dominated the governments of the urban communities perceived in the *Corpus of the Civil Law* that same devotion to rationality and order which informed their own existence. By the last decade of the eleventh century a great school of law had been established in Bologna, which remained the dominant center for education in the civil law through the high middle ages. The *universitas,* or corporation of masters and students, at Bologna was a pioneer in the institutionalization of higher education, one of the most important aspects of twelfth-century intellectual development.

The synthesized and rational qualities of the civil law made it a very suitable subject for academic study. In turn, the academic nature of Roman legal study profoundly affected the outlook of the lawyers of continental Europe in the middle ages. In order to become a member of the legal profession in a country which had received the Roman law, it was necessary to devote many years to formal academic study under a very strict regimen. This helps to account for the fact that the young lawyers of medieval Europe tended to be cut from the same cloth: they were all well educated and zealous, but also generally impecunious, somewhat inhuman, and eager to sell their services to the highest bidder. They made ideal bureaucrats. At the very time that the governments of Europe were beginning to require the services of professional civil servants trained in law, a school had been established in Bologna which commenced the production of a new species of bureaucratic man. The rise of secular administrative governments in western Europe and the emergence of a new class of civil lawyers are thus contemporaneous and intimately related developments. It was not until the second half of the twelfth century that the university of Bologna and the new law schools founded north of the Alps produced enough graduates to satisfy the needs of the European monarchies. But by 1200 the administrations of the powerful continental states were being regularly staffed with faceless *magistri,* the civil lawyers.

The academic presentation of the Justinian code followed educational lines long used in the study of the Bible. The professors read the text to their students and added their comments and explanations by way of marginal glosses; hence the twelfth-century commentators on the Justinian code are called the Glossators. Eventually the glossed text was published and became an authority which all who wished to be expert in the civil law had to study carefully. The most famous pioneer of this method of legal study was the Bolognese scholar and teacher Irnerius (d. 1125), who drew students from all over Europe. Irnerius' glosses were empirical as well as scholarly, for he was not satisfied merely to explain the meaning of the text under discussion, but also attempted to apply the law to contemporary situations. The leading disciples of Irnerius, commonly called the Four Doctors, continued this integration of the civil law into twelfth-century civilization. By the time of Irnerius' death students from France, England, and Germany were streaming to Bologna to acquire the new legal science which offered them not only a rigorous intellectual discipline but also entry into a new profession.

Frederick I Barbarossa, the German emperor in the 1160's, was the first important transalpine ruler to take advantage of the recovery of the civil law and the availability of the new professional lawyers. Civil law was attractive to him for two reasons. He could use the lawyers in his government and administration, and furthermore the Justinian code provided him with an ideology to replace the old sacred kingship which had been undermined during the investiture conflict. By laying claim to the legal prerogatives of the Roman emperor, Barbarossa justified political absolutism and the enhancement of his authority in Germany; in addition, he could use the evidence of the Justinian code to assert his sovereignty over the Italian cities. When he first entered Italy on his great expedition of reconquest, he summoned an assembly at which civil lawyers in his service presented the juristic basis of his claims to absolute authority over the Italian community. Naturally the north Italian oligarchs were not happy at the use which the German emperor was making of the revival of Roman law, the study of which had been originated with their support. But Frederick's enthusiasm for the Justinian code indicated how the work of the Glossators might be turned to the advantage of the monarchies of northern Europe. Although the strong native traditions of Germanic law in the empire precluded the immediate application of the Roman legal system on the local level, by the end of the fourteenth century the reception of the civil law was well under way in Germany, and its procedure remains the basis of the German legal system to the present day.

Because of Barbarossa's early association of the Roman law revival with his own policies and ideology, the Capetian kings of the late twelfth century were wary of the introduction of the civil law into France. But by 1200 the king of France had discovered that the civil lawyers were the most suitable personnel for his expanding administration. As, during the thirteenth century, the civil lawyers came to dominate the French government, the introduction of the civil law into France was not long delayed. An important law school was established at the university of Montpellier. The civil lawyers who dominated the royal judiciary slowly wore down local vestiges of feudal and Germanic law and made the Justinian code more and more the foundation of the expanding jurisdiction of the royal courts. By the middle of the thirteenth century Roman procedure had been adopted by the French courts, which still retain a strongly judge-centered character. The Capetian monarchy overcame its initial distrust of the Justinian code as its value in the legal unification of the kingdom became more apparent. Furthermore, the French king discovered that he was able to use the principles of the civil law in support of his absolutist political doctrine in much the same way that the German king had. The French legal scholars interpreted the imperial office of the Justinian code in a generic way and arrived at the conclusion that every "king is an emperor in his own kingdom," that is, he possesses the prerogatives of legal absolutism which the *Corpus Juris Civilis* attributes to the Roman emperor.

The revival of the Justinian code profoundly affected the nature of the legal systems not only of France and Germany but also of the church itself. The canon law of the church in its formative period in the first half of the twelfth century was strongly conditioned by the concepts and procedures of the civil law. In the middle of the eleventh century church scholars had begun to try to systematize and eventually codify the canon law out of the disorganized mass of pronouncements and traditions left over from the early middle ages. The originators of this difficult work were two northern bishops, Burchard of Worms and Ivo of Chartres. In 1050 the law of the church consisted of a heterogeneous group of pronouncements made by the Bible, patristic writers, church councils, popes, and bishops. In the early middle ages various unofficial collections of canon law were made, of which the most famous was the one falsely attributed to St. Isidore of Seville and hence known as the Pseudo-Isidorian Decretals. The first generation of canon lawyers encountered an enormous body of material put together according to no critical or rational principle, containing legal propositions which contradicted each other and even some flagrant forgeries. The pioneering northern canonists of the eleventh century were, however, extremely able and dedicated scholars, and there is no doubt that they could have carried through the codification of the church law to a successful conclusion. But they were not allowed to do this by the Gregorian papacy. Hildebrand and his colleagues in the college of cardinals were apprehensive that the synthesizing of the ecclesiastical law by northern scholars would not be entirely favorable to the kind of papal absolutism they advocated, but would instead draw upon early medieval usage to give the episcopate considerable autonomy. The papacy therefore directed its own codification of the canon law, and by the beginning of the twelfth century this work was largely carried on under papal auspices by Italian scholars strongly inclined to the doctrine of papal plenitude of power.

The progress in the study of the civil law helped the Roman canonists to complete their work. They envisaged the legal position of the papacy in the church as identical with the emperor's in the state. All legislative power in the church was deemed to reside in the will of the supreme pontiff, and the Roman curia was held to be the supreme court of the church, with full appellate jurisdiction over any other ecclesiastical court in Europe. From the first decade of the twelfth century the canon lawyers were all trained extensively in the civil law, and they were inclined to see the pope as an absolute emperor in his own international, ecclesiastical kingdom. The intensive work of codification of the canon law came to fruition in the *Decretum* of the Italian, papally commissioned legist Gratian, published in 1140. Gratian drew upon the synthesizing of the canon law which had been in progress for a century, upon the principles of the civil law, and upon the new dialectical method which was being developed by the philosophers in the French universities. The alternative title of his treatise, *The Concordance of Discordant Canons,* indicates the method Gratian employed. He placed one contradictory principle next to another, that is, thesis against antithesis, and then argued toward a logical resolution of the conflicts. In every instance of disagreement in his sources he decided in favor of the plenitude of papal authority. The *Decretum* was given canonical status by the papacy, and it remains the foundation of the canon law to the present day. It was supplemented during the ensuing century by the commentaries of the Decretists (as the glossators on Gratian's text were called), by the pronouncements of Popes Alexander II and Innocent III, and finally by the *Collections* of Pope Gregory IX, an additional textbook of canon law published in 1234.

The creation of a comprehensive and systematic code of church law facilitated the creation of a great international, ecclesiastical, judicial system centered on the papal court during the twelfth and thirteenth centuries. The support which the canon law afforded the doctrine of papal plenitude of power was bound to be very helpful to the papacy in its relations with the great transalpine churchmen. It would, nevertheless, be an error to assume that every statement in a canon-law textbook or a Decretist's gloss was fully in accord with medieval reality. The canon lawyers were inclined to engage in wishful thinking and to describe as the inflexible, universal law and custom of the church what was only an ideal and potential. In countries such as England, where the great ecclesiastics were closely associated with powerful monarchies, many provisions of the canon law remained largely inoperative. It has become fashionable with some historians in recent years to accept all the pronouncements of the canon lawyers as fully reliable accounts of medieval life. This shoddy methodology can lead only to the creation of fanciful myths about the real position of the church during the high middle ages.

In two special ways did the civil-law revival affect the church in the twelfth century. First of all it gave the canon lawyers the procedure they used in ecclesiastical courts. The church so fully adopted the practices of the Roman imperial courts, as set down in the Justinian code, that historians now frequently talk about the Romano-canonical procedure of the twelfth and thirteenth centuries as a single system. The fact that the civil law advocated a judge-centered court with absolute powers given to the juristic representatives of the emperor appealed to the canonists, with their inclinations toward papal absolutism. There was nothing, therefore, very novel about the procedure used by the famous papal Inquisition of the thirteenth century. The Inquisition was a special *ad hoc* court commissioned by the papacy to deal with heretics. It basically followed civil-law procedure, and there was certainly nothing original in its use of torture as far as the history of Roman law is concerned.

The second special contribution of the Roman-law revival to the development of the high-medieval church was its provision of trained personnel for the growing papal administration. The papacy required men educated in law to staff its courts and bureaucratic offices, and the new schools of civil law provided this personnel in the same way they staffed the growing administrations of the European monarchies. A graduate in law from a medieval university could therefore enter into the service of a secular ruler, or else he could, in effect, undergo postgraduate training in canon law and enter the service of the church. If he followed the former course, he might someday become the chief minister of a powerful king in conflict with the papacy; if he pursued the latter course, he might end his career by ascending to the throne of Peter itself. The original choice of the young law-school graduate was usually made on simple professional grounds. By the second half of the twelfth century the papacy was recruiting nearly all its administrators from among the products of the European law schools, and with scarcely an exception every pope from 1150 to 1300 received his initial training in canon law. This meant that the papal administrators of the twelfth and thirteenth centuries were well trained and skillful, but this homogeneous legalistic background of the leaders of the papal curia also had less fortunate consequences. It partly accounts for the great difficulty which the high-medieval papacy experienced when faced with the problem of channeling and controlling the new popular piety. The lawyer-popes of the twelfth and thirteenth centuries were far more successful in fulfilling the administrative than the spiritual responsibilities of their office. Their juristic education and bureaucratic experience did not tell them how to cope with the emotional religiosity and heretical inclinations of the urban communities.

England was the only European country whose legal system did not come heavily under the influence of the Justinian code. While the civil law was beginning to penetrate into the juristic systems of Germany and France in the twelfth century, English law went off in another direction, developing both institutions and principles which were remarkably different from the theory and procedure of Roman law. This departure had a profound effect

on both the later government and law of England, and it constitutes one
of the outstanding ways in which the intellectual changes of the twelfth
century influenced the subsequent course of European history. Therefore, no
study of the twelfth century can avoid the question of why England developed its own non-Roman legal system. Many English historians have
completely ignored this problem, simply assuming that the channel sufficed
to cut England off from the great changes that were taking place on the
continent. This is not, however, a safe assumption, because twelfth-century
England was a cultural satellite of France. English art, literature, and
religious development in the twelfth century were heavily under French
influence; then why was English law excluded from this general cultural
impact?

It is simply not true that the Justinian code was unknown in England.
One of the outstanding Bolognese scholars was teaching in England as
early as the 1140's, and many of the royal administrators from the latter
part of the reign of Henry I received their education in France and Italy.
Most of Henry II's judges were churchmen who had been given the usual
indoctrination in Romano-canonical procedures and principles, and they
certainly had sufficient familiarity with Roman law to introduce it into
England. It was assumed by liberal English historians of the nineteenth
century that the Germanic legal tradition, descending from the Anglo-Saxon
period, was so pure and powerful that Roman law had no chance to over-
whelm it. There is some merit in this view, but it does not take into account
the real facts of the situation. While Roman vulgar law was completely
obliterated by the Anglo-Saxon invasion and the Germanic legal system
exclusively dominated English juristic practice and doctrine during the
preconquest period, the Anglo-Norman rulers had no vested interest in preserving it. No English king after 1066 had reason to be enthusiastic about
the political implications of Germanic law, which was biased in the direction of the power of local communities and against strong central government. The legal absolutism and centralism enshrined in the Justinian code
were far more in conformity with the policy of the Anglo-Norman and
Angevin monarchs than was the old Germanic system. On a priori grounds
Henry II should have eagerly imposed the civil law on England; it was as
amenable to his general inclinations as it was to Barbarossa's or the
Capetian monarch's. It must finally be pointed out that the existence of
pristine Germanic law in the empire did not discourage or ultimately
prevent the German rulers from introducing the civil law into their
country. Henry II's power over England was far greater, and he certainly
could have effected the imposition of the Justinian code on his kingdom;
yet he did not do this, and the question remains: Why did England, for all
practical purposes, remain outside the area of the Roman legal system?

The answer emerges from the historical timetable of the twelfth century. Precisely because the Anglo-Norman monarchy was at least half a century ahead of every other government in Europe in the development of strong centralizing institutions, it ultimately refrained from the reception of the Roman law. During the founding period of English royal power, between 1066 and 1135, the text of the Justinian code and the new personnel for administrative bureaucracies which the law schools were to provide were not yet available north of the Alps. The aggressive royal government had to make do with whatever was at hand, although it was by no means as suitable for establishing royal centralism and absolutism as the materials which the Capetian monarchy could draw upon at the end of the twelfth century. The Anglo-Norman rulers allowed the shire and hundred courts, the descendants of the old Germanic folk moots, to stand with their procedure and juristic principles fundamentally unchanged. The domination of the court by the prominent men of the neighborhood or county, the strictly oral pleading, and the use of the ordeal as a prime method of proof in criminal proceedings were perpetuated. The royal government sought to exercise a general supervision over the workings of the local courts by dispatching panels of itinerant justices to preside during the court days. But the function of the justices was merely to see that the correct procedure was followed, to impose sentence, and to collect the fines and amercements. The local English courts remained community courts, and their procedure preserved the Germanic principle that law belonged to the community and that it could not be changed without the assent of the political nation, the important classes in society.

The feudal law followed by the central *curia regis* reinforced this Germanic tradition. The king presided at and dominated the royal court, but did not exert an absolute control over it. Changes in the law were made with the consent of the magnates, conforming to the Germanic tradition of the legislative power of the people, and in suits between the king and one of his vassals the decision was rendered by the assembled lords. William the Conqueror ameliorated the archaic and inefficient Germanic procedure by introducing the Frankish-Norman inquest into England and by commissioning his justices to use it in civil suits, but here again the fundamental doctrine of Germanic law only received reinforcement. The institution of the inquest required the justices to place even greater reliance on the opinions of the leading men of the community, for it was they who comprised the juries and whose testimony was instrumental in deciding the lawsuits in civil matters. The success of the inquest in strictly legal matters encouraged the royal government to use it for purposes of administration as well. If juries could give testimony on such matters as the income of local landlords, which was needed for tax purposes, the government would be freed from the necessity of assigning royal agents to these tasks. In the days before the European law schools began turning out their flood of graduates, reliable administrative personnel were hard to find. Thus, by the 1130's the English monarchy became accustomed to using unpaid representatives of the local communities for a great part of the work of both law and administration in the counties.

When Henry II became king in 1154, he found a legal system in operation composed of Germanic, feudal, and additional elements which had been fused together by the royal justices after half a century into a common law for the whole realm. This peculiar system had certain deficiencies. It still relied exclusively on oral pleading, which made it archaic in relation to the civil-law systems which were spreading throughout Europe. It had no concept of equity, no way of suspending the law in a particular case in the interests of abstract justice, and in fact, while it was devoted to peace and order, it had no idea of justice. In criminal proceedings common-law procedure was strongly biased against the defendant, especially if he came from the lower classes in society. The man who was "ill-famed" in his community had little chance where the opinion of the neighborhood was the determining factor in criminal proceedings and where the investigation of evidence by the court was unknown. As a cosmopolitan Frenchman and one of the best-educated kings of the twelfth century, Henry II was fully aware that the common law compared unfavorably in several respects with the Roman system, nor were his justices, trained in Romano-canonical procedures, blind to this fact. Yet the government of Henry II decided to leave the common law in operation and not to undermine it by the introduction of civil-law institutions and principles. The common law was already in existence; it worked smoothly enough and was popular. Above all, it found favor in Henry's eyes because it was cheap. It required very few judges in comparison with the Roman system and yet returned a steady profit to the crown. Furthermore, the use of the jury for administrative purposes at the local level allowed the English government to operate with a minimum of bureaucratic personnel and, instead of an expensive host of royal agents, to make use of the unpaid services of the local nobility. One historian has called this system "self-government at the king's command." If these peculiar English institutions had not been already in operation in 1154, there is no doubt that Henry II would have introduced the Roman kind of centralized law and administration which the Capetian monarchy established at the end of the twelfth century. Henry satisfied himself with improving English legal procedure through expanding the use of the jury in civil suits and introducing the indicting grand jury in criminal pleas. Ordeals were still used as proof in criminal cases, but this was terminated by action of the Fourth Lateran Council of 1215, and in the thirteenth century the English common law assumed its full recognizable institutional form with the development of the jury of verdict.

The preservation of the common law, with its strong Germanic overtones, was thus a consequence of simple convenience to the government of Henry II. Henry and his ministers were not unaware of the fact that the political theory of the common law was much less favorable to royal absolutism than the Justinian code. But the general advantages of the common law more than compensated for this absence of a theoretical foundation for royal power. Henry believed that he could achieve a practical absolutism through the effective exploitation of existing English institutions. While he was to succeed in this aim to a very remarkable degree, the common law preserved for future generations in England the idea that the law of the land resided in the legislative power of both the king and the community and that it was not simply an expression of royal will. Thus, while in the Justinian code "the will of the emperor has the force of law," in English juristic theory the king was as much subject to the law as any member of the community. A thirteenth-century English jurist remarked that in England law rules and not will. For England as well as for France, Germany, and the Catholic church, the heritage of twelfth-century law makes its effect felt to the present day.

III. A Great Generation: Five Leaders of Twelfth-Century Thought and Feeling

A student at the embryonic University of Paris in the year 1140 would have encountered directly or indirectly the five great leaders of European thought and expression at the high tide of twelfth-century cultural creativity. There is a peculiar rhythm in intellectual history which, after long ages of gestation and merely derivative thinking, brings together several creative geniuses in a single, marvelously creative generation, and which furthermore connects their most vital work to one center of civilization. Periclean Athens, Shakespeare's London, the Paris of Voltaire and Diderot spring immediately to mind. It is a lesson of history that genius does not appear in either physical or intellectual deserts, but requires the challenge and protection of an appreciative environment and the fellowship of other great minds and personalities. Medieval civilization exhibited such a creative moment and place in the Paris of the fourth and fifth decades of the twelfth century. Five masters of thought and feeling crossed one another's paths along the banks of the Seine, and between them they represent and

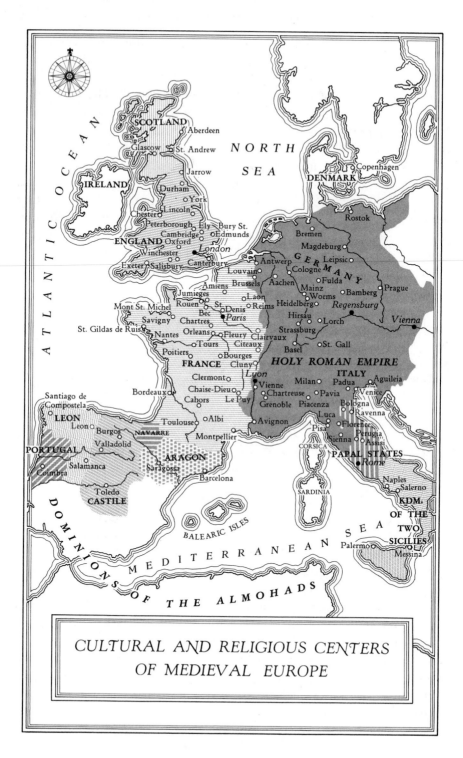

ATLANTIC OCEAN

NORTH SEA

SCOTLAND
Aberdeen
Glascow ○ ○St. Andrew
○Jarrow
IRELAND
Durham○
○York
Chester○ ○Lincoln
Peterborough○ ○Bury St.
Cambridge○ ○Edmunds
ENGLAND Oxford○
Winchester○ *London*
Exeter○ ○Salisbury ○Canterbury

Copenhagen
DENMARK

Rostok

Bremen○
Magdeburg○
Leipsic○
Antwerp○ **GERMANY** Cologne○ ○Fulda
Louvain○ Aachen○ ○Bamberg Prague○
Amiens○ Brussels○ Mainz○ *Regensburg*○
Jumieges○ ○Laon Heidelberg○ Vienna○
Mont St. Michel○ Rouen○ ○St. Reims○ ○Worms
Savigny○ Bec○ *Paris* Hirsau○ ○Lorch
St. Gildas de Ruis○ Chartres○ Strassburg○
Nantes○ Orleans○ ○Fleury ○St. Gall
Poitiers○ ○Tours Citeaux○ Basel○
FRANCE ○Bourges Cluny○ **HOLY ROMAN EMPIRE**
Clermont○ Lyon○ **ITALY**
Bordeaux○ Chaise-Dieu○ Vienne○ Milan○ Padua○ Aguileia○
Cahors○ Le Puy○ Chartreuse○ ○Pavia Venice○
Grenoble○ Piacenza○ Bologna○
Toulouse○ ○Albi Avignon○ Luca○ ○Ravenna
Santiago de Pisa○ ○Florence
Compostela○ Montpellier○ Sienna○ ○Perugia
LEON NAVARRE Assisi○
Leon○ ○Burgos CORSICA **PAPAL STATES**
PORTUGAL Valladolid○ *Rome*
Coimbra○ Salamanca○ **ARAGON**
Saragossa○ Naples○
Toledo○ Barcelona○ Salerno○
CASTILE SARDINIA **KDM.**
OF THE
BALEARIC ISLES **TWO**
Palermo○ **SICILIES**
Messina○

MEDITERRANEAN SEA

DOMINIONS OF THE ALMOHADS

CULTURAL AND RELIGIOUS CENTERS
OF MEDIEVAL EUROPE

350

also dominate every aspect of important cultural change in the period. The subsequent history of medieval thought could be viewed with considerable plausibility as the working-out of their immensely rich cultural legacy. The two later critical periods of medieval intellectual development, between 1240 and 1270 and between 1300 and 1325, were largely concerned with meeting the challenge of ideas and emotions which the great twelfth-century leaders imparted into the mainstream of medieval thought. Four of these twelfth-century intellectual leaders—Suger, Abelard, Otto of Freising, and St. Bernard—died in the 1140's or 1150's, and they may be regarded as belonging roughly to the same generation. The fifth, John of Salisbury, was of a younger generation and lived until 1180, but he did most of his important intellectual work before 1160 and can therefore be viewed as the intellectual contemporary of the other four. Three of the men were French, one was German, and one English, but a student at Paris would have discovered their physical and intellectual tracks all around him, and he would have experienced that rare, intoxicating satisfaction that comes with the sense of having been privileged to study in the vital center of an emerging, new cultural era.

Through the narrow, crooked streets of Paris, where wolves still sometimes appeared in winter, students from all over western Europe were making their way in 1140 toward the diocesan cathedral in the "Latin Quarter." Under the patronage and protection of the bishop of Paris a school of higher studies had been established. Out of this cathedral school and others such as Chartres, which was probably the first to be organized, the universities of northern Europe were to grow in the twelfth century. In a technical sense a cathedral school required only the incorporation of the masters into a *universitas,* or guild, to make this advance. The scholars who had been licensed by the bishop of Paris to teach in his school dealt with subjects which had no place in the circumscribed intellectual world of the monastery. Using the new intellectual tools of dialectic, which they derived from that part of Aristotle's logic which had been translated by Boethius into Latin in the sixth century, they were prepared to analyze and resolve the persistent problems of western thought: the nature of the world, of man, and above all, of the deity, and the relations between them. Very little of such speculation had been undertaken since patristic times; a world which was fighting for physical survival, where the preservation of literacy itself was a constant struggle, or even, as was the case in the ninth and tenth centuries, a world which was establishing the foundations of social order had to concern itself with more immediate problems and could not release its best minds for speculative thinking. In the late eleventh century Europe could afford the luxury of higher thought, and under the protection of the wealthy and sophisticated bishops of northern France, first at Chartres and then at other places such as Laon and Paris, the great intellectual quests of western civilization resumed. For two or three decades the debates over the nature of a Christian world order diverted the attention of many of the best minds from philosophy, science, and theology, but the termination of the investiture conflicts freed the surplus mental energy of Europe for speculative ratiocination.

It was difficult to slake the intellectual thirst of the generation which came to maturity about 1100. From the obscure corners of France, England, Italy, and to a lesser degree Germany, young clerical scholars took the roads in pursuit of some famous teacher whose reputation had dimly penetrated into their homelands. In the 1060's a certain Bérengar of Tours appeared as the first of a soon-to-be-familiar type of intellectual master who drew the most brilliant of the younger generation to him by the magnetic quality of his mind and personality. Bérengar's fall into doctrinal heresy confirmed the suspicions of anti-intellectuals such as Damiani and more cautious theologians such as Lanfranc that dialectic could easily be put to dangerous and irresponsible uses, but this in no way impeded the spread of the new intellectual movement or the proliferation of Bérengar's imitators. In a world growing more ordered, wealthy, populated, and literate, mastery of the well-tilled Biblical-patristic tradition of the early middle ages could not satisfy the best minds of the rising generation. Their restless intellectual quest shattered the framework within which Alcuin, Bede, and even Augustine had worked, and reached back across silent centuries to seek the guidance of Greek philosophy and science.

No one in 1100 or even 1140 was sure of the ultimate tendencies of the new learning; no one could clearly perceive the reconstruction of the Christian thought-world which would result from the new investigations into philosophy, science, and theology. Yet no one, not even those who doubted the validity or social usefulness of the new pursuits, could afford to ignore the new investigations undertaken by the masters and students in the cathedral schools of northern France. In the early twelfth century it was becoming more apparent every day that knowledge was power; without much consideration of the enormity and difficulty of the task they had assumed or even to what specific use they could put the new learning, many of the most brilliant minds of the new generation which came to maturity about 1100 set off for the new cathedral schools to participate in the intellectual revolution. Outstanding contemporaries who found the new dialectical methods temperamentally unpalatable and who were concerned by their long-range effect on the traditional Christian thought-world came forward with alternative systems drawn from extensions of the early-medieval Neoplatonic tradition, from classical humanism, or from the emotional resources of the new piety. This did not stem the intellectual upheaval in which the universities were engaged. It added other facets to it, enriching and intensifying its impact. These other approaches which were offered helped to make the intellectual expansion of the twelfth century a more comprehensive and complex movement, affecting all important aspects of higher culture, and helped to increase the variety and magnitude of the problems with which later generations of medieval thinkers had to deal.

On their way through Paris to the cathedral school many students in the 1140's had to pass the great abbey of St. Denis, the royal abbey of France. They were astonished at the results of the reconstruction of the old Carolingian church of St. Denis, which had been carried out under the close supervision of abbot Suger. The abbot had dared to make a radical departure from the church architecture of northern Italy and Constantinople, whose style, the so-called Romanesque, had hitherto dominated western art. Students who came to Paris from England or Normandy thought they saw in the abbot's work the influence of the Norman cathedrals, which had begun a shift from the Romanesque emphasis on the horizontal lines to the perpendicular plane and introduced ribbed vaulting. But many aspects of Suger's reconstruction could not be paralleled anywhere; here was a new French style, as novel and startling as the new ideas discussed in the cathedral schools. Over the entrance to the church of St. Denis had been placed a stained-glass rose window, whose manufacture had taxed the ingenuity and skill of the craftsmen employed by the abbot. The sides of the church had been raised to emphasize the perpendicular lines, and, in sharp contrast to the solid masonry wall of the Romanesque church, large windows had been cut through the stone to allow a uniform light to suffuse into the hitherto obscure interior and illuminate the altar.

At first look Suger seems a most improbable candidate for the role of inaugurating the first really new architectual style in 1700 years. Superficially he appears to be a typical figure of the early middle ages, more at home in the Cluniac culture of the tenth century than in the revolutionary intellectual world of twelfth-century Paris. His whole life was spent in the monastery of St. Denis, which had been associated with the French monarchy since the seventh century. As an affiliate of Cluny and as the keeper of the regalia of the French crown, the monastery of St. Denis was intimately involved with the affairs of the royal dynasty. The close association of St. Denis with the Capetian family is symbolically rendered in the sculptured facade of Suger's church. Abbot Suger became the chief minister and then biographer of Louis VI, and until the abbot's death in 1151 he continued to render extremely valuable services to young Louis VII, whom he had tutored. While Louis was absent on his ill-fated crusade, Suger served as his regent and capably directed the Capetian government. Thus it can be said that the abbot of St. Denis was the last of the great monastic statesmen of the middle ages, the successor of St. Boniface, Alcuin, and Lanfranc of Canterbury. Certainly his background sharply distinguishes him from the chief servants of the French monarchy in the thirteenth century.

Suger's culture also seems to mark him off as an early-medieval man, a conservative thinker out of touch with the intellectual currents of his day. His philosophy of art, by which he justified the style of the reconstruction of his church, is expressed entirely in the Neoplatonic terminology of the early middle ages. He is heavily indebted to the mystical writings of Pseudo-Dionysius, the anonymous fifth-century Syrian monk whom he identified with St. Denis, the disciple of St. Paul, and the apostle of France to whom his church was dedicated. The Dionysian Neoplatonic philosophy has for Suger canonical authority; its mystical identification of the deity with light is used by him to explain that the function of the new windows of his church is to illuminate the altar with divine emanation.

These aspects of Suger's career and doctrines, which appear to be archaic survivals of an earlier age, are balanced by other qualities which reveal him as one of the leaders of a great generation of innovators. While certainly more conservative than the lawyers who came to dominate the Capetian administration in the following half century, he resembles these *magistri* in his application of critical intelligence to the problems of medieval government. Although French kings were still crowned and anointed in the old Carolingian manner, Suger did not urge upon his royal masters the continued assertion of theoretical claims which had resulted in humiliation for the early Capetians and even for Louis VI. Instead he advocated the more sensible and realistic policy of the careful building-up of royal power in the Île-de-France. The concentration upon the resources of the royal domain as the starting point for the expansion of royal power, which became a fundamental policy of the Capetian monarchy in the later years of Louis VII, seems to have been first adumbrated by the abbot of St. Denis.

Suger's quotations from the Pseudo-Dionysian writings should not preclude us from understanding the radical significance of his artistic innovations. The purpose of his architectural reconstruction was to create a more inspiring place of worship. He regarded St. Denis as not merely a chapel for the monks but a church where the populace of Paris could feel emotionally closer to the deity than they could in the dark and squat ecclesiastical buildings of the early middle ages. Behind the austere exterior of the monastic statesman can be perceived a devout but shrewd intelligence keenly aware of the new popular piety and the yearning of zealous layman for a more intimate relationship with the Lord. In his treatise on the reconstruction of the church of St. Denis, Suger describes in detail his plans for the enriching and beautification of the interior of the church. His account of his search for magnificent liturgical vessels and jewels for the altar, taken together with his architectural innovations which illuminated the interior of the church, reveals a profound sense of the popular educational function of religious art.

In yet another way does Suger's work make him a worthy contemporary of the masters and students of the Paris school. With almost no precedent he had conceived and executed a new style of ecclesiastical architecture. This innovating spirit involved a bold departure from the intellectual attitudes of the early middle ages, which sought the preservation of the best traditions of the past. Suger's confidence in the validity of his own judgments and his boldness in pursuing the consequences of these judgments distinguish him as one of the new kind of self-reliant and progressive thinkers of the twelfth century. The work and care involved in effecting the reconstruction of the church of St. Denis were enormous. Suger had to risk spending a great part of the accumulated wealth of his abbey. He had to recruit and consult with master masons and masonic architects, and he had to find and supervise scores of stonemasons, glass cutters, and common laborers in order to get the kind of building he wanted. After all this expenditure of money and time there was no certainty that, when completed, the rose window and clerestory would not go crashing down onto the heads of the congregation. This intellectual self-confidence and organizing skill is far more important as the background to the new style than Suger's Neoplatonic philosophy of art, which had been in existence for 900 years before his time without producing anything that even remotely approximated Gothic architecture. There is an obvious parallel between Suger's work and the philosophic and theological investigations which were being pursued in his day a few miles from St. Denis at the cathedral school of Paris. In the embryonic university the masters and students were also applying an old doctrine to new ends; like abbot Suger they were optimistically creating a new structure such as had never existed before and whose feasibility and permanence could not be determined for certain before its completion. The audacity, enterprise, and pragmatic intelligence of the mid-twelfth century has no more outstanding representative than the abbot of St. Denis.

Suger was an old-fashioned social type who unself-consciously created an artistic revolution. John of Salisbury was in every respect the type of new man which the intellectual and educational revolution was producing. But in spite of this, or perhaps because of it, he was painfully conscious of the growing separation of contemporary culture from the early medieval thought-world. He tried to preserve the older values in the face of the rapid change and sought the means of controlling the effects of the new learning and power of the twelfth century. John was an English cleric of obscure and probably modest social background who came as a very young man to study in the new schools of Chartres and Paris in the 1130's. He sat at the feet of the great dialecticians and theologians of the day, and his vivid accounts of his teachers and fellow students provide us with some of our most valuable information about the beginnings of the French universities. He went to Rome in search of employment and became the secretary of the English pope Adrian IV (Nicholas Breakspear) in the early 1150's, whose educational background was the same as John's. It was the only time in history when an Englishman conducted papal affairs; Cardinal Robert Pullan, also an English product of the French schools, was another prominent servant of Adrian IV. In 1153 John returned to England to become the secretary of Archbishop Theobald of Canterbury. He inevitably became a close associate of Thomas Becket, yet another English cleric who had studied in France, who was the head of the archbishop's chancery. John witnessed the advancing power of the English state in the early part of Henry II's reign, and on one occasion he seems to have incurred the wrath of the king, who regarded him as a papal agent. In the 1160's John experienced at first hand the struggle between Henry II and Thomas Becket, by now archbishop of Canterbury after having served the king as his chancellor. John was Thomas' secretary and accompanied Becket into exile. He wrote the Canterbury martyr's biography, but he was not blind to the faults of his master's character. As a widely respected churchman and writer John was summoned back to France to spend his last years before his death in 1180 as bishop of Chartres, where he had gone almost a half century before as an unknown cleric to study in the cathedral school. No other twelfth-century figure was personally involved with so many and such a variety of important developments. Yet John of Salisbury was much more a thoughtful spectator of these events than a leading participant in them. His disposition, contemplative rather than active, compassionate rather than critical, his enormous erudition, and his solid common sense fitted him ideally for the task of observing and considering the implications of the great changes of his era.

John was well educated in the new logic, philosophy, and theology of the French schools, but he became one of the most prominent critics of the new intellectual trends. He considered the work of the teachers at Paris and Chartres to be at best useless—he describes how, after returning to Paris after several years' absence, he found the masters and students pursuing the same debates with no appreciable progress except an increase in arrogance—and at worst dangerous to the foundations of the Christian thought-world. In this respect John was in agreement with the anti-intellectual attitudes of Damiani and his own great contemporary St. Bernard. But he did not go along with their substitution of a mystical for a dialectical road to the deity. The fact is that John of Salisbury's mind was that of a moralist; he was temperamentally unsuited for either the scientific or emotional approaches to life. In his view there was no need to discover truth, for that was already known; the question was how to inculcate it in the rising generation. Everywhere around him he could see the corrupting effects of the new learning, wealth, and power, the undermining of the old values. John of Salisbury is therefore, if not the originator, at least one of the most eloquent spokesmen for one of the primary educational doctrines of western civilization: the function of education is not intellectual but moral. The purpose of the schools, he claimed, should be to preserve and teach the traditional values, to counter the corrupting effects of intellectual, financial, and political power, to teach men how to live rightly. John was deeply grieved to see the liberal arts declining in importance and taking a secondary place in the new universities of the arrogant and irresponsible masters of dialectic. He believed that it was precisely in the great literature of the classical heritage, which was coming to be neglected in favor of its philosophical and scientific aspects, that the means could be found for teaching men the principles of right conduct. Virgil, Livy, Cicero, and other great Latin belletristic writers had presented to their contemporaries these principles of human decency and self-restraint which were more and more ignored in the twelfth century. John of Salisbury's teaching was the purest form of Christian humanism which had yet appeared. More clearly than any of his contemporaries he realized the corrupting influence of power, and the use made of the classical heritage in conditioning the moral outlook of the European ruling classes from the fifteenth to the twentieth centuries plausibly demonstrates the large degree of utility in his proposed educational remedy. But his contemporaries, engrossed by the prizes which learning, wealth, and power appeared to offer, were not willing to listen to him. The liberal arts steadily declined in importance in the universities, and the Christian humanism of John of Salisbury found its disciples not in the twelfth- and thirteenth-century thinkers but in Petrarch, Erasmus, and More. John's moralistic outlook resembles the doctrines of the Renaissance humanists in every way, both in its primary emphasis on the preservation of humane values in society through classical education, and in its failure to understand the possibilities and advantages of science and speculative thought.

The evil in contemporary society which most concerned John of Salisbury was the corrupting effect of political power—the degradation of the human spirit resulting from the authority which one man or group of men held over large groups of people. He was by no means blind to the emergence of this condition within the church. He bitterly criticized avaricious and venal ecclesiastical lords, and on one occasion he frankly told Adrian IV that he was disturbed by what he had found at Rome: evidence of a self-sustaining and arrogant bureaucracy impervious to growing criticism. It was only, however, when he returned to England in the 1150's and encountered the secular engine of the Angevin state that the consequences of power were first fully brought home to John of Salisbury. The result was the publication in 1159 of the *Policraticus,* a treatise on the right ordering of the political life. Few works in the history of political theory have so frequently been misinterpreted. What has impressed most students of the *Policraticus* is its general support for the traditional political theory of the church. John views the whole of society as a body and gives the church the position of the heart and the state that of the head. Thereby he restates the traditional hierocratic theory: the state must serve the church, which, as the spiritual organism, is superior. This recapitulation of old doctrine is hardly significant; John had spent his whole life in the service of the church and had just returned from several years at Rome, and he knew no other political theory. What is significant are his quiet hesitations and his qualifications of the hierocratic doctrine in the face of contemporary political experience in Angevin England.

No dispassionate observer of England at the end of the 1150's, such as John was, could deny the fact that the leader of English society was not the church but monarchy. The royal government, through its legal and financial institutions, was coming more and more to impose its will on the people and to obliterate the effectiveness of any competing jurisdictions. Lord, bishop, knight, and peasant—all were steadily being drawn into the nexus of royal power. These realities of social life cast grave doubts on the empirical value of the old political Augustinianism, and John's sensitivity drove him to try to integrate the existence of secular power and leadership with the old political ideals of the church. The *Policraticus* is an interior dialogue; John was trying to tell himself that the emergence of the state had not shattered the framework of the old order. He was not very convincing in his arguments, and the resulting ambiguity of his work is evident. Along with the traditional hierocratic theory he admits that the end of the state is the perception of truth and the rewarding of virtue, with the implication that when the state pursues moral ends, it has a sanction in and of itself. This is a subtle but highly significant departure from political Augustinianism; John's modification of hierocratic doctrine would have infuriated Gregory VII. It is the earliest example of the shift from a pessimistic to an optimistic view of the state, which was to be the fundamental theme of political thought for the next hundred and fifty years. John was the first ecclesiastical political theorist to face the consequences of the political changes of the high middle ages, and his exasperation and quiet desperation are reflected on almost every page of the *Policraticus.* He could neither abandon the traditional hierocratic theory nor, as an intelligent and extremely sensitive observer of the mores of his time, ignore the new leadership exercised in society by the state. The only solution was to ascribe moral qualities to the state, thereby preserving, in theory, the ethical foundations of the social order. But to do this was to give the state moral sanctions and to implicitly increase its authority. John was not blind to radical implications of his doctrine. He tried to resolve the problem by emphasizing the distinction between king and tyrant, and to give his discussion a tone of plausibility he speculated on the possibility of justifiable tyrannicide. He fully realized, however, the dangerous consequences to social order of such a principle and came to no definite conclusion on the question. John's treatise is the result of a painful and reluctant adjustment of a moralist and traditionalist to the realities of political life; what is most significant is not his pain and reluctance but his adjustment at all. It marks the beginnings of an upheaval in European political thought.

John's contemporary, Bishop Otto of Freising (d. 1158), carried considerably further this transformation in the political consciousness of Europe. In Otto's writings the dichotomy between the old and the new is sharper and the movement from pessimism to optimism more explicit, and cautious recognition of contemporary reality is replaced by an ominous, almost hysterical celebration of the moral potentialities of secular leadership.

Whereas John of Salisbury's social origins were modest, Otto was a scion of one of the most aristocratic families in Europe, the princely German house of Hohenstaufen. The heterogeneous appeal of the new learning and new piety is dramatically demonstrated by the fact that Otto studied in the Paris school from 1127 to 1133 and then became a Cistercian monk and abbot. He was elected bishop of Freising in 1137 and applied his vast erudition and considerable literary skill to two historical works of a highly sophisticated and philosophic nature. The first of these, published in 1146, *The Two Cities,* is an extremely pessimistic survey of world history written from the standpoint of Augustinian theology. Otto undertook to demonstrate the conflict between the earthly and the heavenly cities on the stage of world history, which Augustine believed was fully apparent to God alone. Nevertheless, Orosius, in his immensely popular *Seven Books Against the Pagans,* already had presumed to see the particular working of divine providence in history, and the common historiographical inclination of the middle ages was to pick out the course of the heavenly and earthly cities on the plane of world history. While Otto does not fully subscribe to Augustine's doctrine of meta-history, and while he attempts to reveal the actual development of the two cities in world history, his general world view is conditioned by Augustinian pessimism, in particular with regard to secular power. In *The Two Cities* the bishop of Freising can see almost no good in the history of earthly kingdoms. Their lugubrious annals are almost exclusively a record of sordid crime, and the history of the earthly city, as viewed by Otto, is virtually identified with the development of monarchy. *The Two Cities* is an historiographical presentation of the Augustinian pessimism and hatred for secular power which looms in the doctrines of Gregory VII. The experience of his own day gave Otto no cause to mitigate his harsh judgment of the propensities of secular power; writing in Germany two decades after the investiture conflict, he could see no moral value in the imperial office.

A comparison of *The Two Cities* with Otto's other important historical work, *The Deeds of Frederick Barbarossa,* on which he was working at the time of his death and which was completed by his secretary, Rahewin, produces a startling contrast. It is difficult to believe that these two works were written by the same historian. We pass suddenly from the Augustinian denigration of the state to an extremely optimistic, highly emotional celebration of the moral and messianic potentialities of imperial authority. The fact that Frederick I Barbarossa, who ascended the imperial throne in 1152, was Otto's nephew and confidant cannot be discounted. But *The Deeds of Frederick Barbarossa* is not simply dynastic propaganda; Otto was far too austere and independent a man and too dedicated to the welfare of the Christian world order to prostitute his learning in such a way. He sincerely believed that Frederick's policy of reconstructing the imperial power inaugurated a new and better era for Christian society. The interests of the heavenly city were now to be furthered by secular power. Augustinian pessimism could not long withstand twelfth-century civilization's disposition to creativity and improvement. The spirit of the age was constructive, forward-looking, bold, optimistic. Augustinian pessimism could not resist the pragmatic claim made by success and achievement, in government no less than in architecture, for the moral approval of society. Hence Frederick Barbarossa appears in Otto's history as the charismatic hero who will not only rebuild the authority of the German crown, but will also bring closer the triumph of the heavenly city. The devout church scholar and Cistercian monk relegates the papacy to a secondary position in this heaven on earth which Barbarossa was establishing. The bishop of Rome is regarded in Otto's work as an alien official, respected but remote.

What appears, therefore, in John Salisbury's *Policraticus* in an inferential and implicit way emerges with startling clarity in Otto's outlook: the twelfth-century state is absorbing into itself moral, emotional, and even divine qualities to buttress legal absolutism and administrative power. These additional sanctions were all that the new monarchies of western Europe needed to establish themselves as self-sustaining and irresponsible entities. Otto's history inaugurates the reversal of the effects of the investiture conflict—the regaining of moral and quasi-sacred attributes by royal power. John of Salisbury reluctantly admits the moral sanction of the state; Otto of Freising advocates it. The next hundred and fifty years were to witness an ever increasing repetition, on the part of the churchmen of northern Europe, of Otto's attitude to monarchy and the papacy. He is the prophet of the morally shrouded, self-righteous, sovereign state of the thirteenth century.

Suger, John of Salisbury, and Otto of Freising are very important, but still not the most central and seminal figures in the intellectual expansion of twelfth-century Europe. That accolade belongs jointly to Peter Abelard and his self-appointed antagonist, St. Bernard of Clairvaux. It would be an exaggeration, but not an entirely implausible one, to assert that the subsequent history of medieval thought and feeling constitutes a series of appendices to the work of Abelard and Bernard.

The reputation of Peter Abelard (1079–1142) has undergone many vicissitudes among historians. In the nineteenth century he was hailed as a forerunner of Protestantism. In the first half of the twentieth century it was the fashion to underrate and ignore much of the significance of his work. In recent appraisals of medieval thought his crucial importance has begun to be perceived, but a comprehensive study of his work is still lacking.

Abelard was the son of a minor lord in Brittany, a wild frontier region which was accustomed to produce savage warriors but not scholars and philosophers. The tremendous social impact of the new learning may be gauged by the attractions it presented to this obscure nobleman. He made his way to the new schools of philosophy and theology at Chartres and Paris. He was recognized from the beginning as an exceptionally brilliant student, and he mastered the new dialectical methods rapidly, but he was also a difficult person, entirely inner-directed, arrogant, disagreeable, hypercritical, and gauche. After completing a course, it was his custom to set himself up as a lecturer on the subject in competition with his former teacher. He was not the kind of scholar who makes a pleasant academic colleague; such a type was as bound to get into trouble in the twelfth century as in the twentieth. Nevertheless, it was a personal scandal which, by his own account, if it may be believed, got him into trouble. He seduced a certain Héloise, the niece of a prominent cathedral canon in Paris. He tells us that her family punished him by "cutting off those parts of my body with which I had done that which was the cause of their sorrow." The rest of his career was a series of unhappy crises. He assumed the office of abbot of a Breton monastery, but gave it up when he discovered that the monks were all thugs. He entered the monastery of St. Denis where, as might be expected, he was miserable and restless. He was denounced by St. Bernard for publishing heretical doctrines, and he was subsequently summoned before a church council, where he was forced to recant. Abelard spent the last year of his life in retirement at Cluny, where he was well treated. The Cluniac monks, like all true aristocrats, did not hold grudges.

Beyond all doubt Abelard was a genius of the first rank. Everybody who met him was impressed by the force of his personality and the power of his intellect. His stormy career may reflect a psychological instability resulting from a failure to find a suitable environment in which he could fully exercise his unusual talent. Abelard's personal troubles seem to stem largely from the fact that he lived a century too soon, as it were. He was a pioneer in the rigorous use of the Aristotelian dialectic and the ruthless pursuit of rational truth. Other men were doing the same thing, but far less effectively, and Abelard's preeminence made him the obvious scapegoat for those who suspected the consequences and implications of the new logic. As a contemporary of Thomas Aquinas he might have aroused some concern, but he would have appeared far less singular or peculiar. In the thirteenth and fourteenth centuries he would have been able to follow a normal academic career, to have held a professorship in a great university, and to have avoided the unhappiness and personal misery which marked his life.

The two most important aspects of Abelard's thought were his rediscovery of personality and his views on the problem of universals. In both cases he was undermining the Platonic structure of early medieval thought. From the third century on there had been little or no recognition of individual personality. The real person, with his unique characteristics, had been obliterated by the Platonic concern with ideal types. Early-medieval culture had very little appreciation for personality; only the representative type seen under the aspect of eternity and religion was portrayed in literature. Autobiography disappeared entirely, because literate men found their lives significant only to the extent that they conformed to an ideal pattern. The description of personal idiosyncracies would be regarded as proud, sinful arrogance. Augustine's *Confessions* was the last autobiography written before the twelfth century, and even it is not strictly an autobiography, for the bishop of Hippo was concerned with revealing himself only as Everyman. In the early middle ages there was very little biographical writing worthy of the name. A mass of hagiographical literature followed conventional patterns, forcing its subjects into preconceived molds and turning them into plaster saints. Kings were generally portrayed by their secretaries in accordance with the ideal pattern of a Christian monarch as set down in the prototype *Life of Constantine* by Eusebius of Caesarea. When the characteristics of a real personality did break through in these royal biographies, it was the result of a failure in artistic consistency; the writer was unable to sustain his typological motif.

Twelfth-century creativity produced a new appreciation of individual accomplishment and with it the beginning of the attempt to describe the details of particular lives. It came to be doubted that depicting men as merely conforming to an ideal type fully captured the significance of lives known for singular achievement. Thus the secretary of St. Anselm, the theologian and archbishop of Canterbury, early in the second decade of the twelfth century produced two biographies of his master. One was a piece of conventional hagiography; the other gives many details of Anselm's episcopate. In the former work Anselm appears as a conventional saint, but in the latter as a real person who occasionally loses his temper, becomes discouraged, suffers anguish, falls ill, etc. In the 1120's a French monk undertook to write his autobiography, and in the same decade the Anglo-Norman historian, William of Malmesbury, published two collections of biographies, one of the English kings and the other of the bishops and abbots of his day. The latter book is so circumstantial in its account and contains so many unflattering details that William was forced to publish an expurgated edition. In the following half century a radical change in attitude toward personality occurred, and European writers discovered the art of biography. By the 1180's this development had reached the point where a Welsh clerk filled four volumes with accounts of his experiences and reminiscences, giving us a vivid and at times hilarious account of the court of Henry II, the crooked intricacies of ecclesiastical politics, and the uncouth customs of the Irish.

Abelard's autobiography, *The History of My Calamities,* was the critical turning point in the twelfth-century rediscovery of personality. It goes to the opposite extreme from early-medieval typology. Abelard revels in his idiosyncrasies and delights in revealing to the world the peculiar facts of his own life, even those which could not be socially approved. In fact, like so many later biographers, he may have made his experiences appear more dramatic and startling in retrospect than they actually were. His account of his affair with Heloise does not always ring true. It was certainly his intention to titillate and shock his readers, although it is unlikely that he made up the story out of whole cloth. The important point is that Abelard wished to reveal himself to the world as a unique individual whose biography could not be confused with anyone else's. It is not the universal and ideal that he wishes to portray but the particular and individual. *The History of My Calamities* is thus a direct attack on the Platonic absorption of the individual into the universal.

Abelard's iconoclasm and individualism were a reflection of the fact that he was an urban personality, a city man. One of the most important aspects of medieval universities was their emergence in urban areas. Monastic schools had existed in rural society, isolated and without much occasion for the personal exchange of ideas. In rural society, with its strict class lines and conventional pattern of life, there was little or no opportunity for unique and original ways of life. Men were born into a certain class and followed the mores suitable to their status. But "city air made men free" not only in the legal sense meant by the nineteenth-century German historian who coined the phrase, but also in the sense of providing the environment for the creation of an original personality and pattern of thought. This was even truer of the academics than of the businessmen. The masters and students in the embryonic universities lived in an extremely competitive society. If a teacher did not appear interesting and important, he would lose his students, and if a professor was successful, it was due to the impression made on his audience by his mental and other qualities. Even in the more organized universities of the thirteenth and fourteenth centuries an excellent teacher was a celebrity who attracted students from all over Europe to his crowded lecture hall. In Abelard's day the academic lived entirely by his own wits; if he could not attract students, he had nothing to fall back on, and his career would terminate in miserable failure and poverty. When a great scholar such as Abelard found students from every corner of Europe pondering his every word, he could not help but be greatly impressed by the quality of his own mind and become a strong egoist. It is true in any case that self-love and grandiose self-esteem are the most general psychological characteristics of an outstanding teacher. In the peculiar circumstances of Abelard's academic world the teacher was bound to conceive of himself as a charismatic individual. The awe with which he was regarded by his students was transferred to his own conception of himself, until he felt that every aspect of his life, even his calamities, were worthy of revelation to the world. The extreme individualism and egoism which in later centuries were to be the peculiar characteristics of the artistic temperament appeared in Abelard's day as a quality of academics. While the great architects and artists of the twelfth century, men worthy in every way to be ranked with Michelangelo and da Vinci, were still faceless men about whom we know next to nothing, the Paris masters thought of themselves as great personalities.

Abelard's contribution to the debate on the nature of universals was as important in shaping the intellectual tendencies of his age as was his emphatic revelation of himself as a distinct individual. In fact, these two aspects of his thought are related, for in both instances he was challenging the Platonic doctrine that the general and universal is everything while the particular and individual is nothing, which had dominated western thought since the third century A.D. The debate on the nature of universal concepts or abstract ideas began in the late eleventh century and continued intermittently, now quietly, now acrimoniously, into the fourteenth and fifteenth centuries. The debate was carried on in academic institutions and in highly technical philosophical language which requires knowledge of logic and metaphysics for complete understanding. This does not mean, however, that the debate had no relevance to the general problems of medieval civilization; on the contrary, the stability of the Christian thought-world depended on the outcome of this philosophic controversy. The Italian Renaissance humanists had no taste for logic and the more technical aspects of metaphysics; not being able to understand the debate on universals, they made fun of it and dismissed it as obscure nonsense. They claimed that medieval philosophers had been so foolish as to debate the question of how many angels could dance on the head of a pin. As a matter of fact, debates on a subject much like this were held in medieval universities, and they were by no means insignificant or absurd, except to the ignorant. The angel-dancing proposition was a way of expressing the problem of infinity, one of the central problems of logical and mathematical thought. The Italian humanists could no more understand, and therefore appreciate, medieval philosophy than the twentieth-century layman can comprehend Einstein's physics. For four hundred years the greatest minds of Europe debated the nature of universals, and learned society waited with bated breath for the resolution of this controversy, and justifiably so. The outcome of this philosophic debate profoundly affected the medieval conception of man's relation to the deity, the nature of the church, the sacraments, and the priesthood, and the relationship between science and dogmatic faith.

The dispute on the nature of universals was the form taken in the middle ages by the most persistent problem in western philosophy, which still commands the attention of some of the most acute minds in the world today. The problem is, Do the general concepts in our minds, such as justice, truth, beauty, God, church, state, etc., or even simpler ones, such as the generic idea of tree, chair, horse, etc., have a reality outside our own minds? Are they purely mental images and convenient terms or are these images and terms expressive of a metaphysical reality outside individual minds? When men speak of the idea of justice or the idea of chair, are they merely using vague terms, or are they describing a self-subsisting universal which has an existence apart from human speech and thought? In the early middle ages there was no debate on these questions, because before the eleventh century all medieval thinkers subscribed to Platonic philosophy. Plato's system was founded on belief in the reality of universal ideas. He claimed that our own idea of justice or chair was but a vague reflection of a pure, self-subsisting, eternal, metaphysical form. In fact, Plato contended that we have a knowledge of justice or chair only because of these eternally existing metaphysical realities outside our own minds. This is one of the two fundamental extreme forms which the answer to the problem of universals can take. In modern philosophy the followers of Plato are called idealists because they believe that ideas are real; in the medieval schools, taking the other end of the same proposition, they were called realists. They believed that ideas are *res,* things, and therefore that universals have an independent reality outside individual human minds.

At the beginning of the twelfth century the validity of Platonic realism was questioned for the first time. If the early-medieval men had had available to them the metaphysical writings of Aristotle, they would have found Plato's doctrines seriously challenged by the other master of Greek thought. But Aristotle's metaphysics was not translated into Latin until the second half of the twelfth century; until then, only that part of his logic that was translated into Latin by Boethius was known in Latin-Christian Europe. This intellectual tool, fully taken up and used by the vigorous and critical minds of the late eleventh and first half of the twelfth centuries, was sufficient to provide a method for scrutinizing the merits of Plato's doctrine. The new logicians were not satisfied to accept Platonism as the canonical philosophy divinely inspired, but they wished to put it to the test of rigorous dialectical inquiry. From the first, this endeavor aroused concern and uneasiness in more conservative minds. It was not simply that the prevailing Biblical-patristic tradition was heavily influenced by Platonism; even more important was the relevance of the question of the reality of the universals to Christian knowledge. It had been comforting to believe that human reason could arrive at those same universal concepts of God, immortality, justice, and the church which had been initially revealed by the

Bible and dogmatic faith. If, however, philosophers concluded that it was impossible for human reason to maintain the reality of those concepts, then faith would have to stand alone as the source of Christian knowledge, and its alliance with rational thought, which Platonism made possible, would be dissolved. As early as the 1060's Peter Damiani had well understood the dangerous implications of the new logic. He sensed that the reckless inquiry into the reality of universals could end in a growing separation and eventually a dichotomy between the world of reason and the world of faith, between the new learning and revelation, which was bound to result in disparagement and humiliation for the latter.

Damiani's warning about the course that philosophic thought was taking failed to impede the inquiry into the validity of the Platonic doctrine of universals. The great cardinal's suspicion of dialectic appeared to be groundless because the initial consequence of the pursuit of the new logic strongly confirmed the validity of Platonism. In the first decade of the twelfth century St. Anselm of Canterbury maintained that it was possible for "faith to seek understanding" through rational philosophy and science. He showed how realism could be used to prove the existence of God. His so-called ontological argument for the existence of God (which was rejected by Thomas Aquinas in the thirteenth century but later revived by Descartes and Leibnitz) contended that since ideas are *res* and since we have on our minds an idea of "that which nothing greater can be thought," or God, then God must exist. Anselm's immense prestige as a scholar and saint gave additional weight to his argument and momentarily indicated that realism would not be threatened by the new philosophic inquiry.

The emergence of a contrary philosophic doctrine was not long in coming, however. In the second decade of the twelfth century one of the most outstanding teachers in the French schools, Roscelin, took a position diametrically opposed to the realist view and negated Anselm's assumptions. He declared that universals were not *res* but merely *voces,* words, or *nomina,* names. Universals were terms used for convenience in human intercourse, but they had no independent existence outside individual human minds. This fundamental position came to be known as nominalism, the doctrine directly contrary to realism. The corollary of Roscelin's teachings was that while universals might indeed exist, they do not necessarily exist because we think about them. In other words, their reality could not be established by reason, but was only known to us through revelation. On the surface there was no cause for alarm at the nominalist position; the early nominalists' skeptical attitude toward the potentialities of reason increased the exclusive importance of faith. Only through revelation could the universal concepts of the Christian faith be known. By negating the power of reason, Roscelin's and his followers' nominalism ended in extreme fideism. It was hard for anyone to deny Roscelin's orthodoxy, for, if anything, he had enhanced the importance of revelation; it, was, in his view, the only source of Christian knowledge. Against the background, however, of the Platonic tradition of the early middle ages, which had offered rational support for dogmatic faith, the nominalist view signified the disappointing radical diminution of the foundations of Christian knowledge.

In the 1130's an intense debate raged in the French schools between the realist and nominalist positions, between the supporters of Anselm and Roscelin, while sensitive and well-informed churchmen throughout Europe looked on with apprehension as to its outcome. The position which Abelard would take was of the greatest moment and was bound to cause a sensation. As the most outstanding teacher of his day, as both the most brilliant mind and most forceful personality in the new schools, his opinions were bound to be very influential. Abelard had, in fact, been a pupil of Roscelin, but he had also listened to the lectures of those who took the realist side. He was fully conscious of the importance of the debate and his contribution to it, and in stating his views he avoided his accustomed extremism. Abelard concluded that universals were "confused general images," that is, they were general images developed in the mind through extrapolation from particular impressions. Therefore, in his view universals were neither things nor terms; they were conceptions, useful but not necessarily real. It was a moderate position, but it leaned toward the nominalist side, and it certainly cast doubt upon the validity of rational support for the teachings of revelation, although it did not absolutely deny this possibility. If Abelard had not towered above contemporary philosophers and if he had not been an aggressive and unusual person with a great following among the students, his moderate nominalism would not have attracted much attention. As it was, he seemed to be leading the attack on the Platonic foundations of traditional Christian thought, and, beyond doubt, to a considerable degree the implications of his philosophy were in that direction. Even when Abelard expressed his conclusions in a qualified and moderate way, the general tendency of his worldview to conflict with the Biblical-patristic tradition was immediately evident to sensitive observers. Abelard was not helped by the radical and volatile propensities of his students, who were eager to criticize all sorts of long-standing traditions and aroused wide-spread fears that Abelard was leading the younger generation to overthrow the Christian order. One of Abelard's students, a certain Arnold of Brescia, later fomented a social revolt in Rome and was executed by Frederick Barbarossa. Such notorious disciples could only serve to enhance Abelard's reputation among the leaders of society as a monstrous subverter of Christian ideals and a devilish corrupter of the younger generation.

Abelard was a marked man, and his fall was not long in coming. He seems to have had a perverse inclination to give his enemies everything they needed to destroy him. He undertook to publish a work on the nature of the trinity, a subject which western thinkers had always avoided because of the heresies into which Greek-Christian theologians had stumbled when they tried to define philosophically the relations between God the Father, God the Son, and God the Holy Spirit. When Abelard's book appeared, the worst fears of conservative churchmen were confirmed. He had already antagonized them by the publication of an earlier book, *Sic et Non,* which placed in dialectical juxtaposition, for and against, the opinions of various church fathers on theological problems. Gratian employed this same method in his *Decretum,* as did the standard mid-twelfth century orthodox textbook on theology, Peter Lombard's *Sentences,* and Thomas Aquinas' *Summa Theologica* was also to use this dialectical manner of argument—with the important difference that they resolved the contradictory propositions, whereas Abelard allowed them to stand without resolution. He seemed to be mocking the church fathers and now questioning the validity of the greatest Christian mystery. His condemnation as a heretic and the ruination of his academic career inevitably followed. His subsequent personal miseries prevented Abelard from carrying further his investigation into the nature of universals. In any case, the reception into western thought in the half century after his death of Aristotelian corpus broadened and somewhat altered the terms of the realist-nominalist debate as it existed in the first half of the twelfth century. Abelard's doctrine was inevitably outmoded by the tremendous impact on western thought of Greek and also, to some extent, Arabic philosophy. This fact does not substantially diminish his central position in the higher culture of the middle ages. He was the most important spokesman of the movement away from the Platonic realism which had cemented the thought-world of the early middle ages. The next two centuries of Christian thought were devoted to struggling with the implications of this intellectual upheaval.

The prosecutor at Peter Abelard's trial for heresy was St. Bernard, abbot of Clairvaux, the self-appointed conscience of the mid-twelfth-century church. He had from the first been hostile to the work of the Paris school. He suspected those who learned "merely in order that they may know"; "such curiosity," he said, "is blamable." He accused Abelard and men like him of wishing "to learn for no other reason than that they may be looked upon as learned, which is ridiculous vanity." As the great successor in medieval culture to Peter Damiani, he had no appreciation for the utility of the new learning. The only secular knowledge to which he was willing to ascribe any value was the liberal arts, and even then only for the traditional, limited, functional purpose of service in clerical education. Bernard claimed that literacy and learning offered no road to God. All that was needed for salvation was a "pure conscience and unfeigning faith." These pronouncements seem to mark St. Bernard as the conservative leader of his generation, and he liked to think of himself in this way. But when his ideas are examined as a whole, they appear to be no less a radical challenge to the early medieval thought-world than the doctrines of Abelard, although, of course, from a different direction. St. Bernard was the spokesman for the new piety of the twelfth century, as Abelard was the protagonist of the new learning. Far from being conservative, the Bernardine vision looms as the most potentially revolutionary doctrine of the twelfth century.

Bernard's reputation, like Abelard's, has undergone many vicissitudes. In the middle ages he was greatly revered and frequently portrayed (although not by those who knew him personally) as the prototype of the angelic saint. His emotionalism and uncompromising conviction have not made him popular with modern writers. He has been depicted as querulous, overbearing, and neurotic. The only strongly favorable biography of Bernard which has appeared in the twentieth century was one published on the eight-hundredth anniversary of his death in 1153 by his own Cistercian order. His intolerance and fanaticism make his character unpalatable to modern tastes, but the more medieval culture is studied, the more far-reaching and complex does his influence appear. It is not easy to love Bernard, but it is impossible to ignore him or even, indeed, to exaggerate his importance in the development of medieval civilization.

Bernard was the product of one of the higher ranks of the French nobility. His young manhood was devoted to the life of the aristocractic warrior, but, as was later the case with St. Francis and St. Ignatius Loyola, whose social background was similar, he experienced a revulsion against the mores of his class and underwent a powerful conversion experience which impelled him toward the religious life. In medieval parlance, he became "a soldier of Christ," a monk. He joined the new Cistercian order, the leader north of the Alps of the new ascetic tendencies in western monasticism, taking some of his noble friends with him. Eventually Bernard was appointed to the abbacy of the Cistercian monastery of Clairvaux. He was by far the most famous member of his order, and his reputation contributed greatly to the rapid expansion of the Cistercian movement. In actuality, however, Bernard had erred in his calling; he was temperamentally unsuited for the contemplative life. He was too complex and vital a man to be a twelfth-century monk, and his bad temper and querulous disposition were largely the consequence of his inability to remain under the restraints of the Cistercian rule and the feelings of guilt which developed when he spent the greater part of the last two decades of his life away from his monastery.

Bernard's reputation as the leader of the much admired Cistercians, his dynamic personality and eloquence, and his position as the unofficial spokesman of popular piety gave him the opportunity to play a great role in society. Between 1125 and 1153 he seems to have dominated the western church. He made popes, harangued kings, preached crusades, advised churchmen, condemned Jews and then prohibited pogroms, and generally made a nuisance of himself. An example of his conduct was the papal election dispute of 1130, which was the consequence of a split in the electoral college. A slight majority elected Anaclete II, but the more prominent cardinals chose Innocent II. Bernard announced that votes should be weighed, not counted, and secured the papal throne for Innocent II. While this view of majority rule was common in the twelfth and thirteenth centuries, contemporaries were not blind to the fact that he had scarcely acted in a disinterested way, for Innocent II was one of his disciples. A careful reading of Bernard's voluminous correspondence reveals many similar instances of arbitrary judgment. He was particularly severe in criticizing the older Cluniac monasticism. He took it upon himself to castigate the architecture of Cluny, which he found too ornate and not sufficiently austere, and he did not refrain from lecturing abbot Suger of St. Denis, whom he accused of associating with bad company and thereby endangering his soul. Many churchmen were secretly delighted when the second crusade, which Bernard had preached, ended in disaster. Bernard wondered why God had humiliated him in this way, but this did not stop him from continuing to act as the arbiter of Europe. It has sometimes been said that he was the leader of Christian Europe during his lifetime. He certainly had great influence, and he undoubtedly viewed himself in this way, but his control over the lay and ecclesiastical princes was more apparent than real. Kings, popes, and bishops came to feel that a letter or lecture from St. Bernard was a regular ordeal that they had to endure, but they did not often do what he bid them, at least for any length of time.

What Bernard wanted was the moral reformation of Europe, the strict ordering of life according to Christian teachings. No less than Humbert and Hildebrand, he was a puritan who wished to create the City of God on earth, but he was accepted because, unlike them, he confined himself to using moral persuasion to achieve this end. This is why the leaders of society were willing to tolerate him: he was a great religious, universally respected, and an extremely eloquent preacher who had assumed the role of the moral conscience of Europe. But he had no official authority, he was not the pope, he excommunicated no one, and he had no power to depose kings. Consequently kings and churchmen were willing to listen to his harangues, because he interfered in no substantial way with their endeavors to increase their power or to pursue their normal policies.

It was not for his appeals to the leaders of society that St. Bernard was really important, but rather for his religious doctrines and his tapping of the vast emotional resources of the new piety to accelerate the transformation of medieval Christianity. In this respect he carried on the work of Damiani, greatly intensifying the emotional qualities of European religiosity, and prepared the way for St. Francis of Assisi. Like Damiani, he was an anti-intellectual who bitterly criticized the masters of the French schools for trying to establish a rational avenue to divine knowledge, but no more than Abelard was he satisfied with the single approach to the deity through the traditional means of revelation and the sacraments. He believed in a direct religious experience, the union between the loving, self-abnegating God and the Christian soul. The end of religion, he said, is "to know Jesus, and to know Jesus crucified"—not Christ in majesty, but in self-sacrifice. Bernard's theology, for the first time in medieval Christianity, clearly makes love greater than faith. In Bernard's view the union between God and man is greatly abetted by the intercession of the Divine Mary, "the Virgin that is the royal way, by which the Savior comes to us." She is the "Flower upon which rests the Holy Spirit." St. Bernard played the leading role in the development of the Virgin cult, which is one of the most important manifestations of the popular piety of the twelfth century. He was not the inventor of Mariology; medieval churchmen had found this doctrine implicit in the Gospels themselves. But in early medieval thought the Virgin Mary had played a very minor role, and it is only with the rise of emotional Christianity in the eleventh century that she became the prime intercessor for humanity with the deity. She was held to be the loving mother of all, whose infinite mercy offers the possibility of salvation to all who seek her assistance with a loving and contrite heart. St. Anselm and some of his disciples made important contributions to the rapid expansion of the Virgin cult at the end of the eleventh century, but it was St. Bernard who made Mariology a cardinal doctrine of the Catholic faith and one which passed beyond the dimensions of strictly religious teaching to enrich deeply the artistic and literary vision of the high middle ages.

In Bernard's teaching the Virgin Mary thus becomes an additional aspect of the deity and aids the Son and the Holy Spirit in uniting men to God. But there is a more direct approach to the deity possible: the mystical way of the beatific vision. The Bernardine doctrine fulfills the mystical tendencies of Damiani's theology. The abbot of Clairvaux was by no means the only spokesman for the mystical way to union with God in the mid-twelfth century. In the emotionally charged religious atmosphere of the age the idea of the direct experience of divine will was bound to become prominent. In Bernard's own day certain writers at the monastery of St. Victor at Paris were producing an extensive mystical literature, but Bernard was the most powerful advocate for the mystical approach to the deity between Damiani and Francis. With his usually acute perception, Dante, in the final cantos of the *Divine Comedy,* makes the abbot of Clairvaux the representative of the beatific vision in medieval Christianity. The mystical union with God is for Bernard far more possible of human attainment than it is for Augustine and the church fathers. He says that if anyone is so filled with an earnest longing for union with Christ that he "desires it vehemently, thirsts for it ardently, and without ceasing, dwells upon the hope of it," then he shall feel himself inwardly embraced by the bridegroom and "shall receive a sweet inpouring of the Divine Love." His soul shall "die the death which belongs to the angels." He shall escape not only from the desire for things corporeal but even from their haunting ideas and images and shall attain the contemplative ecstasy; he shall enter into pure relation with "the image and likeness of purity."

This mystical doctrine constitutes the most profound revolution in Christian thought, for if the soul can in the present life thus escape from its human bondage, what is any longer the necessity and utility of the church and the sacramental way to salvation? The church and sacraments are still necessary as a preparation for the beatific vision, Bernard would reply, and for those who are incapable of the pure life of the spirit. But those who have followed the spiritual exercises which Bernard proposes have in effect dispensed with the necessity of the ecclesiastical means of grace; they have entered into a direct relationship with the deity; they have died the death of the angels; they have become the heavenly pure. And when these angelic saints have momentarily descended from their spiritual Sinai— when they have, for the moment, left the embrace of the Divine Bridegroom—who is to tell them what is the truth, who is to exercise authority over them? Is it to be the official ministers of Christ, the ordained priesthood? How many of the latter have attained the beatific vision and experienced the heavenly embrace? Can such as these presume to govern angels? These are the momentous questions raised by the Bernardine vision, and not only by implication. For St. Bernard, whose only office in the church was that of the abbot of a small Cistercian monastery, presumed himself to judge the church and the ministers of Christ of his day. He discovered "a contagious corruption creeping through the whole body of the church," the more desperate of cure as it was universal, and the more dangerous because so deeply seated. "The plague of the church is inward, and it is incurable," proclaimed Bernard from his angelic standpoint. The churchmen of his day, with their "meretricious splendor" and "infamous traffic" in offices, have betrayed the Lord. "They are advanced to honor upon the goods of the Lord, and to the Lord they render no honor at all." The great bishops are "ministers of Christ and they are serving Antichrist." The church has become the province of "the Demon of noonday," the Antichrist, who "has without question swallowed up the rivers of the learned and the torrents of those who are powerful." Only the final apocalyptic age remains when the Lord Jesus will destroy the Antichrist "with the brightness of his coming."

Compared to these ominous pronouncements by the abbot of Clairvaux, the most extreme statements of Abelard appear moderate in their import. In Bernard's sermon on the church the new piety becomes uncontrollable and turns upon the established order. No one ever thought of accusing Bernard of doctrinal error, but his writings are the most obvious and prestigious source of many of the doctrines disseminated by the movements of popular heresy in the latter part of the twelfth and again in the fourteenth century. In all these movements the power of the angelic saint is placed over and above the official authority of the church hierarchy, and individual morality overrules sacerdotal office. Without intending to subscribe to Donatism, St. Bernard opened the way for the proliferation of Donatist principles in the late twelfth century. His doctrines prefigure in every way the radical teachings of the south Italian monk and archheretic Joachim of Flora a half century later. Bernard never says that the pope is the instrument of Antichrist, but he denounces every other rank of the hierarchy in the church from archbishop to archdeacon as the servants of the "Demon of noonday." Joachim only had to add that the Vicar of Christ is really the vicar of Antichrist to arrive at his full-blown revolutionary theory. Even the eschatological idea that the world had entered the age of Antichrist, soon to be followed by the coming of the Lord, upon which Joachim develops his theology of history, is already fully explicit in Bernard's writings.

The ambiguous character and many-sided consequences of the intellectual expansion of Europe are vividly illustrated in the Bernardine vision. An archconservative in some respects and an anti-intellectual, he saw the dangers of the new learning and fully understood the ominous implications of Abelard's personality and philosophy, but on his side Bernard directed the new piety in directions which the church of the late twelfth century could not control. By raising the puritan saint above the ministers of Christ and by his presumptuous moral judgment of the priesthood as instruments of Antichrist, he enunciated the doctrines which were to form the common ethos of the popular heresies. Bernard gave to medieval Catholicism a new emotional dimension which enriched and revitalized it, but at the same time he must be regarded as the gravedigger of sacerdotal authority.

IV. Literature and Society in the Twelfth Century

The intellectual expansion of the twelfth century involved belletristic literature as much as other forms of thought and feeling. The century witnessed an enormous increase in literacy, the development of important new literary motifs which exercised a powerful influence on European belles-lettres until the twentieth century, and the creation for the first time on any large scale of vernacular literatures. No early-medieval writer, with the exception of St. Augustine, possibly Boethius, and a few Anglo-Saxon poets, is read today for any purposes except purely historical ones. The twelfth century, however, produced French, Spanish, and German poets whose works are still celebrated by literary critics and command a substantial audience. These works, most of them in the vernacular languages, present a vivid picture of the ideals and mores of European society, particularly the landed classes. No aspect of the acceleration of cultural change in the twelfth century is more difficult to assess than the intellectual and social implications of the new literary forms.

What kind of people wrote the literature of the twelfth century? The great majority of writers, even in the vernacular languages, were still churchmen. But instead of the predominance of monastic authors, which characterized the period before 1100, the twelfth century exhibits prolific writing on the part of secular clerks, most of them attached to cathedral chapters. A novel group of writers were the university students, who, north of the Alps, were at least nominally churchmen. In addition to the clerics, who produced the bulk of twelfth-century literature, secular people for the first time in the middle ages were making contributions to European literature. Many of the nobility, particularly in northern Italy, southern France, and by the end of the century also in western Germany, were highly literate, and some French and German aristocrats became productive authors in their vernacular languages. The exigencies of their work required many bourgeois to be able to read and write in order to do accounts and engage in business correspondence. It was only about 1200, however, that a distinctly bourgeois literature begins to appear.

Latin was still, in the late twelfth century, the exclusive language for technical and intellectual subjects: philosophy, theology, law, and the documents of church and state. Latin remained the international academic language until the eighteenth century, and the affairs of the Catholic church are still conducted extensively in the Roman tongue, but after 1200 the vernacular began to be employed in the administrative work and law courts of the developing national monarchies. In the twelfth century there was still an extensive belletristic writing in the Latin tongue, and some of the greatest Latin poem's were produced after 1100. The Catholic liturgy received a rich heritage from the twelfth century, as, for instance, the Gregorian chant in the form we know it today and the devotional lyrics and hymns of St. Bernard and the Paris Victorines.

The twelfth century also saw the appearance of what has been called "secular Latin poetry," i.e., lyrics which deal with themes that are to a considerable extent nonreligious. They were mostly poems written by the so-called wandering scholars, by which is meant university students. In this poetry is expressed the typical *Weltschmerz* of the undergraduate of any era: his frustrated ambitions, his superficial cynicism, his amorous affairs, and his drinking bouts. The best of the surviving student poems were actually written by two middle-aged alumni: the Archpoet, a cleric in the entourage of Frederick Barbarossa's chancellor, and the Primate, a prominent canon of Orleans cathedral. These lyrics are often referred to as Goliardic poetry, because many are dedicated in jocular fashion to a certain Golias, or Goliath, presumably a synonym for the devil. These "devilish" poems, urging the attractions of dissolute life, have sometimes been interpreted (especially by sentimental women scholars) as accurate accounts of the life and ideals of medieval university students. This view is no more valid than would be a similar interpretation of the contents of contemporary American undergraduate journals. Wine, women, and song, even less than today, were only a peripheral part of twelfth-century student life.

The cynical attitude toward the church hierarchy prevalent in the Goliardic poems has some significance, but it must be remembered that the authors themselves were frequently church officials. Obviously the Goliardic poems are more secular than Bernard's hymns to the Virgin, but their youthful pessimism does not preclude at all an underlying deep devotion to the traditional faith of the middle ages. In assessing the social significance of the Goliardic and similar student poetry of the twelfth century, it must be emphasized that these same writers who declared that it was their resolution to "drop down dead in the tavern" also listened in rapt attention to the lectures of Abelard and the sermons of St. Bernard. After the Archpoet has finished describing his dissolute life as a toper, gambler, and woman chaser, he implores God to grant him grace and absolution and looks forward to greeting "angels without measure/ Singing requiems for the souls/ In eternal leisure." The Goliardic poetry expressed the variety and complexity of twelfth-century life, but it can scarcely be taken as evidence of a genuine secularist attitude. On the contrary, this literature shows how the new piety blunted and inhibited the effects of undergraduate rebellion and how it helped to transform the young bohemians of the Latin Quarter into responsible men of affairs, whose student escapades survived only in the form of romantic nostalgia.

The achievements of twelfth-century Latin literature have been overshadowed by the prolific vernacular works of the period. Lay society in the early middle ages commonly used vulgar tongues in ordinary conversation. But the only vernacular literature written before 1100, or at least 1050—there is great difficulty in dating the earliest work—consisted of Anglo-Saxon poetry, of which *Beowulf* is the greatest example. The French language, which had distinctly appeared as early as the ninth century out of the *lingua romana,* the debased popular form of classical Latin, produced its first literary works two or three decades before or after the year 1100. The Iberian romance dialects began to be used for literary expression at about the same time or probably a little later. German vernacular literature makes its appearance at the end of the twelfth century, and in Italy, where Latin naturally exerted the strongest hold on popular letters, the vulgar tongue began to be used by writers in the second half of the thirteenth century. The cultural effects of the Norman conquest and the subsequent transformation of England into a cultural appanage of France precluded the development of English vernacular literature until the fourteenth century. In fact, as late as the middle of the fifteenth century a bastardized French was still used in English legal and governmental records.

The most important vernacular literature of the twelfth century, both by the criteria of the number of its works produced and the seminal importance of its motifs and techniques, was that produced in the northern and southern French dialects. Any reader of the prolific French literature of the twelfth century will instantly see mirrored therein some important facets of intellectual and social change, but there is great disagreement among scholars as to the degree of immediacy and accuracy in this reflection. Literary historians often take the accounts in their sources at face value and accept them as accurate pictures of the ideals and mores of the ruling class of twelfth-century society; the older political historians did their best to ignore the literary accounts, regarding them as at best a distorted view and at worst so distant from the realities of medieval life as to be useless as historical evidence. Recent historical scholarship, more attuned to a broad social perspective, and as sensitive to states of consciousness as to institutional forms, has found in twelfth-century literature indications of profound changes in feeling that affected important groups in the medieval world.

The mass of French vernacular poetry of the twelfth century falls into three distinct categories: the *chanson de geste,* the troubadour lyrics, and finally the romantic epic, which is a result of the confluence of the first two forms. The *chansons de geste* were long epic poems indigenous to northern France that portrayed deeds of heroism and other aspects of the life of the feudal nobility. They were certainly meant to entertain aristocratic courts, and they were probably stories which had circulated orally and been slowly expanded over three centuries before being written down at the end of the eleventh century or early twelfth century. They were based upon incidents, some of them known from historical sources, which occurred in Carolingian times. These epic poems, written for the entertainment of the French feudal nobility, presumably portray the great lords of northern France in the way they liked to think of themselves. The result is an idealized picture of feudal life but one which is recognizable from, and in many instances vividly confirms, what we know about feudal life from nonliterary sources. Iberian-Christian literature begins about the middle of the twelfth century with the great Spanish epic *The Cid,* an account of the deeds of a famous eleventh-century Spanish warrior. The ideals and attitudes expressed in *The Cid* are the same as in the French *chansons de geste.*

The *chansons de geste* portray the feudatories as the leaders of society: the emperor-king is at best distant and at worst appears as weak and crooked, churchmen are merely assistants to the feudal nobility, peasants are a negligible social force who have no other function except to toil for their lords and be massacred during feudal wars, and the bourgeois hardly exist at all in the pages of these epics. The cohesive force in the world of the *chanson de geste* is loyalty, and the theme around which the poem is built is always some question of vassalage, its fulfillments or its violations. Thus, in the *Song of Roland,* the earliest work of French literature through which so many generations of modern students have had to toil, the hero is a count who fulfills his oath of loyalty to Charlemagne even though it involves his certain death. *Raoul de Cambrai,* which is the most valuable of the epic poems for the social historian, is built around the troubles and violence which result when the emperor does not reward one of his leading vassals with the fief which he claims by inheritance. In *Raoul* the bellicose disposition of the feudal nobility is starkly revealed; the wronged hero engages in bloody rebellion and the massacre of innocent churchmen and bourgeois. Apparently the aristocratic audience enjoyed such incidents, and, in certain backward frontier regions such as Brittany and the Massif Central, even in the year 1200 such violence was still common. These manifestations of feudal disorder are intertwined in the same poem with reflections of the new popular piety. A poem which takes as its subject the career of a certain lord called Robert the Devil describes how the hero, after several years of banditry and pillaging of monasteries, suffers remorse, goes to Rome and obtains papal absolution for his sins, and ends up as a saintly monk himself. The combination of violence and piety in the *chanson de geste* is confirmed by our general knowledge of the mores of the twelfth-century nobility. There is, however, an additional element, a certain mawkish sentimentality in the poems which does not fit in with our general historical picture of the northern French nobility at the beginning of the twelfth century. Thus when Charlemagne informs Roland's betrothed of the hero's death, she immediately faints and dies of a broken heart, and we are told that the tragedy causes the great nobles in Charlemagne's court to weep profusely. This effeminate sentimentality conflicts strongly with the rough masculinity of the landed classes of northern France at the time the *chansons de geste* were written. If it has any historical base, it indicates only that within the narrow confines of some feudal courts a new sensibility had made its appearance by the early twelfth century.

Sensibility, emotion, and effeminate sentiment are not, however, generally characteristic of the *chansons de geste.* The intrusion of these romantic attitudes into the outlook of the European nobility, insofar as it ever did become important, which is a moot question, originated not in the northern feudal principalities but in the rather different social environment of southern France. Here, in Provence, Aquitaine, and Toulouse, there was a culture which looked southward toward the Mediterranean world and which in the twelfth century was little affected by the north. The military vigor of the southern nobility was diminished and their way of life fully altered by several factors working together. The boundaries of the feudal principalities in the south were well settled and there was scarcely any opportunity for baronial wars. Many of the nobility of Languedoc, the country of the southern dialect, took up residence in the cities, and their attitudes were slowly transformed by bourgeois animadversions on violence and disorder. The new piety had a profound effect on the world-view of the southern nobility; their new enthusiasm for the saints and the Virgin made the old code of the warrior class no longer satisfactory to the more intelligent members of the nobility.

The social life of the southern French nobility came to center in the court of the count or duke, and its confining circumstances gave the great aristocratic ladies the opportunity to educate the nobles in genteel and sentimental mores. The term "court," whose meaning heretofore was almost exclusively legal and governmental, began to take on the additional connotation of an aristocratic social center, and "courtly" became a synonym for "refined" and "sophisticated." Finally, romantic attitudes which had long existed in the courts of Moslem princes, such as are described in the *Arabian Nights,* may have penetrated into southern France from the neighboring Arabic-Spanish principalities. All these elements have been used to explain the sentimental ideals which are found in the troubadour lyrics of southern France in the late eleventh and first half of the twelfth century. Some of the troubadours were professional poets and minstrels at princely courts. Others were members of the nobility themselves, including some of the powerful dukes of Aquitaine. The troubadour ideals are the first clear expression of what has been called the code of chivalry. The term is not a very good one; the ideas and sentiments involved were too loose and vague even to be as clearly defined a code as vassalage, and the term "chivalry" is ambiguous, for by itself it really means nothing except the way of life of the chevalier, or knight. But whatever the term used, it is possible to perceive something new in the outlook of the aristocrats of southern France in the early twelfth century.

Chivalry has both a broad and a specific meaning. The broader sense of the term implies that the customs of a warrior class were coming to be replaced by the mores of aristocratic gentlemen. In the long intervals between wars the southern nobility engaged in various pastimes at court which could not be imitated by any other class in society, and these expensive and intentionally impractical recreations—ceremonies, dinners, hunting, falconry, tournament jousting, singing, troubadour recitals, etc.—served to preserve the identity of a class which for the most part had lost its military function. In a more limited and specific way, chivalry has been identified with the ideals and practices of courtly love. In the troubadour lyrics ladies are addressed in a sentimental and gentle manner unknown to the rough lords of the early middle ages, who looked upon women as instruments for physical pleasure and the breeding of children. Carried to the northern court of Champagne from Aquitaine in the middle of the twelfth century, courtly love developed a whole special code of its own, which was written down by a certain Andreas Capellanus, i.e., Andrew the Chaplain. This code was based on the principle of romantic love, that is, love involving a man and woman of the aristocracy who are not married and never can or even want to be, for love is presumed to exist only outside of marriage. The romantically entwined go through elaborate rituals of exchanging encouraging messages, vows, and tokens. The woman becomes for the nobleman the ideal lady who symbolizes for him all virtue and beauty and in whose name he performs valorous and other worthy deeds.

Historians of medieval civilization have had a very difficult time interpreting the significance of the courtly love of Aquitaine and Champagne. It has been viewed as a central motive in aristocratic life throughout western Europe, being, for instance, supposedly carried to the Île-de-France and then to England by the ubiquitous Eleanor of Aquitaine. It has been viewed as a dangerous heresy imported from the Moslem world, which undermined traditional Christian morality. It has also been interpreted as the secularized form of the Virgin cult and the Bernardine vision of divine love, and as such it is believed to have made an outstanding contribution to western culture by raising the dignity of women and enriching European literature with a new romantic strain. It has also been regarded as a nebulous factor in European life, existing only in the minds of a few idle court poets who were heavily under the influence of Ovid's *Art of Love,* a popular book in the twelfth century. It has even been suggested that Andrew the Chaplain's handbook of courtly love was meant as a joke or as a clever satire.

It is clear that many more people talked about courtly love than really practiced it, and even those who talked about it consisted of a handful of aristocratic ladies and their literary sycophants. But courtly love does represent, in its most extreme form, the new sentimentality and gentility which came to be adopted by European aristocracy whenever and wherever its traditional military functions were atrophied. Scarcely any of the European nobility of the twelfth century, even in Champagne and Aquitaine, were actually lovers, but more and more the members of the aristocracy acted in a civilized and restrained manner, and if they still thought nothing of assaulting peasants or insulting bourgeois, they were "courteous" to each other and especially to the women of their own class. This slow transformation in the social attitudes of the nobility was greatly encouraged by the growth of the European monarchies, whose governments placed severe limitations on violence and thuggery and thereby forced the nobility to develop a more pacific way of life.

The average member of the twelfth-century landed class took seriously the teachings of the church and exhibited the accoutrements of popular piety. He attended church services, adored the saints and the Virgin, respected monks, contributed to ecclesiastical endowments, and joined pilgrimages and sometimes, when called upon, crusades to the Holy Land. But a small minority of the nobles of the higher ranks were influenced more strongly by sentiment and sensibility than was normal in this typical behavior of the feudal class. For them a romantic code of honor replaced the old code of loyalty. Such genuine chivalric types did not fare much better in the twelfth century than they would today. The sentimental Robert Curthose lost his duchy of Normandy to his more tough-minded brother, Henry I of England, and the extremely generous Stephen of Blois, who tried to gain the English throne in the 1130's, was singularly inept as a soldier and statesman. The most famous chivalric knight of the twelfth century was the English king Richard the Lionhearted. The dramatic incidents of his career were celebrated by troubadours and minstrels, but he was easily made a fool of by the distinctly unchivalrous king of France; the greatest service he rendered his long-suffering people was to remain out of England for almost his whole reign, and nothing became his life so much as his manner of leaving it. He had no sooner returned to England from captivity in Germany than he dashed off to France, pennants flying, to besiege the castle of a minor vassal who refused to surrender to the king a negligible treasure trove. A stray arrow dispatched from the besieged castle wall by an idle bowman prematurely cut off the flower of European chivalry.

We may gauge the more normal outlook of the European aristocracy of the twelfth century by the character and career of Richard's contemporary, William Marshal (d. 1223), the most universally admired nobleman of his day. His family thought him so worthy of general emulation that they hired a cleric to write his biography. It is the Horatio Alger story of the twelfth century and provides illuminating insight into the actual code of conduct of a twelfth-century chevalier. William Marshal was a landless knight who began his career without even a horse and armor. His only possibility for advancement lay in his kinship to a wealthy nobleman in Normandy, who outfitted him as a knight and sent him out on the tournament circuit. As described in the history of William Marshal, the tournaments of the late twelfth century did not usually involve individual combats by valorous knights dedicated to the service of fair ladies; they were simply war games. Two groups of knights in full armor lined up on opposite sides of a large field, charged into a general melee, and hacked away at each other. Each knight's object was to unseat as many of his opponents as possible so that he could hold them for ransom. William Marshal proved to be particularly adept at these disordered combats, to which he took a highly mercenary attitude. He even had a clerk accompany him to the tournaments in order to keep an accurate record of the sums which his defeated opponents owed him. His many victories made him wealthy and gained him a reputation as a great fighter, which won him a position in the household of Henry II as military tutor to the royal heir. He was eventually rewarded for his services to the Angevin family by being married to the richest heiress in England, who was a ward of the crown, and he thereby became the most powerful earl in the realm. In the last years of his life he was the regent of England, admired and respected by all members of the English ruling class. Assuredly William was a civilized character, shrewd and capable in government and administration, and undoubtedly courteous to ladies, but there is no evidence that he had either the time or the inclination for the complex code of courtly love. William Marshal's biography shows that in 1200 the ideal nobleman was neither a robber baron nor a chivalric knight. The European feudal lords were being transformed by many pressures—political, religious, as well as intellectual and economic—into the European aristocracy in the form it was to maintain until the nineteenth century. This class enjoyed certain privileges and entertainments which were forbidden the bourgeois and peasantry, but they also had heavy responsibilities and obligations—in the case of the ordinary nobleman, toward his family and patrimony, and in the case of a few great aristocrats such as William Marshal, toward society as a whole.

The troubadours of Aquitaine and Champagne ultimately impinged on the style of life exhibited by an aristocrat like William Marshal by contributing to the formulation of a new system of values which gave much greater primacy to individual feelings and needs. And this individualism and self-consciousness was absorbed in muted form into the aristocratic way of life. The prime medium of the education of the aristocracy in this system was a new form of vernacular literature that developed after 1130, first in England and France and then in Germany.

The romantic motifs of the troubadour lyrics impinged on the northern *chanson de geste* in the second half of the twelfth century and transformed it into the adventure-romance, an extremely sentimental, idealized, and imaginative epic poem. The "affairs of France," the Charlemagne cycle, did not offer the authors of the adventure-romance sufficient opportunity for exercise of their remarkable inventive powers; consequently they experimented with stories based on the Trojan War or on legendary exploits of Alexander the Great, but even these did not allow them full play of their romantic imaginations. They found the subject they needed in the "affairs of Britain," the King Arthur cycle.

The inaugurator of the Arthurian legends, to whose refinement so much of the literary ingenuity of the later twelfth and thirteenth centuries was devoted, was a secular clerk, Geoffrey of Monmouth, writing under the patronage of the bishop of Lincoln. In 1136 Geoffrey published his *History of the Kings of Britain,* which he claimed, perhaps facetiously, to have discovered in an old manuscript at Oxford, but which obviously consists of tales which had circulated for a long time in Geoffrey's Welsh homeland. Arthur was probably a real historical figure of the fifth century, a British Christian prince who had died fighting the invading Anglo-Saxon heathens. His compatriots, hiding out in the Welsh mountains through the long cold centuries, transformed Arthur into a Christian hero of superhuman prowess. The Arthurian legend spread eastward through Europe almost as fast as a medieval plague, growing more complex and sentimental as it went. The most important contributions to the expansion of the Arthurian cycle were made by Chrétien de Troyes, a contemporary and compatriot of Andrew the Chaplain, of courtly-love fame. It was Chrétien who highlighted the subsidiary characters in the Arthurian legend, such as Lancelot, and introduced the motif of the search for the Grail.

From Champagne the Arthurian cycle reached western Germany at the end of the twelfth century. It was the creative period of vernacular German literature, the age of the minnesingers, as the German troubadours were called. The most famous of these was the extremely versatile lyric poet Walther von der Vogelweide, who worked under the patronage of the royal Hohenstaufen dynasty. The German poets, such as Gottfried of Strassburg, who was a bourgeois, and Wolfram von Eschenbach, a nobleman, produced adventure-romances in which the Arthurian cycle is suffused with religious mysticism and, in the opinion of many critics, carried to its highest art form.

The Arthurian romances, like the poems of Chrétien de Troyes and Wolfram von Eschenbach's *Parzifal,* have as their theme the two forms of love, religious and secular, which are closely related. The romantic yearning of the hero for his unattainable beloved appears as the earthly counterpart of the mystic yearning for the unattainable union with the deity, and the exertions of the chivalric knight are the mundane counterpart of the spiritual exercises of the holy mystics. The knight's lady is as mysterious, distant, and gracious as the Virgin Mary herelf. The blending of the sacred and secular worlds also appears in the motif of the Holy Grail. A young romantic hero, inspired by high idealism, undertakes a quest for the Grail and cannot be turned aside by any kind of physical or social obstacle. In mundane form, the Grail was the chalice from which Jesus drank at the Last Supper. But in the subtle imagination of the romantic poets it came to symbolize the ineffable ideal, the perfected and unattainable condition of human happiness whose quest was the purpose and joy of life.

In the Arthurian cycle a whole dimension is opened up for European literature, that of romantic love, which only intermittently appears in the literature of the ancient world and which is by and large an original contribution of the twelfth century to western civilization. This romanticism receives its highest social significance in the formulation of a liberation ethic that expressed a profound revulsion against the existing feudal-ecclesiastic complex and its ideological counterpart, the hierarchic view of the world that ignored and suppressed self-consciousness and individual feelings. Romantic love is an intensely personal and individual attitude that proclaims a value system based on emotional needs against inherited status and bureaucratic political power. The romantic hero's quest for the Grail gives primacy to the individual's quest for self-realization and rebels against the static nature of feudal and ecclesiastical hierarchy. In general, the courtly and aristocratic authors of these poems wanted to liberate the individual human personality from the stultifying subjection to authority and tradition. The new romantic literature demonstrates the uncompromising dissatisfaction with the traditional ecclesiastical culture on the part of highly sensitive and literate minds. And the long-range impact of the romantic rebellion on European thought and higher culture is inestimable in its ramifications.

It is hard to believe that the nobility who formed the audience for these adventure-romances understood clearly the extremely subtle interweaving of religious and mundane love and the other romantic symbolism. What they got out of the poems was mostly—but not only—the involved and imaginative plot into which the extremely perceptive and skillful authors wove their emotional doctrines and symbols. If the original audience of the adventure-romances missed some of the finer shades of meaning, none who read or heard the poems could fail to glimpse the new horizon in human experience which was opened up by the Arthurian cycle. The romantic literature taught the late-twelfth-century aristocracy that personal feelings and individual quests were values that deserved to be recognized and reconciled with the individual's obligations to the demands of social order.

The romantic literature also instructed the aristocracy that the sensibility which had hitherto been regarded as a mark of feminine inferiority was now made into a virtue practiced by heroes such as Lancelot, Parsifal, and Tristan. By making feminine qualities heroic, the romantic poets enhanced the dignity of woman and made her a being with distinctive and valuable qualities. The teaching of the fourth-century church fathers on sex and marriage was the first stage in the emancipation of women in western civilization. The romantic ethos of the twelfth century marked the second stage.

But if on the one hand the adventure-romances contributed to the partial emancipation of women, on the other hand they laid the intellectual foundations for the double standard of sexual morality which existed in western civilization until the twentieth century. The chief basis for the double standard was not intellectual but rather social and legal. In a society in which landed property and title descended by primogeniture and in which illegitimacy was the bar sinister to inheritance there were inevitably different standards of sexual conduct for husband and wife. The lord could have as many mistresses and bastards as he wished or could afford, because the consequences of his promiscuity were evident to the world, but the opposite was true of his wife, whose adulterous behavior could not so easily be detected. The mere suspicion of promiscuity in the lady of a feudal household, and the doubts about the legitimacy of her children which therefore arose, could result in interminable lawsuits and destroy a great patrimony. It was therefore necessary for the noble to keep his wife under very close surveillance to preclude any suspicions of bastardy in his line. The romantic conception of women fomented by the troubadour lyric, the notion of courtly love, and, above all, the adventure-romances provided an intellectual justification for the double standard and the seclusion of women. Noblewomen were held to be frail, sentimental creatures who could not be allowed the freedom accorded the male sex. They had to be both protected and virtually imprisoned.

The growth of vernacular literature in the twelfth century thus profoundly affected the dimensions of higher culture and had some effect on the conditions of social life. It had also played a part in the development of the national monarchies. For the proliferation of rich vernacular literatures in the twelfth century secured the place of the vulgar tongues in European society, and this entrenchment of the vernacular tongues made the European peoples more conscious of separation from each other, decreased the cosmopolitan attitudes of the European nobility, and encouraged xenophobia, which became common in the thirteenth century. This linguistic, intellectual, and social Balkanization of European society, which was well under way by 1200, was the necessary precondition for the emergence of nationalism in the thirteenth and fourteenth centuries.

Chapter Sixteen

MOSLEM AND JEWISH THOUGHT: THE ARISTOTELIAN CHALLENGE

I. The Problem of Learning

Learning, piety, and power, through their great expansion in the twelfth century, all came by 1200 to challenge the leadership of the church in western society. The implications of the great intellectual, religious, and political changes of the twelfth century required the church to reconsider and readjust its policies and institutions in order to deal successfully with the consequences of European creativity and improvement. The destiny of medieval civilization after 1150 was predicated first on the implications of learning, piety, and power, then on the ways in which the church reacted to these implications, and finally upon the effectiveness of the church's readjustment.

The strongest challenge which the old order faced from the side of the new learning consisted of Aristotelian philosophy and science. The work of Abelard in the 1130's had already demonstrated how new modes of thinking derived from Aristotelianism could act as a powerful solvent of the early-medieval thought-world with its heavily Platonic basis. Abelard had had available to him only a small portion of the vast Aristotelian corpus: that part of the peripatetic logic which had been translated by Boethius. But Aristotle had also produced not only other works on dialectic but also the most comprehensive scientific philsophy of the ancient world, involving cosmology, metaphysics, ethics, psychology, and political theory. In the second decade of the twelfth century the onerous work of preparing Latin translations of the Aristotelian knowledge had been inaugurated, and by the middle of the century it was well under way. Yet only at the end of the twelfth century, after an initial period of digestion and consideration of the Aristotelian doctrines, did Latin scholars begin to try to integrate this vast new body of science with the Biblical-patristic tradition. It was a formidable and momentous undertaking and one which many conservative churchmen believed would end in disaster for the traditions of the church. If Abelard, with only a small part of the Aristotelian logic, could cause such trouble, then how much more dangerous and revolutionary would be the effect of the reception of all Aristotelian science! It was a turning point in the history of western thought, a genuine "crisis of conscience" paralleled only by the later impact of Newtonian science and Darwinism.

The Aristotelian corpus and other works of Greek science became available in the west through the medium of translations prepared in Spain, Sicily, and to a lesser degree in Provence. Until the last quarter of the twelfth century the translations were made from Arabic versions of the Aristotelian writings and not from the original Greek. A Christian scholar worked together with a Moslem translator in Spain and Sicily or, as in the case of Provence, sometimes with a Jewish translator. In view of this awkward procedure, producing translations twice-removed from the original, it was amazing how accurate were the final versions. In the first three quarters of the twelfth century there were scarcely any western scholars who knew Greek, and the assistance of the Arabic-speaking translators had to be sought. By 1200 a new set of translations of the Aristotelian writings, directly from Greek into Latin, was under way. Thomas Aquinas, in the middle of the thirteenth century, was the first Christian philosopher who had available to him the completed new translation. It was, of course, more accurate than the original secondhand Latin versions of the Aristotelian corpus, but the differences between the two translations were not remarkable.

The work of the twelfth-century translators was not organized by any central authority. A few translators enjoyed the patronage of bishops and princes, but by and large it was a matter of individual scholars inspired by their training in the universities, undertaking the arduous and thankless tasks of translation so that the philosophy and science of western Europe could be greatly enriched by the new material. It is indicative of the new dimensions of European thought that it is only in the twelfth century that a concerted effort was made to obtain from the Arabic world the Greek science and philosophy which had been available there for several centuries.

Translation is generally a self-sacrificing endeavor; the translator makes knowledge available to others, who use it in their own intellectual work. But the twelfth-century translation of the Aristotelian corpus was a particularly heroic undertaking. The translators received little or no remuneration and enjoyed scarcely any fame; there was no other motive for their work than devotion to truth and knowledge. The translators' work was made harder by their high degree of isolation from one another, which occasionally resulted in wasteful repetition with the same work being independently rendered into Latin by two or three scholars.

Aristotle was by no means the only Greek author translated into Latin in the twelfth century. Every Greek contribution to philosophy and science that the Latin scholars could find in the Mediterranean world was translated. By the end of the century an enormous amount of information about natural science, medicine, and cosmology, which had heretofore been unknown, had flooded into the universities of western Europe. In a sense the translators did their work too well, for they made available such an amount and variety of material that original and critical thinking on the part of the philosophers of Christian Europe was inhibited for more than half a century. The western thinkers were too busy reading Aristotle and the other Greek writers to engage in critical, original, and systematic speculation of their own. This is assuredly one reason why close to a century went by before western Europe again produced thinkers of Abelard's stature. Yet European scholars could no more afford to reject the opportunity of acquainting themselves with the intellectual riches of Greek civilization than legal scholars could have turned their backs on the Justinian code. Greek philosophy and science were the best products of the western mind in these fields; before continuing to work out their own systems, it was first necessary for medieval thinkers to absorb and comprehend the best that previously had been thought and said in the world.

Sicily was the important center for the translation of words in more technical subjects: medicine, natural sciences, and mathematics. The heterogeneous culture of Sicily, with its mixed Greek, Moslem, Italian, and Norman population made it an ideal center for the transmitting of knowledge from Mediterranean to western Europe. Spain was the provenance of the translations of Greek philosophy and ethics. In order to carry out this work, Christian scholars had to take up residence in Cordoba and other Moslem cities, which, in view of the almost continuous wars between the two faiths on the Iberian peninsula, involved some risk to their personal safety. Provence was the third and least prolific center of transmission of knowledge. The work here seems to have been effected largely through cooperation between Christian and Jewish scholars.

When the Aristotelian corpus began to be available to western thinkers in the second half of the twelfth century, they discovered that it had not come from the Arabic world unaccompanied but rather trailing clouds of Moslem and Jewish commentaries behind it. The western thinkers discovered that they were not original in trying to deal with the problem of the relation between science and revelation. Some of the greatest minds in the Moslem world, such as Avicenna and Averroes, and Jewish scholars such as Maimonides had either already dealt with the consequences of Aristotelianism for their traditional faiths or were in the course of doing so in the twelfth century. The ways in which the greatest minds of the Moslem and Jewish cultures met the challenge of Aristotelian philosophy is significant in two ways. First, some of the doctrines proposed by the Moslem and Jewish commentators influenced the positions taken by western thinkers. Averroism is in fact an important stream in thirteenth- and fourteenth-century Christian thought. Second, the doctrines of the Moslem and Jewish scholars are worthy of consideration because they offer interesting parallels and contrasts with the western reactions to the intellectual crisis engendered by the introduction of Aristotelian science and thereby provide an illuminating background to the intellectual history of thirteenth-century Europe.

Islam, Judaism, and Christianity were all theistic and providential religions. Because of their common nature, the challenge which Aristotelian doctrines offered to one was bound to be repeated with respect to the others. The difficulties which Aristotelianism presented to any believer in Islamic, Jewish, or Christian revelation were threefold. Instead of the theistic and providential God whose will constantly determines the course of the universe, Aristotle posits a mechanistic God who is simply a prime mover. He inaugurates the course of universal events, but He does not participate actively after He has inaugurated the long chain of being. The Aristotelian conception of the deity tends to preclude belief in providence and to make prayer useless. These views seemed to conflict sharply with the teachings of the Bible and the Koran. The second stumbling block which Aristotelianism offered the scholars of the three faiths was its denial of the creation of the world *ex nihilo*. Instead, Aristotle assumed the eternity of matter, and this contradicted the Judaeo-Christian and Moslem belief that in the beginning there was nothing but God. The third difficulty which Aristotle presented to those thinkers who wished to show the compatibility of science and revelation was his failure to support the doctrine of the immortality of the individual soul. Plato had argued eloquently for the existence of personal immortality, and this is one reason why Platonism had been so acceptable to Christian thinkers before the twelfth century. But

Aristotle leaned toward a doctrine of general rather than individual immortality, that is, he indicated that the individual human intelligence survived after death through the union with the general intelligence of the universe. It was very difficult to establish a compatibility between Aristotle's view and the traditional dogma of personal immortality. The Aristotelian conflicts with the teachings of revelation thus occurred at crucial points. The Moslem and Jewish thinkers of the eleventh and twelfth centuries, like their Christian successors in the thirteenth and fourteenth, had the choice of rejecting Aristotelianism in its entirety, of separating the world of science from the world of faith, or of trying to prove the ultimate compatibility of reason and revelation.

II. Reason and Revelation in Moslem and Jewish Thought

The pattern which Moslem and Jewish thought took in meeting the challenge of Aristotelianism was determined, as it also was in Christian Europe, not only by the achievements of certain great minds but by the general social environment in which they had to work. In sharp contrast with both the Christian and Jewish worlds, Islam had always maintained a dichotomy between the religious authorities and the teachers and scholars in the fields of philosophy and science. The leaders of the Islamic religion were either fundamentalists and religious legalists, who derived all their knowledge of theology and ethics from the Koran and the Traditions of the Prophet, or they were mystics (Sufists), who through direct religious experience discovered an additional road to knowledge and divine truth. But the leaders of the Islamic religion had never attempted to construct a rational theology by taking into account the implications of Aristotelian science. The speculative thinkers of the Islamic world were independent men who made their livings as physicians, civil servants, lawyers, or professional teachers. This peculiar social background of the higher thought of the Arabic world meant, on the one hand, that its speculative thinkers could afford to be especially bold, since they were not inhibited by having to worry immediately either about the compatibility of reason and revelation or about whether they would lose their jobs for preaching heresy. On the other hand, however, there was a grave threat to the long-range development of Islamic philosophy in this separation between the religious and intellectual leadership. If the fundamentalists and mystics felt that the traditional religion was actually in danger of subversion by the speculative thinkers and if they could obtain the cooperation of the state, they would simply silence the expression of rational thought. This is, in fact, what began to happen in the latter part of the eleventh century, and after 1200 scientific thought in the Islamic world was dead. This unfortunate development offers an illuminating contrast with the course of speculative thought in the Christian world. Because all the important philosophic work in high-medieval Europe was carried on in educational institutions which were subject to ecclesiastical authorities, and because all the important western philosophers were at least in a nominal sense churchmen, the western thinkers were at first more conscious of the painful conflict between reason and revelation, and they moved more slowly than the Arabic writers; but their work was, on the whole, protected from destruction at the hands of fanatics precisely because it was carried out under church auspices.

The Aristotelian corpus was translated into Arabic in the eighth century in Syria by Moslem scholars relying extensively on the assistance of heretical-Christian clerics. The text of the translations spread slowly throughout the Moslem world and in the tenth century reached Spain, where it was intensively studied in the great schools of philosophy and science in Cordoba and other cities. The first of the two greatest Arabic commentators on Aristotle was a Persian whom the Latins called Avicenna, but whose Arabic name was Ibn Sina (d. 1037). He was an extremely prolific writer, and his contributions to medicine were very popular in western Europe in the twelfth and thirteenth centuries. In philosophic thought he represented an older tradition in which Aristotelianism had not yet entirely pushed out Neoplatonism, resulting in a peculiar system drawing elements from both traditions. Avicenna believed that God does not concern himself with individuals. He creates an Intelligence, a sort of Platonic idea which engenders all other things. The result is a combination of the hierarchical universe of Plato and the mechanistic cosmos of Aristotle. It is an extremely ingenious philosophic system, but one which runs contrary to some of the fundamental precepts of Islam. Avicenna's philosophy destroys the omniscience of God and with it the efficacy of prayer. He further negated the creation of the world and denied personal immortality, contending that the human soul found an after-life only through reunion with the universal Intelligence.

Substantially the same conclusions were arrived at by the greatest of the Moslem philosophers, a Spaniard named Ibn Rushd (d. 1198), whom the western church called Averroes. Although he did not know Greek, he imbibed the whole Aristotelian system from translations and became the leading interpreter of Aristotle to the Arabic world and also to a very considerable extent, to the Latin Christian world. Thomas Aquinas refers to him as "the commentator" on Aristotle. Averroes does not flinch from the prospect of the separation of the world of science as represented by Aristotle and the world of revelation as represented by the Koran. Science inexorably demonstrates that God is the mechanistic mover of the universe; He is a machine entirely removed from interference in human life. Science upholds the eternity of the world and denies the Islamic doctrine of creation. Finally, Averroes is explicit in denying personal immortality and in upholding the doctrine of general Intelligence, or the universal soul. This completely Aristotelian system did not imply for Averroes the abandonment of his Islamic religion. He professed himself to be a devout Moslem and met the contradiction between science and revelation by the frank recognition of the existence of a "double truth." There is one truth for science and another for revelation, and it is beyond the powers of the human mind to establish their compatibility. The ignorant must have their faith. The learned have knowledge of this double truth. Averroes' teachings infuriated the champions of Moslem orthodoxy. Although he certainly never denigrated the validity of Koranic doctrine, his conclusion that it was contradicted by science and his placing of rational knowledge alongside revelation seemed to be an attempt to insult and undermine the faith. Since the eleventh century the political power in Moslem Spain had passed to groups who had emigrated from North Africa and who exhibited a fanaticism and puritanism new to the Moslem principalities in the Iberian peninsula. It was not hard for the defenders of the traditional avenues to truth by way of revelation and mystical experience to convince the Moslem princes to take measures against the continuance of free speculation. The great schools declined, Averroism was condemned, and the Arabic mind passed under the long tyranny of fanaticism and ignorance. But the teachings of Averroes, brought into the west along with the translated text of the Aristotelian corpus, were to live on, having a long history in Latin Europe and exerting a powerful influence on the course of Christian philosophy in the thirteenth and fourteenth centuries.

The relation between reason and revelation in medieval Jewish thought in some respects offers a closer parallel to the intellectual history of Christian Europe than the Moslem experience. The dichotomy between the world of science and the world of faith was not as evident among medieval Jews as among the Moslems. The great majority of rabbis were as narrowly fundamentalist and legalistic as their Moslem counterparts. But the best minds in medieval Jewry, who were also in many instances leaders of their religious communities, tried to establish a compatibility between science and revelation and work out a rational theology. They exhibited the same concern with bridging reason and faith which exercised the intelligence and imagination of Latin thinkers, and Maimonides' thought foreshadowed Thomism.

At the beginning of the Christian era there were already large Jewish communities outside of Palestine in the cities of the eastern Mediterranean and in Mesopotamia. The destruction of the Jewish community in Palestine which followed unsuccessful rebellions against Roman rule in the second half of the first century A.D. augmented the size of these Jewish communities in the Diaspora, as the Jews called all the lands outside of their homeland. The two most important communities were the so-called Babylonian, or Mesopotamian, and the large Jewish population in Alexandria. They represented sharply contrasting approaches to the question of the relationship between Judaism and secular culture. The Alexandrian Jews found their spokesman in the great philosopher Philo, who demonstrated the compatibility between Judaism and Platonism and advocated a kind of Jewish religion which in every way resembles twentieth-century reform Judaism. The Babylonian rabbis pursued a diametrically opposite tendency. They shut out secular culture from Jewish life and preserved Pharisaic Judaism by building a vast wall of religious and moral law around the Jewish believer. This traditional and legalistic approach to Judaism was expressed through the Talmud, an enormous commentary on the Pentateuch which drew upon the precepts of Biblical Judaism to provide a legalistic system which completely cut off the Jews from intellectual intercourse with the gentile world. Every aspect of the daily life of the Jewish believer was regulated by the Talmud; the effect was to make the Jewish community a world within a world, and the only intercourse which the Talmudic Jew was allowed to have with his gentile neighbors was in indispensable economic relations. This conflict between diametrically opposite conceptions of Jewish life, first presented by Alexandrian and Talmudic Judaism, constituted the main internal theme of Jewish history until the latter part of the nineteenth century.

The Jews of western Europe came gradually under the influence of the Talmudic form because of the decline of the Alexandrian Jewish community under Christian persecution between the time of Philo and the liberating Moslem conquest in the seventh century. The Jews prospered in early-medieval Europe because of their position as merchants and bankers in an agrarian society. They played an important role in whatever international trade still existed between western Europe and the Mediterranean after the sixth century. They suffered occasional persecution, particularly in Visigothic Spain, but by and large the Germanic kings found their services as merchants and moneylenders too useful to allow fanatical bishops to foment pogroms against them. The Jews especially prospered under the Carolingian rulers, who appreciated the economic services they rendered to the underdeveloped society of the ninth century. It is by no means true that the Jews in early medieval Christian Europe made their living exclusively as merchants and moneylenders. In some places they were allowed to become landlords, and by the early eleventh century some of them held extensive estates in the wine-growing regions of southern France.

The dividing line in the history of the Jews in Christian Europe comes in the mid-eleventh century. The new militancy of Latin Christianity and the growth of popular piety contributed to a tremendous increase in Judophobia, which was dramatically expressed in the pogroms committed by the crusaders in the 1090's. Furthermore, changes in economic and political life resulted in a deterioration of the Jews' position. The proliferation of feudal institutions made it difficult for them to hold land, because they could not enter into the necessary oaths involved in vassalage. The growth of the merchant guilds, which came to control international commerce, resulted in the exclusion of Jewish entrepreneurs from business by their gentile competitors. By the early twelfth century their main economic recourse was usury. The Jewish rabbis took the Biblical injunction against usury to mean that this referred only to relations between members of the Jewish community and that usurious practices were permitted between Jew and gentile. Christian ecclesiastical leaders, in effect, arrived at the same conclusion. They interpreted the same Biblical statements as prohibiting usurious practices among the brotherhood of Christians (although in reality this prohibition was violated with the greatest frequency), and they legalized usurious relations between gentiles and Jews. It was not really a doctrinal question but a social and economic one. The Jews had capital, and they had no other way of making a living except through lending money. The developing European commerce and industry needed their services, as well as did profligate nobles, bankrupt churchmen, and, above all, the expanding royal governments. The Jewish usurers charged enormously high interest rates—as much as 50 per cent of the principal. This is not because they were a tribe of Shylocks but because enormous risks were involved. It was very difficult for them to collect on their loans since their debtors had status in the law courts which they lacked. They were lucky if they could secure a return on half the money they lent. Non-Jewish moneylenders charged rates of interest which were just as high. Nevertheless, the Jews' activity as usurers increased.

Incessant and violent anti-Semitism stems from the age of the Gregorian reform and the first crusade. By the middle of the twelfth century the appearance of the blood libels—the myths which held that the Jews had a propensity for engaging in the ritual slaughter of Christian children—and other manifestations of popular hatred led to repeated pogroms. The only protection which the Jews had against massacre came from kings and princes, and this was dearly bought. By 1200 the Jews in western Europe were in effect the slaves of royal and ducal governments. They were allowed to engage in usurious practice and to preserve their religion, and they were protected from mass murder, but in return they were mercilessly taxed by royal treasuries which used them as parasites to draw money out of the outraged populace.

Even before the great deterioration of their economic and social position, the internal life of the Jewish communities in Christian Europe was gradually coming to be conducted according to the precepts of Talmudic Judaism, but it was not until the end of the eleventh century that Jewish thought was completely severed from the classical heritage and general secular culture. By this time the Jewish communities in Christian Europe had assumed a common pattern. The community was governed by a small elite of rabbinical or capitalist families who governed the mass of the Jewish population, which consisted of artisans and small tradesmen. Excluded from Christian society and culture, the elite sought to strengthen the corporate nature of the Jewish community by the systematic application of Talmudic law. The outstanding and representative thinker of this Jewish elite was Rashi (Rabbi Solomon ben Isaac, d. 1105), who was in his day the head of the Jewish community in Troyes. He worked entirely within the Talmudic tradition, adding another commentary on the Pentateuch in order to relate its moral and legal precepts to contemporary Jewish needs. Rashi's Biblical commentary still has canonical status for orthodox Jews, and his marginal glosses are still commonly printed alongside the Hebrew text of the Bible. His commentary is distinguished by an empirical and common-sense attitude which contrasts strongly with the highly allegorical interpretation originated by Philo and extensively employed by Christian scholars. For this reason some Christian scholars in the twelfth century found Rashi's work curious and illuminating. Rashi's mind was urbane and shrewd, and he was obviously aware of the problems of daily life which his coreligionists faced. He tried to show them how they could maintain the moral and legalistic precepts of the Bible in the midst of rapidly deteriorating circumstances. He thus performed a valuable service to the European ghettos of the next eight centuries. But as an intellectual document Rashi's commentary on the Bible is mediocre and insignificant. It is distinguished neither by mysticism and deep piety nor by any attempt to relate Judaism to science and philosophy. It demonstrates all too clearly the intellectual poverty of the Jews who lived in medieval Christian Europe.

The Jewish situation in Christian Europe steadily deteriorated during the twelfth and thirteenth centuries. The Fourth Lateran Council of the Church of 1215 prescribed their absolute ghettoization and decreed that all Jews should wear a yellow label as an emblem of their pariah status. With the emergence of Christian financial institutions, the service which Jewish capitalists could render steadily declined. The orthodoxy promulgated by the rabbinical elite was increasingly fundamentalist and hostile to philosophical thought. Under these conditions it is not surprising that there was some apostasy to the Christian faith. But the number of Jews who escaped from their bondage and persecution by conversion represented a tiny minority. Whereas in the twentieth century persecuted Jews could not escape from the trammels of anti-Semitism, in the Middle Ages they were offered their freedom through conversion. And yet there were few conversions for three reasons. First, the Jews' sense of providence and eschatology led them to believe that the age of persecutions heralded the coming of the Messiah and their imminent redemption. Second, the pluralistic, corporate nature of medieval society left converts who had forsaken their family and community with a very bleak prospect once they had left their social group and gone out into the Christian world. Third, while the Church welcomed Jewish converts and even rewarded them, the lay population was generally hostile to them since they feared economic competition from Jewish converts.

In the 1290's the kings of both England and France expelled the Jews from their territory, partly to satisfy the demands of popular hatred, and partly to enrich their treasuries by seizing Jewish property. Many of the Jews who were expelled moved eastward into Germany where there was a substantial Jewish population in the fourteenth and fifteenth centuries. Here the Jews acquired the German language, which with the addition of Hebrew words and written in the Hebrew script, became the modern Yiddish. And here also they again suffered the ravages of pogroms. This precipitated a further eastward Jewish migration into Poland and Russia where yet further agonies awaited them.

The Jews were undoubtedly the most literate ethnic or linguistic group in medieval society. Their separation from general European culture after the eleventh century, partly in response to persecution and ghettoization, and partly the result of dictates of narrowly orthodox rabbis, represents an incalculable loss to the intellectual life of the medieval world and a substantial impediment to the progress of western civilization. The magnitude of this loss can be shown by comparing the meager Jewish contribution to culture in the rest of Europe with their achievements in Moslem Spain.

The position of the Jews in Moslem Spain until the end of the eleventh century was more favorable than in any other part of western Europe. The Arab princes virtually accepted them as equals, and Jews rose to high positions in the government and prospered in commerce and in the learned professions, particularly medicine. During the tenth and eleventh centuries a highly cultured, quite secularized Jewish court aristocracy flourished in the centers of Moslem rule. For the only time between Philo's Alexandria and the eighteenth century a large community of Jews was accepted into society and given the opportunity to participate in all aspects of life. As a

consequence, the Jewish scholars of Spain became attracted to secular culture, and they made the only important contributions of any members of
their faith to the general culture of the high middle ages. There was
almost as great a variety in the Jewish approach to learning and knowledge
as there was in the Christian world. Some of the Jewish thinkers held to a
strict Neoplatonism; the most outstanding spokesman of this school was
Avicebrol (Solomon Ibn Gabirol, d. 1058). His most important work, *The
Fountain of Life,* was translated into Latin and widely read in Christian
Europe. Avicebrol's Neoplatonic thesis is purely philosophic, and there is
nothing in it to identify its author as a Jewish scholar. In fact, the authorship of this treatise was not established until the nineteenth century;
medieval Latin scholars assumed it was written by a Christian.

Another aspect of Spanish-Jewish culture was represented by the greatest
Hebrew poet of the middle ages, Judah Halevi, who died around 1140. His
earlier work is concerned with themes of secular love similar to those which
inspired the Provençal troubadours and also the Arabic poets of the
period. A homosexual motif is common in these poems. The tone of
Halevi's work becomes, however, steadily more anti-intellectual, didactic,
and nationalistic in outlook. Living in a wealthy society in which many Jews
had become completely assimilated into the mores and ideals of their
environment, he became concerned with the preservation of the identity
of the Jewish people. Halevi became an eloquent spokesman for the moral
grandeur of traditional Judaism and the implacable enemy of a secularized
Jewish culture. He was too much of a humanist, however, to adopt the
legalistic outlook characteristic of Talmudic Judaism. Halevi's greatest
book, *The Kuzari,* is inspired by a kind of romantic nationalism, a distinctive proto-Zionism that celebrates not only the Jewish law and religious
tradition but also the moral superiority of the Jewish people. *The Kuzari*
was favorite reading among nineteenth- and twentieth-century Zionists, and
for good reason: "If we bear our exile and degradation for God's sake, as is
meet, we shall be the pride of the generation which will come with the
Messiah, and accelerate the day of deliverance we hope for. . . . The
gentiles merely serve to introduce and pave the way for the expected Messiah, who is the fruition, and they will all become His fruit. Then, if they
acknowledge Him, they will become one tree. . . . Jerusalem can only be
rebuilt when Israel yearns for it to such an extent that they embrace her
stones and dust." Not only was Halevi's style powerful and attractive, but
the ideals propounded in his later work offered that distinctive tone of
intense romanticism and aggressive nationalism which inspired modern
Zionism. It might be said, however, that Halevi came eight centuries too
soon. His death on a pilgrimage to the Holy Land ended the attempt to
establish not a Talmudic or a Philonic but a third new force in Jewish life.

Neither Avicebrol nor Halevi nor any other Spanish-Jewish writer gained so much attention from his contemporaries and so much posthumous fame as Maimonides ("Rambam," Rabbi Moses ben Maimon, 1135–1204). He was the scion of a prominent rabbinical family in Spain, and he was the greatest Talmudic scholar of his day and, in the opinion of many, of all time. At the same time, he had early become interested in Greek philosophy and science, and he was concerned with examining the relationship between Aristotelianism and Judaism and with demonstrating that his faith was compatible with the highest precepts of reason. He set out, therefore, to bridge the gap between Talmudic knowledge and Aristotelianism. It was a most difficult undertaking, and his enterprise gained the full attention of Jewish scholars. Maimonides was an extremely vigorous and independent man, and nothing could dissuade him from carrying out his chosen task, not even personal misfortune. In the twelfth century Jews were suffering persecution at the hands of Moslem fanatics who had come to power in the Iberian principality. The religious militancy which had hurt the Jews so much in the Christian world was now beginning to attack them in Moslem countries as well. Maimonides and his family escaped to North Africa, where the learned rabbi formally made obeisance to Islam while secretly maintaining his Judaism. In later years he could see nothing wrong with his conduct, painful as it is for Maimonides' modern biographers - to contemplate. From North Africa his family emigrated to Egypt, where Maimonides became a physician to Saladin's vizier. This did not prevent him from continuing his work of commentary on the Bible or from trying to establish the relationship between Aristotelianism and Jewish revelation.

The result of Maimonides' work was a new, massive commentary on the Old Testament and, much more important for the general pattern of medieval thought, *The Guide for the Perplexed.* The latter work was intended to assist those educated Jews who were faced with the contradictions between the teachings of science and revelation. Maimonides, like Thomas Aquinas after him, rejected the Averroist double-truth doctrine. He claimed that behind science and revelation there was one single God-given truth. It was a noble sentiment, but Maimonides had a very hard time maintaining it; his book seems to have perplexed more Jews than it guided. In order to arrive at the conclusions he wanted, he had to water down Aristotle's doctrines and engage in the kind of allegorizing of the Bible which Philo had used to show the compatibility of Judaism and Platonism. Maimonides contended that God was indeed a prime mover, but that the Aristotelian conception of the deity only dealt with part of His nature; he is also the theistic God of Judaism who interferes continuously in human affairs. Maimonides tried desperately to show that the creation of the world could be supported by reason, but he had to admit that his proofs were only probable and not certain. This was enough to arouse bitter criticism from the leaders of traditional Talmudic Judaism. It was when he came to discuss immortality, however, that he got himself into the greatest difficulty. Ironically, Maimonides himself had played a leading role in making the immortality of the soul a cardinal principle of the Jewish faith. There is no such doctrine in the Jewish Bible. It had been imported into Judaism in the first century B.C. from Persia by the Pharisees and had always been cautiously regarded by Talmudic scholars. But after making immortality an article of faith, Maimonides became involved in the question of personal, as against general, immortality, which had bothered the Moslem Aristotelians. In the end he seemed to support the Averroist doctrine of immortality through union with universal Intelligence. His specific teachings and the generally rationalist attitude he adopted in *The Guide for the Perplexed* roused the ire and fears of the leaders of rabbinic Judaism. He was denounced as a heretic, and while his compendium of Jewish law became authoritative, his philosophic works were prohibited, totally neglected, and not studied by Jewish scholars until the nineteenth century. Some of his critics in Provence, where there was a great school of Talmudic Judaism, opposed him so bitterly that they asked the Inquisition to burn his philosophic treatises, a request with which the inquisitors gladly complied. In defense of the Provençal rabbis, it can be said that they feared that the dissemination of Maimonides' Aristotelian treatise would allow the inquisitors to blame the Jews for instigating Christian heresy.

In both Moslem and Jewish thought, the attempts of great thinkers to deal with the relationship between revelation and the new Aristotelian science thus ended in defeat and disaster at the beginning of the thirteenth century. Islam turned away from science because it was considered heretical by religious leaders who were able to obtain the assistance of fanatical princes to destroy rational speculation. The general decline of vigor in Islamic civilization undoubtedly also played a part in the termination of the great scientific and philosophic movement in the Arabic world. Judaism at the same time turned its back on science and secular thought, partly again because of the hostility of orthodox religious leaders and also because of the ghettoization of European Jewry which began in the twelfth century. This separated Jewish scholars from the science and philosophy of western civilization for another six hundred years and played into the hands of the Talmudic obscurantists. In later Islamic culture and also in Judaism only mysticism was allowed to stand as an addition to the prime avenue to truth found in revelation. After 1200 only the thinkers of Christian western Europe were afforded the opportunity to establish a new intellectual system which would take into account the challenge of Aristotelian science.

Chapter Seventeen

VARIETIES OF RELIGIOUS EXPERIENCE

I. The Problem of Piety

By the end of the eleventh century the church had achieved the imposition of its ideals on society. Christianity was taken seriously by the landed classes, by the bourgeois, and even, on a much lower level of intelligence, by the peasants, into whose villages the Christian faith was at last being actually carried by the spread of the parish system. The problems of religion were ever-present realities to the people of western Europe, and since they took God seriously, they tried in various ways to conform to Christian ideals. Their search for satisfactory expression of their devotion profoundly affected many facets of medieval civilization. The architecture, pictorial art, Latin poetry, and liturgical music of the twelfth century were monuments to this profound piety. But the channeling of religious feeling into controllable forms became more and more a cause of grave concern to the leaders of the late eleventh- and twelfth-century church. The expression of the new piety had been a relatively simple matter before 1050. Devout men and women who felt a strong call to live a regular religious life and who were able to dissociate themselves from their families became members of the ever growing Benedictine community. Those who were not able to become monks assisted the Cluniacs and other Benedictines with various kinds of services and gifts. But after the middle of the eleventh century the forms of religious experience become much more varied. The Cluniac form of monasticism did not satisfy the ascetic impulses of many people inspired by the new piety, and they sought new institutional expressions for the ascetic impulse. The result was the tremendous proliferation of new monastic orders in the late eleventh and twelfth centuries. Many devout people who did not participate in this new wave of ascetic withdrawal from the world, especially among the urban population of western Europe, found satisfaction in an intense religious individualism whose doctrines were disseminated by popular preachers. By the end of the twelfth century ecclesiastical leaders were faced with the unprecedented and dismaying tasks of controlling the proliferation of new religious orders, of directing the ascetic impulse into the channels which would make it useful to church and society, of finding new ways to satisfy the spiritual yearnings of devout laymen, and of overcoming the schisms fomented by popular heresy.

II. *The Institutionalization of Asceticism*

Northern Italy at the end of the tenth century was the scene of the first stirrings of a profound revolution in western monasticism. New ascetic concern and eremetic tendencies began to come to the forefront of religious life. The hermit had never been as important a figure in Latin monasticism as he had been in the Greek Christian world. Extreme ascetic practices had not been a quality of Benedictine life in the original Rule, and even less so in its Carolingian and Cluniac forms. The emergence of an urban civilization in northern Italy in the late tenth century, with the attendant opportunities for wealth and comfort, provided in Europe for the first time the temptation of luxurious living against which the ascetic hermit could revolt. About the year 1000 the figure of the hermit-saint made his appearance in northern Italy; he withdrew from the world to escape spiritual degradation attendant upon life in princely courts and wealthy cities, but he periodically returned to preach a moral and spiritual revival to the urban populace. These strongly ascetic and eremetic impulses and the ubiquitous hermit-saints were to be a central current in north Italian religiosity over the next three centuries.

By the middle of the eleventh century the new monasticism had assumed the character of a widespread spiritual movement in the area between Rome and the Alps, and some of these ascetics had formed monastic communities which offered strong contrasts with the prevailing Benedictine life. The order of Camaldoli founded a monastic community of hermits who lived in individual cells. The monastery of the order of Vallombrosa, near Florence, consciously revolted against Cluniac life and aimed at the strict observance of the pristine Rule of St. Benedict. In the fulfillment of this aim Vallombrosa included within its community uneducated lay brothers as well as clerics who could perform liturgical offices. This separation of the order into clerical and lay brothers, giving uneducated men from the lower ranks of society the opportunity to assume the monastic habit, was a radical departure which was to be imitated by several of the new religious orders of the twelfth and thirteenth centuries.

North of the Alps a similar ascetic impulse appeared in the middle of the eleventh century, although it never went as far as Italian monasticism in accentuating the eremitic life. The first significant change appears to be the founding in 1043 of "The House of God," not far from Lyons, by a former Cluniac monk dissatisfied with the religious life in western Europe's leading monastery. During the following half century there were several such rejections of the Cluniac model in favor of a more rigorous religious life within monastic communities that were less involved with society and its attendant obligations and temptations than had been the case for several centuries. The spread of the internal colonization movement in Europe undoubtedly played a part in encouraging men of ascetic inclinations to establish little cells in frontier regions and to live entirely on their own resources. In the Rhineland and southern France the ominous figure of the itinerant saintly preacher also appears before the end of the eleventh century, as is fully attested by the history of the people's crusade of 1095.

The vicissitudes of the Gregorian reform movement strongly contributed to the growth and influence of these new tendencies within western monasticism. The Gregorians had drawn their initial inspiration and all their leadership from the new ascetic impulses and movements of the eleventh century. In the Gregorian reform, asceticism adopted its puritanical form; it tried to create a world which would be a suitable environment for the undisturbed pilgrimage to the City of God. The reform movement's failure showed clearly that asceticism could not hope to impose its ideals on society, to turn the world into a monastery with a universal abbot demanding obedience from all rulers. The Hildebrandine papacy had brought to the church not peace but a sword, not greater strength but deep divisions, confusions, and doubts. Hence, many of the best spirits of the first three decades of the twelfth century turned from the world and sought their peace with God outside the world in new communities and orders which aimed at complete withdrawal. Many of the older monasteries, even Cluny during the abbacy of Peter the Venerable in the second quarter of the twelfth century, came to some extent under this new impetus toward withdrawal.

These critical changes within western monastic life were made possible by the decline of the regular clergy's usefulness to society. In the late eleventh and first half of the twelfth century the services which the Benedictine monks had for centuries rendered to European civilization were no longer required. The first, and ultimately the most decisive, development along these lines was the monks' loss of control over higher education. The monastic school had admirably served the compelling educational need of society before the eleventh century—the preservation of a basic literacy through the cultivation of the liberal arts and the Biblical-patristic tradition. But the monastic school was too limited in its interests and too restricting in its organization to be a suitable haven for the new intellectual elite of the early twelfth century or to be the center for the tremendous achievements in speculative thought and in law during the following decades.

The monks' loss of leadership in education contributed to the decline of their importance in political life. The municipal schools of northern Italy and the cathedral schools of northern France, which provided homes for the new higher learning, began to turn out shrewd, well-educated, and frequently quite ruthless secular clerks and civil lawyers who displaced monastic scholars as the literate servants of the European monarchies during the twelfth century. Simultaneously, with the decline of the monks' importance in education and their displacement as royal ministers by a new kind of professional bureaucrat, the great religious houses were becoming less useful in another way to the more powerful monarchs. In the latter half of the eleventh century the Norman and German rulers' dependence on the military resources of the monasteries declined markedly as these able and aggressive rulers found new sources of recruitment for their armies. The imposition of new knight service on the Norman monasteries ended by 1050 and similarly stopped in England by 1080. Not only was the knight service from lay fiefs now available in sufficient amount, but also the Norman rulers, using the proceeds from feudal taxation and later also from scutage, extensively employed mercenaries. Similarly, the Salian kings relied heavily on their own *ministeriales* for military forces. By the second quarter of the twelfth century the main social obligation of the Benedictine monk was that of acting as intercessor for lay society with Christ, the Virgin, and the saints. This sufficed in the twelfth century to continue to make the Benedictines popular with laymen, although they were bitterly criticized by the cathedral clergy, who coveted the black monks' centuries-old privileges and possessions. But even in the religious sphere the importance of the Benedictine community markedly declined. The cathedral and the parish church became more and more the centers for expressing the religious devotion of the populace in town and country, and the fervent admiration which the Benedictines had evoked in the early middle ages was, in the twelfth century, accorded the new religious orders.

The increasing tendency after 1100 to dispense with the educational, political, military, and even, to some degree, religious services of the regular clergy to society gave impetus to the emergence of new religious orders devoted to ascetic withdrawal. Among the many obscure French monasteries founded in the late eleventh century was that of Cîteaux, whose leading spirit was a saintly Englishman named Stephen Harding. Cîteaux rapidly attracted outstanding young men of strongly ascetic leanings, among them Bernard, the greatest religious mind of the twelfth century. Cîteaux was soon able to establish daughter houses and to absorb into her order independently founded communities. By the 1130's the Cistercians had become the major new monastic order, second in size only to the Benedictines. The Cistercian way of life was from the first consciously and stridently at variance with the prevailing Benedictine pattern, and this was signified by the wearing of a white, instead of black, habit. The Cistercians asked their secular patrons to grant them rights of settlement only in uninhabited regions, because they were especially eager to avoid the privileges and obligations that had come to the great Benedictine houses from their possession of cultivated and settled domains. The white monks claimed that manorial estates worked by dependent serfs encouraged monastic avarice and luxury and precluded the apostolic poverty which was a necessary aspect of the true religious life. By the 1120's St. Bernard, the most eloquent spokesman for the new order, although by no means a typical Cistercian, was violently criticizing Cluny's wealth, comforts, and even artistic beauty, and similar open attacks were made on the Benedictines by other leaders of the white monks. The harassed Benedictines replied in an equally bitter vein. They contended that it would be unjust to expect the faithful to endure the privations that the Apostles had suffered in the midst of heathen hostility and persecution now that the church had vanquished its enemies. They pointed out that the Cistercians, in their ostentatious self-righteousness, had not escaped the snares of pride, and they claimed that among the many white monks who had a genuine contempt for the world there were also "many hypocrites and seducing pretenders."

Both the religious and social circumstances of the twelfth century favored the triumph of the Cistercians and the extremely rapid expansion of their order. All over Europe there were devout and serious young men concerned for the safety of their souls in a world which was steadily growing more urbanized and wealthy, and hence one which, in their eyes, was fraught with ever greater danger to the achievement of the spiritual life. The desire to assume the Cistercian habit was virtually a mass movement in the twelfth century, and after 1150 the order also established convents for women of similar calling. By the late thirteenth century there were no fewer than seven hundred Cistercian establishments in Europe. Landlords everywhere greeted the Cistercians with the greatest enthusiasm, and they were very eager to allow the white monks to settle in previously uncultivated lands within their domains in order to open up these frontier areas for later settlement. All over Europe in the twelfth century the Cistercians acted as pioneers in the colonization movement. They were particularly active in this respect in eastern Germany, where they played an important part in developing the new method of working the land in large blocks instead of in strips. It was the twelfth-century Cistercian monasteries which developed sheep raising in the hitherto unproductive hilly wastelands of northern England. This innovation was immediately imitated by the secular landlords of Yorkshire, and it opened up this frontier region. In the thirteenth century the export of wool to the Flemish weaving cities was the staple of English foreign trade.

The enormous popularity which the Cistercians gained with all classes of twelfth-century society still left room for the creation of several smaller orders with very similar aims and attitudes. The Carthusians were a small, highly selective, austere order which eventually won renown for two things: their order of Chartreuse never experienced the vicissitudes of other Catholic orders, so that the Carthusians were later able to claim that they never had needed to be reformed; and they played an important part in the invention of brandy, the first European hard liquor, during the thirteenth century. The order of Fontrevault, which had forty houses by 1200, was primarily designed for nuns, although it included an attached group of monks to perform religious service and to do hard physical labor. Fontrevault was sharply different from early medieval nunneries (which were high-toned aristocratic places) in that it accepted women from all classes and was particularly a refuge for fallen women, destitute widows, etc., of whom there were an inordinate number in medieval Europe. The emergence of these and other smaller orders alongside the Cistercians indicates the ubiquity of piety in twelfth-century Europe and also the increasing tendency to organize religious movements into distinct corporate orders. The early medieval Benedictines had by no means been homogeneous in their outlook, but the varying groups among the black monks had not considered it necessary to constitute themselves into separate orders. Even the Cluniacs had not been, in a constitutional sense, a separate order. The legalistic spirit and organizing impulse of the twelfth century affected even monastic life and encouraged the proliferation of several distinct orders.

All the new ascetic orders were involved with romanticized and highly emotional forms of Christianity, particularly the Virgin Cult. The tendency of the new forms of monasticism was away from an intellectualized

Christianity and toward an intensely personal kind of religious experience. This further separated the new monastic orders from the achievements in philosophy and science which were being pursued by secular clerks in the universities. But it brought their religious attitudes into conformity with the main trends in lay piety and gained for the Cistercians and their imitators a still higher degree of social approval. Yet by 1200 it was becoming apparent that the Cistercians' withdrawal from the world had not altogether succeeded, and the extravagant praise which the white monks had received in the first half century of their existence was frequently replaced by sardonic criticism, such as the black monks had already experienced.

The Benedictines steadily lost social approval during the second half of the twelfth century, and it is easy to see why. Ensconced behind the walls of their comfortable establishments and living off their vast income, they no longer contributed anything to society. They were simply there, and they continued to attract new members, but by no means many of the finer spiritual minds of the age. Their importance in liturgical prayer was on the decline, and they no longer had any other social functions. Here and there a Benedictine *scriptorium* would still produce a valuable illuminated manuscript, or a black monk would, as in times past, devote himself to writing the history of his times. But by and large, by the late twelfth century, the Benedictines were no longer making any contributions to European civilization and in view of the fact that they did not attract the more devout religious, it is not suprising that many black monks were beset by the terrible sin of *accidia*—simple boredom. We have a graphic and detailed account of one of the largest, oldest, and wealthiest English Benedictine abbeys, Bury St. Edmunds, in the *Chronicle* of Jocelyn of Brakelond, the abbot's secretary. Abbot Samson appears in Jocelyn's description as a hard-working and sincere administrator, but one who completely lacked a real interest in the contemplative life. Jocelyn remarked that the abbot "commended good officials more than good monks." Yet Jocelyn regards his abbot as an outstanding monastic leader!

The Cistercian order did not suffer as much from ossification as from corruption. The later history of the Cistercians is one of the most disillusioning themes in medieval history, and by 1200 contemporaries were well aware of it. The Cistercians seemed to have demonstrated the truth of the aphorism that nothing fails like success. They had taken the lead in the monastic withdrawal from the world, but the world followed and they were unable to resist its temptations. The Cistercian monasteries had been established in uninhabited frontier regions. But by 1200 these areas were among the most flourishing in Europe. The Cistercians' laborious improvement of their lands had made them prominent landlords. They technically abided by their vow not to use the labor of serfs, but they got around its spirit by leasing their estates to secular lords for high rents. Many Cistercian houses built up large amounts of capital, and their abbots used it to become moneylenders to the local nobility and less fortunate churchmen. By the early thirteenth century the Cistercians had become notorious for their business acumen and their similarity to Jewish usurers. The order of the white monks became sharply divided into a more zealous group, who wanted to return to the original ideals of Stephen Harding, and the more moderate majority, who were prepared to accept their prosperity as the grace of God. The later history of the white monks was marked by bitter internal controversies; in the seventeenth century the radical ascetic wing broke away and formed the Trappist order. The failure of the Cistercians to provide a satisfactory institutional form of piety was partly the result of inadequate government. The order grew far too fast and was too modest in its admission requirements. The abbot of Cîteaux was supposed to supervise carefully the affairs of the daughter houses, but this became a practical impossibility because of the vast number of Cistercian monasteries. This inadequate administration and lax discipline allowed the intrusion into the ranks of the white monks of men who betrayed the ascetic ideals of the founders of the order. In addition, the Cistercians had the misfortune of choosing a way of life which perfectly satisfied the economic needs of the twelfth century. They had been organized as a religious order which engaged in complete withdrawal from society, but the Cistercian program was such that they opened up the frontier regions, and society followed. The Cistercians had neither the organization, the experience, nor the leaders to deal with the situation in which they had become landlords and capitalists in what had once been their areas of ascetic retreat. The white monks had no traditions of either learning or worldly sophistication; they were anti-intellectuals who also lacked the Benedictines' familiarity with government and lordship They were inevitably overwhelmed by their involvement with the world, and their withdrawal from society, which had been such a glorious chapter in twelfth-century religiosity, ended in a mixture of tragedy and paradox.

The failure of both puritanism in the eleventh century and monastic withdrawal in the twelfth to achieve their aims encouraged the increasing prominence of a new kind of religious order which was a compromise between the two extreme variants of asceticism. This new institutionalized form of asceticism allowed its adherents both to undertake a regular religious life and the traditional vows of chastity, poverty, and obedience and at the same time to work in the world and to make a direct personal contribution to the welfare of society. Various experiments with this new kind of religious order provided the background for the emergence in the thirteenth century of the Franciscan and Dominican friars, which marked the most important stage in the development of the Catholic orders since the Rule of St. Benedict. The new orders working in the world eventually constituted the institutional means by which the ascetic impulse was used to meet the challenge of the intensive religiosity of the urban population of Europe.

The primary twelfth-century experiments with the new kind of religious order were undertaken by the regular canons and the military orders. The cathedral canons in the early middle ages had been notorious for their lack of devotion to their calling. The early twelfth-century development of the additional institution of the prebend, by which each cathedral official was given a fixed endowed income, only acerbated this situation. It made the cathedral canons financially independent of the bishop, and their offices particularly tempting for the younger sons of the nobility. The founding of the order of Prémontré in France in the 1120's was an attempt to remedy this situation. Its aim was an order open to both men and women who would take monastic vows but who would be free to work in the world as did cathedral canons and other secular clergy; hence the designation of "regular canons." In some ways the Premonstratensian order was inspired by the same ideal which influenced the early Cistercians. Prémontré, the original establishment of the order, was built in a desolate place which had been "shown out" by the Virgin. But whereas the white monks fled from the world, the regular canons were active in the growing urban areas in their philanthrophic, charitable, and hospital work and as parish clergy. In the twelfth century another group of monks working in the world, the Austin (Augustinian) canons, achieved prominence, particularly in England.

The regular canons foreshadowed, both in their institutional form and in their aims, the great orders of friars founded in the thirteenth century. But they did not have the impact which the Dominicans and Franciscans exercised on thirteenth-century civilization. The value of religious orders working in society, particularly in the urban areas, was not sufficiently perceived by the papacy until the beginning of the thirteenth century. The regular canons could have had much the same impact on twelfth-century Europe as the friars were to have a little later, but there was simply not enough of them for this purpose. The twelfth-century popes were able and sincere administrators, but they were remarkably insensitive to the currents of lay piety, and they offered no organized program to counter the more revolutionary implications of urban religiosity. The regular canons were forced to work with very little assistance from the leaders of the church, and it was not until the pontificate of Innocent III in the first decade of the thirteenth century that the significance of their new institutionalized form of asceticism was fully perceived at Rome.

It would have been fortunate for the church and for European civilization in several respects if some of the energy and wealth which was given to supporting the crusading military orders in the twelfth century had been accorded instead to the regular canons. The military orders were the consequence of an attempt to apply the spirit and institutions of corporate monasticism to crusading ends. They are the most extreme expression of the militant stream in twelfth-century Christianity. It seemed to all kinds of people in the twelfth century in Europe that it was not only appropriate but desirable that men who had taken vows dedicating themselves to divine service should accomplish this by killing infidels. The military orders were particularly attractive to those members of the nobility who wanted to assume the monastic life but who wanted to continue to make use of their military skills. There had always been a psychological affinity between monastic and military discipline, and the regular clergy were commonly referred to as the soldiers of Christ. In the military orders this term took on a more than metaphorical significance.

The earliest crusading orders were initially founded as welfare agencies, to provide secondary services for crusaders and pilgrims, but they rapidly formed themselves into effective and powerful paramilitary organizations. The Knights Templars (the Poor Brothers of the Temple of Jerusalem) originated around 1120 in the efforts of a few French knights to protect pilgrims on the way to the Holy Land. St. Bernard formed these knights into a corporate religious order dedicated to fighting in the Holy Land. There was a threefold division within the ranks of the Templars: the aristocratic soldiers, the clergy, and the lay brothers of lower-class background who assisted the highborn knights as squires and grooms. The Knights Hospitalers (Order of St. John of Jerusalem) were the great rivals of the Templars. The original aim of the Hospitalers was to serve as the medical corps of the crusaders, but they rapidly became a military order and competed with the Templars for prestige and influence in the affairs of the Latin Kingdom of Jerusalem. The internecine feuds of the monastic soldiers contributed to the weakness of the crusading state in Palestine.

The later history of the Templars exhibits that same yielding to the temptations of Mammon that corrupted the Cistercian order. In the midst of the twelfth-century economic expansion it was very hard for any effective corporate group *not* to make money, and if the corporation was also dedicated to divine service, it received endowments from all sides. As a result of the great success of their fund-raising drives the Templars became involved with the techniques of the accumulation and transfer of capital, and by the thirteenth century they were the greatest bankers in Europe, with the papacy and the French kings as their clients. The thirteenth-century Templars did not kill many Moslems, but they were expert at increasing their capital, and they set up the headquarters of their bank in Paris. The popular attitude toward the Templars changed from fervent admiration to cynicism and jealousy, but the leaders of the order did not seem to mind. They insisted that their banking activities were ultimately in the service of God and pursued them with ascetic dedication. The history of the Templars constitutes one documented case of religion playing a part in the rise of capitalism.

If, in the case of the Templars, institutionalized asceticism ended in the creation of a bank, the Teutonic Knights, founded in 1190, provided what the nineteenth-century German nationalist historian Heinrich Treitschke called the origins of Prussianism. At the time of the third crusade some German lords formed a military order to fight in the Holy Land. But within thirty years they had transferred their area of operations from the middle east to Germany's eastern frontier, and they came to play a leading part in the *Drang nach Osten,* the eastward movement into the Slavic lands which had begun a century before. The original spiritual ideals of the order were subordinated to political ambitions. The Teutonic Knights indiscriminately attacked Christians and heathens in eastern Europe. They were fundamentally a state in the guise of a religious order. But their monastic form imbued them with corporate efficiency and fanatical zeal and greatly contributed to their long string of victories. They conquered Prussia from the Slavs and ruled it until the late fifteenth century. They pushed into Lithuania, Estonia, and Russia, where their advance was finally stopped shortly after 1400. In a sense the Teutonic Knights constituted one of the most successful variants of the institutionalized piety of the twelfth century. They remained dedicated to their vows and firm in their organization and were great soldiers and administrators for nearly three centuries after their founding.

By the late twelfth century, as a result of the work of the regular canons and the military orders, the idea of monks working in the world had become a familiar and popular one. In the last decades of the century there was, in fact, a proliferation of obscure orders based on the principle of serving society while at the same time pursuing the ascetic life. The Order of Bridgebuilders, for instance, was organized in France in 1189 to contribute to human welfare by improving communications. The Roman curia was disturbed by the dispersion of the ascetic impulse into so many distinct orders, and at the Fourth Lateran Council of 1215 it decreed the cessation in the licensing of new orders by the papacy. But almost immediately the church found it necessary to constitute the new orders of friars to meet the challenges of urban piety and popular heresy. The original contribution of twelfth-century institutionalized asceticism was its compromise between the puritan and monastic extremes and its direction of spirituality toward service to Christian society. Out of this background emerged the religious orders which were to be indispensable in the church's struggle to maintain its leadership in European civilization.

III. The Dimensions of Popular Heresy

Anticlericalism and antisacerdotalism were the two modes of thought which in the second half of the twelfth century threatened to undermine the traditional position of the church in medieval society and forced the papacy, under Innocent III and his successors in the early decades of the thirteenth century, to undertake a desperate struggle for the reaffirmation of ecclesiastical leadership. Anticlericalism prepared the ground for the rise of antisacerdotalism, but they are per se distinct attitudes and doctrines. Anticlericalism is criticism of the clergy for not fulfilling the duties of their office and, as such, is not an error in the faith. Antisacerdotalism denies to the clergy the power of their office and claims that the sacraments which they administer have no efficacy. This view, of course, is the Donatist heresy and contradicts the fundamentals of Catholicism.

The common tendency of medieval thinkers to vulgarize St. Augustine's conception of the city of God and to identify the heavenly community with the church provided an intellectual basis for the growth of antisacerdotalism. For if the church is the city of God, then assuredly its leaders are the most saintly of men and the ministry of Christ ought to be founded on personal holiness rather than on the impersonal, official authority of the priesthood.

Anticlericalism can, and in the twelfth century did, contribute to the growth of antisacerdotal movements. Constant and protracted criticism of the personal qualities of the church hierarchy and the insistence upon a discrepancy between their ideals and their practices eventually raised doubts in the minds of some devout people as to whether the priesthood were the ministers of God in the first place. But it must be emphasized that criticism of the clergy as lazy and corrupt in and of itself does not constitute heresy. In fact, such criticism may be the necessary precondition for reform and revitalization of the church. Thus it is possible to have two men speaking unfavorably about the clergy, but with their attitudes fundamentally different. One wants the clergy to exercise the full powers of its office in accordance with the highest ideals of the church, while the other holds that the church hierarchy has no religious authority. The former represents an act of criticism, the latter of denial. The second half of the twelfth century was marked by a thunderous chorus of attacks on the clergy, and the papacy was faced with the difficult task of evaluating the merit of these criticisms and making a distinction between those who wanted a better Catholic hierarchy and those who wanted to destroy the Catholic church and substitute new kinds of sectarian religious communities.

With each passing decade of the twelfth century, criticism from all quarters of the conduct of the clergy became more intense. Some of the severest criticism came from within the church itself. Monks attacked the cathedral clergy as corrupt and materialistic; the canons claimed that the monks were useless and selfish; and competing religious orders made derogatory remarks about each other. St. Bernard and his disciples denounced the soft living of ecclesiastical princes in the severest terms, and Pope Innocent III castigated the higher clergy of southern France as "dumb dogs who can no longer bark." In the later decades of the century it was fashionable for poets, university students, and courtly writers to produce clever satires depicting the clergy as greedy and corrupt. The circle of any king who was in trouble with Rome, such as the German Hohenstaufens, attributed the grossest motives to the pope and cardinals. The German minnesinger Walther von der Vogelweide supported his Hohenstaufen patron by denouncing the papacy as a ravenous wolf, and he did not refrain from dragging up old legends that Sylvester II had been a sorcerer. Since the twelfth century almost everyone who had lost a case in the Roman court was inclined to attribute this to the cardinals' love of gold; the secretary of the angelic St. Anselm of Canterbury had made such a claim as early as 1095. Papal legates were fair game for all satirists and critics north of the Alps since they were frequently alien Italians who interfered in the affairs of the territorial churches of northern Europe. The Italian legates were deemed to be devious, mendacious, and unprincipled; one English writer, for good measure, asserted that a cardinal legate had a penchant for consorting with prostitutes. The picture of the clergy as ignorant, stupid, and lecherous given in Boccaccio's fourteenth-century stories can already be found in the bourgeois literature of the thirteenth century, which in turn reflects the impressions which many of the educated townsmen had of their bishops and priests before 1200.

From all this literary evidence it is possible to build up the blackest image of the late twelfth-century clergy. This was done in the 1920's in the work of the fiercely anti-Catholic historian G. G. Coulton, who indicted the medieval clergy for a sordid failure to live up to its profession. There is certainly plausible evidence for the truth of such an indictment, and the records of bishops' inspections of their dioceses, which were required after 1215, provide documentation for almost every conceivable kind of wrong-doing on the part of members of both the regular and secular clergy. On the other side of the case, however, is the fact of the magnificent achievements and vitality of the twelfth-century church and the hundreds of churchmen all over Europe, from bishop and abbot to the humblest monk and parish priest, whom we know to have been capable and zealous and even self-sacrificing in the fulfillment of their duties. In the assessment of the cause of the sharp rise in anticlericalism in the late twelfth century, the evidence points much more strongly to social and intellectual change rather than to a decline in the morality and quality of the clergy as the key to the problem.

In 1200 there were more dedicated members of the ecclesiastical hierarchy than ever before, but the standards the laity expected of their clergy became ever higher from the middle of the eleventh century, and the church simply did not have sufficient personnel to meet these demands. Particularly in urban areas, where there was an unprecedented degree of literacy and an intense piety among laymen, the church was pressed to provide clergy of the greatest learning and dedication, and there was a limited number of such men available. The association between the growth of capitalism and religious attitudes which Max Weber attributed to the sixteenth century can more certainly be identified in the twelfth. The twelfth-century merchant or craftsman necessarily had a very strong sense of calling. He knew that if he did not fulfill the possibilities of the vocation he had chosen, he would be condemned to miserable poverty. This made him very jealous of other groups in society who did not have to rely entirely on their own efforts—not only nobles, but also the churchmen. The medieval bourgeois was obstreperous and intolerant, and he tended to judge other people by the criteria of his own way of life. He felt that every clergyman should work for a living and that the cleric should not enjoy the powers and privileges of ecclesiastical office unless he demonstrated by his personal life that he was truly a minister of Christ. The burgher should be a businessman and the priest a saint; everyone should fulfill the obligations of his calling in life. But when the burgher applied this iron standard of rationality to the world around him, he discovered that many clergymen were not doing a good job and in fact were perhaps less worthy of their offices than the burgher himself would be. This made him angry and disillusioned with the priesthood.

The fault of the twelfth-century papacy was not that it permitted monstrous scandals with impunity, but rather that it did not adjust with sufficient rapidity and energy to the consequences of far-reaching social change. The church at the end of the twelfth century was still primarily organized for a rural society, and its attempts to satisfy the religious needs of the urbanized areas of Europe were halfhearted at best and perfunctory at worst. This situation left the bourgeois, particularly in the numerous and wealthy cities of northern Italy and southern France, to work out their own resolution of their religious problems. They wanted a faith which could provide an intense personal experience and involve them emotionally with Christ, the Virgin, and the saints. They had contributed to the building of magnificent municipal cathedrals all over Europe because they wanted a place to worship where they could feel a close association with the divine spirit. But a great many of the priests who worked in urban areas could not or would not pursue this intensely personal approach to the Christian faith. The old kind of cathedral cleric or parish priest believed that his function as a Christian minister should be confined to administering the sacraments, hearing confession, and performing the traditional liturgical offices. They were not prepared to give long and inspiring sermons, which served for the bourgeois as both the staple of their religious diet and their chief source of diversion amid the ruthless, overregulated, and cramped life of the medieval cities.

The social and religious milieu of northern Italy, the Rhineland, and southern France had already in the eleventh century produced itinerant preachers of saintly reputation who offered to the bourgeois the sermons and other accoutrements of personal religious experience they could not find in ordinary church services. After 1150 this kind of popular spiritual leader began to exercise greater and greater influence and to command formidable followings. The church was very slow to perceive the dangers inherent in such an unfamiliar situation. The new preachers appeared to be merely perpetuating and disseminating the new piety as expressed by Damiani and Bernard. But with each passing decade it became more evident that many of these popular religious leaders were going beyond this. They were advocating antisacerdotal and antisacramental doctrines which the fourth-century church had condemned as the Donatist heresy and which, although revived momentarily by Cardinal Humbert in 1059, had after 1080 been again anathematized by the church. Bored and disappointed by their dull clergy, many of the townsmen had come to doubt the value and efficacy of the sacraments and offices of the church. They were eager to listen to the itinerant saints who claimed that it was holiness of life and personal devotion to God which determined the members and leaders of the fellowship of Christ. This doctrine pleased the zealous burghers, who felt themselves in many cases superior in morality and intellect to their priests, while at the same time it gave the itinerant preachers the position of leadership over the new heretical communities. The Latin church had, of course, encountered heretical doctrines before in isolated instances, but since the Donatist heresy of the fourth century it had not been troubled by any which had a large popular following and which were associated with mass social and intellectual discontent. Before the end of the twelfth century the papacy did not discover how to deal with this grave threat to the unity of the church and the authority of the priesthood.

By the nature of its doctrine antisacerdotalism implied a sectarian rather than ecumenical religion. There were a number of sects devoted to their saintly leaders, but there was little or no cooperation among them. The only one of the late twelfth-century antisacerdotal sects which took on the character of more than an isolated local movement was the Waldensians. They take their name from Peter Waldo, a saintly merchant of Lyons in south-eastern France. Lyons and its environs had for a long time been distinguished by extremely ascetic religious leaders. Near Lyons in the 1040's was established the first of the anti-Cluniac monasteries to be founded north of the Alps. The archbishop of Lyons in the 1080's and the 1090's was the most devoted disciple that Gregory VII had in northern Europe. Waldo and his disciples called themselves the Poor Men of Lyons. They preached not only antisacerdotal, antisacramental, and Donatist doctrines but also the corollary theory of the apostolic poverty of the church which later influenced the policy of the radical Gregorian pope, Paschal II, in the second decade of the twelfth century. The church, as seen by the Waldensians, was not the prevailing Catholic institution but the purely spiritual fellowship of saintly men and women who had experienced divine love and grace. The Waldensian sect spread to the cities of northern Italy, where it had the greater part of its adherents by the later twelfth century. The followers of Peter Waldo were proto-Protestants who, for the first time, clearly presented the doctrines to which the more radical Protestant sects of the sixteenth and seventeenth centuries subscribed. And their doctrines contain that same combination of freedom and authoritarianism, of personal religious experience and the rule of the saints, which distinguishes the sixteenth-century Anabaptists and the seventeenth-century English Puritan sects who were their ultimate disciples. Although later driven from the cities of northern Italy by the church, they survived in very small numbers in Alpine valleys until the seventeenth century; they are the "slaughtered saints" of whom John Milton speaks in his famous sonnet.

The apocalyptic and eschatological tone of the antisacerdotal movements was given emphasis and greater content by the prolific speculations of an obscure south Italian abbot, Joachim of Flora, at the end of the twelfth century. His treatises received remarkably wide and rapid circulation. Following suggestions already made by St. Bernard, Joachim claimed that the world had entered the age of Antichrist, which immediately preceded the Second Coming and the Last Judgment. But whereas Bernard had satisfied himself with denouncing archbishops and bishops as the captives of the devil, Joachim identified the papacy itself with Antichrist. This revolutionary doctrine, which turned hierocratic theory on its head, proved to be enormously popular with all heretical movements up to and including the Protestant leaders of the sixteenth century. It made simpler the heretics' denunciation of the church and allowed them to indulge in an unqualified hatred of the Catholic priesthood. Subscribers to this doctrine could dismiss even the most zealous and moral acts of the papacy as merely the treacherous wiles of Antichrist. Their eschatological convictions gave the adherents of Joachimism the strength to withstand any counterattack on the part of the church. They alone were the true disciples of the Lord who would gain their triumph at His imminent coming. Men who held convictions such as these were not liable to be moved by appeals either to tradition, reason, or common sense.

The dualism implicit in Joachim's speculations comes out much stronger and in an absolute form in the heretical movement which won an enormous number of adherents in southern France: the religion of the Cathari (Pure Ones, Saints), or the Albigensian religion (after the town of Albi in Toulouse, where the heretics were particularly strong), or medieval Manicheanism, as it is sometimes called. Both the origins and the exact teachings of this most famous of twelfth- and thirteenth-century heresies—and the one which offered the greatest threat to the preservation of the unity of Latin Christendom—are somewhat obscure and the subject of debate among scholars. The thirteenth-century church eventually destroyed them with such efficiency that almost all that we know about the Cathari comes from the descriptions of their orthodox enemies and from the records of the church courts which tried and condemned them. The basic fact is that at the end of the twelfth century the wealthy bourgeois and many of the nobility of Toulouse and Provence, and perhaps even the count of Toulouse and his family, were members of an heretical church whose doctrines closely resembled, and perhaps were the perpetuation of, that fourth-century Manicheanism to which St. Augustine had for a time subscribed and then, after he had become a Christian, denounced in the severest terms. Many of the people of southern France who were not actually members of the Albigensian church seem nevertheless to have admired its saintly leaders;

the count of Toulouse most likely fell into this category. Considering the wealth of this part of Europe and the vitality of its culture, its increasing defection from the Catholic church threatened a schism in the Christian world of the greatest significance. In the eyes of the papacy and other orthodox believers everywhere in 1200, the Albigensian domination of southern France constituted a cancer in the body of European civilization which had to be rooted out at all costs.

The origins of the Cathari movement are not certainly known. In the late eleventh century it makes a dim appearance in the towns of both northern Italy and southern France. It disappeared in the former but slowly gained adherents in the latter, and after 1150 it came out in the open and brazenly and successfully challenged the church. The clergy of southern France were notoriously incompetent and corrupt; this situation both provided fertile ground for the growth of popular heresy and accounts for the initially perfunctory and totally inadequate efforts made to stop the steady expansion of the Albigensian church. The twelfth-century papacy must be convicted of the charge of ignoring too long the Albigensian threat and of being too conservative and timid in its remedy, which was simply to preach against the Cathari. An heretical movement which struck such deep roots into society was not going to be destroyed by even the most eloquent homiletics and apologetics. Yet the appearance of a popular schismatic church on such a great scale was a new thing in Latin Christianity. The well-meaning lawyers who dominated papal government did not realize until after 1200 that novel and radical methods would be needed to destroy the Albigensian heresy.

It has been asserted by Steven Runciman and other outstanding scholars that there is a direct line of transference of ideas stretching back from the twelfth-century Cathari to the fourth-century Manichees. This view holds that while Manichean doctrines disappeared in the Latin world, they invaded the Byzantine empire from their place of origin in Persia and were carried into Bulgaria in the tenth and eleventh centuries. There was indeed a Manichean sect called the Bogomils in the Balkans, and it has been suggested that its doctrines were spread to western Europe along trade routes in the late eleventh and twelfth centuries. This is a plausible thesis, although there is no documentary evidence for it. It was, however, possible to derive the dualist theology, which is the heart of Manicheanism, from the Neoplatonism which dominated early-medieval philosophy and theology. The Manichees believed that there are two gods, the god of good and the god of evil, of light and of darkness, who struggle for victory in the world. Man is a mixture of good spirit and evil matter. The Cathari are the ascetic "perfects" who have achieved a pure spirituality; those who do not live the fully ascetic life may nevertheless assure themselves of salvation by recognizing the leadership of the Cathari. These "auditors" of the true faith receive a sacrament on their deathbed which wipes away their previous sin and allows the reunion of their souls with the Divine Spirit. It is possible to arrive at this theology via a perversion of Neoplatonism, which similarly views God as the fountain of spirit to which the mystic returns by catharsis. Assuming that the possibility of receiving the grace of God through the ministry of the Catholic priesthood is denied, the Christian would have to conclude that catharsis is the only approach to God and would have to posit the mystic's sharp antithesis of spirit and matter. The Albigensian theology, then, seems to be the result of the combination of antisacerdotalism with Neoplatonism, and even if some pristine Manichean ideas did filter into Europe from the Balkans or Byzantium, it was the strength of these two doctrines in twelfth-century Europe which prepared the ground for the eastern heresy and provided the intellectual stimulation behind its growth.

The thirteenth-century persecutors of the Albigensian sect attributed to them several other beliefs aside from this basic dualist theology. It was claimed that they rejected the incarnation of Christ because it involved the imprisonment of the deity in evil matter. And it was asserted that the Catharist conviction that matter was evil led to bizarre ideas and social mores. The Albigensians were said to be opposed to marriage, believing that this perpetuated the monstrosity of the human race in which the divine spirit was encased in the gross and evil body. They were said, however, to permit any kind of sexual promiscuity, presumably as long as procreation was avoided. They advocated as virtuous both racial and individual suicide; they exposed babies, and their "perfect" saints starved themselves to death. They believed that whatever the auditors (laity of the Albigensian church) did before they received the final purifying sacrament was of no account. Consequently it was claimed that the Albigensian laity engaged in the most profligate and dissolute living, for no morality is necessary if the human body is innately evil and a sacrament suffices to free the spirit.

It is very hard, in view of the dearth of evidence, to decide whether these accusations are merely canards thought up by orthodox churchmen to discredit the Albigensians or whether they are substantially true indictments. Many anti-Catholic or sentimental modern writers, as well as self-appointed protectors of the underdog in all times and places, especially lady novelists of the twentieth century, have dismissed these indictments as totally false and have pictured all the Albigensians as extremely devout and ascetic saints, which is undoubtedly true of the perfects. All those who opposed the Cathari have been depicted as blackguards and enemies of free thought who acted from the vilest of motives. But the charges made against the Albigensians are entirely within the realm of plausibility. The descriptions given of the basic Manichean theology ring true from what we know of twelfth-century thought; we can see in it elements of Neoplatonism and anti-sacerdotalism, and the central figure of the saintly leader the Albigensians have in common with all the popular heresies of the twelfth century. The additional and reprehensible doctrines and practices attributed to them are logical deductions from the principles of their religion. These peculiar ideas and mores were compatible with, and partly encouraged by, the luxurious and romanticized milieu of southern France, the wealth and independence of its burghers, and the effeminate qualities of its tamed and urbanized nobility.

The Albigensians were not Christian heretics as much as they were members of a different religion. It was a sick religion, the product of a sick civilization. It was a civilization sick enough to call for the exposure of babies, suicidal enough to believe in destroying itself. In the febrile environment of southern France piety could produce strange and perverse results, leading to a religion which threatened not only the unity of Christendom and the authority of the priesthood but the moral order of European civilization.

Chapter Eighteen

THE ENTRENCHMENT
OF SECULAR LEADERSHIP

I. The Problem of Power

The investiture controversy had shattered the early-medieval equilibrium and ended the interpenetration of *ecclesia* and *mundus*. Medieval kingship, which had been largely the creation of ecclesiastical ideals and personnel, was forced to develop new institutions and sanctions. The result, during the late eleventh and early twelfth centuries, was the first instance of a secular bureaucratic state whose essential components appear in the Anglo-Norman monarchy. The intellectual expansion of Europe in the twelfth century, which was largely the work of churchmen, was in some ways more beneficial to the growth of secular power than to ecclesiastical leadership. The improvements in education, law, and even the increase in piety all came to serve the aims of monarchy. The rise of the universities produced a new kind of administrative personnel for royal government. The great increase in legal knowledge gave kings a way of implementing their control over society. It also gave them a juristic ideology to replace the early-medieval tradition of theocratic kingship, which had been divested of its effectiveness by the attacks of the Gregorian reformers. The explosive effects of the new piety also contributed to the entrenchment of secular power. The widespread criticism of the clergy made it easier for royal government to assert its own leadership in society. The many problems arising from the new piety also distracted the hierarchy from paying close attention to what was happening in political life and gave kings greater freedom to pursue their own interests without ecclesiastical interference.

The twelfth-century Roman Curia had only one firm policy with regard to the kings of western Europe: the northern rulers were not to threaten the independence of the papacy by invading Italy. Otherwise the popes took a flexible and pragmatic attitude toward the European kings, trying to win from them limited concessions, such as recognition of the papal curia as the central appellate court of the church. The calm in church-state relations allowed monarchy to make use of the new learning for improvement in its administrative techniques, bureaucratic personnel, and ideology and to entrench its leadership in society. Especially in England and Capetian France, by 1200 all classes and groups were becoming accustomed to the regular exercise of royal power in law and taxation. The central importance of the royal government in the lives of nobles, bourgeois, and the higher clergy was becoming routinized. Given a dramatic and strong personality on the throne, the engine of royal power would become an extremely formidable one which would be difficult for the papacy to control. Two such charismatic royal figures appeared in the second half of the twelfth century, namely, Henry II of England and Frederick Barbarossa of Germany. By the last decade of the century the advance of royal power was a matter of deep concern to the Roman curia. On all sides the success of monarchy was being demonstrated, and the papacy was now faced with the problem of learning to deal with the kings who, in one way or another, had established vast reserves of wealth and military strength and in some cases inspired as well an emotional loyalty on the part of their subjects.

II. The Value of Charisma

The strength of the medieval state was determined by three essentials: the personal qualities of the ruler, the ideology of kingship, and the effectiveness of administrative, legal, and financial institutions. In the earliest stage of medieval monarchy the king's power had depended almost exclusively on his own personality. If he was a formidable warrior, he commanded loyalty, at least within his immediate circle; and if he did not exhibit the characteristics which the warrior class admired, royal property and power were usurped with impunity by local lords, and the king was neglected and insulted. From the eighth until the end of the eleventh century the church buttressed the inadequate foundations of monarchy with moral and religious sanctions, and the kings of the period had come to depend heavily on ideology to sustain the loyalty of lay and ecclesiastical lords, with varying degrees of success. They also made painful experiments in the development of effective administrative institutions, and after the Gregorian papacy had delivered a mortal blow to the old doctrine of sacred kingship, the institutional basis of royal power was accentuated, while the kings also sought to find new moral and theoretical sanctions for their power. The twelfth-century monarchies made use of administrative institutions and ideology in varying degrees, but the personal qualities of the king could still contribute strongly to the growth of royal power. Where a self-perpetuating and self-conscious bureaucracy existed, governments could now sometimes get by with little or no decrease in authority for a considerable period, even if the throne's occupant did not make an impressive and attractive figure. But the effectiveness of even the most skilled bureaucracy would be weakened by the long reign of a king who was inept in war and government. The personality of the king still counted for much in the affairs of states. And if the king was a charismatic figure, great in the arts of war and peace, an admired leader in the eyes of the landed classes, then royal power would enjoy an immediate growth. A king of charismatic qualities, even without the assistance of centralized administrative traditions, could make a profound impression upon society.

For four decades after 1150 political life was dominated by two charismatic figures, Henry II of England and Frederick Barbarossa of Germany. They both exhibited a rare combination of qualities which made them appear almost superhuman figures to contemporaries: longevity, boundless ambition, extraordinary organizing skill, and greatness on the battlefield. They both came to the throne in the prime of manhood; they were handsome and proficient in courtly gestures, which some members of the nobility now found attractive, without being in any way softened by courtly ideals. They were both benefited at critical points in their careers by outstanding strokes of good luck. Henry and Frederick were men of active, not scholarly, disposition. But they keenly appreciated the potential uses of the new learning, especially in the field of law, to royal government. They were adept at selecting educated men who served them with intense loyalty. Henry and Frederick were formally devout, but they were not greatly moved by the piety of the twelfth century. They were ruthless in pursuit of their aims, and they were not charitable toward their enemies. They believed mostly in themselves and never questioned the identity of the amelioration of society with the advancement of their own power.

When Henry II (1154–1189), the first of the Angevin line, became king of England, he was already duke of Normandy, count of Anjou, and the most powerful prince in northern France. The condition of England in 1154 was favorable for the achievement of Henry's ambitions. The feudal lords had just experienced two decades of exhausting civil war, and they wanted the restoration of the peace and good government of the Anglo-Norman kings. This Henry gave them. He completed the work of his grandfather, Henry I, making the shire court into a royal court presided over by an itinerant justice who carried the king's commission. He effectively destroyed the jurisdiction of the private feudal courts and brought the civil cases involving land disputes, which had previously been tried in the feudal courts, before his own justices. He greatly expanded the use of the sworn inquest, or jury, in civil suits, and he introduced the indicting grand jury in criminal cases. The reign of Henry II constitutes the most important era in the creation of the institutions of the common law. It was therefore fashionable among Victorian writers to hail Henry II as the founder of liberal English institutions and constitutional monarchy. Nothing could have been further from his mind. His aims were no different from those of contemporary rulers such as Frederick Barbarossa of Germany and Philip Augustus of France: he wanted as much power for himself as possible. Henry and his judges did not make much use of Roman law, and he did not formulate a theory of juristic absolutism on the basis of the Justinian code. But this is because English legal institutions had already gone in a different direction from those on the continent, and Henry found it cheaper and more convenient to preserve the prevailing system, systematizing and improving it. In accordance with political traditions which he found in existence in England, Henry recognized that he had to rule, at least formally, with the advice and consent of the lay and ecclesiastical magnates. He introduced his improvements in the English common law not by royal decree but rather by "assizes" (establishments), that is, improvements in the prevailing law with the consent of the magnates, in accordance with the Germanic ideal of legislation which still prevailed in England. Some of Henry's courtiers addressed him in terms of Roman absolutism and even those of the archaic traditions of theocratic monarchy, but he made no attempt to formulate an ideology of royal absolutism in England. He was satisfied with the exercise of an effective control over society through royal, legal, and financial institutions and through his position as feudal liege lord; his was a practical absolutism, as J. E. Jolliffe has called it.

Henry's marriage to Eleanor of Aquitaine brought him a principality which, when joined to his other possessions, made him the ruler of most of the western half of France. He was an extremely energetic man who spent a great deal of time attending to the affairs of his continental principalities. In England he was content to achieve order, wealth, and power; he did not concern himself deeply with the ideological foundations of his rule. The tone and efficiency of Henry's government can be seen in *The Dialogue on the Course of the Exchequer,* the first great administrative treatise written in the middle ages. It was the work of Richard FitzNeal, the head of Henry's exchequer, and also, as a reward for his services, bishop of London. Richard's treatise is an admirably organized and informative work written in the dialogue form so popular in the twelfth century. The philosophy of administration set forth in the preface to the work is highly significant. FitzNeal tells the novice in the exchequer, for whom his treatise was especially intended, that it is the function of the exchequer officials to exercise royal policy, not to decide on its merit. Here is already, full-blown, the secular bureaucratic attitude which knows no sanction beyond the king's will.

The advance of royal power in England in Henry II's reign was facilitated by the absence of any organized opposition. The lesser members of the feudal class, who were called knights in England, benefited from the increase in royal power, because they were more likely to get justice in the king's court than in the private feudal courts of their lords. The great nobles were loath to quarrel with a king who commanded such vast resources and who could simply destroy them with the twin engines of law and taxation. Henry was very popular with the English bishops, who in any case, for the most part, had begun their careers as royal clerks and were personally grateful to the king. The attention of the papacy was completely distracted from English affairs by its struggle with the German emperor. The only opposition which Henry ever experienced came from an unexpected source: his own appointee as archbishop of Canterbury, the former royal chancellor Thomas Becket. The archbishop's motives in trying to limit the king's authority over the English church and his willingness to engage in a bitter quarrel with his former patron and friend were the cause of much speculation by contemporary writers as well as by modern historians and dramatists. Clearly, Becket was a psychologically disturbed person, but his neurotic tendencies do not detract from the significance of his struggle against the advance of secular power and his position as the first martyr to the Leviathan state.

Becket was the son of a poor knight who had gone into trade in London. Thomas was therefore a bourgeois who rose to very high position in ecclesiastical and royal government, which was as yet unheard of in his day north of the Alps. His father had great ambitions for his precocious son and sent him to be educated in the new French schools. On his return to England he became the principal secretary of the archbishop of Canterbury, then royal chancellor, and finally, on the archbishop's death, he was made the primate of the English church by Henry II. He proceeded to struggle against royal power in as vehement a manner as he had previously served it, much to Henry's surprise and chagrin. As a bourgeois who had risen very high in circles which were as yet open only to the landed classes, Becket had a very strong feeling of insecurity and inferiority, for which he compensated by the most zealous fulfillment of his duties. He determined to become as great a servant of the church as he had been of monarchy. But this led him to take a stand which ran contrary to the long tradition of royal control over the English church. He began to propound doctrines which had not been heard in Europe since the time of Gregory VII and which were regarded as archaic even in Rome. His colleagues in the English episcopate were as annoyed as the king by the archbishop's stand. The bishop of London, an excellent scholar and administrator, made cruel allusions to Becket's bourgeois background, and the bishops generally regarded the archbishop as either a fool or a madman. The issue upon which Henry II and Becket quarrelled most bitterly was whether clergymen accused of crimes should be tried in royal or ecclesiastical courts; Becket saw this as part of the larger issue of whether the English church should be subjected to the legal supremacy which the royal government was imposing on the whole realm. He refused to surrender on this issue and, receiving no support from his ecclesiastical colleagues, fled to exile in France and appealed to Rome for help. Becket's conduct greatly embarrassed the pope. It was hard to deny the theoretical validity of the archbishop's argument, but the papacy had no inclination to arouse the ire of one of the two strongest kings in Europe, especially while it was engaged in a struggle against the other. Becket finally returned to England and pursued his quarrel in a reckless manner that could end only in disaster for himself. He proceeded to excommunicate some of his opponents among the English bishops, and finally the exasperated king remarked to his court that he wished someone would rid him of this nuisance. Four knights who overheard this careless statement, wishing to court Henry's favor, took him at his word and rode off to Canterbury to slay the archbishop. Becket appears to have expected this end, and he certainly welcomed his martyrdom, which would be an unusual achievement for a bourgeois and would fulfill his desire to be an ideal churchman. He waited calmly for his executioners at the high altar of Canterbury cathedral, objecting only that one of his assassins happened to be his vassal and was therefore violating his oath of homage in killing his lord.

Becket was far more useful to the church dead than alive. The querulous archbishop immediately became the Canterbury martyr, whose shrine attracted thousands of pilgrims over the next three centuries. The papacy, which had largely ignored Becket when he was alive, found his martyrdom to be useful as a lever for winning concessions from the dismayed English king. In order to gain absolution for his part in Becket's death, Henry had to surrender on the question of criminous clerks. This resulted in the peculiar institution of "benefit of clergy," which lasted until the Reformation. If a man, indicted in a royal court, could prove that he was a member of the clergy, the case was transferred to the jurisdiction of an ecclesiastical court; in practice, however, the royal judges frequently proceeded to try the case before the defendant could prove his clerical status. The most important concession which Henry made to Rome was recognizing that all English churchmen could have freedom of appeal to the papal court in ecclesiastical disputes, including cases of disputed elections of bishops and abbots. This was the first instance of the penetration of some form of effective papal jurisdiction over the English higher clergy. The fact that it took the assassination of the archbishop of Canterbury to achieve this indicates the degree of royal control over the English church since the time of William the Conqueror. Henry's concession was the entering wedge of papal influence in English ecclesiastical affairs, but by and large, royal power suffered very little from reactions to Becket's death. During the next three decades the king continued to appoint bishops and abbots as before, to receive the homage of these spiritual lords, and to tax the English church heavily. The loyalty of the English higher clergy to the crown was unaffected by the Becket interlude.

Henry II's power was based on the combination of a charismatic personality with administrative skill. His two sons who followed him on the English throne, Richard I the Lionhearted (1189–1199) and John (1199–1216), exhibited only one or the other of their father's qualities, and even then only to a limited degree. Richard had the reputation as the greatest chivalric warrior in Christendom, which made him personally popular with the nobility, but he was inept in government and law. It is probably fortunate for English royal power that he spent nearly all his reign in overseas ventures and left the government in the capable hands of his father's bureaucrats. John, on the other hand, was something of an administrative genius and made some important contributions to the technique of royal administration. He was, however, a paranoiac who suspected treachery everywhere and flagrantly abused the processes of the common law in order to vent his hatred against certain noble families whom he suspected of treason. Eventually these families were driven to become rebels as the only way of saving themselves from ruin. He was furthermore susceptible to manic-depressive tendencies, at times exhibiting frenetic energy and then, particularly at crucial moments when his presence was required on the battlefield, becoming totally incapable of action. The third weakness of John's personality, his lecherous proclivities, inaugurated the chain of events which brought about his crushing defeat by the Capetian monarchy. He took as his queen the daughter of a minor French count, whose father had already betrothed her to another obscure feudatory. The enraged lord, whose intended had been stolen from him in violation of contemporary custom by the English king, appealed to the king of France. Since John was technically the vassal of the king of France for Normandy, Anjou, and Aquitaine, Philip Augustus was the mutual overlord of both parties to the dispute. John was in one of his deep funks, and he refused to answer the summons to the French court. He was declared a contumacious vassal by Philip Augustus' court and held to have forfeited Normandy and Anjou to the French crown. Had John quickly put his army into the field, he would likely have prevented Philip from seizing Normandy and Anjou. But John did nothing—did not even give instructions to his captains in Normandy. Thus the original homeland of the English kings fell to the Capetian monarch with scarcely a blow being struck.

The loss of Normandy was a disaster not only for the Angevin family but also for many of the English nobility who had held fiefs across the channel. They henceforth had to confine their interests to England, and they necessarily became more and more concerned with John's use of royal, legal, and financial institutions. Any medieval king who was defeated on the battlefield was bound to lose the respect of his people and find his authority challenged at home. John was simply employing in a more relentless and severe manner the institutions of royal power which had developed in his father's day. But his complete lack of an attractive and imposing personality removed from the English political situation the factor which had previously compensated for the stringency of Angevin institutions.

The charismatic personal qualities of the king, which in England in the reign of Henry II contributed to the growth of royal power, in Germany during the same period was the chief resource of monarchy. The reign of Frederick I Barbarossa (1152–1190) was a magnificent performance, a fantastic juggling act in which the king tried to overcome the enormous obstacles to the revival of imperial authority. His formidable enemies defeated him on almost every side, yet in the end, by what appeared to be an incredible stroke of good luck but was partly the consequence of his unceasing efforts, he emerged triumphant. When Frederick came to the throne, the prospects for the revival of German imperial power were extremely thin. During the previous half century the great German princes had steadily increased their territorial sovereignty, and the king was left with only his family domains and the vestige of control over some bishoprics and abbeys. For a quarter century before Frederick's accession the holders of the German throne had done nothing to reverse the disastrous consequences of the investiture controversy. They were too involved in the great feud which had broken out between the descendants of the Salians, the Hohenstaufen dukes of Swabia, and the Welfs, first dukes of Bavaria and then, as a result of a marriage alliance, also dukes of Saxony. When the Salian line died out with Henry V in 1125, the princes refused to give the crown to his nephew, the duke of Swabia, fearing that he would try to regain the power which the German monarch had lost during the investiture controversy. Their choice, the duke of Saxony, Lothair (1125–1137), found himself embroiled in a bitter feud with the Hohenstaufens, and for protection he allied himself by marriage with the Welfs. One of the Hohenstaufen princes gained the throne as Conrad III (1137–1152) on Lothair's death, but the struggle between the two great dynasties continued unabated.

When Frederick Barbarossa succeeded his uncle in 1152, there seemed to be excellent prospects for ending the feud, since Frederick was a Welf on his mother's side. But the Welf duke of Saxony, Henry the Lion, could not be appeased; he remained the implacable enemy of Hohenstaufen monarchy. Barbarossa had the force of his own personality, the duchies of Swabia and Franconia, and very little else to begin with. The German crown still enjoyed some vestiges of its former control over the German bishoprics and abbeys, but this could not provide the additional resources that Frederick needed to crush the Welfs and the other great princes. He tried for a time to make additions to his family holdings and to build up a royal domain in the Rhineland, but he quickly realized that this would be a very long task and would not in the end give him the resources he needed. His only hope lay in asserting his effective control over northern Italy and taxing the Italian communes heavily. Only then would he have the wealth to defeat the great princes. It was a risky plan, since the Italian cities were bound to put up stiff resistance to real, instead of merely nominal, imperial control, and such a plan might arouse the pope's fears. But Frederick could find no alternative if he wished to regain royal power in Germany. The prospect of asserting imperial domination in Italy also appealed to Frederick's personal inclinations. He had a very high sense of the dignity and potential powers of his office as set down in Roman law, and he tended to envision himself as a successor to the Roman emperors. He was strongly under the influence of the new juristic absolutism, and he could not bear to see the perpetuation of the discrepancy between the prevailing weakness and the potential glory and autocracy implicit in his office.

Frederick made his first expedition to Italy in 1154–55. He wanted to make a show of strength, to assert personally German hegemony, and to get himself crowned emperor by the pope. He accomplished all these aims, partly because the pope was having trouble with the communal movement in Rome led by a fiery disciple of Abelard, Arnold of Brescia, who combined intellectual and social radicalism. Arnold and the commune proclaimed the independence of the city and appealed for support to the German king. But Frederick had no sympathy with the Italian urban leaders and their ideal of the city-state; the latter was contrary to the achievement of his ultimate aim to rule northern Italy. Frederick captured Arnold of Brescia; he had him burned and his ashes scattered into the Tiber.

There were three parties in the northern Italian situation: the emperor, the communes, and the papacy. On his visit to Rome Frederick had been disturbed by the pope's insistence that he officially perform the office of papal groom in accordance with the Donation of Constantine. But Barbarossa's first expedition to Italy indicated to him that he and the pope were natural allies against the city-states and their principles of self-government. He returned to Germany to prepare for a great expedition which would bring the riches of northern Italy under his control. Meanwhile, a great debate was waged in papal circles as to whether the papacy ought to ally itself with Frederick against the communal movement or to join ranks with the city-states and revert to the traditional papal policy of trying to keep the emperor out of Italy. It was a hard decision to make. The north Italian burghers were notorious for their frequent quarrels with bishops and for their anticlerical and even antisacerdotal views. The pope certainly did not want a commune in Rome. Should the papacy throw in its lot with the scurvy bourgeois? It was a difficult choice to make, and there was division among the cardinals. Those who opposed Frederick tried to foment a split between emperor and pope by means of provocative tactics. A papal legate addressing Frederick's court in 1157 claimed that the emperors received their power from the pope, which he knew would greatly anger the young and ambitious ruler. Adrian IV, the only English pope, slowly moved toward alliance with the communes against the German ambassador, and when in 1159 the cardinal who had intentionally aroused the emperor's wrath was elected to the throne of Peter as Alexander III, it became evident that the die was cast and that another great imperial-papal struggle was inevitable.

During the next two decades Frederick made three great expeditions against the north Italian cities. He won some initial victories, including the defeat and humiliation of the obstreperous burghers of Milan. The professors of the law school in Bologna proclaimed at a diet, or assembly, on the Roncaglian plain in 1158 that the emperor's claims to appoint the chief officials of each city and to impose taxes were in accordance with Roman law. Frederick was helped at first by the fact that there were deep divisions among the oligarchs who ruled the Italian cities. Some, called the Ghibellines, after the Italianized form of Waiblingen, one of the Hohenstaufen possessions, were willing to surrender to Frederick's demands and the juristic arguments of the civil lawyers; but the majority, who came to be called the Guelphs, after the Hohenstaufen enemy in Germany, determined to devote all their resources to a struggle to retain their independence. For a few years the emperor managed to subject some of the Italian cities to his absolute authority, but after two decades it became apparent that the alliance of the papacy and the commune was too much for him. The pope contributed organizing ability and leadership and managed to unite most of the cities, who had always fought each other with delicious hatred, into the Lombard League (1167). In 1174 the armies of the Lombard League inflicted a complete defeat on the imperial forces at the battle of Legnano, and Frederick decided to cut his losses and sue for peace. Alexander III, having achieved his aim of keeping the emperor out of Italy, could afford to be generous; he forgave the emperor for setting up an anti-pope in accordance with the traditional technique of imperial-papal struggles. The peace of Constance of 1183 allowed Barbarossa to save face but nothing more. His loose suzerainty over northern Italy was recognized, but he was denied the right to appoint the city officials and collect taxes. In other words, after two decades of war Frederick had failed to gain control over northern Italy, which he felt was the first great step toward the restoration of imperial authority over the German princes.

When Frederick returned to Germany after his defeat in northern Italy, he was a bitter and exhausted man. The princes, far from being subordinated to royal control, were intensifying their hold on wealth and power in Germany and entrenching their positions as the leaders of society by their direction of the great eastward movement of the German people. In the 1130's the Germans again, for the first time since Otto II's reign, began to press against the Slavic world to the east. They crossed the Elbe and in the twelfth century created a "new Germany" stretching eastward to the Oder and even beyond. They opened up the Baltic seacoast and founded great commercial centers, such as Lübeck. The "old Germany" west of the Elbe was the creation of the church and the Germany monarchy, but the new Germany was largely settled and civilized at the direction of great princes who had understood the significance of the colonization movement and had rushed to put themselves at the head of it. Dukes and margraves who already had great fiefs in the old Germany now carved out vast domains in the east, thereby completely upsetting the balance of power in

BALTIC SEA

C. OF HOLSTEIN

D. OF
SLAVINIA

DUCHY OF
POMERANIA

Konitz

PRUSSIA

MARCH OF BRANDENBURG

Oder R.

Vistula R.

Spree R. Berlin

HOLY

M. OF
LAUSITZ

Posen

Warthe R.

KDM.

OF POLAND

DUCHY
OF
SAXONY

Elbe R.

TO BRANDENBURG

Dresden

DUCHY OF SILESIA

Breslau

Oder R.

Cracow

Eger R.

Elbe R.

Prague

ROMAN

KDM. OF BOHEMIA

Moldau R.

M. OF MORAVIA

March R.

KDM. OF
HUNGARY

DUCHY

DUCHY
OF BAVERIA

OF AUSTRIA

Veinna

Pressburg

Danube R.

DUCHY OF CARINTHIA

EMPIRE

KDM. OF
ITALY

D. OF
STYRIA

D. OF CARNIOLA

Venice

REP. OF
VENICE

Trieste

CROATIA

"THE NEW
GERMANY"

Boundary of the Accession of
Frederick Barbarossa, 1152

Boundary in the Early 13th
Century

Church Lands

432

Germany and making the existing Hohenstaufen power relatively less significant. The dukes' direction of the *Drang nach Osten* involved no consideration for the Slavs, who were massacred or subjugated, but it was very clever and efficient. The princes attracted peasants from the Low Countries and western Germany, especially those experienced in the new techniques of colonization, by offering very favorable terms of settlement. The immigrants of the eastern frontier were promised freedom from the old manorial dues and services and large blocks of land instead of the meager manorial strips. These attractive offers, when combined with the fertility of the soil and the protection the peasants received from the princes, induced a steady eastward movement in the twelfth century, resulting in the creation of the new Germany. Frederick Barbarossa played no part in this development. He allowed it to go on without making any attempt to intervene, and the princes greatly increased their domains and power by default. Modern writers have criticized Frederick for his blindness in getting involved in the morass of Italian politics while ignoring the opening-up of eastern Germany, where the Hohenstaufens would have been able to create the royal domain they needed if they had early assumed the direction of the movement. In retrospect this was a grave miscalculation which, in the long run, greatly conditioned the future history of the German monarchy. But it is hard to be severe with Frederick for making this fatal error. At the beginning of his reign the eastward movement was still a modest development; Frederick believed that he needed an immediate increase in his resources, and Italy appeared to be the only place he could obtain this; the creation of new, wealthy domains in the east seemed a far-off prospect. Frederick's gamble failed, and by the end of the 1170's he was in some ways worse off than when he started, but under the circumstances he had made the most plausible choice of the alternatives open to him.

When the aging and disappointed king returned to Germany, he vented his anger on his old Guelph enemy, Henry the Lion. One slim hope of victory seemed open to Frederick: the use of the feudal resources of the crown in the manner which the Norman and Angevin rulers of England had done for more than a century and which the Capetian kings were to follow just a quarter of a century later. German feudalism was by no means English feudalism. The feudal pyramid in the empire was truncated, and while the great dukes were the emperor's vassals, their subvassals did not recognize the king as their liege lord. But Henry the Lion, as Frederick's vassal, could still be impleaded in his lord's court and, if found guilty by his peers, declared in forfeit of his feudal duchies of Saxony and Bavaria. On this legal basis Frederick inaugurated his great feudal trial against his Guelph enemy, charging him with failure to render his lord military service in the Italian campaigns and with other felonies. The princes were not reluctant to see the great duke of Saxony brought low, and when Henry refused to appear in Frederick's court to answer the indictment brought against him, they declared his fiefs forfeit. Frederick was able to drive Henry out of Saxony and Bavaria and leave him only his eastern principalities, which were not fiefs of the crown, but the princes would not let the emperor absorb the forfeited duchies into his own domain; he had to infeudate the Guelph principalities to other princes. The trial of Henry the Lion was the decisive moment in German feudalism; Frederick's failure to gain the lands of his Guelph enemies meant that the emperor could not use feudal law to increase his power, which had been the case in England for more than a century and was also soon to be attempted successfully in France.

In the last years of his life the aging emperor finally had to abandon the prodigious efforts and great wars of his younger days. He took the Cross and died en route to the Holy Land in 1190. But the great emperor was able to die with the comforting knowledge that his son would have the resources to achieve the triumph of imperial power that he had lacked. By an incredible combination of circumstances Frederick's son, who had already been crowned Henry VI before Barbarossa's departure on the third crusade, found himself the ruler of the Norman kingdom of Sicily, one of the wealthiest countries in the Mediterranean world. Four years previously Barbarossa had married his son to the Norman Sicilian princess Constance, but this did not appear significant, because Constance's chances of inheriting the throne were slim; if this had not been the case, the pope would never have allowed the marriage. The year before Barbarossa's death Constance, due to unexpected deaths in her family, inherited the Norman Sicilian crown, and her husband came into possession of the kind of domain that Barbarossa had striven unsuccessfully for three decades to obtain. Yet the decisions of fortune had been prepared by the indomitable will of the emperor. He had tried one method after another to achieve his grand design, and all had failed. His last effort, a dynastic union with the Norman house in the hope that someday one of his successors might gain the throne, had an almost immediate result in the ascendancy of the Hohenstaufens.

It was Frederick's enormous reputation as one of the greatest men in Christendom that induced the Norman Sicilian king, the traditional ally of the papacy against the German emperor, to agree to an alliance of the northern and southern ruling dynasties. Barbarossa's long struggle with the pope did not in any way lessen the intense popular admiration which he evoked. The sort of enthusiasm with which he had been greeted by his uncle, Bishop Otto of Freising, in the early part of his reign, continued all through his life and long afterward. He became a folk hero, a kind of messianic figure who, it was said, would return some day and lead the Germans to new glories. This emotional response transcended the severe institutional limitations of the German monarchy and gave the Hohenstaufens the aura of majesty and virtue which, it seemed in 1190, had brought them to the threshold of the power they had sought for so long.

But Henry VI's temperament and character differed even more strongly from Barbarossa's than Richard's and John's did from Henry II's. Barbarossa appeared to contemporaries to be a man with greatness of soul; Henry IV was singularly lacking in this quality. He was pompous, calculating, ruthless, a schemer and a bully. It took him until 1194 to enter fully into possession of southern Italy. Almost immediately he began an attack on the cities of northern Italy and scored initial successes. Henry could not refrain from making extravagant announcements of how the Hohenstaufen family would achieve western and, in fact, world supremacy. He terrified the German princes, the northern Italian cities, and above all the papacy, which found itself on the verge of being surrounded by the Hohenstaufen power it had fought twenty years to keep out of Italy. Henry VI's only miscalculation was not to take into account the effects of the unsalubrious Italian climate, which had carried off in their prime some of his wife's family and had made him king of Sicily. Henry died suddenly in 1197, leaving a three-year-old child as his heir and the affairs of Germany and Italy in a turmoil. This act of God favored the enemies of the Hohenstaufens even more than a similar stroke of fortune, eight years previously, had given Barbarossa most of what he had wanted. It is difficult for a modern German historian to write a book on the twelfth or thirteenth centuries without expatiating on the misfortune of Henry VI's early death and attributing to this one event the subsequent troubles and final collapse of the medieval German empire. Yet, the fact that Henry VI's death was such a great calamity demonstrates the almost exclusive reliance which the German monarchy had to place on the person of the king due to its lack of administrative institutions. Nothing in medieval history illustrates more graphically both the value and the limitation of charisma than the history of the German empire in the second half of the twelfth century.

III. *The Capetian Ascendancy*

The seizure of Normandy and Anjou in 1204 and their incorporation into the royal domain of the French monarchy was a great turning point in the history not only of France but generally of Europe as well. The kingdom of

France, which was ruled by the Capetians in a direct line of succession until 1328 and then by the cadet branches of the family, the Valois and the Bourbons, until the nineteenth century, was to be the most important European state at least until 1700 and, in the opinion of some historians, until 1870. If the lands lying between Flanders and the Pyrenees and between the Atlantic and the Rhine could be brought under an effective central government, the result was bound to have a profound impact on European civilization, for this government would then have at its command a larger population and more intellectual, economic, and military resources than any other state in Europe. The conquest of Normandy signaled the emergence of such a state, but a century before there was no France; it was merely a geographical expression. It was a large, diverse land with neither topographical, political, economic, linguistic, nor cultural unity. The people of north and south spoke different Romance dialects. Northern France was the classic land of feudalism and was largely a rural area; its dominant figure was the feudal baron. The culture, society, and language of southern France had much more in common with Christian Spain and Italy than with northern France. Languedoc, the region of the southern dialect, had a vibrant urban civilization and a literate bourgeois class. Its aristocracy was also becoming urbanized; like the north Italian nobility they had town houses, and they enjoyed the intellectual benefits of town life. The third area of what later became France, the Rhineland region, tended to look eastward toward the German empire, to which many of its bishoprics, principalities, and cities technically belonged, and many of the people in this area spoke German rather than one of the French dialects. In central France there was a mountainous region which served as a hangout for robber barons and made travel between north and south very difficult. Thus, in 1100 France was not naturally or even potentially one country. It was the Capetian monarchy of the twelfth and thirteenth centuries which created France. It need not have existed; there was no national destiny of France before the rise of the French monarchy. But if the country could ultimately be subjected to royal power, then the kings would have at their disposal wealthy cities, a large feudal warrior class, and universities and their graduates—a formidable combination.

The history of the Capetians before the twelfth century gave no promise of the later success of the dynasty. The Capetians gained the French crown in 987, but until 1108 the French kings were nonentities who had no control over the great dukes and counts who were their nominal vassals. They did not even have unchallenged power in their own domain of the Île-de-France. Paris was surrounded by the castles of robber barons, and the French king was sometimes afraid to go outside the walls of the city. The first Capetian monarch to make a contribution to the institutional foundation of royal power was Louis VI the Fat, or the Wideawake (1108–1137). Because of the information provided by Louis' biography, written by his chief minister Abbot Suger of St. Denis, he is much more of a real person to us than any of his predecessors, who are completely faceless men, renowned only for piety or personal scandal. One of the mistakes of the early Capetians was their involvement in grandiose attempts at the expansion of their authority when they were not even strong in the Île-de-France. Under the wise and patient guidance of Suger, Louis VI generally pursued a policy which was both much more limited and more effective. He was not free from his predecessors' delusions of grandeur; he made a stab at conquering Flanders, which ended in humiliation when his army was routed by the Flemish burghers. But usually he stayed close to home and succeeded in destroying the power of the petty lords and robber barons in the Île-de-France, thereby providing a secure base of operations for his successors.

The very long reign of his son Louis VII (1137–1180) was the turning point in the development of Capetian institutions and the beginning of the exercise of some royal jurisdiction over the great feudal princes. Louis was a devout, hard-working, and rather colorless figure who suffered the terrible humiliation and great loss attendant upon his divorce from Eleanor of Aquitaine. Some historians have said that Louis VI made such an impression by his work of building royal power in the Île-de-France that the extremely wealthy duke of Aquitaine deigned to marry his daughter to the heir of the French throne. This is a possibility, but it may have been simply the result of whimsy on the part of the troubadour duke of Aquitaine. In any case, Louis VIII lost the vast accretion in the territory of the royal domain which Eleanor had brought with her, and this duchy passed under the rule of Henry II, Eleanor's second husband. As a consequence, Louis faced the grim fact that his nominal vassal ruled the western half of France and, even without England, was immensely more powerful than Louis himself. Yet, by the end of Louis' reign the Capetian king was beginning to exercise some leadership among the great princes who were his nominal vassals.

The court of the French king, as the overlord of the great feudatories, was technically the high court of the realm. But before the reign of Louis VII this was merely a theoretical possibility. The dukes and counts ignored the king's court in their dealings with each other, and the king had no power to compel his vassals to give him suit at court in accordance with feudal law. In the latter half of Louis' reign the great vassals began to bring cases in the royal court for the first time. This was partly because by the middle of the twelfth century there was a balance of power among the great feudatories and therefore little possibility of settling their disputes by the old method of feudal warfare. They knew that they would receive a fair judgment in the court of the peaceful and pious Capetian king. The French feudal princes also turned toward Paris for the first time because of their fear of the overwhelming power of Henry II. By his vast holdings the Angevin ruler had made himself the most obvious threat to the future independence and security of the other dukes and counts, and as a reaction they looked with greater favor on the Capetian king as a counterbalance to Henry II. In the long run Louis VII benefited greatly from Eleanor of Aquitaine's marriage to Henry II. For the first time the value of the Capetian monarchy in the affairs of France became evident to the great feudatories.

The French royal demesne had been traditionally administered by *prévôts*, local lords who paid the king a lump sum for the privilege of farming the demesne in his area. This primitive system was indicative of the general ineptitude of the early Capetians. The *prévôts* cheated the king, ruthlessly abused the populace, and tried to turn their jurisdictions into hereditary patrimonies. Furthermore, by delegating his local authority in this way, the king lost the opportunity to impress the local areas with the tradition of royal leadership. Louis VI by and large continued this ruinous system of local administration, but in the latter part of his reign there are indications that he was experimenting with sending out officials directly from the royal court to supervise the local administration of the royal demesne.

His son Philip II Augustus (1180–1223) turned these experiments into the creation of a distinctive local administrative system, whose essentials were perpetuated to the end of the *ancien régime.* The third of the great rulers of the later twelfth century, alongside Henry II and Frederick Barbarossa, Philip was singularly lacking in their glamorous and attractive qualities. He was a miserable, crafty hunchback totally without scruples. His high-sounding appellation was probably intended to mean "the augmentor" rather than to associate him with the Roman emperors. Yet Philip's devious qualities were the only ones that could have led to a great increase in the French royal demesne. By the late twelfth century the political borders of Europe had been drawn, and in France the division of the country among the feudatories had a long tradition behind it. The rearrangement of the political map of France could not be accomplished without craft and guile, qualities in which Philip excelled. But he was also an extremely industrious and ingenious administrator who prepared for the expansion of the royal demesne by creating the *bailli,* the local financial, legal, administrative, and military representative of the French monarchy.

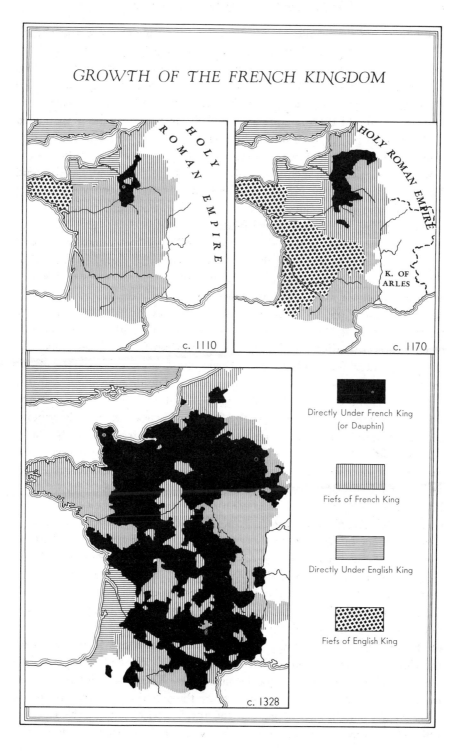

GROWTH OF THE FRENCH KINGDOM

c. 1110

HOLY ROMAN EMPIRE

c. 1170

HOLY ROMAN EMPIRE

K. OF ARLES

c. 1328

Directly Under French King
(or Dauphin)

Fiefs of French King

Directly Under English King

Fiefs of English King

In England the local officials of the royal government were the sheriff, who acted as the general administrative officer and was in charge of tax collection in the shire, and the itinerant justices who presided over the county courts. The *bailli* combined both these offices, carrying out all the administrative, judicial, and financial services on behalf of the king. The English sheriff and his assistants were wealthy members of the local landed classes with strong interests in the shire where they worked. This meant that in the long run the monarchy had to preserve the good will of the county families who were its agents or suffer the paralysis of local government. This was not so evident in the reign of Henry II due to his overwhelming popularity and power, but after 1200 it became more and more apparent in England that royal government could only be effectively carried on with the assent and cooperation of the leading families of the county. The social and political characteristics of the *bailli* were very different. He was a paid official sent out by the royal government, and he had no roots in his area of jurisdiction. He was a true bureaucrat whose whole income and social status depended on his position as a royal servant. He was therefore fanatically loyal to the king and was concerned only with the full exercise of royal power. Unlike the English county families from whose ranks were drawn the sheriffs and other local officials, the *bailli* never took it into his head to question the merit of the royal policy. The difference between the French *bailli* and the English sheriff was not so much the result of prescient wisdom on the part of the French monarchy; rather it was determined by geographical and social circumstances. The territory which Philip Augustus initially had to administer was only the size of one of the larger English counties. He did not need many officials to govern this small area, and he could afford to dispatch reliable and experienced men directly from his court. In fact, the institutional term designating the French local official was simply that of bailiff, a generic word used all over Europe to mean a personal agent or steward. In the beginning the *bailli* only differed in degree from the bailiff who managed the estate of a great manorial lord. But by the end of the twelfth century the *bailli* had become more of a public than a private institution of the monarchy. It would have been very difficult for the Capetian kings to perpetuate this institution and to apply it to the new areas then conquered if it had not been for the educational revolution of the twelfth century. It was the universities which provided them with the clerks and lawyers who filled the office of *bailli,* and these were the ideal personnel to serve as local bureaucrats. They were intelligent, industrious, and well educated, and few of them had any prospects in life other than what they could gain in the royal service. During the reign of Philip Augustus several of the *baillis* were already *magistri,* university graduates who were sent out to administer the new areas which were absorbed into the French royal domain and to incorporate them fully into the royal jurisdiction. The same institution was extended in the thirteenth century to Languedoc when the southern principalities came under French rule. In southern France the *bailli* was called the seneschal, another old generic term for the agent of a feudal lord which was now given a new meaning as the local paid representative of the French monarchy. By the middle of the thirteenth century the *baillis* and seneschals had become a self-sustaining corporate group and in some ways were more fanatical supporters of the extension of royal power than the king himself. It was they who subordinated local customs and institutions and brought the disparate regions of France under a common government. It is no exaggeration to say that France was the creation of a bureaucracy which began to assume its characteristic form at the beginning of the reign of Philip Augustus, perhaps even a little earlier.

The advance of royal power in France was conditioned by the king's relations with the bourgeois and the church. It is a nineteenth-century myth that the king of France realized the importance of the new urban development and that he allied himself with the new class against the feudal nobility. Even if this were true, it would not have secured his triumph, because the towns of northern France were too few and, aside from Paris, too small in size and wealth to affect profoundly the power structure. In reality Louis VII and Philip Augustus were not much more sympathetic to the ambitions of the burghers than were the lay and ecclesiastical princes. The towns on the royal domain received only meager communal privileges, and even then only after a long struggle and heavy payments to the royal treasury. But the townsmen generally favored the advance of royal power as a counterbalance to the feudal lords and because they were able to win more concessions of urban self-government from the king than from the local magnates, even though they had to pay dearly for them.

The relation between the Capetian monarchy and the church played a much more important part in the eventual Capetian triumph. The backwardness and also the insignificance of the eleventh-century Capetian monarchy is demonstrated by the fact that the French king held on to some of the accoutrements of theocratic monarchy long after the papacy had forced the abandonment of such traditions in the much more powerful monarchies of Germany and England. From the late eleventh century the papacy generally looked on the French monarchy as its ally and supporter, if for no other reason than that the pope had to have some support among the kings of Europe. The pope was intermittently embroiled with the German emperor and feared the consequences of his claims over northern

Italy. In view of the power of the English monarch, his hold over the church in his territory, and the distance of England from Rome, the papacy could not ally itself with the Norman and Angevin kings. The French king remained the only possible candidate, and he appeared so weak and innocuous that it seemed impossible that he would ever threaten the authority of the papacy. The Capetian kings, furthermore, had a great reputation for piety; even in the twelfth century they were already known as the "very Christian" kings. Therefore Gregory VII was unusually moderate in his relations with the Capetian monarch. During the late eleventh and twelfth century France became a common place of refuge for the popes driven from Rome by the German emperor. Urban II went to France to get away from the armies of Henry IV and to preach the first crusade, and Alexander III sought the protection of Louis VII in the 1160's when Frederick Barbarossa for a short time held Rome. The sympathetic attitude of the papacy allowed the French kings to perpetuate some of the archaic traditions and rituals of early-medieval kingship. There was a very close association between the Capetian dynasty and the royal abbey of St. Denis. The regalia of the French crown were kept there, and much later than monastic statesmen played a leading role in other European governments, abbot Suger of St. Denis, in the reigns of Louis VI and VII, continued to be the chief minister of the royal administration. Whereas in Germany and in England the ceremony of anointment was becoming a mere formality, in France the religious and emotional qualities of this ceremony were still accentuated. The association of the church with the French monarchy was particularly emphasized during the long reign of Louis VII. Louis, who was personally very devout, exhibited great friendship for both the pope and the higher clergy all over France. He received Alexander III with the greatest deference, and he took the side of bishops and abbots in their struggles with local lords. In so doing he was, of course, helping the advance of royal power as well as satisfying his own devout inclinations. Louis' attempts to aid the higher clergy were part of his general effort to expand the jurisdiction of the royal court. The Capetian king's reputation as the friend and ally of the papacy could not but help to contribute to his prestige in France and might eventually prove useful in his relations with the great feudatories and the other kings of western Europe.

The moral and religious traditions of the very Christian Capetian monarchy were valuable to Philip Augustus. They provided the necessary facade behind which he could undertake his depredations and pursue his crooked schemes. He gained the northern county of Artois by his marriage and then turned upon the vast domains of the Angevin ruler in northern France. He fomented the rebellion of Henry II's sons against their father and made miserable the great king's last years. He was continually plotting against Richard and John, and by 1204 he had achieved his great triumph. He had incorporated all of northwestern France into the royal domain, leaving the English king with only Gascony and part of Poitou, the most distant of the former French possessions of the Angevin house. In the first two decades of his reign Philip clearly demonstrated for his successors how the territory of the French crown might be expanded: by dynastic marriage, by political and diplomatic chicanery, by feudal forfeiture, and by outright conquest. The old innocuous royal ally of the church had suddenly become a great power in northern Europe, and not the least of the problems facing the thirteenth-century papacy was the kind of adjustment it should make to this new situation.

Part Seven

Single rulers have single provinces, and single kings have single kingdoms; but Peter rules them all. . . .

—Innocent III

We loved to live in poor and abandoned churches and we were ignorant and submissive to all.

—St. Francis of Assisi

The state is a perfect community.

—St. Thomas Aquinas

THE SEARCH FOR A NEW EQUILIBRIUM

Earlier and Mid-Thirteenth Century

Chapter Nineteen

THE PEACE
OF INNOCENT III

I. The Reaffirmation of Papal Leadership

It is a tradition in the history of the papacy that the cardinals often oscillate between choosing strong and weak popes in order to obtain alternate cycles of aggressive, reforming, and then calm, conservative pontificates. Since the death of Alexander III in 1181 the papal throne had been held by a succession of well-meaning but weak men who seemed to have been paralyzed into a state of immobility by the vast problems affecting the church as a consequence of the twelfth-century changes in learning, piety, and power. Papal leadership was becoming such a negligible factor in European life that the cardinals went to the other extreme in 1198. They chose the ablest member of the college of cardinals, Lothario Conti, who took the title of Innocent III (1198–1216). At the time of his accession Innocent was only thirty-seven years old, phenomenally young for a pope. Innocent III came from one of the leading families of the Roman aristocracy. He was a man of limitless energy, high intellectual capacity, and unusual gifts as a leader and administrator. He was a canon lawyer of great ability, and he could have gained a distinguished reputation as a theologian if he had had the time or inclination. He was fully aware of the problems that the papacy faced on all sides, and he had no doubt that he could find ways to deal with them. The unusually high degree of self-confidence which characterizes men of his superior qualities was combined in Innocent's case with his high sense of the traditions and power of the papal office. He believed that "everything in the world is the province of the pope," that St. Peter had been commissioned by Christ "to govern not only the universal Church but all the secular world." Innocent was fond of alluding to hierocratic theory, in which the spiritual sword was superior to the earthly sword, in which the subordination of monarchy to the priesthood was likened to the moon's dependency on the sun. Innocent's was not a revolutionary temperament, however, but that of a constructive conservative; he was not another Gregory VII. He did not intend to launch an apocalyptic attack on the forces that threatened to terminate the leadership of the church in medieval society; rather, by a great variety of methods he intended to exert papal influence on the changed society of western Europe and to control the effects of twelfth-century learning, piety, and power. He wished to direct these new forces into channels which would restore ecclesiastical influence in Europe. Innocent wanted a new equilibrium between the church and the world which would bring political, intellectual, and religious order to a society seething under the impact of new ideas and institutions. The greatest tribute to his ability, good judgment, and inflexible determination is the high degree of success he had. When he died, exhausted from his labors, papal leadership in Europe had been reaffirmed and the church was counterattacking on every front against heresy, intellectual disorder, and secular power. By the end of the 1230's a new consensus and optimism had entered European life. The forces dissolving the medieval world order seemed to have been stopped and turned aside by the peace of Innocent III.

The necessary foundation of all the other achievements of his pontificate, as seen by Innocent, was the reconstruction of the administration of the church. This involved a general rationalization and tightening of central control so as to make more real the canonist's doctrines of the plenitude of power of the absolute papal monarchy in the church. The reforms which Innocent introduced all through his pontificate were summed up and confirmed by the decrees of the Fourth Lateran Council of 1215, one of the three most important ecumenical councils of the Catholic church, the other two being the Council of Nicea in 325 and the Council of Trent in the sixteenth century. The Lateran Council set the number of Christian sacraments at the seven which still obtain in the Roman church: baptism, confirmation, marriage, and extreme unction (which mark the stages in the life of man) and the Eucharist or mass, confession, and the ordination of priests (the ones which are at the heart of sacerdotal Christianity). Only a bishop can perform confirmation and ordination of priests. The early-medieval church had never clearly defined the number of the sacraments. Damiani had at one point listed eleven, including the ordination of kings.

The twelfth-century standard textbook on theology, Peter Lombard's *Sentences,* had listen seven, and this view was accepted by the Lateran Council. The council decreed that every member of the church was to confess his sins to a priest and to receive the Eucharist at least once a year and as often as possible. This was a reassertion of the authority of the priesthood over the laity and was intended as a direct challenge to the doctrines of the antisacerdotal heretics. As a way of further inhibiting the corrosive effects of the new piety, the Lateran Council further announced that there were to be no new saints and relics without papal canonization and that the proliferation of religious orders was to cease.

The system of papal legates was greatly expanded by Innocent as a way of bringing the bishops of western Europe under closer control by Rome; and whereas the twelfth-century popes, in order not to offend national feelings, had frequently appointed the metropolitans in various countries as legates, Innocent chose Italian cardinals as his representatives to the territorial churches. In turn, the bishops were to give much greater attention to the affairs of their dioceses, particularly to the quality of the clergy under their rule. The bishops and their adjutants were to engage in annual visitation of the monasteries in their dioceses and to inspect carefully the cathedral and parish clergy to make sure they merited their offices. Innocent asserted with a high degree of success the right of the pope to appoint bishops in special cases: in the event of a disputed election whose resolution was appealed to Rome, if an episcopal or other church office was vacant for six months, and if the previous bishop died while on a visit to Rome. The frequent disputes over episcopal elections and the notoriously unsalubrious climate of Rome gave the thirteenth-century papacy many occasions to claim that the power of appointment had "devolved" upon the Roman Curia. The pontificate of Innocent III thus witnessed a general increase in the legal powers of the papacy as the high court of Christendom and the refinement of the legal institutions of the church. This general tightening of the administrative system of the church and the increase of centralized control had the immediate effect of improving the quality of both the higher and the lower clergy. Thirteenth century episcopal visitation turned up hundreds of cases of incompetence and dereliction of duty by the monastic and parish clergy, and in turn the episcopate came under constant pressure and scrutiny from Rome to fulfill its pastorate. Innocent demonstrated that the effects of the new piety had got out of control in large part because of lax administration and that the best way to wean men away from their enthusiasm for heretic saints was by presenting to the world a Catholic clergy that was conscientious, zealous, and well informed.

The vast administrative structure of the papal monarchy, like that of any other government in Europe, needed a large amount of money to keep the machine going. The cardinals were furthermore princes of the church; they often came from prominent families of the Italian aristocracy and were accustomed to living well; and in any case the papal court, as one which claimed to be the most important in Christendom, could not appear impoverished and niggardly in comparison with the establishments of rulers north of the Alps. In addition, the pope had to find the money for the support of diplomatic and military ventures if he was to deal effectively with the entrenched secular powers of Europe.

Where was the money for these purposes to come from? Like any king, the pope had his demesne in the form of the papal states, but this was not enough to maintain the papal administration, diplomacy, court, and army. Like the kings of western Europe, he had to devise new forms of taxation. Special papal tithes levied for the third crusade had demonstrated both the vast wealth that could be obtained by a general tax on the clergy and how relatively easy it was to administer the tax, in view of subordination of the clergy to papal authority and the church's supply of loyal and literate tax officials. Accordingly, in 1199 Innocent levied the first general income tax on European churchmen for papal needs. Its great success made it the first of a variety of taxes levied by the thirteenth-century papacy on the clergy. This steady income not only facilitated the improvement of the papal administration; it gave the pope the added resources which were needed for his complex involvements in European politics.

A prime necessity for the freedom of papal action with regard to the kings of northern Europe had always been the security of the papacy in Rome. From the beginning of his pontificate Innocent worked hard to strengthen papal control over the city of Rome and over the papal states, which he sought to expand, while the power of the emperor to intervene was rendered negligible by the sudden death of Henry VI and the consequent dispute over the German throne. Innocent had a hard time asserting his complete control over the government of the eternal city; the jealous nobility and the commune fought him step by step, but by 1205 he had firmly established his authority in his own city. Since Rome lived largely off the business of the Curia, it could not long withstand the demand of the pope to control its municipal government. Innocent had even greater success with the patrimony of St. Peter, and during his pontificate the papal states attained the dimensions which they retained until the middle of the nineteenth century.

Secure at home, Innocent was able to devote his superb political talents to defining the pope's relations with the great northern monarchies. "The imperial business," as it was called in papal circles, was the most pressing political matter. Henry VI had terrified the papacy, and it was Innocent's intention to separate the kingdom of Sicily from Germany once more and to preclude the papacy's ever again being faced with the threat to its independence which Henry VI had presented. He was given a great opportunity to achieve this aim by the renewal of the feud over the German throne between the Hohenstaufens and the Guelphs which plunged Germany into civil war after Henry's death. The Hohenstaufens and their supporters chose as king Henry's brother Philip of Swabia, while some of the German nobility who had come to fear the Hohenstaufen family, joined in the election of Otto IV of Brunswick, the son of Henry the Lion. Both parties ignored the rights of the child Frederick II, Henry's son, who remained in Sicily with his mother. Both parties tried to gain Innocent's support because only the pope had the authority to make one of the rival kings emperor. Innocent waited three years to render his decision, intentionally allowing the civil war to deplete further the power of the German crown. Finally, in 1200, he rendered his decision, to no one's surprise, in favor of Otto, who recognized the boundaries of the papal states, surrendered what remained of royal authority over the German church, and promised not to intervene in Italy. Innocent appeared to have completely removed the German threat to the papacy, but in 1208 Philip was assassinated in a personal quarrel, and Otto married his daughter and established an unchallenged claim to the German throne. Almost immediately Otto took up the traditional policy of the German kings and moved upon northern Italy. Innocent was angry and disappointed, but not dismayed, for the Welf king was a colorless and incompetent leader who was no match for the pope. In 1212 Innocent recognized young Frederick II as king of Germany, after first extorting from Frederick the promise that he would abdicate as king of Naples and Sicily when he established his effective rule in Germany. Innocent then devoted himself to organizing a great coalition between the papacy, Frederick II, and Philip Augustus of France against Otto and King John of England, who was allied by marriage with the Welf house. This was the first great example of the clash of international alliances in European history. The conflict was decided at the battle of Bouvines in 1214, which had a profound effect on the political development of thirteenth-century Europe. Philip Augustus inflicted a crushing defeat on Otto and thereby opened the way for Frederick's gaining of the German throne. At the time of Innocent's death in 1216 the pope was again firmly convinced that he had permanently solved the German problem. Frederick II, whom Innocent personally admired and trusted, was obtaining the support of the German nobility, and Frederick had promised to abdicate the Sicilian crown as soon as he fully gained their loyalty. Furthermore, it did not appear that the

German emperor would be much of a threat to the papacy in the future. Two decades of civil war and sweeping concessions of territorial sovereignty made to the German princes by the various claimants to the throne had further diminished the power and resources of the monarchy and had undone all the work of Frederick I and Henry VI.

Innocent's triumphs in the imperial business were paralleled in his relations with the English and French monarchies. He humiliated the powerful Angevin king and improved the prospects of the French papal ally. The papacy had always been extremely wary of becoming involved in a struggle with the English king, but Innocent pressed such a contest and won a complete victory. The quarrel between the pope and King John arose over a disputed election to the see of Canterbury which, in accordance with the new provisions of canon law, was appealed to Rome. Innocent rejected the candidates offered him and appointed instead Stephen Langton, an Englishman who had been a theologian at Paris and was at the time a cardinal in the Roman Curia. John regarded this as a gross violation of the traditional royal authority over the English church; he furthermore regarded Langton as a papal agent, and he refused to recognize the archbishop-elect and forbade him to enter England. A bitter conflict ensued in which both pope and king used extreme measures. Innocent placed England under an interdict, which suspended church services, and John seized a great part of the landed wealth of the English church. Finally Innocent encouraged Philip Augustus to prepare for the invasion of England under the papal banner, and John, terrified that he would lose England to his great enemy as he had lost most of his continental possessions abnegated himself before the pope. He not only accepted Langton as archbishop, but he became the pope's vassal and made England the fief of the papacy. These sensational events seemed to demonstrate that no king could withstand for long the will of the papacy.

Even the pope's ally, Philip Augustus, incurred Innocent's wrath. They disputed a private matter, but Innocent, as the guardian of the faith and morals of Europe, used all the moral and religious powers at his command to force Philip's accedence to the papal will. Philip had entered into a marriage contract with a Danish princess named Ingeborg in order to obtain the assistance of the Danish fleet for one of his ventures against the Angevins. When the titanic northern princess arrived in France, Philip changed his mind and refused to accept her as his wife. The affair dragged on for years until Innocent became pope and adopted his accustomed drastic measures, including the leveling of a papal interdict on France which forced Philip to give way. Eventually a compromise settlement favorable to all parties was reached. This strange incident demonstrates

Innocent's supreme self-confidence in the power of the papacy and his willingness to use all the weapons at the pope's command even in minor matters. In general, Innocent's relations with France were greatly to the benefit of the Capetian monarchy. The alliance he established with Philip Augustus against Otto IV and John intensified the long association of the papacy with the Capetian monarchy and cloaked Philip's expansionist policies and devious methods in an aura of morality. The greatest boon which the French monarchy received from the papacy, however, was the Albigensian crusade, which opened up southern France to penetration by the north and eventual incorporation into the French crown. Philip Augustus did not participate in the Albigensian crusade, and it is possible that he did not fully perceive its significance. But the crusade destroyed the power of the nobility of Languedoc and made inevitable the subjection of southeastern France to the Capetian king.

Innocent had originally hoped to bring the Albigensian heretics back into the church by sending in outstanding preachers to demonstrate the Cathari errors. This approach had little success; the Albigensian doctrines had penetrated too deeply into the social and intellectual milieu of southern France. The murder of a papal legate in 1208, in which the count of Toulouse was thought to be implicated, induced Innocent to take a more drastic measure, namely, the launching of a crusade against the heretics. Innocent had already become familiar with the use of the crusading ideal for some special purpose favorable to the Roman church. The fourth crusade of 1204, which Innocent had proclaimed, had been turned by the Venetians from its initial aim of fighting the Moslems to the attack and capture of Constantinople. Innocent readily accepted the change in plans, because he saw the Latin Kingdom of Constantinople as the means of bringing the Greeks back into union with the Latin church and under the authority of the papacy. If a crusade could be directed against Constantinople, then assuredly it could be directed against heretics whose insidious doctrines, perverse morality, and stronghold in southern France threatened the unity of Latin Christendom. The northern French barons enthusiastically responded to Innocent's proclamation of the Albigensian crusade. They looked upon it as a heaven-sent opportunity to carve out fiefs for themselves in the rich lands of the Languedoc. The Albigensian crusade took on the qualities of a land grab. The northern barons, led by one Simon de Montfort, a lord from the Île-de-France, indiscriminately attacked the heretics and the orthodox and perpetrated blood baths in the Southern cities. As a consequence the southern nobility, whether or not it sympathized with the Cathari doctrine, bitterly resisted the crusaders, and the king of Aragon, who was very far from being a heretic, came to the assistance of the count of Toulouse.

At the battle of Muret in 1213 the southern forces were decisively defeated, and while it took another dozen years to end all resistance, the victory of the north in the long run was assured. By his launching of the Albigensian crusade Innocent prepared the way for the gaining of the wealthy lands of Languedoc for the French crown, which took place finally in the 1220's. Innocent was criticized by the southern nobility in his own day and also by many modern writers, for preaching of this crusade against the Cathari. It has been said that he perverted the crusading movement and that he destroyed a brilliant civilization in the south of France. There is some truth in both indictments, but he had no alternative if he was to cut out of the body politic of Christendom the cancerous sore of Catharism.

With his typical thoroughness Innocent could not leave the heretics to be rooted out and judged by diocesan officials in southern France, whom he greatly distrusted anyway. He sent in legates commissioned to establish courts for dealing with heretics. Out of these precedents developed the general papal Inquisition which was officially established in 1233. The main lines of its work and procedure were already set down by Innocent: it would use Roman-canonical procedure, which allowed the use of torture to ferret out the heretics, and those who refused to recant or, having recanted, were discovered to have relapsed would be "relaxed to the secular arm" to suffer the death penalty of burning. The bias of the Inquisition against the defendant was typical of any Roman law court which came to deal with a case involving conscience.

Nothing, as Innocent said, was outside the province of the papacy, and he felt compelled to legislate not only on the matter of heretics but also on the treatment of the Jews. He forbade attempts to convert them to Christianity by force, but he advocated ghettoization—their exclusion as social pariahs from European society. The Fourth Latern Council decreed that Jews should wear a yellow label so that these outcasts could easily be distinguished. This requirement was to have a long and illustrious history in western Europe. Some writers have attempted to whitewash Innocent's Jewish policy; they claim that he wanted to ostracize the Jews in order to save them from further pogroms, which were becoming endemic in European life as a result of the dissemination of the blood libels. It seems most unlikely that Innocent was motivated by humanitarian reasons. He shared in the militant Christianity of his time, and the threat to the church from the great wave of antisacerdotalism tended to make ecclesiastical leaders even more intolerant and severe in their dealings with those who dissented from the Catholic faith. Innocent would not have been flattered by attempts to make him out to be a liberal. He had an unmitigated belief in the truth of the Catholic faith and the validity of the hierocratic tradition, the Petrine theory, and the Donation of Constantine. Both his doctrine and his personality were authoritarian. For eighteen years Innocent devoted his magnificent administrative and leadership qualities to furtherance of these doctrines, with far-reaching results.

Yet Innocent realized that his own methods could have only a limited impact in meeting the problems of piety and learning. He had reorganized the church, humiliated kings, and caused the taking up of the sword against the worst of the heretics, but none of these could resolve the struggle in men's minds that followed from the effects of the new piety and the challenge of Aristotelian science. It is not the least of Innocent's accomplishments as an administrator and leader that he was sensitive to the need for a more positive kind of approach than he himself could take and that he realized the significance and value of the work of St. Dominic and St. Francis.

II. The Dominican and Franciscan Ideals

The founding of the Dominican and Franciscan orders demonstrates the continued vitality of medieval civilization in the early thirteenth century. The product of the institutionalization of asceticism in the twelfth century —the religious orders working in the world—was used to meet the consequences of the new piety and the new learning and to reassert the leadership of the church in European society, thereby completing the bases of the new consensus that Innocent had set out to construct. The Dominican order met the forces which challenged the medieval order by teaching the truths of Catholic dogma and demonstrating their compatibility with science; the Franciscan approach was emotional rather than intellectual. It appealed to men's hearts rather than to their reason. It was founded on the premise that profound individual religious experience could strengthen faith rather than undermine. The development of thought, religion, and culture in the thirteenth century was largely in terms of the working-out of the implications of Dominican and Franciscan ideals.

The Order of Preachers, to give its official name, was a product of the struggle against the Albigensians. A Spanish priest named Dominic, working as a preacher against the heretics in Languedoc, gathered around him a group of like-minded disciples who aimed to live saintly lives, to be as ascetic as Cathari perfects, and at the same time to engage in homiletics and apologetics. In 1216 St. Dominic secured the pope's approval of a new order which would follow rules derived from the Austin canons and the Premonstratensians. The order attracted from the first a steady stream of young men who fitted its very high standards: the candidates had to be men of both ascetic persuasion and first-class intellectual powers. In the Dominican order ability counted for everything and overrode even the prescriptions of seniority. The officials of the order were responsible to meetings of the general chapter, and the representatives sent to these meetings were elected in order to assure that the best man would most likely be chosen, irrespective of his age or length of time in the order. Like Dominic himself, the members of the preaching order were men who subordinated entirely their own personalities and characteristics so that their talents could be fully put to the service of the church. The Dominicans were the intellectual shock troops of the thirteenth-century church. These were the ideal clergy to administer the new courts directed against heresy, and in the thirteenth century the Inquisition was largely a Dominican institution. Similarly, the aims, organization, and personnel of the new order made it eminently suitable for undertaking the task of meeting the Aristotelian challenge. For three or four decades the Aristotelian texts had steadily been coming in from the Arabic world, and the philosophy and theology faculties of the University of Paris and, to a lesser degree, other institutions had been deeply involved in trying to relate this new science to the older Biblical-patristic tradition, with indifferent results. The Dominicans assumed this task eagerly, and by the middle of the century they had come to dominate the University of Paris. As scholars and intellectuals they were convinced that revelation and science were ultimately one truth. As the official apologists for church doctrine, they deeply sensed the necessity for a philosophic defense of Christian doctrine, and it was one of the Dominican professors at Paris, Thomas Aquinas, who definitively formulated this kind of intellectual system in the third quarter of the thirteenth century.

The Dominican message was addressed to educated people; it was the Franciscans who undertook the hardest task of trying to come to terms with the impact of piety on the ordinary townsman, of trying to control the direction of that urban religiosity which produced the great anti-sacerdotal movement. It was not the idea of St. Francis of Assisi (1182–1226) that his disciples should be organized into a corporate order along the lines of the Dominicans. He simply called on all men to live the life of Christ as fully as they could. And the saintly lives of his disciples, the *fratres minores,* "the little brothers," would suffice to stir men's hearts by example and convert them to better ways. It was the most direct possible approach to the problem of converting society. The walls of pride and hatred which had been created by the complexities of social life could only be breached by manifestations of Christian love. It was both the simplest and the most profound message possible, and its implications troubled the leaders of the church as much as they admired the greatest saint which medieval civilization produced, the man who most perfectly followed in the steps of the Lord.

St. Francis' life was as simple and pure as his teaching. His father was a wealthy merchant of Assisi in northern Italy, and his mother came from the urbanized nobility. He was a rich, spoiled youth who read chivalric romances and dreamed of himself as another Lancelot. But when he tried to become a knight, he was wounded and disgraced. He passed through one of those great conversions which other great religious minds of Christianity have experienced—St. Paul, Augustine, Ignatius Loyola, Luther; he felt the grace of God coming unto him, and instead of mundane love, the most exalted kind of religious love became the inspiration of his life. He determined to live as Christ had lived—a mendicant, a teacher, a healer, the friend of all creatures, the preacher of the simplest and the most sublime truths. He wandered around the cities and villages of northern Italy existing solely as a beggar, and yet with the most complete faith in God's grace to provide for him. He ministered to the poor, the sick, even the lepers, whom no one else would approach. He tried to lead the rich and the powerful to live more fully Christian lives, and he was never discouraged by the insults directed at him. He celebrated the glories of God's creation with a magnificent lyric addressed to the sun, and he preached to the birds, whom he regarded also as his brothers.

The figure of the itinerant preaching saint had been familiar in the cities of northern Italy for two centuries, and such men had played a great role in fomenting the heretical movements of the twelfth century. But St. Francis seemed to go beyond any of these previous saints by the perfection of his life. His complete fulfillment of the life of Christ was confirmed by the appearance on his body of the stigmata, the wounds of Christ, it was said. He soon gathered men and also women around him, whom he sent out along the dusty roads of Italy to bring the Christian gospel to the laity in the way that he had done. The rules he set down for his Little Brothers were general statements of principles, not the specific code of a corporate order. Francis' basic requirement of his disciples was that they live and preach Christ and pursue their pilgrimage to that City of God with complete faith in divine beneficence, "taking nothing for the way." The Little Brothers were to be poor in every sense of the word: poor in spirit, in possessions, in offices, and in learning. The kingdom of God within man was all they needed. The friars were, in accordance with the example of the apostolic church, to hold no property either individually or corporately. They were to live in abandoned churches, caves, or anywhere they could find shelter. Their physical labor was to earn them their keep, and if this did not suffice, they were to be mendicants. They were to obtain no privileges from the pope, and they were not to be ordained priests. They were not to seek learning, because it was a snare and a distraction; to know that they should adore and serve God was enough.

These ideals bore some striking similarities to the attitudes of the Waldensian heretics, and Innocent and other ecclesiastical leaders were at first deeply concerned by the implications of what St. Francis was teaching. But there was something more, and this made all the difference: St. Francis was not an antisacerdotalist but a firm believer in the authority of the priesthood and the efficacy of the sacraments, and he fully subordinated himself and his Little Brothers to the hierarchy. The priests alone, Francis told his followers, could minister the Eucharist which made salvation possible. He said that he had such faith in the priesthood and the sacraments that he would have faith even in the ministration of the sacraments by a bad priest. This constituted an explicit negation of the Donatist heresy and allowed Innocent to give his approval to Francis to continue his work and to found his little society of Friars Minor. Innocent shrewdly perceived that St. Francis was supplying the necessary supplement to the pope's own work of restoring the prestige and leadership of the church. The Franciscan movement would make the positive contribution of inspiring the religious feelings of Europe, which could not be done by cardinal legates and Inquisitors. Innocent, who was a very different kind of man from the saint of Assisi, nevertheless glimpsed how useful his work was to the church. The Franciscan movement was the rallying point for all those laymen who were no longer satisfied with the church hierarchy but who did not want to break with the church and go off into the uncharted wastes of heresy. The teaching of St. Francis allowed those who wanted an intense personal religious experience to remain within the church. This was the best of all possible spiritual worlds, and it profoundly satisfied the religious yearning of the thirteenth century. The great enthusiasm which greeted St. Francis and his disciples, which so deeply moved the laity of the thirteenth century, revivified their attachment to the church, and brought about the rapid spread of the Franciscan movement over Europe, was not simply the result of the saintly disposition of these angelic men. It was because the Franciscans were both saints and Catholics. St. Francis was the product of mass psychology; the laity of his time wanted and needed such a figure, and they were fortunate in finding a man who so perfectly fitted their ideal.

The papacy after Innocent III determined to harness the Franciscan movement more firmly as an agent of clerical leadership by turning it into a corporate order on the model of the Dominicans. St. Francis only reluctantly agreed to these changes, and most of them were carried out while he was absent in the Levant trying to convert the Moslems. After his death the Franciscan order's leaders, with papal encouragement, proceeded to violate some of Francis' most fundamental rules. The Franciscans, and the Dominicans as well, became priests and were given the authority to wander over the countryside and through the towns, hearing confession, and administering the sacraments, much to the chagrin of the jealous parish priests and cathedral clergy. The Friars Minor came to hold property corporately, and Franciscan scholars became as outstanding as Dominicans for their work in philosophy and science. By the last quarter of the thirteenth century Franciscan professors dominated Oxford as much as Dominicans took the lead at Paris. These changes were to produce grave disputes within the order, but did not detract from the new devotion and respect for the church which the Franciscans gained during at least the first half of the thirteenth century. Among Innocent III's many decisions none was as important as allowing Francis of Assisi to send out his Little Brothers into the cities and villages of Europe.

Chapter Twenty

THE NEW CONSENSUS
AND ITS LIMITATIONS

I. The Cathedral of Intellect

The pontificate of Innocent III initiated a half century of renewed peace
and apparent stability in European life. There were no important wars from
the battle of Bouvines in 1214 until the 1290's. The first three quarters of
the thirteenth century were the concluding stage in the long period of population growth and economic boom which had marked European economic
history since the middle of the tenth century. Innocent III's success in dealing with kings of western Europe was continued by the popes who followed
him. The rulers of France and England were saintly men who appeared
deferential toward the papacy, while a renewed struggle with the Hohenstaufen house ended in the complete triumph of the church. The half
century that followed Innocent's death was also the period of balance and
consensus in intellectual life, a period when the thinkers of western Europe
tried to work out the implications of twelfth-century creativity and to
demonstrate the relationship between revelation and science as part of a
single body of truth. The resulting ambitious constructions of the mind
are paralleled by a new consensus in the realm of piety. The attack of the
Inquisition on heresy, reinforced strongly by enthusiasm for the Franciscan
ideal, brought about a very sharp decline in the influence of the antisacerdotal movement which had shaken the medieval world order to its
foundations at the end of the twelfth century. By 1260 popular heresy
seemed to be a negligible factor in European life. The Franciscans and

their followers succeeded in channeling the intense spirituality which now characterized all groups in society, but especially the townsmen, toward the enriching and fulfilling of Catholic Christianity. Some of the greatest achievements of medieval art and literature remain as monuments to the new harnessing of popular piety in the interests of the church.

The new architectural style which had originated in the middle of the twelfth century in the Île-de-France and which later, by a pejorative misnomer, came to be called Gothic had gone on from triumph to triumph since its experimental beginnings in Abbot Suger's day. The great bishops of northern France—Chartres, Paris, Orleans, Amiens, Sens—in the century after Suger engaged in a great competition to erect vast cathedrals in the new style, with wide portals, high clerestories, soaring buttresses, pointed arches, ribbed vaulting, rose windows, and magnificent sculptured façades. They strained the vast resources of their sees and the architectural ingenuity of Europe to create yet greater and higher edifices, and they ended by erecting, in the shape of crosses, buildings which had the greatest amount of uninterrupted and undivided interior space western man had ever known. The new French style spread rapidly to England and Germany and even influenced Italian architecture, where the previously dominant Romanesque form had originated. It was in the Île-de-France, however, that Gothic architecture achieved its greatest triumphs.

The lord, bourgeois, or peasant who entered Notre Dame or Chartres was given his most effective impression of the nature of heaven. All arts were employed, all senses were stirred, to render a momentary insight into the indescribable glory of the heavenly life. The stained glass refracted the Divine Light and bathed the altar in a myriad of miraculous colors. The worshippers, standing in their thousands to see and hear the celebration of the mass with all the visual and musical pomp of an imperial church, could not tell from inside the cathedral how its walls were held up. As the choir intoned the complex harmonies of its hymns and chants, as the bishop or his adjutant stood before the altar in his golden vestments, as the Savior, Virgin, and saints blazed forth from the glass mosaics in the clerestory and were made to stand out below in sculptured roundness from the surrounding gloom by the falling light, it was easy to imagine the angelic host as the supporters of this divine temple.

These supreme moments of faith were made possible only by an enormous amount of planning, money, and labor. It was a great task to build a Gothic cathedral, requiring the best efforts of hundreds of men over many years. The cathedrals of France of the late twelfth and thirteenth centuries were not put together by a few clerics and pious laborers while they sang hymns to the Virgin. They were built by guilds of masons who had to be well paid for their work. The bishop not only used his own income, but raised funds from kings, nobility, and burghers. The townsmen's municipal pride led them to support the building of the episcopal cathedral, even though they frequently were engaged in a bitter quarrel with the bishops over their communal rights. The bishop was not always inspired by the highest of motives; the cathedral was in a sense his monument, and the same prelate who cared nothing for the sufferings of peasant and proletarian and who was stingy in his charity to the sick and the helpless could achieve both contemporary and posthumous renown as a cathedral builder. Even with all this effort, the completion of a Gothic cathedral within thirty years was considered very good time, and in some instances the construction lagged over a century or more. All sorts of obstacles could arise: the original bishop could die and his successor care less about the work; the money could run out; the architects and builders could run into technical problems. Erecting a Gothic-style cathedral even today is a very expensive and difficult proposition—there has been one a-building in New York City for sixty years—and it was not less so in the thirteenth century. There was a ready supply of stonecutters then, which is lacking today, but medieval construction machines were simple and thirteenth-century knowledge of civil engineering crude.

The Gothic architect worked his plans by geometric proportions. He could not determine exactly the stress at any point in the walls of his building, and he had to take great risks, with not always happy consequences. The more strident the ambitions of his episcopal employer, the greater the chance he had to take, and the larger structures of the thirteenth century had to be supported, as a measure of security, by projecting flying buttresses. Under these conditions it is not surprising that good architects, who rose from the ranks of the master masons, were highly valued and remunerated. They were a small professional elite, the more successful of whom were deluged with commissions and often took on several jobs at the same time.

The architect's task was not only to plan and execute the construction of the cathedral but also to supervise its decoration. He was responsible for the direction of the craftsmen, whose stained-glass windows, sculptured statues, friezes, and ornaments were considered as necessary to a cathedral as illuminations to a good manuscript. In obscure corners of the cathedral or very high on the exterior walls, where the details of decoration were invisible to the viewer on the ground, the craftsmen were sometimes allowed to use their imagination, and they created all sorts of weird and grotesque figures in accordance with vulgar humor or popular myth. But the iconography for the sculpture and stained glass was carefully worked out in advance and designed to the smallest detail by the supervising architect. At times the bishop or abbot who had commissioned the building would make specific suggestions of the motifs and symbols he wanted depicted in his church, or scholars in the patron's service would advise the architect. It is possible that more learned architects worked out motifs themselves. But it is also clear that much of the symbolism in Gothic art was not the result of conscious thought, but merely the adaptation of traditional Christian iconology that can be traced back for centuries through illuminated manuscripts. The often overcommitted and hard-pressed architects borrowed ideas extensively from churches already in existence. The sketchbook of an early thirteenth-century French architect, Villard de Honnecourt, has survived. It reveals that he had gone around to various cathedrals and made extensive copies of both the architectural and iconographical work he liked.

If all aspects of art were not as much the product of conscious thought as some enthusiastic modern writers have believed, the cathedrals of northern France nevertheless remain as the monumental symbols of the intellectual tendencies of the first seven decades of the thirteenth century. If the leitmotif of twelfth-century thought was creativity and originality, that of the earlier and mid-thirteenth century was order and discipline. As the Gothic cathedral combined all the artistic and engineering resources of the thirteenth century to create a house for the divine spirit, the thinkers and writers of the period tried to create a cathedral of intellect. The heterogeneous and sometimes conflicting currents of twelfth-century thought were subjected to the scrutiny of ordered intelligence, its bewildering twists and turns straightened out into systematic patterns, and its open ends circumscribed and marked off by visible limits. Thirteenth-century thought resembles the form of the Gothic cathedral in another way, however: the structure is dominated by a central nave and transept open for all to see, spacious, finished, magnificent, but it also contains less prominent and rather obscure side chapels and rooms, and there was a pressure on the walls of this great intellectual edifice which sometimes worried its architects.

Thirteenth-century civilization had a compulsive urge to collect and systematize all forms of knowledge. There was an underlying feeling that if all the known information in a certain field could only be brought together in a regular pattern within the pages of a large book, the gnawing doubts and confusions would go away, and educated men could feel secure and happy. It was a natural reaction against the centrifugal tendencies of twelfth-century culture. Prodigious effort and fine intelligence went into the making of such systematic compendia, and they were very popular at all levels and in all fields of thought. There was a *summa* for every interest and taste; the most comprehensive, if not the most profound, was the gigantic *Speculum Maius* (Greater Mirror) of Vincent of Beauvais, a French Dominican. Theology and philosophy and law of every kind, whether civil, canon, feudal, or common, had its great systematizers. There were textbooks on cosmology describing the universe on the basis of the theories of Ptolemy, Aristotle, and the Arabic scholars, all presenting variants of an earth-centered universe, which fitted in so well with the book of Genesis and the obvious central place of man in God's creation. For the less learned there were encyclopedias of all knowledge, some of them written in the vernacular, enthusiastically received by nobles of courtly inclination and burghers trying to improve themselves. Bestiaries were very popular, not least because they described and pictured animals no one had ever seen.

The thirteenth-century penchant for systematization of all knowledge in summaries and encyclopedias was paralleled by its incorporation of all important intellectual activity within the life of academic institutions. Not again until the twentieth cenutry would the universities of the western world so dominate the life of the mind, and the academics held an even greater monopoly in the thirteenth century. Thirteenth-century thought was "scholastic," that is, academic. All the important writers on theology, philosophy, law, and science were "scholastics," that is, they were professors in the schools, the universities, and they were devoted to the use of the dialectical method of reasoning and exposition which had become common in the twelfth century. The institutional milieu in which they worked inevitably conditioned their outlook in other ways. It was an intensely serious, competitive, and confined environment, one that was probably better for refinement of prevailing doctrines than for the breaking away from accepted patterns and the opening of new lines of thought. Medieval professors and students have sometimes been depicted as jovial and serene characters; this was generally not the case. It would be more accurate to typify them as unhappy, compulsive, and aggressive.

The medieval university, which grew out of the early twelfth-century French cathedral schools and the Italian municipal schools, was a distinctive and original contribution to the institutionalization of higher education. It was organized for the dissemination of many branches of knowledge to a large number of students as cheaply and as systematically as possible, and as such, it was superior to the academies and schools of rhetoric of the ancient world. The medieval system was designed to get students through prescribed programs and to give them degrees certifying a minimum proficiency; this is still the basic idea of a university in western civilization. The medieval university also developed a new teaching method involving lectures and the use of textbooks which is still, for better or worse, substantially in use today. The medieval lecture was literally "a reading"; the professor read a passage from a text such as the Justinian code, the Bible, or one of Aristotle's works and developed his interpretation by glossing the text. Since books could only be produced by manuscript, they were extremely expensive, and only the wealthier students could buy standard editions of the textbooks. Three or four students would get together to buy a book and to write down the professors' glosses on the text. There was little or no discussion between professor and student. The only Socratic dialogue in the medieval university was among the professors; they occasionally offered competing courses on the same text, and they engaged in great public debates on disputed theses.

The universities were organized as special guilds for manufacturing learned men. North of the Alps the teachers acted like the masters of any other guild; they set the length and time a student had to serve as an apprentice and journeyman, and they established the conditions under which he could enter into the ranks of the master-teachers and receive his final degree. All such degrees, whether the graduate was called master or doctor, were technically licenses to teach, even though most university graduates did not become teachers. They were certificates of competence in the craft pursued by the corporation. The intellectual standards and length of study required by the undergraduate were severe. (A medieval student took as long, or longer, to train himself for a learned profession as students in American universities take today.) In the schools of Italy, which specialized in civil law in the north and medicine in the south, the guild was in the hands of the undergraduates, or bachelors, who hired the teachers and set rules requiring the lecturers to finish the commentary on the prescribed texts before the end of the term of study. This is the bourgeois attitude toward education at work. Examinations in the medieval university were given orally; they were comprehensive and difficult.

The guilds of masters in the northern universities were licensed by the bishop in whose city they taught. Occasionally he intervened in the university if he was concerned by the doctrinal implications of what was being said or written by one of the professors. The papacy and the king also exercised supervision over the universities. As a consequence, professors were occasionally silenced and their doctrines condemned. But what is remarkable is the large degree of freedom which the thirteenth-century professor had even in the fields of theology and philosophy. The discipline and control to which the professor was subjected were largely intramural. His colleagues constantly competed with him for intellectual distinction, the best professorships, and the devotion and sometimes the fees of the students. Any slipshod or revolutionary thinking would be stiffly challenged. Furthermore, many of the professors were members of religious orders, particularly the Dominican and Franciscan, which exercised a further control over their work.

It is a myth that most students in a medieval university were zealots who wanted to become theologians. Actually there was not a much greater proportion of the thirteenth-century university students studying theology than there is today. Among the students the most popular faculty by far was law, and for the same reasons that this study attracts large numbers today. It was the road to good jobs in the church and the state. On the other hand, the study of theology, although it might be hailed as the queen of the sciences, was very long and difficult and offered little employment opportunity on completion of the degree. The medieval student's life was always hard and frequently desperate. Most of the students came from families of lesser knights, who could offer their children little in the way of a patrimony, or from the burghers, for whom the system presented a way of escaping from their class and entering the service of the church or the state. The students' impecunious condition was made worse by the exorbitant prices and the inadequacy of the food and lodging available in university towns such as Paris and Oxford. Occasional fights between townsmen and students, and even large-scale riots, were the natural result. The king and bishop were supposed to protect the students from exploitation, but their work was not very effective in this regard. The University of Cambridge was founded in the early thirteenth century by masters and students who left Oxford in disgust after a particularly violent "town and gown" riot. During the thirteenth century certain wealthy benefactors, including a Robert de Sorbon at Paris, began to establish communal houses or "colleges" for the students. At Oxford the colleges became more and more important in the teaching life of the university. It was also traditional at Paris to divide the students into certain "nations" according to their provenance. A student found his studies long and hard, the cost of living high, and the discipline to which he was subjected severe. It is not surprising that he occasionally vented his unhappiness in drinking, gambling, and street fighting. It is also not surprising that some of the most illustrious thinkers in thirteenth- and fourteenth-century academic life were querulous and disagreeable men and rather unstable personalities.

The arts faculty provided the basic preliminary studies in the medieval university, from which the students proceeded, as rapidly as possible, to their advanced work in law, theology, or medicine. The teachers in the arts faculty were generally not the better minds in the medieval university, and their treatment of the classics totally lacked the humane values which John of Salisbury had found in the cultivation of the liberal arts. John had feared that humanism could not prevail in the dialectical atmosphere of the university, and the subsequent development of the study of the liberal arts proved the keenness of his intuition. The thirteenth-century scholastics wanted to find the truth, but they did not appreciate great literature either for its esthetic qualities or as a teacher of morality. The teachers in the arts faculty approached the classics in a very analytical way; they looked upon the ancient texts as a body of knowledge to be subjected to the tools of dialectic. Its word structure and rhetoric were to be dissected and then systematized. But their narrowly utilitarian approach left no room for either the ideas or values of the classical tradition. The ancient world meant nothing to them; they were self-consciously separated from it. In its anti-humanist attitude thirteenth-century thought was at its weakest, and this failure in the long run was to be very important in later medieval culture. The perpetuation of the classical tradition, which since the sixth century had been the task of ecclesiastical schools, moved out of the university and joined up with the romantic literary tradition. It was the Italian poets of the late thirteenth and early fourteenth centuries who revived humanist values and were the true successors of John of Salisbury. The hostility which the Renaissance humanists frequently expressed toward scholasticism and the universities, even though many of them were university graduates, was the result of the rejection of the humanist tradition by the thirteenth-century schoolmen.

The scholastics believed that their dialectical method and great store of Christian and Greek learning prepared them to answer all problems. They, for instance, devoted considerable time and ingenuity debating whether the taking of usury was compatible with Christian doctrine and what was the "just price" which the ecclesiastical authorities should permit the merchant to charge. While the scholastics concluded that there were moral limitations to capitalist enterprise, they nevertheless allowed the business entrepreneur a comfortable return on his investment and labor. In actual practice the scholastic limitations on profit-taking were generally ignored with impunity by merchants and bankers.

The greatest demand which society, and particularly the church, placed upon the scholastics fell in the areas of logic, metaphysics, epistemology, and theology. The intellectual problems which had been left over from the twelfth century, and which became even more pressing and crucial as a result of the absorption of the Aristotelian corpus and its Arabic commentators, were the ones which fully exercised the dialectical skill and unsurpassed mental powers of the thirteenth-century scholastics. By the middle of the century there was great confusion and controversy among the philosophers and theologians as competing and sharply different intellectual systems contended against one another. There were still those who supported the older Augustinianism and Neoplatonism and a strongly realist position. A member of the arts faculty of Paris, Siger of Brabant, was openly advocating the Averroist position, whose strict determinism and denial of creation *ex nihilo* and the individuality of the soul were as much a contradiction of Christian revelation as of Arabic. A German Dominican at Paris, Albertus Magnus, was attempting to establish a Christian Aristotelian position, but with little success.

At this point another Paris Dominican, Thomas Aquinas (1225–1272), began to work out his distinctive system. The completion of his work in the *Summa Theologica* was the major turning point in thirteenth-century thought, a breakthrough of first importance. But it was one which startled and disturbed as many of his contemporaries as it satisfied. Nothing is further from the reality of thirteenth-century culture than to imagine that Thomism was immediately acclaimed by all as the answer to the intellectual problems of the church. Modern Catholicism may regard Thomism as the official philosophy of the church, but this is very far from the attitude which prevailed in St. Thomas's own day and for the next two centuries. Thomas was regarded by many as a radical, highly speculative, and very tendentious thinker. Yet the importance of his work was recognized from the first even by those who criticized it. He had created a vast, complex, subtle, and ordered system which integrated to the fullest possible degree Aristotelian science and the Christian revelation. The question remained, however, whether such a system was philosophically valid or theologically desirable.

Aquinas was not disturbed. The criticism which he received both within and without his university did not upset his usual serenity. He was attacked not only by some of his colleagues but also by the bishop of Paris and the leading contemporary Dominican philosopher at Oxford. But he went on with his teaching and writing, adding bit by bit to his intellectual structure, which the art historian Erwin Panofsky has said exhibits all the qualities of a Gothic cathedral. It was not for nothing that Aquinas became known as the "angelic doctor." Thomas Aquinas' personality, remarkable for self-confidence, serenity, and moderation in debate, often has been regarded as typical of the medieval scholastic; these qualities, on the contrary, make him the great exception. His intellectual pre-eminence partly accounts for his serenity, but this quality must also be attributed to his famous obesity and above all to his class background. While most of the schoolmen came from modest and even obscure backgrounds, Thomas was the scion of an aristocrat Neapolitan family, and he retained in his intellectual work the unshakable self-confidence of the high-born.

The Christian philosophy of Thomas Aquinas may be said to be founded on a magnificent paradox: he tried to arrive at most of the conclusions of Augustine and the Neoplatonists by using most of the science and logic of the Averroists. This was an extremely bold and risky undertaking, and it is no surprise that he startled and stunned contemporaries by daring and completing it in a vast systematic treatise. Thomas' basic assumption was that Aristotelianism need not lead to the conclusions that Averroes, "the Commentator," had derived from Aristotle, "the Philosopher." Although his critics unjustly accused him of being close to Averroism because of his use of Aristotelian science as the basis of his philosophy, he wanted above all to negate the double-truth theory of the great Arabic thinker. There was not one truth in science and another in faith; it was possible to prove the essential doctrines of Christian theology by rational logic. It is his Aristotelian epistemology which allows Aquinas to work his way to this conclusion. His whole system rests on the principle that our knowledge comes not from the illuminating participation of the mind in pure and divine ideas, as was held by Augustinian Platonism, but rather that it is primarily built up out of sense experience. As an Aristotelian he cannot accept the Platonic theory of forms; to him this is not scientific, and any Christian philosophy which is based on this false epistemology will fail, as the twelfth-century realists had failed, in the face of the nominalist attack. If, however, the origin of human knowledge is in the senses, then the constructions of the mind have a secure foundation, and we can proceed by reason to consider the nature of reality. Aquinas, therefore, arrives at a conclusion which may be termed "moderate realism," but he gets there from an Aristotelian, non-Platonic starting point. He admitted that there are certain ultimate areas of the Christian faith to which reason cannot penetrate: it is impossible to prove the miracle of incarnation or the trinity. But it is possible to prove rationally the existence and many of the attributes of God. Aquinas presents five proofs for the existence of God; they are all based on the Aristotelian argument for the existence of a first cause. There cannot be an infinity of causation; there must be an original, unmoved mover, which Aquinas identifies with God. Thus far, however, he has only proved the existence of the deterministic deity of Aristotle and Averroes, not the Christian providential God. He proceeds to argue, with a validity that was doubted by many, that from this premise can be derived the Christian attributes of God as perfect, omniscient, omnipotent, and free. Similarly, he proceeds from Aristotelian causality by way of logical argument to prove creation *ex nihilo,* and similarly from Aristotelian psychology to the human soul, and from Aristotelian ethics to Christian virtue.

Aquinas believed that he had come very close to the ultimate principles of Augustinian teaching. He had arrived there, however, by a new route;

the discredited trail of Platonism had been replaced by the new and secure highway of Aristotelian science. The critics of Thomism fell into two groups. The Averroists and other keen students of Aristotle claimed that he had misused the work of the philosopher and had perverted Aristotelian causality and logic. Those who were inclined to the older Neoplatonist and Augustinian position denied that he had come out at the Augustinian deity at all. Rather, they claimed that Aquinas had blundered off into the dead end of Aristotelian determinism. They said that the Thomistic deity was mechanistic and not omnipotent and free—a machine, not Christ. They claimed that the Thomist ordered universe had been achieved at the price of rejecting Augustine for Aristotle. It was claimed that Thomas was undermining the distinction between the Greek and Christian world views that Augustine had drawn. The great church father had emphasized the primacy of will over intellect; Thomas had achieved his ordered world by subverting will to the supremacy of intellect.

The latter criticism of Thomism was presented by the Franciscan philosophers who, at the time of Aquinas' death, were coming to dominate the theology faculty at Oxford. Already Thomas' contemporary, the Italian philosopher St. Bonaventura (1221–1274), who was also the head of the order of the Friars Minor, had published a great treatise which reasserted the Platonic-Augustinian position against the new Aristotelianism. In Bonaventura's system the Platonic realist theory that it is universals which individuate matter is joined with a strongly Augustinian theology which was compatible with the outlook of the disciples of St. Francis. The primacy of will, and therefore love, over intellect was again predicated, and the majesty and grace of God was emphasized against the mechanistic deity of Aristotle.

St. Bonaventura's attempt to present a philosophic statement of the Franciscan ideal was an expression of a deep anti-intellectual current in thirteenth-century culture which could not long remain quiet in the face of the implications of Thomism. The Franciscan movement had brought back within the church the current of piety which in the twelfth century had overflowed ecclesiastical banks and threatened to destroy sacerdotal supremacy. But if piety once again recognized the authority of the church, it nevertheless had a very definite conception of God, and it was not that which appears in the *Summa Theologica*. Even when Thomas wrote a hymn on *Corpus Christi*, it was a rather old-fashioned celebration of "the everlasting Father, and the Son who reigns on high, With the Holy Ghost proceeding forth from Each eternally." Profoundly different is the spirit of the two great Franciscan hymns of the thirteenth century, Jacopone da Todi's *Stabat Mater* and Thomas of Celano's *Dies Irae.* Between them they illustrate the twin themes of the Franciscan world view: religious love and the majesty of God:

> O thou Mother, fount of love,
> Touch my spirit from above,
>   Make my heart with thine accord!
> Make me feel as thou hast felt;
> Make my soul to glow and melt
>   With the love of Christ my Lord.
>
> Thou giv'st leave, dread Lord, that we
> Take shelter from Thyself in Thee,
> And with the wings of Thine own dove
> Fly to the sceptre of soft love.

The influence of the Franciscan movement in the mid-thirteenth century was amply demonstrated by the tremendous popularity of the cult of the Poor Man of Assisi, as expressed in the *Little Flowers,* the biographical and legendary accounts which circulated immediately after his death, and in many other ways. The importance of the Franciscan movement was also illustrated by the number of outstanding minds it attracted, although St. Francis himself had opposed learning as a dangerous temptation. By 1270 the intellectual life of Europe, in which the incomparable edifice of Thomism loomed so large, was marked also by the rise of a group of Franciscan philosophers who were beginning to put into philosophical form their dissatisfaction with the Dominican integration of science and revelation. In other words, a dangerous dichotomy was just beginning to make its appearance in the ordered thought-world of the thirteenth century.

As an offshoot of mid-thirteenth-century Franciscan thought, like a flying buttress projecting from a French cathedral, is the dim beginning of modern science. The subject is made more obscure by our lack of unanimity on what constitutes the essential nature of modern science. Can science be defined as the observation of nature? It can be said that this is too vague and fails to distinguish the novel factor which separates modern from earlier science. Then is it the quantification of nature, the expression of natural phenomena in mathematical terms? This seems to be a good definition, except for the fact that mathematics does lie about nature sometimes; it posits relationships which do not always exist in nature. One may identify modern science with the experimental method. There is, however, some confusion about the nature of the experimental method, although it may be accepted that it has something to do with inductive reasoning.

Whatever may be regarded as the proper definition of the nature of science, the work of Robert Grosseteste (1175–1253), bishop of Lincoln and protector of the English Franciscans, and the Oxford friar Roger Bacon (d. 1292) may be said to apply. In both cases there is a gain of new knowledge through observation in such fields as optics and astronomy, where little equipment was needed, and some understanding of the value of the inductive as well as the deductive method. Grosseteste further asserted the need to express natural phenomena in terms of mathematical propositions. The penetration of Arabic mathematics into western Europe was for the first time opening up to European thinkers the mathematical dimension in human thought. Bacon's writings are furthermore distinguished by a tone of intellectual aggressiveness and independence which may be associated with the general attitude of the modern scientist. The most important question which rises from the work of these two men is why the first steps to modern science should come from the Franciscan movement and not from Thomism. The answer lies partly in the nature of Aristotelianism and partly in the tendencies of the Franciscan intellectual movement. The Aristotelian science was the best yet known in the world, and that is why Thomas thought it was necessary to integrate it with Christian revelation. But since it was based on a system of deductive reasoning from certain premises, it was fundamentally an intellectual cul-de-sac, as Bacon was the first to see clearly. By his integration of Aristotelian science with revelation Thomas in any case made it into a closed system which could not move in new directions. The Franciscan movement, with its emotional religiosity, might seem an odd starting point for modern science, but it had certain characteristics that proved fruitful in this regard. It was Plato who had claimed that the cosmos operated in terms of ideal mathematically proportioned forms, and the early Platonic cast of the Franciscan philosophy, as expressed in Bonaventura's work, led Grosseteste toward his theory of the quantification of nature. Bacon, writing a little later, is already under the influence of the general Franciscan revolt against Aristotelianism which threatened in the late decades of the thirteenth century to break apart the scholastic cathedral of intellect.

II. The Moral Authority of the State

St. Thomas Aquinas' attempt to bring all the problems of the human mind within an ordered system led him to develop a political theory which was as significant and as bold as his philosophy and theology. Just as in his interpretation of divine and human nature he broke definitively with the Platonic tradition of the early middle ages, so also, in political thought, he created a revolution. The political doctrine of the early-medieval thinkers was strongly conditioned by Augustine's hostility to the state and by his denial of independent moral sanction to political authority. Augustinian philosophy had established the primacy of will over intellect in defiance of the Socratic teaching; similarly, political Augustinianism had negated the Greek view of the state as a moral being whose existence was necessary for the fulfillment of human potentialities. The Greeks could not conceive of man living apart from the state, but to Augustine it was only the interior and not the social man that counted, only the relationship between the human soul and the all-powerful deity which gave meaning to human life. In the Augustinian view the state in and for itself was only a band of robbers, without moral quality, and the state received a sanction only insofar as it furthered the ends of the City of God. Turned into more specific doctrine, Augustinianism became the political theory of the church before the twelfth century, which made the state the servant of the church and gave the state a moral sanction only insofar as monarchy subjected itself to the commands of the hierarchy and particularly the papacy. Political Augustinianism reached its fullest form in the radical aspects of the Gelasian doctrine, in the Donation of Constantine, and in the pronouncements of Gregory VII. In the twelfth and thirteenth centuries the canon lawyers, who worked under papal auspices, perpetuated this ecclesiastical political theory, giving it a new format by their juristic doctrines of the plenitude of absolute papal power.

The actual entrenchment of secular leadership in society more and more contradicted the established hierocratic tradition, however, and from the middle of the twelfth century a new current in political speculation among the leading thinkers of Europe began slowly to come to the fore. Without abandoning the theory of the ultimate supremacy of the church, they tried to delineate a theory of the state which would conform more realistically to actual social conditions, in which the leadership of royal government was rapidly becoming indispensable. John of Salisbury and Otto of Freising, in the twelfth century, took the first steps in this new direction, and it remained for Thomas Aquinas, in this as in other fields of thought, to fulfill and formulate in a precisely defined doctrine the novel tendencies of twelfth-century speculation.

As was the case with his philosophical and theological work, Thomas found the starting point for his political doctrine in Aristotelian science. He was as impressed with the merits of the Philosopher's *Politics* as he was with his metaphysics, epistemology, and ethics. Consequently he was prepared to accept the Greek view of the moral necessity of the state and Aristotle's doctrine that man was a political being whose potentialities could only be fulfilled in political society. The political doctrine of Aquinas, therefore, constituted a revolution against the tradition of political Augustinianism and a reversion to the Greek idea of the moral integrity of the authority of the state. But as he attempted to do in his theological works, while rejecting the spirit and methodology of Augustinianism, Thomas did not want to throw aside the authoritative church father's conclusions. He wanted to arrive in political thought at a point not far distant from the Augustinian tradition, but only by making use of the truths of Aristotelian science. In other words, Aquinas wanted to maintain both the moral quality of the state, in conformity with the teachings of Aristotle, and the continued ultimate supremacy of the church in society. This extremely bold and provocative integration of the old and the new in medieval political thought Aquinas attempted to achieve through his philosophy of law. He asserted that the law of the state had to be in conformity with natural law, which in turn was a reflection of divine law, and when the positive law of the state was in this way in conformity with the law of God, its moral sanction was complete and unmitigated. By this legal doctrine Aquinas thought that he had given to political authority its necessary moral quality and at the same time had subordinated it to the hierocratic agency of divine will. He believed that he had recognized the value of secular leadership in Christian society and yet had maintained fundamentally inviolate the traditional Gelasian doctrine.

The delicate balance and integration of hierocratic and secular authority which distinguishes political Thomism conformed in many ways to the relations between monarchy and the church in the mid-thirteenth century. Undoubtedly the realities of contemporary political life encouraged Aquinas to formulate his departure from the Augustinian theory of the state; what was happening in England, France, and Germany in his day seemed to confirm his political philosophy to a marked degree. The English king, Henry III, was a saintly and docile man who continued the deferential attitude toward Rome that his father, King John, had been forced to adopt in his later years. An even more impressive confirmation of Thomist doctrine could be found closer to home, in Paris itself, in the personality and attitudes of Louis IX, who must have seemed to Thomas the incarnation of his political ideal. Louis was renowned as a self-sacrificing crusader and a righteous persecutor of heretics and hater of Jews. His popular image is revealed in the biography of the king written by a prominent Champagne nobleman, the Lord of Joinville, which was the first medieval royal life produced by a layman. In Joinville's account Louis is a saintly but brave man who has no other ambitions than service to God and the furtherance of the welfare of his people. He endures without complaint great suffering during his ill-fated crusade in Egypt and ends his life in martyrdom in Tunis while attempting, like St. Francis, to convert the infidel. In France Louis bears without rancor ill treatment by his mother when she is regent of the kingdom and turns aside the rebellion of obstreperous barons without a thought of vengeance. He insists that his government fulfill the highest ideals of Christian justice, and to assure this the king sits under an oak tree and personally renders his judgment in cases brought by his adoring subjects. The angelic doctor and the saintly king were almost exact contemporaries, and in both instances there were already strong movements for their canonization under way before their deaths. St. Louis seemed to be political Thomism in action.

Aquinas' ideal of church-state relations was confirmed in other ways as well. The German emperor Frederick II warred against the papacy in Italy, but the hierocratic representative of divine law emerged completely triumphant from this struggle, and during Aquinas' own lifetime the contumacious Hohenstaufen family, as befitted tyrants, were wiped from the face of the earth and their Italian possessions handed over by the pope to the brother of the ideal Christian monarch Louis IX. The integration of papal and royal authority was amply demonstrated during the thirteenth century by grants to royal governments of a share of clerical taxation when the kings undertook some venture favored and encouraged by Rome. This was also illustrated by the increasing involvement of the papacy in clerical appointments all over western Europe on the basis of a maze of canon-law precedents. In order to maintain unchallenged their own predominant control over clerical appointments, secular rulers found it expedient to give the pope the right to designate and make "provision" for the filling of certain clerical offices within their realms.

Thomas's political philosophy, while in some ways radical and provocative, thus seemed to be an expression of a new political consensus in European life which fulfilled the work of Innocent III during the half century following his death. The policy of the great pope with regard to the European monarchies was perpetuated by his able successors, particularly Gregory IX (1227–1241) and Innocent IV (1243–1254), who resembled Innocent in their legal background, diplomatic and administrative expertise, and intransigent defense of papal interests. They gained some remarkable triumphs and generally strengthened the edifice of papal power which Innocent had delineated. There were, however, certain aspects of Rome's relations with the English, French, and German monarchies which the papal curia found deeply disturbing even during the lifetimes of Thomas Aquinas and St. Louis. The new political consensus, so imposing in many respects, was not without definite limitations and weaknesses.

There were discrepancies between the Thomistic ideal order and the realities of political life which the angelic doctor could not well perceive from the vantage point of the Paris schools. Changes were occurring in the institutions and ideology of thirteenth-century kingship whose significance was not fully apparent until the later decades of the century.

The English political situation from the last years of John was one that was peculiarly exasperating to the papacy. The English king had finally been brought low, but the Italian cardinals were puzzled and annoyed to discover that royal power no longer seemed to dominate English life. The papacy now had a vassal in the person of the English king, but one who could not keep order in his own house. Instead, the English barons, with the encouragement and assistance of some churchmen, engaged in revolts aimed at establishing institutional controls over the king's government. They propounded legal theories subjecting the king to the due processes of law which, they claimed, could only be changed by consent of what was called "the community of the realm." To the leaders of the papal curia, steeped in the Roman-canonical traditions of absolutism, news of these political experiments and constitutional ideas made strange reading. Not only was the cardinals' sense of right order offended, but also the power of the papal vassal and therefore, indirectly, the effectiveness of Roman intervention in England, was threatened. As a consequence, for six decades after John made his subservience to the papacy, the curia was invariably in favor of royal authority in England and hostile to the novel constitutional experiments and ideas, with profound consequences for Anglo-papal relations.

In 1214 John suffered his second great humiliation and defeat at the hands of his archenemy Philip Augustus of France. He had allied himself with his relative, Otto IV, to foment a two-front attack on the Capetian kingdom. Otto was supposed to come down from Germany through Flanders by a route which would become familiar to German armies in the nineteenth and twentieth centuries, while John pushed upward from Poitou to complete a great pincers movement. John won some initial successes, but he was overcome by one of his periodic fits of depression. He stood idly by while Philip deployed most of the French army against Otto and inflicted a crushing defeat on the German emperor at Bouvines. This second military disaster was the signal for the crystallization of baronial revolt against Angevin power in England. John had for a long time been using the prerogatives of the crown, such as relief, wardship, and scutage, in an unusually severe manner in order to increase royal income from taxation. John's government was very hard-pressed; the king had a growing administration, and he was engaged in far-flung diplomatic and military ventures, and with the general introduction of heavy plate armor and other improvements in military technology, the costs of warfare were steadily increasing. The baronial leaders did not, however, sympathize with John's predicament; they did not want to be subjected to very heavy taxation for the support of a king who was a failure on the battlefield, who had lost them their lands in Normandy, and who furthermore had corrupted the law courts in order to obtain judgments against baronial families which John suspected, in many cases on little or no grounds, of disloyalty. The king had furthermore been defeated and humiliated by the pope, and he had entered into a position of vassalage to the papacy, which was a flagrant turnabout in Anglo-papal relations as they had existed since the time of William the Conqueror.

The majority of the great barons, led by members of certain northern families who had particularly suffered from arbitrary procedures in the royal courts, prepared the first real rebellion against the royal liege lord in England since the Norman invasion. The baronial movement appears to have been given defined and conscious aims by the archbishop of Canterbury, Stephen Langton, who, far from being the papal sycophant that had been expected, turned out to be a man of strong and independent opinion. Ignoring the fact that John was the pope's vassal, Stephen aligned the English church alongside the lay magnates in what was a little later to be called the community of the English realm. It appears to have been Stephen who suggested to the barons that they stipulate their grievances in the form of a "great charter," which they forced the king to approve and seal in 1215. Stephen took as a precedent for Magna Carta the coronation charter of promises made to the English church and people by Henry I in 1100. Magna Carta contained a long list of baronial rights and privileges which the king promised not to infringe. It was, of course, a document which was biased in favor of the interests of the baronial class, but it was a class which claimed, and on the whole had the right, to speak for the "whole people of England." Magna Carta placed severe limitations on the exercise of the financial powers of the Angevin monarchy; many such provisions were eliminated in the final issuance of the document by the government of Henry III in 1225. It is highly significant, however, that the barons did not try to destroy the common-law system which Henry II had perfected nor to regain from the royal courts the independent powers and jurisdictions of the private feudal courts which had been lost to royal justice. Nor did any of the great nobles try to gain special concessions for themselves; they spoke as a group whose liberties were homogeneous throughout the realm. This was a consequence of one hundred and fifty years of powerful central government in England which had so unified the country that the great magnates, while they wanted to limit royal authority, could not conceive of depriving themselves of the benefits of efficient royal administration and law. It did not even enter their minds to establish autonomous principalities.

The greatest importance of Magna Carta lies in the theory of law implied in the statement that the king should observe "the law of the land" and that he cannot proceed against anyone without following the due processes of the common law. If the king wished to do something beyond the prevailing law of the land, such as imposing a new tax, he could only do so with the consent of the community of the realm. Magna Carta thus reasserted the Germanic constitutional principle which had been incorporated into the common law: as a great thirteenth-century English lawyer later expressed it, "in England law rules and not will." It is because it expresses the ideal of the supremacy of the law over the will of the king that Magna Carta became such an important rallying cry for later generations of Englishmen struggling against royal power. During the thirteenth and fourteenth centuries, dissatisfaction with the arbitrary quality of royal government came to be expressed in demands for royal confirmations of Magna Carta. The seventeenth-century English common lawyers saw in Magna Carta the bastion of English liberty against royal despotism. They even said that Magna Carta confirmed trial by jury in the full meaning of the term. Although the jury of verdict was not actually developed until the later thirteenth century as a result of the Fourth Lateran Council's prohibition of ordeals as a method of proof, the seventeenth-century interpretation of Magna Carta was not as absurd as many modern critics have said. The fundamental doctrine of Magna Carta was that the king could not proceed against any free man in the realm except by the prevailing due process of the common law, whatever its institutions might be.

The last clause of Magna Carta provided for a general feudal *diffidatio* and barons' revolt against the king if he failed to keep his promises. They almost immediately had cause to make this provision operative. John appealed to his overlord, Innocent III, to absolve him from his vows to the barons, which he claimed he had made under duress, and the pope, who did not like the theoretical implications of the great charter nor the diminution of his vassal's power, immediately complied. Innocent furthermore censured Langton for his participation in the drafting of Magna Carta and suspended the archbishop from the exercise of his office. The barons took up arms against the king and called in the son of Philip Augustus to help them, but John's death made possible the restoration of peace between the royal government and the magnates. However, John's heir, Henry III (1216–1272), who was still a minor at the time of his father's death, was not any more successful in the exercise of royal leadership. After he came of age in the 1220's, crisis after crisis developed in his relations with the leaders of the community of the realm until, in 1258, a committee of barons took over the management of the royal administration. In 1264 Henry tried to resume direction of control over the royal administration, but he was defeated in open battle by the barons and captured.

The constitutional crisis of Henry III's reign was a product of both his weakness as a king and the further development of the constitutional ideas reflected in the provisions of Magna Carta. Henry was an extremely devout man with fine aesthetic tastes, and he was largely responsible for the building of Westminster Abbey in its present form. But he was a failure as a soldier; he lost Poitou to Louis IX, his wife's brother-in-law, whom he greatly respected and treated with deference. Henry was even more subservient to the pope and allowed himself to be involved in papal plans for replacing the Hohenstaufen ruler with a more pliant king. The pope offered Sicily to one of Henry's sons in return for very large payments, which the king supplied out of the royal revenue. The only way the royal government could obtain extraordinary revenue for this and other purposes was by the development of new forms of taxation. John's administration had already experimented with the exploitation of the old principle of the feudal "gracious aid." This was a special tax which vassals might give to their lord for a certain purpose, but only with their specific consent. As the liege lord of all the English magnates, John was able to obtain consent for an aid to fight the French king, and this precedent was used several times by Henry III's government in order to obtain consent for a tax on the revenue and property of the magnates and their subvassals. The unpaid county officials were made responsible for assessing and collecting the tax, and the techniques they used were modeled on those employed in the implementation of a tithe levied by the church in 1188 for support of the third crusade. As the magnates became more and more dissatisfied with Henry's government, the king was unable to obtain their consent to the imposition of new taxes, and he had to default on his payments to Rome, whereupon the pope handed Sicily over to the brother of the French king. This placed Henry in a most disadvantageous position. His treasury was bankrupt, and the baronial class was strongly critical of his administration. They were angry at his deferential attitude to Rome and his gifts of royal and ecclesiastical offices to his French relatives and their supporters. As in 1215, baronial discontent in England was given direction by some churchmen, including the head of the Franciscan order in England. Many ecclesiastical leaders felt neglected, deprived, and mistreated by the Roman curia, which had struck bargains with the king for the taxation of the clergy and which filled up lucrative offices in the English church with Italians.

The barons and the discontented churchmen were inspired by an incipient nationalist feeling which took the form of both xenophobia and a greater emphasis on the need to control the royal government by the representatives of the community of the realm. But the magnates alone could no longer presume to speak for the whole country. The lesser nobility, the knights of the shire (or the gentry, as they were called in later centuries), were now taking the leading part in the administration and taxation of the shire. They were becoming a distinct group, or estate, in the realm, and the great barons could no longer claim to represent them. Similarly, the burgesses, particularly in London, made distinctive commercial contributions to the life of the country. Although their legal and social status was still inferior to that of landholders, it was useful because of their wealth to associate them with the baronial movement. In 1265 the leader of the barons, probably with the advice of his Franciscan friends, summoned representatives of the knights of the shire and the burgesses for a meeting of the great council of the realm, which heretofore had been attended exclusively by the lay and ecclesiastical magnates. This was the first joint assembly of the groups who, by the end of the thirteenth century, were regularly coming together in those occasional meetings of the great council of the realm called "parliaments." In 1265 the knights and burgesses were summoned merely for propaganda purposes, but the fact that they were invited at all indicates a new consciousness on the part of the barons that they could not themselves speak for the whole community of the realm. The baronial constitutional doctrine was that, in matters that concerned the whole realm—taxation, legislation, foreign policy—the king had to act with the consent of the whole realm, and the knights and burgesses were summoned to give verisimilitude to this view.

Representative institutions were common all over western Europe in the thirteenth century. They were used in provincial meetings of magnates in France, in the Spanish Cortes, or assembly of estates, and in town government. It has been suggested that this development was the result of the dissemination of the Roman-law idea of proctorship and attorneyship. England was the country in Europe in which representative institutions, beginning in the 1260's, played their most important role in political life; yet England was precisely the country which remained outside the area of Roman-law influence. The English judges before the end of the thirteenth century were mostly churchmen who were familiar with civil and canon law, and it is possible that the idea of representation filtered into the realm through these legists. But while the idea of attorneyship may have helped to give more formal shape to English representation, it is apparent that this institution had strong indigenous roots in England. In the workings of the common law the grand jury was supposed to speak for the whole "country" of the shire, and juries brought the record of cases from shire to central royal courts and similarly represented the county before the royal judges. A meeting of the great council of the realm was technically an expanded meeting of the *curia regis*. Hence, when the baronial leaders in 1265 wanted to hold an augmented meeting of the great council, they had both the idea and the experience of representation in the workings of the common law ready to hand. A parliament in the thirteenth century was a special meeting of the royal court to deal with great matters of state, and to it could be summoned representatives of the knights of the shire and of the burgesses, too, in order to use this grand occasion for gaining the approval of all groups within the community of the realm for the policy of the central government.

The leader of the barons in 1265 was Simon de Montfort, a son of the French lord of the same name who had led the Albigensian crusade. Simon had become an English earl by inheritance through his grandmother, he married the king's sister, and his intelligence, ability, and friendship with the Franciscans qualified him to be the leader of the baronial movement. Many of the other magnates, however, lacked his superior qualities, and once they had gained control of the central administration, they found the work hard and boring. The baronial movement therefore began to break up almost on the morrow of its victory, as several of the magnates turned away from the affairs of the central government to pursue more private interests. In 1265 a royal army led by Henry III's heir, Edward, defeated and killed Simon de Montfort, and Henry regained control of his administration. His troubles, however, had constituted a salutary lesson to his son, who came to the throne as Edward I in 1272. Edward had seen what failure as a military leader and servility to Rome had done to ruin his father. He also had become conscious of the corporate and national feelings of the country, and he determined to channel these attitudes toward the reconstruction of royal authority in England.

In the half century after Innocent III the papacy had enjoyed the unfailing devotion and loyalty of the English king, which stood in sharp contrast with Anglo-papal relations during the previous hundred and fifty years. But the curia was disappointed to discover that this great advantage was in large part rendered nugatory by the peculiar internal conditions of England, in which all groups in society, including many of the churchmen, wanted the great limitation of royal authority. The pope's relations with the empire during this period differed in almost every way. In this direction the curia had to struggle against an extremely able enemy in the person of an emperor who brought back the terrifying days of Henry VI. This struggle terminated in the most complete victory over monarchy which the medieval papacy ever attained.

The settlement of the imperial problem which Innocent III had regarded as definitive did not last very long. He had given Frederick II (1215–1250) the imperial crown upon the condition that he would abdicate his kingdom of Sicily when he gained the full recognition of the German princes. This was achieved in 1218 when Otto IV, who had been Innocent's original candidate for the German throne, finally died. But Frederick had no intention of giving up Naples and Sicily, which were the real strongholds of his power. He was, in fact, completely uninterested in Germany, and he visited it only to make sweeping concessions to the German princes, bishops, and towns, recognizing their full territorial sovereignty and completely undoing what was left of the centralizing work of Frederick Barbarossa and Henry VI. Frederick was an Italian, and he wanted to make himself the ruler of all of Italy, bringing the great cities of the north, which had successfully resisted his grandfather, under his full domination. He was vague about whether he would recognize the integrity of the papal states, and the Roman curia by the middle of the 1220's found itself again facing the prospect of the papacy being swallowed up in a Hohenstaufen Italy.

Frederick claimed that his aim of conquering northern Italy would not endanger the independence of the papacy, and he may have been sincere in this profession. But the Roman curia did not intend to put it to an empirical test, for Frederick was a strange man, the "wonder of the world" who seemed to stand outside the moral order of his day. He had been raised as an orphan in Sicily by various princes, and he had been badly treated as a youth. Innocent III had been his official guardian, but the pope had done little to protect the personal welfare of his ward. Frederick grew up to be a handsome and extremely talented man: a great soldier, a patron of the arts and sciences, the author of a formidable treatise on falconry. But he was a megalomaniac who considered himself beyond the ethical standards of Latin Christianity. It is entirely appropriate that Frederick was idolized by the Nazis in the 1920's and 30's, and that the most popular and probably best modern biography of him, published in Germany in 1927, carries a swastika on its cover. Frederick II was a sort of intellectual Fascist, a man of learning and fastidious tastes but a brute and a bully nevertheless. The organization and atmosphere of his court and administration were conditioned by oriental despotism. He had been strongly influenced by Arabs and Greeks, who lived in great numbers in his kingdom, and the flattery and subservience with which rulers were traditionally greeted in the Moslem countries went to his head. Frederick not only envisioned himself as the reincarnation of the

Roman emperors, but as a leader of messianic qualities. He and his court propagandists did not refrain from the sacrilege of drawing parallels between Frederick's life and that of Christ.

Given these attitudes, personality, and resources, Frederick was bound to be a formidable enemy, and the papacy, after moving slowly for two decades, by the 1240's had been plunged into a maelstrom of violence in its attempts to deal with him. The initial skirmishing between Frederick and the papacy was on a peripheral matter and was not free from elements of farce. In order to gain Innocent III's support, Frederick had taken the cross, but he was reluctant to carry out his vow because he was eager to inaugurate his campaign in northern Italy. Finally, in 1227, he actually did go to the Holy Land while he was under excommunication from Rome for previous failure to fulfill his crusading vows. He merely went through the motions of fighting the Moslems and then hurried back to southern Italy, where a papal army had invaded his lands, although with little success. A truce was patched up between the emperor and the pope, but it broke down after Frederick won a great victory over the Lombard League in 1239, and his mastery of the whole peninsula became a grim possibility. The Italian cities were no longer as united against imperial domination as they had been in Frederick Barbarossa's time. In many cities there were oligarchic families who were Ghibellines, as the pro-imperial party in the Italian cities was called. Faced with this danger, Gregory IX put to work all the resources which the papacy commanded. He excommunicated the emperor and denounced him as a heretic, for which there was plausible grounds, and he summoned a church council in Rome to give greater effect to this denunciation. An emperor who regarded himself as standing beyond good and evil was not one to be greatly worried by religious sanctions. He commanded his admiral to sink or capture many of the ships bringing churchmen to Rome from other parts of Europe. This monstrous act convinced the papacy that only the most extreme measures would succeed against Frederick. In 1245 Innocent IV held a council at Lyons, on safe ground just outside the border of Louis IX's kingdom, and preached a crusade against the emperor. This was a departure from the original idea of a crusade, but it was not quite, as it has sometimes been called, "a political crusade." Frederick had murdered churchmen and offended the moral sensibility of Christendom, and his personal beliefs were certainly very close to heresy if they were not, indeed, outside the Christian faith altogether. Innocent IV's preaching of a crusade against Frederick was an extreme measure, but under the circumstances there appeared to be no alternative, and it could be doctrinally justified.

It was one thing, however, to declare a crusade against Frederick; it was another to get any important ruler in Europe to risk his armies against the emperor, who controlled a great part of the resources of Italy. In the remaining five years of Frederick's life the crusade against him was largely a desultory affair, for the most part a propaganda war. When the superman of the thirteenth century finally passed from the scene in 1250, the papacy determined to continue the crusade and make it into a war against the whole Hohenstaufen family in order that such a monster as Frederick should never again arise to threaten the vicar of Christ. Frederick's only legitimate son, Conrad IV (1250-1254), put up a very stiff resistance, however. His premature death, leaving only a child as his heir, terminated the Hohenstaufen line on the imperial throne. There was an unseemly squabble for a few decades among the German princes and various other European rulers who also offered themselves as candidates for the elective German throne. The interregnum was finally terminated in 1273 with the election of count Rudolph of Hapsburg as king. He was a minor prince with modest ambitions. For all practical purposes Germany during the next two centuries was to consist of a variety of independent states.

In Sicily the Hohenstaufen line was perpetuated by Frederick II's illegitimate son Manfred (1254-1266), who turned out to be as able a leader as his father. Finally, the papacy, in desperation, offered the Sicilian crown to the brother of Louis IX, Charles of Anjou, who arrived in Italy with a formidable army and in a swift campaign defeated and killed Manfred, the last of the Hohenstaufen rulers in Sicily. Two years later, in 1268, Conrad IV's young son Conradin appeared in southern Italy with a small army, which was easily routed by the new French ruler. Conradin was captured and, with papal permission, publicly executed in Naples.

The papal struggle against Frederick II and the last of the Hohenstaufens is significant in several ways. In the first place, it ended with a dramatic and total victory which demonstrated the power of the papacy to destroy a monarchy which violated the moral law and flouted the supremacy of the church. In this respect it confirmed political Thomism by seeming to demonstrate that even the most powerful of royal families which challenged the vicar of Christ would go down to defeat before the combined spiritual and material swords, which, in accordance with the Gelasian dotcrine, were both ultimately in the hands of the pope. But some men could draw another implication from the same series of events. For twenty-five years a king had withstood every kind of weapon at the disposal of the papacy. Was, after all, the imposing structure of papal monarchy which Innocent III and his successors had created vulnerable to royal power? The third consequence of the struggle between empire and papacy in the thirteenth century was the injection of a new attitude of reckless violence into contemporary life which began the poisoning of the moral atmosphere of Europe. First the emperor and then also the pope had used the most extreme and morally dubious methods, which even their most eager partisans had difficulty in justifying. The emperor had murdered bishops, and the pope had hunted down Frederick's descendants to the man and had exercised a blood vengeance on the last youthful remnant of the house of Hohenstaufen. As is often the case in long and desperate wars, the defender, in his harassed struggle for survival, came to employ the ruthless methods of the aggressor.

The designation by the papacy of Charles of Anjou as ruler of southern Italy and Sicily was the second boon which the Roman Curia gave to its ally, the French monarchy, in the thirteenth century. The first had been the gift of nearly all of southern France, which was a consequence of Innocent III's Albigensian crusade. The latter event was the greatest turning point in the history of the Capetian monarchy. Philip Augustus, by his own efforts, had made himself the ruler of northern France, but without the papal crusade against Languedoc it would have been an enormous and probably impossible task for the Capetians to conquer the wealthiest and most thickly populated part of France. Philip had not participated in the crusade itself, but the need for royal leadership arose in 1218 when the leader of the northern barons who were carving out fiefs for themselves in Languedoc, the elder Simon de Montfort, was killed and the force of the crusading movement momentarily faltered. The nobility of southern France, who were now fighting more for personal and national reasons than for religious ones, made their last important stand. This brought into the war prince Louis, heir to the French throne, whose army immediately carried out an atrocious massacre in one of the southern cities. During his short reign as Louis VIII, from 1223 to 1226, this fierce warrior inaugurated the incorporation of the southern provinces under the French crown. The Dominican inquisitors and the French seneschals arrived together, and in the following quarter of a century destroyed whatever was left of the independent spirit of the once great culture of southern France. In 1249 a brother of the French king became the count of Toulouse, and the Capetian monarchy, which a century before had not even been strong in the Île-de-France, fulfilled its self-appointed destiny of extending to the Mediterranean.

The last opportunity for the French feudatories in the thirteenth century to stop the advance of Capetian power came during the early years of the reign of Louis IX (1226–1270), when the king was still a minor and the government was under the regency of his mother, Blanche of Castile, the first of that incomparable breed of Spanish princesses who influenced the political life of Europe over the following five centuries. The young Henry

III of England joined the rebellious dukes and counts of the north of France in a feeble attempt to undo the work of the previous half century. They were no match for Blanche and her son. For his pains Henry lost more French territory, and, with the exception of the wild duke of Brittany, the French princes, including the leader of the rebellion, the courtly count of Champagne, demonstrated that even when they had the Capetians at a disadvantage, they did not have the will to stem the advance of royal power.

The saintly mien of Louis IX was what the royal government needed during the following half century to develop its institutions and to entrench its control over the remaining pockets of feudal power in both north and south. By the middle of the thirteenth century the French *curia regis* had begun to differentiate into distinct financial and legal branches. Out of the latter developed the Parlement of Paris; it consisted of a professional judiciary which encouraged appeals from all over the realm, thereby extending royal legal jurisdiction and further diminishing the importance of baronial courts. The Parlement similarly asserted its superiority over ecclesiastical courts. The royal bureaucrats also worked hard to decrease the autonomy of the French towns, whose number and wealth had greatly increased as a result of the southern conquests. The dissatisfaction in many cities with the narrow and corrupt oligarchies who dominated the communal governments gave the royal administration the pretext for intervention and closer subordination to the central authority. The characteristic personnel of the French bureaucracy, which had already made its appearance in the reign of Philip Augustus, was perpetuated as its responsibilies and size increased. It was a largely self-sustaining group of lawyers whose sole guiding principle was the expansion of that royal power with which they identified themselves and which they furthered by every legal subterfuge that their learning and ingenuity could devise. This astringent attitude was probably the only way to build the French state. The many provinces which had been rapidly appended to the French crown contained such an amalgam of provincial traditions, conflicting feudal jurisdictions, of local laws and customs, of episcopal and bourgeois privileges, that the only common rationale for constructing the semblance of a political entity was that right always ran with the king. A saint on the throne was the ideal moral façade behind which the guile and force of the royal clerks worked to create the most powerful despotism in Europe. The baron, the bishop, and the burgher, who experienced the incessant evaporation of their old privileges, could always feel comforted by the fact that St. Louis was sitting under an oak tree and dispensing justice. Did the king ordain or even understand what his ministers were doing? It appears that he was by no means entirely a figurehead. He sent out "investigators," among whom Franciscan friars were prominent, to find out what his *baillis* and their assistants were doing in his name and to make a record of the complaints of the people they ruled. These investigations turned up almost every kind of subtle chicanery and ruthless severity known to human ingenuity. St. Louis appears to have sympathized with his subjects, but the methods of the royal servants did not change.

If the expansion of Capetian power over the whole realm was largely the work of harsh *magistri* over whom St. Louis appears not to have exercised a very close supervision, his personal direction of royal policy toward the church and the papacy is readily apparent. It was a policy which, while it allied the French government ever more closely with the Roman curia, by no means made the French monarchy the deferential servant of Rome. Louis IX's relative, Henry III of England, was far more pliable in his relations with the papacy. In no instance did St. Louis ever sacrifice the interests of the French monarchy in his ecclesiastical policy. He strongly asserted the rights of jurisdiction of the French crown over the clergy. He refused to help bishops confiscate the property of barons who had been excommunicated. He spoke sharply to prominent members of the higher clergy whom he regarded as having failed to fulfill the duties of their office. For his crusade against Egypt he made heavy demands for financial support from the pope and the French church. He did not answer Innocent IV's appeal for a crusade against Frederick II. It was an ominous sign of St. Louis' conception of church-state relations that he was made uneasy by this use of the crusading ideal to attack a duly constituted monarch. He even protested against papal taxation of the French clergy to support the crusade. He allowed his brother to invade southern Italy only after obtaining his own terms for such a venture. The pope who conceded to Charles of Anjou full rights over what had been Frederick II's kingdom was a Frenchman, as was his immediate predecessor on the papal throne. By the end of Louis' reign there was a strong French party among the cardinals, who inevitably looked to Paris for leadership.

The Angevin domination of southern Italy was the concluding stage in the rise of French power in Europe, which had begun with Philip Augustus' conquest of Normandy in 1204. A change of fundamental importance had by 1270 taken place in the European balance of power. The German monarchy had been totally eliminated as a factor in European politics. Its place was taken by the old ally of the papacy, the Capetian kingdom. The papacy, who had so long fought to keep the German emperor out of Italy, had eagerly established the brother of the most powerful king in Europe in the Italian realm in place of the hated Hohenstaufens.

With the resources of the wealthiest state in Europe, the loyalty of the French clergy, a French stronghold in Sicily, and with a French party in the college of cardinals itself, the Capetian ruler had the power to dominate the papacy more thoroughly than any king since the middle of the eleventh century. But in 1270 the papacy was not concerned about its potential vulnerability. On the contrary, it led the universal acclaim for a king who seemed the perfect Christian monarch. There was no cause to fear a ruler who confirmed the Thomistic confidence in the moral quality of the state.

III. *The Interests of Society*

While the intellectual, ecclesiastical, and political leaders of thirteenth-century Europe sought to meet the challenge of twelfth-century creativity, lord, burgher, and peasant also sought to adjust as best they could their private interests and destinies to social change. Until very recently, it was easy for historians to describe the pattern of the social and economic order of the thirteenth century. They wrote about the life of *the* noble, *the* medieval city, *the* manor. Henri Pirenne was the most typical and the best of this kind of older social historian of the middle ages. This approach was based upon a very limited amount of research and information and a great deal of imaginative extrapolation of ideal social types. During the last two or three decades the tendency in medieval social history has been away from broad generalizations and toward intensive regional and local studies. This has been mainly the work of French scholars inspired by Marc Bloch. As is the case with the general development of sociology in the twentieth century, the movement has been away from the bold speculation about ideal social types toward the intensive accumulation of data, from a broad horizontal view of the whole structure of medieval society toward vertical, empirical soundings into the details of economic and social life in a given region, county, or town. The major consequence of this kind of intensive and specific research has been to bring into question the old stereotyped patterns and to give the impression of the enormous variety and heterogeneity of medieval social life. The old generalizations have been brought into question, and new ones have been very slow in making their appearance. It is not yet certain how much of this apparent variety and heterogeneity is simply the result of the extremely empirical methodology currently fashionable—whether the attack on the validity of the pattern of medieval economy and society built up by the older historians may not be largely due to a reluctance to generalize and a penchant for emphasizing minor differences rather than more important similarities. The recent work on thirteenth-century society has, however, at least had the salutary effects of cautioning against the facile creation of stereotypes and of demonstrating the existence of strong regional differences in the lives of the lord, burgher, and peasant.

All classes and groups in all regions of thirteenth-century Europe found their lives conditioned by four common factors. The first was a great increase in social control due to the expansion of government and of legal institutions. Second, a transition was under way from a society based on status to one based on money. Birth still counted a very great deal in determining a man's life; it was hard in many parts of Europe for even the wealthiest burgher to enjoy certain privileges which the son of a lord took for granted. But on the other hand, status was not enough for a happy and secure life. No matter how impressive a man's pedigree might be, bad financial management resulted in hard times. The third factor was related to the second. The first seven or eight decades of the thirteenth century marked the final stage in a long period of boom, population growth, and inflation which had characterized the European economy since the middle of the tenth century, and this general economic condition profoundly affected the interests of all groups in society. Finally, the thirteenth century was the age of the long peace, which would not be experienced again for many centuries, perhaps not in the same degree until the period between 1815 and 1914. From the Battle of Bouvines in 1214 until the beginning of the long and ruinous struggle between England and France in the 1290's there was no major war in western Europe, and this condition of peace had important and varying consequences for the classes of society.

Neither in government nor in economy nor in war were the nobility, the landed class descended from the feudal lords of the tenth century, as important as they had been before 1100. But they were still, taking everything into account, easily the dominant class in society, a position they were to retain in Europe until the nineteenth century. There was a growing heterogeneity in the life and organization of the nobility, both horizontally and vertically. It is possible to establish definite regional types. In Italy and southern France the nobility was marked by its high degree of urbanization and involvement in city life. The German lords were, as a group, closer to the early-medieval warrior class: the disintegration of Germany into a maze of petty principalities gave the German nobility many opportunities for acting independently and serving in local wars. Urbanization had had no appreciable effect on the landed classes of northern France and England. They held themselves completely aloof from the burgher class, whom they condemned as social inferiors. There was a growing polarization at work among the nobility between the great aristocrats and those of more modest means. The former were becoming a closed caste of superior blood and self-conscious mores and rituals, while the latter were becoming local gentlemen, in many cases as rustic and ignorant as the peasants among whom they lived.

The thirteenth-century lord was circumscribed, especially in England and France, by ever more efficient systems of government, law, and taxation. He was a very different person from the thugs of the tenth century, and even from most of the men who fought in the first crusade. This was, of course, especially true of the upper strata of the nobility. They frequently had a limited amount of literacy and education—enough to write letters in the vernacular and read chivalric romances or little treatises on the life of a gentleman or estate management. Most of this noble literature was written in French, which had become the international language of the aristocracy as it was to remain until the twentieth century. At least three members of the thirteenth-century French nobility were highly literate and sophisticated men. William de Lorris wrote the first half of the *Romance of the Rose,* a sort of encyclopedia of romantic allegory which was very popular with aristocratic readers and is still regarded by some people as a great work of literature. Another French nobleman, Villehardouin, wrote a graphic and honest account of the ill-fated fourth crusade, in which he was a participant. Joinville's *Life of St. Louis* is a personal memoir by an intimate of the great king. In some respects it is almost as idealized as previous medieval royal biographies written by ecclesiastics, but it presents a large number of circumstantial details, and it is still the only biography of Louis IX worth reading. A minor lord of mid-thirteenth century England, Sir Walter of Henley, produced a treatise on estate management for the benefit of his son. It is well organized and full of common sense about crops, sheep raising, and manorial administration. The thirteenth-century lords were educated at home for the most part. But some of the urbanized nobility of northern Italy and southern France received a university education and became civil lawyers. From the end of the thirteenth century in England it became fashionable for county families to send their sons to the schools of common law in London, called the Inns of Court, to obtain a rudimentary knowledge of law, which would later stand them in good stead in their almost incessant lawsuits over proprietary rights. Many younger sons of the nobility, of course, were destined for the church and were sent to the universities; a few became great scholars and professors.

Fighting was the original *raison d'être* of the nobility, but during the long peace of the thirteenth century there were limited opportunities inside Europe for the exhibition of military skill. A slow revolution was taking place in military life. The cavalryman, the armored knight on horseback, was becoming a more and more expensive commodity as plate armor formed an increasing proportion of his equipment. Consequently, the knight who could afford to equip himself was very much in demand. When a king had to fit out a whole army, he found it a great drain on his resources. As a result, the practice of calling out the feudal vassals declined and the hiring of professional mercenaries increased. At the beginning of the thirteenth century the heavily armored knight was the almost exclusive staple of warfare. By the end of the century, while the knight was still the backbone of any army, his strategic importance was being challenged by the increased use of massed infantry. The appearance of new weapons began the slow process of obsolescence which steadily diminished the value of the knight over the following two centuries. Flemish and Swiss mercenaries showed in the late decades of the century that well-disciplined peasants armed with pikes could break a feudal charge. In the thirteenth century it was also demonstrated that armor could be penetrated by a metal bolt fired from a crossbow. All over the continent military leaders added contingents of crossbowmen to their armies. The great weakness of the crossbow, however, was that it had to be mechanically loaded and that once the crossbowman had "shot his bolt," he was usually out of the battle; the effect of this terrifying new weapon, in some ways the ancestor of the gun, was also diminished by its short range and poor accuracy. In the mid-thirteenth century English armies, fighting in Wales, came up against the longbow, a rapid-fire and long-range weapon which they adapted for their own use against the French in the fourteenth century. The shaft fired from the longbow did not often penetrate armor, but it made possible a massive salvo which created havoc among knights charging into battle. In response to these changes in military technology armor became heavier and horses larger, but this did not maintain the previous exclusive military importance of the knight. By the end of the thirteenth century he was rendered immobile, after being thrown from his horse, by the sheer weight of his armor.

While a decline was under way in the military importance of the knight, it was still unthinkable to go to war without having the nobility as officers. The nobility, in spite of technological change, maintained their stranglehold on war because of social traditions and values. The old feudal sub-vassals were becoming obsolete; it was a risky proposition to go to war with an army composed of men who owed only forty days' service a year and who in any case might be ill-equipped and ill-trained. The mercenary had, by the middle of the thirteenth century, become the staple unit in European military life. But it was the more prominent nobility whom the king commissioned to raise and equip his mercenary contingents. Because of the long peace of the thirteenth century, however, there was not any great demand for aristocratic services of this kind before the 1290's, a situation which the aristocrat found frustrating and inhibiting. He knew a little bit about a great many things—government, law, literature, agriculture—but only in warfare was he an expert.

The inability of the greater nobility of the thirteenth century to demonstrate their military superiority over other groups in society encouraged them to find social and ceremonial expressions of their status. By the end of the thirteenth century the aristocracy had become a closed, self-conscious class with specific conventions and rituals in which the rustic lords and common knights could not participate. A whole science of heraldry and genealogy developed, expressing the belief that nobility was a matter of blood and not of service. The ritual of knighthood and chivalry became steadily more elaborate, and a code of gentility more universal, among the great lords. The boy of gentle birth was sent off at the age of seven or eight to be a page in the household of a great aristocrat, where he was given his rudimentary education. Seven years later he became a squire and was trained in arms, and finally, if he could afford the expense, he "took on him the order of knighthood" in a great ceremony during which he made chivalric vows and was dubbed by the great lord. These and similar rituals, which in the popular mind have been so often associated with feudalism, were actually the products of its declining stage. They are the means by which an old ruling class, whose importance in society is atrophying, attempts to preserve its former status, substituting class exclusiveness for social utility.

The rise in the population curve and the inflationary cycle which prevailed during most of the thirteenth century made it a good period for landlords. However, the landed classes were plagued by personal indebtedness, and this was particularly true among the great nobles. The maintenance of an aristocratic household and the extravagant style of living expected of a great lord was beyond even his lavish resources in many cases. In a sense, monarchy corrupted the nobility. The king had great means, he could use income from taxation as well as his private estates to maintain his household, and he was able to put on a splendid show. The nobility ran into debt trying to imitate the monarchy, and lesser lords, imitating the great aristocrats, ruined themselves trying to keep up establishments which were beyond their means. Another cause for the economic troubles of the nobility was simply poor management of their resources. Some of them were very good at husbandry, but most of the great nobility were too caught up in the diurnal round of court and tournament to give close attention to how their stewards were maintaining their vast holdings. It seems probable that many of the hard-pressed nobility of the thirteenth century were mining their already unfertilized and nearly exhausted lands in a desperate effort to meet their financial obligations. This expedient only intensified their economic problems. By the end of the thirteenth century, in England, Germany, and France, once fertile agricultural lands had been played out and could no longer be cultivated.

The political interests of the thirteenth-century nobility varied greatly from country to country. In Italy the political life of the great aristocracy was inevitably involved with urban development. When, at the end of the thirteenth century, the burghers discovered that they could not effectively administer their own governments, they were often willing to pay the price of calling in members of the nobility and accepting them as despots in order to achieve a modicum of peace and order. This is the origin of the famous "Renaissance princes." The political disintegration of Germany provided many opportunities for the advancement of great and even petty lords. There was always some small court where an intelligent, literate, and aggressive nobleman of even modest means could find an important place. This remained the prevailing political and social condition of Germany until the nineteenth century. In France and in England the lives of the nobility were more and more dominated by the institutions of national monarchy. The thirteenth-century French nobility found their feudal jurisdictions evaporating and themselves circumscribed at every turn by the relentless royal administration. But royal taxation was not heavy, and the crown established a greatly increased measure of peace, order, and security which those lords less proficient in warfare found advantageous to their interests. For the more aggressive kind of thirteenth-century French nobleman there were outlets for his energy, particularly the Albigensian crusade and the conquest of Sicily. Because of the size and provincial traditions of the country, the French aristocracy never became a politically homogeneous group. It was the royal government that was able to envision the unity of the realm, but the nobility continued to think of themselves as Normans, Bretons, Burgundians, etc. There were no general assemblies of the French nobility until the first meeting of the Estates General in the early fourteenth century, and this was merely a propaganda show and not the beginning of an effective institution. The only important assemblies of the French nobility were local, provincial, and regional. The Capetian government did not bring the nobility together to obtain their consent to taxation; it dealt with them in this fragmented way, which was a reflection of the fact that the nobility tended to think in terms of their own problems rather than of the realm. The situation in England was very different. Partly because it was a much smaller country and partly because of the much longer tradition of the unity and homogeneity of royal power and common law over the whole realm, and partly also because the greater nobles frequently held estates in two or even more counties, the English nobility thought of themselves not so much as the men of Kent or Devon or Yorkshire but as the leaders of the community of the whole realm. From the time of the Norman conquest they had been summoned from every corner of the kingdom to attend great meetings of the *curia regis,* and this tradition naturally led to advice and common consent on taxation and legislation by the higher nobility in the thirteenth century. The English aristocracy knew much more about the workings of royal government than members of the same class across the channel, and this in part accounted for their attempts to take over the direction of the royal administration in the reign of Henry III.

The bourgeois of England and northern France were embittered by the continued domination of the nobility in society and by the continued exclusive political and legal privileges of the great lords. Their literature is marked by cynical and critical pictures of the nobility and churchmen who enjoyed the advantages of traditional status which, in bourgeois eyes, they did not deserve. Thinly disguised allegories, such as the extremely popular fables concerned with Reynard the Fox, bitterly vented the burghers' feeling that they had been ill used. Their outlook on life was necessarily more rational and less romanticized than that which prevailed in chivalric literature. This rationalism and cynicism distinguishes the second part of the *Romance of the Rose,* written by Jean de Meun, a university-educated French bourgeois, from the courtly idealism of the earlier part of the work. The thirteenth-century bourgeois generally could not afford to take a romantic view of life; he had to depend on his own talents and energy to avoid helpless poverty. The walls of the medieval town enclosed a society which was extremely competitive, in spite of the efforts made by the old craft guilds to control economic life, and in which there was very little charity for the weak and the incompetent. Yet the same merchant or craftsman who was critical, skeptical, and without illusion was intensely pious and emotional in his religious attitudes. This was the means of escape from the restraint and disappointments of urban life. The burgher supported the construction of great municipal churches, and he was intensely devoted to the religious leadership of the Franciscan friars. He stood for hours listening to the friars' harangues or watching miracle and morality plays, whose leading characters and plots were based on Biblical stories. He made crude jokes about the clergy, but heaven and hell were extremely real and concretized places for him. The crowded and unsalubrious medieval cities, and the political and legal limitations against which the burgher struggled, made for repressed people who oscillated between the extremes of cynicism and religious devotion.

During the thirteenth century there was a continued increase in urban wealth and institutions, but these brought in their wake new problems to plague bourgeois life. In the cities of Flanders and in northern Italy, which were engaged in large-scale production and international trade in woolen textiles, there was an increasing polarization of wealth and the intensification of a class struggle. In every guild there was hard feeling between the masters who controlled the corporation and the subordinate journeymen and apprentices. There was hostility between the wealthier guilds devoted to the international cloth trade and the more ordinary guilds who produced goods for local consumption. In the Flemish textile cities such as Ghent and in the Italian industrial centers, particularly Florence, a large proletariat had emerged by the thirteenth century. At the other end of the social scale were great entrepreneurial oligarchs who endeavored to dominate the town governments and to secure regulations suitable to their own interests, and finally there was a bitter struggle for power among these ruling families. The larger the medieval city, the more bitter became its class and political struggles. The atmosphere was one of continual distrust and mutual hatred.

The bourgeois of the thirteenth century made great progress in strictly economic development. The volume of trade in the Mediterranean, in the Baltic, and with the middle east, central Asia, and Russia was steadily increased. The merchants of northern Italy used their experience in international exchange to develop banking institutions, and they became even wealthier as the financial agents of the papacy. In the middle of the thirteenth century Europe revived extensive use of gold coinage in international trade, and the gold florin first minted in 1252 to serve the needs of Florentine merchants became a monetary standard for Europe. The burghers achieved a very high level of general literacy, and this was reflected not only in belletristic literature, first in France and then in Italy, but also in the development of the professional notary to draft the myriad of documents necessary in a highly literate and commercial society.

But the burghers could not solve their political problems, and the cities suffered from continual internal instability. Because the cities were so faction- and class-ridden, their electoral systems became extremely indirect; nobody trusted anybody else to cast an honest vote. By the end of the thirteenth century many of the Italian towns were giving up their communal freedom, which they had struggled for centuries to obtain, a development which has been much bemoaned by modern liberal historians. Political power was surrendered by the burghers to a *podestà*, a dictator who came

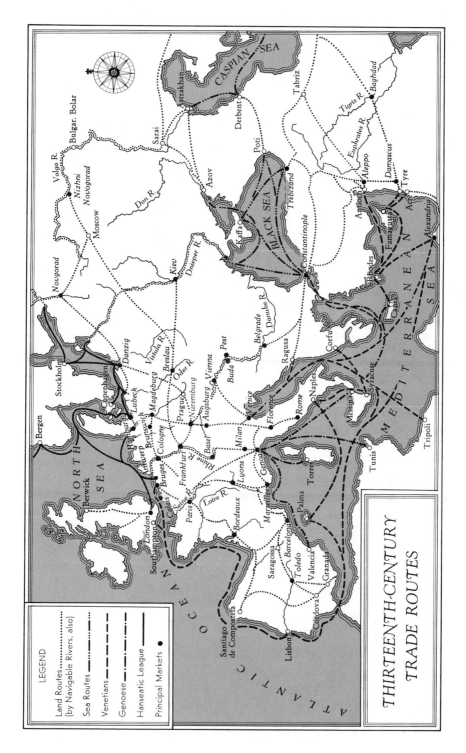

THIRTEENTH-CENTURY
TRADE ROUTES

LEGEND

Land Routes...............
(by Navigable Rivers, also)

Sea Routes ·—·—·—·

Venetians ——————

Genoese —··—··—··—

Hanseatic League ————

Principal Markets ●

497

from the ranks of the local aristocracy and whose family became hereditary princes in the wealthy commercial centers.

In some parts of Europe the communes maintained their independence. There were still "free cities" in the German Rhineland in the fourteenth century. The most outstanding group of independent communes were the German Baltic commercial cities who comprised the Hanseatic League. The north German merchants not only engaged in far-flung trade stretching from Russia to England, but they formed political and military alliances and fought Scandinavian kings for hegemony in the Baltic. Wherever there was strong royal power, the burghers had little political autonomy. The French towns in the thirteenth century, including some in the south and along the Rhine, which had enjoyed communal privileges, were brought under the expanding royal administration. In England the political and legal privileges of the bourgeois lagged behind those on the continent. The London merchants, until almost the end of the thirteenth century, were exasperated by the exchequer's insistence that their legal status was scarcely different from that of peasants on the royal demesne and that all burgesses were subject to arbitrary taxation.

One of the fundamenatl facts of thirteenth-century civilization was the failure of the industrial and commercial classes to make use of their economic and intellectual importance to achieve a measure of political leadership in society. By 1300 even the Italian communes were losing their political freedom. The governments of the emerging national monarchies were in the hands of the landed classes and university graduates, who, although in many cases of bourgeois provenance, had no interest save that of their royal masters. It was still kings, lords, churchmen, and scholars who were the leaders of European society. The economic importance of the bourgeois was not translated into political and social leadership until the late eighteenth and nineteenth centuries.

The largest class in medieval society, comprising certainly a majority of the total population, was mute. There is no thirteenth-century peasant literature, and it is only in the fourteenth century that there is any kind of writing which we can identify as representing the peasants' outlook. *Piers Plowman* was probably written by one of the poor English parish priests, who were themselves often drawn from the peasant class. Its anguished, bitter, and apocalyptic tone indicates that the peasant was very conscious of his exploitation by the ruling classes in society, and he was at the same time devoted to the teachings of the church, which had been brought to him by the spread of the parish system and the preaching of itinerant friars. We have no way of knowing for sure how typical of peasant attitudes are the opinions of William Langland, the author of *Piers Plowman.*

Economic historians tell us, from their study of manorial and legal records, that the economic condition of the peasants was improving in most parts of Europe in the thirteenth century, particularly in France and Germany. The combined impact of a money economy and the colonization movement allowed the peasants to escape from the servile dues and services of the old manorialism. Some carved out "new villages" from former wastelands, while others joined the movement to the eastern frontier, where the German lords gave them favorable terms of settlement. Those who remained in their old open-field villages were often able to reach an agreement with their usually hard-pressed lords to commute the old manorial services into money rents. Thus, in France and Germany the serf was becoming a small, independent farmer. He was still exploited and abused by the local lords, he was contemned by the bourgeois, he was ignored by prelates, but he was better off than he was two centuries before.

There appears to have been great horizontal and vertical differentiation in the status of the peasant. The English serfs were less successful in gaining manumission, probably because the English knights, or gentry, were rustic characters who stayed at home and gave more careful attention to management of their lands than did the French seigneurs; England was also a country less affected by capitalism than were France and western Germany. In Italy the peasantry suffered from the economic domination of the bourgeois capitalists, who bought up land and exploited them mercilessly. There was an extensive gradation within the peasant class itself— from those wealthy peasants with their own plows, animals, and farms, down to landless day laborers whose existence was always marginal.

The general amelioration in peasant conditions during the thirteenth century should not blind us to the fact that they were the "dark people" of medieval life. The peasant had little surcease from the endless course of birth, labor, and death. Because he did not have enough fodder to winter all of his livestock, he had to slaughter most of them in December. After he had gorged himself on his twelve-day Christmas feast, he did not have any fresh meat until the spring, and during many years the specter of starvation loomed over his filthy cottage. His major diversions were the Sunday-morning service given by a half-literate parish priest or the sermons of a wandering friar. Between this dumb brutish peasant, in whose dim and impenetrable mind a spark of intelligence only occasionally flickered, and the magnificent cathedrals of intellect which the schoolmen were building in not far-distant university towns there yawned almost the whole of human evolution.

Part Eight

Whoever works for the good of the state, works with right as his end.

—DANTE ALIGHIERI

Any Catholic is allowed to appeal the decision of an heretical pope.

—WILLIAM OF OCCAM

THE BREAKDOWN

Later Thirteenth and Early Fourteenth Centuries

Chapter Twenty-One

THE FAILURE OF THE
NEW CONSENSUS

I. *The Death Wish of Medieval Society*

In 1270 the ideal Christian monarch, Louis IX of France, went to his heavenly reward, to be followed two years later by Henry III of England, the compliant servant of the papacy. A new severity and intransigence crept into the policies of their successors during the next two decades. In 1272 the angelic doctor, Thomas Aquinas, also passed from the scene, and while his Dominican disciples at Paris continued to dominate the theology faculty of the university, they were hard pressed to defend the integration of revelation and Aristotelianism that Thomas had created. In 1277 the bishop of Paris, in a rash and ill-considered moment, published a condemnation of several propositions which he denounced as erroneous Averroism but which in some instances could be interpreted to cover some of the Thomistic teachings; it is apparent that this implication was fully intended. Some of the younger Franciscans at Oxford, over whom restraint had lapsed with the death of St. Bonaventura in 1274, took the condemnation of 1277 as the starting point for an attack on Thomism and began to move closer and closer to a radical nominalist position. In the 1270's, or shortly thereafter, the population growth and inflationary boom that had marked the European economy since the mid-tenth century petered out, and Europe north of the Alps slid into a long and baffling depression that lasted until the middle of the fifteenth century, bringing with it the social discontent and rebellion common to the deflationary phase of the business cycle.

These events distinguish the 1270's as the last great dividing line in medieval history. They inaugurated a catastrophic period of breakdown and violence which endured for half a century and did not fully run its course until the later fifteenth century. By 1325 the work of centuries had crashed in pieces, and both the intellectual and the moral order of medieval society had disintegrated. During this half century the French monarchy turned on its ally (and to some degree its creator), the medieval papacy, and simply assassinated it, destroying within a few years its prestige and power. The greatest minds of the half century that followed the death of Thomas Aquinas not only revolted against the ordered intellectual world he had created; they attacked the authority of the church and the hierarchy and adored the state as the only leader of European society. By 1325 the whirlwind of popular heresy which had apparently been stilled in the mid-thirteenth century was again sweeping over Europe. Medieval civilization received its mortal wound between 1270 and 1325, and there remained only the long death agony of chaos and malaise during the next hundred and fifty years.

Why did medieval civilization, which had been the creative work of so many centuries, disintegrate so suddenly and quickly? It is possible to attempt a very empirical answer: the errors in papal policy, the overriding ambitions of certain kings, the intellectual vagaries of certain outstanding minds. If St. Louis and St. Thomas were still dominating the medieval political and intellectual worlds, this disaster would never have happened! But the fact is that the leaders of medieval society, in the half century after 1270, had different aims and different methods from those of their immediate predecessors. They were not less able than the angelic doctor and the saintly king, but they wanted to act in different ways. The Cleopatra's-nose approach merely avoids the great question of history: why did the leaders of society in a given period choose the values and the course of action they did? Why did the leaders of European society in 1300 differ so strongly in their attitudes from the great generation of the mid-thirteenth century?

It is possible to give a deterministic answer based on the proposition that civilizations are organisms which pass through a life cycle and then perish. Every civilization experiences a birth, youth, maturity, old age, and death, the philosophers of the ancient world believed—or as Spengler and many other twentieth-century writers have expressed it, a spring, summer, autumn, and winter. A civilization does indeed appear to be an organism which runs its course and then is gone, although it may have a powerful impact on the ideas and institutions of later civilizations and, through its legacy, become immortal. The deterministic interpretation of history is at fault in its denial of human freedom. It is not to be thought that humanity lacks the power to control its own destiny, and to perpetuate a civilization which human creativity has brought into existence. The deterministic approach to history is plausible, but it offends against morality.

A civilization, like a human being, has a will to live, but it may also arrive at the neurotic condition of having a will to die. Medieval civilization in the half century after 1270, by its violence, extremism, and suicidal destruction of its fundamental values, manifests such a will to destroy itself, just as in the early middle ages, against enormous material obstacles, it had exhibited a will to live. What was the origin of the neurotic death wish of medieval society? As is the case with the neuroses of individuals, it was the result of repression. The continual repression of difficult and insoluble problems may eventually reach a point where these become no longer conflicts which can be put aside, and the consequence is a sudden and debilitating breakdown. This is what happened to medieval civilization. The creativity of the twelfth century had posited certain conflicts of the most fundamental kind which have never been resolved in human society and thought: the conflict between revelation and science, the conflict between sacerdotal authority and the freedom of individual religious experience, the conflict between hierocratic authority and the sovereign state. During the first seven decades of the thirteenth century medieval civilization made the most strenuous efforts possible to resolve these conflicts. The result was a consensus which produced a momentary calm but did not end these conflicts.

The greatest work of thirteenth-century French literature, the second part of *The Romance of the Rose,* written in the late 1270's by a university-educated French bourgeois, Jean de Muen, demonstrates on every page that the peace of Innocent III and the compromise of Thomas Aquinas did not satisfy the intellectuals of his generation. The romantic idealism of the twelfth century has turned cold and sour: "So degenerate is all the world that it has put up love for sale." On all sides de Muen sees greed, corruption, and rottenness. Scholars and lawyers, he says, "sell their skill for cash." Although he was himself a bourgeois, de Muen saw no redemptive qualities in his own class. "No merchant ever lives at ease; he has for life enlisted in the war of gain, and never will acquire enough." De Muen has only contempt for the leadership of medieval society. Kings and princes have "brought despotism to pinch and rob the folk." On all sides he sees "bad divines who overrun the earth, preaching to gain favor, honor, wealth." The Franciscan ideal has also failed miserably. "Poverty . . . is unloved and vilified by all." In de Muen's eyes all the efforts to achieve a Christian commonwealth that were made in the twelfth and thirteenth centuries had proved futile. His poem heralds the frustration, bitterness, anger, and dismay of the late thirteenth century.

The men of the new generation of the later thirteenth century found it impossible to maintain the slender web of subtle compromise which the two previous generations had painfully constructed. The new world order which had been created in the early and middle thirteenth century was so finely balanced that they found it impossible to sustain. Nor was there any need to sustain it, because it had failed to provide for human happiness. They wanted to end the exhausting repression of conflict which had been built up from 1198 to 1270; they sought an aggressive breakthrough to a clear and affirmable extreme. They wanted science *or* revelation, personal piety *or* sacerdotalism, the sovereign state *or* hierocratic supremacy. They wanted to end the complexity, the subtleties, the compromises, the intricacies of medieval civilization. They wanted to affirm some fixed and identifiable extreme which could be a new starting-point for faith and love. Finding that the subtle balances and difficult compromises of the Thomist era had not rid society of greed and corruption, the generation, particularly the intellectuals among them, of the later thirteenth century seem to lay the blame for the moral failing of their society upon the Thomist synthesis itself. In the previous century and a half, so much had been studied, so much had been thought, so much had been felt, and yet human happiness and the Christian commonwealth had not been achieved. By adhering to one of the polarities, one of the extremes rather than to the center which had failed them, the men of the later thirteenth century hoped to find a new love and a new idealism. In their yearning for the simplicity of the extreme, they sought the death of medieval civilization, which had become an impossible burden, one they could no longer bear.

II. The Dissolution of the Medieval Thought-World

The Dominicans established Thomism as the official doctrine of their order in 1284. They sought to gain for it acceptance as the official theology of the church. They believed that Aquinas' system had solved the intellectual problems of the thirteenth century. St. Thomas, they claimed, had brought Aristotelianism, the best science known to man, into harmony with the truths of the Christian religion. He had vindicated the orthodox Christian faith at the bar of reason. He had shown that man stands at the head of the natural order and yet is in touch with the supernatural and that "the end of man is the contemplation of truth." Yet this imposing system did not satisfy the best minds of the rising generation. In both northern Italy and in England during the half century after Thomas' death the outstanding thinkers undermined and then openly attacked the Thomistic system and came forward with doctrines of a very different nature. They ended by separating science and revelation, by elevating the state outside and above the moral order as a law unto itself, by denying the foundations of hierocratic theory, and by reviving the teachings of twelfth-century popular heresy. In other words, they abandoned the cathedral of intellect of Thomist theology and brought about the dissolution of the medieval thought-world.

The beginnings of the revolt against Thomism can be seen in the ambiguous and many-sided thought of Dante Alighieri (1265–1321), the most famous name in medieval literature. Dante has often been depicted as the poet who put the *Summa Theologica* in verse, as a fervent disciple of Thomas Aquinas. There are plausible grounds for this view; undoubtedly Dante was heavily influenced by Thomistic doctrine. But he was also sympathetic to some of the views of the Averroists, and in his approach to political thought there is a new note of radical voluntarism which strongly contradicts Thomistic political doctrine. Dante was a man of prodigious learning and deep piety. But the radicalism of the north Italian communes is also manifested in his work. He was reaching out toward new intellectual horizons which were not yet clearly perceptible. He oscillated between the extremes of traditional medieval doctrine and audacious radicalism, signifying the dilemma of the new generation of medieval thinkers.

Dante was a Florentine who spent the last twenty years of his life in exile from his native city, which he loved deeply, as a consequence of one of those interminable political feuds which poisoned the life of the north Italian communes. He was the creator of the Italian vernacular as a literary language. He brought into Italian literature the romantic motifs which had prevailed in French poetry for over a century, and in his lyrics there is that same subtle intertwining of mundane and spiritual love upon which the French and German romances had already been built. He venerated Virgil and the great names of classic Latin literature and was a pioneer in uniting humanism with romanticism.

Dante's most ambitious work, *The Divine Comedy,* has generally been regarded as the greatest medieval poem. It is an allegorical epic based upon prodigious learning and almost incomparable literary craftsmanship. It has been viewed as the summation of medieval orthodox religious thought and also as a presentation in allegorical and poetical form of the chief tenets of Thomism. There is much to commend this interpretation. Dante describes how he was led on a journey from the depths of Hell, through Purgatory and Heaven, to the glory of the beatific vision. His three guides on this journey symbolize the three ascending stages of knowledge. Virgil takes

ITALY IN THE
EARLY FOURTEENTH CENTURY

PIED-MONT
Vercelli Milan
K.D.M.
MARCH OF TREVISO
MARCH OF FRIULI
Treviso
Asti
Verona
Padua
REPUBLIC
MONT-FERRAT
OF
Venice
OF VENICE
Genoa
ITALY
Ferrara
Savona
EMILIA
ROMANIOLA
Bologna
Ravenna
RAVENNA
Pisa Florence
DUCHY
MARCH
Ancona
OF
Arezzo
OF
DUCHY
Assisi OF ANCONA
OF
SPOLETO
TUSCANY
PAPAL STATES
CORSICA
ABRUZZI
PATRIMONIUM
Rome
K.D.M.
Ceprano
Benevento OF
Naples
Bari
Melfi APULIA Taranto
SARDINIA
NAPLES
ADRIATIC SEA
TYRRHENIAN SEA
CALABRIA
Palermo Messina
KDM. OF
SICILY
Syracuse
Tunis
MEDITERRANEAN SEA
TUNIS

him through the circles of Hell to the lower stages of Purgatory; the Roman poet whom Dante idolized is meant to represent reason, which by its own efforts can sufficiently educate men in the good life to escape damnation. Dante is guided through the higher stages of Purgatory and all but the highest circles of Heaven by a certain Beatrice. A woman of this name did play an important part in Dante's life, although they seldom met and she became the wife of a wealthy Florentine banker. She came to symbolize for Dante the romantic ideal of secular and spiritual love, and in *The Divine Comedy* she is meant to represent Grace or Divine Love, that is, revelation or the church, whose sacraments are the only way to salvation and admission to Heaven. Finally, to come face to face with the Divine Spirit, the guidance of St. Bernard, who symbolizes the mystical experience, is necessary. There is a rough parallel between this scheme of religious pilgrimage and Thomistic doctrine. At least St. Thomas and Dante are in agreement on the ability of reason to show men the rudiments of the good life and the necessity of the church for the fulfillment of this potentiality and the understanding of the higher truths. Dante's designation of Bernardine mysticism as the highest form of knowledge is derived from Franciscan teaching much more than from Dominican Thomism. Appropriately, St. Francis and St. Dominic appear in the same circle of Heaven, and the poem ends with a prayer to the Virgin.

There are. some aspects of *The Divine Comedy,* however, which are sharply at variance with its generally orthodox and traditional teaching. Siger of Brabant, the Averroist antagonist of St. Thomas Aquinas, turns up in Dante's Heaven. There are many expressions of hostility to the claims of the papacy. Dante puts into the mouth of St. Peter a bitter condemnation of the "rapacious wolves, in garb of shepherd" who have betrayed their office, and he was particularly uncomplimentary to his contemporary Boniface VIII, whom he consigned to Hell. In Dante's view it is regrettable that Constantine ever made his Donation to the pope and thereby involved the vicar of Christ in worldly matters. There is a more profound limitation to Dante's orthodoxy, and it lies in the scheme of salvation which he presents. His literary concretization of traditional medieval religiosity, its vision of Hell, Purgatory, and Heaven, reflects an overfamiliarity with this doctrine of salvation and the beginnings of its ultimate exhaustion. The poetic construction of such a detailed picture of religious cosmology indicates that the traditional doctrines have lost their freshness and vitality and have become conventional stereotypes. That is not to say that Dante did not believe in the Catholic view of salvation, but he so internalized these doctrines that the line between literary imagination and theological reality became indistinct.

The radical implications of Dante's thought are more pronounced in his treatise on *Monarchy*. It was ostensibly written to advocate the rights and powers of the emperor in Italy, to whom Dante looked as the rightful ruler of Italy and also as the restorer of his personal fortunes. As a matter of fact, the German king Henry VII did come down into Italy during his lifetime, but he immediately turned around and went back again without doing anything to end Dante's exile from his beloved Florence. The significance of the work does not lie in its traditional arguments from law and historical tradition on the superior authority of the Roman emperor in the world, but rather in its novel attitude. Dante makes favorable allusions to the Averroist doctrine of the collective immortality of the soul, which stand in strange contradiction to his view of personal immortality upon which *The Divine Comedy* is based. He debates the traditional papal interpretation of the Petrine Biblical text, claiming that from Christ's words to Peter "it does not follow that the pope can loose or bind the decrees of the empire." He denies the validity of papal claims based on the Donation of Constantine because "Constantine had no power to alienate the imperial dignity, nor had the church power to receive it." Most significant of all is Dante's argument for imperial authority, not only on the basis of tradition, law, and Biblical texts but also from a simple and radical doctrine of pragmatic necessity: the welfare of the human race, he says, is best advanced under monarchical rule. This represents a new departure in medieval political thought. The implication of Dante's argument is that political power is based upon the sanction not only of divine and natural law but also of social necessity.

The pragmatic and voluntarist theory of law suggested by Dante receives its clearest possible statement in the *Defender of the Peace,* published in the 1320's by Marsilio of Padua (d. 1343), another product of the communal life of northern Italy. What is only implicit in the *Monarchy* is argued in great detail by Marsilio. He argues that the essence of law lies in its imperative and coercive character. Law does not have an ethical content; it is the will of the legislator which makes the law. Marsilio thus rejects in the clearest terms the Thomistic doctrine that the power of the state is subject to an eternal and absolute order of values which gives to positive law its sanction. To Marsilio law has no other sanction than the absolute will of the state. He thereby comes close to the doctrine of sovereignty expressed by Bodin in the sixteenth century and Hobbes' relativist theory of law in the seventeenth century. The church, like any other corporation in the state, is subject to law. Marsilio thus turns the hierocratic doctrine of the plenitude of papal power upside down. Instead of the state being subject ultimately to the moral sanction of the church, it is the church which is subject to the absolute will of the state. Allowing the church any legislative power whatsoever is "incompatible with the peace of men." In the work of Marsilio of Padua the radicalism of the Italian communes attains definitive intellectual form and expresses a political doctrine which attacks in the strongest terms the association of the state with moral authority, which St. Thomas had advocated; the *Defensor Pacis* makes the state a law unto itself.

Behind Marsilio's separation of the state from the moral and divine order is an underlying Averroist radicalism. Averroes' double-truth theory, his dichotomy of the world of science and the world of revelation, appears in political philosophy in Marsilio's pragmatic and voluntarist theory of law. Marsilio had come under the influence of Averroism in the universities of northern Italy, which, by the early fourteenth century, were infected with the teachings of the Arabic philosopher. During the next two centuries Averroism was to be an important current in medieval thought, radiating from Italy northward to the rest of Europe.

The double-truth doctrine of Averroes, against which St. Thomas had devoted all his efforts, as it spread northward from Italy after 1300 was confirmed by a similar separation of faith and reason propounded by the leaders of the Oxford Franciscan school. But these thinkers were not Averroists; in fact, the starting point for their intellectual development was the condemnation of Averroism by the bishop of Paris in 1277. Yet half a century later the Franciscan school had arrived at the same conclusion which the Averroists propounded: reason and revelation belonged to two separate worlds and could not be integrated.

The Franciscan philosophers had from the first been unhappy with Thomas Aquinas' Christian Aristotelianism. In conformity with the general attitude of their order, they looked more toward the older Augustinianism than the new Aristotelianism. St. Bonaventura had presented a doctrine which was a restatement of the early-medieval philosophic tradition. He upheld St. Augustine's Platonic theory of the illumination of the intellect by divine ideas, and as a corollary of this Platonic theory of knowledge, St. Anselm's realist philosophy was also affirmed by the Franciscan philosopher. Bonaventura believed that this Augustinian Platonist-Realist philosophy provided a firmer base than Aristotle's determinism and intellectualism for Franciscan insistence on the majesty of God and the primacy of the will. His successors pursued the same aim, and they too rejected St. Thomas' Christian Aristotelianism. But they abandoned also Bonaventura's conservative Platonic realism and arrived at a revolutionary nominalist and empiricist conclusion.

Bonaventura's death in 1274 was in every respect a dividing line in the history of the Franciscan order. He was the dominant philosopher among the Franciscans, and his removal from the scene gave the intellectual radicalism of the younger Franciscan philosophers free rein. They were profoundly stirred by the condemnation of Averroism in 1277, which they also took to imply a severe criticism of Thomism. They believed that the omnipotence of God and the freedom of the human will had, in Thomism, been subjected to the mechanistic order of Aristotelian determinism. They therefore set out to separate philosophy and science from faith and revelation. Bonaventura, however, had been not only the leading Franciscan philosopher; he was also the master-general of his order and the leader of the majority "Conventual" party among the Friars Minor. The Conventuals accepted the changes in Franciscan life which the papacy had encouraged, the most important of which was allowing the order to own property. A minority group in the order who came to be called the "Spirituals" refused to accept these departures from the original teachings of St. Francis, and a bitter struggle slowly began to divide the order into a conservative and a radical wing. From insisting on the poverty of their order, the Spirituals began to demand the apostolic poverty of the whole church and to question in particular the secular power and material possessions of the papacy.

In the 1250's the Italian Spirituals revived the heretical speculation of Joachim of Flora, which had long been condemned by the church as the most dangerous of doctrinal errors. They applied Joachim's ideas to the current situation in their order, claiming that the pope was Antichrist and the Conventuals were his agents. They proclaimed the coming of the reign of the Holy Spirit, which would overthrow Antichrist and bring to an end the imperfect rule of the priesthood. A new mendicant order, apparently an outgrowth of the Spiritual Franciscans, would be formed and would bring in the new age of the Holy Spirit. The Spirituals' devotion to the original Franciscan ideal and the revival of the doctrine of the apostolic poverty of the church and the Joachimist heresy produced serious disorders among the Friars Minor. In 1257 the minister-general of the order was condemned for sympathizing with the doctrines of the Spirituals and was deposed. He was succeeded by St. Bonaventura, who accepted the Conventual position but tried to mollify the Spirituals and restore unity to the order. A legal subterfuge was arranged by which the pope held the property of the Franciscans on their behalf so that technically the Friars Minor could maintain their mendicant status. In the last quarter of the thirteenth century the disintegration of the order which was so instrumental in regaining prestige for the church among the laity was avoided. Many of the Spirituals withdrew to hermitages, and the Conventuals remained in control of the order. But the Spirituals had not surrendered belief in their radical doctrines. They had on their side some of the ablest men in the order, and after 1300 the current of spiritual radicalism among the Friars Minor joined forces with the philosophic radicalism of the Oxford Franciscan doctors.

The advance of the Oxford Franciscans toward nominalism was begun by Duns Scotus (1266–1308), probably the greatest of medieval logicians. As his name implies, he was born in Scotland; he joined the Franciscan order, studied at Paris, and taught theology at Oxford. He begins with an extremely searching inquiry into the power of the human intellect to abstract from sense data and arrives at a conclusion contradicting Thomist optimism, which had believed it possible to build up a rational knowledge of God on an epistemological foundation of sense experience. Scotus concludes that the human mind cannot penetrate to God's being through ratiocination. God is infinite, but human reason is finite. God is absolutely omnipotent and free to follow His own will; the human mind cannot work out a train of causation so as to be able to know rationally the inner being of God. Scotus was not trying to undermine faith but rather to enhance its exclusive importance; he was trying to make revelation the only source of knowledge of divine being. He thought that he had protected the majesty of God and the freedom of the will from the limiting effect of Thomistic determinism.

Duns Scotus died at the height of his intellectual powers and before he could complete his work. The major implications of Scotus' doctrine were worked out by William of Occam (d. 1350), another Oxford Franciscan of extreme precocity who developed his system by 1320, when he was not more than thirty years old. Occam effected a revolution in scholastic philosophy by a complete separation of logic and metaphysics. This had already been suggested by Scotus, but Occam makes the distinction absolute. He maintained that logic does not deal with being as such, with propositions from the standpoint of the accordance with fact or existence. Intellectual propositions are purely forms of thought divested of all metaphysical content, of any connection with ultimate truth. "Their being is their being understood." Logic, then, deals only with the analysis of modes of signification, or "terms," but when we ask if metaphysical knowledge is possible, if man can know ultimate truth rationally, Occam's reply is in the negative. Universals are merely intellectual symbols, far removed from ultimate reality, which are formed by the mind out of repeated sensations and confused memory and which only dimly stand for individual things. Our conceptions of causality are contingent upon this mental process and have no reality outside the mind. Occam thereby arrived at an extreme nominalism which is very close to the radical empiricism of Hume and some twentieth-century philosophers.

Occam's purpose was the same as that of Scotus; he wanted to uphold the Franciscan claim that knowledge of God can come only through revelation and intuition and that divine being cannot in any way be known rationally, which for him would imply a limitation of divine being. He used philosophy to destroy the importance of philosophy and to uphold the Franciscan approach to the deity as the only way. His extreme nominalism, or "terminalism," argued with enormous subtlety and force, immediately had a powerful effect on the schools which by the 1330's were the scene of a great debate between the Occamist "modernists," as they are called, and the supporters of the Thomist "ancient way."

Occam believed that he had used the dialectical weapons of the schools against the schoolmen. He had demonstrated that philosophy itself supported the teachings of St. Francis concerning the intuitive knowledge of God. Occam's devotion to St. Francis made him susceptible to the doctrines of the radical wing of the Friars Minor. At the end of the thirteenth century the Spirituals had again become active, and they openly preached the apostolic poverty of the church and the apocalyptic heresies of Joachim of Flora. Not satisfied with his onslaught on Thomism, Occam began to attack the temporal power of the papacy and to demand the apostolic poverty of the church. He fell under the censure of Pope John XXII and spent the last years of his life at the court of the German king Louis of Bavaria, who was also at odds with the pope. Occam was joined in his flight to seek royal protection by the minister-general of the Franciscans, who had sided with the Spirituals and thereby finally opened the split within the order which had been threatening since the middle of the thirteenth century. In 1323 the papacy condemned the doctrine of the apostolic poverty of the church as a heresy, and the more extreme members of the Spirituals in Italy, known as the Fraticelli, were hunted down by the Inquisition. These conflicts inaugurated a sharp decline in the vitality of the Franciscan order and its leadership of European piety.

At the court of Louis of Bavaria Occam met Marsilio of Padua, who had also fled there to seek protection against the papal wrath. They continued their work with impunity, and Occam seems to have accepted Marsilio's doctrine of the authority of the state over the church. Occam claimed that not only the pope but even a general council of the church could err. Thereby he made individual conscience the ultimate religious authority and greatly enhanced the power of the state. For his denial of the infallibility of pope and general council left the sovereign state as the dominant corporate force in society. Religious individualism and the sovereignty of the state were opposite sides of the same intellectual coin.

Thus the two streams of revolutionary thought came together. Marsilio had begun with the Averroist separation of science and revelation, and Occam ended with a similar double-truth doctrine, denying the possibility of knowing divine being by reason. Both currents of intellectual radicalism denounced the temporal power of the papacy, made the church into a purely spiritual institution, and allowed the exclusive power of the state in society. The dominant movements in European thought in the half century after Thomas Aquinas' death attacked his cathedral of intellect from every direction by emphasizing the primacy of will—the primacy of human will over human intellect, the primacy of God's unlimited and incomprehensible will over the necessary and rationally comprehended first cause of Thomism, the primacy of the will of the state over the moral order.

III. *The New Violence*

Marsilio of Padua's withdrawal of the state from an overriding moral authority was the theoretical formulation of the chief political events of his day. In the half century that followed the death of St. Louis the medieval state, which had assumed its definitive form in the French and English monarchies, became a law unto itself. It refused to recognize the moral sanction of the church and the leadership of the vicar of Christ, and the government of Louis IX's grandson undertook the sordid assassination and ruthless subjugation of the medieval papacy. The leading political entities of European civilization—England, France, and the international ecclesiastical state which the papacy had created—had, by the closing decades of the thirteenth century, fully developed their institutions and defined their ideologies. But they found that their aims were mutually exclusive. The expansionist tendencies of the English and French monarchies led to an irreconcilable conflict between the two great powers of Europe. The drive of royal government to sovereignty over all groups within the realm contradicted papal claims to jurisdiction over territorial churches and to an ultimate position of moral authority in society. Conciliation and compromise were abandoned as means of solving these disputes. England and France, in the last decade of the thirteenth century, engaged in a ruinous war which ended the long peace of the thirteenth century. This was to go on intermittently for a hundred and fifty years, and ended in political and social chaos and the degradation of both monarchies. The conflict between the papacy and the French monarchy was settled by the use of physical violence against the pope himself in the first decade of the fourteenth century, the most immoral act in the long history of the relations between the church and medieval kingship.

Thus the leaders of European society in the late thirteenth century tried to settle their problems by only the most extreme and reckless measures. An attitude of intransigence and violence conditioned the actions of the leaders of both state and church during the period. It is not the violence stemming from primitivism, which had been common in the early middle ages, but the violence which comes from the disintegration of civilized order and the collapse of moral standards. It is not the violence of the barbarians but the violence of the "terrible simplifiers," in Jacob Burckhardt's phrase, who can no longer endure the compromises and conflicts of civilized life and can find satisfaction only in the aggressions of organized brutality.

The medieval state reached its apogee in England and France in the late thirteenth and early fourteenth centuries, and Europe was not again to see such exercise of sovereign power until shortly before 1500. The troubles of the English monarchy during the first seven decades of the thirteenth century were largely the consequence of the inadequate personal quality of the king, and in Edward I (1272–1307) the royal government again found a leader to make use of the institutional power of the English monarchy which had been created by the Norman and Angevin kings. Edward I differed from his father, the devout and inept Henry III, in almost every way. The new king's piety was the formal kind, which provided a useful façade for an aggressive policy without inhibiting its exercise. Edward was a handsome crusader and a great soldier who commanded enthusiasm from all groups in English society. He won a great triumph by bringing Wales for the first time securely under the English crown, and he made an attempt at the conquest of Scotland, which was less successful but enhanced his reputation as a soldier.

Edward had learned well the miserable lesson of his father's inability to control the barons and the community of the realm. Instead of reverting to the arbitrary practices of John's reign, he determined to make use of the constitutional experiments which the rebellious barons had undertaken in order to exercise their control over the royal administration. But he aimed to use these institutional innovations to enhance, rather than diminish, royal power. He continued Simon de Montfort's practice of calling a special meeting at the royal court, at which the great council of the magnates was augmented by the summoning of representatives of the knights of the shire and the burgesses. These special occasions came to be called parliaments, and by the end of his reign they had been used so frequently and with such great success that they had become an indispensable royal institution —the king holding his court in his council in parliament.

The parliament of Edward I had a fourfold function: judicial, legislative, financial, and propagandistic. It was technically the high court of parliament, and as such it was the highest judicial body in the realm, where great suits could be held between the king and the magnates and between great lords, and at which the knights and burgesses could present petitions asking for redress of grievances. As an institution which brought together representatives of all estates in the kingdom, parliament could be regarded as expressing the will of the community of the realm. Hence, in accordance with the political and juristic theory of Magna Carta, it could be used to obtain consent to changes in the common law. In a series of great statutes Edward resolved many of the confusions and filled many of the lacunae in the common law, which had suffered from lack of royal attention during the previous reign. Similarly, parliament was used to obtain the necessary consent to new taxation, and even taxes which legally belonged to the royal prerogative, such as customs duties and levies on the burgesses, now received parliamentary approval. It was much easier to administer a tax which had previously received the consent of the representatives of the community of the realm, particularly in view of the fact that the tax assessors and collectors were for the most part unpaid knights of the shire who could not easily be suborned to carry out unpopular royal policy. The final function of parliament probably seemed to Edward one of its more important ones. It provided an easy way of informing the country about royal policy and allowed the king's ministers to harangue the assembled lords, spiritual and temporal, and representatives of the knights and burgesses and even of the lower clergy, whose representatives were occasionally summoned, on the merits of the king's proposed course of action. By the 1290's Edward had made himself the most powerful English king since Henry II. He was able to reduce further the power of the barons under a statute requiring them to show by what warrant they still held vestiges of private feudal jurisdiction, which they had great difficulty in doing in the law courts.

Edward's reassertion of royal leadership in England gave him the resources he needed to enter a war against France in 1294. The war arose out of the designs which both the English and French monarchies had on the wealthy county of Flanders, but Edward defended his policy to the community of the realm on the grounds that the French king was the enemy of English culture. This was a rather extravagant claim in view of the fact that the English king and his magnates usually spoke French, but it is indicative of Edward's conception of himself as a national monarch.

The French government welcomed the challenge from the English king. They hoped to be able to gain the last English continental province of Gascony and thus to complete the expansion of the French state to what had come to be regarded as the natural frontiers of the realm. Champagne and Navarre had come into the royal domain as a result of a marriage alliance, and Lyons and other previously independent cities in the Rhineland were subverted by the legalistic chicanery at which the royal administrators were adept. St. Louis' son Philip III (1270–1285) was a lethargic man who left the government largely in the hands of his chief ministers and allowed them to continue unhindered the draconic measures which not even St. Louis had contravened. The subordination of the old feudal, episcopal, and municipal jurisdictions to the national financial and legal institutions of the crown was continued without ceasing, and any lord or corporation who resisted the royal will was harassed and impleaded until surrender was the only way out. The royal government was not able to overcome the intensely provincial attitudes of the French magnates, with the result that it could not obtain consent to taxation in a single assembly, as was the case in England. Even when the Estates General was first called in 1302, it was strictly for propagandistic purposes, and it did not have any of the other functions of the English parliament. While the French kingdom was much wealthier and more heavily populated than England, the Capetian government could not tax its financial resources as fully or as quickly as the English king was allowed to do in his realm through the use of parliamentary taxation. But the obtaining of consent through provincial assemblies of magnates and negotiations with the town governments brought in enough money to make the French king the wealthiest in Europe. The French treasury was able, furthermore, to gain a share of papal taxation of the clergy on the pretext that the money was to be used exclusively for crusading purposes.

The enormous power which the French monarchy enjoyed at the accession of Philip IV the Fair (1285–1314) had a corrupting effect on the personnel of the royal bureaucracy, especially the chief ministers of the crown. These were men of modest background, of knightly or bourgeois provenance, who had made their way in the world because of their legal knowledge and administrative ability after a hard early struggle in life. The vast resources which they controlled in the king's name and their almost unlimited power to ruin men born to a much higher social status made them into arrogant and unprincipled scoundrels. Since the time of Philip Augustus the French bureaucracy had been known for its harsh attitudes, and this was to some degree a political necessity if the country was ever to be really united under the crown. But the megalomania of

Philip the Fair's ministers was something new. To severity and chicanery was now added slander, blackmail, and extortion. The government of late thirteenth-century France discovered the technique of the "big lie": the more fantastic the accusation, the easier it would be to destroy helpless opponents. It learned how the processes of law could be easily perverted into an invincible agency of despotism. The royal administration always acted against its helpless victims with a parade of legal formalities; it discovered that if governments will only use a façade of juristic institutions, the most extreme and groundless accusations will begin to take on the coloration of truth in the dim minds of the populace. It is not easy to discern what part the king played in all this—to what extent he actually directed this vicious policy or was merely the dupe of his ministers. The latter is the more probable. Personally devout and brave, Philip was also silent and stupid, the perfect façade behind which the bureaucracy could work its plans. His ministers were monsters of cynicism, but the king seems actually to have believed their big lies. They had no trouble convincing him of the legality of their attacks on anyone who stood in their way, including the vicar of Christ himself.

After the death of St. Louis the papacy found itself in greater and greater difficulties. Its legal and financial institutions were the object of criticism all over Europe, and not least by churchmen who found themselves heavily taxed by Rome and frequently impleaded in the papal courts. The cardinals were well educated and good administrators, but they had gained a bad reputation for nepotism and venality. The extreme measures taken against the Hohenstaufens had disturbed sensitive minds, who doubted that the keeper of the keys of Heaven should use methods which better suited petty Italian despots. The Spiritual Franciscans sowed confusion by raising the claim that the papacy had failed to emulate the poverty of the apostolic church. Once again anticlericalism, this time directed chiefly against the papal "wolf," became a leitmotif of western literature. There were, in addition, grave problems within the Curia itself. Intermittently since the tenth century the throne of Peter had been embroiled in the feuds of the ambitious Roman families, who regarded the papal tiara and the cardinal's hat as the entry to new dynastic riches. In addition to the parties maintained by leading families of the Roman aristocracy within the college of cardinals, there was also a minority group of French cardinals who were sensitive to the demands of the Capetian government and the Angevin ruler of southern Italy. Under these conditions of a faction-ridden cardinalate, every papal election produced a minor crisis and scandalous rumors. By the early 1280's the papacy was in an extremely vulnerable position if any major issue arose in Europe which affected its interests and tested the mettle of the curia. Such an issue arose out of a strange and mysterious series of events in Sicily, and the papacy was found wanting in the effectiveness of its reaction to this crisis.

Angevin rule in southern Italy and Sicily was from the first very unpopular with the native population. Charles of Anjou, unlike the previous Hohenstaufen rulers, had no claim to descent from the original Norman house, albeit he had seized this wealthy land with papal authorization. His treatment of the people he had conquered was not much better than that which the northern French nobility had accorded to Languedoc early in the century. It was another land grab by the French nobility, who had no concern for the welfare and the dignity of the people they had conquered. Angevin rule in southern Italy marked the beginning of the long descent of this previously prosperous region into miserable poverty. It is unlikely that anything would have come out of the Italian hatred for the French if it had not been for Charles of Anjou's ambitions against Constantinople. In 1261 the Latin Kingdom of Constantinople, which was the creation of the fourth crusade, finally tottered to its demise, and the princely Byzantine dynasty of Palaeologus gained the throne of Constantinople. The resources of the revived Byzantine state were meager, and it was all the Greeks could do to hold off the Turks until the Moslems finally took the Golden City on the Bosporus in 1453. Innocent III's plan for the reunion of the Roman and Greek churches, as a result of the Latin conquest of Constantinople, thereby ended in failure. For another two decades the Byzantine ruler bought protection against a western counterattack by agreeing to a formal union of the two churches, but in 1281 this pretense was denounced by Charles of Anjou, who made plans to attack Constantinople. The Greeks had forgotten how to fight, but not how to conspire. Byzantine agents and gold gave direction to the bitter hatred of the Sicilians, and in 1282 they arose and massacred the French garrison in a savage rebellion which came to be known as the Sicilian Vespers. The exact details of the organization of the Sicilian Vespers have baffled historical researchers; the conspiratorial genius of the Sicilian people was first clearly demonstrated in 1282. But it is apparent that the Byzantines had taken the lead in fomenting the uprising. The Sicilians gave their loyalty, however, to the king of Aragon, whose wife was the daughter of Manfred, Frederick II's illegitimate son and the last Hohenstaufen ruler. The Spanish king accepted the crown of Sicily, and after landing on the island prevented Charles of Anjou from reconquering it.

The papal throne at the time of Sicilian Vespers was occupied by a Frenchman who was the tool of Charles of Anjou. He not only devoted the financial resources of the papacy to helping Charles in his war of reconquest, but he announced that the throne of Aragon was forfeit and proclaimed a crusade against its ruler. There was no moral or religious justification for this extreme measure. It had been one thing to launch a crusade against the Albigensian heretics—and even the crusade against the Hohenstaufens had plausible grounds—but the crusade against Aragon was purely political and manifested the grossest debasement of the crusading ideal. The kings of Aragon had always been among the foremost Christian soldiers; now the Aragonese ruler found himself, for purely political reasons, treated as though he were an enemy of the church. In order to insure French response to the political crusade against the Spanish ruler, the pope conferred the title to the throne of Aragon on the son of Philip III and furthermore offered to the Capetian king the income from a crusading tax levied on the French clergy. Philip III advanced on Aragon while Charles warred against the Sicilians and Spaniards to regain Sicily. Partly due to the effectiveness of the Sicilian and Spanish fleets and partly due to disease which broke out in Philip's army, and above all due to the courage and military skill of the Spaniards, the French suffered ignominious defeat on both fronts.

The crusade against Aragon was the second act of the tragedy which led to the destruction of the medieval papacy. In the following two decades the papacy exhausted its finances in its desperate effort to regain Sicily for its Angevin ally. And finally it had to acknowledge the separation of southern Italy into the two kingdoms of Aragonese Sicily and Angevin Naples. Philip III had died on his way back from the ill-fated crusade against Aragon, and his son's ministers, chagrined at the first defeat of Capetian arms in the thirteenth century, decided to make the papacy the scapegoat. They claimed that the curia had failed to fulfill its obligation of supporting the French enterprise, and they convinced Philip the Fair of the truth of these allegations. After 1285 the attitude of the French government toward Rome became more and more severe and intransigent; it appears that the royal ministers were waiting only for a suitable opportunity to crush the papacy as they had subordinated everything in their own country.

They did not have long to wait. The feuds within the college between the Roman aristocratic families made every papal election increasingly difficult and scandalous. Finally, in 1292, when the papal throne was vacant, the factions in the college of cardinals canceled each other out, and no candidate could gain the necessary two-thirds majority. For two years, while Christendom looked on in dismay, the cardinals quarreled and plotted and the see of Peter remained unfilled. A temporary compromise was reached in 1294 when all factions agreed to the election, as Celestine

V, of a famous Italian hermit and spiritual leader. Celestine was completely bewildered by the duties of his office, and after a few months of confusion in the papal curia he abdicated. Celestine's "great refusal," as Dante called it, was a sensational scandal and the cause of bitter controversy, for no pope had ever abdicated, and many sincere people claimed that the heir of St. Peter could not resign his office, since theoretically the pope had been designated by divine grace. Celestine said that he had been told to abdicate by an angelic voice, although it was rumored that this message really came from Cardinal Benedict Gaetani, the leader of one of the factions in the cardinalate, by means of a secret speaking tube. Substance was given to this by Gaetani's election as Pope Boniface VIII (1294–1303), and when Celestine died shortly afterward, it was claimed that he had been poisoned at Gaetani's order.

The scandal which marked the beginning of the pontificate of Boniface VIII was exceeded only by the outrage which brought it to an end. The papacy in 1294 was in an extremely vulnerable position. Its moral authority in Christendom had been greatly vitiated, and the monarchies of northern Europe had developed to the point where any disagreement with the pope would be translated immediately into animosity and violence toward Rome. But Boniface was so mesmerized by the theory of plenitude of papal power and by the institutions of Roman autocracy that he could not bring himself to face the realities of the situation and restrain himself from provocative action. In many ways he was as extreme and irresponsible as any minister of the king of France. He was a skilled lawyer and an excellent administrator and sincere in his devotion to the authority of the church. His conception of the papal office was not fundamentally different from that of Innocent III; but he lacked Innocent's political skill and diplomatic tact, and he actually faced a situation which in some respects was potentially more dangerous to the papacy than that with which Innocent had to cope. Neither in his own time nor since has Boniface had a good reputation, and some of the criticisms directed against him have been unfair. It is not exactly his fault that the French government was dominated by cynical and ruthless men whose amorality was something new in the Christian world. But he was at fault for failing to have recognized the existence of this new situation and of failing to adjust papal policy to meet it. Instead he pushed recklessly forward, making the most extreme claims (although not by any means unprecedented ones) for papal authority, and he suffered terrible defeat.

In 1294 the inevitable war between the expansionist French and English monarchies had begun. No major war had been fought in Europe in eight decades, and both governments soon discovered that they had underestimated their military expenditures and their financial resources were severely strained. They looked around for expedients to increase royal income. The most obvious source was taxation of the clergy, for which there was a dubious precedent in the several occasions on which the church had given royal governments large shares of the income from crusading taxes. Both the English and the French royal governments claimed that this gave them the right to tax the clergy for any war purpose whatsoever, and there was a plausible argument for this view. There seemed, after all, to be little difference between taxing French churchmen for a war against Aragon and requiring them to support a war against England. The big difference was, however, that the pope did not authorize the new tax, and Boniface regarded it as a flagrant violation of canon law. He published the bull *Clericis Laicos,* which prohibited all clerical taxation by lay rulers without papal permission on pain of excommunication. The bull was marked throughout by an extremely bellicose and intransigent tone. Its opening statement asserted that "the laity have been from the most ancient times hostile to the clergy," a palpable untruth in view of the enormous enthusiasm and devotion which laymen had shown and were still showing to many clergymen. Boniface's lack of restraint and moderation conclusively drew the lines between papal authority and royal sovereignty, and the kings of England and France proceeded to reply to his challenge in a similarly definitive manner. Edward I terrified the English clergy by withdrawing from them the protection of the common law, and Philip the Fair's ministers demonstrated their mettle by a full-scale campaign of harassment and vituperation in which they were so experienced. They banished the Italian bankers from France and cut off the export of money from the realm so as to deprive the papacy of a considerable part of its resources. They launched a shower of pamphlets against Boniface, asserting the sovereign power of the king over his subjects and the obligation of the clergy to contribute their share for the defense of the kingdom. The French episcopate was suborned into telling the pope that the clergy would be regarded as enemies of the state if they did not pay taxes to support a national war. Boniface was bewildered and frightened, and he rapidly gave way, acknowledging that the king of France, and by implication all secular rulers, had the right to tax their clergy for the defense of the realm. This was a clear admission on the part of the papacy of the sovereign power of the state over the national church. It was Boniface's second mistake, for it showed Philip the Fair's ministers that the pope could easily be forced into submission, and it gave them a taste for even more extreme measures.

The opportunity for new violence came in 1301. The previous year had been a great jubilee year for the church. Thousands of pilgrims had made their way to Rome and acclaimed the pope in religious festivals. These demonstrations restored to Boniface his confidence and his arrogance. If the people of Europe were so loyal to the vicar of Christ, what did he have to fear from mere kings? He was ready to engage in a new struggle with the French monarchy, and this time he would not give in. The royal administration had found one of the bishops of Languedoc recalcitrant and troublesome; this prelate was a fiery southerner who hated the men of the north for subjugating his land. Philip's ministers decided to make an example of the dissident bishop. Using their accustomed methods of extravagant slander and legal niceties, they had him arrested on a charge of treason, and with their usual cynical audacity they demanded that the pope remove their prisoner from his episcopal office in order that he might be punished for his alleged crime. Boniface replied to the provocations in an equally extreme manner. He suspended his previous concession to the French king on clerical taxation, severely criticized Philip for the immoral conduct of his administration, and summoned the meeting of a council of French clergy to Rome to reform the church in Philip's realm. In 1302 he issued another inflexible statement of hierocratic doctrine, the bull *Unam Sanctam,* claiming that both the spiritual and temporal sword were ultimately held by Christ's vicar on earth, that if a king did not rightly use the temporal sword which had been lent him he could be deposed by the pope, and concluded with an unmitigated assertion of papal authority: "We declare, proclaim, and define that subjection to the Roman Pontiff is absolutely necessary for the salvation of every human creature."

One of Philip the Fair's ministers is said to have remarked, on reading Boniface's latest pronouncement, that "my master's sword is of steel, the pope's is made of verbiage." The king himself appears to have been momentarily shaken by Boniface's salvo, but his ministers were not frightened. They had complete confidence in the effectiveness of their techniques of despotism, which had crushed so many opponents of state power in the previous two decades, and they now directed against the pope the venomous method of the big lie. The leading force in the royal administration was now William de Nogaret, a violently anticlerical lawyer from Languedoc who seems to have reacted against the work of the Inquisition in his home country with impassioned hatred for the church. At what later came to be regarded as the first meeting of the Estates General he read a long list of charges against Boniface, accusing him of every crime from heresy and murder to personal immorality and black magic. The pope was depicted as the enemy of the church, and it was asserted that it was the duty of the "very Christian king" of France to rescue the church from this monster. The lay population believed Nogaret's charges, and the clergy also went along with these fantastic lies, partly because they were bewildered by the violence of the accusation and partly because they were frightened. For half a century Europe had become more and more inured to intemperate language and extravagant denunciations which were exchanged between secular rulers and the papacy and even among churchmen themselves. This legacy of reckless charges had so increased the credulity of even sincere and intelligent men, and the incessant use of slander and calumny in debate had so debased the moral currency of Europe, that men were prepared to accept the most outlandish accusations, even against the pope. When Nogaret said that he had evidence for his claim that Boniface was a heretic in the fact that the pope had once declared that he would rather be a dog than a Frenchman, implying that Boniface did not believe in the soul, devout and honest men gravely nodded their assent.

Boniface was driven to the wall by the French government; he had left only the ultimate weapon in the spiritual armory of the papacy. He repaired to his family's palace at Anagni to prepare a bull of excommunication and deposition against the king of France. But he had not anticipated the physical violence which the royal government was prepared to bring against him. Nogaret had been dispatched on a secret mission to Italy to capture the pope and bring him back to France for trial. With the support of personal enemies of Boniface and his family among the Italian nobility, and the secret connivance of some cardinal, Nogaret took the pope prisoner at Anagni and started northward. It is difficult to see how Nogaret could have hoped to get Boniface back to France, but in any case the people of Anagni and the pope's aristocratic relatives freed Boniface and escorted him back to Rome, where he died a broken man almost immediately. The poet Dante, who had condemned Boniface and refused to regard his election as legal, perceived that the events at Anagni were a momentous turning point in the history of civilization. "The new Pilate," he said, had imprisoned Christ in the person of His Vicar and allowed him to be done to death. All Europe waited anxiously for the next act of this fantastic tragedy.

The church now needed another Innocent III or Gregory VII; instead it got Benedict XI, a timid Dominican who excommunicated Nogaret but exonerated Philip and then expired. For a year there was a bitter struggle between the pro-French and anti-French factions in the college of cardinals. A fatal compromise led to the election of the archbishop of Bordeaux as Clement V (1305–1314), who was supposed to be Boniface's devoted disciple but who had secretly established liaison with the French royal administration. He was in any case afraid of the French King and was almost continually ill during his administration, probably with cancer. It would be hard to imagine a worse choice; Clement turned the tragedy of Anagni into a permanent disaster for the papacy. He never even went to Rome, but instead, on the pretext of the disturbed political conditions in the papal states, took up residence with his curia in the little city of Avignon, which was technically within the German empire but was just across the Rhone river from France and completely within the sphere of influence of the Capetian monarchy. The "Babylonian Captivity" of the papacy, which was not fully to end for over a century, precipitated a great decline in papal prestige throughout Europe. The English government, in particular, looked upon the Avignon papacy as the mere tool of the French monarchy, which it was. And this encouraged the increasing withdrawal of the English church from effective papal authority. But Philip's ministers were not satisfied with this humiliation of the head of the church. They threatened to try Boniface posthumously unless Clement fully acceded to their demands. The pusil-lanimous pope exonerated Nogaret, annulled *Unam sanctam*, and even re-stored to their offices the cardinals who had connived in Nogaret's capture of Boniface. Nogaret and his adjutants, free from any possible papal inter-ference, proceeded to use their weapons of slander, blackmail, and legalism to secure the destruction of the Templars in order to gain the holdings of the Templar bank in Paris for the royal treasury. The Templars were accused of heresy and sodomy, and the Dominican inquisitors, on the testimony of perjured witnesses, were persuaded to convict the leaders of the order. Clement V fulfilled his puppet function by dissolving the order while the French treasury quietly expropriated the resources of the largest bank in northern Europe in order to gain more income for the war against England.

By the end of the first decade of the fourteenth century the European state had thus gained a sovereign status and had achieved the destruction of the medieval papacy. The church was powerless to stem the will of the French and English monarchs, who were now exercising their authority over their people without the limitations of moral sanctions. Yet the kings of England and France did not long enjoy their Leviathan authority. Ed-ward I and the ministers of Philip the Fair had seriously miscalculated and overestimated their resources. The engines of despotism were new things in medieval civilization, and men were not yet experienced in their control. The war between the kings of England and France turned out to be ruinous to both parties. The extremely heavy taxes which had to be im-posed on the population at last encouraged discontent and rebellion. In his later years Edward I encountered stiff opposition from the magnates who protested bitterly against his attempts to levy new and heavier taxes, and his successor, Edward II, discovered that the new institution of par-liament could be used as a means of limiting royal power as well as of manifesting it. In 1311 a committee of the barons momentarily took over the management of the royal administration in much the same way as the magnates of Henry III's reign had done. In 1315, the year after Philip the Fair's death, provincial assemblies of disaffected nobles forced the new king to issue charters confirming their feudal privileges. The history of both England and France in the fourteenth and fifteenth centuries was marked not by the continued expansion of royal power but rather by the resurgence of aristocratic privilege and the revival of the leadership of the greater nobility in society. The aristocracy learned from late thirteenth-century monarchy its violent attitudes and ruthless techniques and used them against royal power. Because the royal leaders of society had demolished moral standards, it became generally fashionable to adopt a cynical and selfish outlook. The European state at the end of the thirteenth century had gone too far; by its violation of all standards of decency and honesty it had corrupted the moral basis of social life and induced men to be completely self-seeking and brutal in their relations with the royal government. The leaders of European society had to learn the bitter lesson that unrestrained power is self-destructive, for no society can long endure the absence of some moral order without descending into chaos and despair.

PART NINE

In Italy. . . . Man became a spiritual in-dividual and recognized himself as such.

— JACOB BURCKHARDT

The fifteenth century in France and the Netherlands is still medieval at heart. . . . But all these forms and modes were on the wane. . . . The tide is turning, the tone of life is about to change.

— JOHAN HUIZINGA

AN END AND A BEGINNING

Fourteenth and Fifteenth Centuries

Chapter Twenty-Two

BETWEEN TWO WORLDS

I. "Autumn" and "Renaissance"

The era which stretches from the second quarter of the fourteenth century to the late fifteenth century has been called both the later middle ages and the age of the Renaissance. The latter term was very popular among historians in the later nineteenth century and was unchallenged until four decades ago. This view of the period from 1325 to 1500, so widely held, was strongly conditioned by one book, Jacob Burckhardt's *Civilization of the Renaissance in Italy,* published in 1860. Urbane, aesthetic, learned in most fields of higher culture but never a pedant in any, Burckhardt was himself the reincarnation of *der Renaissancemensch* he admired so much. This scion of the Basel aristocracy prized individuality, the free expression and development of the mind, over all other values, and he thought he saw in fourteenth- and fifteenth-century Italy the place and the moment when individuality was freed from medieval civilization's limitation, which was the result of subjecting individuality to the corporate and the general. The Italian city-states, Burckhardt said, created a new kind of social elite who thought of themselves entirely as individuals and not as members of a corporate group. The Italians found kindred spirits in the men of antiquity, the products of a similar civic life, and they used the classical heritage as a guide to the knowledge of the physical and intellectual worlds, with the result that they cast off the "fantastic" and "childish" medieval world-view and "rediscovered man and the world." Burckhardt's interpretation was not entirely original; part of his conception of the history of the fourteenth and fifteenth centuries can be found in the writings of the early nineteenth-century French Romantic, Jules Michelet, and, of course, in the opinions of the Italian humanists themselves. The great fourteenth-century Italian humanist, Petrarch, was strongly conscious of a cultural break between his own day and the "dark ages."

Burckhardt's interpretation has been the subject of bitter controversy among historians for many years; for a time hardly a year passed in which the American Historical Association did not schedule a session on "The Renaissance—Was It or Wasn't It?" at its annual meeting. Medievalists were sensitive to the pejorative scorn of Renaissance historians and were eager to show that the great period of cultural achievement came in the twelfth century rather than in the fourteenth and that the later middle ages, far from being an age of glorious rebirth, was a period singular for disintegration, confusion, gloom, and failure. The greatest of Burckhardt's critics was the Dutch historian and sociologist, Johan Huizinga, who resembled his predecessor by his possession of a vivacious style and his tendency to construct his study around ideal types extrapolated from the context of the period. Huizinga's *The Autumn of the Middle Ages* (translated into English as *The Waning of the Middle Ages*) attracted little attention when it was first published in the 1920's; historians were then completely under the sway of positivism, and they were not inclined to appreciate a scholar who used belletristic literature and pictorial art as evidence. A quarter of a century after its initial publication the importance of Huizinga's masterly essay and the validity of his method is widely recognized. Huizinga claimed that, in examining fifteenth-century France and the Low Countries, he could not find evidence to support Burckhardt's views on the Renaissance; instead he found despair and defeat everywhere. The Dance of Death, for instance, was a very popular motif in late-medieval literature and art. Huizinga's study of the court of Burgundy revealed to him an aristocracy pursuing a completely stylized way of life totally lacking in individuality; the court of Burgundy was in fact remarkable for the pursuit of outmoded traditions, a sure sign of cultural ossification. Even the more naturalistic style of fourteenth- and fifteenth-century art, Huizinga contends, does not substantiate the claim made for a renaissance. Naturalism, which began to a limited degree with Giotto at the end of the thirteenth century in Italy and culminated in late fifteenth-century Flemish art, is actually a symptom of cultural disintegration—of the fact that European society can no longer hold symbols in common.

It is not necessary to go to the other extreme from Burckhardt and attribute no originality to the fourteenth and fifteenth centuries, as some medievalists have done, to understand the lines of development in the period. And in doing so, it is inescapable that the fact of primary importance is that north of the Alps there is an older civilization going to pieces rather than a new one making a strong appearance. The dominant tone of life is one of despair and disappointment, not one of creativity and the will to succeed. This does not mean that the latter indications are absent; rather, they are much less important than the former. Italy appears to be a special case, albeit a highly significant one, since its economy and political institutions augur the emergence of the pattern of modern civilization. In the Italian cities the development of capitalist institutions and the growth of devotion to the state proceeded with only a slight decrease in momentum. North of the Alps the situation was very different. In France, England, Germany, and Flanders it is the death agonies of medieval civilization which predominate over the birth pangs of the modern world. The fourteenth and fifteenth centuries in general compromise an era which looks in two directions, like the fourth century A.D.

It does not detract from the significance of certain ideas and attitudes prevalent in the north Italian cities—which, if not new, at least do look toward the modern world—to describe the general pattern of later medieval development as distinguished by war, violence, disease, social upheaval, political instability, and a general malaise and unhappiness. The research of the last two decades has indicated that economic troubles were an underlying condition for the discontent and bitterness which is so apparent in the later medieval period. In England, Germany, and France there was a long depression from the last third of the thirteenth century to shortly after 1450. The population curve, which had been steadily rising since the middle of the tenth century, suddenly leveled off and probably declined even before the bubonic plague carried off as much as a quarter of Europe's population in the Black Death of the mid-fourteenth century. Cities no longer built new suburbs and walls; it is probable that the volume of international trade was actually less in 1400 than in 1300, at least north of the Alps. Certainly land went out of cultivation in England and Germany, as statistical studies have shown. This seems to have been jointly caused by soil exhaustion and the population decline.

The long depression explains the short temper and restlessness of the men of later medieval Europe; lords found their rents declining in value, and burgesses also had a hard time making a living. Knowing the explosive consequences of the great depression of the 1930's, we are not surprised that the men of the fourteenth century resorted to all sorts of desperate expedients as a way of finding a solution to their troubles, whose ultimate root was much more mysterious to them than the economic collapse of our century to us. They betrayed, deposed, and murdered kings; they engaged in savage wars against each other; they tried to summon divine assistance through mystical experiences or by joining heretical cults; they burned witches. But nothing seemed to help.

The world, to the men of the later middle ages, as to the Romans of the third and fourth centuries, seemed to be growing old. The troubles of their day seemed the preparation for the end of the world, for the last things, for the Last Judgment and the coming of the Lord to slay Antichrist. It was a time for the proliferation of mystical, eschatological, apocalyptic, and heretical doctrines. Some historians have talked about "the rise of the lay spirit" in the fourteenth century. The era is indeed marked by the entrenchment of a secular culture,-but paradoxically it was also a time that exhibits most intense and heterogeneous religious experience. Medieval men once again sought escape from their failures and miseries in government and economics by fleeing to the kingdom of God within. They were eager to listen to new religious teachers, avid for emotional sermons, deeply moved by religious art. As violent and as crooked as they were in many social relationships, so intense and devout were they in their relationship to God; this is characteristic of an ambiguous, tortured era, an age of transition and breakdown, a moment when values are either thrown aside or adhered to fanatically.

The church needed an Innocent III and a St. Francis to control these new wellsprings of medieval religiosity, but ecclesiastical leadership was totally inadequate for the great task at hand. This was by no means entirely the fault of the church. The papacy had been imprisoned at Avignon and been made the puppet of the French monarchy. The result was an immediate relaxing of discipline; the great edifice which Innocent III had created steadily cracked and fell apart. With the vital center gone there was a general slacking all along the line. Ecclesiastical visitation was neglected; bishops were allowed to pursue private interests, and their parish priests were in many cases not supervised; the orders, even the Franciscans and Dominicans, lost much of their zeal and their reputation. Some historians have tried to rehabilitate the Avignon papacy; some historians will try to rehabilitate anything. The Avignon papacy was indeed Antichrist come to plague the church; the Avignon popes were skilled administrators but they were also selfish, shortsighted men who cared for little beyond the filling of their treasury with the proceeds of clerical taxation, usually gained by cynical bargains with royal governments. But worse was to come. In 1378 some of the cardinals went back to Rome and elected another pope while the Avignon papacy continued, and the Great Schism now scandalized Christendom and sowed doubt and confusion in all directions. The schism was only ended in the early fifteenth century through a reforming expedient which had long been discussed by canon lawyers and also by critics of papal absolutism: the calling of a general council to end the schism and reform the church. The Council of Constance (1414–1418) did end the schism, but it was unable to reform the church; no sooner did it choose a single vicar of Christ than he reasserted papal absolutism. The German emperor, at the urging of the conciliarists, called another ecumenical council, but he was easily outflanked by the pope, who won the support of kings against the conciliar movement in return for concordats recognizing the national character of churches under their rule. In the mid-fifteenth century the papacy, having returned to Rome, fell again under the domination of Roman aristocracy, which transformed the holder of the keys of heaven into a Renaissance Italian despot, no worse but no better than others of that ilk.

These scandals and failings on the part of ecclesiastical leadership gave vent to a torrent of anticlericalism which, as in the twelfth century, easily and rapidly spilled over into antisacerdotalism. But heresy no longer had to rely entirely on poor itinerant preachers to define its doctrines; it now found its ablest spokesmen among the greatest minds in Christendom and in the universities. The disintegration of the medieval thought-world which had been proclaimed by the work of William of Occam was intensively developed by his successors. Occamism dominates the intellectual history of later medieval Europe, and especially of England and Germany. It should not be surprising to find that Martin Luther, not the simple monk he is sometimes regarded, but a professor of theology at a second-rate German university, proclaimed that he was an Occamist. The intellectual heritage of the great English Franciscan lies heavily over the culture of the fourteenth and fifteenth centuries and reaches out in many directions: to ruin philosophy, bring science to the verge of its great breakthrough, and inspire mysticism and heresy.

The sterile quality of fifteenth-century scholasticism was mainly the consequence of Occam's doctrines. His insistence that logic was the only valid form of philosophy, that metaphysics and rational theology had no validity, caused his "terminist," or nominalist, successors to devote themselves exclusively to abstruse, esoteric logic-chopping and to lose touch completely with the problems that excited the imaginations and aroused the interests of intelligent men. It is no wonder that the scholastics came to be regarded with contempt by the humanists, who turned from dialectic toward the more belletristic works of Plato for guidance.

Yet while the humanists' derision of the scholastics as fools and triflers was largely justified, their attack on the schoolmen in one respect resembled the inability of the layman to comprehend the scientist and to see the value of his apparently impractical ratiocination. Occam did not end in complete egocentricity; he believed that certain kinds of human knowledge are attainable. He eliminated metaphysics, but established the epistemological foundations for modern science toward which his Franciscan predecessors Grosseteste and Roger Bacon had been working. Occam concluded that while relations between individual things are mental products, the individual things themselves do exist and furthermore are knowable. Through simple sensory data the human mind can learn to perceive these individual, permanent things in nature, which are extended, quantitative and measurable. Occam thus glimpsed that universe of discourse, based on the quantification of nature, which made the thought-world of Galileo, Copernicus, and Newton possible. The Oxford Franciscan himself suggested the law of inertia, although among his contemporaries only a small group of natural philosophers at Merton College, Oxford could understand what he was saying. In the latter half of the fourteenth century the Parisian Occamist school, following their master's rejection of metaphysics and advocacy of the observation and analysis of individual things, advanced to the threshold of modern mechanics, physics, and analytic geometry. Nicholas of Oresme, undoubtedly the most outstanding member of this school, suggested the principle of the daily rotation of the earth before Copernicus and discovered the law of falling bodies before Galileo.

Occam's disciples thus had all the intellectual equipment to achieve the great scientific breakthrough of the sixteenth and seventeenth centuries. Why did they not proceed with their work? Why did these scientific studies decline so completely in the fifteenth century that it has taken the most thorough research of modern scholarship to discover the work of Nicholas of Oresme and his colleagues? The answer lies in the social background in which these men worked. No one in the fourteenth century, not even the scholastic scientists themselves, perceived the empirical value and social utility of the law of falling bodies. The men who pursued these new studies did so on their own time; they had no social encouragement. There were no chairs in science in the universities, but there were many in dialectic and theology; it was much more profitable to pursue the latter disciplines than to engage in scientific research which no one, outside a very small circle, appreciated. It was a change in military technology which eventually made mechanics a socially useful subject and encouraged the revival of research in the sixteenth century. Gunpowder was just coming into use in the fourteenth century, and Europeans were still very unskilled and amateurish in its use. By the sixteenth century armies had become sufficiently adept at firing cannonballs so that someone who could devise a formula for falling projectiles could make a contribution whose empirical value could be understood.

The second factor that frustrated the great scientific movement of the fourteenth century was a deficiency in mathematical knowledge, particularly algebra. The late medieval thinkers knew that natural science required the quantification of natural phenomena, but they could only implement this goal in a fragmentary way. The additional reason for the aborting of the scientific breakthrough in the fifteenth century lies in the humanists' hostility to the scholastics and their refusal to look beneath the surface and find out what was valuable in the work of the best minds among the schoolmen. Many of the humanists in Italy did receive a university education, but they had no knowledge of the most valuable work done at Oxford and Paris. The humanists, by the end of the fifteenth century, had in their ranks the outstanding thinkers and scholars in Europe; their lack of sympathy for academic thought was a contributing factor to the failure of European culture to achieve a breakthrough into science even when Occam and his disciples had a good view of that new intellectual dimension, the one which was so markedly to distinguish European from other civilizations.

It is indicative of the intense religiosity of later medieval Europe that society derived from Occamism not an understanding of the possibility of quantifying nature but rather an encouragement toward religious individualism. Occam had begun with an assumption diametrically opposed to Averroes' philosophical presuppositions, but he had arrived at virtually the same conclusion: reason cannot ascend to the majesty of God, and it can say nothing sure about theological matters. The effect of Occamism's rejection of reason as a road to understanding the deity was to emphasize individual mystical experience as a buttress for the truths received through revelation. Thomas à Kempis' *Imitation of Christ,* with its pietism and hostility to the snares of reason, was in accord with Occam's teaching. Especially was the "ignorant teaching" of Nicholas of Cusa the inevitable corollary of nominalism. Nicholas maintained that the right attitude of man to God was one of awe and humility; we must wait patiently in the darkness for the "vision of God." All over western Europe in the later middle ages mystical literature received its most prolific and eloquent expression. It does not seem to be an accident that these doctrines of individual religious experience were especially popular in England and Germany, where Occamism also found its greatest support. Occamism and mysticism had a close intellectual affinity.

The late-medieval mystics were generally loyal to the church and the priesthood, but, as in the twelfth century, the heavy emphasis on a direct relationship with the deity encouraged devout men who had experienced the beatific vision to criticize the clergy, and it emboldened some eventually to deny the efficacy of ecclesiastical authority. Occam himself had claimed that the pope and even a general council could err, and he seems to have concluded that the only infallible source of truth was the Scriptures. This view carried the revolutionary implication of leaving religious authority with individual consciences. The doctrine of the authority of the Bible was made much more important by the archheretic of the fourteenth century, John Wyclif (1320–1384), an outstanding professor of theology at Oxford. Wyclif was an embittered, unhappy, and apparently neurotic person but a man of prodigious learning and polemical skill. He was not an Occamist but a Platonist; it is indicative of the extent of dissolution of the medieval thought-world that the great heretical thinker of the late fourteenth century was a realist. He seems to have conceived of the Scriptures as the emanation of the divine mind, the reflection of the spiritual Form, which had overriding authority. From there he went on to produce an encyclopedia of the heretical doctrines of the previous two centuries, combining the teachings of Peter Waldo, Joachim of Flora, and Marsilio of Padua. He denied the authority of the priesthood and the efficacy of transubstantiation, attacked the pope as Antichrist, and called for the creation of a purely spiritual church through the secularization of church lands. This last principle naturally pleased the English government and nobility, and the church was unable to carry out a prosecution against him. But Wyclif did more than publish a small library of heretical theology; he translated the Bible into English and inspired and personally encouraged itinerant saintly preachers, called Lollards, to travel up and down the country spreading his doctrines. By the 1380's England, which in the previous century was so free from heresy that the Inquisition had never been established there, was the center of the most powerful heretical movement in Europe.

There is nothing, or almost nothing, in the writings of Martin Luther or of any of the Protestant reformers of the sixteenth century that cannot be found in fourteenth-century literature. The question is not why the Protestant Revolt and schism came in the sixteenth century, but why it did not come a hundred or a hundred and fifty years before. This is perhaps the most important question which can be asked with regard to the later middle ages. Five reasons can be given for the failure of the heretical movement of the fourteenth century to produce a schism in Christendom. In the first place, the fourteenth century did not have the printing press, which did not come into use until just before 1500. It was very hard for the heretical theorists to disseminate their doctrines. In the early sixteenth century the same ideas spread like wildfire across Europe. Wyclif's doctrines were carried into Bohemia, presumably as the result of a dynastic marriage and consequent relations between England and that distant country, but he did not gain disciples in France and Germany. Second, the long depression of the later middle ages, while it produced discontent, sapped men's energy and distracted their interests, making them unlikely to get involved in a major struggle with ecclesiastical authority. Third, there is the paradoxical fact that the papacy was so weak in the fourteenth century that it did very little to combat the heretical movements. By not forcing the issue, the papacy allowed the new wave of heresy to run its course.

The last two reasons are undoubtedly the most important. The wealthier classes in Europe were frightened by the apparent social implications of heresy. It seemed to foment social revolt, and this led them around 1400 to turn against the heretical movements. The fourteenth century was the era of the first social revolts in medieval Europe. The industrial proletariat spawned by the textile industry in Flanders and Florence engaged in bitter, and ultimately unsuccessful, struggles against the oligarchies who dominated urban life. Even the peasant, whose economic position had been ameliorated in many parts of Europe because of a labor shortage, lifted up his head for the first time. Wherever the hitherto docile and mute peasant thought he was being ill-treated or the new freedom which seemed to be coming his way impeded by desperate landlords, he resorted to savage rebellion—the Jacquerie in France, the Peasants' Revolt in England. The English peasant uprising certainly was encouraged, and perhaps even led, by itinerant heretical preachers, and this caused the English government and nobility to turn against Wyclif's disciples. Similarly, the proto-Protestants of Bohemia made their doctrines into a national religion, raised armies, and terrified Germany. Even after the heretical leader John Hus had been burned by order of the Council of Constance, his disciples continued to harass southern Germany. What happened, then, was that the heretical movements unleashed feelings of social discontent and national hatred, as they were to do in the sixteenth century. But there was no Luther in the late middle ages to stem the tide of reaction and dissociate the religious radicalism from social and political extremism. Antisacerdotal doctrines did not entirely disappear in the fifteenth century, but they had been discredited by such terrifying events as the Peasants Revolt and the Hussite wars, and they were driven underground for another century.

The final reason why the Reformation did not occur in the fourteenth or early fifteenth century is that the royal governments were so inept and distracted by other problems that they failed to take advantage of the religious situation as many sixteenth-century kings were to do. In the first decade of the fourteenth century the national monarchies of France and England appeared destined for continual and unlimited accretion of power, but the next one hundred and fifty years turned out to be disastrous for the royal goverments in both countries. Europe had to wait until the late fifteenth century for the territorial sovereign state to secure its position of leadership in European society. In the interval the aristocracy was given a final chance to dominate the governments of the two most centralized states; but the great lords exhibited only greed and laziness in their role as the dominant force in fourteenth- and fifteenth-century political life. The result was a degree of social disorder not experienced in Europe since the tenth century.

The French and English monarchies were largely to blame for the perilous circumstances in which they found themselves by 1400. They squandered both their material and moral resources and made just about every error which could open the way for aristocratic resurgence. Edward I and Philip the Fair had pushed a little too far, had acted in extreme and unscrupulous ways, particularly in the case of the French royal government, with bitter consequences for their successors. Monarchy which had been so popular in the thirteenth century faced moral bankruptcy by the end of the reigns of Edward I and Philip the Fair. It was obvious that the royal administrations were simply out for the main chance, so if the kings found themselves in difficulty, why should anyone not get as much for himself as he could? Edward's son, Edward II, was a bad soldier and a homosexual; he was forced to abdicate and was then murdered by a cabal of lords working in collaboration with his French queen. The Capetian line ran out finally in 1328; their Valois cousins were weak and inept. In the 1330's both the English king, Edward III, and the French ruler, Philip VI, were foolish chivalric knights who blundered into war, seeking to win glory on the battlefield and ignoring the problems which a renewed conflict would create. It was bound to deplete further the royal treasuries and make the administration vulnerable to aristocratic rebellion. Furthermore it was likely to make the great lords more important in the country.

During the long peace of the thirteenth century the nobility's military functions had atrophied; in the interminable war that now began they became the indispensable leaders of society. The kings commissioned lords to raise armies; these contingents turned out to be as valuable to the aristocrats at home as they were on the battlefield. Possession of private armies allowed the great lords to bully everyone and to meddle in royal affairs. It was a pernicious political-military system which brought back the worst of the old feudal days; it has aptly been called "bastard feudalism." The

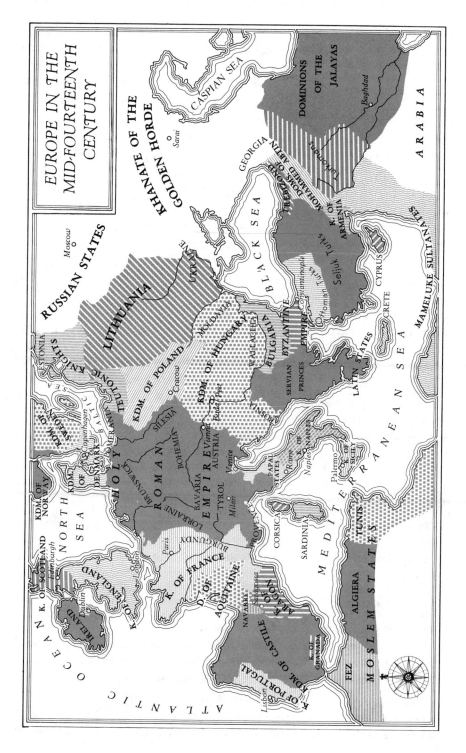

EUROPE IN THE
MID·FOURTEENTH
CENTURY

RUSSIAN STATES

KHANATE OF THE
GOLDEN HORDE

DOMINIONS OF THE
JALAYAS

Baghdad

CASPIAN SEA

Sarai

ARABIA

GEORGIA

K. OF
ARMENIA

MOHAMMED ABTIN

Turcomans

BLACK SEA

Seljuk Turks

Ottoman Turks

BYZANTINE
EMPIRE
Constantinople

CYPRUS

CRETE

MAMELUKE SULTANATE

LITHUANIA

UKRAINE

MOLDAVIA

WALLACHIA

SERVIAN
PRINCES

BULGARIA

LATIN STATES

KNIGHTS
TEUTONIC

ESTONIA

SEA

KDM. OF POLAND
Cracow

KDM. OF HUNGARY
Budapest

TRANSYLVANIA

MEDITERRANEAN SEA

Moscow

KDM. OF
SWEDEN

KDM.
OF
DENMARK

Copenhagen

POMERANIA

BALTIC

SILESIA

BOHEMIA

AUSTRIA

Vienna

TYROL

Venice

K. OF
NAPLES

Rome

PAPAL
STATES

Palermo

K. OF
SICILY

KDM. OF
NORWAY

NORTH
SEA

HOLY
ROMAN
EMPIRE

BRUNSWICK

LORRAINE

BAVARIA

Milan

PROVENCE

CORSICA

SARDINIA

TUNIS

ALGIERA

MOSLEM STATES

SCOTLAND
Edinburgh

K. OF
SCOTLAND

IRELAND

Dublin

K. OF ENGLAND

London

ATLANTIC OCEAN

K. OF FRANCE

Paris

D. OF
AQUITAINE

BURGUNDY

NAVARRE

Bordeaux

ARAGON

KDM. OF CASTILE

K. OF
GRANADA

K. OF PORTUGAL

Lisbon

FEZ

541

aristocrats on their part were only too glad to be given this new leadership in society; they had found themselves driven to the wall by the depression in rural economy, and their only recourse was to engage in pillaging expeditions and to intervene in royal government. In the fourteenth and early fifteenth centuries the French and English aristocracy was given excellent opportunities to participate in politics, to bargain with candidates for the throne, and, in the case of the French lords, also to conspire with the English invaders. Both the French and English governments followed the suicidal policy of allowing large princely domains to be established in their kingdoms. In both countries royal princes were given these privileges; they proceeded to fight one another for the crown. This system of princely appanages was particularly cultivated in France; England was also bothered by large aristocratic holdings in the frontier marches.

When Edward III began the so-called Hundred Years War in the late 1330's, these factors all became operative, and within half a century political and social chaos had resulted in both countries. The English won great victories over the French, partly due to their advanced use of bowmen, but the royal government could not enjoy its new conquests on the continent. It was too busy with aristocratic rebellion and princely wars at home. The armies which the lords had used to beat the French were brought home to pursue private quarrels and to further dynastic ambitions. Parliament, which Edward I had used as an engine of royal power, became the tool of aristocratic faction. In the 1450's these conflicts finally came to a head in the so-called Wars of the Roses, a full-scale civil war among the aristocracy for control of the English throne and royal government. France was for a time even in a worse way. One branch of the royal dynasty threw in its lot with the invaders, the French armies suffered defeat after defeat, and only the internal troubles of the English kingdom saved the crown for the inept house of Valois. The English squabbles provided the opportunity for Valois recovery beginning in the 1430's, and after a century of pillage by English freebooters the French finally agreed on one thing: that the English must be driven out. An hysterical peasant girl named Joan of Arc provided the emotional leadership that was needed. The slow-moving Charles VII finally took advantage of this nationalist feeling to drive back the divided English and re-establish royal power.

To the political, economic, and intellectual problems of later medieval Europe various solutions were offered. Many found comfort in intense religious experience, in personal communication with the deity. The Italian humanists offered an optimistic view of the critical and creative powers of human intelligence, the cultivation of the classical heritage, and a Christian Platonism, as the founts of moral standards which would restore stability in

European life. In the late fifteenth century, as represented by the Dutch scholar Erasmus, this Christian humanism gained adherents among the best minds in northern Europe. But it was the other side of the humanists' program which eventually obtained the fullest realization in European life. The Italian humanists were vehement patriots of their city-states, and their municipal patriotism led them toward the expounding of the doctrine of *raison d'état,* which was to be definitively stated by Machiavelli in the early sixteenth century.

It was to the sovereign state, which knows only its own reason, that the exhausted and disillusioned European peoples turned at the end of the fifteenth century. Edward IV and Henry VII in England and Louis XI in France established the so-called "new monarchies," which actually constituted a return to the governments of Edward I and Philip IV, but with more attention to a moral façade and a greater emphasis on nationalist feeling. After two centuries of chaos the only solution seemed to be the bringing back of the leadership of the state. Humanists exulted in the glory of revived monarchy, which would maintain moral standards and patronize the arts. To scholars profoundly influenced by the classical heritage absolutism seemed the only form of government which could maintain social order and further common welfare. To the many who were infected by various forms of religious individualism the sovereign state was welcome, for the king could stand as a bulwark against sacerdotal power, or whatever was left of it.

In 1500 strong monarchy could not avoid success and popularity. There seemed to be no alternative viable form of social order; submission to the sovereign rule of kings was the only apparent solution to the ills of European society. Thus the Great Leviathan, which had suffered miserable failure in the fourteenth century, returned to be the dominant force in European life.

In the late fifteenth century the prime need in every European country was domestic peace. With the ending of the great depression of the later middle ages, the decline of plague, and the consequent rise in population, prosperity in both town and country was again possible if law and order could be restored. Monarchy seemed to be the only principle of order, and hence there was a new enthusiasm for the prerogatives of kingship. The late fifteenth-century monarchs everywhere operated the same basic pattern of government: a small court and royal bureaucracy pacified the aristocracy, or when this policy failed, fought the great lords in the interests of the national community.

Nineteenth-century historians thought the rise of the "new monarchies" was effected by a grand alliance between the king and the bourgeoisie. But this view is not tenable on close examination. England, France, and Spain, where monarchy flourished, were predominantly landed societies. The bourgeoisie's money was useful to the kings in building up mercenary armies, but the merchants and bankers were of small importance in political life. The struggle was between royal court, council, and bureaucracy on the one side and the aristocracy on the other. All other groups in society—the vast majority of the population—remained outside the political nation. They applauded kings because the restoration of royal power implied peace and order, but they had very little to say about the course of political change.

The king's relations with the aristocrats was an ambiguous one. He shared their outlook and style of life, and if they were content with positions in the court and government, he was eager to cooperate with them and give them their accustomed place at the head of society. Only when the great lords threatened the efficacy of royal law and taxation, and particularly when great nobles exhibited ambitions on the throne itself, was the late-fifteenth-century king inclined to turn his mercenary armies against the chateaus and castles of great landed families. The political and social structure of the northern monarchies, with the exception of England, did not fundamentally change during the next two centuries.

At the end of the fifteenth century there was a widespread feeling that social order required the subjection of all classes, groups, and corporations to the ultimate sovereignty of royal government and law. The political trend of the twelfth and thirteenth centuries was thereby resumed and accentuated. Nevertheless, there were in 1500 severe practical limits on the exercise of royal authority, no matter what theorists might say about the divine right of monarchy. Communications and transportation in 1500 were not substantially improved over conditions that prevailed in 1300. The underdeveloped character of the communications network still meant that royal government, no matter how authoritarian its ideology, could do very little to affect the daily lives of the vast majority of the population. The king provided legal justice in his law-courts, collected taxes, and led armies against national enemies. But Europe was still almost as far in 1500 from the centralized, authoritarian, and welfare states of the modern industrial world as it had been in 1300. Only to a very limited degree had the autonomy of families, groups, corporations, and local communities been diminished and the individual brought more directly in contact with the sovereign state. What still counted in the lives of 95 per cent of the population was constantly these immediate, subordinate institutions. The majesty of the state rarely entered into the lives of ordinary men, for good or ill. In this sense, Europe in 1500 was still a pluralistic, fundamentally medieval society, and the great transformation in political and social order did not come until the Industrial Revolution.

In the Italian cities, the state was inevitably closer to men's lives because of the small size of these political entities, but this peculiar situation was not very significant for Europe as a whole. What Italy did contribute to the European civilization of 1500 was a new kind of secular culture, which may be called humanism. The Italian Renaissance was an important development in European life because it established the educational system and style of life that became common to the aristocracy and the high bourgeoisie throughout western Europe during the sixteenth and seventeenth centuries. To be a member of the elite neither inherited status nor wealth, however gained, was sufficient: one had to be educated in the classics and exhibit a high literacy, one had to have good taste in art, music, and dress, and one had to show a highly refined and rhetorical way of speaking. The Italian bourgeoisie had borrowed this ethos from the French aristocracy of the thirteenth century, and imbibed it as their own to prove their right to belong to the elite of European civilization. But they extensively refined and enriched the old aristocratic style, to the extent that the northern aristocracy of the late fifteenth century had to take lessons in how to live and be a superior person from the Italian humanists.

It is easy enough to denigrate this humanistic culture as the ideology of the upper classes, but this definition misses the significance of the Italian Renaissance and its extension northwards in the late fifteenth century. In the first place, this humanistic culture was the *only* acceptable one, the only style that was self-conscious and perpetuated by the educational system. It was not until the Industrial Revolution and the development of mass literacy that, particularly in the United States, another self-conscious and integrated literate culture was evolved in western civilization. Second, while both the Italian and northern humanists were devout Christians, the humanistic ethos was genuinely secular in character: the good man fulfilled the Christian pieties, but his dignity, his value, in society had little to do with hierarchy and theocracy. The criterion of membership in the elite was the secular side of man—his literacy, his style, his manners, which, of course, were only open to the wealthy. Even more than the decline of papal leadership and the rise of royal power, the emergence of this secular ethos signals the ending of medieval civilization and the dawn of a new era. Finally, it must be stressed that the humanistic ethos, although it departed from the church-centered ethos of the middle ages, was a product of medieval culture itself, and was ultimately a consequence of the intellectual expansion and romantic revolution of the twelfth century.

While humanistic culture was the ideology of the ruling classes of 1500, it did mark a great advance in the history of the West: for it did stress individual values, the cultivation of personal excellence, the realization of a finely tuned and sensitive mentality. One of the great themes of the history of the past century is whether this individuality and personal dignity and cultivation can be taught to the masses, or, to put it another way, whether the refinements of the human mind and temperament that the Italian Renaissance made the province of the wealthy few can be transformed into the common heritage of all mankind.

II. Concluding Thoughts on Medieval History

It is fashionable to end surveys of the history of medieval Europe with stirring accounts of "the medieval legacy." Authors are at pains to point out how many of the institutions and attitudes which emerged in medieval Europe are still with us today: the Catholic church, representative government, the university, romanticism, experimental science, capitalist institutions, and other things we hold dear. It is true that the medieval presence is with us far more than is the ancient heritage, and our lives are ultimately conditioned in many ways by the medieval legacy. But on the other hand, all these institutions and ideals whose origins we can find in the middle ages have been subtly changed since the thirteenth century, and we have to recognize the fundamental differences between our own civilization and the world of Thomas Aquinas and St. Louis. This may be summed up by pointing out that if we could be transported back into the thirteenth century, we would find medieval men really a different breed from ourselves. We would be astounded by the foul odors of their bodies, their glut-and-famine eating habits, their lack of physical comforts, their fanatical piety, gross superstition, and also the violence and cruelty of everyday life. This is another way of saying that medieval civilization was in many respects a pre-industrial society. Medieval civilization did not achieve the full application of science to technology which has made possible our mass-consumption economy, and therein lies the most apparent dividing line between medieval men and ourselves. Nevertheless, we are closer to medieval people than to any other civilization in the past. We *can* share in their experiences far more than in the life of ancient man or that of oriental peoples. The middle ages *were* a very long and decisive experience in the development of western civilization, and are therefore very much worth studying. Understanding the medieval past is indispensable for self-knowledge.

There is, however, another reason for studying medieval history: the lessons we can learn from examining the whole course of medieval civilization. The philosopher Santayana expressed one of the most profound truths when he remarked that those who ignore the past are condemned to repeat it. What is there in the history of medieval Europe that we can take to heart and either emulate or try to avoid? Fortunately we know more about medieval civilization than any other that is dead and gone; we can, with confidence in the probable nature of our knowledge of historical change, examine the pattern of development of medieval Europe and learn from this study both inspiring and sobering lessons. Medieval history teaches us that tremendous achievements are within the grasp of a small elite group guided by high ideals and capable of willing the realization of those ideals. The finest delight in studying medieval history comes from the contemplation of the personalities and work of those great men who bestrode Europe like colossi for so many centuries—from Constantine, to Gregory VII, to St. Louis—those men who dared and achieved great things because they took God seriously.

Medieval history also has a lesson to teach about breakdown of a civilization, and we can ignore this lesson only at great peril to our own culture and society. Medieval civilization was created, after a struggle of five centuries' duration, on the basis of a complex and sophisticated compromise between spirit, represented by the church, and the world, represented mainly by kingship. We have seen in this book how this equilibrium was shattered in the eleventh century when it offended the moral and religious principles of some zealous men who then tried and failed to reconstruct society in accordance with their own puritan ideals. A less complete, but still viable, equilibrium was worked out in the thirteenth century, taking into account the consequences of creativity in learning, piety, and power. But this new consensus involved such a fine and critical balance between extremes that it proved intolerable to many people. The result was a social neurosis and the seeking of satisfaction by terrible simplifiers who broke apart the constituent elements of the medieval world order.

The study of medieval history therefore teaches us that civilization is the result of a complex interpenetration of spirit and power, of moral and material resources; that this delicate compromise is not easy to maintain, that its preservation requires mature intelligence, sophisticated moderation, and constant vigilance; and that the enemies of civilization, apart from the uncomprehending primitives, are the socially irresponsible zealots and the neurotic simplifiers.

A READING GUIDE TO MEDIEVAL HISTORY

PREPARED IN COLLABORATION WITH THOMAS W. HUBER

This annotated bibliography attempts to summarize the most significant and current works of scholarship dealing with each chapter. Works in foreign languages are cited only when there is no equivalent book in English.

For those students with a deep interest in the Middle Ages this bibliography is merely a beginning. Several comprehensive and standard bibliographical collections can provide the more advanced student a starting point for cultivation of his interests. These include: *American Historical Association's Guide to Historical Literature,* ed. G. F. Howe et al., 1962; Dahlmann-Waitz, *Quellenkunde der deutschen Geschichte* 9th ed., 1931; G. Franz, *Bücherkunde zur deutschen Geschichte,* 1951. Important periodicals and reviews for medieval history include: *American Historical Review, English Historical Review, Review Historique, Deutsches Archiv, Historische Zeitschrift, Annales, Speculum,* and *Viatur.* Important original source collections include: J. P. Migne, *Patrologia Graeco-Latina; Monumenta Germanicae Historica; Melanges Historiques;* and *The Rolls Series.* A standard comprehensive history of the Middle Ages, now somewhat out of date, is the *Cambridge Medieval History.* For economic matters begin with *The Cambridge Economic History* with many excellent articles.

PART ONE: THE ROMAN DESTINY

Chapter One: Decline and Fall

*Bury, J. B. *History of the Later Roman Empire.* New York: Dover, 1957. Absorbing political history.
*Gibbon, Edward. *The Decline and Fall of the Roman Empire.* D. Saunders, ed. New York: Viking, 1974. After 200 years, still an insightful narrative.
Jones, A. H. M. *The Later Roman Empire.* 3 vols. New York: Harper & Row, 1968. An excellent comprehensive account of all aspects of late Roman society.
Rostovtzeff, M. I. *The Social and Economic History of the Roman Empire.* London: Oxford University Press, 1957. A work of genius; the class struggle in the Roman world.
*Walbank, F. W. *The Awful Revolution.* Toronto: University of Toronto Press, 1969. Suggestive, interesting.

Sources

*Apuleius. *The Golden Ass.* R. Graves,

trans. New York: Farrar, Straus & Giroux, 1954. A Roman picaresque novel that exposes the undercurrents of unrest in the late empire.

*Casson, L., ed. *Selected Satires of Lucian.* New York: Norton, 1968. The poverty, philosophical sterility, and religious enthusiasm of the later empire bear the brunt of Lucian's wit.

Chapter Two: Christian Empire and Christian Church

Alfoldi, A. *The Conversion of Constantine and Pagan Rome.* London: Oxford University Press, 1948. Constantine as a sincere Christian; pious but interesting.

Burckhardt, I. *The Age of Constantine the Great.* New York: Pantheon, 1949. Constantine as a cynical, egotistical political opportunist; a nineteenth century masterpiece, perpetually condemned but never forgotten.

*Jonas, H. *Gnostic Religion.* Boston: Beacon, 1963.

*Lietzmann, H. *History of the Early Church.* 4 vols. Cleveland: World Publishing, 1961. A thorough account of the emergence of Christianity; conservative.

*MacMullen, R. *Constantine.* New York: Harper & Row, 1971. A subtle, thoroughly interesting biography stressing the complexity of Constantine's character and policies.

Momigliano, A. *The Conflict Between Paganism and Christianity in the Fourth Century.* London: Oxford University Press, 1963. Original, insightful essays.

*Nock, A. D. *Conversion.* New York: Cambridge University Press, 1961.

Piganiol, A. *L'empire chrétien.* Paris: Presses Universitaires de France, 1933. A brilliant, succinct analysis.

Sources

The New Testament of the Jerusalem Bible. Garden City, N.Y.: Doubleday, 1974. The source of much of medieval thought and an important historical document in its own right; a modern Catholic translation.

*Eusebius, Bishop of Caesarea. *Ecclesiastical History.* Grand Rapids: Baker Books, 1974. Church history as seen through the eyes of one of its most important bishops; the ideology of the Constantinian monarchy.

Chapter Three: The Making of Latin Christianity

*Bolgar, R. R. *The Classical Heritage and Its Beneficiaries.* New York: Cambridge University Press, 1954. The social value of classicism in the medieval world; very important.

Brown, P. R. *Religion and Society in the Age of St. Augustine.* London: Faber, 1972. Useful survey of the Patristic world.

———. *St. Augustine of Hippo.* Berkeley: University of California Press, 1967. Readable but superficial biography.

*Cochrane, C. N. *Christianity and Classical Culture.* London: Oxford University Press, 1959. A provocative work contending Christianity replaced the arid values of classical culture with a new and more realistic view of man; reflects the neo-Augustinianism of the 1930s when it was written; still a masterpiece.

Ladner, G. B. *The Idea of Reform.* Cambridge, Mass.: Harvard University Press, 1944. Massive, turgid study of patristic thought; important.

Meer, F., van der. *Augustine the Bishop.* New York: Sheed & Ward, 1962. Informative, interesting.

Mommsen, T. E. *Medieval and Renaissance Studies.* Ithaca, N.Y.: Cornell University Press, 1959.

*Morey, C. R. *Christian Art.* New York: Norton, 1962.

*Nygren, A. *Agape and Eros.* New York: Harper & Row, 1969. An absorbing study of the place of human and divine love within Christianity.

Palanque, J. R. *Saint Ambroise et l'empire romain.* Paris: L. de Bocard, 1933. St. Ambrose as an ecclesiastical statesman.

*Prestige, G. L. *God in Patristic*

Thought. 2nd ed. Naperville, Ind.: Allenson, 1952. Insightful, succinct.

*Smalley, B. *The Study of the Bible in the Middle Ages.* Notre Dame, Ind.: University of Notre Dame Press, 1952. Occasionally brilliant, always interesting survey.

Wolfson, H. *The Philosophy of the Church Fathers.* 3rd ed. Cambridge, Mass.: Harvard University Press, 1970. A monumental study, very important.

Sources

*Saint Augustine. *The City of God.* D. Knowles, ed. Baltimore: Penguin, 1972. The most influential and profound of medieval books.

*Saint Augustine. *Confessions.* F. Sheed, trans. New York: Sheed & Ward, 1942. The fascinating psychological and spiritual pilgrimage of the greatest doctor of the Western Church.

PART TWO: THE TRANSFORMATION OF EUROPEAN GOVERNMENT AND SOCIETY

Chapter Four: The Age of the Barbarian Invasions

*Bury, J. B. *The Invasion of Europe by the Barbarians.* New York: Norton, 1967. An excellent political narrative.

Chadwick, H. M. *The Heroic Age.* Cambridge: Cambridge University Press, 1926. Stimulating comparison of Germanic and Homeric worlds.

Courcelle, P. P. *Histoire literaire des grands invasions germaniques.* Paris: Hachette, 1948. Persuasive, original inquiry into Germanic culture; an important, underrated study.

Dopsch, A. *The Economic and Social Foundations of Europe.* New York: H. Fertig, 1969. Dense, tedious argument that the invasions caused little economic and social dislocation; Nazi historiography at its best.

Latouche, R. *Les grands invasions et le crise d'occident au Vie siècle.* Paris: Aubier, 1946. The best history of the cataclysmic process of invasion and social disruption; a wonderfully learned and succinct study.

*Lott, F. *The End of the Ancient World and the Beginning of the Middle Ages.* New York: Harper & Row, 1974. One of the standard works on this chaotic period, written in the second decade of the twentieth century, and showing its age; a monument to the Third Republic.

Salin, E. *Le civilisation merovingienne.* 5 vols. Paris: A. et J. Picard, 1959. Attempts to demonstrate through the use of archeological, numismatic, and literary evidence that the invasions were an unmitigated catastrophe.

*Wallace-Hadrill, J. M. *The Barbarian West.* New York: Harper & Row, 1952. Pedestrian.

Sources

Beowulf. M. Alexander, trans. Baltimore: Penguin, 1973. One of the finest examples of the Germanic folk-hero genre; a very complicated book.

Gregory, Bishop of Tours. *History of the Franks.* L. Brehaut, trans. New York: Norton, 1969. The chaos, violence, and cruelty of Frankish Gaul as seen through the eyes of an aristocratic bishop; wonderful.

*Tacitus. *Germania.* H. Mattingly, ed. Baltimore: Penguin, 1971. A Roman aristocrat's view of primitive German folkways—or an attack on Roman decadence?

Chapter Five: Justinian and Mohammed

BYZANTIUM

*Baynes, N., and Moss, H. *Byzantium: Introduction to Eastern Roman Civilization.* New York: Oxford University Press, 1948.

*Diehl, Ch. *Byzantium: Greatness and Decline.* New Brunswick, N.J.: Rutgers University Press, 1957. A fine introduction to Byzantine civilization.

Ostrogorsky, G. *History of the Byzantine State.* New Brunswick, N.J.: Rutgers University Press, 1969. An absolutely superb history of the Byzantine empire with extensive annotated bibliographies.

*Vasiliev, A. A. *History of the Byzan-

tine Empire. 2 vols. Ann Arbor: University of Michigan Press, 1968. Dull, but detailed and useful.

Sources

Hull, D. B. *Digenes Akritas, The Two-Blood Border Lord.* Athens: Ohio University Press, 1972. The great Byzantine hero epic.

*Procopius. *The Secret Histories.* R. Atwater, trans. Ann Arbor: University of Michigan Press, 1964. Unvarnished portraits of Emperor Justinian and Empress Theodora.

The Institutes of Justinian. T. C. Sandars, trans. 7th ed. London: Longmans, 1948. The greatest law code ever assembled; a world of its own; it turned on twelfth-century Europe.

ISLAM

Gibb, H. *Mohammedanism.* 2nd ed. London: Oxford University Press, 1953. Masterly.

Goitein, S. D. *Studies in Islamic History and Institutions.* New York: Humanities, 1966. A collection of extremely interesting essays on important aspects of Islamic life.

*Grunebaum, G. von. *Medieval Islam.* 2nd ed. Chicago: University of Chicago Press, 1953. The finest book ever written on Medieval Islamic intellectual history; a work of genius.

*Hitti, P. K. *A History of the Arabs.* 10th ed. New York: St. Martin, 1970. Partisan but useful.

Rodinson, A. *Mohammed.* New York: Pantheon, 1971. A biography of the prophet by a French leftist; interesting.

Saunders, J. *A History of Medieval Islam.* New York: Barnes & Noble, 1965.

Watt, W. M. *A History of Islamic Spain.* Chicago: Aldine, 1965. A useful history of one of the most brilliant periods of Islamic civilization.

Sources

Arberry, A. J. *The Koran Interpreted.* New York: Macmillan, 1964. The sacred book of Islam; as important to Islam as the Bible to the West.

The Life of Mohammed; A translation of Ishāq's Sirat Rasūl Allāh. A. Guillaume, trans. London: Oxford University Press, 1968.

Chapter Six: The Advance of Ecclesiastical Leadership

Casper E. *Geschichte des Papstums.* 2 vols. Tübingen, West Germany: Mohr, 1930. The most authoritative history of the papacy through the sixth century; a classic work; incredibly learned, subtle, insightful.

Dudden, H. *Gregory the Great.* 2 vols. London: Russel, 1967. Dull but useful.

Schmitz, P. *Geschichte des Benedicktinerordens.* Zurich: Benziger, 1960. Massive partisan survey.

Ullman, W. *The Growth of Papal Government in the Middle Ages.* London: Methuen, 1965. A work that conceives the expansion of the Latin Church as an organic process; partisan, idiosyncratic, important.

Sources

*Gregory the Great. *The Life of St. Benedict.* M. L. Uhlfelder, trans. Indianapolis: Bobbs-Merrill, 1966.

The Rule of St. Benedict—Excerpts from the Holy Rule of St. Benedict. St. Charles, Ill.: St. Charles House, 1974.

*Waddell, H. *The Desert Fathers.* Ann Arbor: University of Michigan Press, 1957.

PART THREE: THE FIRST EUROPE

Chapter Seven: The Making of Carolingian Kingship

Bieler, L. *Ireland Harbinger of the Middle Ages.* London: Oxford University Press, 1966. Neat introduction.

*Blair, P. N. *Introduction to Anglo-Saxon England.* New York: Cambridge University Press, 1954. A good survey.

Chadwick, N. *Celtic Britain.* New York: Praeger, 1963. Often original, valuable.

Hanning, R. *The Vision of History in*

Early Britain. New York: Columbia University Press, 1966. Brilliant, provocative, original.

Hodgkin, R. H. *A History of the Anglo-Saxons.* London: Oxford University Press, 1967. Absorbing, comprehensive account of England to A.D. 800.

Hughes, K. *The Church in Early Irish Society.* Ithaca, N.Y.: Cornell University Press, 1966. A work that demonstrates the creativity, vitality, and originality of the Celtic Church in Britain and Europe.

Levison, W. *England and the Continent in the Eighth Century.* Oxford: Clarendon Press, 1955. An exploration of the cultural interchanges in the eighth century; a careful, balanced, important work.

Schieffer, T. *Winfred Bonifatius und die Christliche Grundlagen Europas.* Freiberg, Germany: Herder, 1954. Important study of ecclesiastical culture.

Whitelock, D. *The Beginnings of English Society.* Hammondsworth, Eng.: Pelican, 1950. A very useful introduction to Anglo-Saxon England.

Sources

*Bede. *The Ecclesiastical History of the English People.* L. Shirley-Price, trans. Baltimore, Penguin, 1974. The finest historical work of the early Middle Ages.

Chapter Eight: Culture and Society in the First Europe

Bronsted, J. *The Vikings.* Baltimore: Penguin, 1973. Sympathetic, well-informed.

Burns, C. D. *The First Europe.* London: Allen and Unwin, 1947. Original, insightful, exciting, underrated.

Coulburn, R. *Feudalism in History.* Princeton, N.J.: Princeton University Press, 1957.

*Fichtenau, H. *The Carolingian Empire.* P. Munz, trans. New York: Harper & Row, 1963. An important antiromantic analysis; overrated but valuable.

*Ganshof, F. *Feudalism.* P. Grierson, trans. New York: Harper & Row, 1961. A succinct introduction to the nature and problems of feudalism; narrow, useful.

*————. *Frankish Institutions Under Charlemagne.* New York: Norton, 1970. A collection of essays on various aspects of the Carolingian Empire.

Halphen, L. *Charlemagne et l'empire carolingien.* Paris: A. Michel, 1949. The best book on the subject; beautiful synthesis.

*Hinks, R. *Carolingian Art.* Ann Arbor: University of Michigan Press, 1962. Superficial but useful introduction.

Laistner, M. L. W. *Thought and Letters in Western Europe.* Ithaca, N.Y.: Cornell University Press, 1966. Dull but valuable.

*Latouche, R. *The Birth of the Western Economy.* London: Methuen, 1961. An intelligent, balanced survey.

*Pirenne, H. *Mohammed and Charlemagne.* New York: Norton, 1939. A landmark work concerning the impact of Islam on Western Europe by one of the greatest scholars of Medieval History; read but do not necessarily believe.

Turville-Petre, G. *The Heroic Age of Scandinavia.* New York: Hutchinson's University Library, 1951. Peculiar, interesting.

*White, L. *Medieval Technology and Social Change.* New York: Oxford University Press, 1966. An exasperatingly near-brilliant analysis of the impact of warfare technology on European social organization; important.

Sources

*Einhard and Notker the Stammerer. *The Lives of Charlemagne.* L. Thorpe, trans. Baltimore: Penguin, 1966. Two interesting portraits of the greatest king of the early Middle Ages.

Lupus of Ferrier. *Collected Letters.* G. W. Regenos, trans. The Hague: Martinus Nijhoff, 1967. An absorbing collection of letters from a minor member of the "Carolingian Renaissance."

PART FOUR: THE EARLY MEDIEVAL EQUILIBRIUM

Chapter Nine: Ecclesia and Mundus

*Barraclough, G. *The Origins of Modern Germany.* New York: Putnam, 1963. The classic apologetic account of the ways in which Germany's Middle Ages influenced its development; the Germans love it; a near-masterpiece.

*Focillon, H. *The Year 1000.* F. D. Wieck, trans. New York: Harper & Row, 1969. The influence of the millennial aspirations of the tenth century on medieval art; thought-provoking.

Kantorowicz, E. *Laudes Regiae.* Berkeley: University of California Press, 1958. The ideology of theocratic kingship; unusual, important.

Schramm, P. E. *Kaiser, Rom, und Renovatio.* Berlin: B. G. Teubner, 1929. The classic study of Ottonian culture; brilliant, baroque, a monument of the Weimer world of the 1920s.

*Tellenbach, G. *Church, State, and Christian Society at the Time of the Investiture Contest.* New York: Harper & Row, 1970. The best study of the ideological bases of politics in the eleventh century; the one book to read on the Gregorian Reform.

Thompson, J. W. *Medieval Germany.* Chicago: University of Chicago Press, 1928. Out of date but useful.

Chapter Ten: Byzantium, Islam, and the West

Geanakoplos, D. J. *Byzantine East and Latin West.* New York: Harper & Row, 1966.

*Grabar, A. *Byzantine and Early Medieval Painting.* New York: Viking, 1973.

Hussey, J. *Church and Learning in the Byzantine Empire.* New York: Russell & Russell, 1963. A collection of essays devoted to the relation of scholarship, religion, and politics in the Byzantine world.

*Lewis, B. *The Arabs in History.* New York: Harper & Row, 1966. Easy reading; good insights.

Obolensky, D. *The Byzantine Commonwealth.* London: Weidenfeld, 1972. Valuable, frequently original insights into Byzantine culture and its Balkan affiliations.

Southern, R. W. *Western Views of Islam in the Middle Ages.* Cambridge, Mass.: Harvard University Press, 1962. Subtle, disturbing.

Sources

Comnena, Anna. *Alexiad.* A. S. Dawes, trans. New York: Barnes & Noble, 1967. A Byzantine princess regards the barbaric West during the age of the Crusades.

Hitti, P. K. *Usamah ibn-Mundiqh; An Arab-Syrian Gentleman and Warrior in the Period of the Crusades.* New York: Columbia University Press, 1929.

ibn-Khaldûn. *Muqaddimah.* F. Rosenthal, trans. Princeton, N.J.: Princeton University Press, 1967. A work adjudged by some to be the finest work of history written during the Middle Ages.

PART FIVE: THE AGE OF GREGORIAN REFORM

Chapter Eleven: On the Threshold of the High Middle Ages

*Bloch, M. *Feudal Society.* L. Manyan, trans. Chicago: Phoenix Books, 1966. A superlative flawed, unfinished work of enormous scope and erudition with great evocative power and exceptional analytic insight by one of the greatest scholars of the twentieth century.

Brooke, Z. N. *A History of Europe 911–1198.* London: Methuen, 1938. A very solid political introduction to the period.

Duby, G. *Rural Economy and Country Life in the Medieval West.* C. Postan, trans. London: E. Arnold, 1968. An exceptional work that captures the textures of social life with clarity and elegance; very French.

Focillon, H. *The Art of the West in the Middle Ages*. 2 vols. New York: Phaidon, 1969. A tedious but very useful summary.

Hallinger, K. *Gorze-Kluny*. Rome: Studia Anselmiani, 1950. Monastic reform.

*Kern, F. *Kingship and Law in the Middle Ages*. S. B. Chrimes, trans. New York: Harper & Row, 1970. A superb elegant discussion of the theories of kingship, customary law, and medieval legislative theory.

*Leclerq, J. *The Love of Learning and the Desire for God*. New York: Mentor, 1962. A monk's sensitive and perceptive account of the traditions and concerns of Benedictine monastic scholarship.

Lopez, R. S. *The Birth of Europe*. New York: M. Evans, 1967. Learned, wide-range, good on economic and social history.

Sackur, E. *Die Cluniacenser*. Darmstadt, Germany: Wissenschaftliche Buchgesellschaft, 1968. The most influential and thorough work ever written on the impact of monastic reform in the eleventh century; breathtaking in its scope and learning. (First edition 1911.)

Sources

The Song of Roland. D. L. Sayers, trans. Baltimore: Penguin, 1968. The epic poem embodying the aristocratic-warrior and shame culture ethos of the eleventh century.

Chapter Twelve: The Gregorian World Revolution

Fliche, A. *Le Reforme grégorienne et la reconquête chrétienne*. Paris: Bloud et Gay, 1950. Although over fifty years old, still one of the finest and most comprehensive accounts of the Gregorian reform papacy, by a conservative catholic.

Fournier, P., and LeBras, G. *Histoire des collections canoniques en occident*. Paris: Sirey, 1932. Canon law.

Klewitz, H. W. *Reformpapstum und Kardinalkolleg*. Darmstadt, Germany: H. Genter, 1957. A brilliant study of the effect of conflicting ideologies in the college of cardinals.

Morrison, K. F. *Tradition and Authority in the Western Church*. Princeton, N.J.: Princeton University Press, 1969. Subtle, learned, important.

*Prinz, J. *Popes from the Ghetto*. New York: Schocken, 1968. An interesting, problematical account of the Jewish convert family that allegedly financed and supported the Gregorian Reform movement.

*Tierney, B. *The Crisis of Church and State*. Englewood Cliffs, N.J.: Prentice-Hall, 1964. A useful introduction to the issues and problems of the Investiture Controversy.

Whitney, J. P. *Hildebrandine Essays*. Cambridge: Cambridge University Press, 1932. Somewhat out of date but perceptive, valuable.

Sources

The Correspondence of Gregory VII. E. Emerton, trans. New York: Norton, 1966. The eloquent, passionate, and often ferocious letters of the greatest of the reform popes.

Chapter Thirteen: The Anglo-Norman Monarchy and the Emergence of the Bureaucratic State

Brooke, Z. N. *The English Church and Papacy from the Conquest to the Reign of John*. Cambridge: Cambridge University Press, 1939.

Cantor, N. F. *Church, Kingship, and Lay Investiture in England*. New York: Octagon Books, 1967.

*———, ed. *William Stubbs on the English Constitution*. New York: Crowell, 1966. Selections from a classic nineteenth-century work, still very important.

Davis, R. H. C. *King Stephen*. Berkeley: University of California Press, 1967.

*Douglas, D. C. *William the Conqueror*. Berkeley: University of California Press, 1964. An authoritative, well-written biography of one of the most brilliant and energetic kings of England.

*Haskins, C. H. *The Normans in European History*. New York: Norton,

1966. An admiring study of the energy, resourcefulness, and ability of the supermen of the eleventh century; naive but interesting.

John, E.. *Orbis Britanniae.* New York: Humanities, 1966. Perceptive essays dealing with topics in late Anglo-Saxon England.

Knowles, D. *The Monastic Order in England.* Cambridge: Cambridge University Press, 1940. A monumental work dealing with every aspect of monasticism in England; a world of its own; delightful reading.

Maitland, F. W. *Domesday Book and Beyond.* Cambridge: Cambridge University Press, 1907. A masterpiece of legal and social history.

Richardson, H., and Sayles, G. O. *The Governance of Medieval England.* Edinburgh: Edinburgh University Press, 1963. Heavy-handed but valuable.

*Sayles, G. O. *The Medieval Foundations of England.* New York: A. S. Barnes, 1950. Good survey, clear and concise.

Sources

The Ecclesiastical History of Odericus Vitalis. M. Chibnall, trans. and ed. Oxford: Clarendon Press, 1964. An absolutely charming and perceptive history of the Norman dukes from the early eleventh century through 1154.

Chapter Fourteen: The First Crusade and After

Alphandery, P., and Dupont, A. *La Chrétienté et l'idée de croisade.* Paris: A. Michel, 1954–59. Suggestive, interesting.

Erdman, C. *Die Entstehung des Kreuzugsgedankens.* Stuttgart: Kohlhammer, 1965. A brilliant, profoundly disturbing study of the origins and debasement of the crusading ideal; a masterpiece.

Krey, A. C. *The First Crusade.* Gloucester, Mass.: Peter Smith, 1955.

*Runciman, S. *A History of the Crusades.* 3 vols. New York: Harper & Row, 1955. An exhaustive and au-

thoritative study of the entire crusading movement.

Throop, P. A. *Criticism of the Crusades.* Amsterdam: N. Swets and Zeitlinger, 1940.

Sources

Gesta Francorum. R. Hill, ed. Camden, N.J.: Nelson, 1962. The First Crusade as seen and experienced by a minor knight.

Joinville, Jean de, and Villehardouin, Geoffri de. *Chronicles of the Crusades.* M. Shaw, ed. Baltimore: Penguin, 1963. The crusades as grand, noble, knightly adventures, tinged with sadism and decadence.

PART SIX: LEARNING, PIETY, AND POWER

Chapter Fifteen: The Intellectual Expansion of Europe

*Cantor, N. F. *The Meaning of the Middle Ages.* Boston: Allyn & Bacon, 1973. A sociological analysis.

*Chenu, M. D. *Nature, Man, and Society in the Twelfth Century.* Chicago: University of Chicago Press, 1968. Learned assessment of the new vision of man in the twelfth century.

Chodorow, S. A. *Christian Political Theory and Church Politics.* Berkeley: University of California Press, 1972. Canon law theory; useful.

*Curtius, E. R. *European Literature and the Latin Middle Ages.* New York: Harper & Row, 1963. Masterful survey.

Denomy, A. J. *The Heresy of Courtly Love.* Gloucester, Mass.: Peter Smith, 1965. An important controversial study of the implications of the ideals of courtly love.

Dronke, P. *Medieval Latin and the Rise of the Love Lyric.* New York: Oxford University Press, 1966. A superb study of the origins, development, and themes of courtly poetry; a masterpiece.

Ghellinck, J. de. *L'essor de la literateur latine au XII ie siècle.* Brussels: Desclee de Brouwer, 1955.

Gilson, E. *A History of Christian Philosophy in the Middle Ages.* New York: Random House, 1955. Careful, detailed, immensely valuable.

————. *The Mystical Theology of Saint Bernard.* New York: Sheed & Ward, 1955. An important analysis of St. Bernard's theological positions.

*Heer, F. *The Medieval World.* New York: Mentor, 1964. An exciting, commendable attempt to integrate politics, religion, and thought in the twelfth century.

Kuttner, S. *Harmony from Dissonance.* Latrobe, Pa.: Archabbey Press, 1960. An attempt to understand the formation and structure of the Canon Law.

LeBras, G., Lefebvre, C., and Rambaud, J. *L'âge classique.* Paris: Sirey, 1965. Canon law and society; thick.

*Leff, G. *Medieval Thought.* Chicago: Quadrangle, 1959. A subtle discussion of the major trends in medieval philosophy and theology.

*Lewis, C. S. *The Allegory of Love.* New York: Oxford University Press, 1967. Disjointed but illuminating.

Loomis, R. S. *The Grail.* New York: Columbia University Press, 1963.

Morris, C. *The Discovery of the Individual.* London: S.P.C.K., 1972. Valuable introduction; occasionally original analysis.

Panofsky, E. *Abbott Suger and the Abbey Church of St. Denis.* Princeton, N.J.: Princeton University Press, 1948. Suger speaks; fascinating.

Sikes, G. *Peter Abelard.* New York: Russell & Russell, 1965. A good biography of one of the intellectual leaders of the twelfth century.

*Southern, R. W. *The Making of the Middle Ages.* New Haven: Yale University Press, 1953. A powerful neoromantic evocation of the best of medieval culture; a classic.

Vinogradoff, P. *Roman Law in Medieval Europe.* New York: Barnes & Noble, 1968. Useful, sound.

*Wolff, P. *The Cultural Awakening.* New York: Pantheon, 1968. A thoughtful interpretation of the twelfth century.

Sources

*Abelard, Peter. *Historia Calamitum.* Toronto: Pontifical Institute, 1964. The triumphs and tragedies of one of the greatest minds of the Middle Ages; psychohistory.

*Eschenbach, Wolfram von. *Parzival.* New York: Random House, 1973. The zenith of medieval romanticism; perhaps the most imaginative of all medieval books.

John of Salisbury. *The Statesman's Book.* J. Dickinson, trans. New York: Russell & Russell, 1963. The finest example of the medieval humanist tradition; a radical conservative.

The Letters of St. Bernard. B. S. James, trans. Chicago: Regenery, 1953. The correspondence of Europe's self-appointed conscience.

Chapter Sixteen: Moslem and Jewish Thought: The Aristotelian Challenge

Baron, S. *A Social and Religious History of the Jews.* 9 vols. New York: Columbia University Press, 1952. An authoritative history of the Jewish people from Biblical times to the early modern world.

*Husik, I. *A History of Medieval Jewish Philosophy.* New York: Atheneum, 1966. Valuable, perceptive.

*Katz, J. *Tradition and Crisis.* New York: Schocken, 1971. An excellent examination of the problems of Jewish life in the later Middle Ages.

Peters, F. E. *Aristotle and the Arabs.* New York: New York University Press, 1968.

Sharif, M. M. *A History of Muslim Philosophy.* 2 vols. Wiesbaden: Harrassowitz, 1966. A very good history of the problems, schools, and developments in Islamic philosophy into the twentieth century.

Sources

Averröes. *On the Harmony of Religion and Philosophy.* G. Hourani, trans. London: Luzac, 1967. A very influential attempt to reconcile Aristotle with the truths of revealed religion by the greatest of medieval Moslem thinkers.

Halevi, Judah. *The Kuzari.* Intro. by H. Slonimsky. New York: Schocken, 1964. Antirationalist and nationalistic.

*Maimonides, Moses. *The Guide for the Perplexed.* M. Friedlander, trans. New York: Dover, 1904. Jewish aristotelianism.

Chapter Seventeen: Varieties of Religious Experience

Borst, A. *Die Catherer.* Stuttgart: Hiersemann, 1953. Important, thorough.

*Cohn, N. *The Pursuit of the Millennium.* New York: Oxford University Press, 1970. A sociological study of apocalyptic movements in premodern Europe; unreliable but exciting.

Grundmann, H. *Religiose Bewegungen im Mittelalter.* Hildesheim, West Germany: G. Olm, 1961. Comprehensive but not profound.

Koch, G. *Frauenfrage und Ketzertum.* Berlin: Deutsche Verlag, 1966. A socioeconomic analysis of the place of women in heretical movements.

*Lea, H. C. *Inquisition of the Middle Ages.* New York: Harper & Row, 1974. The old classic, still valuable.

Leff, G. *Heresy in the Later Middle Ages.* New York: Barnes & Noble, 1967. A thorough discussion of the major heretical groups and their beliefs.

*Runciman, S. *The Medieval Manichee.* Cambridge: Cambridge University Press, 1955. A good introduction to the history of heresy.

Russel, J. B. *Witchcraft in the Middle Ages.* Ithaca, N.Y.: Cornell University Press, 1972. Not way out, but sober and thoughtful.

Thouzellier, C. *Catharisme et valdensianisme en Languedoc.* Louvain, Belgium: Nauwelaerts, 1966. A very difficult but important work that attempts the re-creation of heretical beliefs from inquisitorial sources.

Wakefield, W. *Heresy, Crusade, and Inquisition in Southern France.* Berkeley: University of California Press, 1974. The best introduction to the subject; judicious, learned.

Sources

Evans, A. P., and Wakefield, W., eds. *Heresies of the High Middle Ages.* New York: Columbia University Press, 1969. A vast, immensely valuable collection of source material.

Chapter Eighteen: The Entrenchment of Secular Leadership

*Cantor, N. F. *The English.* New York: Clarion, 1967. An effort to relate politics, society, and culture.

Chrimes, S. B. *An Introduction to the Administrative History of England.* Oxford: Oxford University Press, 1962. Convenient survey.

*Fawtier, R. *The Capetian Kings of France.* New York: St. Martin, 1960. A clear, concise history of the Capetian dynasty.

Hyde, J. K. *Society and Politics in Medieval Italy.* New York: St. Martin, 1973. Well-informed, succinct, valuable.

Kantorowicz, E. *The King's Two Bodies.* Princeton, N.J.: Princeton University Press, 1957. Original, sophisticated, important.

*Kelly, A. *Eleanor of Aquitaine and the Four Kings.* Cambridge, Mass.: Harvard University Press, 1950. Delightful, illuminating.

Jolliffe, J. *Angevin Kingship.* London: A. and C. Black, 1963. A persuasive analysis of political conflict.

Knowles, D. *Thomas Becket.* London: British Academy, 1949. Engrossing; beautifully written.

Lot, F., and Fawtier, R. *Histoire des institutions françaises au moyen age.* Paris: Presses Universitaires de France, 1957. A vast compendium.

*Maitland, F. W., and Pollock, F. *The History of English Law.* 2 vols. Cambridge: Cambridge University Press, 1973. A brilliant and complex study of English law and society in the Middle Ages; a classic.

Muntz, P. *Frederick Barbarossa.* Ithaca,

N.Y.: Cornell University Press, 1969. Authoritative, engrossing, important.

*Painter, S. *French Chivalry*. Ithaca, N.Y.: Cornell University Press, 1957.

*————. *William Marshall*. Baltimore: Johns Hopkins University Press, 1933. The engaging biography of a prominent knight of the late twelfth century.

Schramm, P. E. *Der König von Frankreich*. Weimar: H. Böhlaus, 1960. Watch on the Rhine.

Warren, W. L. *Henry II*. Berkeley: University of California Press, 1973. Careful and well-informed.

Sources

FitzNeale, Richard. *The Course of the Exchequer*. C. Johnson, ed. Camden, N.J.: T. Nelson, 1950. The medieval bureaucratic mind.

John of Salisbury. *Historia Pontificalis*. M. Chibnall, trans. Camden, N.J.: T. Nelson, 1962. Dirty politics in Rome; marvelous.

PART SEVEN: THE SEARCH FOR A NEW EQUILIBRIUM

Chapter Nineteen: The Peace of Innocent III

Brentano, R. *The Two Churches*. Princeton, N.J.: Princeton University Press, 1968. The realities of ecclesiastical politics.

Jungmann, J. *The Mass of the Roman Rite*. New York: Benziger, 1955. Medieval liturgy; a massive survey.

Lambert, M. *Franciscan Poverty*. London: S.P.C.K., 1961. An inquiry into the issue that created and ultimately dismembered the Franciscan order; important.

Luchaire, A. *Innocent III*. 5 vols. Paris: A. Picard, 1925. Out of date but valuable.

Mortimer, R. *Western Canon Law*. Berkeley: A. and C. Black, 1953. Useful summary.

Packard, S. R. *Europe and the Church Under Innocent III*. New York: Russell & Russell, 1968.

Poole, A. L. *Lectures on the History of the Papal Chancery*. Oxford: Clarendon Press, 1922. A study of the machinery of the papal monarchy.

Powicke, F. M. *Stephen Langton*. Oxford: Clarendon Press, 1928. A masterful study of the enigmatic papal legate under Innocent.

Sabatier, P. *Saint Francis of Assisi*. New York: Scribner, 1894. A neo-romantic study of the dominant religious figure of the thirteenth century.

Sources

*Brown, R., ed. *The Little Flowers of St. Francis*. Garden City, N.Y.: Doubleday, 1971. Franciscan ideology and myth; bourgeois guilt culture; powerfully evocative of the Franciscan impact on urban society.

Chapter Twenty: The New Consensus and Its Limitations

*Baldwin, J. W. *The Scholastic Culture of the Middle Ages*. Lexington, Mass.: Heath, 1972. Neat survey.

*Branner, R. *Gothic Architecture*. New York: Braziller, 1961. Incisive.

Carté, M. H. *Realists and Nominalists*. New York: Oxford University Press, 1947.

*Carsten, F. L. *The Origins of Prussia*. New York: Oxford University Press, 1954. A study of the German *Drang nach Osten* movement.

*Copleston, F. *Aquinas*. Baltimore: Penguin, 1955. Useful study of the life and thought of the greatest philosopher of the thirteenth century.

Cromble, A. *Robert Grosseteste and the Origins of Experimental Science*. Oxford: Clarendon Press, 1962.

Easton, S. *Roger Bacon*. New York: Columbia University Press, 1952. Interesting, provocative.

Gilson, E. *The Philosophy of St. Bonaventure*. Paterson, N.J.: St. Anthony Guild Press, 1965.

Gimpel, J. *The Cathedral Builders*. C. F. Jones, trans. New York: Grove, 1961.

Grabmann, M. *Die Geschichte der Scho-*

lastichen Methode. Berlin: Akademie Verlag, 1966. Massive.

*Holt, J. C. *Magna Carta.* New York: Wiley, 1969. An excellent modern work discussing the problems and interpretations of Magna Carta.

Homans, G. *English Villagers of the Thirteenth Century.* London: Russell & Russell, 1960. A remarkable sociology of the common man in medieval Europe.

Kantorowicz, E. *Frederick II.* E. O. Lorimer, trans. New York: Ungar, 1957. Medieval fascism.

*Leff, G. *Paris and Oxford Universities in the Thirteenth and Fourteenth Centuries.* Grand Rapids, Mich.: Krieger, 1968. A brilliant synthesis of all aspects of university life; masterly.

*Luchaire, A. *Social France at the Time of Philip Augustus.* New York: Harper & Row, 1970. Out-of-date but interesting account of the modes of life in the early thirteenth century.

*Mâle, E. *The Gothic Image.* New York: Harper & Row, 1973. A classic study written in the 1920s; suggestive, elusive.

McKechnie, W. S. *Magna Carta.* New York: Franklin, 1958. An extremely thorough and detailed account of Magna Carta, somewhat out of date.

Noonan, J. T. *The Scholastic Analysis of Usury.* Cambridge, Mass.: Harvard University Press, 1957. A thorough discussion of scholastic analysis and its techniques; important.

*Painter, S. *The Reign of King John.* Baltimore: Johns Hopkins University Press, 1941. A first-rate political history.

*Panofsky, E. *Gothic Architecture and Scholasticism.* New York: World Publishing, 1967. An incisive exploration of the effects of the scholastic habits of mind upon architecture; a controversial classic.

Powicke, F. M. *Henry III and the Lord Edward.* Oxford: Clarendon Press, 1950. Detailed, illuminating.

Powicke, F. M. *The Thirteenth Century.* Oxford: Clarendon Press, 1962.

Rashdall, H. *Universities in the Middle Ages.* E. Emden and F. M. Powicke, eds. Oxford: Oxford University Press, 1936. An exhaustive study of universities and university life in the Middle Ages.

Sarton, G. *An Introduction to the History of Science.* Baltimore: Williams and Williams, 1927.

*Simson, O. von. *The Gothic Cathedral.* New York: Pantheon, 1962. The classic work on the gothic cathedral; very German.

Steenbergen, F. van. *Aristotle in the West.* Louvain, Belgium: Nauewelaerts, 1955. A valuable survey.

Strayer, J. R. *The Albigensian Crusade.* New York: Dial, 1971. An excellent, thoughtful history of religious heterodoxy and the ugly face of Capetian imperialism in Southern France; a small masterpiece by a great American medievalist.

*Temko, A. *Notre Dame of Paris.* New York: Viking, 1955. A wonderful, imaginative account.

Thorndike, L. *A History of Magic and Experimental Science.* New York: Macmillan, 1941. Bewildering but illuminating.

*Waddell, H. *Wandering Scholars.* Garden City, N.Y.: Doubleday, 1955. Excellent translations of the works of the radical scholar-poets known as the Goliards.

Young, K. *The Drama of the Medieval Church.* Oxford: Clarendon Press, 1967. Learned, careful, massive.

Sources

*Lorris, Gillaume, and Meun, Jean de. *Roman de la Rose.* S. G. Nichols, ed. New York: Appleton-Century-Crofts, 1967. Part I is a summary statement of the courtly ideal; Part II is an exciting revelation of the disintegration of medieval culture and society; very important.

Pegis, A. C., ed. *The Basic Writings of St. Thomas Aquinas.* New York: Modern Library, 1945. Well-edited compendium of the Thomist canon; still worthy of a lifetime's study.

PART EIGHT: THE BREAKDOWN

Chapter Twenty-One: The Failure of the New Consensus

Boase, T. S. R. *Boniface VIII*. London: Constable and Co., 1933. Out of date but useful.

Hilton, R. *Bond Men Made Free*. London: Smith, 1973. Valuable Marxist account of medieval peasant rebellion.

Leff, Gordon. *Heresy in the Late Middle Ages*. Manchester: University Press, 1967. Dissent and revolution; important.

*Macfarlane, K. B. *John Wycliffe and the Beginning of English Non-conformity*. London: English Universities Press, 1952. A subtle study of a central dissenter to the medieval consensus.

Mollat, G. *The Popes of Avignon*. Camden, N.J.: T. Nelson, 1963. A useful study of the nadir of the medieval church.

*Perroy, E. *The Hundred Years War*. New York: Putnam, 1965. A work that succeeds in capturing some of the disorder and violence spawned by the Hundred Years war.

Runciman, S. *The Sicilian Vespers*. Cambridge: Cambridge University Press, 1958. Beautifully written.

Ullmann, W. *The Origins of the Great Schism*. Hamden, Conn.: Archon Books, 1967.

*Wilkins, E. H. *The Life of Petrarch*. Chicago: University of Chicago Press, 1961. A perceptive biography of the first of the humanists.

Sources

*Dante Alighieri. *The Divine Comedy*. D. L. Sayers, ed. 3 vols. Baltimore: Penguin, 1954. Usually regarded as the greatest work of medieval literature—a work that epitomizes the medieval tradition while looking forward to a new age.

*Froissart. *The Chronicles of England, France, and Spain*. C. W. Dunn, ed. New York: Dutton, 1961. Powerful evocation of decadence and disaster.

*Marsilius of Padua. *Defender of the Peace*. A. Gewirth, ed. New York:

Harper & Row, 1964. A trenchant radical attack on the prerogatives and claims of the medieval church; the new secularism.

*Petrarch. *Selected Sonnets, Odes, and Letters*. F. G. Bergin, ed. Northbrook, Ill.: AHM Publishing Company, 1966. Beloved by Humanists.

PART NINE: AN END AND A BEGINNING

Chapter Twenty-Two: Between Two Worlds

*Baron, H. *The Crisis of the Early Italian Renaissance*. Princeton, N.J.: Princeton University Press, 1966. An intriguing inquiry into the political forces that generated the flowering of Florence.

Bloomfield, M. *Piers Plowman as a Fourteenth Century Apocalypse*. New Brunswick, N.J.: Rutgers University Press, 1962. Religious currents in the fourteenth century; a masterpiece.

*Brucker, G. *Renaissance Florence*. New York: Wiley, 1969. An excellent account of one of the centers of the Italian renaissance; strong on politics and society.

*Burckhardt, J. *The Civilization of the Renaissance in Italy*. New York: New American Library, 1974. A nineteenth-century masterwork arguing for the Renaissance's new vision of man; still a controversial classic.

Burke, P. *Culture and Society in Renaissance Italy*. New York: Scribner, 1972. Brilliant structuralist interpretation; original, very important.

Calmette, J. *The Golden Age of Burgundy*. New York: Norton, 1963.

Chrimes, S. B. *Lancastrians, Yorkists, and Henry VII*. New York: Macmillan, 1967. Suggestive, useful.

Clagget, M. *The Science of Mechanics in the Middle Ages*. Madison: University of Wisconsin Press, 1961. Almost the scientific revolution.

DuBoulay, F. *An Age of Ambition*. New York: Viking, 1970. A brilliant, provocative study of society, culture, and politics in late medieval England; important.

Ferguson, W. K. *The Renaissance in Historical Thought*. Boston: Houghton Mifflin, 1948. Somewhat pedestrian, but important.

*Hay, D. *The Italian Renaissance in Its Historical Background*. New York: Cambridge University Press, 1961. A succinct overview of the Italian renaissance.

*Huizinga, J. *The Waning of the Middle Ages*. Garden City, N.Y.: Doubleday, 1924. An absorbing work that explores the perpetuation of archaic medieval patterns of thought and behavior into the fifteenth century; an impressionistic evocation of late medieval decadence; a masterpiece.

*Lewis, C. S. *The Discarded Image*. New York: Cambridge University Press, 1968. A brilliant discussion of the thought patterns, symbols, and imagery of the late Middle Ages; a small masterpiece.

*McLuhan, M. *The Gutenberg Galaxy*. New York: New American Library, 1969. Suggestive, illuminating, important.

*Meiss, M. *Painting in Florence and Siena After the Black Death*. New York: Harper & Row, 1964. A careful examination of the effects of social cataclysm upon imagination; valuable.

Oberman, H. *The Harvest of Medieval Theology*. Cambridge, Mass.: Harvard University Press, 1963. The intellectual crisis of the late Middle Ages.

Oman, C. *The Great Revolt of 1381*. Oxford: Clarendon Press, 1906.

Owst, G. *Pulpit and Preaching in Medieval England*. Cambridge: Cambridge University Press, 1926. Suggestive, valuable.

Robertson, D. W., Jr. *A Preface to Chaucer*. Princeton, N.J.: University Press, 1963. A provocative, controversial, original study of the structure of late medieval literature; very important.

Stadelmann, Rudolf. *Vom Geist des Ausgehenden Mittelalters*. Stuttgart: Fromman, 1966. Written in the 1920s, this remains the classic survey of late medieval culture.

Tierney, B. *Foundations of the Conciliar Movement*. Cambridge: Cambridge University Press, 1955.

Sources

*Boccacio, Giovanni. *The Decameron*. G. H. McWilliam, trans. Baltimore: Penguin, 1972. An example of the secular Italian spirit.

*Chaucer, Geoffrey. *Chaucer Reader*. C. W. Dunn, ed. New York: Harcourt Brace Jovanovich, 1952. Generally regarded as the greatest of all medieval English poets.

*Thomas a Kempis. *Imitation of Christ*. L. Shirley-Price, trans. Baltimore: Penguin, 1973. A sensitive work of late medieval religiosity.

*Langland, William. *Piers Plowman*. Goodridge, J. F. Baltimore: Penguin, 1966. A biting commentary on late medieval society; the voice of the common man; very important.

CHRONOLOGICAL LISTS

THE MEDIEVAL POPES[1]

314–335	Sylvester I	642–649	Theodore I	885–891	Stephen V
336	Mark	649–655	Martin I	891–896	Formosus
337–352	Julius I	654–657	Eugenius I	896	Boniface VI
352–366	Liberius	657–672	Vitalian	896–897	Stephen VI
355–365	*Felix II*	672–676	Adeodatus	897	Romanus, Theodore II
366–384	Damasus I	676–678	Donus		
384–399	Siricius	678–681	Agatho	898–900	John IX
399–401	Anastasius I	682–683	Leo II	900–903	Benedict IV
401–417	Innocent I	684–685	Benedict II	903	Leo V
417–418	Zosimus	685–686	John V	903–904	*Christopher*
418–422	Boniface I	686–687	Conon	904–911	Sergius III
422–432	Celestine I	687–701	Sergius I	911–913	Anastasius III
432–440	Sixtus III	701–705	John VI	913–914	Lando
440–461	Leo I the Great	705–707	John VII	914–928	John X
461–468	Hilary	708	Sisinnius	928	Leo VI
468–483	Simplicius	708–715	Constantine	928–931	Stephen VII
483–492	Felix III	715–731	Gregory II	931–935	John XI
492–496	Gelasius I	731–741	Gregory III	936–939	Leo VII
496–498	Anastasius II	741–752	Zacharias	939–942	Stephen VIII
498–514	Symmachus	752–757	Stephen II	942–946	Marinus II
514–523	Hormisdas	757–767	Paul I	946–955	Agapitus II
523–526	John I	767–768	*Constantine*	955–964	John XII
526–530	Felix IV	768	*Philip*	963–965	Leo VIII
530–532	Boniface II	768–772	Stephen III	964–966	Benedict V
533–535	John II	772–795	Adrian I	965–972	John XIII
535–536	Agapitus I	795–816	Leo III	973–974	Benedict VI
536–537	Silverius	816–817	Stephen IV	974	*Boniface VII*
537–555	Vigilius	817–824	Paschal I	974–983	Benedict VII
555–561	Pelagius I	824–827	Eugenius II	983–984	John XIV
561–574	John III	827	Valentine	984–985	*Boniface VII*
575–579	Benedict I	827–844	Gregory IV	985–996	John XV
579–590	Pelagius II	844	*John VIII*	996–999	Gregory V
590–604	Gregory I the Great	844–847	Sergius II	997–998	*John XVI*
604–606	Sabinianus	847–855	Leo IV	999–1003	Sylvester II
607	Boniface III	855–858	Benedict III	1003	John XVII
608–615	Boniface IV	858–867	Nicholas I the Great	1004–1009	John XVIII
615–618	Deusdedit			1009–1012	Sergius IV
619–625	Boniface V	867–872	Adrian II	1012–1024	Benedict VIII
625–638	Honorius I	872–882	John VIII	1012	*Gregory VI*
640	Severinus	882–884	Marinus I	1024–1032	John XIX
640–642	John IV	884–885	Adrian III		

[1] *Anti-popes in italics.*

1032–1044 Benedict IX (re-signed)	1144–1145 Lucius II	1294–1303 Boniface VIII
1045 Sylvester III	1145–1153 Eugenius III	1303–1304 Benedict XI
1045 Benedict IX (de-posed)	1153–1154 Anastasius IV	1305–1314 Clement V
	1154–1159 Adrian IV	1316–1334 John XXII
1045–1046 Gregory VI	1159–1181 Alexander III	*1328–1330 Nicholas V*
1046–1047 Clement II	*1159–1164 Victor IV*	1334–1342 Benedict XII
1047–1048 Benedict IX	*1164–1168 Paschal III*	1342–1352 Clement VI
1048 Damasus II	*1168–1178 Calixtus III*	1352–1362 Innocent VI
1049–1054 Leo IX	*1179–1180 Innocent III*	1362–1370 Urban V
1055–1057 Victor II	1181–1185 Lucius III	1370–1378 Gregory XI
1057–1058 Stephen IX	1185–1187 Urban III	1378–1389 Urban VI
1058–1059 Benedict X	1187 Gregory VIII	1378–1394 Clement VII*
1059–1061 Nicholas II	1187–1191 Clement III	1389–1404 Boniface IX
1061–1073 Alexander II	1191–1198 Celestine III	1394–1423 Benedict XIII*
1061–1064 Honorius II	1198–1216 Innocent III	1404–1406 Innocent VII
1073–1085 Gregory VII	1216–1227 Honorius III	1406–1415 Gregory XII
1080–1100 Clement III	1227–1241 Gregory IX	*1409–1410 Alexander V*
1086–1087 Victor III	1241 Celestine IV	*1410–1415 John XXIII*
1088–1099 Urban II	1243–1254 Innocent IV	1417–1431 Martin V
1099–1118 Paschal II	1254–1261 Alexander IV	*1423–1429 Clement VIII*
1100 Theodoric	1261–1264 Urban IV	*1425–1430 Benedict XIV* *
1102 Albert	1265–1268 Clement IV	1431–1447 Eugenius IV
1105–1111 Sylvester IV	1271–1276 Gregory X	*1439–1449 Felix V*
1118–1119 Gelasius II	1276 Innocent V	1447–1455 Nicholas V
1118–1121 Gregory VIII	1276 Adrian V	1455–1458 Calixtus III
1119–1124 Calixtus II	1276–1277 John XXI	1458–1464 Pius II
1124–1130 Honorius II	1277–1280 Nicholas III	1464–1471 Paul II
1130–1143 Innocent II	1281–1285 Martin IV	1471–1484 Sixtus IV
1130–1138 Anacletus II	1285–1287 Honorius IV	1484–1492 Innocent VIII
1143–1144 Celestine II	1288–1292 Nicholas IV	1492–1503 Alexander VI
	1294 Celestine V	

THE LATER ROMAN EMPERORS

161–180 Marcus Aurelius	251–253 Gallus	361–363 Julian "the Apos-tate"
161–169 Lucius Aurelius Verus	252–253 Aemilian	363–364 Jovian
180–192 Commodus	253–259 Valerian	364–375 Valentinian I (West)
193 Publius Helvius Pertinax	259–268 Gallien	364–378 Valens (East)
193–211 Septimius Servus	268–270 Claudius II	375–383 Gratian (West)
211–217 Caracalla	270–275 Aurelian	375–392 Valentinian II (West)
209–211 Publius Septimius Geta	275–276 Tacitus	
	276–282 Probus	379–395 Theodosius the Great
217–218 Macrinus	281–283 Carus	
218–222 Elagabulus	284–305 Diocletian	383–388 Maximus
222–235 Alexander Severus	286–305 Maximian	392–394 Eugenius
235–238 Maximin	305–306 Constantius I	395–408 Arcadius (East)
237–238 Gordian I	305–311 Galerius	395–423 Honorius (West)
238 Marcus Clodius Pupienus	306–307 Severus	408–450 Theodosius II (East)
	306–312 Maxentius	
238 Decimus Caelius Balbinus	311–324 Licinius	425–454 Valentinian III (West)
	311–337 Constantine I, the Great	
238–244 Gordian III	337–340 Constantine II	450–457 Marcian (East)
244–249 Philip	337–361 Constantius II	455 Petronius (West)
249–251 Decius	337–350 Constans	455–457 Avitus (West)

* *Names followed by an asterisk are those of popes of the Avignonese line after the Great Schism of 1378.*

457–461	Majorian (West)	472	Olybrius (West)	473–474	Leo II (East)
457–474	Leo I (East)	473–474	Glycerius (West)	474–491	Zeno (East)
461–465	Severus (West)	473–475	Julius Nepos	475–476	Romulus Augus-
467–472	Anthemius (West)		(West)		tulus (West)

THE BYZANTINE EMPERORS

474–491	Zeno	842–866	Bardas	1203–1204	Isaac II
491–518	Anastasius I	867	Theophilus II	1203–1204	Alexius IV
518–527	Justin I	867–886	Basil I	1204	Alexius V
527–565	Justinian I, the	886–912	Leo VI		*Latin Emperors*
	Great	912–913	Alexander III	1204–1205	Baldwin I
565–578	Justin II	913–959	Constantine VII	1205–1216	Henry
578–582	Tiberius	919–944	Romanus I	1216–1217	Peter de Cour-
582–602	Maurice	959–963	Romanus II		tenay
602–610	Phocas I	963–1025	Basil II	1218–1228	Robert de Cour-
610–641	Heraclius I	963–969	Nicephorus II		tenay
641	Constantine III	969–976	John I	1228–1261	Baldwin II
641	Heracleon	1025–1028	Constantine VIII		*Nicaean Emperors*
641–668	Constans II	1028–1050	Zoë (Empress)	1206–1222	Theodore I
668–685	Constantine IV	1028–1034	Romanus III	1222–1254	John Dukas
685–695	Justinian II	1034–1041	Michael IV	1254–1259	Theodore II
695–698	Leontius II	1041–1042	Michael V	1258–1261	John IV
698–705	Tiberius III	1042–1054	Constantine IX	1259–1282	Michael VIII
705–711	Justinian II (again)	1054–1056	Theodora (Em-		Paleologus
711–713	Philippicus		press)		*The Paleologi*
713–715	Anastasius II	1056–1057	Michael VI	1282–1328	Andronicus II
715–717	Theodosius III	1057–1059	Isaac I	1295–1320	Michael IX
717–741	Leo III	1059–1067	Constantine X	1328–1341	Andronicus III
741–775	Constantine V	1067	Andronicus	1341–1347	John V
775–780	Leo IV	1067–1071	Romanus IV	1347–1354	John VI
780–797	Constantine VI	1071–1078	Michael VII	1355–1376	John V (re-
797–802	Irene (Empress)	1078–1081	Nicephorus III		stored)
802–811	Nicephorus I	1081–1118	Alexius I	1376–1379	Andronicus IV
811	Stauracius	1118–1143	John II	1379–1391	John V (re-
811–813	Michael I	1143–1180	Manuel I		stored)
813–820	Leo V	1180–1183	Alexius II	1390	John VII
820–829	Michael II	1182–1185	Andronicus I	1391–1425	Manuel II
829–842	Theophilus I	1185–1195	Isaac II	1425–1448	John VIII
842–867	Michael III	1195–1203	Alexius III	1448–1453	Constantine XI

THE KINGS OF FRANCE

	Capetian Dynasty	1223–1226	Louis VIII		*Valois Dynasty*
987–996	Hugh Capet	1226–1270	Louis IX (St.	1328–1350	Philip VI
996–1031	Robert II the		Louis)	1350–1364	John II
	Pious	1270–1285	Philip III	1364–1380	Charles V
1031–1060	Henry I	1285–1314	Philip IV the	1380–1422	Charles VI
1060–1108	Philip I		Fair	1422–1461	Charles VII
1108–1137	Louis VI the Fat	1314–1316	Louis X	1461–1483	Louis XI
1137–1180	Louis VII	1316–1322	Philip V	1483–1498	Charles VIII
1180–1223	Philip II Augus-	1322–1328	Charles IV		
	tus				

THE CAROLINGIANS

PEPIN II OF HERISTAL
(Mayor 680–714)

CHARLES MARTEL
(Mayor 714–41)

CARLOMAN
(Mayor 741–47)

PEPIN III THE SHORT
(Mayor 741–51, K. 751–68)

CARLOMAN
(King 768–71)

CHARLEMAGNE
(K. of Franks 768–814,
Emperor 800–814)

LOUIS THE PIOUS
(Emperor, 814–40)

LOTHAIR
(Emperor 840–55)

LOUIS THE GERMAN
(K. of E. Franks 840–76)

CHARLES THE BALD
(K. of W. Franks 840–77,
Emperor 875–77)

LOUIS
(Emp. 855–75)

CHARLES
(K. of Provence 855–63)

LOTHAIRE
(K. of Lorraine 855–69)

CARLOMAN
(K. of Bavaria 876–80)

LOUIS
(K. of Saxony 876–82,
K. of Bavaria 880–82)

CHARLES THE FAT
(K. of Franks 884–87,
Emperor 881–87 dep.)

LOUIS THE STAMMERER
(K. of W. Franks 877–79)

ARNULF
(K. of E. Franks 887–99,
Emperor 896–99)

LOUIS THE CHILD
(K. of E. Franks 899–911)

LOUIS III
(K. of W. Franks 879–82)

CARLOMAN
(K. of W. Franks 879–84)

CHARLES THE SIMPLE
(K. of W. Franks 898–922)

LOUIS IV
(K. of W. Franks 936–54)

LOTHAIR
(K. of W. Franks 954–86)

LOUIS V
(K. of W. Franks 986–87)

THE KINGS OF GERMANY

911–918	Conrad I, of Franconia	1125–1137	Lothair (Saxon)	1292–1298	Adolph I (Nassau)
	Saxon Dynasty		*Hohenstaufen Dynasty*	1298–1308	Albert I
919–936	Henry I, the Fowler	1137–1152	Conrad III	1308–1313	Henry VII (Luxembourg)
936–973	Otto I, the Great	1152–1190	Frederick I Barbarossa	1314–1347	Louis III (Hapsburg)
973–983	Otto II	1190–1197	Henry VI		
983–1002	Otto III	1197–1208	Philip	1346–1378	Charles IV
1002–1024	Henry II, the Saint	1208–1218	Otto IV	1378–1410	Wenceslas
		1215–1250	Frederick II	1410–1437	Sigismund
	Salian Dynasty	1250–1254	Conrad IV	1438–1439	Albert V
1024–1039	Conrad II	1254–1268	Conradin	1440–1493	Frederick III
1039–1056	Henry III, the Black		*Hapsburg and Luxembourg Dynasties*	1493–1519	Maximilian
1056–1106	Henry IV	1273–1291	Rudolf I of Hapsburg		
1106–1125	Henry V				

THE MEDIEVAL KINGS OF ENGLAND

870–899	Alfred the Great	1042–1066	Edward the Confessor	1272–1307	Edward I
899–925	Edward the Elder	1066	Harold Godwinson	1307–1327	Edward II
925–939	Athelstan			1327–1377	Edward III
939–946	Edmund	1066–1087	William I the Conqueror	1377–1399	Richard II
946–955	Edred			1399–1413	Henry IV, of Lancaster
959–975	Edgar the Peaceable	1087–1100	William II Rufus	1413–1422	Henry V
		1100–1135	Henry I	1422–1461	Henry VI
975–979	Edward the Martyr	1135–1154	Stephen—Mathilda	1461–1483	Edward IV, of York
979–1016	Ethelred the Redeless	1154–1189	Henry II	1483	Edward V
1016–1035	Canute	1189–1199	Richard I, the Lion-Hearted	1483–1485	Richard III
1035–1040	Harold	1199–1216	John I	1485–1509	Henry VII, Tudor
1040–1042	Harthacnut	1216–1272	Henry III		

INDEX